Praises for

WHAT'S YOUR MBA IQ?

I often tell the young professional we work with that I learned more in the first two chapters of this book than I did in my first two months at Harvard Business School. This book has become our primary teaching tool for young business managers.
—Ronald Mitchell, CEO & Co-Founder, CareerCore Inc.

This book defines a tough and tangible new standard for what every MBA graduate should know about business. With the degree's credibility under fire, this quality benchmark is just in time. Test yourself and see how you measure up.
—Tim Westerbeck, Managing Director and Principal, Lipman Hearne, Inc.

Kudos to Devi for creating what the business world has always needed – a simple guide and assessment that covers the fundamental business skills all industry professionals need. This should be required reading for all corporate training professionals, business school faculty and students! Devi Vallabhaneni clearly gets it!
—Doug Harward, CEO and Founder, TrainingIndustry.com

As one who has been involved in the hiring and promotion decisions of many professionals over my career, I would recommend this book to those managers who are looking to take their careers to the next level. It gives the reader a broader understanding of business operations which so many companies need in today's challenging and complex market.
—Michael Sprague, Vice President–Marketing & Communications, Kia Motors America

WHAT'S YOUR MBA IQ™?

WHAT'S YOUR MBA IQ™?

A Manager's Career Development Tool

Devi Vallabhaneni

WILEY

John Wiley & Sons, Inc.

Published by John Wiley & Sons, Inc., Hoboken, New Jersey.
Published simultaneously in Canada.

Library of Congress Cataloging-in-Publication Data:

Vallabhaneni, Devi, 1969–
    What's your MBA IQ? : A Manager's Career Development Tool / Devi Vallabhaneni.
        p.   cm.
    Includes bibliographical references and index.
    ISBN 978-0-470-43957-9 (pbk.)
  1. Management–Research.   2. Leadership.   3. Strategy.   I. Title.
    HD30.4.V35 2009
    658–dc22   2009015528

Printed in the United States of America

10 9 8 7 6 5 4 3 2 1

To my parents

By word and by deed, you have showed me that the harder I work today, the easier tomorrow will be.

Well, that tomorrow is now here.

Devi

Contents

Preface		xv
Acknowledgments		xvii
Introduction		xix
Learning Module 1	**General Management, Leadership, and Strategy**	**1**
	Learning Objective 1.1: Understand the Scope and Nature of Corporate Strategies	2
	Learning Objective 1.2: Understand the Importance of Planning and Organizing Skills	10
	Learning Objective 1.3: Understand the Importance of Directing and Leading Skills	14
	Learning Objective 1.4: Understand the Importance of Controlling and Measuring Skills	19
	Learning Objective 1.5: Understand the Importance of Motivating Skills	21
	Learning Objective 1.6: Understand the Importance of Problem-Solving and Decision-Making Skills	23
	Learning Objective 1.7: Understand the Importance of Negotiating Skills	30
	Learning Objective 1.8: Understand the Importance of Communication Skills	32
	Learning Objective 1.9: Understand the Importance of Conflict Management Skills	35
	Learning Objective 1.10: Understand the Various Issues in Organizational Behavior, Culture, Change, Development, Effectiveness, and Decline	38
	Learning Objective 1.11: Understand How to Measure and Manage Business Performance Results	42
Learning Module 2	**Operations Management**	**45**
	Learning Objective 2.1: Understand the Strategic Importance of Demand Forecasting	46
	Learning Objective 2.2: Understand the Production Strategies and Manufacturing Performance Measures	47
	Learning Objective 2.3: Understand the Production-Related Value Concepts	48
	Learning Objective 2.4: Understand the Philosophies of Just-In-Time and Lean Operations	49
	Learning Objective 2.5: Understand the Principles and Techniques of Inventory Management	52
	Learning Objective 2.6: Understand the Principles and Techniques of Supply-Chain and Logistics Management	56

Learning Objective 2.7: Understand the Various Planning Systems Applicable
    to Manufacturing and Distribution Operations   58
Learning Objective 2.8: Understand the Various Short-Term Scheduling
    Systems Used in Production   60
Learning Objective 2.9: Understand the Theory of Constraints in Operations   62
Learning Objective 2.10: Understand the Principles of Production Economics
    and Application of Decision Tools   63
Learning Objective 2.11: Understand the Principles and Techniques of
    Equipment Maintenance and System Reliability   65
Learning Objective 2.12: Understand the Production Process Flows and Metrics 66
Learning Objective 2.13: Understand the Technology Deployed in
    Manufacturing and Service Operations   67

Learning Module 3   Marketing Management   71

Learning Objective 3.1: Understand the Components of Marketing Mix   72
Learning Objective 3.2: Understand the Expectancy-Value Model in Consumer
    Markets   72
Learning Objective 3.3: Understand the Brand Elements and Calculate
    a Brand Value   72
Learning Objective 3.4: Understand Competitor Analysis   73
Learning Objective 3.5: Understand the Pricing Strategies and Methods   73
Learning Objective 3.6: Understand the Marketing Communications Mix   75
Learning Objective 3.7: Understand the New-Product Development Process   75
Learning Objective 3.8: Compute the Customer Retention Rate   76
Learning Objective 3.9: Compute the Lifetime Value of a Customer   77
Learning Objective 3.10: Compute the Customer Conviction in Terms of Net
    Promoter Score   78
Learning Objective 3.11: Compute the Customer Loyalty Score   78
Learning Objective 3.12: Compute the Net Marketing Contribution Amount   78
Learning Objective 3.13: Compute the Marketing Profitability Metrics   80
Learning Objective 3.14: Compute the Market Development Index   80
Learning Objective 3.15: Compute the Market Share Index   80
Learning Objective 3.16: Compute a Product's Lifecycle Cost and Economic
    Value to a Customer   81
Learning Objective 3.17: Compute the Relative Performance, Price, and
    Customer Value of a Product   81
Learning Objective 3.18: Compute a Marketing Channel Intermediary's
    Transaction Value   82
Learning Objective 3.19: Understand the Relationships Among Price, Profit, and
    Market Share   83
Learning Objective 3.20: Understand a Marketing Channel's Performance   83
Learning Objective 3.21: Evaluate the Advertising's Effectiveness with Customer
    Response Index   83
Learning Objective 3.22: Learn How to Conduct a Marketing Portfolio Analysis 85
Learning Objective 3.23: Learn How to Develop a Marketing Budget   85
Learning Objective 3.24: Understand the Financial Performance Metrics Related
    to Marketing   85
Learning Objective 3.25: Understand the Nature of Marketing of Services   86
Learning Objective 3.26: Understand the Strategies in Product Management   87
Learning Objective 3.27: Understand the Stages in a Product Lifecycle   88

Learning Module 4   Quality and Process Management   91

Learning Objective 4.1: Understand the Basic Quality Concepts   91
Learning Objective 4.2: Understand the Various Definitions of Quality   93

Learning Objective 4.3: Calculate the Cost of Quality 94

Learning Objective 4.4: Calculate the Six-Sigma Metric 94

Learning Objective 4.5: Compute the Return-on-Quality Metric 96

Learning Objective 4.6: Apply Quality Tools 96

Learning Objective 4.7: Apply Statistical Process Control Techniques 98

Learning Objective 4.8: Compute Taguchi's Quality Loss Function 100

Learning Objective 4.9: Understand the Role of Inspection and Quality
at Source 100

Learning Objective 4.10: Understand the Process Management Methods
and Tools 101

Learning Module 5   Human Resources Management   103

Learning Objective 5.1: Understand the Human Resources Planning Process 103

Learning Objective 5.2: Understand the Relationship between Job Analysis
and Job Descriptions 104

Learning Objective 5.3: Understand the Recruitment Methods
and Alternatives 105

Learning Objective 5.4: Understand the Employee Selection Process 106

Learning Objective 5.5: Understand the Employee Selection Tests and their
Characteristics 107

Learning Objective 5.6: Understand the Employment Interview Process 108

Learning Objective 5.7: Understand the Pre-Employment Screening Process 108

Learning Objective 5.8: Understand the Employee Training and Development
Process 109

Learning Objective 5.9: Understand the Management Development Process 110

Learning Objective 5.10: Understand the Organization Development Process 111

Learning Objective 5.11: Understand the Career Planning and Development
Process 112

Learning Objective 5.12: Understand the Employee Performance Appraisal
Process 113

Learning Objective 5.13: Understand the Employee Relations Issues 114

Learning Objective 5.14: Compute the Human Capital Metrics 116

Learning Module 6   Accounting   119

Learning Objective 6.1: Understand the Basic Concepts of Financial
Accounting 120

Learning Objective 6.2: Understand the Purpose of the Accounting Cycle 121

Learning Objective 6.3: Understand the Types and Contents of Financial
Statements 122

Learning Objective 6.4: Understand the Intermediate Concepts of Financial
Accounting 128

Learning Objective 6.5: Understand the Advanced Concepts of Financial
Accounting 132

Learning Objective 6.6: Learn How to Analyze Financial Statements 133

Learning Objective 6.7: Understand Various Cost Concepts and Cost
Behaviors 140

Learning Objective 6.8: Understand the Principles and Techniques
of Operating Budgets 143

Learning Objective 6.9: Understand the Application of Transfer Pricing 146

Learning Objective 6.10: Understand the Application of Cost-Volume-Profit
Analysis 148

Learning Objective 6.11: Understand the Meaning and Application
of Relevant Costs 150

Learning Objective 6.12: Understand Various Costing Systems for Products and
   Services   151
Learning Objective 6.13: Understand the Meaning and Application of
   Responsibility Accounting   152

Learning Module 7   Finance   153

Learning Objective 7.1: Understand the Need for Financial Plans and Controls   154
Learning Objective 7.2: Understand the Principles and Techniques of Cash
   Management   157
Learning Objective 7.3: Understand the Techniques of Managing Current
   Assets   160
Learning Objective 7.4: Understand the Various Types of Debt and Equity in a
   Capital Structure   163
Learning Objective 7.5: Understand the Techniques for Evaluating the Cost
   of Capital   169
Learning Objective 7.6: Understand the Principles and Techniques of Capital
   Budgeting   171
Learning Objective 7.7: Understand the Various Types and Risks of Financial
   Instruments   179
Learning Objective 7.8: Understand the Various Types of Valuation Models   182
Learning Objective 7.9: Understand the Nature of Business Mergers
   and Acquisitions   185
Learning Objective 7.10: Understand the Implications of Dividend Policies,
   Stock Splits, Stock Dividends, and Stock Repurchases   187

Learning Module 8   Information Technology   191

Learning Objective 8.1: Understand How to Plan and Manage the Information
   Technology Function   192
Learning Objective 8.2: Understand How Business Application Systems are
   Developed and Maintained   196
Learning Objective 8.3: Understand How Business Application Systems are
   Operated and Improved   198
Learning Objective 8.4: Understand the Need for Contingency Plans to Ensure
   the Continuity of Business Operations   201
Learning Objective 8.5: Understand How Information Technology Operations
   Are Managed   207
Learning Objective 8.6: Understand the Technology Behind Computer
   Network Management   211
Learning Objective 8.7: Understand how to Manage the Information
   Technology Security Function   217
Learning Objective 8.8: Understand How Databases are Designed
   and Managed   223
Learning Objective 8.9: Understand How Electronic Commerce is Facilitated
   and Managed   228

Learning Module 9   Corporate Control, Law, Ethics, and Governance   235

Learning Objective 9.1: Understand the Nature and Types of Corporate
   Control Systems   236
Learning Objective 9.2: Understand the Nature and Types of Corporate Risk   241
Learning Objective 9.3: Understand the Scope and Nature of Business Law,
   Policy, and Ethics, Including Social Responsibility   247
Learning Objective 9.4: Understand the Various Issues in Corporate
   Governance   256
Learning Objective 9.5: Understand the Nature and Types of Corporate Audits   260

Learning Objective 9.6: Understand the Nature and Types of Corporate Fraud 263
Learning Objective 9.7: Understand the Issues in Corporate Law Regarding Agency Problems and Costs 266

Learning Module 10   **International Business**   **269**

Learning Objective 10.1: Understand How to Develop and Manage International Business Strategies 269
Learning Objective 10.2: Understand the Various Issues in International Trade and Investment 271
Learning Objective 10.3: Understand the Nature of International Production Economics 275
Learning Objective 10.4: Understand the Nature of International Trade Laws 276
Learning Objective 10.5: Understand the Various Issues in International Financial Systems 280
Learning Objective 10.6: Understand How to Staff and Manage International Operations 281
Learning Objective 10.7: Understand the Various Issues in Conducting International Business in Cross Cultures 281

Learning Module 11   **Project Management**   **287**

Learning Objective 11.1: Define Project Management and Identify Success Criteria for Projects 287
Learning Objective 11.2: Understand the Various Types of Risks in Project Management 289
Learning Objective 11.3: Understand the Various Types of Project Structures and Organizations 291
Learning Objective 11.4: Understand the Project Management Process, Including its Lifecycles 294
Learning Objective 11.5: Understand the Various Methods in Project Planning, Estimating, Controlling, and Reporting 296
Learning Objective 11.6: Understand the Various Methods in Project Scheduling 303
Learning Objective 11.7: Understand the Project Management Metrics, Problems, and Governance Mechanisms, Including Project Audits 306

Learning Module 12   **Decision Sciences and Managerial Economics**   **311**

Learning Objective 12.1: Learn How to Apply Quantitative Methods to Business 311
Learning Objective 12.2: Understand the Basic Principles and Concepts in Economics 321
Learning Objective 12.3: Understand the Basic Principles and Applications of Microeconomics 322
Learning Objective 12.4: Understand the Basic Principles and Applications of Macroeconomics 325
Learning Objective 12.5: Understand the Basic Principles and Applications of Key Economic Indicators 332
Learning Objective 12.6: Understand the Nature of Economic Business Cycles and Industry Growth Levels 333

References   **337**

Index   **339**

Preface

This is the book I wish I had before I started my MBA at the Harvard Business School.

I thought I would be adequately prepared for the rigors facing me, as I was a CPA and had worked for four years as a consultant at Arthur Andersen in its Chicago, Singapore, and Hong Kong offices. Nevertheless, and despite an undergraduate degree in business, as I began my first year at Harvard, I felt that I didn't have the core building blocks to take full advantage of the curriculum. I felt comfortable with the accounting and finance classes, but I had not been exposed to the vocabulary and concepts of operations management or to the quantitative side of marketing. As a result, I had to work two to three times as hard to keep up with engineers in operations management class and with the Procter & Gamble brand managers in marketing class. In other words, I had to work really hard just to have what I refer to as *Basic* or even *Intermediate* types of discussions while the engineers and the brand marketers were capable of Intermediate or even *Advanced* discussions. Because they had been exposed to the Basic or even Intermediate levels during their previous work experience, they were able to jump in and really dig deep into the coursework, just as I could in the accounting and finance classes.

How fast you move from engaging in Basic level discussions to more Advanced level discussions will determine your success in business school. If you only have minimal awareness of the issues and concepts, then you have a Basic level comprehension in a particular course. As you gain a better working knowledge, perform quantitative analysis, and can solve problems, you now have an Intermediate comprehension level. With an Advanced comprehension level, you can apply the concepts learned in one class to other classes in your MBA program and can begin to visualize the consequences of your analysis and decisions on the rest of the company. See the figure on the next page for further clarification. As you have more exposure to the subject matter, you can transition faster from the Basic types of discussions to the Advanced level discussions.

What surprised me even more was that many of my classmates had even less business experience than I had. They were seeing most of the first-year curriculum for the first time. In general, the majority of MBA aspirants probably is strong in two to three functional areas and will need to work on strengthening themselves in the other areas. For example, an engineer is going to be great at operations and may need to focus on accounting and strategy. An investment banker is strong in accounting and finance and may need to focus on marketing and operations. Your effectiveness in MBA coursework will depend on how fast you can get up to speed in the areas in which you are weak.

The top business schools excel at providing learning opportunities outside the classroom, such as team projects, independent study, job search and interviewing, attending company presentations, and socializing and networking with fellow classmates. If MBA students have to spend too much time just keeping their heads above water with coursework, they are not maximizing all of the learning opportunities that top business schools have to offer.

Earning an MBA is a big investment in time and money, so I encourage you to plan ahead. You prepared for your GMAT/CAT, so take the next step and plan for your MBA coursework. It is often said that the hardest part of the top MBA programs is getting in. I challenge that notion; getting admitted is just the starting point. In today's environment, there is more at stake than ever in doing well at school, so it is imperative that you prepare for what happens

Basic Discussions	Intermediate Discussions	Advanced Discussions
		Can proficiently apply concepts to any company and industry + Can discuss impact of concepts on other parts of the company + Can visualize the consequences of decisions on other stakeholders
	Working knowledge of quantitative analysis + Can solve problems and make recommendations	Working knowledge of quantitative analysis + Can solve problems and make recommendations
Vocabulary + Minimal awareness of issues and concepts	Vocabulary + Minimal awareness of issues and concepts	Vocabulary + Minimal awareness of issues and concepts

with no previous exposure →

with previous exposure →

after you get in. You want to be armed with a solid foundation across the entire curriculum so that you can interact with peers and professors at a higher, more advanced level. The better prepared you are in terms of subject matter from MBA IQ, the more you can get out of the MBA program, ultimately resulting in getting the job you want, which is the primary goal of attending business school.

For those of you who do not want to pursue an MBA, this book and the accompanying online assessment provide a roadmap for further management education irrespective of the MBA degree. Most of the topics covered in the book can be developed further through your corporate training and development department or through third-party training organizations.

My experience over the last nine years as the founder and CEO of Association of Professionals in Business Management (APBM), a nonprofit higher education organization, has enabled me to assemble the range of topics necessary for all business managers, with or without an MBA. Having worked through the dot-com rise and fall, the implosion of Enron, WorldCom, and Arthur Andersen, increased globalization, and the latest financial industry crisis, I am more convinced than ever that all business managers need to be proficient in the topics covered in this book in order to have a job security, career advancement, and a positive societal impact.

My personal story is what inspired me to write this book. However, two other books reinforced the MBA IQ process. Malcolm Gladwell's *Outliers* and Geoff Colvin's *Talent Is Overrated* suggest that exceptional performance in any field, including business, is a result of "deliberate practice." My goal for you is to view the MBA IQ process as deliberate practice to build and develop your career. I don't expect you to master the 12 Learning Modules presented in this book immediately. It may take several jobs and years for you to truly see the interdependencies of these modules. I don't want you to get discouraged at a low initial score. As you gain more knowledge and experience, you will see for yourself how your MBA IQ score progresses over time. That's the whole point. In other words, your MBA IQ will mirror your career development.

This book covers a lot of material—it reflects the increased responsibility placed on today's business manager. I am grateful to be in a position to help managers in their career development efforts.

With no bias intended and for the sake of simplicity, the pronoun "he" has been used throughout the book rather than "he/she" or "he" or "she."

DEVI VALLABHANENI
Chicago, IL
September 2009
www.mbaiq.com

Acknowledgments

I would like to first and foremost thank Sheck Cho of John Wiley & Sons for bringing forth this project. Sheck, thank you for seeing the vision and guiding me through this process. Stacey Rivera and Natasha Andrews-Noel of Wiley, I appreciate your patience in reviewing and editing the very long and detailed manuscript.

Dean Dipak Jain of Kellogg School of Management, Professor Rakesh Khurana of Harvard Business School, and Professor Deborah Ancona of MIT's Sloan School of Management: thank you for your suggestions and input regarding the topics to be covered in this book. Rakesh, a hearty thanks to you for all of our touch-base calls and the tremendous support you have shown over the years.

Dennis Chookaszian, thank you for discussing the various ways the self-assessment can be structured as well as all of the other suggestions you have provided me.

A special thanks to my friends and colleagues (in alphabetical order)—Carol Allen, Peri Altan, Carine Beer, Marie Cohen, Kerry Whorton Cooper, Alison and Greg Deldicque, Jen and Amit Dhadwal, April Diehl, Mark Donofrio, Matt Finick, Lori Flees, Mary Glasser, Melissa Hayes, Barb Hoffman, Karen Klutznick, Mary-Jo Kovach, Alex Lach, William Levacy, Michael Littlejohn, Luba McElroy, Armeen and Zeeshan Mirza, Ron Mitchell, Sharon Novaaaaak, Bill Paladino, Helene Roux, Michael Sprague, Sean Stowers, John Wannamacher, Tim Westerbeck, and Craig Will—thank you for being extremely supportive and for letting me ask you for your opinions and suggestions. Your guidance and patience are very much appreciated. You know that I can get rather focused at times. Lisa Schuble, it's great working with you to educate audiences about the value of this book to their career development.

I'd also like to thank Neal Maillet who, back in January 2007, first inspired in me the idea that I could become an author. You planted the seed that made this book possible. Jon Malysiak and Scott Adlington, thank you for being part of the journey. I hope we can find another project where we can work together. Dad, I really couldn't have completed this project without you. Mom, you made me who I am today.

I am truly grateful for my time at Harvard Business School, where I was convinced of the following: (1) a general management education needs to be accessible to all managers and (2) there is indeed a common body of knowledge that all managers need to know.

Last but not least, I'd like to thank my trusted colleague Karen Murphy who makes my life easier every day!

Introduction

This book provides business practitioners and MBA aspirants with a roadmap to facilitate advanced management education (i.e., MBA or CBM) and provides a structured approach for career development in the management profession.

Scope

An individual's MBA IQ is based on 12 Learning Modules, which reflect the scope of a general management education:

1. General Management, Leadership, and Strategy
2. Operations Management
3. Marketing Management
4. Quality and Process Management
5. Human Resources Management
6. Accounting
7. Finance
8. Information Technology
9. Corporate Control, Law, Ethics, and Governance
10. International Business
11. Project Management
12. Decision Sciences and Managerial Economics

These 12 Learning Modules have been compiled from multiple sources, such as MBA curricula, specialty professional certification programs in business, and corporate training and development programs. These modules together establish a common body of knowledge necessary for all business managers. This book exposes readers to that common body of knowledge.

Studies have revealed a positive correlation between job performance and functional knowledge and competence (i.e., the 12 Learning Modules). Strong job performance is also correlated to higher compensation, greater job security, and increased career opportunities.

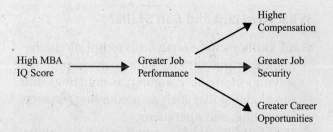

Score

You can compute your MBA IQ through the online self-assessment exercises at www.mbaiq.com. Each of the 12 Learning Modules is divided into specific learning objectives, which are the basis for the self-assessment exercises. The self-assessment exercises have awareness, knowledge, and experience components. In other words, your MBA IQ is a combination of these three components.

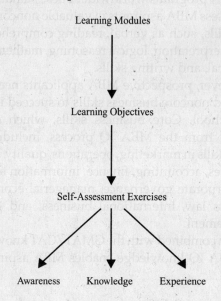

Leadership

In management literature and business media, the term *leadership* has come to connote personal characteristics, or soft skills. I believe the view of leadership needs to be broadened to include and perhaps even emphasize knowledge competencies, or hard skills. Today we need the competency-based type of leader. The competency-based leader is rooted in equal knowledge of hard and soft skills. A figurehead leader who possesses only soft skills is no longer acceptable to direct complex businesses and to lead knowledge workers. This book enables an individual to develop the knowledge, skills, and abilities to become a competency-based leader.

What Are Hard and Soft Skills?

Hard skills include analytical; technical; mathematical or quantitative data analysis; problem solving; strategic planning; negotiating; and functional skills, such as accounting/finance, marketing, and operations.

Soft skills include communication skills; decision-making skills; time-management skills; and people/interpersonal skills, such as motivation, teamwork, conflict management, and leadership skills.

Business School Admissions

The Graduate Management Admission Test (GMAT [worldwide]) and Common Admission Test (CAT [India]) are among the admissions requirements to top MBA programs worldwide. These standardized tests assess MBA aspirants in valuable noncore business skills, such as verbal, reading comprehension, data interpretation, logical reasoning, mathematical, analytical, and writing skills.

However, prospective MBA applicants need both core and noncore business skills to succeed in business school. Core business skills, which can be learned from the MBA IQ process, include functional skills in marketing, operations, quality, human resources, accounting, finance, information technology, corporate governance, managerial economics, business law, international business, and general management.

When combined with the GMAT/CAT knowledge, the MBA IQ knowledge enables MBA aspirants to maximize their coursework due to enhanced business knowledge and to be well prepared to take advanced MBA courses. Furthermore, the MBA IQ self-assessment enables people to cope with and put their best foot forward during the fast-paced MBA program.

GMAT/CAT → Noncore business skills

MBA IQ → Core business skills

GMAT/CAT + MBA IQ = Preparedness for an MBA program

In other words, there is built-in synergy among MBA IQ, GMAT/CAT, and MBA.

Business Practitioners
Career Development

The MBA IQ process is just as applicable to business practitioners who may never pursue an MBA degree because it provides them with a roadmap of hard skills needed to be effective business managers and to help in the transition from business specialists to business generalists.

The MBA IQ score reveals a person's knowledge gaps. We encourage business practitioners to use existing company training programs or third-party training programs in order to actively close these knowledge gaps. For example, if an accountant is strong in accounting and finance and perhaps weak in marketing and human resources (HR), we encourage him to be deliberate in strengthening his marketing and HR skills.

As the business practitioner takes on more assignments, receives promotions, or participates in cross-functional projects, we encourage him to recalculate his MBA IQ so that he actively manages his knowledge competencies. Upward career movement necessitates generalist rather than specialist knowledge. Using the accountant example again, his career trajectory is influenced more by his understanding of nonaccounting issues than by an even deeper level of understanding of accounting. More accounting knowledge and training will strengthen his specialist skills but not his generalist skills.

In the job search and recruiting process, we encourage business practitioners to include their MBA IQ score as part of their resumes, showing potential employers that they are actively managing their knowledge competencies in a generalist fashion. Employers value the fact that potential hires are actively monitoring their knowledge strengths and weaknesses.

Professional Certifications

Regardless of the MBA IQ score, an individual can pursue either the Certified Associate Manager (CABM) Credential or the Certified Business Manager (CBM) Credential. The CBM is a professional certification based on an MBA curriculum while the CABM is based on a pre-MBA curriculum. In other words, the CABM is a stepping-stone for the CBM or an MBA. There is a natural and built-in synergy among MBA IQ, the CABM/CBM Credentials, and the MBA due to a common syllabus.

The MBA IQ self-assessment can be used to satisfy the continuing professional education (CPE) hours required for various professional certifications in business, including the CABM and CBM. There are approximately 100 certifications in various functional areas, so please check with the continuing education requirements of your certification to make sure that the MBA IQ can be used for CPE hours.

Professional management certification options available to business practitioners with MBA IQ include:

Option 1: MBA IQ → CABM
Option 2: MBA IQ → CABM → CBM
Option 3: MBA IQ → CABM → MBA
Option 4: MBA IQ → CABM → MBA →CBM
Option 5: MBA IQ → CABM → CBM →MBA
Option 6: MBA IQ → CBM
Option 7: MBA IQ → CBM → MBA

Business Specialist versus Generalist

Business specialists work in a specific business function handling a single role. They still need to have a full understanding of the inner workings of other functions in order to become effective and efficient in their current jobs. To understand what it means to be a business generalist, please refer to the Generalist Manifesto at the end of this section.

Who Is a Business Specialist?

A business specialist is an individual working in accounting, auditing, advertising, marketing, risk management, project management, operations, supply chain, procurement, human resources, staffing and recruiting, information technology, software development, computer security, product development, sales, finance, treasury, brand management, engineering, program management, manufacturing, management consulting, investment banking, government contracts, quality assurance and control, service management, learning and development, logistics, organizational development, fraud, investment management, research and development, or international business.

At some point in a business specialist's career development, there will be a trade-off between increasing specialization and transitioning into a generalist. The MBA IQ process exposes business specialists to what is required in the transition. An example of how an accountant with CPA credential (a business specialist in accounting) can turn into a vice president of finance (a business generalist) either with CBM credential or MBA is shown next:

CPA + CBM → Vice President of Finance
CPA + MBA → Vice President of Finance

In today's flat organizational structures, resulting from downsizing and restructuring, generalists are prized by employers for their cross-functional knowledge. Management recognizes a business generalist because of his resourcefulness in handling multiple roles and tasks. This is because a generalist is a person who appears to be a specialist to a specialist and a generalist to a generalist.

A business specialist handles one role at a time. A business generalist handles multiple roles at a time.

Very often, business generalists are promoted to business managers, general managers, division/group directors, senior managers, vice presidents, senior vice presidents, executive vice presidents, and presidents due to their strong cross-functional knowledge base, greater core competencies with big-picture focus, and general management skills. In essence, these generalists manage more than one business function at a time in an efficient and effective manner.

The figure below shows why business specialists must move to become business generalists on their career trajectory, moving from an entry-level job to a mid-level to an executive-level position. The MBA IQ knowledge can facilitate a smooth transition among these levels.

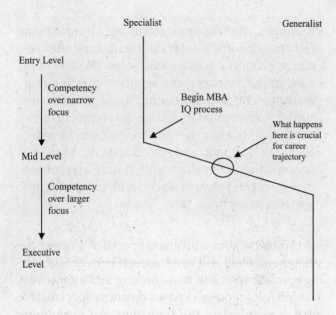

Generalist Manifesto

A generalist:

1. Understands where, when, and how a business function fits into the rest of the organization.
2. Is cognizant of the key drivers of each function as well as the entire organization.
3. Makes decisions that are best for the entire organization, not at the expense of other functions.
4. Has an understanding of the level of impact (i.e., low, medium, and high) of a decision taken by one function on other, interrelated functions of an organization.
5. Appreciates how the rate of business velocities (i.e., sales, inventory, production, finance, human resources, and systems) in a specific business unit affects other business units.

6. Has an understanding of how the Chain of Knowledge is established, maintained, and applied to employees and to the management hierarchy in order to keep the knowledge base consistent and current.
7. Listens to all stakeholder voices at one time instead of listening to one voice at a time and has the ability to integrate all voices simultaneously.
8. Has a greater working knowledge of the industry in which an employee works and a company operates and how that industry knowledge affects the inter- and intra-industries.
9. Filters business noise and understands the implications of management fads and has the ability to select and apply only what is right for the organization.
10. Possesses a strong functional knowledge of all business requirements and has the ability to keep that knowledge current through continuous learning, training, and self-improvement.
11. Solves business problems aimed at the root cause, instead of at the symptom, so that solutions have a far-reaching and positive effect.
12. Possesses a big-picture view of the entire company and the industry in which the company operates.
13. Is viewed by senior management as a potential candidate in the succession planning pool of talent.
14. Maintains an understanding and complies with all applicable laws, rules, and regulations affecting the organization and the industry to reduce or eliminate enterprise-wide risks.
15. Above all, is a person who appears to be a specialist to a specialist and a generalist to a generalist.

WHAT'S YOUR MBA IQ™?

General Management, Leadership, and Strategy

Learning Objective 1.1: Understand the Scope and Nature of Corporate Strategies — 2
Strategic Management Defined — 2
Strategic Management Process — 2
Strategic Planning Process — 5
Competitive Strategies — 6
Blue-Ocean/Red-Ocean Strategies — 7
McKinsey 7-S Framework — 8
Portfolio Techniques to Improve Strategy and Competitiveness — 8

Learning Objective 1.2: Understand the Importance of Planning and Organizing Skills — 10
Management Functions — 10
Planning Defined — 10
Organizing Defined — 11
Characteristics of Organization Structure — 11

Learning Objective 1.3: Understand the Importance of Directing and Leading Skills — 14
Leadership Defined — 14
Leadership Theories — 14
Other Theories of Leadership — 16
Leadership Categories — 16
Management Defined — 17
Management Skills Defined — 17
Management Types — 17
Managerial Roles — 18
Management Assumptions about Employees — 18
Leaders versus Managers versus Entrepreneurs — 19
Mentoring — 19
Delegation — 19

Learning Objective 1.4: Understand the Importance of Controlling and Measuring Skills — 19
Controlling Defined — 19
Management Controls — 20
Measuring Defined — 20

Learning Objective 1.5: Understand the Importance of Motivating Skills — 21
Motivation Defined — 21
Motivation Theories — 21
Motivation Strategies — 22

Learning Objective 1.6: Understand the Importance of Problem-Solving and Decision-Making Skills — 23
Problem Defined — 23
Problem-Solving Process — 23
Impediments to Problem Solving — 23
Reasons Individuals Solve Problems Differently — 24
Tools and Techniques for Problem Solving — 24
Decision Defined — 24
Decision-Making Process — 24
Facets of Decision Making — 24
Decision-Making Models — 24
Types of Decisions — 25
Types of Data Used in Decision Making — 25
Tools and Techniques for Decision Making — 25
Decision Making versus Problem Solving — 25
Group Dynamics — 25
Group Behaviors — 26
Factors Affecting Group Decisions — 26
Manager's Information Processing Styles — 26
Stages of Group Development — 26
Criteria and Determinants of Group Effectiveness — 27
Groups and Individuals — 27
Group Structures — 28
Methods Used in Team Building — 29

Learning Objective 1.7: Understand the Importance of Negotiating Skills — 30
Negotiation Defined — 30
Process of Negotiation — 30
Why Opposition? — 30
What Is Negotiation? — 30
Elements of Negotiation — 30
Modes of Negotiation — 31
Compromise versus Collaboration — 31

Do's and Don'ts of Negotiations	31
Added-Value Negotiating	32
BATNA	32

Learning Objective 1.8: Understand the Importance of Communication Skills   **32**

Communication Defined	33
Communication Chain	33
Formal Communications	34
Informal Communications	34
Barriers to Communication	34
Essentials for Effective Communication	35
Information Communicated by Others	35

Learning Objective 1.9: Understand the Importance of Conflict Management Skills   **35**

Conflict Defined	35
Personal Conflict Prevention and Control Methods	36
Group or Organizational Conflict Prevention and Control Methods	36
Tools for Managing Conflict	37

Learning Objective 1.10: Understand the Various Issues in Organizational Behavior, Culture, Change, Development, Effectiveness, and Decline   **38**

Organizational Behavior Defined	38
Organizational Culture Defined	39
Organizational Change Defined	39
Organizational Development Defined	41
Organizational Effectiveness Defined	41
Organizational Decline Defined	41

Learning Objective 1.11: Understand How to Measure and Manage Business Performance Results   **42**

Productivity Defined	42
Components of Productivity Measurement	42
Effectiveness, Efficiency, and Economy Defined	43
Design of Performance Measurement Systems	43

❑ Learning Objective 1.1: UNDERSTAND THE SCOPE AND NATURE OF CORPORATE STRATEGIES

The scope of this learning objective includes defining strategic management and its processes in terms of grand strategy and strategic planning, implementation, and control. It concludes with describing strategic planning process and competitive strategies.

Strategic Management Defined

Strategic management is the set of decisions and actions used to formulate and implement strategies that will provide a competitively superior fit between the organization and its environment so as to achieve organizational goals. Managers ask questions such as, "What changes and trends are occurring in the competitive environment? Who are our customers? What products or services should we offer? How can we offer those products and services most efficiently?" Answers to these questions help managers make choices about how to position their organization in the environment with respect to rival companies. Superior organizational performance is not a matter of luck. It is determined by the choices that managers make.

Strategic Management Process

Top executives use strategic management to define an overall direction for the organization. The **strategic management process** is defined as a series of activities:

> **Grand Strategy → Strategic Planning → Strategy Implementation → Strategic Control**

Grand Strategy

Grand strategy is the general plan of major action by which a firm intends to achieve its long-term goals. Grand strategies can be defined using four general categories: (1) growth, (2) stability, (3) retrenchment, and (4) global operations.

1. **Growth** can be promoted internally by investing in expansion or externally by acquiring additional business divisions. Internal growth can include development of new or changed products or expansion of current products into new markets. External growth typically involves **diversification,** which means the acquisition of businesses that are related to current product lines or that take the corporation into new areas. The number of companies choosing to grow through mergers and acquisitions is astounding, as organizations strive

to acquire the size and resources to compete on a global scale, to invest in new technology, and to control distribution channels and guarantee access to markets.

2. **Stability,** sometimes called a **pause strategy,** means that the organization wants to remain the same size or grow slowly and in a controlled fashion. The corporation wants to stay in its current business. After organizations have undergone a turbulent period of rapid growth, executives often focus on a stability strategy to integrate strategic business units and to ensure that the organization is working efficiently.

3. **Retrenchment** means that the organization goes through a period of forced decline by either shrinking current business units or selling off or liquidating entire businesses. The organization may have experienced a precipitous drop in demand for its products or services, prompting managers to order across-the-board cuts in personnel and expenditures. **Liquidation** means selling off a business unit for the cash value of the assets, thus terminating its existence. **Divestiture** involves the selling off of businesses that no longer seem central to the corporation. Studies show that between 33 and 50 percent of all acquisitions are later divested. Retrenchment is also called **downsizing.**

4. In today's **global operations,** senior executives try to formulate coherent strategies to provide synergy among worldwide operations for the purpose of fulfilling common goals. Each country or region represents a new market with the promise of increased sales and profits. In the international arena, companies face a strategic dilemma between global integration and national responsiveness. Organizations must decide whether they want each global affiliate to act autonomously or whether activities should be standardized and centralized across countries. This choice leads managers to select a basic grand strategy alternative such as globalization versus multidomestic strategy. Some corporations may seek to achieve both global integration and national responsiveness by using a **transnational strategy.**

Strategic Planning

The overall strategic management process begins when executives evaluate their current position with respect to mission, goals, and strategies. They then scan the organization's internal and external environments and identify strategic factors that might require change. Internal or external events might indicate a need to redefine the mission or goals or to formulate a new strategy at either the corporate, business unit, or functional level.

Strategy formulation includes the planning and decision making that lead to the establishment of the firm's goals and the development of a specific strategic plan. Strategy formulation may include assessing the external environment and internal problems and integrating the results into goals and strategy. This is in contrast to strategy implementation, which is the use of managerial and organizational tools to direct resources toward accomplishing strategic results. Strategy implementation is the administration and execution of the strategic plan. Managers may use persuasion, new equipment, changes in organization structure, or a reward system to ensure that employees and resources are used to make formulated strategy a reality.

Planning (formulating) strategy often begins with an assessment of the internal and external factors that will affect the organization's competitive situation. **Situation analysis** typically includes a search for SWOTs (strengths, weaknesses, opportunities, and threats) that affect organizational performance. Situation analysis is important to all companies but is crucial to those considering globalization because of the diverse environments in which they will operate. External information about opportunities and threats may be obtained from a variety of sources, including customers, government reports, professional journals, suppliers, bankers, friends in other organizations, consultants, or association meetings. Many firms hire special scanning organizations to provide them with newspaper clippings, Internet research, and analyses of relevant domestic and global trends. Some firms use more subtle techniques to learn about competitors, such as asking potential recruits about their visits to other companies, hiring people away from competitors, debriefing former employees or customers of competitors, taking plant tours posing as "innocent" visitors, and even buying competitors' garbage. In addition, many companies are hiring competitive intelligence professionals to scope out competitors.

Executives acquire information about internal strengths and weaknesses from a variety of reports, including budgets, financial ratios, profit-and-loss statements, and surveys of employee attitudes and satisfaction. Managers spend 80 percent of their time giving and receiving information. Through frequent face-to-face discussions and meetings with people at all levels of the hierarchy, executives build an understanding of the company's internal strengths and weaknesses.

Internal strengths are positive internal characteristics that the organization can exploit to achieve its strategic performance goals. **Internal weaknesses** are internal characteristics that might inhibit or restrict the organization's performance. The information sought typically pertains to specific functions such as marketing, finance, production, and research and development (R&D). Internal analysis also examines overall organization structure, management competence and quality, and human resource characteristics. Based on their understanding of these areas, managers can determine their strengths or weaknesses vis-à-vis other companies.

External threats are characteristics of the external environment that may prevent the organization from achieving its strategic goals. **External opportunities** are characteristics of the external environment that have the potential to help the organization achieve or exceed its strategic goals. Executives evaluate the external environment with information about various sectors. The task environment sectors are the most relevant to strategic behavior and include the behavior of competitors, customers, suppliers, and the labor supply. The general environment contains those sectors that have an indirect influence on the organization but nevertheless must be understood and incorporated into strategic behavior. The general environment includes technological developments, the economy, legal-political and international events, and sociocultural changes. Additional areas that might reveal opportunities or threats include pressure groups, interest groups, creditors, natural resources, and potentially competitive industries.

Strategy Implementation

The next step in the strategic management process is **strategy implementation**—how strategy is put into action. Some people argue that strategy implementation is the most difficult and important part of strategic management. No matter how creative the formulated strategy, the organization will not benefit if it is incorrectly implemented. In today's competitive environment, there is an increasing recognition of the need for more dynamic approaches to formulating as well as implementing strategies. Strategy is not a static, analytical process; it requires vision, intuition, and employee participation. Many organizations are abandoning central planning departments, and strategy is becoming an everyday part of the job for workers at all levels. Strategy implementation involves using several tools—parts of the firm that can be adjusted to put strategy into action. Once a new strategy is selected, it is implemented through changes in leadership, structure, information and control systems, and human resources. For strategy to be implemented successfully, all aspects of the organization need to be in congruence with the strategy. Implementation involves regularly making difficult decisions about doing things in a way that supports rather than undermines the organization's chosen strategy.

The difficulty of implementing strategy is greater when a company goes global. In the international arena, flexibility and superb communication emerge as mandatory leadership skills. Likewise, structural design must merge successfully with foreign cultures as well as link foreign operations to the home country. Managers must make decisions about how to structure the organization to achieve the desired level of global integration and local responsiveness. Information and control systems must fit the needs and incentives within local cultures.

Finally, the recruitment, training, transfer, promotion, and layoff of international human resources create an array of problems. Labor laws, guaranteed jobs, and cultural traditions of keeping unproductive employees on the job provide special problems for strategy implementation.

In summary, strategy implementation is essential for effective strategic management. Managers implement strategy through the tools of leadership, structural design, information and control systems, and human resources. Without effective implementation, even the most creative strategy will fail.

Strategic Control

A formal **control system** can help keep strategic plans on track. A control system (e.g., reward systems, pay incentives, budgets, IT systems, rules, policies, and procedures) should be proactive instead of reactive. Control should not stifle creativity and innovation since there is no tradeoff between control and creativity. Feedback is part of control.

The goal of a control system is to detect and correct problems in order to keep plans on target. This means negative results should prompt corrective action at the steps both immediately before and after problem identification. Some examples of corrective actions include updating assumptions, reformulating plans, rewriting polices and procedures, making personnel changes, modifying budget allocations, and improving IT systems.

Strategic Planning Process

The input to the **strategic planning process** is the strategic management process. The output of the strategic planning process is the development of a strategic plan. Its four components include:

1. **Organizational mission.** Every organization exists to accomplish something, and the **mission statement** is a reflection of this. The mission statement of an organization should be a long-term vision of what the organization is trying to become, the unique aim that differentiates the organization from similar ones. It raises questions such as "What is our business?" and "What should it be?" In developing a statement of mission, management must take into account three key elements:
   a. The organization's history
   b. The organization's distinctive competencies
   c. The organization's environment

   The organization's environment dictates the opportunities, constraints, and threats that must be identified before a mission statement is developed.

   When completed, an effective mission statement will be focused on markets rather than products, achievable, motivating, and specific. A key feature of mission statements has been an external rather than internal focus. This means, the mission statement should focus on the broad class of needs that the organization is seeking to satisfy (external focus), not on the physical product or service that the organization is offering at present (internal focus). As Peter Drucker put it, the question "What is our business?" can be answered only by looking at the business from the outside, from the point of view of customer and market.

   A mission statement should be realistic and achievable and should not lead the organization into unrealistic ventures far beyond its competencies. A mission statement is a guide to all employees and provides a shared sense of purpose and strong motivation to achieve objectives of the organization.

   A mission statement must be specific to provide direction to management when they are choosing between alternative courses of action. For example, a mission "to provide the highest quality products at the lowest possible cost" sounds good, but it is not specific enough to be useful. Specific quantitative goals are easier to measure.

2. **Organizational objectives.** An organization's mission is converted into specific, measurable, and action-oriented commitments and objectives. These objectives in turn provide direction, establish priorities, and facilitate management control. When these objectives are accomplished, the organization's mission is also accomplished. Peter Drucker advises at least eight areas for establishing objectives, including: (1) market standing, (2) innovations, (3) productivity, (4) physical and financial resources, (5) profitability, (6) manager performance and responsibility, (7) worker performance and attitude, and (8) social responsibility.

3. **Organizational strategies.** Organizational strategy involves identifying the general approaches a business should take in order to achieve its objectives. It sets the major directions for the organization to follow. Specific steps include understanding and managing the current customer and current products and identifying new customers and new products. Mission and objectives lead an organization where it wants to go. Strategies help an organization to get there.

   The organizational strategy described in terms of a product/market matrix is shown here:

	Current products	New products
Current customers	Market penetration	Product development
New customers	Market development	Diversification

   Market penetration strategy focuses on improving the position of the present product with its present customers. It involves designing a marketing plan to encourage customers to purchase more of a product. It can also include a production plan to produce more efficiently what is being produced at present. **Market development strategy** would seek to find new customers for its present products. With the **product development strategy**, new products are developed for present customers. **Diversification strategy** seeks new products for new customers.

4. **Organizational portfolio plan.** An organization can be thought of as a portfolio of businesses (i.e., combination of product lines and divisions and

service lines and divisions). It is understandable that some product lines will be more profitable than others. Management must decide which product lines or divisions to build, maintain, add, or eliminate.

Competitive Strategies

Porter's **five competitive forces** include (1) threat of new entrants, (2) rivalry among existing firms, (3) pressure from substitute products or services, (4) bargaining power of buyers, and (5) bargaining power of suppliers. All five competitive forces jointly determine the intensity of industry competition and profitability.

1. **Threat of new entrants.** New entrants to an industry bring new capacity and the desire to gain market share, and they often also bring substantial resources. As a result, prices can be low, cost can be high, and profits can be low. There is a relationship between threat of new entrants, barriers to entry, and reaction from existing competitors. For example:
   - If barriers are high and reaction is high, then the threat of entry is low.
   - If barriers are low and reaction is low, then the threat of entry is high.

   There are seven major barriers to entry, including: (1) economies of scale, (2) product differentiation, (3) capital requirements, (4) switching costs, (5) access to distribution channels, (6) cost disadvantages independent of scale, and (7) government policy.

2. **Rivalry among existing firms.** Rivalry tactics include price competition, advertising battles, new product introduction, and increased customer service or product/service warranties. Competitors are mutually dependent in terms of action and reaction, moves and countermoves, or offensive and defensive tactics. Intense rivalry is the result of a number of interacting structural factors, such as numerous or equally balanced competitors, slow industry growth, high fixed costs or storage costs, lack of differentiation or switching costs, capacity increased in large increments, diverse competitors, high strategic stakes, and high exit barriers.

3. **Pressure from substitute products or services.** In a broad sense, all firms in an industry are competitors with industries producing substitute products. Substitutes limit the potential returns of an industry by placing a ceiling on the prices firms can profitably charge. The more attractive the price–performance alternative offered by substitutes, the stronger or firmer the lid on industry profits. Substitute products that deserve the most attention are those that are subject to trends improving their price–performance trade-off with the industry's product or produced by industries earning high profits.

4. **Bargaining power of buyers.** Buyers compete with the industry by forcing down prices, bargaining for higher quality or more services, and playing competitors against each other—all at the expense of industry profits. A buyer group is powerful if the following circumstances hold true: it is concentrated or purchases large volumes relative to seller sales; the products it purchases from the industry represent a significant fraction of the buyer's costs or purchases; the products it purchases from the industry are standard or undifferentiated; it faces few switching costs; it earns low profits; buyers pose a credible threat of backward integration; the industry's product is unimportant to the quality of the buyers' products or services; and the buyer has full information about demand, prices, and costs. Informed customers (buyers) become empowered customers.

5. **Bargaining power of suppliers.** Suppliers can exert bargaining power over participants in an industry by threatening to raise prices or reduce the quality of purchased goods or services. The conditions making suppliers powerful tend to mirror those making buyers powerful. A supplier group is powerful if the following apply: it is dominated by a few companies and is more concentrated than the industry it sells to; it is not obligated to contend with other substitute products for sale to the industry; the industry is not an important customer of the supplier group; the supplier's product is an important input to the buyer's business; the supplier group's products are differentiated or it has built up switching costs; and the supplier group poses a threat of forward integration.

Competitive strategy involves taking offensive or defensive actions to create a better position in an industry and to cope with the five competitive forces in order to achieve a superior return on investment. Porter's **three competitive strategies** include: (1) differentiation, (2) low-cost leadership, and (3) focus.

The **differentiation strategy** involves an attempt to distinguish the firm's products or services from others in the industry. An organization may use advertising, distinctive product features, exceptional service, or new technology to achieve a product that is perceived as unique. This strategy usually targets customers who are not particularly concerned with price, so it can be quite profitable. The differentiation strategy can be profitable because customers are loyal and will pay high prices for the product. Companies that pursue a differentiation strategy typically need strong marketing abilities, a creative flair, and a reputation for leadership.

A differentiation strategy can reduce rivalry with competitors and fight off the threat of substitute products because customers are loyal to the company's brand. However, companies must remember that successful differentiation strategies require a number of costly activities, such as product research and design and extensive advertising.

With a **low-cost leadership strategy,** the organization aggressively seeks efficient facilities, pursues cost reductions, and uses tight cost controls to produce products more efficiently than competitors. A low-cost position means that the company can undercut competitors' prices and still offer comparable quality and earn a reasonable profit. Being a low-cost producer provides a successful strategy to defend against the five competitive forces. For example, the most efficient, low-cost company is in the best position to succeed in a price war while still making a profit. Likewise, the low-cost producer is protected from powerful customers and suppliers because customers cannot find lower prices elsewhere and because other buyers would have less slack for price negotiation with suppliers. If substitute products or potential new entrants occur, the low-cost producer is better positioned than higher-cost rivals to prevent loss of market share. The low price acts as a barrier against new entrants and substitute products.

The low-cost leadership strategy tries to increase market share by emphasizing low cost compared to competitors. This strategy is concerned primarily with stability rather than taking risks or seeking new opportunities for innovation and growth.

With Porter's third strategy, the **focus strategy,** the organization concentrates on a specific regional market or buyer group. The company will use either a focused differentiation or focused low-cost, but only for a narrow target market.

Managers must think carefully about which strategy will provide their company with its competitive advantage. In his studies, Porter found that some businesses did not consciously adopt one of these three strategies and were stuck with no strategic advantage. Without a strategic advantage, businesses earned below-average profits compared with those that used differentiation, cost leadership, or focus strategies.

These three strategies require different styles of leadership and can translate into different corporate cultures. A firm that is "stuck in the middle" is the one that has failed to develop its strategy in at least one of the three directions. The firm stuck in the middle has low profitability, lost high-volume customers, lost high-margin businesses, blurred corporate culture, and conflicting motivational systems. Risks in pursuing the three generic strategies include failing to attain or sustain the strategy and eroding the strategic advantage with industry evolution.

Blue-Ocean/Red-Ocean Strategies

Authors Kim and Mauborgne (Havard Business Review, October 2004) first discussed the concept of **blue-ocean strategy** where its scope encompasses all the industries not in existence today—the unknown market space that is untainted by competition. In blue-ocean strategy, demand is created rather than fought over. There is ample opportunity for both profits and growth created by blue-ocean strategy because it deals with new and uncontested market space that makes competition irrelevant.

On the other hand, **red-ocean strategy** works within the established market spaces that are slowly and steadily shrinking. It deals with old and highly contested market space where competition is relevant, vigorous, and overcrowded. One firm tries to steal a share of demand from other firms, instead of creating its own demand. The following table presents the differences between the red-ocean and blue-ocean strategies:

Red-Ocean Strategy	Blue-Ocean Strategy
Compete in existing market space	Create uncontested market space
Beat the competition	Make the competition irrelevant
Exploit existing demand	Create and capture new demand
Make the value/cost trade-off	Break the value/cost trade-off
Align the whole system of a company's activities with its strategic choice of differentiation or low cost separately	Align the whole system of a company's activities in pursuit of differentiation and low cost simultaneously

It is interesting to note that both the blue- and red-ocean strategies have always coexisted and always will, and the one who separates them and breaks out of the old mold will win big. Practical reality, therefore, requires that corporate management understand the strategic logic of both types of oceans before diving into them.

McKinsey 7-S Framework

The premier management consulting firm, McKinsey & Company, has developed a **7-S framework** as criteria for an organization's success. This framework includes seven elements: **structure, strategy, skills, staff, style, systems,** and **shared values**.

Structure is the way in which tasks and people are specialized and divided and authority is distributed. It consists of the basic grouping of activities and reporting relationships into organizational sub-units. It includes the mechanisms by which the activities of the members of the organization are coordinated. There are four basic structural forms—functional, divisional, matrix, and network, where the functional form is the most common of all.

Strategy is the way in which competitive advantage is achieved. It includes taking actions to gain a sustainable advantage over the competition, adopting a low-cost strategy, and differentiating products or services.

Skills include the distinctive competencies that reside in the organization. They can be distinctive competencies of people, management practices, systems, and/or technology.

Staff includes employees, their backgrounds, and competencies. It consists of the organization's approaches to recruitment, selection, and socialization. It focuses on how people are developed, how recruits are trained, socialized, and integrated, and how their careers are managed.

Style deals with the leadership style of top management and the overall operating style of the organization. Style impacts the norms employees follow and how they work and interact with each other and with customers.

Systems include the formal and informal processes and procedures used to manage the organization, including management control systems; performance measurement and reward systems; planning, budgeting, and resource allocation systems; information systems; and distribution systems.

Shared values are the core set of values that are widely shared in the organization and serve as

guiding principles of what is important. These values have great meaning to employees because they help focus attention and provide a broader sense of purpose. Shared values are one of the most important elements of an organization's culture.

In order to manage the change process and seek improvements needed, organizations are classifying these seven elements into two groups: hard S's and soft S's. Hard S's include strategy, structure, and systems, which are easier to change than the soft S's, and the change process can begin with hard S's. Soft S's include staffing, skills, style, and shared values, which are harder to change directly and take longer to do. Both hard S's and soft S's are equally important to an organization.

Portfolio Techniques to Improve Strategy and Competitiveness

A firm is said to have a **sustainable competitive advantage** over other firms when it has technical superiority, low-cost production, good customer service/product support, good location, adequate financial resources, continuing product innovations, and overall marketing skills.

Portfolio strategy pertains to the mix of business units and product lines that fit together in a logical way to provide synergy and competitive advantage for the corporation. For example, an individual might wish to diversify in an investment portfolio with some high-risk stocks, some low-risk stocks, some growth stocks, and perhaps a few fixed-income bonds. In much the same way, corporations like to have a balanced mix of business divisions called **strategic business units (SBUs).** An SBU has a unique business mission, product line, competitors, and markets relative to other SBUs in the corporation. Executives in charge of the entire corporation generally define the grand strategy and then bring together a portfolio of strategic business units to carry it out.

Portfolio models can help corporate management to determine how resources should be allocated among the various SBUs, consisting of product lines and/or divisions. The portfolio techniques are more useful at the corporate-level strategy than at the business-level or functional-level strategy. Two widely used portfolio models are (1) the Boston Consulting Group (BCG) matrix and (2) the General Electric (GE) model. Each model is presented in the following sections.

BCG Matrix Model

The **BCG matrix model** organizes businesses along two dimensions—business growth rate and market share. **Business growth rate** pertains to how rapidly the entire industry is increasing. **Market share** defines whether a business unit has a larger or smaller share than competitors. The combinations of high and low market share and high and low business growth provide four categories for a corporate portfolio.

The BCG matrix model utilizes a concept of **experience curves,** which are similar in concept to learning curves. The experience curve includes all costs associated with a product and implies that the per-unit cost of a product should fall, due to cumulative experience, as production volume increases. The manufacturer with the largest volume and market share should have the lowest marginal cost. The leader in market share should be able to underprice competitors and discourage entry into the market by potential competitors. As a result, the leader will achieve an acceptable return on investment.

The BCG model (growth/market share matrix) is based on the assumption that profitability and cash flows will be closely related to sales volume. Here, **growth** means use of cash, and **market share** means source of cash. Each SBU is classified in terms of its relative market share and the growth rate of the market the SBU is in, and each product is classified as stars, cash cows, dogs, or question marks. Relative market share is the market share of a firm relative to that of the largest competitor in the industry.

The following list describes the components of the BCG model:

- **Stars** are SBUs with a high market share of a high-growth market. They require large amounts of cash to sustain growth despite producing high profits.
- **Cash cows** are often market leaders (high market share), but the market they are in is a mature, slow-growth industry (low growth). They have a positive cash flow.
- **Dogs** are poorly performing SBUs that have a low market share of a low-growth market. They are modest cash users and need cash because of their weak competitive position.
- **Question marks (problem children)** are SBUs with a low market share of a new, high-growth market. They require large amounts of cash inflows to finance growth and are weak cash generators because of their poor competitive position. The

question mark business is risky: it could become a star, or it could fail.

The following is the desirable sequence of portfolio actions for the BCG model:

- A star SBU eventually becomes a cash cow as its market growth slows.
- Cash cow SBUs should be used to turn question marks into stars.
- Dog SBUs should either be harvested or divested from the portfolio.
- The question mark SBUs can be nurtured to become future stars.
- Unqualified question mark SBUs should be harvested until they become dogs.

GE Model

The **General Electric (GE) Model** is an alternative to the BCG model and it incorporates more information about market opportunities (industry attractiveness) and competitive positions (company/business strength) to allocate resources. The GE model emphasizes all the potential sources of business strength and all the factors that influence the long-term attractiveness of a market. All SBUs are classified in terms of business strength (i.e., strong, average, weak) and industry attractiveness (i.e., high, medium, low).

Business strength is made up of market share, quality leadership, technological position, company profitability, company strengths and weaknesses, and company image. The major components of **industry attractiveness** are market size, market share, market growth, industry profitability, and pricing.

Overall strategic choices include either to invest capital to build position, to hold the position by balancing cash generation and selective cash use, or to harvest or divest. The GE model incorporates subjective judgment, and accordingly, it is vulnerable to manipulation. However, it can be made stronger with the use of objective criteria.

BCG Matrix versus GE Model

Both the BCG matrix model and the GE model help in competitive analysis and provide a consistency check in formulating a competitive strategy for a particular industry. Either model can be used as per the manager's preference. However, if a competitor uses the BCG model because of experience curves, then a company can benefit by using the same model.

The following is a comparison among BCG, GE, and Porter:

- Both the BCG matrix and the GE model focus on corporate-level strategy accomplished through acquisition or divestment of business.
- Porter's five competitive forces and three competitive strategies focus on business-level strategy accomplished through competitive actions.

Despite its widespread use in allocating corporate resources and acceptance by managers, the BCG model has been criticized for:

- Focusing on market share and market growth as the primary indicators of profitability.
- Its assumption that the major source of SBU financing comes from internal means.
- Its assumption that the target market has been defined properly along with its interdependencies with other markets.

❑ Learning Objective 1.2: UNDERSTAND THE IMPORTANCE OF PLANNING AND ORGANIZING SKILLS

Planning and organizing are the first two functions of management, as discussed in this learning objective. Planning sets the direction for the other three functions of management, which are organizing, directing, and controlling.

Management Functions

Management is the attainment of organizational goals and objectives through planning, organizing, directing (leading), and controlling functions. Managers use a multitude of skills to perform these four functions in the process of utilizing an organization's resources in an effective and efficient manner. The correct sequence of management functions is shown here:

Planning → Organizing → Directing → Controlling

Planning Defined

Planning defines where the organization wants to be in the future and how to get there. Planning means defining goals for future organizational performance and deciding on the tasks and use of resources needed to attain them. A lack of planning—or poor planning—can hurt an organization's performance.

Types of plans include strategic, tactical, and operational plans. The time horizon for a **strategic plan** is between three and five years as it deals with the broadest and most complex issues that will have a dramatic impact, both positively and negatively, on the success and survival of an entire organization. The time horizon for a **tactical plan** is between one and two years as it deals with a specific business and its product lines by translating strategic plans. The time horizon for an **operational plan** is *less than a year* as it deals with a specific department and its functions by translating tactical plans. These three types of plans are interconnected.

Planning levels include corporate, business unit, and functional, which are developed by managers at various levels of the company. For example, strategic plans are developed at the corporate level and business unit level. Tactical plans are developed at the business unit level and functional level. Operational plans are developed only at the functional level. The lower levels support the higher levels, meaning that the functional level supports the business unit and corporate levels and that the business unit level supports the corporate level. A corporate-level strategy is concerned with the question, "What business are we in?"; "How do we compete?" is related to business unit–level strategy; and "How do we support our chosen strategy?" is related to functional-level strategy.

The following shows a linkage of planning levels to planning types:

Planning Levels	Planning Types
Corporate Level	Strategic Plans
Business Unit Level	Tactical Plans
Functional Level	Operational Plans

The **planning process** consists of six stages or steps: (1) analyzing external environment, (2) assessing internal resources, (3) establishing goals and objectives, (4) developing action plans, (5) implementing action plans, and (6) monitoring outcomes.

The **planning tools** include portfolio techniques, budgets, and performance goals, resulting from the translation of plans. Portfolio techniques include models to improve portfolio strategy and competitiveness. Budgets are financial goals and include operating budgets (e.g., revenue, expense, and income budgets) and capital budgets (e.g., to acquire long-term, fixed, assets). Budgets can be prepared using (1) either incremental-based or zero-based approach and (2) either top-down or bottom-up approach. Performance goals are nonfinancial in nature and should be specific, realistic, time bound, and measurable.

Organizing Defined

Organizing typically follows planning and reflects how the organization tries to accomplish the strategic plan. Organizing involves the assignment of tasks, the grouping of tasks into departments, and the assignment of authority and allocation of resources across the organization. Organizing is important because it follows from strategy in that strategy defines what to do and organizing defines how to do it. **Organization structure** is a tool that managers use to allocate resources for getting things accomplished.

Characteristics of Organization Structure

The design of an organization structure is important as it affects the success and survival of a company. Important characteristics include the following:

Authority, Responsibility, Accountability, and Delegation

Authority is the formal right of a manager to make decisions, to issue orders, and to allocate resources in order to achieve goals. Authority is vested in organizational position, accepted by the subordinate, and flows down the vertical hierarchy. **Responsibility** is the subordinate's duty to perform the assigned task, which is the flipside of the authority coin. **Accountability** brings both authority and responsibility together and requires the subordinates to report and justify task outcomes to superiors in the chain of command. **Delegation** is a transfer of authority and responsibility from a superior to subordinate, but accountability still rests with the superior.

Organization Charts

An **organization chart** is a visual display of an organization's managerial pyramid. Such charts show how departments are tied together along the principal lines of authority. They show reporting relationships, not lines of communication. Organization charts are tools of management to deploy human resources and are common in both profit and nonprofit organizations. Every organization chart has two dimensions—horizontal hierarchy and vertical

hierarchy—and two types—formal and informal. These two dimensions represent the division of labor and chain of command respectively.

> ### Division of Labor and Chain of Command
>
> **Division of labor** or **work specialization** is the degree to which tasks are subdivided into separate, single, and narrow jobs. Many companies are moving away from specialization and enlarging jobs to provide greater challenge so that employees can rotate among several jobs.
>
> **Chain of command** is an unbroken line of authority that links all employees and specifies who reports to whom. The chain of command is linked to two principles: **unity of command** (one subordinate is accountable to one supervisor) and **scalar principle** (a clearly defined line of authority).

Horizontal hierarchy establishes the division of labor and specialization, such as marketing, production, and finance. Generally, specialization is achieved at the expense of coordination when designing organizations. A workable balance between specialization and coordination can be achieved through contingency design. The horizontal hierarchy does not show responsibilities, cannot show informal organization, cannot show all lines of communication, and does not show reporting channels or hierarchy of authority. A person with a lower job rank may be shown at a higher level on the chart (e.g., administrative secretary or assistant). Networking is accomplished through horizontal hierarchy where the interaction of persons of equal status is taking place for the purpose of professional or moral support.

Vertical hierarchy establishes the chain of command, or who reports to whom. It does not show responsibilities, cannot show informal organization, and cannot show all lines of communication. A person with a lower job rank may be shown at a higher level on the chart (e.g., administrative secretary or assistant).

The **formal chart** is a documented, official map of the company's departments with appointed leaders who get things done through power granted by their superiors. Formal charts have job titles.

The **informal chart** is not documented and is composed of natural leaders who get things done through power granted by peers. Informal charts have no job titles.

Implications of Organization Charts

Job title does not necessarily indicate everything about an employee's level of authority.

Organization charts work in routine and predictable task environments.

Organization charts do not work in nonroutine and unpredictable task environments.

Nominal power lies in formal organization charts.

Real power lies in informal organization charts.

Supervisors and managers need to use the informal power network to get things done.

The formal organization chart may not always keep track of changes in power relationships.

Formal leaders have the nominal power, whereas informal leaders have the real power.

There may be several informal leaders but only one or two formal leaders (natural leaders) in each area of a company.

Span of Control or Span of Management

The **span of control** (or **span of management**) refers to the number of subordinates reporting to a superior and indicates how closely a supervisor can monitor subordinates. It has two dimensions:

1. **Narrow and wide.** The number of people who report directly to a manager represents that manager's span of control or span of management. The optimal size of a span of control in a work area is dependent on the department's function, organizational levels, changes in the nature of the work, and the clarity of instructions given employees. The optimal span of control is not dependent on the total number of employees in the department or company.

Varieties of Span of Control

Narrow span of control means few people to oversee, which in turn creates many hierarchical levels (tall organizations), which in turn requires many managers. The number of subordinates supervised is small. Workers may be geographically dispersed.

Wide span of control means many people to oversee, which in turn creates few hierarchical levels (flat organizations), which in turn requires few managers. Jobs are similar, procedures are standardized, all workers are in the same work area, and tasks are simple and repetitive. An upper limit of the number of employees supervised must exist.

Obviously, a balance between too little and too much supervision is required. The ideal span of control ranges from 4 subordinates at the top of the organization to 12 at the lowest level. The reason for the difference is that top-level managers are supervising people and lower-level managers are responsible for supervising specific tasks.

2. **Tall and flat.** A tall organization has many levels of hierarchy and a narrow span of control. A flat organization structure is one with relatively few levels of hierarchy and is characterized by a wide span of management control.

Varieties of Organization Structure

A **tall structure** has a narrow span, is vertically focused, and has more hierarchical levels.

A **flat structure** has a wide span, is horizontally focused, and has fewer hierarchical levels. The trend is toward wider span of control (flat structure) to facilitate delegation.

Line and Staff Organization Structures

Line and staff organization structure is designed to maximize the unity-of-command principle by giving only the managers the authority to make decisions affecting those in the chain of command. There is no crossover between line and staff organization structure since each structure has its own chain of command.

Line managers have the authority to make decisions and give orders to all subordinates in the chain of command. Staff authority is generally limited to subordinates within its department. There is a natural conflict between these two parties due to power differences and various backgrounds.

One important source of conflict is that line employees have formal authority while staff employees have informal power. Line managers tend to emphasize decisiveness, results, costs, and implementation, whereas staff members advise and prefer completeness, controls, adherence to policies and procedures, and systematic analysis to solve organizational problems. The staff function supports the line function but does not control it.

Differences between Line and Staff Authority

Managers with **line authority** can direct and control immediate subordinates and resources, whereas managers with **staff authority** can merely advise, recommend, and counsel.

Organization Systems and Management Structures

Two organization systems—closed system and open system—and two management structures—mechanistic and organic—are discussed. A relationship between organization systems and management structures is established.

A **closed system** is independent of its external environment; it is autonomous, enclosed, and sealed off from the external environment. It focuses on internal systems only. Its external environment is simple, stable, and predictable. The major issue for management is to run the business efficiently with centralized decision making and authority. It represents a bureaucratic organization. The **traditional view of organizations** has closed-system thinking and assumes that the surrounding environment is fairly predictable and that uncertainty within the organization can be eliminated through proper planning and strict control. The primary goal is economic efficiency. All goal-directed variables are known and controllable.

An **open system** is dependent on its environment to survive; it both consumes resources and exports resources to the external environment. It transforms inputs into outputs. It must continuously change and adapt to the external environment. Open systems are complex, unstable, and unpredictable and internal efficiency is a minor issue for management. It represents a modern organization. The **modern view of organizations** has open-system thinking and assumes that both the organization and its surrounding environments are filled with variables that are difficult to predict or control. The organization interacts continuously with an uncertain environment. The primary goal is survival in an environment of uncertainty and surprise. The modern view deals with more variables that cannot be controlled or predicted.

A **mechanistic structure** is characterized by rules, procedures, and a clear hierarchy of authority. Organizations are formalized and centralized, and the external environment is stable.

An **organic structure** is characterized by a fluid and free-flowing nature, which adapts to changes in the external environment with little or no written rules and regulations and operates without a clear hierarchy of authority. Organizations are informal and decentralized, and responsibility flows down to lower levels. It encourages teamwork and problem solving by letting employees work directly with each other.

Types of Management Structures

A **mechanistic management structure** resembles a closed system of an organization.

An **organic management structure** resembles an open system of an organization.

Centralized, Decentralized, and Matrix Organizations

Two methods of organizing are centralized and decentralized. In a **centralized organization,** decisions are made at higher levels of management. Decisions in a **decentralized organization** are made at lower levels. Authority is delegated to lower levels of the organization.

The extent of an organization's centralization or decentralization is determined by the span of control, the number of levels in the hierarchy, and the degree of coordination and specialization. Centralization is typically used in those organizations that emphasize coordination of decisions that must be applied uniformly to a set of known or common problems. Companies that allow managers a great deal of autonomy are described as utilizing decentralized management.

Departmentalization is the basis for grouping positions into departments and departments into the total organization. The three traditional approaches (e.g., the vertical functional approach, divisional approach, and matrix approach), based on departmentalization, rely on the chain of command to define departmental groupings and reporting relationships along the hierarchy. The three contemporary approaches (e.g., team approach, network approach, and virtual approach), not based on departmentalization, have emerged to meet changing organizational needs in a global knowledge-based business environment.

In a **matrix organization,** people with vertical (down) and horizontal (across) lines of authority are combined to accomplish a specific objective. This design is suitable to a project environment where the project manager is responsible for completing a project without a formal line authority. Under these conditions, project managers tend to use negotiation skills, persuasive ability, technical competence, and the exchange of favors to complete a project in order to compensate for their lack of formal authority.

A matrix organization structure will likely have unity-of-command problems unless there is frequent and comprehensive communication between the various functional managers and project managers.

❑ Learning Objective 1.3: UNDERSTAND THE IMPORTANCE OF DIRECTING AND LEADING SKILLS

Much has been written about leading, and this learning objective will discuss leadership theories and categories and compare leaders with managers and entrepreneurs.

Leadership Defined

Directing (leading) is the third function of management. Providing leadership is becoming an increasingly important management function. **Leading** is the use of influence to motivate employees to achieve organizational goals. Leading means creating a shared culture and values, communicating goals to employees throughout the organization, and infusing employees with the desire to perform at a high level. Leading involves motivating entire departments and divisions as well as those individuals working immediately with the manager. In an era of uncertainty, international competition, and a growing diversity of the workforce, the ability to shape culture, communicate goals, and motivate employees is critical to business success.

One doesn't have to be a well-known top manager to be an exceptional leader. There are many managers working quietly who also provide strong leadership within departments, teams, not-for-profit organizations, and small businesses.

Leadership Theories

The evolution of leadership theory can be presented in four ways.

Trait Leadership Theory

It was once assumed that leaders are born and not made. Later, this assumption was changed to accept that leadership traits are not completely inborn but can be acquired through learning and experience.

One way to approach leadership characteristics is to analyze autocratic (bureaucratic) and democratic leaders. A **autocratic leader** is one who tends to centralize authority and rely on reward, coercive, and legitimate power (position power) to manage subordinates. A **democratic leader** is one who delegates authority to others, encourages participation, and relies on referent and expert power (personal power) to manage subordinates.

Although hundreds of physical, mental, and personality traits were said to be the key determinants of successful leadership, researchers reached agreement on only five traits: (1) intelligence, (2) scholarship, (3) dependability in exercising responsibilities, (4) activity and social participation, and (5) socioeconomic status. Trait profiles do provide a useful framework for examining what it takes to be a good leader.

Behavioral Styles Leadership Theory

Researchers began turning their attention to patterns of leader behavior instead of concentrating on the personal traits of successful leaders. In other words, attention turned from who the leader was to how the leader actually behaved. Subordinates preferred managers who had a democratic style to those with an authoritarian style or a laissez-faire (hands-off) style.

Three popular models that received a great deal of attention are the **Ohio State University Model**, the **University of Michigan Model**, and the **Leadership Grid** developed by Blake and Mouton at the University of Texas.

1. A team of **Ohio State University** researchers defined two independent dimensions of leader behavior as initiating structure (leader getting things organized and getting the job done) and consideration (degree of trust, friendship, respect, and warmth of a leader). It was concluded that high initiating structure combined with high consideration is generally the best all-around style.
2. The **University of Michigan Model** focused on the behavior of effective and ineffective supervisors. The study classified two types of leaders:
   a. **Employee-centered leaders** (effective supervisors), who established high performance goals and displayed supportive behavior toward subordinates.

b. **Job-centered leaders** (ineffective supervisors), who are less concerned about goal achievement and human needs and more concerned about meeting schedules, keeping costs low, and achieving production efficiency.

3. In the **Leadership Grid,** Blake and Mouton remain convinced that there is one best style of leadership. They described this in a grid with two axes, scaling each axis from 1 to 9: horizontal (x) axis representing a concern for production involving a desire to achieve greater output, cost effectiveness, and profits; vertical (y) axis representing a concern for people involving promoting friendship, helping coworkers get the job done, and attending to things that matter to people, like pay and working conditions.

By scaling each axis from 1 to 9, the grid consists of the following five leadership styles:

a. **Authority-compliance management** where primary concern is for production and people are secondary (9,1 style).

b. **Country club management** where primary concern is for people and production is secondary (1,9 style).

c. **Impoverished management** where minimal concern is for either production or people (1,1 style).

d. **Middle-of-the-road management** where moderate concern is for both production and people to maintain the status quo (5,5 style).

e. **Team management** where high concern is for both production and people as evidenced by personal commitment, mutual trust, and teamwork (9,9 style).

Most managers prefer the 9,9 style, regardless of the situation at hand, since this style correlates positively with better results, better mental and physical health, and effective conflict resolution. The 9,9 style represents a high concern for both production and people as evidenced by personal commitment, mutual trust, and teamwork.

Situational Leadership Theory

Situational theory or contingency thinking is based on the assumption that successful leadership occurs when the leader's style matches the situation. It stresses the need for flexibility and rejects the notion of a universally applicable style.

Different approaches to situational leadership include: Fiedler's contingency theory, the path-goal theory, and the Vroom/Yetton/Jago decision-making model.

1. **Fiedler's contingency theory,** which is thoroughly tested, is based on two assumptions. The performance of a leader depends on two inter-related factors: (1) the degree to which the situation gives the leader control and influence to accomplish the job and (2) the leader's basic motivation whether to accomplish the task or have close supportive relations with others (task-motivated leader has a concern for production and relationship-motivated leader has a concern for people).

Fiedler and his colleagues summed up their findings by noting that "everything points to the conclusion that there is no such thing as an ideal leader." Instead, *there are leaders, and there are situations.* The challenge to a manager is to analyze a leader's basic motivation and then match that leader with a suitable situation to form a product in combination. Fiedler believes that it is more efficient to move leaders to a suitable situation than to tamper with their personalities by trying to get task-motivated leaders to become relationship-motivated or vice versa.

2. The **path-goal theory,** which is a derivative of expectancy motivation theory, emphasizes that leaders should motivate their followers by providing clear goals and meaningful incentives for reaching them. *Motivation is seen as essential to effective leadership.*

Path-goal proponents believe that managers need to rely contingently on four different leadership styles since personal characteristics of subordinates, environmental pressures, and work demands on subordinates will all vary from situation to situation. These four leadership styles include **directive** (tell people what to do), **supportive** (treat subordinates as equals), **participative** (consult with subordinates), and **achievement oriented** (set challenging goals). For example, a directive situational leadership style would be appropriate for a subordinate who possesses very low task maturity for a particular assignment.

3. **Vroom/Yetton/Jago decision-making model.**
Vroom helped develop the expectancy theory of motivation based on the assumption that motivational strength is determined by perceived probabilities of success. The term **expectancy** refers to the subjective probabilities (or

expectancy) that one thing will lead to another. Researchers Vroom, Yetton, and Jago (the Vroom model) portray leadership as a decision-making process with five distinct decision-making styles, each of which requires a different degree of subordinates' participation. The Vroom model qualifies as a situational-leadership theory because it prescribes different decision styles for varying situations managers typically encounter.

The makeup of these five decision-making styles is: two are autocratic (low degree of subordinate participation), two are consultative (moderate degree of subordinate participation), and one is group directed (high degree of subordinate participation). In addition, the Vroom model gives managers the tools for matching styles with various individual and group situations.

Transformational Leadership Theory

Transformational leaders are characterized as visionaries who challenge people to achieve exceptionally high levels of morality, motivation, and performance. The transformational leaders are masters of change, have charisma, rely on referent power and can envision a better future, effectively communicate that vision, and get others to willingly make it a reality. A **charismatic leader** is one who has the ability to motivate subordinates to transcend their expected performance. A charismatic leader is also a **visionary leader** who speaks to the hearts of subordinates, getting them to be a part of his vision.

There is a distinction between a transactional leader and a transformational leader. **Transactional leaders** monitor people so they do the expected, according to plan (i.e., maintain status quo). In contrast, transformational leaders inspire people to do the unexpected, above and beyond the plan (fostering creative and productive growth).

Other Theories of Leadership

Several new leadership theories are in place in light of globalization, e-commerce, employee diversity, and virtual organizations. They include the following:

- **Level 5 leader** has no ego as he reaches the highest level in the management hierarchy in terms of knowledge, skills, and abilities (KSAs). He gives credit for successes to his subordinates while taking responsibility for failures.

- **Interactive leader** is one who uses consensual and collaborative process in problem solving and decision making by including subordinates, and his power is derived from relationship building and caring attitudes instead of position power. Female leaders are found to be better than male leaders as interactive leaders because often they can motivate, communicate, and listen better.
- **Virtual leader** is one who is open-minded, flexible, and exhibits positive attitudes that focus on solution instead of problems. He is good at communicating, coaching, building relationships, and caring skills.
- **Servant leader** is one who operates on two levels: (1) to fulfill subordinates' needs and goals and (2) to achieve the organization's mission. He gives away power, ideas, information, recognition, and credit to subordinates. He connects the subordinate's motives to the organization's mission. The servant leadership position is upside down, meaning that the leader serves the subordinates working for him and the organization that he works for. The servant leader is at the bottom and others are at the top.

Leadership Categories

Leadership is of two categories: formal and informal. Effective leadership is associated with both better performance and more ethical performance. According to Chester Schriesheim, James Tolliver, and Orlando Behling, leadership is "a social influence process in which the leader seeks the voluntary participation of subordinates in an effort to reach organizational objectives."

The following list compares formal leaders with informal leaders:

- Formal leaders have a measure of legitimate power because of their formal authority. Informal leaders lack formal authority.
- Both formal and informal leaders rely on an expedient combination of reward, coercive, referent, and expert power.
- Both formal and informal leaders can be an asset or a liability to the organization (asset when they work for the organization; liability when they work against the organization).

Power is needed in all organizations. Power must be used because managers must influence those they depend on. It is powerlessness, not power, that undermines organizational effectiveness.

Power is the ability to manage all types of resources to accomplish something of value to the organization. These resources could be human, material, and informational in content. Power affects organizational members in three areas: decision making, behavior, and situations. Another dimension to power is to distinguish between "power over" (ability to dominate), "power to" (ability to act freely), and "power from" (ability to resist the demands of others).

Experts on power say that power is neutral. It is a tool that can be used in a positive or negative manner. Power exercised for power's sake can be quite dangerous to all parties affected. The five sources of power exhibited by leaders include:

1. Reward power is gaining compliance through rewards.
2. Coercive power is gaining compliance through fear or threat of punishment.
3. Legitimate power is compliance based on one's formal position and parallels formal authority (job title). It can be eroded by its frequent abuse (or overuse).
4. Referent power is compliance based on charisma, personal identification, or attraction and has no relation to job title.
5. Expert power is compliance based on the ability to dispense valued information and is based on the knowledge or skills possessed by a person.

Note that sources 1, 2, and 3 are based on position power while sources 4 and 5 are based on personal power.

Management Defined

Management is the attainment of organizational goals and objectives through four functions: planning, organizing, directing (leading), and controlling organizational resources in an effective and efficient manner.

Management Skills Defined

Management skills can be broadly classified as conceptual, human, and technical. These skills are not exhibited equally across management levels. They vary with the nature of the job, the level of decision making, and the type of interaction with people.

Conceptual skill is the cognitive ability to see the organization as a whole and the relationship among its parts. It involves the manager's thinking, information processing, and planning. It requires the ability to think strategically—to take a broad, long-term view. Conceptual skills are needed by all managers but are especially important for managers at the top. Many of the responsibilities of top managers, such as decision making, resource allocation, and innovation, require a broad view.

Human skill is the manager's ability to work with and through other people and to work effectively as a group member. It includes the ability to motivate, facilitate, coordinate, lead, communicate, and resolve conflicts. As globalization, workforce diversity, uncertainty, and competition for highly skilled knowledge workers increase, human skills become even more crucial. Here, focus is on emotional needs of employees instead of the physical needs related to the job.

Technical skill is the understanding of and proficiency in the performance of specific tasks. It includes mastery of the methods, techniques, and equipment involved in specific functions such as engineering, manufacturing, or finance. These skills are particularly important at lower organizational levels. Many managers get promoted to their first management job by having excellent technical skills. However, technical skills become less important than human and conceptual skills as managers move up the hierarchy.

The following is a highest-to-lowest order of importance of these skills for three types of management levels:

First-line supervisor: technical, human, conceptual
Middle-level manager: human, technical, conceptual
Senior-level manager: human, conceptual, technical

Management Types

Managers use conceptual, human, and technical skills to perform the four management functions of planning, organizing, leading, and controlling in all organizations. But not all managers' jobs are the same. Managers are responsible for different departments, work at different levels in the hierarchy, and meet different requirements for achieving high performance. Two management types include:

1. **Vertical differences.** An important determinant of the manager's job is hierarchical level. Three levels in the hierarchy include top managers, middle managers, and front-line (first-line) managers. **Top managers** are responsible for setting organizational goals, defining strategies for achieving

them, monitoring and interpreting the external environment, and making decisions that affect the entire organization. They share a long-term vision for the organization, shape corporate culture, and nurture an entrepreneurial spirit that can help the company keep pace with rapid change. **Middle managers** are responsible for implementing the overall strategies and policies defined by top managers. They are concerned with the near future and are expected to establish good relationships with peers around the organization, encourage teamwork, and resolve conflicts. **First-line managers** are directly responsible for the production of goods and services. They include titles such as supervisor, line manager, section chief, and office manager. Their primary concern is the application of rules and procedures to achieve efficient production, provide technical assistance, and motivate subordinates. The time horizon is short, with the emphasis on accomplishing day-to-day goals.

2. **Horizontal differences.** The other major difference in management jobs occurs horizontally across the organization. These jobs include functional managers and general managers. **Functional managers** are responsible for departments that perform a single functional task and have employees with similar training and skills. **Line managers** are responsible for the manufacturing (operations) and marketing departments that make or sell the product or service. **Staff managers** are in charge of departments such as finance and human resources that support the line managers. **General managers** are responsible for several departments that perform different functions. **Project managers** also have general management responsibility because they coordinate people across several departments to accomplish a specific project.

Managerial Roles

Henry Mintzberg studied what managers do by focusing on the key roles they play. He criticized the traditional, functional approach as unrealistic in that it does not tell what managers actually do. Mintzberg believes that the functional approach portrays the management process as far more systematic and rational and less complex than it really is.

In his view, the average manager is not the reflective planner and precise "orchestra leader" that the functional approach suggests. Mintzberg used a method called **structured observation**, which included recording the activities and correspondence of a few selected top-level executives. He then isolated ten roles he believed are common to all managers. These ten roles have been grouped into three major categories: interpersonal, informational, and decisional.

1. **Interpersonal** category includes figurehead, leader, and liaison roles.
2. **Informational** category includes monitor (nerve center), disseminator, and spokesperson roles.
3. **Decisional** category includes entrepreneur, disturbance handler, resource allocator, and negotiator roles.

Management Assumptions about Employees

Managers have different assumptions about employees regarding their nature and behavior toward work. Some examples follow:

- Douglas McGregor outlined a set of highly optimistic assumptions about human nature from the manager's perspective **(Theory Y),** that people are creative, energetic, and capable of taking responsibility, and can exercise self-control and self-direction. This is in contrast with the traditional view of people by managers **(Theory X),** that most people are lazy, dislike work, must be coerced, must be directed, and are interested only in job security. He criticized Theory X for being pessimistic, stifling, and outdated.
- William Ouichi discovered a type of organization that exhibited a style of management that effectively combines the traits and cultures of typical American and Japanese companies. He called these hybrid companies **Theory Z** organizations. These companies focus on the employee in areas such as: long-term employment; relatively slow job evaluation and promotion; job rotation; cross-functional career paths; participative and consensus-style decision making; individual responsibility; concern for employees; and emphasis on employee self-control.
- **Theory T** and **Theory T+** are complementary theories based on Southeast Asian assumptions that: work is a necessity but not a goal itself; people should find their rightful place in peace and harmony with their environment; absolute objectives exist only with God; in the world, persons in authority positions represent God, so their objectives should be followed; people behave as members of a family and/or group; and those who do not are rejected by society.

Leaders versus Managers versus Entrepreneurs

An individual may have more of leadership qualities than management qualities and vice versa but ideally should develop a balance of both qualities. Examples of leadership qualities include visionary, inspiring, creative, innovative, imaginative, and change agent. Examples of management qualities include problem solving, analytical skills, authority, and stability.

One of the major differences between management and leadership qualities relates to the source of power and the level of a follower's compliance with it. Power is the ability to influence the behavior of others. Management power comes from position power (e.g., legitimate, reward, and coercive power) while the leadership power comes from personal power (e.g., expert and referent power). It is true that an effective manager must have leadership qualities.

Entrepreneurs are characterized as risk-takers, idea generators and implementers, opportunity grabbers and exploiters, change agents and innovators, go-getters, and value creators. They have a different mindset, are a different breed, and have a bigger mission and vision than managers and leaders to take advantage of uncertainty (risk). Both large and small firms and new and established firms can be entrepreneurial. All managers and leaders should think and act like entrepreneurs.

Mentoring

Mentoring is a relationship in which experienced managers aid employees in the earlier stages of their careers. Such a relationship provides an environment for conveying technical, interpersonal, and organizational skills from the more-experienced to the less-experienced person. Not only does the inexperienced employee benefit, but also the mentor may enjoy the challenge of sharing his wisdom and knowledge. Mentoring exhibits management and leadership skills.

However, mentoring has problems. Young minority managers frequently report difficulty in finding mentors. Also, men generally show less willingness than do women to be mentors. Further, mentors who are dissatisfied with their jobs and those who teach a narrow or distorted view of events may not help a young manager's development. Fortunately, many managers have a series of advisors or mentors during their careers and may find advantages in learning from the different mentors. For example, the unique qualities of individual mentors may help less-experienced managers identify key behaviors in management success and failure. Further, those being mentored find previous mentors to be useful sources for networking.

Delegation

Delegation is the process of assigning various degrees of decision-making authority to subordinates. It is not an all-or-nothing proposition. Authority may be passed along to subordinates; ultimate responsibility cannot be passed along. Thus delegation is the sharing of authority, not the abdication of responsibility. Experts say that it is good to delegate those activities the manager knows best. Delegation exhibits management and leadership skills.

Advantages from Delegation

- Managers can free more of their time for planning and motivating.
- Subordinates will be better trained and developed as future managers.

Barriers to Delegation

- Lack of confidence and trust in subordinates
- Vague job definition
- Fear of competition from subordinates
- Poor example set by superiors who do not delegate
- Reluctance in taking the risks involved in depending on others

❏ Learning Objective 1.4: UNDERSTAND THE IMPORTANCE OF CONTROLLING AND MEASURING SKILLS

In this learning objective, we discuss the types of management controls and different ways of measuring performance. Controlling helps measuring in meeting the established performance standards.

Controlling Defined

Controlling is the fourth and final function of management. Controlling means monitoring employees' activities, determining whether the organization is on target toward its goals, and making corrections as necessary. Managers must ensure that the organization is moving toward its goals. New trends toward empowerment and trust of employees have led many companies to place less emphasis on top-down control and more emphasis on bottom-up control in terms of training employees to monitor and correct themselves (i.e., a self-control).

Information technology (IT) is also helping managers provide needed organizational control without strict top-down constraints. Companies may also use IT to put *more* constraints on employees if managers believe the situation demands it. Organization failure can result when managers are not serious about controls or lack of controls.

Management Controls

Management controls can be divided into feed-forward, concurrent, and feedback controls. A **feed-forward control** is a proactive control and works in anticipation of problems, such as defect prevention through quality control inspection of raw materials and work-in-process (WIP) inventory, pre-employment screening and background checking, training programs, forecasting inventory needs, advance notice of a purchase, and budgeting. It focuses on inputs, affects timely solutions, and hence is important to management.

A **concurrent control** solves problems as they happen and includes direct supervision, total quality management (TQM) principles, just-in-time (JIT) techniques, and employee self-control and teamwork. It focuses on ongoing processes.

A **feedback control** is used to evaluate past activity to improve future performance, and it focuses on outputs. It measures actual performance against a standard to ensure that a desired result is achieved. Examples of feedback controls include customer/employee surveys, variance analysis, and performance measures (e.g., sales per employee). Feedback control has been criticized because corrective action takes place after the fact (reactive). Feedback control can allow costs to build up due to their back-end position. An example is human resource managers holding exit interviews with employees who have resigned to go to work for competitors. Management tabulates the interviewee's responses and uses the information to identify problems with training, compensation, working conditions, or other factors that have caused increased turnover. Other examples include increased finished goods inspections (final quality inspection), monitoring product returns, and evaluating customer complaints, which are too late to take any corrective action.

Measuring Defined

Measuring is identifying whether actual performance meets established standards. Managers should assess what they will measure and how they will define it. Measuring requires the following steps:

Step 1: Establish standards of performance.
Step 2: Measure actual performance.
Step 3: Compare actual performance with the established standards.
Step 4: Take corrective action in cooperation with employees and other stakeholders.

Traditional measurement tools include operating budgets, capital budgets, analyzing financial statements for profitability and liquidity, adapting TQM principles, and complying with international standards organization (ISO) quality standards. Note that budgets can act as both planning and controlling tools.

Contemporary measurement tools include:

- **Economic value added (EVA)** is defined as a company's net operating profit (after-tax) minus the cost of capital invested in the company's tangible assets. EVA captures all the things a company can do to add value from its activities, such as run the business more efficiently, satisfy customers, and reward shareholders. Each job, department, or process in the company is measured by the value added.

- **Market value added (MVA)** measures the stock market's estimate of the value of a company's past and projected capital investment projects. A company's market value is the value of all outstanding stock plus the company's debt. When a company's market value is greater than all the capital invested in it from shareholders, bondholders, and retained earnings, the company has a positive MVA, which is an indication that it has created wealth for its stakeholders. A positive MVA goes hand in hand with a high EVA measurement.

- The **activity-based costing (ABC)** method allocates costs across all business processes, ensuring that the price of a product is more than the cost to produce it. The ABC method enables managers to evaluate whether more costs go to activities that add value or to activities that do not add value. They can then focus on reducing costs associated with non-value-added activities.

- **Open-book management** means sharing financial information and operating results with all employees in the organization, without hiding anything from employees. This sharing of information makes employees feel like a part owner of the company, ties employee rewards to the company's financial success, increases employee's cooperation and communication, and increases efficiency and effectiveness of employee job performance.

- The **balanced scorecard system** is a comprehensive management control system that balances traditional financial measures with nonfinancial measures, such as customer service, internal business processes, and the organization's capacity for learning and growth. Metrics can be a part of the balanced scorecard system.

❏ Learning Objective 1.5: UNDERSTAND THE IMPORTANCE OF MOTIVATING SKILLS

Motivating subordinates is an important function for both managers and leaders and is not an easy task. The use of correct motivation strategies can bring big results to the supervisor.

Motivation Defined

The term **motivation** refers to the psychological process that gives a purpose and direction to human behavior. Motivation theories are generalizations about the *why* and *how* of purposeful behavior. The goal is to move individual employees toward achieving organizational objectives, including job performance, which is defined as follows:

Job Performance = KSAs × Motivation

Knowledge, skills, and abilities (KSAs) and motivation are necessary for effective and efficient job performance. KSAs are acquired through education, training, and on-the-job experience. The individual's motivational factors—needs, satisfaction, expectations, and goals—are affected by challenging work, rewards, and participation. Motivational factors are both inborn and learned.

Motivation Theories

Four popular motivation theories exist:

1. **Maslow's needs hierarchy theory.** Maslow's theory focuses on five needs structured as a hierarchy, from bottom to top, and includes physiological, safety, love, esteem, and self-actualization needs. Individuals proceed up the hierarchy of needs, one level at a time. Higher needs emerge as lower needs are met. A fulfilled need does not motivate an individual. Needs are related to motivation in that unsatisfied needs motivate behavior. Maslow's esteem needs are most closely associated with Herzberg's concept of job enrichment. Maslow's needs theory failed under actual testing since it does not consider individual perceptions.

2. **Herzberg's two-factor theory.** Herzberg's theory was based on employee satisfaction. A satisfied worker is motivated from within to work harder, and a dissatisfied employee is not self-motivated. Herzberg's two factors are satisfiers and dissatisfiers.

   Examples of **satisfiers** include achievement, recognition, work itself, responsibility, advancement, and growth.

   Examples of **dissatisfiers** include company policy and administration; supervision; relationship with supervisor, peers, and subordinates; work conditions; salary; personal life; status; and security.

   Dissatisfaction is associated with complaints about the job context or factors in the immediate work environment. The elimination of dissatisfaction is not the same as truly motivating an employee. Herzberg is convinced that money is a weak motivational tool because, at best, it can only eliminate dissatisfaction. To satisfy and motivate employees, an additional element other than money is required, including meaningful, interesting, and challenging work. Critics argued that his theory was weak on an empirical basis and that individual's perception was secondary. Others argued that one person's dissatisfier may be another's satisfier. Herzberg's biggest contribution is the motivating potential for enriched work.

3. **Expectancy theory.** Individual perception, though secondary in the Maslow and Herzberg models, is central to expectancy theory. The expectancy theory is based on the assumption that motivational strength is determined by perceived probabilities of success. The term **expectancy** refers to the subjective probability (or expectation) that one thing will lead to another. The focus of this model is as follows: one's motivational strength increases as one's perceived effort–performance and performance–reward probabilities increase. This theory has received empirical support from researchers and is based on common sense since

Effort → Performance → Reward. Employees tend to work harder when they believe they have a good chance of getting personally meaningful rewards.

4. **Goal-setting theory.** Goal setting is the process of improving individual or group job performance with clear objectives and high standards. **Management by objectives (MBO)** is an example of goal-setting theory.

MBO states that organizational goals can be better achieved if the goals of superiors and subordinates are integrated with organizational goals. All levels of management should be involved in setting the objectives of the organization in working toward the common goals.

The essence of MBO is close consultation between superior and subordinate in the setting of and agreement on goals. They must agree on the goals to be achieved. Feedback is necessary during the period of working toward the goals and after the goals are accomplished. A key requirement is **unity of command**, which requires subordinates to be evaluated by a single superior—the manager.

Comparisons among Motivation Theories

- Maslow's theory is built around the hierarchy of human needs.
- Herzberg's theory is concerned with job performance and job satisfaction and focuses on maintenance and motivational factors.
- Expectancy theory is based on the concept that people's expectations of rewards are derived from their unique personal motive structure, beliefs, and perceptions.
- Goal-setting theory is based on improving individual or group job performance.

Motivation Strategies

The following four motivation strategies were derived from the motivational theories discussed previously:

1. **Motivation through job design.** Motivation through job design deals with two specific strategies: (1) fitting people to jobs and (2) fitting jobs to people. Three proven alternatives in fitting people to jobs include realistic job previews (written job descriptions and audiovisual presentations about the job), job rotation, and limited exposure to fragmented jobs. The strategy of fitting jobs to people includes job enlargement (adds width to a job) and job enrichment (adds depth to a job).

2. **Motivation through rewards.** Every employee expects to be rewarded in some way for work performed. Rewards may include material and psychological payoffs for performing tasks in the workplace. Managers have found that job performance and satisfaction can be improved by properly administered rewards.

Two types of rewards exist: (1) extrinsic rewards, which are payoffs granted to the individual by other people (e.g., money, employee benefits, promotions, recognition/employee of the month, status symbols, and praise) and (2) intrinsic rewards, which are self-granted and internally experienced payoffs (e.g., sense of accomplishment, self-esteem, and self-actualization). An intrinsic reward is an internally generated benefit or satisfaction resulting from good work performed.

3. **Motivation through employee participation.** Participative management is defined as the process of empowering employees to assume greater control of the workplace. Employees may participate in setting goals, making decisions, solving problems, and designing and implementing organizational changes. Employee participation will not work if individual values and attitudes are not in tune with it. Organizational factors such as job design and corporate culture can also help or hinder the process. Environmental factors such as technological change and competition also affect the participation process.

Two team-oriented approaches to employee participation include quality control circles and self-managed teams. **Quality control circles** are small groups of voluntary, problem-solving employees who meet regularly to discuss quality improvement and ways to reduce costs. To be successful, quality control circles should be introduced in an evolutionary manner rather than by management order.

Self-managed teams (or autonomous work groups) take on traditional managerial tasks as part of their normal work routine. Advocates say self-managed teams foster creativity, motivation, and productivity. The manager's role will be more of a facilitator than an order giver, and supervision tends to be minimal. Hiring, training, and job design need to be skillfully interlocked with self-managed teams, thus driving up front-end costs. Traditional authoritarian supervisors view self-managed teams as a threat to their authority, job security, and power.

4. **Motivation through work schedules and services.** New approaches such as flexible work schedules, family support services, and sabbaticals are aimed at enhancing employee motivation and increasing job performance. While employees like flexible work schedules, employers may not because of greater administrative expense, supervisory resistance, and inadequate coverage of jobs. Alternative approaches were invented such as compressed workweeks (40 hours in fewer than 5 days), permanent part-time jobs (workweeks with fewer than 40 hours), and job sharing (complementary scheduling that allows two or more part-timers to share a single full-time job).

❑ Learning Objective 1.6: UNDERSTAND THE IMPORTANCE OF PROBLEM-SOLVING AND DECISION-MAKING SKILLS

Managers make decisions to solve current problems or to seek future opportunities. In the former case, problems come first, and decisions come next. In the latter case, opportunities come first, and decisions come next. Group dynamics and team building are also discussed.

Problem Defined

A **problem** exists when there is a gap between *what is* and *what should be*. Individuals recognize a problem when they feel frustrated, frightened, angry, or anxious about a situation. Organizations recognize problems when outputs and productivity are low; when quality of products and services is poor; when people are not cooperating, sharing information, or communicating; or when there is a dysfunctional degree of conflict among people in various departments. When the gap between what is and what should be causes anxiety and inefficiency, something needs to be done to solve the problem (see the figure).

Point A	Gap	Point B
"What is" (actual condition)	←——————→	"What should be" (desired condition)

A problem is the gap between where one is and where one wants to be. The process of closing the gap between the actual situation and the desired situation is problem solving. Problems do not solve themselves—people solve problems.

The management principle behind problem solving is Theory Y in that managers will take responsibility for and are interested in solving organizational problems. *Effective written and oral communication skills are prerequisites to effective problem-solving skills.*

Problem-Solving Process

Problem solving is a systematic process of bringing the actual situation or condition closer to the desired condition. Although there are many ways to handle problems, the following four steps can explain the process:

Step 1: Identify the problem.
Step 2: Generate alternative solutions.
Step 3: Select a solution.
Step 4: Implement and evaluate the solution.

Impediments to Problem Solving

Business problems are solved either by individuals or by groups. The most neglected area of problem solving is human resources, the people who participate in the problem-solving group. The group leader can encourage new ideas and creativity in group members by following these guidelines:

- Practice **effective listening** because people think much more rapidly than they speak. Effective listening is the best way to gather information. Try not to be distracted.
- Practice "**stroking**," a concept borrowed from transactional analysis. A stroke is a unit of recognition. Provide recognition to people and ideas. Positive stroking makes people more important and secure and invites more ideas and creativity.
- Discourage "**discounting**" (i.e., not paying attention), another concept borrowed from transactional analysis. When discounting is high, group members will feel reluctant to respond to questions and will be constantly ready to attack or retreat. This is not a healthy climate for successful problem solving, and it encourages dysfunctional behavior and uncooperative attitudes among group members.
- Keep the group members informed about progress and what is expected of them.

Reasons Individuals Solve Problems Differently

Problem-solving skills are different with different people. Five factors influence a person's problem-solving capabilities: (1) value system, (2) information filtration, (3) interpretation, (4) internal representation, and (5) external representation.

Tools and Techniques for Problem Solving

Several major tools and techniques are available for the problem solver to solve problems, including brainstorming, synectics, nominal group technique, force-field approach, and systems analysis. Differences exist among these tools, and all of them do not work equally well in different situations. In any given situation, one or two tools might have a greater probability of leading to the desired outcomes.

- **Brainstorming** encourages uninhibited flow of new ideas—the more ideas, the better.
- **Synectics** is a highly structured approach using excursions, fantasies, and analogies.
- **Nominal group technique** has no real group as it uses a very structured approach.
- **Force-field analysis** identifies inhibiting and facilitating forces.
- **Systems analysis** breaks down a large problem into many smaller problems.

Other problem-solving tools and techniques include imagineering; value analysis; leapfrogging; blasting, creating, and refining; attribute listing; Edisonian; investigative questions; cause-and-effect diagrams; Pareto charts; psychodramatic approaches; checklists; general semantics; morphological analysis; panel consensus techniques; Delphi technique; work measurement; storyboards; humor; operations research; intuitive approach; T-analysis; closure; and TRIZ (a Russian-language acronym to solve inventive problems by reframing the contradicting and competing goals so contradictions disappear).

Decision Defined

A **decision** is deciding on a specific course of action from several choices.

Decision-Making Process

Decision making is a process of choosing among alternative courses of action. The correct sequence of the decision-making process is shown below:

Step 1: Identify the right information.
Step 2: Identify an acceptable level of risk.
Step 3: Identify alternative courses of action.
Step 4: Make a timely decision.

Note the difference between problem-solving and decision-making steps. *Identify an acceptable level of risk* (step 2) does not enter into the problem-solving process. Risk is unique to decision making and is an integral part of it. Decision making reduces or increases the risk, depending on the quality of the decision making and the level of uncertainty.

Facets of Decision Making

Managers and leaders make decisions. The type of decision made depends on the level of that manager in the organization hierarchy. To accommodate this diversity, many facets of decision making exist, including sequential/nonsequential, static/dynamic, structured/unstructured, programmed/nonprogrammed, and routine/nonroutine.

Decision-Making Models

Models are predetermined procedures that specify the step-by-step actions to be taken in a particular situation. Two types of decision models exist: normative and empirical.

Normative decision models prescribe the decision-making process—what *should be*. These models do not describe actual management practice in decision making. Instead, they describe how a decision procedure should be followed. Normative models are programmed decisions. They help lower-level operating management to implement programs such as production scheduling or inventory control.

Empirical decision models do not describe how a decision-maker should go about making a decision. Instead, they describe the actual decision processes followed by a decision-maker—what *is*. Empirical models are nonprogrammed decisions. They help middle to senior management in making strategic decisions such as pricing and new product introduction. *When there is no set of procedures for a decision process, then by definition there is no "model" for it. Examples include crisis handling and leadership.*

Types of Decisions

Decision making is a frequent and important human activity and is a managerial activity. Decisions are not all of one kind. The procedure for making one decision, such as buying a home, is entirely different from making another decision, such as buying a car.

Four general types of decisions exist that require different decision procedures: (1) decisions under certainty, (2) decisions under risk, (3) decisions under uncertainty, and (4) decisions under conflict or competition.

Types of Data Used in Decision Making

Decision making is a process that incorporates the estimating and predicting of the outcome of future events. When specific events are known with certainty, the decision-maker does not use probabilities in the evaluation of alternatives. When specific events are uncertain, the decision-maker uses probabilities in the evaluation of alternatives. The decision-maker often uses the most likely outcome stated in deterministic format rather than incorporating all outcomes in a probabilistic (stochastic) format.

A decision-maker uses two types of data: deterministic data and probabilistic data. **Deterministic data** are known and not subject to any error or distribution of error. They are based on historical data; their environment is stable and predictable. Decision results will be certain with a single unique payoff. There is only a single outcome for each possible action.

Probabilistic data are used by the decision-maker to evaluate decisions under situations of risk and uncertainty. An estimation of distribution of possible outcomes can be made, not an assured or a predictable outcome. The environment is characterized as unstable and unpredictable since each event is assigned a probability of occurrence. Probabilistic data allow for better risk evaluation since sensitivity analysis can be performed on each action to measure the material impact of the various events.

An estimated payoff table or decision tree can be developed for analysis. A drawback of using probabilistic data is the availability and integrity of data to determine multiple courses of action.

Tools and Techniques for Decision Making

These include differential analysis, decision tables, decision trees, payoff tables, flowcharts, cost–benefit analysis, success–failure analysis, discriminate analysis, management science/operations research applications, devil's advocate techniques, reality checks, risk analysis, and activity analysis.

Decision Making versus Problem Solving

Decision making and problem solving are not the same—they have two different time dimensions. The basic difference is that decision making is future oriented and problem solving is past oriented. Decision making deals with major risk, while problem solving deals with resolving a specific issue. Problems come first, and decisions come next.

Examples of decision-making situations include investing in a new product line, buying new equipment, and selecting an employee for a key position. Examples of problem-solving situations include handling a tardy employee, correcting a poor-quality production, and working with a slow-paying customer.

Group Dynamics

Today, groups or committees make many decisions in organizations. There is a link between communication concepts and the subject of group decision making. Since messages are transmitted between members of the group, the effectiveness of this communication process will have a greater impact on the quality of the group's decisions.

Robbins states that groups offer an excellent vehicle for performing many of the steps in the decision-making process. They are a source of both breadth and depth of input for information gathering. If the group is composed of individuals with diverse backgrounds, the alternatives generated should be more extensive and the analysis more critical. When the final solution is agreed upon, there are more people in a group decision to support and implement it. These pluses, however, can be more than offset by the minuses—time consumed by group decisions, the internal conflicts they create, and the pressures they generate toward conformity.

Strengths or assets of group decision making include breadth of information, diversity of information, extensive analysis of alternatives, acceptance of solutions, and legitimacy of processes.

Weaknesses or liabilities of group decision making include time-consuming efforts, pressure to conform, possibility of conflicts, domination of discussions, ambiguous responsibility, and loss of personal accountability.

Group Behaviors

Group psychology studies have revealed that various groups produced contradictory behavior. Sometimes, people did better at their tasks when there were other people around and sometimes they did worse. Groupthink, groupshift, and group polarization are the three byproducts of group decision making, all of which have the potential to affect the group's ability to evaluate alternatives objectively and arrive at quality decision solutions.

Groupthink is related to norms and describes situations in which group pressures for conformity deter the group from critically appraising unusual, minority, or unpopular views. Groupthink is a disease that attacks many groups and can dramatically hinder their performance. Individuals who hold a minority position that is different from that of the dominant majority are under pressure to suppress, withhold, or modify their true feelings and beliefs. Opposition is viewed as disloyal and is discouraged. Groupthink can ignore risks and contingencies. The group leader must remain impartial and play the devil's advocate to come up with new challenges and alternatives.

Groupshift indicates that in discussing a given set of alternatives and arriving at a solution, group members tend to exaggerate the initial position that they hold. Groups move between conservative and risky. Group decision frees any single member from accountability for the group's final choice. Greater risk can be taken because even if the decision fails, no one member can be held fully responsible.

Group polarization can occur when a group decides to take more risks than any individual would have judged reasonable. Groups tend to make more extreme decisions than individuals who are part of the group. Group polarization (high-risk takers) and groupthink (low-risk takers) are two extremes on a risk measurement scale.

Factors Affecting Group Decisions

Many factors affect group decisions, including ownership of the problem either by individuals or by groups (synectics is a good technique to solve these kinds of problems), nature of the problem to be solved either by few or several people, structure of the problem (i.e., routine vs. nonroutine), nature of the group (i.e., implementers vs. nonimplementers),

maturity level of the group (i.e., short vs. long periods of time), the size of the group (optimum is between 6 and 10), and the climate of the group (i.e., passive and active behaviors).

Manager's Information Processing Styles

The quality of a decision is a direct reflection of how the decision-maker processes information. Managers approach decision making and problem solving in very different ways, depending on their information processing styles. Their approaches, perceptions, and recommendations vary because their minds work differently. Researchers have identified two general information-processing styles: (1) the thinking (objective) style and (2) the intuitive (subjective) style. One is not superior to the other.

The **thinking style** manager tends to be analytical, logical, precise, and objective. He prefers routine assignments that require attention to detail and systematic implementation. The manager uses deductive reasoning. The thinking style is good to use in model-building exercises and forecasting involving projections.

The **intuitive style** manager is creative, is comfortable in handling a dynamic and nonroutine environment, follows his hunches, and is mostly subjective. He likes to address broad issues and use inductive reasoning. This manager sees things in complex patterns rather than as logically ordered bits and pieces. The intuitive style is good to use in brainstorming sessions and where traditional assumptions need to be challenged.

In practice, many managers process information through a combination of thinking and intuitive styles.

Stages of Group Development

Effectiveness and efficiency increase as the group matures. Similarly, immature groups are ineffective and inefficient. A significant benefit of group maturity is that a person's individuality strengthens. Also, members of mature groups tend to be emotionally mature.

Kreitner suggests six stages of group development, including (1) orientation, (2) conflict and challenge, (3) cohesion, (4) delusion, (5) disillusion, and (6) acceptance. During stages 1 through 3, group members attempt to overcome the obstacles of uncertainty over power and authority, while during stages 4 through 6, they overcome the obstacles of uncertainty over interpersonal relations. An understanding of group development stages will improve time-management skills of an employee.

Stage 1: Orientation. Group members give the impression to managers and leaders that they want permanent control expressed through wants and needs.

Stage 2: Conflict and change. Group members struggle for control by suggesting alternative courses of action and strive to clarify and reconcile their roles. Many groups do not continue past this stage because they get bogged down due to emotionalism and political infighting. An *I* feeling is dominant at this stage for power and authority.

Stage 3: Cohesion. A *we* feeling becomes apparent at this stage as everyone becomes truly involved in the project, and any differences over power and authority are resolved.

Stage 4: Delusion. Issues and problems are dismissed or treated lightly. Group members work in participation and promote harmony at all costs.

Stage 5: Disillusion. Disillusion sets in as unlimited goodwill wears off and disenchantment grows. Some members will prevail by showing their strengths while others hold back. Tardiness and absenteeism are the norm, which is symptomatic of diminishing cohesiveness and commitment.

Stage 6: Acceptance. Some group members move from conflict to cohesion and act as group catalysts as their expectations are more realistic. Power and authority structure are accepted. Consequently, the group members tend to be highly effective and efficient.

Criteria and Determinants of Group Effectiveness

A **group** is defined as two or more freely interacting individuals who share a common identity and purpose. Individuals join groups for various reasons to satisfy their personal and professional goals. Two kinds of groups exist, including informal and formal groups. An **informal group** is a collection of individuals seeking friendship while a **formal group** is a collection of individuals doing productive work. Individuals can be subjected to ostracism, which is rejection from a group.

Two criteria for group effectiveness include attractiveness and cohesiveness. **Attractiveness** has the outside-looking-in view, while **cohesiveness** has the inside-looking-out view. Cohesive group members

tend to stick together as they focus on *we* instead of *I*. An individual's perception and frames of reference have lot to do with how groups can be attractive or cohesive.

Factors that can *enhance* a group's attractiveness and cohesiveness include cooperative relationships among members, a high degree of interaction among group members, a relatively small-sized group, and similarities among group members.

Factors that can *detract* from a group's attractiveness and cohesiveness include unreasonable demands on the individual, disagreement over work rules and procedures, unpleasant experience with some group members, and destructive competition or conflict.

Groups and Individuals

Every worker has a dual role: as an individual and as a member of a group. Weber states that a group is defined by functional qualities, not by physical properties. A group consists of a minimum of two or more people who interact, communicate with, and influence each other for a period of time. To comprise a group, a collection of people must share more than circumstances. They must share perceptions and goals. Group members must be aware of each other, interact with each other, and exert influence on each other. To communicate with each other, they must both send and receive messages. And they must be engaged in these processes for more than a few moments.

Why do people join groups? Formal or otherwise, there are two common reasons people join groups: goal attainment and needs gratification. By working together, people can accomplish goals that might be difficult or impossible for solitary individuals to achieve. Additionally, group participation addresses many social needs such as access to approval, a sense of belonging, friendship, and love.

People do not inevitably lose their individuality in groups, although groups may help lessen self-awareness and produce a state of de-individuation. In fact, group membership can heighten certain aspects of individual experience. Three important effects of the group on the individual are:

1. **Identity.** Belonging to a group is a form of social categorization in that the group becomes one aspect of social identity (e.g., a member of a professional or trade association). Reference groups are particularly important in defining not only

identity but also aspirations. A reference group is a social network one consults for social comparison. When groups come into contact with each other, individuals may compare their own group favorably to the alternatives available.

2. **Deviance.** Group goals can sometimes override or conflict with individual members' personal goals. When a member breaks with the group's norms to satisfy personal needs, he becomes a deviant. Members of a group are important in validating each other's beliefs. A deviant threatens that validation by defecting and reducing consensus. Ultimately the deviant will most likely be pushed out of the group, thus restoring consensus with one fewer member.

3. **Social impact.** Social impact theory is an explanation of social influence. According to this theory, the degree to which a targeted individual is influenced depends on three factors: (1) the strength of the source of influence, (2) the immediacy of the influence, and (3) the number of sources. Group membership can be seen as having social impact on an individual. Taken factor by factor, a group will have greater influence on each member if it is strong, if the group's influence is immediate, and if the group is large in number.

Group Structures

Groups have tasks such as solving problems, making decisions (task agenda), and meeting the emotional needs and social roles of their members (social agenda). Groups meet these two agendas through several key processes and structures: norms, roles, and cohesiveness.

Norms are rules or guidelines for accepted and expected behavior. Some norms are explicit; members know what they are and can explain them to newcomers. Others are implicit or subtle, occasionally taken for granted until a deviation occurs. Most groups have a norm for how decisions are made. For example, a group of coworkers in a small business may agree that important contracts are to be voted on by all members, with a simple majority of more than half ruling. The coworker who tries to play dictator will be violating norms and may be treated as a deviant until the group restores consensus—or pushes the deviant out.

Roles are sets of norms defining appropriate behaviors. Groups usually involve roles; some are broad (leaders and followers), while others are more specific. Roles differentiate members' functions and contributions within the group. Roles may be organized according to individual talents. Roles can be a source of reward, as well as a source of problems within a group. Group membership offers personal benefits, and group participation achieves goals that solitary individuals may not.

Roles may differ in not only function but also value to the group. **Values** are abstract ideas that shape an individual's thinking and behavior. Roles associated with greater prestige or respect are said to have higher status-position or rank. Status affects the way members of the group communicate and work with each other. For example, high-status members like executives and managers may initiate communication with lower-status members but not vice versa. A manager can interrupt a subordinate worker to ask a question, but a subordinate is not free to enter a manager's office and ask questions without permission. Status can be a reward for specific members, but it carries a cost, since differences in status can be a source of resentment or competition among members.

Two kinds of role conflict commonly occur: (1) person–role conflict and (2) inter-role conflict. **Person–role conflict** is where a person finds his group role difficult to perform. For example, a committee member may be required to criticize other members' work, but he might feel uncomfortable with having to do this. **Inter-role conflict** is where a member belonging to different groups competes for time in balancing the completion of conflicting tasks.

When one's responsibilities within a group are unclear or unstable, the individual suffers the difficulty of role ambiguity. Roles are likely to be ambiguous when a member first joins a group, or when task performance changes. For example, if a small service company shifts from paper recordkeeping to the use of computers, the roles of the file clerk may become ambiguous. It is not yet clear what—if any—function he will have in the organization from this point on.

Cohesiveness is a feeling of attraction and loyalty that motivates members to stay in the group. Members of cohesive groups like each other more and support common goals more strongly than members of less cohesive groups. High cohesiveness can be a source of both benefits and liabilities. Members of highly cohesive groups enjoy their membership and interaction more but are also prone to make mistakes by giving group feeling a higher priority than other group goals.

Anything that makes a group more valuable to its members increases cohesiveness. Competition within the group can reduce cohesiveness, since members fear threats from each other. Another barrier to fellowship is disliking or special preferences among members. When members are drawn to and away from each other, subgroups form that break down organizational unity. Preferential differences in members' feelings are more likely to develop in large groups, and thus group size is negatively related to cohesiveness—the larger the organization, the harder it is to maintain attraction, loyalty, and fairness evenly among all members.

Methods Used in Team Building

After a team has been created, there are distinct stages through which it develops. New teams are different from mature teams. In the beginning, team members had to get to know one another, establish roles and norms, divide the labor, and clarify the team's task. In this way, members became parts of a smoothly operating team. The challenge for managers is to understand the stage of the team's development and take action that will help the group improve its functioning.

Research findings suggest that team development is not random but evolves over definitive stages in sequence. One useful model for describing these stages contains five phases: (1) forming, (2) storming, (3) norming, (4) performing, and (5) adjourning.

Forming → Storming → Norming → Performing → Adjourning

The **forming stage** of development is a period of orientation and getting acquainted. Members break the ice and test one another for friendship possibilities and task orientation. Team members find which behaviors are acceptable to others. Uncertainty is high during this stage, and members usually accept whatever power or authority is offered by either formal or informal leaders. Members are dependent on the team until they find out what the ground rules are and what is expected of them. During this initial stage, members are concerned about such things as "What is expected of me?," "What is acceptable?," and "Will I fit in?" During the forming stage, the team leader should provide time for members to get acquainted with one another and encourage them to engage in informal social discussions.

During the **storming stage,** individual personalities emerge. People become more assertive in clarifying their roles and what is expected of them.

Conflict and disagreement mark this stage. People may disagree over their perceptions of the team's mission. Members may jockey for positions, and coalitions or subgroups based on common interests may form. One subgroup may disagree with another over the total team's goals or how to achieve them. The team is not yet cohesive and may be characterized by a general lack of unity. Unless teams can successfully move beyond this stage, they may get bogged down and never achieve high performance. During the storming stage, the team leader should encourage participation by each team member. Members should propose ideas, disagree with one another, and work through the uncertainties and conflicting perceptions about team tasks and goals.

During the **norming stage,** conflict is resolved, and team harmony and unity emerge. Consensus develops on who has the power, who is the leader, and members' roles. Members come to accept and understand one another. Differences are resolved, and members develop a sense of team cohesion. This stage typically is of short duration. During the norming stage, the team leader should emphasize oneness within the team and help clarify team norms and values.

During the **performing stage,** the major emphasis is on problem solving and accomplishing the assigned task. Members are committed to the team's mission. They are coordinated with one another and handle disagreements in a mature way. They confront and resolve problems in the interest of task accomplishment. They interact frequently and direct discussion and influence toward achieving team goals. During this stage, the leader should concentrate on managing high task performance. Both socioemotional and task specialists should contribute.

The **adjourning stage** occurs in committees, task forces, and teams that have a limited task to perform and are disbanded afterward. During this stage, the emphasis is on wrapping up and gearing down. Task performance is no longer a top priority. Members may feel heightened emotions, strong cohesiveness, and depression or even regret over the team's disbandment. They may feel happy about mission accomplishment and sad about the loss of friendship and associations. At this point, the leader may wish to signify the team's disbanding with a ritual or ceremony, perhaps giving out plaques and awards to signify closure and completeness.

The five stages of team development typically occur in sequence. In teams that are under time pressure or that will exist for only a short period of time, the stages may occur quite rapidly. The stages may also be accelerated for **virtual teams**. For example, bringing people together for a couple of days of team building can help virtual teams move rapidly through the forming and storming stages.

❑ Learning Objective 1.7:
UNDERSTAND THE IMPORTANCE OF NEGOTIATING SKILLS

Negotiating is a soft skill that is important for managers to learn. In this learning objective, we discuss the negotiation process, its elements, and modes of negotiation. Do's and don'ts are also presented.

Negotiation Defined

Negotiation is a decision-making process among different parties with different preferences. Two common types of negotiation include two party (buyer and seller) and third party (buyer, seller, and agent). Traditionally, negotiation takes a win-lose attitude, which is based on power, position, and competition. Here, one person's success is achieved at the expense of the success of others. It takes something from the other party. However, a win-win attitude is based on high principles and cooperation among parties. Here, one person's success is not achieved at the expense of the success of others. Every party gets something.

Process of Negotiation

According to Cohen, negotiation is more than an exchange of material objects and words. It is a way of acting and behaving that can foster understanding, belief, acceptance, respect, and trust between two or more parties. It is the manner of your approach, the tone of your voice, the attitude you convey, the methods you use, and the concern you exhibit for the other side's feelings and needs. All these things comprise the process of negotiation. Hence, the way you go about trying to achieve your objective may, in and of itself, meet some of the other party's needs.

The prerequisite to negotiation is a conflict situation. Conflict is an unavoidable part of life. It occurs when the goals of each party are in opposition. But conflict can arise even if both parties are in agreement about what they want—sometimes the conflict may be centered on how to get it (the means used).

Conflict may arise from differences in experiences, information, or attitudes about the different roles of the negotiators.

Why Opposition?

Opposition is essential because it results in growth and progress. People who are dissatisfied with the status quo generate tension with their different ideas, which often leads to a creative solution.

What Is Negotiation?

Negotiation is gaining the favor of people from whom we want things such as money, justice, status, and recognition. Both technical and nontechnical managers need negotiating skills to obtain help from and support of colleagues, supervisors, peers, customers, suppliers, and even friends and family members.

Elements of Negotiation

Three crucial elements exist in a negotiation: power, time, and information. People can negotiate anything with these three tightly interrelated variables:

1. **Power.** The other side always seems to have more power and authority than you think you have.
2. **Time.** The other side does not seem to be under the same kind of organizational pressure and time constraints you feel you are under.
3. **Information.** The other side seems to know more about you and your needs than you know about them and their needs.

Negotiating is analyzing power, time, and information to affect people's behavior—it is the meeting of two or more parties in order to make things happen to their mutual satisfaction.

A simple test to make sure that you are ready for negotiation is to ask the following three questions. A "yes" answer will indicate readiness.

1. Am I comfortable negotiating in this particular situation?
2. Will negotiating meet my needs?
3. Is the expenditure of energy and time on my part worth the benefits that I can receive as a result of this encounter?

Modes of Negotiation

Two modes of negotiating behavior/conflict resolution exist: the competitive strategy and the collaborative (cooperative) strategy. The style of negotiators can range between these two strategies:

1. **Competitive negotiation strategy** focuses on getting what you want and defeating an opponent (I win, you lose). This may range from intimidation to manipulation. People applying competitive strategy often start with tough demands, get red-faced, raise their voices, act exasperated, delay making any concession, tend to be impatient, and ignore deadlines. When the other party is focusing on a competitive negotiation strategy, it is better to switch to collaborative strategy.

2. **Collaborative negotiation strategy** shifts the effort from trying to defeat an opponent to trying to defeat a problem and to achieve a mutually accepted outcome (I win, you win). With this method, all parties work together to find an acceptable solution or common ground that will meet the needs of both sides. The best way to start a collaborative strategy is to say something like, "I need your help with this problem" or to employ other kinds of tact and exhibit concern for the other's dignity.

Accomplishing mutual satisfaction using the collaborative win-win style involves emphasis on three important activities:

1. Building trust
2. Gaining commitment
3. Managing opposition

Compromise versus Collaboration

Compromise is not synonymous with collaboration. **Compromise** results in an agreement in which each side gives up something it really wanted. Compromise is an outcome where no one's needs are fully met. This is because the strategy of compromise rests on the faulty premise that your needs and the other party's needs are always in opposition. With this thinking, it is never possible for mutual satisfaction to be achieved. Each party starts out with greater (extreme) demands, hoping to compromise at a midpoint. This is not to say that compromise is always a poor choice. Often the strategy of compromise may be appropriate, depending on the particular circumstances.

Successful collaborative negotiations depend upon finding out what the other side really wants and showing them a way to get it, while still getting what you want. It is the definition of win-win.

Do's and Don'ts of Negotiations

To be successful, a manager needs to know what to do and what not to do during negotiations.

Do's of Negotiations:

- Do use phrases such as "I don't know," or "I don't understand it," which can result in negotiating leverage.
- Do approach others and ask for help. It tends to set the climate for a mutually beneficial relationship. At the very least, you will cause the other side to make an investment that ultimately accrues to your advantage.

Don'ts of Negotiations:

- Don't be too quick to "understand" or prove your intellect at the outset of an encounter. Learn to ask questions, even when you think you might know the answers.
- Never give an ultimatum at the beginning of a negotiation. An ultimatum must come at the end of a negotiation, if at all.
- Don't use *hard* ultimatums such as "Take it or leave it," or "It is this way or else!" These attitudes are self-defeating. Use *soft* ultimatums such as, "Your position is valid, but this is all I can do at the moment. Help me."
- Never leave the other side without alternatives. Always allow them to make some kind of choice.
- Don't reduce the other side's stress unless you receive what you are shooting for.
- Don't be abrasive because how you say something will often determine the response you get.
- Avoid using absolutes when responding to people. Learn to preface your replies with, "What I think I may have heard you say. . . ." This "lubricant demeanor" will soften your words, consecrate your actions, and minimize the friction.
- Avoid public embarrassment to the people with whom you deal. Never ridicule anyone in front of others. Even when you are right, shun all opportunities to humiliate people, especially in public.
- Never forget the power of your attitude.
- Never judge the actions and motives of others.

Added-Value Negotiating

Added-value negotiating (AVN) is a value-added process (win-win) involving development of multiple deals with multiple outcomes as opposed to traditional (win-lose) negotiating, which is based on a single outcome with a single winner.

AVN is based on openness, flexibility, and a mutual search for the successful exchange of value. AVN allows one to build strong relationships with people over time. It bridges the gap between win-win theory and practice.

According to Kreitner, AVN comprises the following five steps:

Step 1: Clarify interests. Both parties jointly identify subjective and objective interests so that a common goal is found.

Step 2: Identify options. A variety of choices are developed to create value for both parties.

Step 3: Design alternative deals. Multiple win-win offers are designed to promote creative agreement.

Step 4: Select a deal. Each party selects a mutually acceptable deal after testing the various deals for value, balance, and fit.

Step 5: Perfect the deal. Unresolved details are openly discussed and agreements are put in writing, which strengthens the relationship for future negotiations.

BATNA

The members of the Harvard Negotiation project discovered a new concept in negotiations known as the **best alternative to a negotiated agreement (BATNA)** to establish a standard (i.e., bottom line) against which any proposed agreement should be measured. The BATNA describes the anchor point for both sellers and buyers when negotiations do not produce the desired outcome(s) for each negotiating party in terms of a settlement amount.

Each negotiating party's BATNA is a decision point in terms of accepting or rejecting the offer by the other party. The difference between the seller's BATNA and the buyer's BATNA is known as the **bargaining zone**, which becomes the only basis for further negotiation due to overlapping range of acceptable outcomes. Negotiation is either useless or unnecessary outside the bargaining zone because it is not a common ground for the both parties. Agreement is possible within the bargaining zone and not possible outside the zone. Therefore, estimating one party's BATNA is essential in protecting the negotiating parties from accepting offers that are unfavorable and from rejecting offers that are favorable.

> ### Example of Calculating the Bargaining Zone Given the Seller's and Buyer's BATNA
>
> An item's original price was $400, current appraised value is estimated at $500, its owner is making a final offer to sell the item at $600, and a buyer's final offer to buy the same item is $350. The seller's BATNA is $400 and the buyer's BATNA is $500. What is the bargaining zone in amount and range?
>
> **The bargaining zone amount is Buyer's BATNA minus Seller's BATNA = $500 − $400 = $100.**
>
> The bargaining zone range is $400 to $500.

A realistic BATNA can protect from four decision-making traps, such as framing error, escalation of commitment, overconfidence, and negotiating without a standard, as follows:

- Framing error deals with how information is presented (i.e., positively or negatively), which can lead to bias in behavior and decision making.
- Escalation of commitment is like "throwing good money after bad" dilemma in that managers continue to fund losing projects to save their face.
- A positive relationship exists between overconfidence and task difficulty. Managers exhibit extra courage needed to handle difficult situations, which leads to unreasonable risks. Careful analysis of situations and critical thinking about decision alternatives can help managers avoid overconfidence trap.
- Negotiating parties usually move aimlessly in the dark due to lack of a negotiating standard, which results in accepting unfavorable terms and rejecting favorable terms. A negotiating standard such as BATNA helps in making better decisions because a seller's BATNA becomes the standard for accepting or rejecting offers

☐ Learning Objective 1.8: UNDERSTAND THE IMPORTANCE OF COMMUNICATION SKILLS

Communications can be either formal or informal and include both written and oral. Communication barriers are discussed along with essentials for effective communication.

Communication Defined

One thing that is common to all four functions of management (i.e., planning, organizing, directing, and controlling) is communication. Surveys have shown that 80 percent of a manager's time is spent on communication and 20 percent on other activities. **Communication** involves two or more people. The effectiveness of organizational communication can be increased with clear verbal and written messages with little or no noise. Nonverbal communications (messages sent through actions, not words) and listening skills (the art of receiving messages) are also important.

Noise is not part of the chainlike communication process. It is any interference with the normal flow of understanding of a message from one person to another. Examples of noise include misperception, illegible print, speech impairment, and garbled computer data transmission. Understanding has an inverse relationship with noise—the higher the noise, the less the understanding. Greater amounts of noise in communication not only waste resources (time and money) but also create frustration between the sender and the receiver.

Communication Chain

Kreitner describes communication as a chain made up of identifiable links—sender, encoding, medium, decoding, receiver, and feedback. The communication chain is only as strong as its weakest link.

The following are the identifiable links in the communication chain:

- **Sender** conveys the message to a receiver.
- **Encoding** translates the message from sender.
- **Medium** is the vehicle by which to send or receive a message.
- **Decoding** translates the message from sender to receiver.
- **Receiver** gets the message.
- **Feedback** means the receiver acknowledges the message.

Sender

The **sender** is an individual or a group of people whose goal is to convey or transmit the message to a receiver via the best possible media and in the fastest way.

Encoding

The objective of **encoding** is to translate internal thought patterns into a language or code that the intended receiver of the message will be able to understand. Words (written or oral), numbers, gestures, or other symbols are used in encoding. The purpose of the message affects the medium of encoding. For example, if a manager were proposing a new employee benefit plan, which is a sensitive program, a meeting with emotional appeal and gestures would have a bigger impact than a normal written (cold) report. A meeting conveys personal interest and empathy, unlike the report.

Medium

Many types of media exist to send and receive a message, including face-to-face communications, telephone calls, regular meetings and electronic meetings (videoconferencing), memos, letters, reports, facsimiles, bulletin boards, newsletters, and others. Each media type varies in richness from high-rich to low-rich. **Media richness** is described as the capacity of a given medium to convey information properly and promote learning. *The goal is to match media richness with the situation. Otherwise, mismatching occurs, which can lead to confusion and embarrassment.*

Comparison of Different Media

Examples of **high-rich media** include face-to-face conversation, telephone, or videoconferencing, since they provide multiple information cues (e.g., message content, tone of voice, and facial expressions), facilitate immediate feedback, and are personal in focus. High-rich media are good for discussing nonroutine issues and problems.

Examples of **low-rich** or **lean media** include bulletin boards, reports, company newsletter, memorandums, and letters. These media provide a single cue, do not facilitate immediate feedback, and are impersonal. Low-rich media are good for discussing routine problems.

Decoding

Decoding is the translation of the transmitted message from the sender's language and terminology to that of the receiver. Effective decoding requires that these be the same between the sender and the receiver. The receiver's willingness to receive the message is a primary criterion for successful decoding.

Receiver

The **receiver** is an individual or a group of people whose goal is to acknowledge and receive the intended message sent by a sender. The receiver will take an action based on the message received.

Feedback

The communication process is not complete until the receiver acknowledges the message via verbal or nonverbal **feedback** to the sender. Without feedback, the sender is not sure whether the receiver has received his message. Feedback affects follow-up: if the receiver does not understand the message, follow-up meetings should be scheduled.

Formal Communications

Formal communication channels are those that flow within the chain of command, and include downward, upward, and horizontal communication.

Downward communication refers to the messages and information sent from a higher level to a lower level in the management hierarchy (e.g., goals, strategies, mission, vision, directives, policies, procedures, and performance feedback).

Upward communication refers to the messages and information transmitted from a lower level to a higher level in the management hierarchy (e.g., grievances and disputes, routine progress and performance reports, suggestions for improvement, and problems and exceptions).

Horizontal communication refers to the lateral or diagonal exchange of messages and information among peers or coworkers, occurring within or across departments (e.g., intradepartmental problem-solving requests, interdepartmental coordination on joint projects, and use of task forces and committees). Horizontal communication is important in learning organizations with teams solving problems.

Informal Communications

Informal communication channels exist that do not consider the organization's formal hierarchy of authority and chain of command. Examples include management by wandering around and the grapevine.

Management by wandering around means higher-level employees (e.g., executives and senior managers) talk directly with lower-level employees (e.g., hourly workers at factory, office, or warehouse) to learn about problems and issues confronting them, as well as to share their key ideas and values. These meetings are informal and unannounced.

A **grapevine** is the unofficial and informal communication system. It sometimes conflicts with the formal system and complements and reinforces it at other times. The grapevine will remain in organizations as long as people are working in a group environment. It has both positive and negative sides. From a positive side, the grapevine communication can help management learn how employees truly feel about policies, procedures, and programs—a type of feedback mechanism. On the other hand, a negative consequence to the grapevine is rumors.

Barriers to Communication

It is false to assume that if a person can talk, he can communicate. Talking is different from communicating. There are many barriers that exist between all people, making communications much more difficult than most people seem to realize. The manager needs to know all the barriers that exist that can block effective communication. The negative effect of roadblocks to communication includes diminishing of self-respect in others, triggering defensiveness, resistance, and resentment. This can also lead to dependency, withdrawal, and feelings of defeat or of inadequacy.

Kreitner describes four types of barriers to communication representing extreme forms of noise: (1) process barriers, (2) physical barriers, (3) semantic barriers, and (4) psychological/social barriers.

Communication Barriers = Process → Physical → Semantic → Psychological/Social

The scope of **process barriers** consists of sender barrier, encoding barrier, medium barrier, decoding barrier, receiver barrier, and feedback barrier—links in the communication chain. The scope of **physical barriers** includes physical objects blocking the effective communication (e.g., walls, medium). **Semantic barriers** address the words used in the communication. A manager who uses jargon in his report is likely to encounter the semantic form of communication barrier. **Psychological and social barriers** deal with peoples' backgrounds, perceptions, values, biases, needs, and expectations—all of which differ to varying degrees.

Perception is a process of giving meaning to one's environment and is a vital link in the communication process. It consists of three subprocesses: (1) selectivity, (2) organization, and (3) interpretation. Selectivity is sensory screening and a sorting out process. Organization is mentally creating meaningful patterns from disorganized thoughts. Interpretation is how people understand a message, which is often different for different people.

Essentials for Effective Communication

After presenting 13 barriers to communication (e.g., criticizing, name-calling, diagnosing, praising, finger-pointing, bossing, threatening, moralizing, advising, excessive questioning, diverting, logical argument, and reassuring), Robert Bolton describes three essentials for effective communication:

1. **Genuineness** means being honest and open about one's feelings, needs, and ideas.
2. **Nonpossessive love** involves accepting, respecting, and supporting another person in a nonpaternalistic and freeing way.
3. **Empathy** refers to the ability to really see and hear another person and understand him from his perspective.

Information Communicated by Others

Information can be improperly analyzed and incorrectly interpreted. The causes of poor business decisions can be attributed not only to a lack of information but also to the failure to properly interpret information.

Proper interpretation of information depends largely on the reliability of the source, the manner in which the information is presented, and the personal perception of the person receiving or giving the information. *The return on an investment in information is knowledge, which is difficult to quantify.*

❑ Learning Objective 1.9:
UNDERSTAND THE IMPORTANCE OF CONFLICT MANAGEMENT SKILLS

Conflict is normal between people due to different perspectives and perceptions. Conflict has two sides: benefits and drawbacks. Tools for managing conflict are discussed.

Conflict Defined

Social scientists say that conflict is inevitable between people, and without conflict there is no major personal change or social progress. Conflict management involves accepting or even encouraging constructive conflict as necessary. The key point is to minimize the destructive form of conflict.

Conflict is the medium by which problems are recognized and solved. Conflict is closely related to change and interpersonal dealings. It refers to all kinds of opposition or antagonistic interaction. Not all conflict is bad.

Conflict is based on scarcity of power, availability of resources, social position, and difference in value structure between individuals or groups involved in the situation.

To be human is to experience conflict. This conflict arises due to differences in personal values, opinions, desires, habits, and needs of people. It is impossible for people to rise completely above selfishness, betrayals, misrepresentations, anger, and strain. The best way to depict conflict is on a scale of disruptive and destructive dimensions, as shown in the figure.

Conflict at best is disruptive and at worst is destructive. Once it erupts, conflict is difficult to control. Destructive conflict has a tendency to expand until it consumes all the things and people it touches.

Social scientists make an important distinction between two types of conflict: realistic conflict and nonrealistic conflict.

In **realistic conflict,** which is based on rationality, there are opposing needs, goals, means, values, or interests. Realistic conflict can be resolved by focusing on the emotions first followed by substantive issues and using collaborative problem-solving methods.

Nonrealistic conflict, which is based on irrationality, arises from ignorance, error, tradition, prejudice, win-lose types of competition, hostility, or the need for tension release. Unrealistic conflict creates unwarranted tension between people and can cause unnecessary destruction; it should be handled very carefully as it can be prevented to some extent.

Another way of classifying conflict is between functional conflict and dysfunctional conflict.

- **Functional conflict.** The organizational benefits of functional conflict are increased effort and improved performance, enhanced creativity, and personal development and growth. It is like expressing anger in a constructive manner, without actually showing the anger. Functional conflict is always encouraged, for obvious reasons.

- **Dysfunctional conflict.** The signs and symptoms of dysfunctional conflict include indecision, resistance to change, destructive emotional outbursts, apathy, and increased political maneuvering. The goal of management is to resolve or neutralize dysfunctional conflict, which is always discouraged, for obvious reasons.

Despite its drawbacks, conflict has benefits. It can spur technological development, encourage personal and intellectual growth, and help renew business organizations.

Personal Conflict Prevention and Control Methods

Although it is impossible to totally eradicate conflict, personal conflict prevention and control can avert much needless strife (nonrealistic conflict). Both individuals and institutions need to develop prevention and control methods. Robert Bolton recommends the following:

- One way of diminishing the amount of conflict is to use fewer roadblocks. Ordering (dominating), threatening, judging, name-calling, and other roadblocks are conflict-promoting interactions.
- Reflective listening helps the other person dissipate "negative" emotions when he has a strong need or a problem to address.
- Assertion skills enable a person to get needs met with minimal strife. By asserting when needs arise, one can prevent the buildup of emotions that so often cause conflict. Both assertion and listening skills help to clear up two major sources of conflict: errors and lack of information.
- Awareness of which behaviors are likely to start a needless conflict between people can eliminate many confrontations. Certain words, looks, or actions tend to trigger specific people into conflict. These behaviors may be rooted in early childhood experiences. Some people can sense that a storm is brewing.
- "Dumping one's bucket" of tension without filling the other's bucket is another important conflict prevention and control method. Strenuous exercise, competitive athletics, and meditation also can drain off one's tensions without adding to other people's stress.

- Increased emotional support from family and friends can decrease one's proneness to unnecessary conflict. In general, the more we are loved and cared for, the less we need to fight.
- Heightened tolerance and acceptance of others also tends to diminish unrealistic conflict. Some say that these tolerances and acceptances are conditioned by upbringing and even by genetic factors. But each of us can become more tolerant and accepting than we now are.
- "Issues control" is another important way of managing conflicts. It is often preferable to deal with one issue at a time, to break issues down into smaller units rather than deal with enormous problems with many parts, to start with easily resolved issues (i.e., start with points of agreement), and to define the dispute in nonideological terms. Try to find how your needs and the other's needs can be satisfied (i.e., win-win situation) through jointly identifying the cause of disagreement.
- A careful appraisal of the full consequences and the cost of a conflict may deter you from involving yourself in needless disputes. It is difficult to estimate the cost of a conflict because emotional interactions are unpredictable and frequently get out of hand.

Group or Organizational Conflict Prevention and Control Methods

Individual actions alone are not enough. Group and/or organizational actions are needed to prevent and control the conflict that occurs in the workplace. The way an organization is structured has a bearing on the amount of conflict generated in it. The potential for conflict tends to be greater in centralized, bureaucratic organizations than in decentralized organizations. The more rigid organizations are, the less effective communications are and the less adept they are at managing conflicts constructively.

Bolton suggests the following:

- The personality and methods of the leader are important. Managers who have low levels of defensiveness and who are supportive tend to help people in their organizations avert unnecessary strife. A person who is in a position of power, one who has great charisma, or one who has developed effective communication skills tends to have the greatest influence on the way conflict is handled.
- The climate of a group also influences the amount of conflict it generates. Although some kinds of competition can be healthy, research evidence

suggests that win-lose competition fosters needless conflict and diminishes the ability to resolve disputes effectively. However, cooperating to achieve goals that could not be accomplished without joint effort promotes more genuine harmony.

- Well-conceived and clearly stated policies and procedures that have the understanding and support of the relevant individuals create orderly processes that can help mitigate unnecessary chaos and conflict. When policies and procedures do not match the needs of the organization or its members, when they are arrived at arbitrarily and administered high-handedly, they can add to the level of unrealistic conflict in the organization.
- The degree of change and the method by which change is introduced into a family or an organization influences the amount and severity of disputes in that institution. A certain amount of change is necessary in all institutions, but too rapid a change or changes utilizing inadequate methods of communication can create significant and needless conflict.
- Mechanisms to settle grievances need to be established. A mechanism is practiced when resolving disputes between labor and management of an organization.
- Training for conflict management is necessary both for the prevention of needless conflict and for the resolution of the conflicts that are inevitable in any relationship or organization. The scope of training should include topics such as listening, assertion, and collaborative problem-solving skills.
- Much conflict needs to be faced and resolved at the earliest possible moment. When prevention and control strategies are used improperly and unwisely, they merely postpone the inevitable. The final result is worse than an early, direct resolution of the strife.
- When some people want to dodge conflict altogether, they tend to misuse the prevention and control strategies listed above. Others use denial, avoidance, capitulation, or domination as mechanisms for keeping their lives free of the unpleasantness of strife.

Tools for Managing Conflict

Two sets of tools are available for managing conflict: (1) conflict triggers, which stimulate conflict, and (2) conflict resolution techniques, which are used when functional conflict deteriorates into dysfunctional conflict.

Conflict Triggers

A **conflict trigger** is a factor or circumstance that increases the choices of intergroup or interpersonal conflict. It can stimulate either functional or dysfunctional conflict, where the former should be continued and the latter should be removed or corrected. According to Kreitner, examples of major conflict triggers include:

- Ambiguous or overlapping jurisdictions. (Reorganization will help to clarify job boundary problems.)
- Competition for scarce resources. (This includes funds, personnel, authority, power, and valuable information.)
- Communication breakdowns. (Communication barriers provoke conflict. Clear communications should be practiced.)
- Time pressures. (Deadlines can prompt performance or trigger destructive emotional reactions.)
- Unreasonable standards, rules, policies, or procedures. (These can lead to dysfunctional conflict between managers and their subordinates. The solution is to correct the situation.)
- Personality clashes. (A solution is to separate the antagonistic parties by reassigning one or both to a new job.)
- Status differentials. (Job hierarchy creates status differentials that lead to dysfunctional conflict. This can be minimized by showing a genuine concern for the ideas, feelings, suggestions, and value of subordinates.)
- Unrealized expectations. (Dysfunctional conflict is another by-product of unrealized expectations. This can be avoided by taking the time to discover what people expect from their employment.)

Conflict Resolution Techniques

Managers have two choices in resolving conflict: do nothing, which is not a good strategy, or try one or more of the following five **conflict resolution techniques:**

1. **Problem solving.** Problem solving encourages managers to focus their attention on root causes, factual information, and promising alternatives rather than on personalities or scapegoats. It is a time-consuming process, but it is worth it.
2. **Superordinate goals.** Superordinate goals are highly valued, unattainable by any one group or individual alone, and commonly sought. The

manager brings the conflicting parties together and tries to resolve the dysfunctional conflict.

3. **Compromise.** Everybody wins and loses because compromise requires negotiation, or give and take. Compromise is based on the idea that "something must be given up if anything is to be gained." It is a time-consuming process, and the problem is worked around rather than solved.

4. **Forcing.** Management steps into a conflict and orders the affected parties to handle the situation in a certain manner. It is based on the formal authority and power of superior position. Forcing does not resolve the personal conflict, and in fact it could compound the situation by hurting feelings, fostering resentment, and creating mistrust.

5. **Smoothing.** Smoothing is a temporary, short-term action, which does not solve the underlying problem. It can be useful when management is attempting to hold things together until a critical project is completed, there is no time for problem solving or compromise, or forcing is deemed inappropriate. Smoothing is appropriate in some situations but not all.

❏ Learning Objective 1.10: UNDERSTAND THE VARIOUS ISSUES IN ORGANIZATIONAL BEHAVIOR, CULTURE, CHANGE, DEVELOPMENT, EFFECTIVENESS, AND DECLINE

Organizations go through lifecycles similar to products, projects, and computer systems. The lifecycle of an organization consists of phases or stages such as startup, growth, maturity, and decline. The effectiveness of an organization's behavior, culture, change, and development processes will determine the distance to the decline stage or to its prolonged life.

There are many issues in the organization's internal environment that a business manager should be familiar with in order to work properly within that environment. The scope of these issues includes organizational behavior, culture, change, development, effectiveness, and decline. The more he learns these issues, the better he is prepared to handle his job.

Organizational Behavior Defined

According to Robbins and Judge (Robbins and Judge), practicing managers cannot succeed on their technical skills alone. They also have to have good people skills (i.e., interpersonal skills)—broadly termed as **organizational behavior (OB).** OB studies three determinants of behavior in organizations: individuals, groups, and structure. In addition, OB applies the knowledge gained about individuals, groups, and the effect of structure on behavior in order to make organizations work more effectively.

Organizational Behavior = Individuals + Groups + Structure

Organizational Behavior → Organizational Effectiveness

OB is concerned with the study of what employees do in an organization and how their behavior affects the organization's performance. It emphasizes behavior as related to concerns such as jobs/positions; work assignments and tasks; employee absenteeism, turnover, productivity, and performance; and management—all connected with employment-related situations. These concerns in turn are translated into core topics such as motivation, leadership, communication (written and oral), groups/teams, learning and listening, attitudes, perceptions, change and conflict management, work design, and work-related stress.

An OB model is developed by identifying dependent variables and independent variables to understand employee behavior, where the latter variable impacts the former variable. A dependent variable, which is the focus of OB, is the key factor to explain or predict and that is affected by some other factor(s). Examples of dependent variables include productivity, absenteeism, turnover, deviant workplace behavior, organizational citizenship behavior, and job satisfaction. An independent variable is the presumed cause of some change in the dependent variable. The independent variable is further divided into three levels: individual level (lowest level), group level (middle level), and organization level (highest level).

The individual level deals with issues such as personality and emotions, values and attitudes, ability, perception, motivation, individual learning and decision making, and biographical characteristics (e.g., age and gender).

The group level deals with issues such as group decision making, leadership and trust, group structure, communication, work teams, conflict, group power, and group or organizational politics.

The organization level deals with issues such as organizational culture, human resource policies and practices (e.g., employee selection processes, training and development programs, and performance evaluation methods), and organization structure and design.

In fact, the scope of OB is very broad as it touches most of the learning objectives (2 through 9) addressed in this learning module.

Organizational Culture Defined

According to Robbins and Judge (Robbins and Judge), **organizational culture (OC)** refers to a system of shared meaning held by employees that distinguishes their organization from other organizations. OC provides direction to employees and helps them understand how things are done in the organization. In other words, OC defines the rules of the game.

A strong culture provides stability (asset) to an organization, and at the same time it can become a major barrier to change (liability). Every organization has a culture, and it can have a significant influence on the employees' attitudes and behaviors.

Researchers have identified seven characteristics to capture the essence of an organization's culture: (1) innovation and risk taking, (2) attention to detail, (3) outcome (results) orientation, (4) people orientation, (5) team orientation (team versus individual), (6) aggressiveness (competitive versus easygoing), and (7) stability (status quo versus growth).

Organizational Culture versus Job Satisfaction

- OC measures how employees see their organization.
- Job satisfaction measures affective responses to the work environment.
- **OC** is a descriptive term while **job satisfaction** is an evaluative term.
- Both OC and job satisfaction have some common characteristics.

Culture has two sides: functional and dysfunctional. The **functional aspects** of culture include boundary-defining role, a sense of identity and commitment, stability of the social system through standards, and a control mechanism to guide and shape the attitudes and behaviors of employees. The **dysfunctional aspects** of a strong culture include barriers to change, barriers to diversity, and barriers to acquisitions and mergers.

The content and strength of culture can influence an organization's ethical climate and the ethical behavior of its employees. An OC most likely to shape high ethical standards is one that is high in risk tolerance, low to moderate in aggressiveness, and focuses on means as well as outcomes. A strong OC will exert more influence on employees (e.g., on turnover) than a weak one. If the culture is strong and supports high ethical standards, it should have a very powerful and positive influence on employee behavior. A combination of the following practices can create a stronger and more ethical culture:

- Be a visible role model by taking the ethical high road.
- Communicate ethical expectations through a code of ethics.
- Provide ethics training to address ethical dilemmas.
- Visibly reward ethical acts and punish unethical ones.
- Provide protective mechanisms to employees through ethical counselors, ombudsmen, or ethical officers.

Culture is first formed from the founder's philosophy, which is reflected in hiring employees at all levels. Later, the current top management set the general climate of what is acceptable behavior and what is not. Culture is transmitted to employees through stories, rituals, material symbols, and language.

Culture is shared among employees through widened span of control, flattened organization structures, introduction of teams, reduced formalization, and empowered employees to ensure that every employee is pointed in the same direction to achieve the organization's common goals and objectives.

Culture is made more customer responsive through employee selection, training and socialization, organization structures, empowerment, leadership, performance evaluation, and reward systems.

Organizational Change Defined

Organizations must change to survive in a competitive environment. This requires everyone in the organization believing in and accepting the change. Ideally, managers need to be architects or agents of change rather than victims of change. When introducing changes, managers often are surprised that things do not turn out as planned. This is because the change process is not carried out properly. The change itself is not the problem. When managers are acting as agents of change, their company will be much more responsive, flexible, and competitive.

A corporation can change by reengineering business policies, processes, jobs, and procedures; outsourcing nonstrategic activities; partnering with major suppliers and customers; implementing total quality management programs; redesigning the organizational structure to fit the business strategy; renovating physical plants and facilities; installing computer-based systems and technologies; understanding one's own products, services, markets, and customers and those of competitors; and installing performance measurement methods and reward systems.

Handling of Change

Employees at the top of the organization usually promote change because they have clear vision and better goals to achieve.

Employees at the bottom of the organization usually resist change the *least* because they know how bad things really are at their level.

Employees at the middle of the organization usually resist change the *most* because they neither know top management goals nor know how bad things really are at the bottom. They are in a confused state since they know neither the top nor the bottom.

Types of Organizational Change

Organization psychologists David Nadler and Michael Tushman developed an instructive typology of organizational change describing four types of changes (Kreitner):

	Incremental	Strategic
Anticipatory	Tuning 1	Reorientation 3
Reactive	Adaptation 2	Re-creation 4

Anticipatory changes are any systematically planned changes intended to take advantage of expected situations (e.g., following demographics). **Reactive changes** are those necessitated by unexpected environmental events (e.g., responding to competitor's action). **Incremental changes** involve the subsystems adjustments needed to keep the organization on its chosen path (e.g., adding a third shift in a manufacturing plant). **Strategic changes** alter the overall shape or direction of the organization (e.g., switch from building houses to apartments by a construction contractor).

The four specific resulting types of organizational change from the previous model are tuning, adaptation, reorientation, and re-creation.

Tuning is the most common form of organizational change covering preventive maintenance and continuous improvement. The major thrust of tuning is to actively anticipate and avoid problems rather than passively waiting for things to go wrong before taking action. Managers should seek the change, not just expect the change.

Adaptation, like tuning, involves incremental changes. The difference is that the changes are in reaction to external problems, events, or pressures.

The **reorientation** change is anticipatory and strategic in scope. It is also called **frame bending** because the organization is significantly redirected while continuing its original mission.

Re-creation is a type of change that is reactive and strategic in scope. It is also called **frame breaking** because the new organization is completely different from the past.

Resistance to Organizational Change

Organizational change comes in all forms, sizes, shapes, and with various degrees of impacts and consequences for employees. Among the most common reasons for resistance to change are: surprise, inertia, misunderstanding, emotional side effects, lack of trust, fear of failure, personality conflicts, lack of tact, threat to job status or security, and breakup of work groups. Management faces the challenge of foreseeing and neutralizing resistance to change, as the resistance is both rational and irrational.

Management theorists have offered at least six options to overcome resistance to change: (1) education and communication, (2) participation and involvement, (3) facilitation and support, (4) negotiation and agreement, (5) manipulation and co-optation, and (6) explicit and implicit coercion. Situational appropriateness is the key to success.

Manipulation occurs when managers selectively withhold or dispense information and consciously arrange events to increase the chance that a change will be successful. Co-optation normally involves token participation, and the impact of their input is negligible.

Explicit and implicit coercion is involved when managers who cannot or will not invest the time required for the other strategies force employees to go along with a change by threatening them with termination, loss of pay raises or promotions, transfer, and so forth.

Organizational Development Defined

Organizational development (OD) is a systematic approach to planned change programs intended to help employees and organizations function more effectively. OD combines the knowledge from various disciplines, such as behavioral science, psychology, sociology, education, and management. OD is a process of fundamental change in an organization's culture. For OD programs to be effective, not only must they be tailored to unique situations, but they also must meet the seven common objectives in order to develop trust. Problem-solving skills, communication, and cooperation are required for success.

Social psychologist Kurt Lewin recommended that change agents unfreeze, change, and then refreeze social systems related to three major phases or components of OD:

Unfreezing Phase → Change Phase

→ Refreezing Phase

Unfreezing involves neutralizing resistance by preparing employees for change. Change involves implementing the change strategy. Refreezing involves systematically following up a change program for permanent results.

Unfreezing Phase

The objective of the unfreezing phase is to assess the situation and suggest an appropriate change strategy. The scope of work includes making announcements, holding meetings, and launching a promotional campaign in the organization's newsletter and on bulletin boards. The goal is to deliver a clear message to employees about the change. Management needs to avoid creating unrealistic expectations such as miracles.

During the unfreezing phase, management may choose to diagnose the situation by using several approaches, such as: (1) requiring records (personnel or financial) for signs of excessive absenteeism, cost overruns, budget variances, (2) interviewing employees with specific questions about their job and the organization, (3) mailing survey questionnaires for opinions and suggestions, and (4) observing employees at work since people tend to say one thing and do another. After the data are collected and compiled, it is good to compare the results with past results to see how things have changed. This would help in mapping a future course of action.

Change Phase

The objective of the change phase is to implement the change strategy through enhanced collaboration and cooperation. In this phase of intervention, the wheels of change are set in motion. Intervention here means that a systematic attempt will be made to correct an organizational deficiency uncovered through diagnosis.

Six popular OD interventions designed to increase effectiveness are (1) life and career planning, (2) skill development, (3) role analysis, (4) team building, (5) survey feedback, and (6) OD grid. The OD grid is based on Blake and Mouton's Leadership Grid—a popular OD approach.

Refreezing Phase

The objective of the refreezing phase is to address unanticipated problems and side effects and to maintain positive changes. The effectiveness of change strategy is also evaluated. The scope includes follow-up and monitoring to ensure lasting change.

Organizational Effectiveness Defined

Effectiveness is a measure of whether organizational goals and objectives are accomplished. It is the combined effect of organizational behavior, culture, change, and development.

Organizational Effectiveness
= Organizational Behavior
+ Organizational Culture
+ Organizational Change
+ Organizational Development

The criteria of organizational effectiveness include:

- The effectiveness criterion is prescribed by society in the form of explicit expectations, regulations, and laws, and by stockholders in the form of profits, return on investment, and growth.
- Organizational effectiveness has a time dimension to it (i.e., near future, intermediate future, and distant future) as well as a performance dimension (i.e., productivity, efficiency, and economy).

Organizational Decline Defined

Organizational decline results from management complacency (usually the primary culprit), unsteady economic growth, resource shortages, competition, and weak demand for products and services. The decline typically involves a reduction in the size or scope of the organization. The decline is compounded by lack of effectiveness and efficiency. While effectiveness deals with achieving goals and objectives, efficiency deals with how well inputs (e.g., all resources such as men, materials, machinery, money, information, and energy) are utilized to produce outputs (e.g., products and services).

> Organizational Decline
> = Organizational Ineffectiveness
> + Organizational Inefficiency
> + Organizational Nonperformance
> + Management Complacency

Some ways to prevent organizational decline include taking the following actions:

- Organize the company into definable businesses that have explicit goals.
- Concentrate on the toughest competitors and the most difficult customers.
- Define each job so that it is closely tied to a definable business purpose.
- Promote individual diversity to take risks and experiment with new ideas.
- Strengthen the participative management process.
- Emphasize more effective communication and information flow—downward, upward, and horizontal.

❑ Learning Objective 1.11: UNDERSTAND HOW TO MEASURE AND MANAGE BUSINESS PERFORMANCE RESULTS

Performance is the organization's ability to attain its goals and objectives by using resources in an efficient and effective manner. The scope includes productivity, effectiveness, efficiency, and economy, which are compared and contrasted.

Productivity Defined

Productivity is the organization's output of goods and services divided by its inputs. This means productivity can be improved by either increasing the amount of output using the same level of inputs, or reducing the number of inputs required to produce the desired output.

Two approaches for measuring productivity are total factor productivity and partial productivity.

Total factor productivity is the ratio of total outputs to the inputs from labor, capital, materials, and energy. **Partial productivity** is the ratio of total outputs to a major category of inputs. Productivity measurement is used to indicate whether there is a need for any improvement in the first place. It is often a part of the improvement process itself and is used to gauge whether improvement efforts are making any progress.

Measurement alone has a dramatic impact on productivity since the effects of feedback are so powerful. Measurement helps diagnose productivity needs and can be used to focus improvement resources on the most needed operations. Monitoring of performance, feedback, and regular consideration of performance peaks and valleys as indicated by measurement data are powerful stimuli for change. Productivity measurement strategies must be simple and practical and must be continually reevaluated.

Examples of productivity measurement metrics are:

- Number of customers helped divided by number of customer service representatives
- Number of parts inspected divided by number of inspection hours

Components of Productivity Measurement

Four components of productivity measurement exist: (1) inputs, (2) processes, (3) interim outputs, and (4) final outputs from which all measures of productivity are built.

Input represents the amount of resources consumed in the production of outputs such as clerical time, budget, and labor hours. **Processes** transform inputs to final outputs through **interim outputs**. **Final output** represents some unit of production or results such as number of contracts negotiated and amount of profit per completed contract. Both outputs and inputs must be measurable and quantifiable.

Criteria for Productivity Improvement

In addition to accuracy, four other criteria must be considered as part of the continuous process of productivity improvement:

1. **Quality.** A measure that assesses only quantity of outputs can lead to reduced productivity in the long run. Both quality and quantity must be defined and measured.

2. **Mission and goals.** The measure must be related to an organization's mission and strategic goals. Measures directed to products and services that are not consistent with mission and goals threaten productivity.
3. **Rewards and incentives.** Measures must be integrated with performance incentives, reward systems, and practices. Measures that have no important contingencies will not work to improve productivity.
4. **Employee involvement.** Employees must participate in the definition and construction of productivity measures. When lack of involvement has not resulted in commitment and buy-in, results from the measures are not likely to be received favorably or to have any impact on future productivity.

Criteria for Measurement of Outputs

- Accuracy
- Timeliness
- Quantity
- Customer satisfaction
- Completeness
- Cost performance

Guidelines for Productivity Measurement

Productivity measurement occurs within a dynamic and complex organization. This means that the organization's culture, the values and experience of employees, and the political context all will have a greater impact on the measurement process. The ideal organization is the one that institutionalizes a productivity measurement system as a "way of doing business."

The traditional performance and productivity measurements such as time schedules, on-time delivery, and cost savings continue to be valid. However, new concepts such as benchmarking, continuous process improvement, concurrent engineering, quality circles, self-managed teams, statistical process control, and total quality management should be practiced and complemented with the traditional measurements.

Improving Productivity

When an organization decides that improving productivity is important, there are three places to look: technological productivity, worker productivity, and managerial productivity. Increased **technological** productivity refers to the use of more efficient machines, robots, computers, and other technologies to increase outputs. Increased **worker productivity** means having workers produce more outputs in the same time period. This includes employees working harder, improving work processes, acquiring more knowledge, more resources, improved task or workplace design, and motivating employees. Increased **managerial productivity** simply means that managers do a better job of running the business. Often, the real reason for productivity problems is due to poor management.

Effectiveness, Efficiency, and Economy Defined

Effectiveness is the degree to which an organization achieves a stated goal or objective. **Efficiency** is the use of minimal resources—raw materials, money, and people—to provide a desired volume of output. **Economy** means whether an organization is acquiring the appropriate type, quality, and amount of resources at an appropriate cost.

Effectiveness and efficiency are related to productivity measurement. Effective production is the process that produces the desired results. Efficient production means achieving the desired results with a minimum of inputs. Efficiency and effectiveness must go hand-in-hand in productive organizations. Organizations can temporarily survive without perfect efficiency; they usually die if they are ineffective.

Design of Performance Measurement Systems

Performance measures should be accurately defined, analyzed, and documented so that all interested parties are informed about them. Performance standards should bring meaning to measurements. Employees who are being measured should feel that standards and specific performance measures are fair and achievable. Self-measurement may create confidence and trust and permit fast feedback and correction from employees. But it can also lead to distortions, concealment, and delays in reporting.

One of the design objectives should be that performance standards must be simple, meaningful, comparable, reproducible, and traceable given similar business conditions. Care should be taken to compare items that are alike in terms of units of measurements (pounds, grams, liters, or gallons), timeframes (hours or days), quantity (volume in units or tons), and quality (meeting the requirements).

During the design of performance measurements, the design team should take both human factors and technical factors into account. From a **human factor viewpoint,** ensure that performance measures are not so loose that they present no challenge or so tight that they cannot be attainable. Ideally, both subordinates and superiors must participate in identifying and developing the performance metrics. From a **technical factor viewpoint,** employees should be given proper tools, training, and equipment to do their job. Otherwise frustration will result. Above all, the performance measures should be based on objective measurement instead of subjective measurement to minimize human bias and suspicion of the reported measurements.

Periodically, the performance measurements should be reviewed and updated to ensure their continued applicability to the situations at hand. Evaluations of performance measures should concentrate on the significant exceptions or deviations from the standards. Therefore, exception reporting is preferred. Significant variances (deviations) require analysis and correction of standards or procedures.

The standards should match the objectives of the operation or function being reviewed. Usually the standards can be found in standard operating procedures, job descriptions, organizational policies and directives, product design specifications, operating budgets, trade sources, organization's contracts, applicable laws and regulations, generally accepted business practices, generally accepted industry standards, generally accepted accounting principles, and generally accepted auditing standards.

 Self-Assessment Exercise

Online exercises are provided for the learning objectives in this module. Please visit www.mbaiq.com to complete the online exercises and to calculate your MBA IQ Score.

Operations Management

Learning Objective 2.1: Understand the Strategic Importance of Demand Forecasting 46
Time-Series Models 46
Linear Regression Analysis 47
Correlation Analysis 47

Learning Objective 2.2: Understand the Production Strategies and Manufacturing Performance Measures 47

Learning Objective 2.3: Understand the Production-Related Value Concepts 48
Value Analysis, Engineering, and Research 48
Value Index 49
Value-Stream Mapping 49
Value-Based Location Strategy 49
Product-by-Value Analysis 49

Learning Objective 2.4: Understand the Philosophies of Just-In-Time and Lean Operations 49
Waste 49
Variability 50
Throughput 50
Just-in-Time Strategy 50
Lean Operations 52

Learning Objective 2.5: Understand the Principles and Techniques of Inventory Management 52
Demand 52
Inventory Levels 53
ABC Analysis 55
Cycle Counting 56

Learning Objective 2.6: Understand the Principles and Techniques of Supply-Chain and Logistics Management 56
Supply Chain 56
Logistics Management 57

Learning Objective 2.7: Understand the Various Planning Systems Applicable to Manufacturing and Distribution Operations 58

Master Production Schedule 58
Material Requirements Planning 58
Distribution Requirements Planning 59
Enterprise Resource Planning 59
Customer Relationship Management 59
Capacity Requirements Planning 60
Aggregate Production Planning 60

Learning Objective 2.8: Understand the Various Short-Term Scheduling Systems Used in Production 60
Capacity Planning versus Short-Term Scheduling 61
Scheduling Methods 61
Loading Jobs 61
Job Sequencing 61
Level-Material-Use Schedule 62

Learning Objective 2.9: Understand the Theory of Constraints in Operations 62
Theory of Constraints 62
Drum-Buffer-Rope Scheduling 62
Buffer Management 62
VAT Analysis 62
The Five Focusing Steps 63

Learning Objective 2.10: Understand the Principles of Production Economics and Application of Decision Tools 63
Make-or-Buy Analysis 63
Learning-Curve Analysis 63
Supplier's Breakeven Analysis 63
Outsourcing 64
Machine Selection 64
Plant Selection 64
Decision Tools 64

Learning Objective 2.11: Understand the Principles and Techniques of Equipment Maintenance and System Reliability 65
Equipment Maintenance 65
System Reliability 65

Learning Objective 2.12: Understand the Production Process Flows and Metrics 66

Learning Objective 2.13: Understand
   the Technology Deployed in
   Manufacturing and Service
   Operations   67

Flexible Manufacturing Systems   67
Process Control Systems   68
Point-of-Sale Systems   68
Bar-Coding Systems   68

❑ Learning Objective 2.1: UNDERSTAND THE STRATEGIC IMPORTANCE OF DEMAND FORECASTING

Manufacturing companies generate revenues by producing and selling their products to customers. Service companies generate revenues by providing their services to clients. Since revenues drive expenses, profits, and stock prices of companies, predicting revenue levels is a strategic issue for all levels of management. Revenue forecasts are called **demand forecasts.**

Good forecasts are an essential part of efficient manufacturing and service operations as they deal with predicting future events such as product/service demand to create revenues. Management has a choice in that they can wait and see what happens to actual demand without forecasting the demand (reactive), which is risky, or they can forecast the demand for both short run and long run (proactive). Forecasts reduce uncertainty (risk) about future outcomes because management can plan ahead.

> **Timely Demand Forecasts → Timely Operational Plans**
> **Late Demand Forecasts → Late Operational Plans**

Demand forecasting may involve the use of a combination of quantitative methods (e.g., time-series models, regression analysis, and correlation analysis) and qualitative methods (e.g., executive opinions, Delphi method, sales force estimates, and consumer market surveys). The **Delphi method** uses expert decision-makers (5 to 10) to estimate the sales forecast without face-to-face meetings.

Demand forecasts are prepared for three time horizons: **short-range** (less than three months to one year for planning purchasing, production, budgeting, and job assignments), **medium-range** (from three months to three years for planning sales, production, and cash), and **long-range** (three years or more for planning new products, new plants, new equipment, new offices, new warehouses, and research and development programs).

Demand forecasts drive a manufacturing company's production plans, material requirement plans, capacity requirement plans, and production scheduling and serve as inputs to financial, marketing, and human resource planning. For example, as sales demand is projected higher, more employees need to be hired.

Time-Series Models

Time-series models use past data points to project future data points and have four components, such as **trends** (upward or downward data movement), **seasonality** (data pattern that repeats itself periodically in weeks and months), **cycles** (data patterns that occur every several years that tie into the business cycles), and **random variation** (no data patterns shown as bumps or blips in the data caused by chance and unusual conditions and hence cannot be predicted). Examples of time-series models include naïve (intuitive) approach, moving average, exponential smoothing, and trend projection.

The **naïve approach** assumes that demand in the next period will be equal to demand in the most recent period. The **moving-average** method uses an average of the most recent periods of data to forecast the next period. The **exponential smoothing** method uses a weighted-moving-average technique in which data points are weighted by an exponential function. The **trend projection** method fits a trend line to a series of historical data points and then projects the line into the future.

The following formulas are related to time-series models:

Moving Average = (Sum of Demand in Previous n periods)/n

New Forecast Using Exponential Smoothing = (Last Period's Forecast) + Alpha (Last Period's Actual Demand − Last Period's Forecast)

where **alpha** is a weight (smoothing constant) with a value between 0 and 1. The value of alpha can be high if weighted more for recent data and can be low if weighted more for past data.

Trend Line Using the Least-Squares Method
$$= y = a + bx$$

where y is the intercept (height) and b is the slope (the angle of the line).

Linear Regression Analysis

Linear regression analysis, which is an associative model, considers several variables that are related to the quantity being predicted. The linear regression method is more powerful than the time-series methods that use only historical values for the forecasted variable. Two types of variables exist: the **dependent variable**, which is the forecasted item of interest, and the **independent variable**, which is related to the dependent variable. The **multiple regression method** uses more than one independent variable, whereas the linear regression method uses only one independent variable.

Linear regression analysis using the least-squares method is calculated as follows:

$$y = a + bx$$

where y is the value of the dependent variable, a is the y-axis intercept, b is the slope of the regression line, and x is the independent variable.

Application of Regression Analysis

XYZ Company derived the following cost relationship from a regression analysis of its monthly manufacturing overhead cost:

$$C = \$80,000 + \$12\,M$$

where C is monthly manufacturing overhead cost and M is machine hours. The standard error of estimate of the regression is $6,000. The standard time required to manufacture a case of the company's single product is four machine hours. XYZ applies manufacturing overhead to production on the basis of machine hours, and its normal annual production is 50,000 cases.

Question 1: What is the estimated variable manufacturing overhead cost for a month in which scheduled production is 5,000 cases?

Answer 1: In the cost equation $C = \$80,000 + \$12\,M$, $80,000 is the fixed cost component, and $12 M is the variable cost component. That is, $\$12 \times 5,000$ cases $\times 4$ machine hours per case $= \$240,000$.

Question 2: What is the predetermined fixed manufacturing overhead rate?

Answer 2: Since $80,000 is the fixed component per month, we need to multiply this by 12 to obtain one-year fixed cost. The predetermined overhead rate per machine hour is ($\$80,000 \times 12)/(50,000 \times 4) = \$4.80$.

Source: Certified Internal Auditor (CIA) Exams from the Institute of Internal Auditors (IIA), Altamonte Springs, Florida, USA.

Correlation Analysis

Correlation analysis predicts the cause-and-effect relationships between two variables, whereas regression methods cannot. Two types of correlation measures exist: (1) **coefficient of correlation**, which is a measure of the strength of the relationship between two variables, and (2) **coefficient of determination**, which is the square of the coefficient of correlation. The coefficient of determination is the percent of variation in the dependent variable that is explained by the regression equation.

❑ Learning Objective 2.2: UNDERSTAND THE PRODUCTION STRATEGIES AND MANUFACTURING PERFORMANCE MEASURES

Production strategies deal with transforming resources (raw materials, labor, energy, and machines) into products and services. Four types of production strategies include process focus, repetitive focus, product focus, and mass customization.

1. In a **process focus,** a production facility is organized around processes to facilitate low-volume, high-variety production.
2. In a **repetitive focus,** a production facility is organized around modules, where modules are parts or components of a product that were previously prepared.
3. In a **product focus,** a production facility is organized around products to facilitate high-volume, low-variety production.
4. In a **mass customization,** high-volume, high-variety, rapid, and low-cost production is used to meet constantly changing customer needs. It uses build-to-order systems, which means producing to actual customer orders and not to forecasts.

Examples of tools and techniques used in production strategies include crossover charts, flow diagrams, time-function (process) mapping, value-stream mapping, process charts, and service blueprinting.

A **crossover chart** can be drawn to show costs at the possible volumes for more than one process. However, at any given volume, only one process will have the lowest cost. A crossover point can be determined where the total cost of the processes changes.

A **flow diagram** is used to analyze movement of material or people. A **process mapping** is a flow diagram with the time element added. A **value-stream mapping** deals with adding value in the flow of material and information through the entire production process. A **process chart** uses symbols to analyze the movement of material or people. In **service blueprinting**, the focus is on the customer and the provider's interaction with the customer.

Manufacturing performance measures include both financial and nonfinancial measures, where the latter include **total manufacturing cycle time (MCT)**, **manufacturing cycle efficiency (MCE)**, and **total throughput**. Management should compare actual performance against the target to identify areas needing improvement.

The following formulas apply to manufacturing performance measures:

$$\text{Total MCT} = \text{Value-Added Time} + \text{Non-Value-Added Time}$$

The value-added time is called **process time** or **assembly time,** and the non-value-added time is the time spent in inspecting, waiting, and moving things around in the plant. A cycle is a complete set of tasks included in an operation or a process. **Cycle time** is the number of steps or procedures necessary to complete those tasks.

$$\text{MCE} = \text{Total Hours of Value-Added Time in Production Process}/\text{Total MCT in Hours}$$

or

$$\text{MCE} = \text{Value-Added Time}/\text{Throughput Time}$$

Eliminating or reducing the non-value-added time increases the MCE. As the MCE increases, it decreases the throughput time.

$$\text{Total Throughput} = \text{Number of Good Units Produced}/\text{Total MCT}$$

Throughput Time (velocity of production)
$$= \text{Process Time} + \text{Inspection Time} + \text{Wait Time} + \text{Move Time}$$

Actual Delivery Cycle Time $=$ Throughput Time $+$ Shipping Time

❏ Learning Objective 2.3: UNDERSTAND THE PRODUCTION-RELATED VALUE CONCEPTS

Production-related value concepts include value analysis, engineering, and research; value index; value-stream mapping; value-based location strategy; and product-by-value analysis.

Value Analysis, Engineering, and Research

Value analysis (VA) is the organized and systematic study of every element of cost in a manufactured part, raw material, or service to make certain it fulfills its function at the lowest possible cost. Value is defined as function divided by cost. VA assigns a price to every step of a process and then computes the benefit-to-cost ratio of that step.

The goal of VA is to make improvements in a product while the product is being produced and after deciding that a new product is a success. VA focuses on the production stage to make it better and economical, thus improving a product's value.

VA is related to product or service characteristics such as quality, performance, marketability, maintainability, and reliability. There is a tradeoff involved among these characteristics.

Value engineering (VE) can be applied to two areas: procurement contracts and manufactured products. VE is referred to as function analysis. The terms VA and VE are used synonymously.

Regarding procurement contracts, VE is the formal technique by which contractors may (1) voluntarily suggest methods for performing more economically and share in any resulting savings or (2) be required to establish a program to identify methods for performing more economically. VE attempts to eliminate, without impairing essential functions or characteristics, anything that increases acquisition, operation, or support costs.

Regarding manufactured products, the goal of VE is to improve a new product's design and specifications before a product reaches the production stage.

It focuses on cost reduction and cost-avoidance techniques to improve product value and meet customer requirements in an optimal way. It reduces the complexity of a product with robust design. VE focuses on pre-production design work to improve a product's value.

Value research, which is related to VE, focuses on identifying customers' likes, dislikes, and neutral features in a given product or service. The goal is to correct the dislikes and neutral features through cost reductions and turn them into "likes" features.

Value Index

The **value index** is a ratio of relative importance of a component to a customer to the total cost devoted to that component, both expressed as percentages. The components with a value index of less than 1.0 are candidates for value engineering in terms of reducing costs. The components with a value index of more than 1.0 are candidates for value enhancements, since they need more investment to improve features important to customers.

Interpretation of Value Index

Value index ratio for a component < 1.0: its costs are higher relative to its importance to customers.

Value index ratio for a component > 1.0: its relative importance to customers is greater than its cost.

Value-Stream Mapping

The goal of **value-stream mapping** is to understand the complexities of process design and redesign stages. It focuses on where value is added or not added to a product, starting from the suppliers and manufacturers (producers) and ending with customers. It looks at the production process as well as the management decisions and information systems that support the production process.

Value-Stream Mapping = Suppliers → Producers → Customers

Value-Based Location Strategy

The goal of **value-based location strategy** is to maximize the value and benefit of location to a company.

Location strategies include expanding an existing facility, maintaining a current facility, adding a new facility, closing an existing facility, or moving to another location.

Application of Location Strategy

For a manufacturing company, the location strategy primarily focuses on minimizing costs.

For a retail company, the location strategy primarily focuses on maximizing revenues.

For a distribution company, the location strategy primarily focuses on maximizing the speed of delivery of goods to customers.

Product-by-Value Analysis

Product-by-value analysis lists products in descending order of their individual dollar contributions to the firm. It also lists the total annual dollar contribution of the product. This type of analysis tells managers which products should be eliminated and which products require further investment in research and development and capital equipment. The product-by-value analysis can help management in increasing cash flows, increasing market penetration, and reducing costs.

❏ Learning Objective 2.4: UNDERSTAND THE PHILOSOPHIES OF JUST-IN-TIME AND LEAN OPERATIONS

Operations management primarily focuses on three things: (1) eliminating **waste** by removing non-value-added activities, (2) removing **variability** in product specifications and production processes by removing problems and waste and adding value at each step of the production process, and (3) increasing **throughput** by reducing the total manufacturing cycle time (MCT) and using pull systems. There is a relationship between variability and waste in that the lower the variability in a product, the lower the waste in that product.

Waste

Taiichi Ohno of Japan pointed out **seven wastes (7Ws)** in a production system, and he believes that any activity that does not add value to a customer is waste (muda in Japanese). His seven categories of waste are overproduction (producing early or producing more than orders), queues (idle time, storage time, and waiting time), transportation (moving and handling the same material more than once), inventory (keeping stock on hand), motion (unnecessary movement of material, people, and equipment), overprocessing (unnecessary work performed on a product), and defective product (rework, scrap, product returns, and warranty claims resulting from defective products).

Japanese operations managers have identified **5 Ss** for a neat, orderly, and efficient workplace to reduce waste. These five Ss (5Ss) are sort, simplify, shine, standardize, and sustain. U.S. operations managers added **two Ss** (2Ss), safety and support, to maintain a lean workplace. Operations managers working in a factory, office, hospital, or retail store can use the 7Ss to eliminate waste, so assets are used for productive purposes only.

Variability

A goal of operations management is to deliver a perfect product to a customer on time and every time. Product **variability** does not enable a perfect product. Waste; incomplete design drawings; inaccurate product specifications; poor production processes; producing improper quantities, late, or nonconforming products; poor management; and unpredictable customer demand are factors that contribute to product variability.

Throughput

Throughput is the time required to manage a customer order through the production process, from receipt to delivery. One measure of throughput is total MCT, which is the time that an order takes between receiving of raw materials and shipping a finished product. The goal is to drive down total MCT to increase throughput.

A technique for increasing throughput is a **pull system,** which uses signals to request materials and supplies from upstream to downstream workstations as needed. This is unlike a **push system,** which requests materials and supplies regardless of their need. Hence, the pull system, which is a standard tool of just-in-time (JIT), lowers costs, improves production schedules, enhances customer satisfaction, and increases throughput.

Just-in-Time Strategy

Just-in-time (JIT) strategy is based on management principles such as eliminate waste; produce to demand and one-at-a-time; think long term; develop, motivate, trust, and respect people; and achieve continuous improvement **(kaizen).** This is made possible when the focus is "quality at the source," and the tools used include **statistical process control (SPC)** methods, **failsafe methods** (mistake-proofing and checklists), and **problem-solving methods** using five *whys* (5Ws) to determine the root cause of a problem. Quality at the source means producing perfect parts every time and all the time. An effective JIT strategy encompasses the entire product lifecycle from the acquisition of raw materials to delivery of the end product to the final customer. The major benefits of JIT strategy are (1) improved productivity, quality, service, and flexibility and (2) reduced costs, inventory investment, lead-times, lot sizes, and physical space.

The scope of JIT strategy includes topics such as JIT production, purchasing, production processing, inventory, transportation, partnerships, quality, scheduling, and layout.

JIT Production

JIT production strategy is to continuously improve productivity and quality. It is based on the belief that "small could be better," not "more is better."

JIT Production versus Traditional Production

The pull systems are the prothesis of JIT production.

The pull system is based on a variable-flow manufacturing principle.

The JIT (pull) production system has a "no contingencies" (i.e., no safety stock) mentality.

The push systems are the antithesis of JIT production.

The push system is based on a fixed-flow manufacturing principle.

The traditional (push) production system has a "contingency" (i.e., safety stock) mentality.

JIT Purchasing

JIT purchasing requires a partnership between a supplier and a customer, which is a major departure from traditional purchasing. JIT supplier relations call for long-term partnerships with single-source suppliers who provide certified quality materials while continuously reducing costs. The JIT supplier's manufacturing processes must be under **statistical process control (SPC)** and their capability should be certified by the customer. The SPC charts serve as the documentation to assure that the process stayed in control during the time the parts were made. JIT purchasing is called **stockless inventory** since the customer has no inventory to stock as it is used up in production right after it is received. The major goal is to reduce or eliminate work-in-process (WIP) inventory so that all raw materials are consumed in a timely manner within the production process.

Traditional Purchasing versus JIT Purchasing

Traditional purchasing practices call for infrequent, large-lot shipments.

JIT purchasing practices call for frequent, small-lot shipments.

Traditional purchasing practices call for inspection, since they focus on continuous checking by the customer. These practices are reactive due to their focus on "after the fact."

JIT purchasing practices call for no inspection, since they focus on continuous improvement by the supplier. These practices are proactive due to their focus on "before the fact."

JIT Production Processing

JIT production processing requires setup reduction, focused factory, group technology, uniform scheduling and mixed model scheduling, and the pull system. The objective here is to produce many varieties of products in small quantities on short notice. Manufacturing flexibility is the hallmark of the JIT production processing strategy.

JIT Inventory

A misconception about JIT is that it is just a program to reduce inventory. Fortunately, JIT does more than that. Major components of **JIT inventory** include reducing variability, reducing inventory quantities, reducing lot sizes, and reducing setup costs. Having too much inventory on hand hides the level of variability and bad quality in the production process.

JIT Transportation

While JIT purchasing is the starting point of a JIT cycle, JIT transportation is the execution part of the JIT cycle. **JIT transportation** is the physical linkage between the inside and the outside processes. It is a process that starts at a supplier location and ends at a customer location. It requires the analysis of all transport events and the elimination of non-value-added events. The basic value-added events include: move load to dock at a supplier location, load carrier, move load to customer location, return empty trailer to terminal, unload by the customer, and move load to assigned customer location.

JIT Partnerships

JIT partnerships are needed between suppliers and purchasers of raw materials, parts, and components to remove waste and to drive down costs for mutual benefits. Long-term partnerships are better than short-term, so a few suppliers can invest money to improve quality.

JIT Quality

JIT quality is realized as JIT forces down inventory levels, meaning fewer bad units are produced, which in turn means fewer units must be reworked, thus improving quality. As JIT shrinks queues and leadtimes, it creates an early warning system for quality problems and production errors. As JIT quality is increased, there is less need for safety stock (inventory buffers) to protect against unreliable quality levels and unpredictable customer demand levels.

JIT Scheduling

JIT scheduling improves the ability to meet customer order due dates, reduces inventory with smaller lot sizes, and reduces work-in-process. Two techniques include level schedules and kanban. A **level schedule** means each day's production quantity meets the demand for that day, using frequent small batches. A **kanban system** moves parts through production via a pull signal. Kanban uses a card system giving authorization for the next container of material to be produced.

The following formulas can be used for JIT scheduling:

Number of Kanban Containers

= (Demand During Production Lead Time

+ Safety Stock)/Container Size

Production Lead Time
= Wait Time + Material Handling Time
+ Processing Time
Demand During Production Lead-Time
= Daily Demand × Production Lead-Time

JIT Layout

An efficient **JIT layout** reduces waste in the form of minimizing the movement of materials on a factory floor or paper in an office because these movements do not add value. The benefits of JIT facility include distance reduction, increased operational flexibility, employees working closer to each other, and reduced space and inventory.

Lean Operations

Two Japanese individuals, Toyoda and Ohno, are given credit for the **Toyota Production System (TPS)** with its three components of **continuous improvement, respect for people,** and **standard work practice.** Continuous improvement means building an organizational culture and instilling in its people a value system stressing that processes can be always improved. These values start with job recruiting and job practice and continue with job training. At Toyota, employees are recruited, trained, and treated (respected) as knowledge workers. They receive cross-training to enrich jobs, have few job classifications, and are empowered to stop machines and processes when quality problems exist. Work is specified as to content, sequence, timing, and outcome with simple and direct flows of products and services as they move from one person to another and from one machine to another. Built-in tests are designed to automatically signal problems so that any gaps can be identified and corrected immediately to make the production system more reliable, flexible, and adaptable.

Lean operations means identifying customer value by analyzing all the activities required to produce a product and then optimizing the entire process to increase value from the customers' perspective. The highlights of lean operations include understanding what the customer wants and ensuring that the customer's input and feedback are obtained to increase value to that customer. Lean operations adopt a philosophy of minimizing waste by striving for perfection through continuous learning, creativity, and teamwork, which can be equally applied to manufacturing and service industries.

Both JIT and TPS have an internal focus on jobs, employees, work practices, materials, and training. Lean operations have an external focus on the customer. Lean operations need both JIT and TPS techniques and more.

Pull Systems—Manufacturing and Distribution

In **pull systems**, work is pulled from the manufacturing plant and have the following characteristics: (1) lean manufacturing production schedules are based on actual customer order demand information, resulting in a build-to-order situation, (2) kanban material systems order raw materials, parts, and components based on actual customer order demand information, and (3) replenishing field warehouse inventory decisions are made at the local distribution center.

Push Systems—Manufacturing and Distribution

In **push systems**, work is pulled through the manufacturing plant and have the following characteristics: (1) finished goods production schedules are based on forecasts of customer order information, resulting in a build-to-stock situation, (2) material requirements planning (MRP) systems order raw materials, parts, and components based on expectation of customer demand information, and (3) replenishing field warehouse inventory decisions are made at the central distribution center or manufacturing plant.

❑ Learning Objective 2.5: UNDERSTAND THE PRINCIPLES AND TECHNIQUES OF INVENTORY MANAGEMENT

Manufacturing companies generate revenues by selling their end-products (finished goods) stored as inventory.

Demand

From an inventory management viewpoint, **demand** is of two types: independent demand and dependent demand.

Independent Demand Inventory Systems

Independent demand inventory systems are based on the premise that the demand or usage of a particular item is not related to the demand or usage of other items. Examples include finished goods; spare parts; material, repair, and operating (MRO) supplies; and resale inventories. Independent demand inventory systems are pull systems in that materials are pulled from the previous operation as they are needed to replace materials that have been used (e.g., finished goods are replaced as they are sold). These types of inventory systems answer the question of when to place the replenishment order and how much to order at one time. Reorder point models and fixed/variable order quantity models (e.g., **economic order quantity, EOQ**) are examples of independent demand inventory systems, which can be reviewed either continuously or periodically.

Four possibilities exist, including the following:

1. Continuous review and fixed order quantity
2. Periodic review and fixed order quantity
3. Continuous review and variable order quantity
4. Periodic review and variable order quantity

Dependent Demand Inventory Systems

Dependent demand inventory systems are based on the premise that the demand or usage of a particular item is dependent on the demand or usage of other items. Examples include raw materials, work-in-process inventories, and component parts.

A company manages its inventory by using various methods and approaches (e.g., EOQ). Inventory consists of raw materials, work in process, and finished goods. Efficient inventory management is needed to support sales, which is necessary for profits. Benefits such as high turnover rate, low write-offs, and low lost sales can be attributed to efficient inventory management. These benefits in turn contribute to a high profit margin, a higher total asset turnover, a higher rate of return on investment, and a strong stock price. Inventory management is a major concern for product-based organizations (e.g., manufacturing and retail), since 20 to 40 percent of their total assets is inventory and, as such, poor inventory control will hurt the profitability of the organization.

Inventory Levels

Inventory levels and accounts receivable levels directly depend on sales levels. Receivables arise after sales have been made, whereas inventory must be acquired or produced ahead of sales. Inventory managers have the responsibility to maintain inventories at levels that balance the benefits of reducing the level of investment against the costs associated with lowering inventories. A company's inventory is related to the amount of expected sales. The company's financial forecasting of inventory in the following year would be most accurate when applying a simple linear regression method.

Efficient **inventory management** focuses on three areas: (1) investment in inventory, (2) optimal order quantity, and (3) reorder point.

Investment in Inventory

Investment in inventory depends on the actual level of inventory carried. The relevant question is how many units of each inventory item the firm should hold in its stock. Two types of stock concepts must be understood: (1) working stock and (2) safety stock. The actual level of inventories carried will equal the sum of working stocks and safety stocks.

1. **Working stock (cycle stock)** is needed to meet normal, expected production and sales demand levels. Producing more goods than are currently needed increases the firm's carrying costs and exposes it to the risk of obsolescence if demand should fall. Remember that demand for sales is uncertain. EOQ establishes the working stock amount.
2. **Safety stock** is needed to guard against changes in sales rates or delays in production and shipping activities, resulting in a **stockout** situation. Safety stock is additional stock beyond the working stock and satisfies when demand is greater than expected. The additional costs of holding the safety stock must be balanced against the costs of sales lost due to inventory shortages. Safety stock will not affect the reorder quantities as it is the inventory level at the time of reordering minus the expected usage while the new goods are in transit.

The goal is to minimize both the cost of holding safety stock and the cost of stockouts. EOQ is not relevant to stockouts. Production bottlenecks lead to a stockout. Factors to be considered in controlling stockouts include time needed for delivery, rate of inventory usage, and safety stock.

Effective management requires close coordination and communication among the various functional departments of the organization such as the marketing, sales, production, purchasing, and finance departments. Sales plans need to be converted into purchasing and production plans to produce finished goods and to acquire raw materials; financing plans are needed to support the inventory buildup.

Since inventories need to be available prior to sales, an increase in production to meet increased sales requires an increase in notes payable (a liability account). Since assets (inventories) are increasing, liability (notes payable) must also increase.

Investment in inventory is not complete without discussing the various costs associated with inventories due to their direct relationships. The cost structure affects the amount and type of investment needed. Three types of inventory-related costs are: (1) carrying or holding costs, (2) ordering costs, and (3) stockout costs.

1. **Carrying or holding costs** are the costs associated with carrying a given level of inventory and rise in direct proportion to the average inventory carried or held. The components of carrying costs include the costs of capital tied up in inventory, opportunity cost associated with not being able to use the capital for other investment, warehouse storage and handling costs, insurance premiums, property taxes, depreciation, pilferage, damage, and obsolescence cost.

2. **Ordering costs** are the costs associated with placing an order and are fixed regardless of the average size of inventory. The components of ordering costs include the cost of placing orders, including production setup and shipping and handling costs. Examples include salaries of the purchasers, paper, postage, telephone, transportation, and receiving costs.

3. **Stockout costs** are costs of running short of inventory and require safety stock as a cushion. However, safety stock increases the carrying costs. The components of stockout costs include the loss of sales, the loss of customer goodwill, and problems or delays in production schedules.

Inventory managers face two **decision rules** in inventory management, "how-much-to-order" and "when-to-order," that will result in the lowest possible total inventory cost. The **how-much-to-order decision rule** can be satisfied with the use of an EOQ model. The **when-to-order decision rule** can be satisfied with the use of a reorder point.

The how-much-to-order decision rule involves selecting an order quantity that draws a compromise between (1) keeping smaller inventories and ordering frequently (results in high ordering costs) and (2) keeping large inventories and ordering infrequently (results in high holding costs).

Optimal Order Quantity

Optimal order quantity deals with deciding how many units should be ordered or produced at a given time. Either too much or too little inventory is not good. An optimum inventory level is designed and is found through the use of the EOQ model because it provides the optimal, or least-cost, quantity of inventory that should be ordered.

The focus of the EOQ method is on the quantity of goods to order that will minimize the total cost of ordering and holding (storing) goods. EOQ is a decision model that focuses on the trade-off between carrying costs and ordering costs. It calculates the order quantity that minimizes total inventory costs. Calculus is used in determining the EOQ.

EOQ is appropriate for managing finished goods inventories, which have independent demands from customers or from forecasts. Note that the data needed to calculate EOQ includes the volume of product sales (demand information), the purchase price of the products, the fixed cost of ordering products, and carrying (holding) costs. It does not include the volume of products in inventory, inventory delivery times, delays in transportation, or quality of materials.

If Q is the order quantity, then the how-much-to-order decision involves finding the value of Q that will minimize the sum of holding and ordering costs.

$$Q = \text{EOQ} = \sqrt{\frac{2DCo}{Ch}}$$

where D is annual sales demand in units, Co is cost of placing one order, and Ch is cost of holding (carrying) one unit in inventory for the year.

Due to the square-root sign, a given increase in sales will result in a less-than-proportionate increase in inventories, and the inventory turnover ratio will thus increase as sales grow.

Annual inventory holding cost is directly related to the amount of inventory carried. The EOQ will rise following an increase in the fixed costs of placing and receiving an order.

If a company's cost of ordering per order increases while carrying costs per order remain the same, the optimal order size as specified by the EOQ model would increase.

Two major **assumptions of EOQ** are:

1. The demand for an item is constant. Since the constant demand assumption is not realistic, managers would have to be satisfied with the

near-minimum-cost order quantity instead of a minimum-total-cost order quantity.

2. The entire quantity ordered arrives at one point in time. Again, this may not be realistic because some vendors will deliver partial shipments. Managers usually add a judgmental value-based order quantity to the EOQ suggested order quantity to accommodate unrealistic assumptions of constant demand rate by the EOQ model.

Specific assumptions of the EOQ model include the following:

- Sales can be forecasted perfectly. This is unrealistic.
- Sales are evenly distributed throughout the year. This is not realistic. What about seasonal or cyclical demands?
- Orders are received without delay. This is also unrealistic.
- Fixed costs, carrying costs, and purchase prices are all fixed and independent of the ordering procedures. This is not possible either.

EOQ cost characteristics include the following:

- The point at which the total cost curve is minimized represents the EOQ, and this in turn determines the optimal average inventory level. Here, total cost is the sum of ordering and carrying costs.
- Some costs rise with larger inventories, whereas other costs decline.
- The average investment in inventories depends on how frequently orders are placed.
- Ordering costs decline with larger orders and inventories due to reduced order frequency.

The relationship between EOQ and material requirements planning (MRP) is as follows:

- The EOQ model is focusing on finished goods inventories, which have an independent demand from customers or from forecasts. The EOQ is a deterministic inventory model, which assumes that the rate of demand for an item is constant. On the other hand, probabilistic inventory models assume that the rate of demand for an item is fluctuating and can be described only on probability terms.
- The demand for raw materials and components in the MRP model is directly dependent on the demand for finished goods in the inventory system (i.e., EOQ).

It is good to know how much the recommended order quantity would change if the estimated ordering and holding costs had been different. Depending on whether the total annual cost increased, decreased, or remained the same, we can tell whether the EOQ model is sensitive or insensitive to variations in the cost estimates.

Reorder Point

Reorder point is the point at which inventory should be ordered or produced (i.e., when-to-order decision rule), and at which stock on hand must be replenished. It is also the inventory level at which an order should be placed. The formula is:

$$\text{Reorder Point (RP)} = \text{Lead-Time (LT)} \times \text{Usage Rate (UR)}$$

where **lead-time** is the time lag required for production and shipping of inventory, and **usage rate** is the usage quantity per unit of time (demand). Note that the time period should be the same in both lead-time and usage rate (i.e., days, weeks, or months).

The **cycle time** answers how frequently the order will be placed, and it can be calculated as follows: cycle time is number of working days in a year *divided by* number of orders that will be placed in a year.

A complication in the calculation of the reorder point arises when we introduce the concept of **goods-in-transit.** This situation occurs when a new order must be placed before the previous order is received. The formula for a reorder point when goods-in-transit is considered is

$$\text{Reorder Point for Goods-in-Transit} = (\text{Lead-Time} \times \text{Usage Rate}) - (\text{Goods-in-Transit})$$

ABC Analysis

ABC analysis is a method of classifying on-hand inventory based on usage and value. It applies the **Pareto principle** (20% critical few and 80% trivial many) to inventory. Expensive, frequently used, high-stockout-cost items with long lead-times (Class A items) are most frequently reviewed. Inexpensive and infrequently used items (B and C items) are reviewed less frequently. To classify the inventory based on annual dollar volume, the annual demand of each item is multiplied with its cost per unit.

Class A items (i.e., approximately 20% of stock items) have a high annual dollar volume representing approximately 80 percent of the total dollar usage.

Class B and C items (i.e., together approximately 80% of stock items) have a medium annual dollar volume for Class B items and a low annual dollar volume for Class C items, representing together approximately 20 percent of the total dollar usage.

Cycle Counting

Cycle counting is a continuing reconciliation and audit of inventory items with inventory records. It is an alternative to the annual physical inventory exercise and uses the inventory classifications developed through the ABC analysis. With cycle-counting procedures, stock items are counted, records are verified, inaccuracies are documented, and corrective actions are taken to ensure integrity of the inventory system. The frequency of cycle counting depends on the type of inventory item. The cycle counting policy might be as follows:

Class A stock items may be counted once a month.
Class B stock items may be counted once every three
    months.
Class C stock items may be counted once every six
    months.

The number of stock items of each classification to be counted each working day can be computed as follows:

Stock quantity for A class divided by the cycle-
    counting policy days gives the number of items
    to be counted per working day.
Stock quantity for B class divided by the cycle-
    counting policy days gives the number of items
    to be counted per working day.
Stock quantity for C class divided by the cycle-
    counting policy days gives the number of items
    to be counted per working day.
Add the number of items to be counted per working
    day for A, B, and C classes.

❑ Learning Objective 2.6:
UNDERSTAND THE PRINCIPLES AND TECHNIQUES OF SUPPLY-CHAIN AND LOGISTICS MANAGEMENT

The focus of this learning objective is on managing the supply chain and understanding the functions of warehouse and distribution management.

Supply Chain

The **supply chain** is seen as an equivalent to an input–transformation–output system. In this context, both customer and supplier goodwill are to be viewed as a key asset to an organization. The supply chain becomes a value chain when all of the transforming activities performed upon an input provide value to a customer. The real challenge is to ensure that value is added at every step of the chain to achieve customer satisfaction. Both purchasers and suppliers play a large role in the **value chain**. The following is an example of a value chain:

**Purchasers → Suppliers → Producers
→ Distributors → Customers**

Managing the supply base includes integration of suppliers, involvement of suppliers, supplier reduction strategies, supplier performance, and supplier certification. The purpose of managing the supply base is to manage quality, quantity, delivery, service, and price.

Integrating suppliers means reducing or balancing the number of suppliers available so that they become part of the buyer/purchaser operation to lower inventories, to increase response time and quality, and to decrease total cost.

Early **involvement of suppliers** in the product design process reduces cost, improves quality, and shortens product development cycle time. This is achieved through review of product specifications and production standards by the supplier.

Supplier reduction strategies include deciding who will be single-sourcing or second-sourcing vendor. Approaches to improving **supplier performance** include improved communication, early supplier involvement in the buyer product design, and measuring supplier performance indicators. Improved communication is achieved through designating one or two individuals for all communication that takes place between the buying and supplying firms and conducting supplier conferences and workshops to share information common to both parties (cost, design specifications, and profit).

Supplier performance is measured in terms of quality, delivery, service, and cost/price. **Quality measures** may include incoming defect rate, product variability, number of customer complaints, use of statistical process control, documented process capabilities, and supplier's quality philosophy. **Delivery measures** include on-time delivery, percentage and availability of product within quoted lead-time, and quantity accuracy. **Service measures** include invoice accuracy and length of time required to settle claims, availability of a supply plan, and availability of engineering support. **Cost/price measures** include product cost, price reductions, transportation cost, willingness to participate in price reviews, and minimum buy requirements.

Supplier certification is a process conducted by the purchasing organization so that shipments go directly into use, inventories, or production. The goal of certification is to reduce or eliminate incoming inspection of goods coming from a supplier by a purchaser. Certification involves evaluating the supplier's quality systems, approving the supplier's processes, and monitoring incoming product quality. The advantages of supplier certification are increased product quality, reduced inspection costs, and reduced process variation.

Logistics Management

The scope of **logistics management** includes shipping of inventory items between a factory, warehouse, and customer (see figure). Forward logistics and reverse logistics are also discussed.

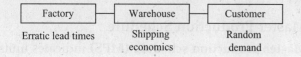

Factory	Warehouse	Customer
Erratic lead times	Shipping economics	Random demand

Warehouses

The functions of warehouse distribution, production, and purchasing are closely interrelated and constantly interacting with each other in a manufacturing firm. The decisions considered during inventory distribution strategy are when, what, and how much of it to ship to a warehouse; when, what, and how much of it to produce at the factory, with what size workforce; and when, what, and how much of it to purchase as inputs to the factory warehouse system.

Warehouses usually stock a very large number of products—the larger the shipment size, the more products are involved, and the greater the problems of controlling inventories of different products in combination. These are some of the considerations involved in decisions to order shipments to warehouses. Two basic types of shipments can take place: (1) periodic shipments and (2) trigger shipments.

The **trigger system** is more responsive to fluctuations in sales than the corresponding periodic system. It has the further advantage that the shipment size is predetermined rather than random; hence, problems of overburdening carrier capacity are minimized. However, the costs of administering the continuous review of inventory position for a trigger system are usually somewhat higher than under the periodic system.

In estimating the cost of alternative shipping carriers, the cost of having valuable inventory tied up while the vehicle is in transit should be considered. While this cost will usually not be large, taking it into account will systematically lower the costs of using faster instead of slower carriers. Additional cost savings associated with fast shipments that may be overlooked come from the fact that time in transit is one component of the lead-time. *Shortening the lead-time allows a reduction in the inventory buffers and hence a decrease in inventory holding costs.*

Distribution System

Inventory in a **distribution system** can be managed through the use of independent demand models such as continuous and periodic review models. The primary advantage of the distribution models is that they allow the various levels in the distribution chain to manage their inventories autonomously. The primary disadvantage of these models is that they ignore the other stages in the supply chain, leading to stockouts and back orders. Excess shipping costs can be incurred since no one is coordinating the movement of materials within the system. Also the demand for replenishment occurs without any regard for what is currently being produced or planned to be produced. Under these situations, the need for an item incurs extra setup costs, lost productivity, and excess transportation costs.

Examples of distribution models include the following:

- The **single-order-point system** basically ignores the fact that the order takes place in a chain and assumes that each element in the distribution system is independent of all other components. This independent behavior can cause large swings due to a phenomenon called "lumpy demand" at the next level down in the distribution chain. **Lumpy demand** comes from lack of communication and coordination between the factory, warehouse(s), distributors, and retailers.

- The **double-order-point system** considers two levels down in the distribution system, hence the "double." For example, if a distributor is quoted a lead-time from the factory warehouse of two weeks and it takes the factory warehouse three weeks to have stock replenished, the reorder point is set based on the demand for a five-week period. It does not produce lumpy demand, as does the single-order-point system. An advantage is that it reduces the risk of stockouts. Increasing the safety stock is its disadvantage.
- In the **periodic review system,** orders are placed on a predetermined time schedule. The advantage is that the order times can be staggered throughout the chain to smooth the demand at each point in the distribution chain. This reduces peaks and valleys caused by several customers ordering at the same time.
- In the **sales replacement system,** the supplier ships only what the customer used or sold during the period. The objective is to maintain a stable inventory level in the system. This does require having enough inventory to cover the potential demand during the replenishment cycle. In essence, the sales replacement system is a periodic review model with variable order quantities.

Forward Logistics and Reverse Logistics

Forward logistics systems move raw materials and finished products from upstream suppliers to downstream customers (e.g., from one supplier to the other and from one customer to the other). The physical (goods) and non-physical (information) flows are forward directed toward the point of consumption.

Reverse logistics systems move products from downstream customers to upstream suppliers for the purpose of returns, repair, remanufacture, refurbishing, and/or recycling. The physical (goods) and non-physical (information) flows are reverse and initiated at the point of consumption. Most manufacturing companies are not fully set up to handle the reverse logistics issues.

Logistics related practices such as reverse purchasing or reverse marketing are discussed, and they are compared with the traditional practices, as follows:

- In **traditional purchasing or marketing**, the supplier approaches the purchaser (buyer) to sell his materials. The supplier establishes prices, terms, and conditions. The buyer takes a reactive, mild, and short-term approach, which does not achieve a competitive advantage to him in the supply chain.

- In **reverse purchasing or reverse marketing**, the buyer approaches the supplier to buy his materials. The buyer establishes prices, terms, and conditions. The buyer takes a proactive, aggressive, and long-term approach to achieve a competitive advantage to him in the supply chain (e.g., reduced supplier inefficiencies, reduced inventory levels, improved demand forecasting accuracy, and increased cost savings). Reverse marketing is also called supplier development.

❑ Learning Objective 2.7: UNDERSTAND THE VARIOUS PLANNING SYSTEMS APPLICABLE TO MANUFACTURING AND DISTRIBUTION OPERATIONS

Planning systems applicable to manufacturing and distribution operations include master production schedule (MPS), material requirements planning (MRP), distribution requirements planning (DRP), enterprise resource planning (ERP), customer relationship management (CRM), capacity requirements planning (CRP), and aggregate production planning (APP).

Master Production Schedule

Master production schedule (MPS) indicates units of finished goods to be produced each time period. The **bill of material (BOM)** defines the components or parts required by each finished product. BOM is a structured components list showing the hierarchical relationship between the finished product and its various components. BOM indicates exactly how many components are needed to produce the quantity of finished goods recommended by the MPS system. The inputs to MPS are forecast orders and/or actual orders.

Material Requirements Planning

Material requirements planning (MRP) systems are used to project inventory stock levels because they depend on the amount and timing of finished goods to be produced and then determine the requirements for raw materials, parts, components, and subassemblies at each of the prior stages of finished goods production. Working backward, each end product is sequentially separated into its necessary components and raw materials (i.e., to project inventory stock levels needed). MRP can also be used for re-source planning (i.e., capacity planning and labor scheduling) and materials planning.

MRP is suitable for managing raw materials, components, and subassemblies, which have dependent demands that may be calculated from the forecasts and scheduled production of finished goods. In other words, the order for component inventory is placed based on the demand and production needs of other items that use these components.

The benefits of MRP include reduced investment in inventory, improved workflow, reduced shortage of raw materials and components, and reliable delivery schedules. Closed-loop MRP system provides information to CRP, MPS, and APP.

Inputs and Outputs of MRP Systems

The inputs to MRP are MPS data, BOM data, and the current inventory data.
The outputs from the MRP system are the planned order releases for production and purchasing.

Distribution Requirements Planning

Distribution requirements planning (DRP) uses a time-phased logic of MRP applied to the distribution system. The purpose of DRP is to forecast demand by the distribution center to determine MPS needs. It uses forecasts and known order patterns from customers in the distribution chain to develop the demand on the master schedule.

Characteristics of DRP

DRP anticipates future needs throughout the distribution chain and plans deliveries accordingly.
The order-point-based distribution system does not anticipate future needs. It simply reacts to the current needs.
DRP pulls inventory through the system from top levels to bottom levels, as it is a stock-replenishment plan for all levels of the supply chain.

Enterprise Resource Planning

Enterprise resource planning (ERP) software can help organizations in optimizing their value chain, which requires integrating business processes across organizational boundaries through information technology (IT).

The value chain is computed as follows:

$$Value\ Chain = Business\ Process\ Reengineering$$
$$+ Change\ Management + ERP$$

Data are entered only once into an ERP system and allow employees to access a full database of information in order to complete their tasks. The information can also be shared with customers and suppliers as needed. All data fields in the database must be defined consistently and correctly to facilitate internal employee access and external sharing of data. The ERP system can track business transactions from their origin (at the customer) to order entry through operations and accounting until the transaction is completed. The objective of ERP systems is to integrate all functions within an organization and to become customer oriented (customer centric). Companies are using the ERP system for increased business competitiveness, as follows:

$$ERP = MRP + Accounting + Finance$$
$$+ Human\ Resources + Supply\ Chain + CRM$$

The advantages of ERP systems include elimination of costly and inflexible legacy systems, improvement of work processes, increase in access to data for operational decision making, and standardization of IT infrastructure (hardware, software, operating systems, and databases). Some disadvantages of ERP systems include expense and time in implementation, difficulty in implementing change in the organization, risks in using one vendor, and difficulty in integrating with other computer systems.

Customer Relationship Management

A **customer relationship management (CRM)** system deals with the customer side of a business, starting from customer order entry to customer satisfaction. It is designed to survive in the customer-centric environment and to establish a one-to-one business relationship with customers. Some define CRM as a call center solution. Some view it as sales force automation; others see it as direct mail, marketing automation, or simply a web page. Many companies see it as a front-end application only, interacting at the point-of-contact, point-of-purchase, or customer support. Others believe the secret to CRM success is in the back-end activities, such as data mining, data warehousing, data distribution, and data sharing. A properly designed and implemented CRM system encompasses all of these and much more. It is better to view the CRM system as a bridge system, not as a front-end system or back-end system.

Capacity Requirements Planning

Capacity requirements planning (CRP) indicates throughput (capacity) of a facility (i.e., plant, warehouse, or office) and measures capacity in three time horizons (i.e., short, intermediate, or long range). Capacity decisions require huge amounts of money, especially in the long range, as it is difficult to modify capacity in the short-range.

1. **Short-range capacity decisions** are concerned with scheduling jobs, employees, and equipment.
2. **Intermediate-range capacity decisions** are concerned with adding equipment, employees, and operating shifts.
3. **Long-range capacity decisions** are concerned with adding facilities and equipment that require a long lead-time.

Utilization and **efficiency** are two performance measures of a facility's capacity. Utilization is the percent of design capacity actually achieved, and efficiency refers to the percent of effective capacity actually achieved. **Design capacity** is the maximum theoretical output in a given period under ideal conditions. **Effective capacity** is expected capacity under the current operating conditions, which is lower than design capacity. **Rated capacity** is a measure of expected output of a facility, which is expressed in terms of effective capacity and percent efficiency. The following formulas are related to capacity:

Percent Utilization = (Actual Output)/
(Design Capacity) × 100

Percent Efficiency = (Actual Output)/
(Effective Capacity) × 100

Expected Output = (Effective Capacity)
× (Percent Efficiency)

Capacity levels must match demand levels. A poor match may mean demand exceeds capacity or capacity exceeds demand. When demand exceeds capacity, management can curtail demand by raising prices, scheduling long lead-times for product delivery, and discouraging marginally profitable business. When capacity exceeds demand, management can stimulate demand through price reductions or aggressive marketing efforts or even initiate employee layoffs and plant/office closings.

Aggregate Production Planning

Aggregate production planning (APP) focuses on an intermediate planning period of 3 to 18 months and is concerned with determining the quantity and timing of production to meet the forecasted demand.

Production (capacity) options may include changing inventory levels; varying workforce size by hiring or layoffs; varying production rates through overtime or idle time; subcontracting; and using part-time workers.

Demand options may include influencing demand through advertising, promotions, personal selling, and price cuts; back ordering during high-demand periods, which could result in lost sales; and counterseasonal product and service mixing (e.g., furnaces and air conditioners and lawnmowers and snow-blowers).

Mixing options may include chase strategy and level strategy. A **chase strategy** sets production equal to demand. A **level strategy** maintains a constant production (output) rate, or workforce level.

A **mixed strategy** uses two or more options from the production options, demand options, and mixed options to achieve the minimum cost goal. Several methods exist to perform APP, including graphical method; mathematical approaches, such as the transportation method of linear programming; management coefficients model based on manager's experience and performance; linear decision rule to optimize production rate, workforce size, and total costs; and simulation methods to minimize cost using a combination of production rate and workforce size.

Yield (revenue) management system is a capacity decision of allocating a company's scarce resources to customers at prices that will maximize profit. It charges customers different prices based on their willingness to pay. Although the aggregate plans are similar to manufacturing and service industries, the yield management system is more applicable to service industries, such as airlines.

❏ Learning Objective 2.8: UNDERSTAND THE VARIOUS SHORT-TERM SCHEDULING SYSTEMS USED IN PRODUCTION

Effective job scheduling means faster movement of goods and services through a plant, office, or a facility to better utilize assets and capacity and to lower costs.

Effective production scheduling may require adding capacity and faster throughput to result in better customer service with faster and more dependable deliveries of goods and services.

Effective production scheduling means parts or finished goods are produced on a just-in-time (JIT) basis with low setup times and costs, little work-in-process (WIP) inventory; high machine utilization; meeting due dates promised to customers; and facing time-based competition.

Capacity Planning versus Short-Term Scheduling

The relation between capacity planning and short-term scheduling is shown here:

Capacity Planning → Aggregate Production Planning → Master Production Schedule → Short-Term Scheduling

Capacity planning focuses on the long term, such as five to ten years, requiring changes in equipment and facilities. **Aggregate planning** focuses on an intermediate term, such as a month or quarter, requiring greater facility utilization and subcontracting work. The master production schedule focuses on the near short term, such as weeks, where the MRP breaks down the aggregate plan. **Short-term scheduling** focuses on days, hours, and minutes, where it deals with a work/process center in terms of job loading procedures and job sequencing/dispatching rules.

Scheduling Methods

The goal of scheduling is to allocate and prioritize demand (forecasts or actual orders) to available capacity. Four types of **scheduling methods** are (1) forward scheduling, (2) backward scheduling, (3) combination of backward and forward scheduling, and (4) scheduling criteria. Regardless of the method used, machine breakdowns, employee absenteeism, product/service quality problems, material shortages, and weather conditions affect job and work scheduling in meeting customer order due dates.

1. **Forward scheduling** method starts the work as soon as the job requirements are known from a customer regardless of the due date, and hence may not meet the due date, thus building up WIP inventory. Forward scheduling means the first operation is scheduled first and the final operation last.

2. **Backward scheduling** method begins with the due date and schedules the final operation first and the first operation last. Backward scheduling means the final operation is scheduled first and the first operation last.

3. In practice, a combination of forward and backward scheduling method is used to meet the promised due dates to customers.

4. **Scheduling criteria** methods include minimizing average completion time per job, maximizing facility utilization, minimizing WIP inventory by minimizing the number of jobs that are in the system, and minimizing customer waiting time by minimizing the number of late deliveries.

Loading Jobs

Loading jobs means assigning jobs to work centers or processing centers. Jobs are loaded using an input–output control technique with Gantt charts and the assignment method of linear programming.

The input–output control technique manages the workflows (i.e., tracks work-added and work-completed). The Gantt chart schedules resources and allocates time. The assignment method loads tasks or jobs to resources (i.e., assigns one job/worker to one machine/project).

Job Sequencing

Job sequencing specifies the order in which jobs should be assigned and completed at each work or processing center. Priority rules need to be established for job sequencing or dispatching, as follows:

1. **First come, first served (FCFS).** The first arriving job is processed first.
2. **Shortest processing time (SPT).** The shortest-time jobs are handled first and completed.
3. **Earliest due date (EDD).** The job with the earliest due date is selected first.
4. **Longest processing time (LPT).** The longest-time jobs are handled first and completed.
5. **Critical ratio (CR).** The job that should be shipped on schedule should be handled first.
6. **Johnson's rule.** A group of jobs are sequenced on two machines (i.e., N jobs on two machines). It minimizes processing time and total idle time.

The CR is an index number computed by dividing the time remaining by the workdays remaining, as follows:

CR = (Time Remaining)/(Workdays Remaining)

where time remaining is due date minus today's date. The CR is used to establish job priority order, as follows:

If CR for a job is less than 1.0, it means the job is falling behind schedule, will be late unless expedited, and should receive first priority.

If CR for a job is exactly 1.0, it means the job is on schedule and should receive second priority.

If CR for a job is more than 1.0, it means the job is ahead of schedule, has some slack, and should receive third priority.

The CR rule is better than FCFS, SPT, EDD, or LPT rules since it is based on the average job-lateness criterion, tracks job progress dynamically, and establishes a relative priority among jobs using a common basis.

Level-Material-Use Schedule

A **level-material-use schedule,** which uses frequent, high-quality, small lot sizes, is appropriate for repetitive production, which requires determining the minimum lot (batch) size first. This scheduling method can shorten the large monthly production runs to weekly, daily, or even hourly cycles, resulting in lower inventory investment, reduced batch size, and increased customer satisfaction through meeting the customer's demand.

❑ Learning Objective 2.9:
UNDERSTAND THE THEORY OF CONSTRAINTS IN OPERATIONS

A **bottleneck** is a constraint in a facility, function, department, or resource whose capacity is less than the demand placed upon it. For example, a bottleneck machine or work center exists where jobs are processed at a slower rate than they are demanded. Another example is where the demand for a company's product exceeds the ability to produce the product.

A bottleneck influences both product profitability and product price. The contribution margin per bottleneck hour or the value of each bottleneck hour should be analyzed. This measure is better than the normal contribution margin per unit. The contribution margin per hour of bottleneck can be used to adjust the product price to better reflect the value of the product's use of a bottleneck. Products that use a large number of bottleneck hours per unit require more contribution margin than products that use few bottleneck hours per unit.

Theory of Constraints

The **Theory of Constraints (TOC)** is an operations strategy that attempts to remove the influence of bottlenecks on a production or service process. According to Dr. Eliyahu M. Goldratt, TOC consists of three separate but interrelated areas: (1) logistics, (2) performance measurement, and (3) logical thinking process tools. **Logistics** include drum-buffer-rope scheduling, buffer management, and VAT analysis. **Performance measurement** includes throughput, inventory and operating expense, and the five focusing steps. **Logical thinking process tools** are important in identifying the root problems (current reality tree), identifying and expanding win-win solutions (evaporating cloud and future reality tree), and developing implementation plans (prerequisite tree and transition tree).

Drum-Buffer-Rope Scheduling

Drum-buffer-rope scheduling is the generalized process used to manage resources to maximize throughput. The drum is the rate or pace of production set by the system's constraint. The buffers establish the protection against uncertainty so that the system can maximize throughput. The rope is a communication process from the constraint to the gating operation that checks or limits material released into the system to support the constraint.

Buffer Management

Buffer management is a process in which all expediting steps in a factory shop are driven by what is scheduled to be in the buffers (constraint/bottleneck, shipping, and assembly buffers). By expediting this material into the buffers, the system helps avoid idleness at the constraint and missed customer due dates. In addition, the causes of items missing from the buffer are identified, and the frequency of occurrence is used to prioritize improvement activities.

VAT Analysis

VAT analysis is a procedure for determining the general flow of parts and products from raw materials to finished products (the logical product structure). A *V logical product structure* starts with one or a few raw materials, and the product expands into a number of different products as it flows through divergent points in its routings. The shape of an *A logical product structure* is dominated by converging points. Many raw materials are fabricated and assembled into a few finished products. A *T logical product structure* consists of numerous similar finished products assembled from common assemblies, subassemblies, and parts. Once the general parts flow is determined, the system control points (gating operations, convergent points, divergent points, constraints, and shipping points) can be identified and managed.

The Five Focusing Steps

The **five focusing steps** is a process to continuously improve organizational profit by evaluating the production system and the marketing mix to determine how to make the most profit using system constraints. The steps consist of:

1. Identifying the constraint to the system
2. Deciding how to exploit the constraint to the system
3. Subordinating all nonconstraints to the system
4. Elevating the constraint to the system
5. Returning to step 1 if the constraint is broken in any previous step, while not allowing inertia to set in

❑ Learning Objective 2.10: UNDERSTAND THE PRINCIPLES OF PRODUCTION ECONOMICS AND APPLICATION OF DECISION TOOLS

The scope of **production economics** deals with make-or-buy analysis, learning-curve analysis, supplier breakeven analysis, outsourcing, machine selection, and plant selection.

Make-or-Buy Analysis

In analyzing **make-or-buy** decision alternatives, relevant costs include direct materials, direct labor, and variable overhead. Allocated fixed overhead should be ignored because it is going to be incurred regardless. A company's fixed costs, which are part of fixed overhead, will not change, whether a part/component is made or bought, or whether a special order is accepted or not. Factors such as product quality, plant capacity, and demand patterns are considered in the make-or-buy decision.

When plant capacity is not fully utilized, it is good to accept a special order that covers all variable costs, to ignore allocated fixed costs, and to not consider profits. This is applicable to short-term decision making only. When plant capacity is fully utilized, the special order has an opportunity cost, and it should recover all variable and fixed costs, including profits.

When buying a part from a vendor, a company is guaranteed only the price charged by the vendor. The buyer has no control, at least in the short term, over product quality, delivery, support, or service.

Learning-Curve Analysis

Learning-curve analysis states that employees get better at their tasks as the tasks are repeated over and over again and take less time to complete those tasks. Applied to the production setting, it takes less time to complete each additional production unit.

Management can use learning-curve analysis to estimate the time required for the remainder of the order, after knowing the labor-hours or labor costs required for a portion of a customer's special-contract production order.

The formula to calculate the time required for the nth unit is:

$$\text{Time Required for } n\text{th Unit} = T \times L^n$$

where T is unit time or unit cost of the first unit, L is learning curve rate (i.e., 80%), and n is number of times T is doubled.

Supplier's Breakeven Analysis

Supplier's breakeven analysis allows a purchaser (buyer) to anticipate a supplier's (seller) pricing strategy during procurement negotiations. The intent of the buyer is to estimate a supplier's expected profit or loss given a supplier's fixed and variable costs. Both the buyer and the breakeven analysis assume that variable costs fluctuate in a linear fashion with respect to volume, and it ignores semivariable costs, which include both fixed and variable costs.

The following formulas can be used in the supplier breakeven analysis:

Breakeven Point in Units = (Total Fixed Costs)/
 (Selling Price per Unit − Variable Cost per Unit)

Contribution Margin (CM) per Unit = Selling
 Price per Unit − Variable Cost per Unit

Net Income or Profit = (Sales Units ×
 CM per Unit) − Total Fixed Costs

Net Income or Profit = Total Revenues −
   Total Variable Costs − Total Fixed Costs

Total Revenue = Sales Units ×
   Selling Price per Unit

Outsourcing

Outsourcing is acquiring non-core products or services from external sources. **Insourcing** is keeping core products or services in-house. Many related terms exist: **offshoring** is moving a business function or process to a foreign country but retaining control of it. **Nearshoring** is choosing an outsource provider located either in the home country or in a nearby foreign country. **Backsourcing** is the return of a business activity to the original firm.

Examples of outsourced functions or processes include information technology; production operations; purchasing; logistics; research and development; training; human resources; accounting and financial services; advertising; legal and tax services; and customer service.

Advantages of outsourcing include cost savings, gaining outside expertise, focusing on core competencies, improving operations and services, and gaining latest technology from outside. These advantages play a role in developing strategies for downsizing and restructuring.

Disadvantages of outsourcing include loss of control, increased transportation costs, negative impact on employees (loss of morale), creating future competition, and trade-off between short-term gains at the expense of long-term objectives.

A breakeven analysis can be applied when a product is identified as a possible candidate for outsourcing by comparing fixed and variable costs for insource and outsource options. The following formula can be used to compute the number of production units that must be outsourced in order to reach a breakeven point in total costs from insource and outsource options:

$$X = (F_{in} - F_{out})/(V_{out} - V_{in})$$

where X is the number of units that must be outsourced, F_{in} is total insource fixed costs, F_{out} is total outsource fixed costs, V_{in} is total variable cost per unit produced at insource, and V_{out} is total variable cost per unit produced at outsource.

If X is less than the expected demand in units, the company should select the source with the lower variable cost and higher fixed cost. If X is greater than the expected demand in units, the company should select the source with the lower fixed cost and higher variable cost.

Machine Selection

Machine selection deals with replacing an old machine with a new one to stay in operation. Equivalent annual costs (EACs) are computed for all new machines under consideration during the selection process, using annuity factors. EAC is total present value of costs divided by the annuity factor. Based on the EAC analysis, management purchases the machine with the lowest EAC.

Plant Selection

Plant selection involves selecting one plant from among several with different capacities. Usually, large plants will incur larger fixed costs. The plant with high fixed costs will have a high breakeven point (BEP) because it takes more sales to recover all fixed costs. The reverse is true with small plants. If a plant has 100 percent of its capacity utilized, there is no safety cushion for expected or unexpected conditions, such as plant downtime, machine breakdowns, holidays, and other unforeseen events. A plant capacity utilization of 80 to 90 percent is desirable.

The following formulas can be used in plant selection:

Plant's BEP in Units = Total Sales Revenues =
   Total Fixed Costs + Total Variable Costs

Plant's Capacity Utilization = (Sales
   Demand in Units)/(Available Production
   Capacity in Units) × 100

A plant with a low BEP and a high capacity utilization percentage should be selected.

Decision Tools

The types of **decision tools** include decision or payoff tables and decision trees.

Decision Table

A **decision table** is a tabular means of analyzing decision alternatives (courses of actions) and states of nature (outcomes). The alternatives are listed on the left side, the states of nature are listed across the top, and the payoffs (i.e., conditional values) are listed in the body of the decision table. A decision-maker uses three methods for dealing with uncertainty of outcomes when he cannot even assess probabilities for each possible outcome. These three methods include maximax (optimistic and best case), maximin (pessimistic and worst case), and equally likely (average and normal case).

1. The **maximax** method maximizes the maximum outcome for every alternative.
2. The **maximin** method maximizes the minimum outcome for every alternative.
3. The **equally likely** method maximizes the average outcome of each alternative.

Decision Tree

A **decision tree** is a graphical means of analyzing decision alternatives and states of nature. The decision tree approach is suitable for multiple sequential decisions, where later decisions are based on the outcome of prior ones. It includes decision alternatives, states of nature with their respective probabilities, and payoff amounts for each combination of decision alternatives and states of nature. The **expected monetary value (EMV)** is computed by working backward, that is, by starting at the right of the tree and working back to decision nodes on the left of the tree. The decision node leading to the state-of-nature node with the highest EMV will be chosen. Decision trees are used in evaluating capacity planning and capital investment decisions.

Decision Table versus Decision Tree

A decision table does not use probabilities.
A decision tree uses probabilities.

❏ Learning Objective 2.11: UNDERSTAND THE PRINCIPLES AND TECHNIQUES OF EQUIPMENT MAINTENANCE AND SYSTEM RELIABILITY

Proper **maintenance** of equipment can remove variability, and variability can destroy a process and create waste. Tactics to improve maintenance include implementing preventive maintenance methods and increasing repair capabilities for the equipment.

Equipment Maintenance

Two types of maintenance exist: preventive and breakdown (emergency). **Preventive maintenance** involves performing routine inspections and servicing work and keeping the equipment and facilities in good working order without interruption. **Breakdown maintenance** occurs when equipment fails and must be repaired on an emergency or priority basis.

Implementing preventive maintenance requires a study of **mean time between failures (MTBF)** distribution, which follows a normal curve pattern. Maintenance work is needed when a machine or process exhibits small standard deviations from the mean (average).

Some firms practice **total productive maintenance (TPM)**, similar to total quality management (TQM), to reduce variability through employee involvement and maintenance records. Use of simulation and expert systems also improves maintenance. TPM is the key to reducing variability and improving reliability.

Preventive and breakdown maintenance costs can be compared when historical data are available on maintenance costs, breakdown probabilities, and repair times.

A measure related to maintenance is availability, in that proper maintenance of a piece of equipment increases its availability for use:

$$\text{Percent Availability} = [(\text{Uptime})/(\text{Uptime} + \text{Downtime})] \times 100$$

Increasing equipment repair capabilities requires trained employees and adequate resources. Repairs can be done in-house by trained and empowered employees or offsite by contractors.

System Reliability

System reliability is the probability that a machine part or product will function properly for a specified time and under stated conditions. Tactics to improve reliability include improving the performance of individual components and providing redundancy. Reliability assures high utilization of facilities, proper scheduling of equipment, low inventory levels, and consistent quality.

A system or piece of equipment consists of parts or components. If any one part or component in a system fails to perform, the entire system can fail. Hence, the key to improving a system's reliability is improving the individual component reliability:

System Reliability = Reliability of Component 1 × Reliability of Component 2 × ⋯ × Reliability of Component n

Other measures of reliability include (1) percent of failures, (2) number of failures per operating hour, (3) MTBF, which is the reciprocal of number of failures per operating hour, and (4) dependability.

Percent of Failures = (Number of Failures)/ (Number of Units Tested) × 100

Number of Failures per Operating Hour
  = (Number of Failures)/(Operating Time)

where operating time is total time minus nonoperating time.

MTBF = 1/Number of Failures per Operating Hour

Percent Dependability = [(Time Available)/ (Time Available + Time Required)] × 100

Redundancy, in the form of backup units, is built into systems to increase their reliability. Backup units are put in parallel with normal units to ensure that if a normal unit fails, the system switches to a backup unit.

System Reliability = (Probability of Normal Unit) + [(Probability of Backup Unit) × (Probability of Needing the Backup Unit)]

where the probability of needing the backup unit is (1 − Probability of Backup Unit).

❑ Learning Objective 2.12:
UNDERSTAND THE PRODUCTION PROCESS FLOWS AND METRICS

Three operational process flow measures include flow time (T), inventory (I), and throughput (R), and they are interrelated in that defining targets on any two of them defines a target for the third:

Inventory (I) = Throughput (R) × Flow Time (T)

The basic managerial levers for process improvement are the following:

- Decrease in flow time
- Increase in throughput
- Decrease in inventory and waiting time

- Control process variability
- Managing process flows and costs

Levers for managing the flow time include decreasing the work content of a critical path by shortening the length of every critical path, as follows:

1. Reduce the work content of an activity on the critical path:
   - Eliminate non-value-adding aspects of the activity (i.e., work smarter).
   - Increase the speed at which the activity is done (i.e., work faster) by acquiring faster equipment and/or by increasing incentives to work faster.
   - Reduce the number of repeat activities (i.e., do it right the first time).
2. Work in parallel by moving some of the work content off the critical path:
   - Move work from a critical path to a noncritical path (i.e., perform work in parallel rather than in sequence).
   - Move work from a critical path to the "outer loop" (i.e., either preprocessing or postprocessing).
3. Modify the product mix:
   - Change the product mix to produce products with smaller work content with respect to the specified activity.

Levers for managing (increasing) throughput of a process include the following:

1. Decrease resource idleness by synchronizing flows within the process to reduce starvation and setting appropriate size of buffers to reduce blockage.
2. Increase the net availability of resources to increase effective capacity by:
   - Improving maintenance policies.
   - Performing preventive maintenance outside periods of scheduled availability.
   - Instituting effective problem-solving measures that reduce frequency and duration of breakdowns.
   - Instituting motivational programs and incentives to reduce employee absenteeism and increase employee morale.
3. Reduce setup waste by reducing the frequency of setups and by reducing the time required for a single setup.
4. Increase theoretical capacity by:
   - Decreasing unit load on the bottleneck resource pool (e.g., work faster, work smarter, do it right the first time, change production mix,

subcontract or outsource, and invest in flexible resources).
- Increasing the load batch of resources in the bottleneck resource pool (i.e., increase the scale of resource).
- Increasing the number of units in the bottleneck resource pool (i.e., increase scale of process).
- Increasing the scheduled availability of the bottleneck resource pool (i.e., work longer).
- Modifying the production mix.

Levers for reducing inventory and waiting time include the following:

1. Reduce cycle inventory (i.e., reduce batch size) by reducing setup or order cost per batch or by reducing forward buying.
2. Reduce safety inventory by:
   - Reducing demand variability through improved forecasting.
   - Reducing the replenishment lead-time and its variability.
   - Pooling safety inventory for multiple locations or products through either physical or virtual centralization of specialization or some combination thereof.
   - Exploiting product substitution.
   - Using common components.
   - Postponing the product differentiation closer to the point of demand.
3. Manage safety capacity by:
   - Increasing safety capacity.
   - Decreasing variability in arrivals and service patterns.
   - Pooling available safety capacity.
4. Synchronize flows by:
   - Managing capacity to synchronize with demand.
   - Managing demand to synchronize with available capacity.
   - Synchronizing flows within the process.
5. Manage the psychological perception of the customers to reduce the cost of waiting.

Levers for controlling process variability include the following:

1. Measure, prioritize, and analyze variability in key performance measures over time.
2. Use feedback control to limit abnormal variability by:
   - Setting control limits of acceptable variability in key performance measures.
   - Monitoring actual performance and correcting any abnormal variability.
3. Decrease normal process variability by designing for processing (i.e., simplify, standardize, and mistake-proof).
4. Immunize product performance to process variability through robust design.

Levers for managing process flows and costs include the following:

1. Manage flows in a plant through:
   - Process structure with cellular layout.
   - Information and material flow using demand pull system.
   - Level production with batch size reduction.
   - Quality at source with defect prevention and decentralized control.
   - Supplier management with partnerships and incentives.
   - Supply consistency through maintenance of safety capacity.
   - Employee involvement and empowerment.
2. Manage flows in a supply chain by:
   - Reducing information and material flow times using technology and efficient logistics.
   - Reducing fixed costs of ordering and quantity discounts.
   - Sharing information on customer demand and product availability.
   - Coordinating forecasts between affected parties.
   - Stabilizing prices.
3. Improve processes through:
   - Continuous improvement and reengineering.
   - Increased visibility; incentives; plan, do, check, adjust (PDCA) cycle; and benchmarking.

❑ Learning Objective 2.13: UNDERSTAND THE TECHNOLOGY DEPLOYED IN MANUFACTURING AND SERVICE OPERATIONS

Topics such as flexible manufacturing systems, process control systems, point-of-sale systems, and bar-coding systems are discussed in this learning objective.

Flexible Manufacturing Systems

Flexible manufacturing systems (FMSs) are computer systems using an automated work cell at each workstation to produce low-volume and high-variety products in an economical manner. FMSs bridge the gap between product-focused and process-focused production strategies.

In a manufacturing environment, **computer-aided design (CAD)** and **computer-aided manufacturing (CAM)** approaches are highly integrated (i.e., **computer integrated manufacturing, CIM**) to produce a quality product in less time. A CAD system is an interactive graphics system suitable for the generation of engineering documentation in both two- and three-dimensional geometry, surfaces, text, or other representation. CAD systems provide engineering drawings and alternative design possibilities, among other things. The major benefit of a CAD system is the productivity gain in comparison to manual drafting. Real estate, municipalities, engineering, and construction industries are some of the major users of CAD systems.

Technologies such as FMS combined with CIM yield several benefits to manufacturers such as reduced machine changeover time, accurate machine scheduling, improved machine utilization, reduced costs, and improved throughput.

Computer-Aided Design + Computer-Aided Manufacturing = Computer Integrated Manufacturing

Computer Integrated Manufacturing + Flexible Manufacturing Systems = Economical and Efficient Production Systems

For example, the electronics industry uses a computer-aided manufacturing (CAM) system to develop integrated circuits and printed circuit-board modules from raw materials and parts. Output from the CAD system would be the input for the CAM system. These systems may even interface with production planning and scheduling systems.

Other examples of integrated manufacturing systems involve master production schedule feeding into a material requirements planning (MRP) system, where the latter explodes raw materials or parts requirements into the lowest detail for placing orders with suppliers. The master production scheduling system also interfaces with the labor-scheduling system and shop-floor control system for scheduling people and machines.

Process Control Systems

In process-oriented manufacturing organizations such as oil-refinery, food-processing, and chemical industries, **process control systems** are heavily used to control the manufacturing process. The raw material flow, work-in-process flow, and final product flow are controlled by these application systems. The exact mixture, content, and timing of the raw materials that go into the manufacturing and mixing process are dictated by these systems.

Point-of-Sale Systems

Point-of-sale (POS) systems are used in the retail industry to collect sales data through cash registers in the store. In most cases, the sales data are collected by in-store processors and then transmitted to a central-host computer via a network. At night, batch processing of sales data is performed to post sales to sales files and to update accounts receivable files for customer-billing purposes. At the same time, sales data are posted to inventory records to adjust inventory levels, which are then used as inputs to the merchandising order system for placing new orders with vendors. The sales staff scans the universal-product-code (UPC) on the merchandise to capture product data and automatic price lookup for each merchandise item to reduce keying time and errors by sales staff.

Other features include help screens, policy lookups, daily-advertising screens, automatic credit approvals, expert system-based credit authorizations, automatic sales tax by store or zip (postal) code, time clock facilities, and perhaps even suggestive selling prompts to the salesperson. This sophistication brings more problems: greater integrity and security controls are needed to prevent honest mistakes and fraudulent transactions.

Bar-Coding Systems

Automated solutions are needed to collect data in real time, at the point of origin, in a way that ensures the captured data are right the first time. One such solution is the use of automatic identification systems, such as bar coding, optical character recognition (OCR), voice recognition (VR), and radio frequency identification (RFID). Bar codes can be used in manufacturing environments such as shop floor and receiving, as well as in office and hospital environments such as purchasing, inventory, billing, accounts payable, payroll time-clocking, and tracking medications in hospitals.

Bar codes are symbols that can be processed electronically to identify numbers, letters, or special characters on a receiving report, invoice, timecard, or part. They are used to improve data accuracy and increase speed of updating the supporting data in all interfacing systems.

Removing the human element from the data collection process greatly improves data accuracy and updating speed.

Bar-code technology supports the JIT production philosophy and continuous improvement (kaizen) program. This is because bar-code technology is paperless, which is one of the goals of JIT. Bar codes support continuous improvement due to increased accuracy of data available in the system and establishment of production standards based on such data. This also improves quality of decision making.

For example, the use of bar codes on raw materials will reduce the amount of paperwork that is required to track inventories. Movement of raw materials, subassemblies, and finished products is monitored electronically using bar codes. In addition to speed, accuracy is increased since there is little or no human involvement in reading and interpreting the bar-code data. Key entry of data is eliminated.

 Self-Assessment Exercise

Online exercises are provided for the learning objectives in this module. Please visit www.mbaiq.com to complete the online exercises and to calculate your MBA IQ Score.

Marketing Management

Learning Objective 3.1: Understand the
Components of Marketing Mix 72
Learning Objective 3.2: Understand the
Expectancy-Value Model in
Consumer Markets 72
Learning Objective 3.3: Understand the
Brand Elements and Calculate a
Brand Value 72
Learning Objective 3.4: Understand
Competitor Analysis 73
Learning Objective 3.5: Understand the
Pricing Strategies and Methods 73
Establishing Prices 74
Price Response Analysis 75
Learning Objective 3.6: Understand the
Marketing Communications Mix 75
Learning Objective 3.7: Understand
the New-Product Development
Process 75
Stages 76
Rating Method 76
Learning Objective 3.8: Compute the
Customer Retention Rate 76
Competitive Markets 77
Calculating the Customer Retention Rate 77
Learning Objective 3.9: Compute the
Lifetime Value of a Customer 77
Calculating the Cost of a Lost Sale 77
Strengthening the Customer Retention Rate 77
Calculating the Lifetime Value of a Customer 78
Learning Objective 3.10: Compute the
Customer Conviction in Terms of Net
Promoter Score 78
Learning Objective 3.11: Compute the
Customer Loyalty Score 78
Learning Objective 3.12: Compute the
Net Marketing Contribution Amount 78
Learning Objective 3.13: Compute the
Marketing Profitability Metrics 80
Learning Objective 3.14: Compute the
Market Development Index 80
Learning Objective 3.15: Compute the
Market Share Index 80

Learning Objective 3.16: Compute a
Product's Lifecycle Cost and
Economic Value to a Customer 81
Learning Objective 3.17: Compute the
Relative Performance, Price, and
Customer Value of a Product 81
Learning Objective 3.18: Compute a
Marketing Channel Intermediary's
Transaction Value 82
Transaction Value 82
Channel Cost per Customer Transaction 82
Learning Objective 3.19: Understand
the Relationships Among Price,
Profit, and Market Share 83
Learning Objective 3.20: Understand a
Marketing Channel's Performance 83
Learning Objective 3.21: Evaluate the
Advertising's Effectiveness with
Customer Response Index 83
Learning Objective 3.22: Learn How
to Conduct a Marketing Portfolio
Analysis 85
Learning Objective 3.23: Learn How
to Develop a Marketing Budget 85
Learning Objective 3.24: Understand
the Financial Performance Metrics
Related to Marketing 85
Learning Objective 3.25: Understand
the Nature of Marketing of Services 86
Service Characteristics 86
Service Quality 86
Overcoming the Obstacles in Service Marketing 87
Learning Objective 3.26: Understand
the Strategies in Product
Management 87
Product Definition 87
Product Classification 87
Product Mix and Product Line 88
Packaging and Branding 88
Learning Objective 3.27: Understand
the Stages in a Product Lifecycle 88
Product Lifecycle (PLC) Concept 88
Product Audit 89

❑ Learning Objective 3.1: UNDERSTAND THE COMPONENTS OF MARKETING MIX

Marketing management develops integrated marketing programs to communicate and deliver value for customers through four major components—product, price, promotion, and place—called the **marketing mix,** which represents the seller's view of the marketing tools available for influencing buyers.

1. **Product** includes variables such as product variety, quality, design, features, brand name, packaging, sizes, services, warranties, and returns.
2. **Price** includes variables such as list price, discounts, allowances, payment periods, and credit terms.
3. **Promotion** includes variables such as sales promotion, advertising, sales force, public relations, and direct marketing.
4. **Place** includes variables such as channels, coverage, assortments, locations, inventory, and transport.

A firm can change only a few variables in the short run, such as price, sales force size, and advertising expenses. A firm can develop new products and modify its distribution channels only in the long run.

A complementary theme with marketing mix is to answer questions that a customer may have using dimensions such as solution, information, value, and access (SIVA):

Solution: How can I solve my problem?
Information: Where can I learn more about it?
Value: What is my total sacrifice to get this solution?
Access: Where can I find it?

❑ Learning Objective 3.2: UNDERSTAND THE EXPECTANCY-VALUE MODEL IN CONSUMER MARKETS

Consumers go through a rational process before deciding to purchase a specific brand product based on consumer attitudes and beliefs, called **expectancy-value model (EVM).**

The EVM focuses on a consumer's positive and negative values for an attribute about a specific brand product and on assigning an importance level to each attribute in order to arrive at an overall perceived value:

Brand A = (Attribute 1 Value × Importance Level)
    + (Attribute 2 Value × Importance Level)
    + (Attribute 3 Value × Importance Level)
    + ⋯

Brand B = (Attribute 1 Value × Importance Level)
    + (Attribute 2 Value × Importance Level)
    + (Attribute 3 Value × Importance Level)
    + ⋯

Brand C = (Attribute 1 Value × Importance Level)
    + (Attribute 2 Value × Importance Level)
    + (Attribute 3 Value × Importance Level)
    + ⋯

The consumer will choose a brand that gives her the highest perceived value.

One way to build value to a customer is to focus on order winners and order qualifiers. An **order winner** (i.e., order-getting power) is a criterion that differentiates the products or services of one firm from another, including low prices. An **order qualifier** is a screening criterion that permits a firm's product or service to be considered as a possible candidate for purchase. Note that these criteria may change over time, meaning an order winner today may become an order qualifier tomorrow.

❑ Learning Objective 3.3: UNDERSTAND THE BRAND ELEMENTS AND CALCULATE A BRAND VALUE

Brand elements identify and differentiate a brand in the marketplace with consumers. A brand element that provides a positive contribution and value to a customer builds positive brand equity and vice versa.

Brand-building elements include memorable, meaningful, and likable, and **brand-defensive elements** include transferable, adaptable, and protectable. Brand-building elements bring consumer awareness, which leads to brand equity, whereas brand-defensive elements deal with leveraging brand equity in the face of competition and constraints.

In addition to brand names, logos and slogans lead to building brand equity.

Brand equity is measured as follows:

1. With a brand audit done internally and annually
2. By collecting data from consumers through brand-tracking studies

Brand equity is different from brand valuation, where the latter deals with assigning a dollar value to a brand.

A **brand value** can be calculated as follows:

Brand Intangible Earnings = Brand Revenues
  −Operating Expenses − Taxes
  −Charge for Invested Capital

Net Present Value (NPV) of a Brand Value = Brand Intangible Earnings × Brand Discount Rate

The higher the NPV, the greater the brand value and vice versa. The NPV of a brand value can be calculated for several years, reflecting the ability of a brand to generate future earnings.

❏ Learning Objective 3.4: UNDERSTAND COMPETITOR ANALYSIS

A company cannot survive in the long run if it does not analyze its competitors' strengths and weaknesses (external analysis) along with its own strengths and weaknesses (internal analysis).

Attack action plans, whether offensive or defensive, can be developed based on this internal and external analysis of strengths and weaknesses.

A company should monitor three variables when analyzing its competitors: competitor's share of market, competitor's share of mind, and competitor's share of heart.

The **share of competitor's market** is computed mathematically based on total target market demand in units and a competitor's sales in units:

Competitor's Share of Market = (Competitor's Sales in Units)/(Total Target Market Demand in Units)

The **share of competitor's mind** is assessed based on a customer-survey question such as, "Name the first company that comes to your mind in this industry."

The **share of competitor's heart** is assessed based on a customer-survey question such as, "Name the company from which you would prefer to buy the product."

There is a relationship between mind share and heart share and market share and profits:

Gains in Mind Share and Heart Share → Gains in Market Share and Profits

A company can also improve market share through benchmarking with its competitors and other world-class companies.

A company can select its competitors with a competitive analysis by dividing them into groups such as strong versus weak, close versus distant, and good versus bad.

A company can select its customers to conduct customer value analysis by dividing them in terms of whether a customer is valuable and vulnerable and to decide which ones to retain or lose. A 2 × 2 matrix can be developed for in-depth analysis:

Customer is...	Vulnerable	Not vulnerable
Valuable	Unhappy and profitable—retain	Loyal and profitable—maintain
Not valuable	Not loyal—defect or lose	Happy and unprofitable—change customer into valuable or vulnerable

❏ Learning Objective 3.5: UNDERSTAND THE PRICING STRATEGIES AND METHODS

Companies establish prices for their products and services in a variety of ways: some by owners, some by division and product-line managers, and some by finance managers. Others who influence prices include senior management, marketing and sales management, and production management.

There is no right way of setting prices since there are multiple factors, including government regulation; production, marketing, and other costs; consumer psychology; company's profit and market share goals; product demand and supply conditions; consumer's personal income levels; and competitors' prices and prices of substitutes. Pricing decisions are very complex and uncertain, to say the least.

The pricing continuum is as follows:

Low Price → Floor Price → Ceiling Price → High Price
(No Profit)   **(No Sales)**

Companies may set target profit margins by applying a target return-on-sales percent to the sales revenue from their product mix. The target cost is determined as follows by subtracting the target profit from the target sales price for each product:

Target Cost = Target Sales Price − Target Profit

Some major corporations establish a Pricing Council made up of pricing leaders from each business unit that looks for the best pricing practices across the company.

The chief marketing officer (CMO) reporting to the chief executive officer (CEO) should lead the pricing initiatives, monitor the pricing practices, and control the pricing outcomes.

For any organization, there should be a systematic strategy and structured approach to establishing, adapting, and changing prices.

Establishing Prices

Six popular methods exist to establish prices, including markup pricing, target-return pricing, perceived-value pricing, value pricing, going-rate pricing, and auction-type pricing.

1. The **markup pricing method,** also known as the **cost-plus pricing method**, is popular, easy to determine, and fairer to both buyers and sellers. This method results in similar prices when all firms in the industry use the same approach, and price competition is, therefore, minimized. Basically, this method takes all costs of producing a product and adds a standard markup for profit as the desired return on sales.

    A manufacturer's unit cost is computed as follows:

    Manufacturer's Total Unit Cost = (Variable Cost per Unit) + (Total Fixed Costs/Expected Unit Sales)

    Percent Markup on Cost = (Unit Price − Total Unit Cost)/Total Unit Cost

    A standard markup percentage is added to the total unit cost (fixed cost per unit plus variable cost per unit), giving the markup price:

    A Manufacturer's Markup Price = (Total Unit Cost)/(1 − Percent Markup)

    Percent Markup on Price = (Unit Price − Total Unit Cost)/Unit Price

The interrelationships between price and cost are as follows:

 Percent Markup on Price = (Percent Markup on Cost)/(1 + Percent Markup on Cost)

 Percent Markup on Cost = (Percent Markup on Price)/(1 − Percent Markup on Price)

Both marketers and accountants determine the selling price of a product as follows:

 Percent Markup on Cost = (Desired Profit + Total Fixed Costs)/Total Variable Costs

 Unit Price = Total Unit Cost + Percent Markup on Cost

    Wholesalers, dealers, and retailers will add their own markup to the manufacturer's markup price, thereby increasing the manufacturer's markup price significantly.

2. The **target-return pricing method** seeks a desired return on invested capital, which is based on an economic concept. The formula is:

    Target-Return Price = (Total Unit Cost) + [(Desired Return × Invested Capital)/ Expected Unit Sales]

    A breakeven point (BEP) in units can be computed and compared to the expected unit sales to determine how much effort is needed to reach the expected sales level to make the desired profit. The BEP can be decreased, resulting in less risk to the company, through lowering fixed and variable costs.

    This method ignores external factors such as price elasticity and competitors' prices because it is based on internal factors such as costs and profits.

3. **Perceived-value pricing method** is based on what the customer, not the company, thinks about the value of a product. Organizations use advertising and sales force to communicate and enhance perceived value in buyers' minds. The goal is to deliver more value to a customer than the competitor and to demonstrate this value to prospective buyers. Market research methods such as focus groups, surveys, judgments, and experimentation are used to determine the value of a product to customers.

4. **Value pricing method** purposefully charges a low price for a high-quality product with cost savings

realized from reengineering the production processes and becoming a low-cost producer without sacrificing quality. The cost savings are passed on to value-conscious customers through programs such as everyday low pricing, high–low pricing, and extreme everyday low pricing.

5. **Going-rate pricing method** focuses on meeting or beating competitors' prices. Some companies adopt a follow-the-leader strategy, meaning changing the price when the competitor changes its price, not when the company's demand or cost structure changes. This method is appropriate when costs are difficult to estimate and when competition is uncertain.

6. **Auction-type pricing method** uses the Internet as the primary medium to transact between buyers and sellers. The items that are auctioned include excess inventories and used goods of all kinds. Bids are exchanged between various members such as one seller and many buyers, one buyer and many sellers, and one buyer and many suppliers as in procurement of supplies. In general, online auctions are giving greater overall satisfaction to buyers and sellers due to a large number of bidders, greater economic stakes, and less visibility in pricing.

Price Response Analysis

Price response analysis is the study of the effects of price decreases and price increases on profits. Price response coefficients are usually collected from market research studies. Generally, price and sales volume varies inversely. This means that higher prices should result in a small number of units sold and vice versa. For example, a price response coefficient of -2.0 means that if price falls by 5 percent, sales would be expected to increase by 10 percent. Similarly, a price response coefficient of $+1.5$ means that if price falls by 6 percent, sales would be expected to decrease by 9 percent.

Marketing management can determine additional net income or loss from operations resulting from price decrease or increase:

Additional Increase or Decrease in Net Income from Operations = Expected Price Decrease × Sales Response Coefficient × Current Net Sales × Accounting Contribution Margin Ratio

❑ Learning Objective 3.6: UNDERSTAND THE MARKETING COMMUNICATIONS MIX

Marketing communications represent the voice of the company and its brands in building relationships with consumers. Marketing communications, such as advertising and celebrity endorsements, contribute to building brand equity through the memory and image it creates in the consumers' minds, which in turn drives sales and profits.

Marketing Communications → Brand Equity

The **marketing communications mix** consists of eight major modes of communication, such as advertising, sales promotion, events and experiences, public relations and publicity, direct marketing, interactive marketing, word-of-mouth marketing, and personal selling.

Brand equity drives sales in many ways through brand awareness, brand image, brand responses, and brand relationships. Brand equity is closely related to the number of customers who are devoted to a brand. Some brands have a higher degree of awareness, acceptability, and preference than others. Although brand equity is not shown in a company's financial statements, similar to human equity, it is reflected in the acquisition price of a company as a premium the brand commands in the market.

Brand dilution occurs when consumers no longer associate a brand with a specific product. It is closely related to **brand extension**, and it is a risk. **Cobranding** and **dual branding** occur when two or more well-known brands are combined in a merger and acquisition (M&A) offer. Competitors benefit from brand dilution because the offering company has a weak position in the market. The more narrow its focus, the stronger the brand.

❑ Learning Objective 3.7: UNDERSTAND THE NEW-PRODUCT DEVELOPMENT PROCESS

Companies need to grow their revenues in the long run by developing new products and services and expanding into new markets because new products and services are the lifeblood of successful firms.

Companies are adopting a structured and standard method of developing new products to minimize the risk of low success rates of new products and services. There is an opportunity cost involved here due to the alternative uses of funds spent on product failures and the time spent in unprofitable product development activities.

Companies are using reverse innovation, incremental innovation, and disruptive technologies and developing a unique, superior product to increase the success rate of new products and services.

Dow Chemical uses a "**reverse innovation**" approach to improve its odds of success in developing new products by starting with the customer. The goal is to learn what customers want and need but cannot get from existing products, and then go back to R&D lab with "invent to order."

Traditional Innovation Approach → R&D Lab
→ Customers

Reverse Innovation Approach → Customers
→ R&D Lab

Marketing management needs to develop criteria (i.e., standards/norms) for success that new products must meet if they are to be considered possible candidates for launching. Possible areas for standards development include profits, costs, use of plant capacity, and market share.

The reasons for a new-product failure are many, including unmet customer needs, misinterpreted or ignored market research results, inadequate marketing intelligence efforts, poor design, wrong price, high development costs, incorrect positioning of a product, poor quality, low value, faulty market testing, improper distribution channels, unexpected changes in the market and the economy, unexpected reactions from competitors, poor timing of product introduction, and ineffective advertising.

Stages

A new-product development process goes through eight major stages, starting with idea generation, idea screening, concept development and testing, marketing strategy development, business analysis, product development, and market testing, and ending with commercialization.

In the idea screening stage, there are two types of errors that must be avoided. These include:

1. **Drop-error,** meaning the company rejects a good idea as a bad one

2. **Go-error,** meaning the company accepts a bad idea as a good one and allows it to move into the product development and commercialization stages

The purpose of screening is to drop poor or bad ideas in the early stages when the costs are lower instead of waiting until the subsequent stages where the costs are higher.

Rating Method

Companies use a product-idea rating method to determine a new product's success rate early, as follows:

Success Factors	Relative Weight	Product Score	Product Rating
	(a)	(b)	($c = a \times b$)
A			
B			
C			

The product ratings are weighted and added to reach an overall rating score, which is then compared to the minimum score required. A reject or accept decision is made.

After a new product's rating score is accepted, and as the new idea moves through the development stages, the company needs to revise its estimate of the product's overall probability of success, using the following formula:

Overall Probability of Success = (Probability of Technical Completion) × (Probability of Commercialization Given Technical Completion) × (Probability of Earning Profit Given Commercialization)

These three probabilities are multiplied, and the result is compared with the target before proceeding with further development.

❑ Learning Objective 3.8: COMPUTE THE CUSTOMER RETENTION RATE

Organizations often use customer surveys to estimate the customer retention rate and customer life in years with a specific product or brand. Customer retention and customer satisfaction are related to each other to some extent and mainly depend on the competitive conditions in the market.

Competitive Markets

In less competitive markets, customers are more easily retained even with poor levels of customer satisfaction because product substitutes are few or product-switching costs are high.

In utility markets (e.g., telephone, water, electricity, gas, and hospital/medical care), where choices are limited, customers stay even when dissatisfied.

In highly competitive markets for frequent purchases (e.g., food stores, gas stations, restaurants, and banks), customers defect quickly when they are dissatisfied. In these markets, higher levels of customer satisfaction are needed to retain higher percentages of customers.

In highly competitive markets for infrequent purchases (e.g., computers, automobiles, appliances, and electronics), customers defect eventually when they are dissatisfied. In these markets, higher levels of customer satisfaction are needed to retain higher percentages of customers.

Calculating the Customer Retention Rate

The **customer retention rate**, expressed as a percentage, is calculated as the percentage of customers surveyed who answered the question "How likely are you to buy this product or brand again on your next purchase?" (i.e., intention to repurchase), multiplied by the probability of repurchase, added together to result in the overall customer retention rate.

Note that each customer may answer the same question differently depending on his experience with the product and the company that makes the product.

The average life expectancy of a customer for a specific product (i.e., customer life) in years can be computed given the rate of customer retention using the following formula:

$$\text{Customer Life in } N \text{ Years} = 1/(1 - \text{CR})$$

where CR is the customer retention rate.

The customer retention rate can also be computed given the customer life in years, as follows:

$$\text{CR} = 1 - (1/N)$$

where CR is the customer retention rate and N is the customer life in years.

☐ Learning Objective 3.9: COMPUTE THE LIFETIME VALUE OF A CUSTOMER

A lost customer is expensive because a new customer has to be attracted to replace the lost customer. The cost of keeping a current customer satisfied is relatively small when compared to the cost of replacing the lost customer.

Calculating the Cost of a Lost Sale

Losing a sale has a minor impact, while losing a customer has a major impact on the selling company. The cost of a lost sale, expressed as lost gross profit amount, is computed as follows:

Lost Sales Percent = 100 − Repurchase Percent

Estimated Lost Sales = Number of Lost Customers × Lost Sales Percent × Average Annual Purchase Amount per Customer

Lost Gross Profit Amount = Estimated Lost Sales × Gross Profit Percent

It has been said that it costs five times more to replace a lost customer than to keep a current customer satisfied. In other words, the higher the rate of customer retention, the longer the average customer life, and the greater the lifetime value of the customer to a company.

Strengthening the Customer Retention Rate

A company with a high customer turnover rate has a high rate of acquisition and a high rate of defection. Establishing high switching costs or creating strong barriers and delivering high customer service can strengthen the customer retention rate. Merely reducing the **defection rate** will not improve the retention rate. The most effective method for reducing the customer defection rate is listening to the customer. This creates loyalty and customer satisfaction and turns defecting customers into retained customers. Relationship marketing can also create a strong customer loyalty base.

The first year of acquiring a new customer results in a negative cash flow (loss) to a company in setting up the new account, and it may take one year or more to start seeing a positive cash flow (profit) to a company.

Calculating the Lifetime Value of a Customer

The **lifetime value of a customer** is calculated as follows:

Step 1: Compute the cash flows generated by a customer for each year for a given period of time in years.

Step 2: Multiply the cash flows for each year with the net present values obtained from a table of present value of $1 for each year.

Step 3: Add these present values for each year to result in a total net present value (NPV) of cash flows. This total amount can be a positive or a negative number, which reflects the worth of this customer to the company in today's dollars.

The higher the NPV of cash flows, the greater the value of the customer to the company.

Another formula used to find the customer's lifetime value is:

Lifetime Value = Number of Years to Become a Loyal Customer × Average Revenue per Customer × Gross Profit Margin Percent

❑ Learning Objective 3.10: COMPUTE THE CUSTOMER CONVICTION IN TERMS OF NET PROMOTER SCORE

A customer's loyalty to a product or brand depends on that customer's conviction about that product or brand. When a customer recommends a product or brand to others, it is a positive sign of that customer's conviction and a reflection of its value. When current customers promote a company's products to potential customers, it leads to sales growth and higher profits.

A company can sample its customers to determine how many customers would recommend a specific product or brand to others (promoters), how many would not likely recommend (passive or indifferent), and how many would not recommend for certain (detractors or captive customers).

The **net promoter score**, which is expressed as a percentage, is computed as:

Net Promoter Score = Percentage of Promoters − Percentage of Detractors

The net promoter score for a company can be compared with the same company's score over a time period as well as with the other companies that compute and publish the same score. The score is a reflection of **customer advantage point,** which translates into sales growth and higher profits.

❑ Learning Objective 3.11: COMPUTE THE CUSTOMER LOYALTY SCORE

Customer loyalty depends on three factors: customer satisfaction, customer retention, and customer recommendation. Each of these factors affects profitability in different ways, some positive and some negative.

The customer loyalty factor is an accurate reflection of overall customer commitment to the company. A low level of customer loyalty sends a red flag to management for positive actions. A low level of customer satisfaction may have a high customer retention rate due to high product-switching costs. A low level of customer recommendation yields a low level of customer loyalty.

Customers are surveyed to obtain their input as to their satisfaction, retention, and recommendation rates. The customer satisfaction levels vary from very satisfied to very dissatisfied, and everything in between. A customer **satisfaction index (CSI)**, a **customer retention rate (CR)**, and a **customer recommendation rate (CM)** is calculated for each of these satisfaction levels.

The overall customer loyalty score (CLS) is calculated as follows:

Step 1: Calculate the loyalty score = CSI × CR × CM.
Step 2: Calculate the overall CLS = loyalty score multiplied by the percent of customers surveyed falling into each of the customer satisfaction levels to reach a weighted-average overall CLS.

The higher the CLS, the greater the customer loyalty to the company. The overall customer loyalty score can be used as a benchmark to compare internally and externally.

❑ Learning Objective 3.12: COMPUTE THE NET MARKETING CONTRIBUTION AMOUNT

The **net marketing contribution (NMC)** concept to marketing is as important as the accounting contribution margin (ACM) to accounting. The NMC can be calculated in many ways:

- Net profit for a manufacturing corporation is sales revenues minus cost of goods sold minus operating expenses.
- Gross profit for a manufacturing corporation is sales revenues minus cost of goods sold.
- Gross profit for a manufacturing corporation can also be measured as a percent of sales revenues using a percent margin number, where margin is (price per unit – cost per unit)/price per unit.
- Net profit for a manufacturing corporation can also be calculated as gross profit minus operating expenses.
- ACM is sales revenues minus all production variable costs.

Operating expenses can be separated into marketing expenses and other (nonmarketing) expenses to show marketing's contribution to profit, called net marketing contribution (NMC).

ACM and NMC are different numbers because ACM focuses on all variable costs related to production, whereas NMC includes both variable and fixed costs of operating the marketing department. ACM comes before the gross profit line item and NMC comes after the gross profit line item on the income statement. The ACM is a higher number than the NMC.

NMC makes marketing management accountable for its part in increasing sales revenues, decreasing marketing expenses, and increasing overall net profit. Marketing expenses can be expressed as a percent of sales.

NMC can be calculated in different ways depending on the data available:

NMC = (Sales Revenues × Gross Profit Percent) – Marketing Expenses

NMC = (Sales Volume in units × ACM per unit) – Marketing Expenses

where sales volume in units is total market demand in units multiplied by the percent market share for the company and ACM per unit is price per unit minus variable production cost per unit.

NMC can be calculated with either a product focus or a customer focus:

NMC with Product Focus = Sales Revenues × Percent Profit Margin – Marketing Expenses

where sales revenues equals market demand in units times market share percent times average selling price per unit times net channel discount. The net channel discount is computed as (1 – CD percent),

where CD is the channel discount given to channel intermediaries for commissions.

NMC with Customer Focus = Sales Revenues × Percent Profit Margin – Marketing Expenses

where sales revenues equals total number of customers times percent market share of customers times average revenue per customer times net channel discount.

The net channel discount is computed as (1 – CD percent), where CD is the channel discount given to channel intermediaries for commissions.

NMC can also be calculated based on marketing strategies:

NMC = Market Demand × Market Share × Average Selling Price × Channel Discount × Percent Profit Margin – Marketing Budget

where market demand strategies are aimed at growing the market demand; market share strategies are aimed at growing the market share; average selling price strategies are aimed at increasing the average selling price; channel discount strategies are aimed at decreasing the channel costs; percent profit margin strategies are aimed at increasing the profit margin; and marketing budget strategies are aimed at decreasing the marketing budget or increasing the marketing efficiency in using the budget.

NMC can also be calculated for a market segment:

Segment NMC = Segment Market Demand in Units × Segment Market Share in Percent × Price per Unit × Percent Profit Margin – Segment Marketing Expenses

DV Knowledge Corporation

Net Marketing Contribution Statement

Gross sales

 Less: Returns and allowances

Net sales

 Less: Variable cost of goods sold

Accounting contribution margin

 Less: Fixed costs of goods sold

Gross profit or margin

 Less: Marketing expenses
  Fixed expenses
  Variable expenses *(Continued)*

Net marketing contribution

    Less: Other operating expenses
        Fixed expenses
        Variable expenses

Operating income

Notes: Cost of goods sold includes wages, materials, rent, supplies, and utilities to manufacture goods, classified as fixed or variable. Operating expenses include selling, general, administrative, lease, and depreciation expenses, classified as fixed or variable. Marketing expenses include both fixed and variable types. Marketing expenses, which are part of operating expenses, are not shown separately in the formal income statement. Net marketing contribution (NMC) is gross profit minus all marketing expenses. Operating income is same as earnings before interest and taxes (EBIT) or simply net profit before taxes.

❏ Learning Objective 3.13: COMPUTE THE MARKETING PROFITABILITY METRICS

Examples of marketing profitability metrics include **marketing return on sales (MROS)** and **marketing return on investment (MROI)**. Both MROS and MROI can be calculated in many ways:

- MROS is related to net marketing contribution (NMC) and sales revenues.
- MROS is also related to gross profit and marketing expenses, both expressed as a percent of sales.
- MROI is related to NMC and marketing expenses.
- MROI is also related to MROS and marketing expenses.

Both MROS and MROI will make marketing management accountable in improving an organization's overall profit.

    The MROS is computed as:

$$\text{MROS} = (\text{NMC/Sales Revenues}) \times 100$$

$$\text{MROS} = (\text{Percent Gross Profit})$$
$$- (\text{Percent Marketing Expenses})$$

where both gross profit and marketing expenses are expressed as a percent of sales.

    The MROI is computed as:

$$\text{MROI} = (\text{NMC/Marketing Expenses}) \times 100$$

$$\text{MROI} = (\text{MROS/Marketing Expenses}) \times 100$$

where both MROS and marketing expenses are expressed as a percent of sales.

❏ Learning Objective 3.14: COMPUTE THE MARKET DEVELOPMENT INDEX

Market potential indicates the overall size of the market demand. Market demand means the maximum number of customers that can enter the market with maximum number of units purchased and the maximum number of dollars spent. The market demand sets an upper limit on sales volume. Unit sales are market demand in units times percent market share. A **market development index (MDI)** is related to current market demand and market potential.

    The MDI is calculated as:

$$\text{MDI} = (\text{Current Market Demand in Units})/$$
$$(\text{Market Potential in Units}) \times 100$$

where

Market Potential = Maximum Buying Customers $\times$ Percent Buying Ceiling $\times$ Percent Repurchase Rate per Year $\times$ Purchase Quantity per Customer

Marketing management can use the MDI to develop strategies for market growth in terms of increasing its market size and share. An MDI of less than 33 percent indicates great potential for growth. An MDI of between 33 and 67 percent indicates need for increasing benefits to customers and reducing prices to attract them. An MDI of more than 67 percent indicates room for growth, which could be difficult to reach due to competitive moves and other external forces (e.g., regulation).

❏ Learning Objective 3.15: COMPUTE THE MARKET SHARE INDEX

Market share index (MSI) will help in achieving the desired market share for an organization. Actual MSI and potential MSI are calculated and their relationships to share development index (SDI) are shown in the following.

    The MSI focuses on five elements of a marketing mix: promotion, product, price, place, and service. The MSI will increase as the customer response to these elements increases and vice versa and is calculated as:

$$\text{MSI} = (\text{Promotion} \times \text{Product} \times \text{Price}$$
$$\times \text{Place} \times \text{Service}) \times 100$$

Marketing management can use the MSI to develop strategies (1) to identify the major causes of lost market share opportunities and (2) to determine how improving poor-performance areas can lead to increased market share positive changes.

Customers can be surveyed to determine actual responses and potential responses to the marketing mix elements so that performance gaps can be identified and improved. **Performance gap** is calculated as:

$$\text{Performance Gap} = \text{Actual Responses} - \text{Potential Responses}$$

The actual MSI is based on the actual responses and the potential MSI is based on the potential responses from customers. Actual MSI or potential MSI, both expressed as percent, are calculated as:

Actual MSI = Product Awareness × Product Attractiveness × Price Affordability × Product Availability × Service Experience

Potential MSI = Product Awareness × Product Attractiveness × Price Affordability × Product Availability × Service Experience

The **share development index (SDI)**, which indicates the level of market share that a company has achieved, can be computed using actual MSI and potential MSI as:

$$\text{SDI} = (\text{Actual MSI}/\text{Potential MSI}) \times 100$$

The ideal goal is to reach an SDI of 100.

The market development index (MDI) can be combined with the SDI to reveal growth opportunities for different products, such as low growth or high growth. Then, marketing strategies can be developed to concentrate on market development or share development or both.

❑ Learning Objective 3.16: COMPUTE A PRODUCT'S LIFECYCLE COST AND ECONOMIC VALUE TO A CUSTOMER

A **product's lifecycle cost** includes many elements, such as direct price paid by a customer; product acquisition cost in terms of materials and labor; production cost in terms of labor, materials, and overhead; installation cost in terms of labor and material; delivery cost in terms of freight and shipping cost for labor and materials; ownership cost in terms of interest and insurance; usage and maintenance cost in terms of repairs and warranties; and disposal cost in terms of recycling packaging materials.

A company should identify all of its product's lifecycle cost and compare it to its competitor's product's lifecycle cost for each product in the market. The difference between a company's total cost and its competitor's total cost provides an **economic value to its customer**, computed as:

Economic Value to a Customer = Competitor Product's Lifecycle Cost − Company Product's Lifecycle Cost

The goal is to assign a positive economic value to a customer during a product's lifecycle. To achieve this goal, companies need to reduce all costs for a product ranging from product design to product disposal using value engineering methods, industrial engineering techniques, and cost reduction and cost avoidance approaches.

❑ Learning Objective 3.17: COMPUTE THE RELATIVE PERFORMANCE, PRICE, AND CUSTOMER VALUE OF A PRODUCT

Marketing management wishes to evaluate the relative performance of competing products that provide value to customers based on a product's features and functions but not necessarily based on total cost of purchase. This is because performance of certain products is based on their features, functions, safety, comfort, and convenience, which are difficult to quantify, unlike total costs.

Companies should determine **relative performance** and **relative price** information for their products and compare them against the competing products. This comparative information can be obtained from reports published by external and independent organizations (e.g., Consumers Union). Relative performance and relative price are computed as:

Relative Performance = (Company's Product Performance Rating)/(Average Performance Rating from All Reported Companies) × 100

Relative Price = (Company's Product Price)/ (Average Price from All Reported Companies) × 100

The purpose is to measure whether products are above or below average in performance and price. The difference between relative performance and relative price yields **customer value**:

$$\text{Customer Value} = \text{Relative Performance} - \text{Relative Price}$$

Customers may decide to purchase a product with a positive customer value and may not purchase a product with a negative customer value, barring other considerations. These customer values should be used as input into the marketing plans for improvement.

Value is the ratio between what the customer gets (benefits) and what the customer gives (costs). Value equals benefits divided by costs. Value can also be defined as the combination of benefits received and costs paid by the customer. The **value/price ratio** is value divided by price. The higher this ratio, the better for the customer, and the lower this ratio, the worse for the customer.

❏ Learning Objective 3.18: COMPUTE A MARKETING CHANNEL INTERMEDIARY'S TRANSACTION VALUE

Retailers are among the marketing channel intermediaries when they sell a manufacturer's products at the retail store to retailer customers. The retailer's goal is to connect producers with consumers at the store for a profit.

Transaction Value

Transaction value for the retailer is derived from a combination of factors such as profitable use of space allocated to a product, inventory turnover for the product, and the marketing expenses incurred to promote the product in that space.

Marketing expenses can be classified in terms of pull and push strategies. In a **pull strategy**, advertising enables consumers to pull branded products from retailers through the marketing channel system. In a **push strategy**, manufacturers push branded products to retailers through the marketing channel system with the help of trade allowances, in-store displays, product promotion costs, sales staff training costs, and personal selling efforts.

The retailer's goal is to maximize the transaction value, which is affected by the manufacturer's product quality, market demand for the product, product margin, and overall marketing policies.

Manufacturers often carry products in their warehouse and deliver them to the retailer as needed in a just-in-time (JIT) manner to reduce the retailer's investment in inventory. This manufacturer's practice increases the transaction value to the retailer. This practice also benefits the manufacturer due to access to a number of consumers who shop at the retail store.

A **marketing channel intermediary's transaction value** is computed as:

$$\text{Transaction Value} = \text{Retail Space Value} \times \text{Inventory Turnover per Year} - \text{Marketing Expenses}$$

$$\text{Retail Space Value} = \text{Profit Margin per Square Foot} \times \text{Total Square Footage Allocated to Hold the Inventory at the Store}$$

The higher the transaction value, the greater the profit to the channel intermediary.

Channel Cost per Customer Transaction

Each channel intermediary will produce a different level of sales and incur a different level of costs. Marketing management of the selling company will try to align customers and channels to maximize demand at the lowest total cost of selling. All else being equal, marketing management prefers to replace high-cost channels with low-cost channels. Two channel choices to perform economic analysis include manufacturer's sales agency and company's own sales force. The goal is to compute the **selling cost per customer transaction** for each of the channel choices at different sales levels. The total selling costs include variable costs such as sales commissions and utilities and fixed costs such as rent and salaries. The lower the cost per customer transaction at a given sales level, the greater the profits to the channel and to the selling company. These costs should not include a product's purchase price and its inventory carrying and holding costs.

The **channel cost per customer transaction** is calculated as:

$$\text{Total Selling Costs} = \text{Total Variable Selling Costs} + \text{Total Fixed Selling Costs}$$

$$\text{Channel Cost Per Customer Transaction} = \text{Total Selling Costs}/\text{Total Number of Customer Transactions}$$

❏ Learning Objective 3.19:
UNDERSTAND THE RELATIONSHIPS AMONG PRICE, PROFIT, AND MARKET SHARE

The goal of a pricing strategy should be to increase profits, not to increase sales or volume. Lowering the price can increase sales revenues, but it may not increase profits because fixed costs stay relatively constant. The first question to ask is how much market share is needed to maintain the current level of profits before asking how much to lower or raise the price. Increasing the market share is difficult, whereas lowering or raising the price is relatively easy. Also, competitors closely follow a company's pricing strategy, whether up or down. The market share needed to maintain the current level of profits, expressed as a percent, is calculated as:

Market Share Needed = (Desired Gross Profit)/ (Market Demand) (Unit Price − Unit cost)

A **breakeven market share**, expressed as a percent, is a good indicator of judging profit potential and risk of loss, and is calculated as:

Percent Breakeven Market Share = [(Breakeven Volume in Units)/(Market Demand in Units)] × 100

where

Breakeven Volume in Units = (Total Fixed Expenses)/(Accounting Contribution Margin per Unit)

The percent breakeven market share indicates how close it is to or far it is from a company's actual market share in realizing a greater profit potential or facing a risk of loss, respectively.

Philip Kotler recommends a useful way to analyze market-share movements in terms of four components: customer penetration, customer loyalty, customer selectivity, and price elasticity. The market share of a company is the product of these four components. The market share can be increased by increasing advertising efforts, increasing price, dropping small and unprofitable dealers, and enhancing product features—all to increase the profit margin on products.

❏ Learning Objective 3.20:
UNDERSTAND A MARKETING CHANNEL'S PERFORMANCE

A marketing channel's performance is based on three areas: **customer reach**, **channel operating efficiency**, and **customer service quality**. All three areas must do well to reach the desired levels of sales and profit goals. Similarly, poor performance in any one of the three areas causes the overall channel to do poorly.

If a channel's performance is poor, the ability to reach customers is inhibited. If a channel's operations are inefficient, the cost of serving its customers will be too high, regardless of how many customers it attracts and its quality of service levels.

If customer service quality is poor, customer satisfaction will decrease, and customer retention rate will also decrease, regardless of higher levels of customer reach and operating efficiency.

A company may have direct channels and indirect channels to serve its customers. Usually, a direct marketing channel generates higher margins, but the channel costs and marketing expenses are higher. E-marketing channels are an example of indirect channels to reach smaller and hard-to-reach customers. For example, online buying can save significant amounts of money to organizations in procurement of products and services. Usually, an indirect marketing channel generates lower margins, but the channel costs and marketing expenses are lower. Marketing management should evaluate whether direct or indirect marketing channels are profitable.

Net marketing contribution (NMC) for a direct or indirect marketing channel is calculated as:

NMC for a Direct Channel = [Sales Volume in Units × (End-User Price per Unit × (1 − Channel Discount Percent))] − Cost of Goods Sold − Marketing Expenses

NMC for an Indirect Channel = [Sales Volume in Units × (End-User Price per Unit × (1 − Channel Discount Percent))] − Cost of Goods Sold − Marketing Expenses

❏ Learning Objective 3.21:
EVALUATE THE ADVERTISING'S EFFECTIVENESS WITH CUSTOMER RESPONSE INDEX

A strong marketing channel system combined with a well-positioned product providing higher levels of customer value cannot achieve full marketing success without a good marketing communications program, which includes advertising.

A customer's value increases when perceived benefits are greater than perceived costs. A company's sales level cannot increase if target customers are largely unaware of the product and its benefits, costs, and value.

The effectiveness of advertising can be measured in a hierarchical set of customer-response effects, starting with exposure (low-level), awareness, comprehension, intention, and purchase (high-level).

Awareness is the first step in a new customer acquisition process. Increasing awareness levels increase customer retention rates and average lifetime value of a customer, which in turn increase customer loyalty and company profits.

A decision tree diagram is used to facilitate the calculation of **customer response index (CRI)**, consisting of five levels, as follows:

CRI = Percent Exposed × Percent Aware
    × Percent Comprehend × Percent Intention
    × Percent Purchase

Marketing management can compute the CRI at the current level and plan for an improved level by changing the percentages of one or more of these five levels:

Incremental CRI = CRI at the Improved Level
    − CRI at the Current Level

Gross rating points (GRPs) measure the extent to which a television advertisement reached the target market and how often the target customers saw the advertisement. GRPs are a better measure of advertising effectiveness than the dollars spent on advertising. GRPs are computed as:

GRPs = Percent Reach × Message Frequency

GRPs are the same as the total number of exposures (E), which is reach (R) times frequency (F). The weighted number of exposures (WE) is reach (R) times the average frequency (F) times the average impact (I).

Total Number of Exposures = $E = R \times F$

Weighted Number of Exposures = $WE = R \times F \times I$

Advertising elasticity is the responsiveness of consumers to advertising expenditures. Marketing management estimates the advertising elasticity needed

to maintain current marketing profits, which is NMC. The goal is to determine the increase in sales in relation to an increase in the advertising expense, computed as:

Advertising Elasticity = (Percent Change in Sales)/
    (Percent Change in Advertising Expense)

Higher advertising elasticities are preferred over the smaller, and a company can compare these elasticities from time to time and among products. The "growth" stage of a product lifecycle yields greater sales gains using advertising than the "introductory," "mature," or "decline" stages.

The effects of advertising can be seen in both the short run and long run, where the latter has a carryover effect. This means that advertising done in the current sales period will produce results not only in the current period but also in the subsequent sales periods, as shown in the following.

Advertising carryover coefficients range from 0 to less than 1, with the average of 0.5, and the coefficient doubles the following period:

Advertising period	0	1	2	3
Carryover effect	0	0.5	0.25	0.125

Total sales impact of the advertising expense can be calculated as:

Total Sales Effect = (Incremental Sales)/
    (1 − Carryover Effect)

The **advertising effectiveness ratio** is actual share of market percentage divided by share of voice percentage. The ratio of 100 means an effective level, below 100 means an ineffective level, and above 100 means a very effective level.

Advertising response analysis, expressed as a coefficient, indicates how an increase in advertising budget increases the sales volume. For example, an advertising response coefficient of +0.3 means a proposed 50 percent increase in advertising budget will increase the sales volume by 15 percent (i.e., 50% × 0.3). The increase in gross profit amount resulting from advertising response coefficient is computed as:

Increase in Gross Profit = Increase in Advertising
    Budget × Advertising Response Coefficient
    × Current Net Sales × Gross Profit Percentage

The major objective of the **marketing public relations (MPR)** function in a firm is to serve the marketing department in areas such as launching of new products, building of customer interest in a product category, and repositioning of a mature market. The return on the MPR investment can be calculated as follows:

Return on MPR Investment = Contribution Margin Due to MPR/MPR Investment or Cost

Learning Objective 3.22: LEARN HOW TO CONDUCT A MARKETING PORTFOLIO ANALYSIS

A **portfolio analysis** is an evaluation of a business unit, specific product, or market segment regarding market attractiveness and competitive position to decide upon a suitable strategic marketing plan. The goal is to increase sales, market share, and profits for a given amount of investment.

Two strategic market plans emerge from a portfolio analysis—offensive and defensive plans:

1. **Offensive plans** focus on investing to grow the market or market share, investing to improve the competitive position, and investing to enter new attractive markets or develop new-product markets.
2. **Defensive plans** focus on investing to protect or hold the market share and competitive position, optimizing the price-volume relationship to maximize profits position (optimize), managing the market position for maximum cash flow with limited resources (monetize), and managing the product for maximum short-run cash flow or minimum losses (harvest/divest).

A company can develop two types of plans (offensive—grow share or defensive—hold share) to determine the best course of action. Year 1 (Y1) will be the base year, as follows:

Actual—Y1	Offensive Plan—Y2	Defensive Plan—Y2
Sales Revenues	Sales Revenues	Sales Revenues
Gross Profit	Gross Profit	Gross Profit
NMC	NMC	NMC
MROS	MROS	MROS
MROI	MROI	MROI

where

Sales Revenues = Market Demand × Market Share

Gross Profit = Sales Revenues × Percent Margin

NMC = Gross Profit − Marketing Expenses

MROS = (NMC/Sales Revenues) × 100

MROI = (NMC/Marketing Expenses) × 100

Learning Objective 3.23: LEARN HOW TO DEVELOP A MARKETING BUDGET

Whether to hold current market share or to grow market share requires financial resources in the form of a **marketing budget**, which is based on the strategic market plan and the marketing-mix strategy.

Three kinds of marketing budgets exist: percent-of-sales, customer-mix, and bottom-up.

1. **The percent-of-sales budget** is based on previous years' data and experience levels, adjusted higher for the growth strategy and lower for the harvest strategy. This kind of budget is simple to develop but the accuracy is low.
2. **Customer-mix budget** includes the cost of acquiring new customers and the cost of retaining current customers. This kind of budget is logical to develop, but the cost data are difficult to obtain. This budget amount can be expressed as a percent of sales for comparative purposes.
   The customer-mix budget can be prepared as:

   Customer-Mix Budget = (Marketing Administration Costs) + (Acquisition Cost per Customer × Number of New Customers) + (Retention Cost per Customer × Number of Retained Customers)

3. **Bottom-up budget** requires specifying each marketing task required and determining the amount needed to accomplish that task. It is good to divide the budget into personnel expenses and non-personnel expenses to facilitate comparison between time periods. This budget amount can also be expressed as a percent of sales for comparative purposes.

Learning Objective 3.24: UNDERSTAND THE FINANCIAL PERFORMANCE METRICS RELATED TO MARKETING

Organizations with marketing-orientation and customer-focus should look at financial data related to customers since they are the major source of cash flows and profits.

Some examples of financial performance metrics related to marketing are shown here:

Financial Performance Metrics Related to Marketing

Customer Volume = Market Demand in Total Number of Customers × Percent Market Share

Customer Margin = Net Revenue per Customer − Cost of Goods Sold per Customer

where net revenue per customer is average revenue per customer times channel discount percent.

Gross Profit = Customer Volume × Customer Margin

Net Marketing Contribution (NMC) = Gross Profit − Marketing Expenses

Net Profit = NMC − Non-Marketing Operating Expenses

Marketing Expenses = Marketing Personnel Expenses + Marketing Non-Personnel Expenses

Marketing Return on Sales (MROS) = (NMC/Sales Revenues) × 100

Marketing Return on Investment (MROI) = (NMC/Marketing Expenses) × 100

Customer Value = Relative Performance − Relative Price

Accounts Receivable Investment = Customer Volume × Net Revenue per Customer × Percent Days Outstanding

Inventory Investment = Customer Volume × Cost of Goods Sold per Customer × Percent Days of Inventory

---

❑ Learning Objective 3.25: UNDERSTAND THE NATURE OF MARKETING OF SERVICES

This learning objective discusses service characteristics and service quality along with overcoming obstacles in services marketing.

Service Characteristics

The definition of what constitutes a service remains unclear. Both products and services have the following common variables that comprise the marketing mix:

- The product or service itself
- The price
- The distribution system
- Promotion
- Marketing research

Yet, services possess certain distinguishing characteristics and have unique problems that result in marketing mix decisions that are substantially different from those found in communication with the marketing of goods. These characteristics include intangibility, inseparability, fluctuating demand, a highly differentiated marketing system, and a client relationship:

- **Intangibility** arises when a service firm is actually selling an idea or experience, not a product. It is often difficult to illustrate, demonstrate, or display the service in use. Examples include airline or hotel service.
- **Inseparability** arises when a service cannot be separated from the person of the seller. In other words, the service must be created and marketed simultaneously. An example is an insurance agent who is selling a policy.
- **Fluctuating demand** occurs when services fluctuate either by season (tourism), days (airlines), or time of day (movie theaters). One example of stimulating demand or unused capacity is when downtown hotels (or those that are used predominantly by business travelers) offer significant discounts for a weekend stay.
- **Highly differentiated marketing systems** offer different service approaches for different services. For example, the marketing of banking or financial services requires a different approach than the marketing of computer services or airline services.
- **Client relationships** exist between the buyer and the seller, as opposed to a customer relationship. Examples include physician–patient and banker–investor relationships. The buyer follows the suggestions provided by the seller.

Service Quality

Poor service quality and nonperformance are two major reasons, and high price is a minor reason for switching to the competition. **Service quality** is measured against performance, which can be very difficult to ascertain. In general, problems in the determination of good service quality are attributable to differences in expectations, perceptions, and experiences regarding the encounter between the service provider and the service user.

It is easier and cheaper to keep an existing customer than to find a new one. Product quality can be measured against accepted standards, which is tangible, while service quality is measured against expected performance, which is intangible.

Service quality is the gap between expected service and perceived service. The following is a list of determinants of service quality, which can help marketing managers to avoid losing customers:

- Reliability involves dependability and consistency of performance.
- Responsiveness concerns the willingness or readiness of employees to provide service.
- Competence means possession of the necessary skills and knowledge to perform the service.
- Access involves approachability and ease of contact.
- Courtesy involves politeness, respect, consideration, and friendliness of contact personnel.
- Communication means keeping customers informed in language they can understand. It also means listening to customers.
- Credibility involves trustworthiness, believability, and honesty.
- Security is freedom from danger, risk, or doubt.
- Understanding the customer involves making the effort to understand the customer's needs.
- Tangibles include the physical evidence of the service.

Overcoming the Obstacles in Service Marketing

In view of the size and importance of the service economy, considerable innovation and ingenuity are needed to make high-quality services available at convenient locations for consumers. Actual services offered by service providers often fall behind the opportunities available due to the following obstacles: a limited view of marketing, a lack of competition, a lack of creative management, a concept of "no obsolescence," and a lack of innovation in the distribution of services.

❑ Learning Objective 3.26: UNDERSTAND THE STRATEGIES IN PRODUCT MANAGEMENT

Product management strategy is a part of the marketing mix (i.e., product, price, place, and promotion). Other parts include promotion strategy, distribution strategy, and pricing strategy. There are many decision areas in product management, including product definition, product classification, product mix and product line, and packaging and branding.

Product Definition

The way in which the product variable is defined can have important implications for the survival, profitability, and long-run growth of a firm. A product can be viewed in several ways:

- Tangible product focuses on physical object itself.
- Extended product focuses on physical object and service.
- Generic product focuses on essential benefits to be received from the product.

A classical example of improper definition can be found in railroad passenger service, where it defined itself as being in the railroad business instead of in the transportation business. A reasonable definition of **product** is that it is the sum of the physical, psychological, and sociological satisfaction the buyer derives from purchase, ownership, and consumption.

Product Classification

Product classification is an analytical device to assist in planning marketing strategies and programs. A basic assumption underlying such classifications is that products with common attributes can be marketed in a similar manner. In general, products are classified according to two basic criteria: (1) end use or market and (2) degree of processing or physical transformation required.

Examples of product classification include agricultural products, raw materials, industrial goods, and consumer goods. The market for industrial products has certain attributes that distinguish it from the consumer goods market. For certain products there are a limited number of buyers, known as a **vertical market,** which means that it is narrow (customers are restricted to a few industries) and that it is deep (a large percentage of the producers in the market use the product). Some products, such as office supplies, have a **horizontal market,** which means that goods are purchased by all types of firms in many different industries.

Product Mix and Product Line

The **product mix** is the composite of products offered for sale by the firm's product line. It refers to a group of products that are closely related in terms of use, customer groups, price ranges, and channels of distribution. There are three primary dimensions of a firm's product mix, including width, depth, and consistency.

Width of the product mix refers to the number of product lines the firm handles. **Depth** of the product mix refers to the average number of products in each line. **Consistency** of the product mix refers to the similarity of product lines. Product line plans take into account consumer evaluation of the company's products (strengths and weaknesses) and objective and accurate information on sales, profits, and market share (actual and anticipated levels).

Packaging and Branding

Distinctive or unique packaging is one method of differentiating relatively homogeneous products, such as toothpaste or soap. The design of packaging should focus on the size of the product, how easy it is to open, how strong the packaging should be in protecting the product, the attractiveness of the packaging, and costs.

Many companies use branding strategies to increase the strength of the product image. Factors to be considered include: product quality, whereby products do what they do very well; consistent advertising, in which brands tell their story often and well; and brand personality, where the brand stands for something unique (e.g., Xerox and Kodak). A good brand name can evoke feelings of trust, confidence, security, and strength.

Marketing management needs to analyze **direct product profitability** for each product because handling costs among products can vary, thus affecting the true gross margin/profit of a product. A product's **handling costs** can include receiving costs, storage costs, warehouse loading costs, and paperwork costs from the time it reaches the warehouse until a customer buys it in the retail store. This means that some high-volume products with higher handling costs are less profitable and deserve less shelf

space in the store than some low-volume products with lower handling costs. **True gross margin** is computed as:

True Gross Margin = Gross Margin Before
Handling Costs − Handling Costs

❑ Learning Objective 3.27: UNDERSTAND THE STAGES IN A PRODUCT LIFECYCLE

A firm's product strategy must consider the fact that products have a lifecycle—phases or stages that a product will go through in its lifetime. This lifecycle varies according to industry, product, technology, and market. In general, product growth follows an S-shaped curve, although shown as linear, due to innovation, diffusion of a new product, and changes in the product and the market.

Product Lifecycle (PLC) Concept

There are four phases that a typical product goes through: (1) introduction, (2) growth, (3) maturation, and (4) decline. Some products skip a phase, such as introduction or maturity, while some products are revitalized after decline, thereby not going through the S-shaped pattern. Each phase is described in the following (see the figure).

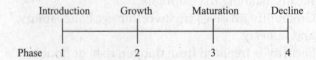

Introduction phase (phase 1) incurs high production and marketing costs. Profits are low or nonexistent. This phase is flat due to difficulties of overcoming buyer inertia and stimulating trials of the new product.

Profits increase and are possibly correlated with sales during the **growth stage** (phase 2) as the market begins trying and adopting the product. As the product **matures** (phase 3), profits do not keep pace with sales because of competition. Penetration of the product's potential buyers is eventually reached, causing the rapid growth to stop and level off. Price concessions, increasing product quality, and expanding advertising will be planned to maintain market share.

At some point, sales will **decline** (phase 4), and the seller must decide whether to drop the product, alter the product, seek new uses for the product, seek new markets, or continue with more of the same. Growth will eventually taper off as new substitute products appear in the market. The advice for the decline phase is not to invest in slow or negative growth or unfavorable markets but instead to pull the cash out.

Due to changing conditions, the marketing mix has to be changed in line with PLC changes. The PLC concept can help in forecasting, pricing, advertising, and product plans. The difficult part of the PLC concept is estimating the exact time periods for these four phases in that it is hard to know when one phase begins and ends. The duration of each phase varies from product to product, which diminishes the usefulness of the PLC concept as a marketing planning tool.

Product Audit

The **product audit** is a marketing management technique whereby the company's current product offerings are required to ascertain whether each product should be continued as is, improved, modified, or discontinued. The product manager, who is responsible for his product, should ensure that the product audit is performed at regular intervals as a matter of marketing policy. One of the major purposes of the product audit is to detect "sick" products for possible discontinuation. Some critical factors to be considered in this area include sales trends, profit contribution, and product lifecycle stage.

- **Sales trends.** How have sales moved over time? Why have sales declined?

- **Profit contribution.** What has been the profit contribution of this product to the company?
- **Product lifecycle stage.** Has the product reached a level of maturity and saturation in the market? Has the product outgrown its usefulness? The product discontinuation issue is a hard one because it involves consideration of its negative impact on employees, keeping consumers supplied with replacement parts, disposing of inventory, and providing repair and maintenance services.

One of the objectives of the product audit is to determine whether to modify or improve the product or to leave the product as it is (status quo). Modifying the product requires changes in product features, design, packaging, promotion, price, and channels of distribution. Product improvement suggestions often come from advertising agencies, consultants, sales staff, consumers, and intermediaries, and involve many functions such as engineering, manufacturing, marketing, and accounting. Market research is advised when a product improvement is planned because it is not always clear how consumers will react to improvements or changes.

 Self-Assessment Exercise

Online exercises are provided for the learning objectives in this module. Please visit www.mbaiq.com to complete the online exercises and to calculate your MBA IQ Score.

Quality and Process Management

Learning Objective 4.1: Understand the Basic Quality Concepts   91

Learning Objective 4.2: Understand the Various Definitions of Quality   93

Learning Objective 4.3: Calculate the Cost of Quality   94

Learning Objective 4.4: Calculate the Six-Sigma Metric   94

Design for Six Sigma   95
Six-Sigma Players   96

Learning Objective 4.5: Compute the Return-on-Quality Metric   96

Learning Objective 4.6: Apply Quality Tools   96

Seven Quality Control Tools   97

Seven Quality Management Tools   97
Other Tools   97

Learning Objective 4.7: Apply Statistical Process Control Techniques   98

Process Variation   98
Process Capability   99

Learning Objective 4.8: Compute Taguchi's Quality Loss Function   100

Learning Objective 4.9: Understand the Role of Inspection and Quality at Source   100

Learning Objective 4.10: Understand the Process Management Methods and Tools   101

❑ Learning Objective 4.1: UNDERSTAND THE BASIC QUALITY CONCEPTS

Quality planning focuses on developing products, services, systems, processes, policies, and procedures needed to meet or exceed customer expectations. Quality planning is a part of the Japanese Hoshin planning method where it involves consensus at all levels as plans are cascaded throughout the organization, resulting in actionable plans and continual monitoring and measurement.

Quality assurance focuses on the inputs to a process or product, rather than the traditional controlling mode of inspecting and checking products at the end of operations, *after* errors are made (i.e., quality control).

Quality control is an evaluation to indicate needed corrective action, the act of guiding, or the state of a process in which the variability is attributable to a constant system of chance causes. It compares and acts on the difference between actual performance and target performance (goal). Quality control includes the operational techniques and activities used to fulfill requirements for quality. Often, quality assurance and quality control are used interchangeably, referring to the actions performed to ensure the quality of a product, service, or process, but they are different in meaning in terms of timing.

Quality engineering focuses on combining product design engineering methods and statistical concepts to reduce costs and improve quality by optimizing product design and manufacturing processes. For example, Taguchi's **quality loss function (QLF)** is connected with quality engineering.

Quality audit is a systematic, independent examination and review to determine whether quality activities and related results comply with planned arrangements and whether these arrangements are implemented effectively and are suitable to achieve the objectives. Quality planning, quality assurance, and quality engineering focus on the front-end of a process, whereas quality control and quality audit focus on the back-end of a process.

Quality circles refer to a team of employees (6 to 12) voluntarily getting together periodically to discuss quality-related problems and issues and to devise strategies and plans to take corrective actions. Quality circles should be introduced in an evolutionary manner, so employees feel that they can tap their creative potential. Quality circles are a part of employee empowerment. Ishikawa is known as the "Father of Quality Circles."

Quality council is a prerequisite of implementing a total quality management (TQM) program in the organization. The quality council is similar to an executive steering committee.

Quality improvement or **continuous improvement** is an ongoing activity where problems are diagnosed, root causes are identified, solutions are developed, and controls are established to improve quality.

Plan-Do-Check-Adjust (PDCA) cycle is related to continuous improvement, where an improvement plan is developed (Plan), implemented (Do), monitored and evaluated (Check), and modified or refined (Adjust). Deming's PDCA cycle is a core management tool for problem solving and quality improvement, which can be used for planning and implementing quality improvements.

Just-in-time (JIT) philosophy reduces the cost of quality (COQ) and improves quality. It is related to continuous improvement.

Jidoka (a Japanese word) means stopping a production line or a process step when a defect or problem is discovered so that it will not cause additional or new problems further down the production line. Jidoka requires employee training and empowerment to stop the running production line. A production worker and/or a programmed machine can accomplish the jidoka goals.

Kaizen is an ongoing process of unending improvement, that is, establishing and achieving higher goals of improvement all the time. PDCA, JIT, and kaizen are related to quality or continuous improvement. Journalist tools such as Five Ws and One H can be used to understand a process deeply and to improve a process continuously. These tools include Who, What, Where, When, Why, and How. Answers to these six questions help guide the problem solving and quality improvement process.

Poka-yoke is an approach for mistake-proofing a production or service process using automatic devices (failsafe methods) to avoid simple human or machine errors in order to improve quality. It is based on two aspects: prediction and detection of a defect or error. It is a simple, creative, and inexpensive method to implement and in part achieves zero defects as suggested by Crosby.

Stakeholder empowerment means involving employees in every step of a production or service process to solicit their input. It is based on the idea that employees who are close to the action would better know the shortcomings of a system, machine, or process than those who are not. Quality circles are part of employee empowerment. Similarly, inviting suppliers and customers to participate in a product or service design to improve quality and features is also a part of stakeholder empowerment.

Sequential engineering (traditional engineering or over the wall engineering) is an approach to product development process where each stage is carried out separately and where the next stage cannot start until the previous stage is completed. The entire process takes time and costs money because the communication and coordination flows are only in one direction and all changes and corrections are relayed back to the beginning of the process or previous stages. The time-to-market for a new product is longer, expensive, and inefficient with sequential engineering. Concurrent engineering approach is an improvement over the sequential engineering approach as the former approach improves timing, communication, and coordination problems encountered in the latter approach.

Concurrent engineering is defined as a systematic approach to the integrated and overlapping design of products and their related processes, including design, manufacturing, and support. It requires that, from the beginning, all elements of a product's lifecycle be evaluated across all design factors to include user requirements, quality, cost, and schedule.

Industrial engineering, also known as management engineering, ensures the economical, efficient, and effective utilization of an organization's resources in manufacturing and service industries.

Industrial engineers (management engineers) are known as efficiency experts in manufacturing or service firms as they deal with the five-M of a company's resources: men, machines, materials, methods, and measurements. Specifically, industrial engineers participate in the design of jobs, products, and processes; schedule machines for greater utilization; schedule operators for maximum productivity; measure material-usage efficiency; measure labor productivity through motion and time studies; measure energy-usage efficiency; participate in layout design for equipment and facilities; analyze materials handling and warehousing operations for efficiency; analyze work steps to identify value-added and non-value-added activities; review product specifications for accuracy and improvement; and enhance production systems, methods, and procedures to eliminate waste and duplication. They approach production or service activities with an eye towards continual improvement using integrated systems, methods, and procedures.

The International Organization for Standardization **(ISO) 9000 standards** address quality system processes but not product performance specifications. In other words, ISO 9000 covers how products are made but not necessarily how they work. ISO 9000 focuses on processes, not on products or people. It is based on the concept that one will fix the product by fixing the process. ISO 9000 is a standard by which to judge the quality of suppliers. It assumes that suppliers have a sound quality system in place and are following it. ISO 9000 can be used as a baseline quality system to achieve quality objectives.

Two kinds of ISO 9000 standards exist: product standards dealing with technical specifications and quality standards dealing with management systems. Four quality measures for ISO 9000 are: (1) leadership, (2) human resource development and management, (3) management of process quality, and (4) customer focus and satisfaction.

Environmental quality engineering means designing products and their processes that are environmentally friendly using green manufacturing techniques, such as design for reuse (recycling), design for disassembly (repair), design for rework, and design for remanufacturing (restoration).

Design for recycling is an investment recovery and environmental improvement effort to recover revenues and reduce costs associated with scrap, surplus, obsolete, and waste materials. In design for repair, a nonconforming product is fixed so that it will fulfill the intended usage requirements, although it may not conform to the originally specified requirements. A repaired product retains its original identity and only those parts that have failed or badly worn out are replaced or serviced. In design for rework, a nonconforming product is taken back to production line to fix it in order to meet the originally specified requirements. In design for remanufacturing, worn out products are restored to like-new condition.

Green manufacturing uses a lifecycle design-approach that focuses on incoming materials, manufacturing processes, customer use of the product, and product disposal.

Complying with environmental quality standards such as ISO 14000 and 14001 is a part of the environmental quality engineering scope. The goal is to reduce the potential legal liabilities and respond to regulatory requirements (e.g., EPA in the U.S.) addressing human safety and health issues.

The **ISO 14000 environmental standards** are divided into two broad categories: (1) environmental management systems consisting of environmental performance evaluation and environmental auditing and (2) lifecycle assessment consisting of environmental labeling and environmental aspects in product standards.

The **ISO 14001 environmental standard** is a framework for planning, developing, and implementing environmental strategies in an organization. The framework includes a policy, a planning process, organizational structure, specific objectives and targets, specific implementation programs, communications and training programs, management review, monitoring, and corrective action in terms of environmental audit.

Total quality management (TQM) is an umbrella term and concept that focuses on doing things right in the first place, whether in producing goods or providing services. TQM encompasses the entire organization both internally from higher-lever employees to lower-level employees and externally from suppliers to customers. A TQM strategy or program includes several elements such as quality concepts and tools, continuous improvement (kaizen), PDCA, JIT, stakeholder empowerment, benchmarking, ISO, Six-Sigma, statistical process control (SPC), and Taguchi's quality loss function. Contrary to the popular belief, quality decreases costs and increases profits.

Drivers of quality include customers; suppliers; employees; products; services; organizational culture; organizational policies, procedures, and standards; and total organizational focus and commitment.

Big Q, little q is a quality-contrasting term where big Q focuses on all business products and processes in the entire company and little q focuses on all or parts of products and processes in one factory or plant.

❑ Learning Objective 4.2: UNDERSTAND THE VARIOUS DEFINITIONS OF QUALITY

Quality has many definitions because it is viewed differently from many perspectives.

Judgment-based criteria are synonymous with superiority or excellence, which is abstract, subjective, and difficult to quantify.

Product-based criteria assume that higher levels or amounts of product characteristics are equivalent to higher quality and that quality has a direct relationship with price.

User-based criteria define that quality is fitness for intended use or how well a product performs its intended function. It is basically dictated by user wants and needs.

Value-based criteria focus on the relationship of usefulness or satisfaction of a product or service to price. This means a customer can purchase a generic product at a lower price if it performs the same way as the brand-name product.

Manufacturing-based criteria mean conformance to specifications (e.g., engineering or manufacturing) that are important to customers. Taguchi opposes the manufacturing-based definition of quality due to built-in defects to be produced at a higher cost.

Customer-driven quality is meeting or exceeding customer expectations. This definition is simple and powerful; hence, most companies use it.

A Japanese professor, Noriaki Kano, suggested three classes of customer requirements in understanding customer's needs in the marketplace: dissatisfiers, satisfiers, and delighters. Customers are **dissatisfied** when the features that they assumed or expected are not present in a product. Customers are **satisfied** when the features that they wanted are present in a product, although those features are not expected. Customers are **delighted** when the features that they did not assume or expect are present in a product because the features exceed their expectations.

Critical-to-quality (CTQ) is a quality measurement technique that dictates a product's output specifications in terms of a customer's needs, wants, and expectations, whether the customer is internal or external to an organization. CTQ focuses on customer requirements, design and test parameters, mistake-proofing, quality robustness, and control charts.

☐ Learning Objective 4.3: CALCULATE THE COST OF QUALITY

The **cost of quality (COQ)** means the price of nonconformance to standards, policies, or procedures. COQ is the cost of doing things wrong, which results in poor quality of products or services. COQ is really the cost of poor quality.

Four categories of COQ are:

1. **Prevention costs** are associated with reducing the potential for producing defective products or rendering poor-quality services in the first place. Examples include quality improvement programs, employee training and education, investment in equipment and facilities, operator inspection costs, supplier ratings, supplier reviews, supplier certification, product design reviews, pilot projects, prototype tests, vendor surveys, quality-related design costs, purchase-order technical data reviews, and quality department review costs.

2. **Appraisal costs** are associated with evaluating products, processes, parts, or services. Examples include material testing, product testing, production line inspection, quality checks, purchasing appraisal costs, qualifications of supplier product, equipment calibration, receiving and shipping inspection costs, production tests, and product quality audits.

3. **Internal failure costs** are associated with producing defective products or rendering poor-quality services before delivering them to customers. Examples include repair, redesign, reinspection, rework, retesting, sorting, scrap, waste, machine downtime, employee fatigue, and employee carelessness.

4. **External failure costs** are associated with correcting defective products or poor-quality services after delivering them to customers. Examples include product returns, product warranty charges, product recalls, liability suits resulting from damage to customers, field service staff training costs, lost customer goodwill, and poor reputation to a firm.

A $1.00 investment in a prevention category will reduce many dollars of internal and external failure costs, which in turn will improve overall product or service quality many times over.

Quality costs can be reported as an index—the ratio of the current value to a base period value—and expressed as a percentage or as a fraction. The **quality cost index** increases the understanding of the underlying cost data. Some common measurement bases include direct labor cost, manufacturing cost, sales dollars, and units of production.

☐ Learning Objective 4.4: CALCULATE THE SIX-SIGMA METRIC

Six-Sigma is a statistical concept to describe accuracy and quality levels in a process, product, or service, which can lead to a competitive advantage in the marketplace. The word **sigma** is associated with a statistical term, **standard deviation,** which is the distance from the mean (average).

Six-Sigma is a strategy, discipline, system, program, and tool to achieve quality improvement continuously, to solve problems, to improve functions and features of a product or service, to reduce cost and time, and to increase customer satisfaction.

Meaning of Different Sigma Levels

- Three-Sigma means 66,800 defects in a million parts produced.
- Four-Sigma means 6,210 defects in a million parts produced.
- Five-Sigma means 230 defects in a million parts produced.
- Six-Sigma means 3.4 defects in a million parts produced.
- The goal of reaching Six-Sigma from Three-Sigma is a challenging one as it is a nonlinear process to reach the goal.

Six-Sigma follows an improvement model called **DMAIC,** which stands for define, measure, analyze, improve, and control stage. D defines the project's purpose, scope, and outputs, M measures the process and collects data, A analyzes the data to ensure repeatability and reproducibility, I improves or redesigns the existing process, and C controls the new or modified process for increased performance.

Implementing a Six-Sigma program requires a strong commitment from employees and management in terms of time, training, and expertise.

Six-Sigma redefines quality performance as **defects per million opportunities (dpmo)** and is calculated as:

dpmo = (Defects per Unit)

$\qquad$ × 1,000,000/Opportunities for Error

where

$\qquad$ Defects per Unit = Number of Defects Discovered/Number of Units Produced

Tools and Techniques Used in DMAIC Model

Examples of tools and techniques used in the Define stage include brainstorming, cause-and-effect diagram, and process mapping.

Examples of tools and techniques used in the Measure stage include cause-and-effect diagram and process mapping.

Examples of tools and techniques used in the Analyze stage include regression and correlation analysis and process mapping.

Examples of tools and techniques used in the Improve stage include brainstorming, simulation, design of experiments, and process mapping.

Examples of tools and techniques used in the Control stage include mistake-proofing (Poka-yoke), statistical process control, and control charts.

Design for Six Sigma

Design for Six-Sigma (DFSS) is a proactive approach in preventing problems from occurring in the first place and/or in resolving problems after they occur. The focus is on functional and quality improvement at the early design stage. An approach to DFSS is established in terms of **DCOV** model, which stands for define, characterize, optimize, and verify.

Tools and Techniques Used in DCOV Model

Examples of tools and techniques used in the Define stage include Kano model, quality function deployment (QFD), and regression and conjoint analysis.

Examples of tools and techniques used in the Characterize stage include design of experiments and TRIZ (a problem-solving tool).

Examples of tools and techniques used in the Optimize stage include design of experiments, simulation, mistake-proofing, and control charts.

Examples of tools and techniques used in the Verify stage include design walkthroughs and reviews and product tests.

DFSS is similar to other design concepts such as design for manufacturability (e.g., lean production and standard parts), design for low cost (e.g., overhead costs, supply-chain costs, and quality costs), design for faster production (e.g., flexible manufacturing and concurrent engineering), design for faster marketing (e.g., time-to-market, quality function deployment, and voice of the customer), design for safety and ergonomics (e.g., safe products and human factors), design for a better environment (e.g., pollution control and recycling), and design for serviceability (e.g., post-sales activities such as ease of repair and maintenance).

Six-Sigma Players

Several **Six-Sigma players** exist in the planning and implementation of the Six-Sigma program in an organization, including White Belts (at the bottom), Green Belts, Yellow Belts, Black Belts, Master Black Belts, Project Champions, and Senior Champions (at the top of the Six-Sigma hierarchy). All of these players assume defined roles and responsibilities and need specific training with varying lengths to make the Six-Sigma program a success.

White Belts are hourly employees needing basic training in Six-Sigma goals, tools, and techniques to help Green Belts and Black Belts on their projects.

Green Belts are salaried employees who have a dual responsibility in implementing Six-Sigma in their function and carrying out their regular duties in that function. They gather and analyze data in support of a Black Belt project and receive a simplified version of Black Belt training. **Yellow Belts** are seasoned salaried employees who are familiar with quality improvement processes.

Black Belts are salaried employees who have a full-time responsibility in implementing Six-Sigma projects. They require hard skills and receive extensive training in statistics and problem-solving and decision-making tools and techniques, as they train Green Belts. Black Belts are very important to Six-Sigma's success.

Master Black Belts are also salaried employees who have a full-time responsibility in implementing Six-Sigma projects. They require soft skills, need some knowledge in statistics, and need more knowledge in problem-solving and decision-making tools and techniques, as they train Black Belts and Green Belts.

Senior Champions are sponsors and executives in a specific business function and manage several **Project Champions** at the business unit level, who in turn manage specific projects. Senior Champions develop plans, set priorities, allocate resources, and organize projects. Project Champions deploy plans, manage projects that cut across the business functions, and provide managerial and technical guidance to Master Black Belts and Black Belts. All champions require soft skills.

Which Six-Sigma Player Does What?

White Belts help Green Belts and Black Belts.
Green Belts help Black Belts.
Black Belts help Master Black Belts.
Master Black Belts help Project Champions.
Project Champions help Senior Champions.
Senior Champions decide *what* gets done while Project Champions, Master Black Belts, and Black Belts decide *how* to get it done.

❑ Learning Objective 4.5: COMPUTE THE RETURN-ON-QUALITY METRIC

Return on quality (ROQ) is similar to return on investment (ROI) in terms of measurement, requiring the same attention as ROI. Quality improvement initiatives have a direct financial impact, which cannot be ignored.

ROQ is similar to COQ in terms of measurement except that COQ takes an internal perspective such as costs and defects and ROQ takes an external perspective such as revenues and customer satisfaction.

Comparison among COQ, ROQ, and CTQ

COQ takes an internal perspective.
ROQ takes an external perspective.
CTQ takes both internal and external customer perspectives.

ROQ measures expected revenue gains against expected costs associated with quality improvement initiatives. ROQ is computed as net present value (NPV) of benefits resulting from quality improvement initiatives divided by NPV of costs associated with quality improvement initiatives minus 1.0.

Return on quality (ROQ), expressed as a percentage, is computed as:

$$ROQ = [(\text{Net Present Value of Quality Benefits})/(\text{Net Present Value of Quality Costs})] - 1.00$$

The result is multiplied by 100 to get the percentage.

All benefits and costs are multiplied with the corresponding present value factors to result in NPV of benefits and costs respectively.

❑ Learning Objective 4.6: APPLY QUALITY TOOLS

Several **quality tools** exist that can be used to analyze processes, prioritize problems, report the results, and evaluate the results of a corrective action plan. Quality tools consist of quality control tools and quality management tools.

Seven Quality Control Tools

Check sheets are used for collecting data in a logical and systematic manner.

A **histogram** is a frequency-distribution diagram in which the frequencies of occurrences of the different variables being plotted are represented by bars.

A **scatter diagram** is a plot of the values of one variable against those of another variable to determine the relationship between them. These diagrams are used during analysis to understand the cause-and-effect relationship between two variables. Scatter diagrams are also called **correlation diagrams.**

A **Pareto diagram** is a special use of the bar graph in which the bars are arranged in descending order of magnitude. The purpose of Pareto analysis, using Pareto diagrams, is to identify the major problems in a product or process or, more generally, to identify the most significant causes for a given effect. This allows a developer to prioritize problems and decide which problem area to work on first.

A **flowcharting** tool can be used to document every phase of a company's operation, for example, from order taking to shipping in a manufacturing company. It will become an effective way to break down a process or pinpoint a problem. Flowcharting can be done at both the summary level and the detailed level serving different user needs.

One form of a **cause-and-effect (C&E) diagram** is used for process analysis when a series of events or steps in a process creates a problem and it is not clear which event or step is the major cause of the problems. Each process or subprocess is examined for possible causes; after the causes from each step in the process are discovered, significant root causes of the problem are selected, verified, and corrected. The C&E diagram is also called a **fishbone** or **Ishikawa diagram,** invented as a problem-solving tool.

Stratification helps the C&E diagram because it is a procedure used to describe the systematic subdivision of population or process data to obtain a detailed understanding of the structure of the population or process. It is not to be confused with a stratified sampling method. Stratification can be used to break down a problem to discover its root causes and can establish appropriate corrective actions, called **countermeasures.**

A **control chart** assesses a process variation. The control chart displays sequential process measurements relative to the overall process average and control limits. The upper and lower control limits establish the boundaries of normal variation for the process being measured.

Seven Quality Management Tools

An **affinity diagram** is a data-reduction tool that organizes a large number of qualitative inputs into a smaller number of major categories. These diagrams are useful in analyzing defect data and other quality problems and useful in conjunction with cause-and-effect diagrams or interrelationship digraphs.

A **tree diagram** can be used to show the relationships of a production process by breaking it down from few larger steps into many smaller steps. The greater the detail of steps, the better simplified they are. Quality improvement actions can progress from the rightmost of the tree to the leftmost.

A **process decision program chart** is a preventive control tool that prevents problems from occurring in the first place and mitigates the impact of problems that do occur. From this aspect, it is a contingency planning tool. The objective of the tool is to determine the impact of the "failures" or problems on project schedule.

A **matrix diagram** is developed to analyze the correlations between two groups of ideas with the use of a decision table. This diagram allows one to systematically analyze correlations. Quality function deployment (QFD) is an extension of the matrix diagram.

An **interrelationship digraph** is used to organize disparate ideas. Arrows are drawn between related ideas. An idea that has arrows leaving it but none entering is a root idea. More attention is then given to the root ideas for system improvement. The digraph is often used in conjunction with affinity diagrams.

Prioritization matrices are used to help decision-makers determine the order of importance of the activities being considered in a decision. Key issues and choices are identified for further improvement. These matrices combine the use of a tree diagram and a matrix diagram.

Activity network diagrams are project management tools to determine which activities must be performed, when they must be performed, and in what sequence. These diagrams are similar to program evaluation and review technique (PERT) and critical path method (CPM), the popular tools in project management. Unlike PERT and CPM, activity network diagrams are simple to construct and require less training to use.

Other Tools

Process mapping is flowcharting of a work process in detail, including key measurements.

Design of experiments deals with planning, conducting, analyzing, and interpreting controlled tests to evaluate the factors that control the value of a parameter (e.g., design specification tolerance).

Quality function deployment (QFD) is a structured method in which customer requirements are translated into appropriate technical requirements for each stage of product development and manufacturing. Input for the QFD process comes from listening to the **voice of the customer (VOC)**. The **house of quality (HOQ)** is a diagram that clarifies the relationship between customer needs and product features. It helps correlate market or customer requirements and analysis of competitive products with higher-level technical and product characteristics. The diagram, which makes it possible to bring several factors into a single figure, is named for its house-shaped appearance but sometimes is referred to as QFD, a sign of the connection between the three approaches of VOC, QFD, and HOQ.

☐ Learning Objective 4.7:
APPLY STATISTICAL PROCESS CONTROL TECHNIQUES

Management's goal is to reduce causes of process variation and to increase process capabilities to meet customer expectations.

Process Variation

Variation is present in every process as a result of a combination of four variables: (1) operator variation (due to physical and emotional conditions), (2) equipment variation (due to wear and tear), (3) materials variation (due to thickness, moisture content, and old and new materials), and (4) environmental variation (due to changes in temperature, light, and humidity). Variation is either expected or unexpected, and it results from common causes, special causes, or structural causes.

Variation affects proper functioning of a process in that process output deviates from the established target **Common causes** of variation affect the standard deviation of a process and are caused by factors internal to a process. These causes, which are present in all processes, are also called **chance** (random) **causes.** Chance causes are small in magnitude and are difficult to identify. Examples of common random causes include worker availability, number and complexity of orders, job schedules,

equipment testing, work-center schedules, changes in raw materials, truck schedules, and worker performance.

Special causes affect the standard deviation of a process and are factors external to a process. Special causes, also known as **assignable causes,** are large in magnitude and are not so difficult to identify. They may or may not be present in a process. Examples of special (assignable) causes include equipment breakdowns, operator changes, new raw materials, new products, new competition, and new customers.

Structural causes affect the standard deviation of a process; they are factors both internal and external to a process. They may or may not be present in a process; they are a blend of common and special causes. Examples of structural causes include sudden sales/production volume increase due to a new product or a new customer, seasonal sales, and sudden increase in profits.

A **control chart** is a statistical tool that distinguishes between natural (common) and unnatural (special) variations. The control chart method is used to measure variations in quality. The control chart is a picture of the process over time. It shows whether a process is in a stable state and is used to improve the process quality.

Natural variation is the result of random causes. Management intervention is required to achieve quality improvement or quality system. It has been stated that 80 to 85 percent of quality problems are due to management or the quality system and that 15 to 20 percent of problems are due to operators or workers. Supervisors, operators, and technicians can correct the unnatural variation. Control charts can be drawn for variables and attributes.

The control chart method for variables is a means of visualizing the variations that occur in the central tendency and dispersion of a set of observations. It measures the quality of a particular characteristic, such as length, time, or temperature.

A **variable chart** is an excellent technique for achieving quality improvement. True process capability can be achieved only after substantial quality improvements have been made. Once true process capability is obtained, effective specifications can be determined. The figure shows the sequence of events taking place with the control chart.

Variable chart → **Quality improvement**
→ **Process capability**
→ **Specifications**

To improve the process continuously, **variable control charts** can be used to overcome the limitations of the attribute control charts. Continuous process improvement is the highest level of quality consciousness. Control charts based on variable data reduce unit-to-unit variation, even within specification limits. Variable data consist of measurements such as weight, length, width, height, time, and temperature. Variable data contain more information than attribute data. Variable control charts can decrease the difference between customer needs and process performance.

The **attribute chart** refers to those quality characteristics that conform to specifications (specs) or do not conform to specifications. It is used where measurements are not possible, such as for color, missing parts, scratches, or damage. Quality characteristics for a product can be translated into a **go/no-go decision,** as follows.

Go/No-Go Decision for Product Quality

Go conforms to specifications.
No-go does not conform to specifications.

Two types of **attribute control charts** exist: (1) the chart for nonconforming units and (2) the chart for nonconformities. A **nonconforming unit** is a product or service containing at least one nonconformity. A **nonconformity** is a departure of quality characteristic from its intended level that is not meeting a specification requirement.

Two types of statistical errors in quality can occur, leading to incorrect decisions, as follows: **Type I error** is called producer's risk (alpha risk), which is the probability that a conforming (good quality) product will be rejected as poor quality product and not sold to customers. This product meets the established acceptable quality level. This results in an incorrect decision to reject something when it is acceptable. **Type II error** is called consumer's risk (beta risk), which is the probability that a nonconforming (poor quality) product will be accepted as good quality product and sold to customers. This results in an incorrect decision to accept something when it is unacceptable. Type II error occurs when statistical quality data fails to result in the scrapping or reworking of a defective product.

Stable and unstable processes are defined as follows. When only chance causes of variation are present in a process, the process is considered to be in a state of statistical control (i.e., the process is stable and predictable). When a process is in control (stable), there is a natural pattern of variation, and only chance causes of variation are present. Small variations in operator performance, equipment performance, materials, and environmental characteristics are expected and are considered to be part of a stable process. Further improvements in the process can be achieved only by changing the input factors, that is, operator, equipment, materials, and environment. These changes require action by management through quality improvement ideas.

When an assignable cause of variation is present in a process, it is considered to be out of statistical control (i.e., the process is unstable and unpredictable). When an observed measurement falls outside its control limits, the process is said to be out of control (unstable). This means that an assignable cause of variation is present. The unnatural, unstable variation makes it impossible to predict future variation. The assignable causes must be found and corrected before a natural, stable process can continue.

Process Capability

Process capability is a production process's ability to manufacture a product within the desired expectations of customers. The **process capability index (PCI)**, which indicates whether a process is capable of meeting customer expectations, must be equal to or greater than 1.00 to meet customer expectations. A PCI of less than 1.00 means that the process does not meet customer expectations.

The PCI is computed in several ways:

$$PCI = (UL - LL)/(6 \times \text{Standard Deviation of a Process})$$

where UL is **upper specification limit** and LL is **lower specification limit**. Upper specification limit means some data points will be above the central line in a control chart. Lower specification limit means some data points will be below the central line in a control chart.

Capability ratio (Cp) is specification tolerance width divided by the process capability. Specification tolerance width refers to variability of a parameter permitted above or below a nominal value. Cp is a widely used PCI.

❏ Learning Objective 4.8: COMPUTE TAGUCHI'S QUALITY LOSS FUNCTION

Taguchi believes that variation in a production process can be reduced by designing products that perform in a consistent manner, even under conditions of varying or adverse use. He emphasizes proactive steps at the design stage instead of late, reactive steps at the production stage.

Taguchi believes in pushing a process upstream to focus on product and process design, which is called **offline quality control**. This is contrary to **online quality control**, where traditional quality control activities take place in downstream with the focus on final inspection procedures, sampling methods, and statistical process control (SPC) techniques. Offline quality control methods reduce costs and defects.

Taguchi uses quality engineering and statistical experimental design methods to reduce all process and product variations from the target value with the goal of producing a perfect product.

Taguchi views **quality engineering** as composed of three elements: system design, parameter design, and tolerance design.

Taguchi developed three related concepts using statistical experimental design: quality robustness, quality loss function (QLF), and target-oriented quality. The QLF measures quality in monetary units that reflect both short- and long-term losses.

Quality robustness means products are consistently produced despite adverse manufacturing and environmental conditions. The goal is to remove the effects of adverse conditions, which is less expensive to do, instead of removing the causes, which is more expensive to do. It is assumed that small variations in materials and process do not destroy the overall product quality.

A **QLF** identifies all costs associated with poor quality and shows how these costs increase as the product moves away from the target value. Examples of costs included in the QLF are customer dissatisfaction costs, warranty costs, service costs, internal inspection costs, equipment or product repair costs, scrap costs, and overall costs to society due to bad reputation and loss of goodwill. The QLF concept can be equally applied to products and services.

Target-oriented quality is a philosophy of continuous improvement, where the goal is to bring the product exactly on target, instead of falling within the tolerance limits, where the latter is too simplistic and costly to customers. Traditionally, products are manufactured using conformance-oriented specifications with tolerance limits allowed. Taguchi opposes conformance to specification limits due to built-in tolerance range, which allows defective products to be produced. He advocates manufacturing a perfect product at the desired specifications, with no tolerance limits and at a relatively low cost.

The QLF is computed as:

$$L = D^2 \times C$$

where L is loss to society, D^2 is the distance from the target value, and C is cost of the deviation at the specification limit. The smaller the loss, the more desirable the product. However, the farther the product is from the target value, the greater the loss. QLF is zero when a product is produced at the target value and rises exponentially as the product is produced to meet the tolerance limits.

❏ Learning Objective 4.9: UNDERSTAND THE ROLE OF INSPECTION AND QUALITY AT SOURCE

Inspection is a means of ensuring that an operation or a process is producing at the expected quality level. The best processes have little variation from the standard level. Three basic issues relating to inspection (audit) are what to inspect, when to inspect, and where to inspect. The audit can take place at several places and several times:

- At supplier's plant while the supplier is producing goods such as raw materials, ingredients, parts, or components
- At company facility upon receipt of goods from the supplier
- During the company's production processes, either in-house or outside
- Before delivery to the customer

Source inspection means individual employees are checking their own work with proper training and empowerment before they pass their work to the next employee, who is considered an internal customer. Inspectors may be using a checklist, a sampling plan, and controls such as failsafe devices (Poka-yoke) for mistake-proofing.

Inspection rules help inspectors to prioritize where inspection should be performed. The **inspection priority index** is computed as:

Inspection Priority Index = Cost of Inspection/ Cost of Failure

If the index is less than 1.0, that item should be inspected first; if the index is greater than 1.0, that item should be inspected last.

Two other inspection methods include **in-process inspection,** where all work is inspected at each stage of the production process, and $N = 2$ **technique,** where the first and last pieces in a supplier's shipment lot are checked to see whether they meet the specification. If they do, then the entire shipment lot is accepted. The $N = 2$ technique is an alternative to **acceptance sampling**, where a lot is accepted if two or fewer defects are found and rejected if more than two defects are found.

Quality at the source is a defect- or error-prevention technique with greater visibility of immediate results and with a decentralized control where the first and local action is taking place. The source could be (1) where raw materials, ingredients, parts, and components are inspected as they are received, used, or stored, (2) where purchased parts and components are fabricated, or (3) where fabricated parts and components are assembled into a finished product with other items. It is always better to detect the defects and errors at the beginning rather than at the end of a process. Quality at the source, which means finding defects or errors and taking immediate corrective action, requires employee training and empowerment.

❏ Learning Objective 4.10: UNDERSTAND THE PROCESS MANAGEMENT METHODS AND TOOLS

Process management methods include business process reengineering (BPR), business process improvement (BPI), continuous process improvement (CPI), and business process redesign (BPD).

BPR identifies, analyzes, and redesigns an organization's core business processes with the aim of achieving dramatic improvements in critical performance measures, such as cost, quality, service, and speed. BPR recognizes that an organization's business processes are usually fragmented into subprocesses and tasks that are carried out by several specialized functional areas within the organization. Often no one is responsible for the overall performance of the entire process. Reengineering maintains that optimizing the performance of subprocesses can result in some benefits, but cannot yield dramatic improvements if the process itself is fundamentally inefficient and outmoded. For that reason, reengineering focuses on redesigning the process as a whole in order to achieve the greatest possible benefits to the organization and their customers. This drive for realizing dramatic improvements by fundamentally rethinking how the organization's work should be done distinguishes reengineering from business process improvement efforts that focus on functional or incremental improvement.

BPI tends to be more of an incremental change that may affect only a single task or segment of the organization. The concept of fundamental or radical change is the basis of the major difference between BPR and BPI. Quite often BPI initiatives limit their focus to a single existing organizational unit. This in itself breaks one of the tenets of BPR, which is that BPR must focus on redesigning a fundamental business process, not on existing departments or organizational units. While BPR seeks to define what the processes should be, BPI focuses more on how to improve an existing process or service.

CPI focuses on both incremental and dramatic improvements to provide better product and service quality but also on the need to be responsive and efficient in achieving a competitive advantage in the marketplace. Two types of CPI are proactive and reactive tools. Examples of **reactive tools** include check sheets, histograms, scatter diagrams, Pareto diagrams, flowcharts, cause-and-effect diagrams, and control charts. Examples of **proactive tools** include the five principles of Kawakita Jiro (KJ): 360-degree view, steppingstone approach, unexpected situations, intuitive capability, and real cases and personal experiences.

BPD focuses on both internal and external customers to increase sales, cut costs, increase profits, and improve service. It dictates what processes should be redesigned (changed) and in what sequence. Once a process is redesigned, it must be continually monitored, reassessed, changed, and improved in order to meet changing demands on the organization

Process management tools include **benchmarking** and **best practices**, which involves selecting a demonstrated standard of products, services, costs, processes, or practices that represent the very best performance in an industry and following them in an organization. It is a standard of comparison between two or more organizations. There are many types of benchmarking, including internal, competitive, industry, best-in-class, process, and strategic.

Which Benchmarking Does What?

Internal benchmarking looks downward and inward.

Competitive benchmarking looks outward.

Industry benchmarking looks for trends. It provides a short-run solution and a quick fix to a problem.

Best-in-class benchmarking looks for the best all around. It provides a quantum jump in improvement.

Process benchmarking is specific.

Strategic benchmarking is broad with big impact.

Self-Assessment Exercise

Online exercises are provided for the learning objectives in this module. Please visit www.mbaiq.com to complete the online exercises and to calculate your MBA IQ Score.

Human Resources Management

Learning Objective 5.1: Understand the Human Resources Planning Process 103

Learning Objective 5.2: Understand the Relationship between Job Analysis and Job Descriptions 104

Learning Objective 5.3: Understand the Recruitment Methods and Alternatives 105

Learning Objective 5.4: Understand the Employee Selection Process 106

Learning Objective 5.5: Understand the Employee Selection Tests and their Characteristics 107

Learning Objective 5.6: Understand the Employment Interview Process 108

Learning Objective 5.7: Understand the Pre-Employment Screening Process 108

Learning Objective 5.8: Understand the Employee Training and Development Process 109

Learning Objective 5.9: Understand the Management Development Process 110

Learning Objective 5.10: Understand the Organization Development Process 111

Learning Objective 5.11: Understand the Career Planning and Development Process 112

Learning Objective 5.12: Understand the Employee Performance Appraisal Process 113

Learning Objective 5.13: Understand the Employee Relations Issues 114

Learning Objective 5.14: Compute the Human Capital Metrics 116

❏ Learning Objective 5.1:
UNDERSTAND THE HUMAN RESOURCES PLANNING PROCESS

Human resources (HR) planning is part of an organization's strategic planning. The **HR planning process** is a systematic approach of matching the internal and external supply of people with job openings anticipated over a specified period of time. Specifically, it includes three major elements: (1) forecasting HR requirements, (2) forecasting HR availability, and (3) comparing HR requirements with HR availability.

In **forecasting HR requirements,** the demand for employees is matched against the supply of employees. If they are equal, no action is necessary. Several methods exist to forecast the HR requirements, including zero-based forecasting, bottom-up approach, simulation models, and relating sales volume to the number of employees needed.

In **forecasting HR availability,** the number of employees with the required skills and at the required locations is determined. The needed employees may be found internally, externally, or a combination. If a shortage is forecasted, the needed employee may come from developing creative recruiting methods, increasing compensation incentives to employees, conducting special training programs, and using different selection standards, such as lowering employment requirements in terms of hiring an inexperienced employee and providing on-the-job training to that employee.

In **comparing HR requirements with HR availability,** a situation of surplus workers may exist. This surplus can be handled through various reduction methods such as restricted hiring, reduced work-hours, encouraging early retirements, mandatory layoffs, or even downsizing the department or the company.

Downsizing, also known as **restructuring** and **rightsizing,** is a reduction in the number of people employed. It occurs for several reasons, such as offshoring; outsourcing; merging with other companies; acquiring other companies; closing or relocating plants, offices, and warehouses; or restructuring the organization to meet or beat competition and to increase efficiency, productivity, and profitability. Excess employees will be laid off, which is dictated by **bumping procedures** if the company is unionized. Bumping procedures are layoff procedures based on job seniority where the least senior employee will be laid off first. Non-union companies should document layoff procedures prior to facing downsizing decisions.

Positive aspects of downsizing include increased efficiency, productivity, and profitability, and meeting competition. Negative aspects of downsizing include (1) cost of termination and severance pay for laid-off employees, (2) employees seeking better job opportunities elsewhere due to low morale, loss of loyalty, and job insecurity, (3) loss of controls, culture, institutional memory, and knowledge, (4) difficulty in getting promoted due to few layers of management left, (5) more work is spread among few remaining employees, resulting in stress, (6) higher costs to bring back former employees as independent contractors when sales are increasing, and (7) increased number of discrimination lawsuits if a disparate treatment is proved in courts due to race, age, and gender violations, unless protected by employee performance evaluations.

Outplacement is a proactive response on the part of company management to soften the negative impact of job displacement where it will provide job assistance to laid-off employees in finding employment elsewhere. This outplacement service provides a positive feeling to both laid-off and remaining employees because it indicates that the company does in fact care about its employees. Typical outplacement services include career guidance, effective resume writing practices, successful interviewing techniques, self-assessment of current knowledge, skills, and abilities (KSAs), and retooling the KSAs needed for a new job or career.

❑ Learning Objective 5.2: UNDERSTAND THE RELATIONSHIP BETWEEN JOB ANALYSIS AND JOB DESCRIPTIONS

A **job** consists of a group of tasks that must be performed to achieve defined goals. A **position** is the collection of tasks performed and responsibilities assumed by one employee. There should be a definite position for every employee in an organization.

Job analysis is the systematic process of determining the skills, duties, and knowledge required for performing a specific job. Timeliness of conducting the job analysis is critical as new jobs are created and old jobs are redesigned or eliminated.

Job analysis provides a summary of a job's duties and responsibilities; its relationship to other jobs; the knowledge, skills, and abilities (KSAs) required; and working conditions under which a job is performed. Job facts are gathered, analyzed, and recorded as the job exists now, not as the job should exist. Industrial engineers and HR analysts often design jobs in terms of determining how a job should exist.

Job analysis is conducted after the job has been designed, an employee has been trained to do the work, and when that employee is performing the job (i.e., working).

Job Design → Employee Training and Working → Job Analysis

Job design is the process of determining the specific tasks to be performed, the methods used in performing these tasks, and how the job relates to other jobs in an organization. Job design should apply motivational theories for improving employee productivity and satisfaction, which are achieved through job simplification, job rotation, job enlargement, and job enrichment.

Typically, job analysis is performed on four occasions: (1) when a job analysis program is initiated for the first time in a company, (2) when new jobs are created, (3) when current jobs are changed due to new technologies, procedures, or systems, and (4) when the nature of a job is changed.

Several methods exist to perform the job analysis, including questionnaires, observations, interviews, employee recordings of daily work activities, and a combination of these methods.

Different types and amounts of information are needed to conduct a thorough job analysis, including (1) work activities, such as procedures used on the job, (2) worker-oriented activities, such as actions and communications required for the job, (3) work facilitating tools used, such as machines, equipment, and work aids, (4) job-related information, such as materials processed, products made, services rendered, and related knowledge required, (5) work performance levels, such as standards and measurements, (6) job context, such as work schedules and working conditions, and (7) personal requirements, such as experience, education, and training needed.

The output of the job analysis is used as input to prepare job descriptions and job specifications, where job specifications can be a part of the job description document. The **job description** document contains essential functions performed and tasks, duties, and responsibilities required of the job. The **job specification** document contains the minimum acceptable qualifications (e.g., skills, education, and experience) an employee should possess in order to perform a specific job. Normally, both of these documents are combined into one document with an effective date and expiration date listed to identify job changes.

$$\text{Job Analysis} \rightarrow \text{Job Descriptions} \rightarrow \text{Job Specifications}$$

Job descriptions must be relevant and accurate in terms of what employees are expected to do on the job, how they do the job, and the conditions under which the job duties are performed. Both job analysis and job description documents must be shared with the employee and his supervisor to ensure that they are clear and understandable to both parties and to ensure employee empowerment. This sharing will make the employee more productive and cooperative with others.

Major reasons for conducting job analysis and developing job descriptions and job specifications include (1) providing input into the HR planning process, (2) providing input into employee recruitment and selection process, (3) planning employee training and development programs, (4) conducting employee performance appraisals, (5) setting employee compensation systems, (6) developing employee health and safety programs, (7) handling employee and labor relations in terms of promotion, transfer, or demotion, and (8) supporting the legality of employment practices to defend decisions involving terminations, promotions, transfers, and demotions. These major reasons in turn become major benefits to all.

Four job design approaches are as follows:

1. **Job simplification** focuses on task efficiency by reducing the number of tasks an employee must do. Tasks must be designed to be simple, repetitive, and standardized. However, this leads to job dissatisfaction due to boredom, resulting in employee sabotage, absenteeism, and unionization.
2. **Job rotation** is moving an employee from one job to another, thereby exposing him to a variety of jobs and to their complexity.
3. **Job enlargement** is increasing the number of tasks a worker performs, with all of the tasks completed at the same level of responsibility. Job enlargement provides job variety and challenge and is a response to dissatisfaction found in job simplification.
4. **Job enrichment** is change in the content and responsibility level of a job so as to provide greater control and challenge to the worker. Job enrichment leads to employee recognition, opportunities for learning and growth, decision-making, motivation, and job satisfaction.

Job Enlargement versus Job Enrichment

Job enlargement adds width to a job.
Job enrichment adds depth to a job.

❑ Learning Objective 5.3: UNDERSTAND THE RECRUITMENT METHODS AND ALTERNATIVES

Recruitment is the process of attracting qualified individuals on a timely basis and in sufficient numbers to fill required jobs, based on job descriptions and job specifications.

External factors such as labor market considerations (e.g., demand and supply) and legal considerations such as nondiscriminatory practices (e.g., gender, race, and ethnicity) affect an organization's recruitment efforts. Similarly, **internal factors** such as promotion policies (e.g., promotion from within) also affect recruitment efforts.

External recruitment sources include high schools and vocational schools, community colleges, traditional colleges and universities, graduate schools, competitor companies, former employees, unemployed, military personnel, and self-employed workers.

External recruitment methods include media advertising, employment agencies, company recruiters, job fairs, internships, executive search firms, professional associations, unsolicited applicants, open houses, event recruiting, and high-tech competitions using electronic games.

Internal recruitment sources and methods include job posting, job bidding, employee referrals, and employee enlistment.

Online recruitment sources and methods include Internet/cyber recruiter, virtual job fairs, corporate career web sites, weblogs (blogs), general employment recruiter web sites, contract/contingent worker web sites, and hourly workers' job web sites.

Alternatives to recruitment include outsourcing, contingent/contract workers, employee leasing, and overtime to meet short-term workload fluctuations.

Recruitment for diversity focuses on equal employment legislation, which outlaws discrimination of protected groups in employment based on race, religion, sex, color, national origin, age, disability, and other factors. This requires that recruiters must be trained in the use of objective, job-related standards, such as use of employee selection devices that predict job performance and success. Two important concepts are at work here: disparate treatment and adverse impact. **Disparate treatment** means that an employer treats the protected groups less favorably than others. **Adverse impact** occurs when women and minorities (protected groups) are not hired at the rate of at least 80 percent of the best-achieving group, computed as:

Adverse Impact = (Hiring Rate for Protected Group of Applicants)/(Hiring Rate for Best-Achieving Group of Applicants)

where the hiring rate for the protected group of applicants is calculated by dividing the number of the protected group hired by the total number of qualified protected group of applicants available in a period. Similarly, the hiring rate for the best-achieving group of applicants is calculated by dividing the number of the best-achieving group hired by the total number of qualified best-achieving group of applicants available in a period.

Recruiting costs are expensive, especially when external recruiting sources and methods are used. **Recruiting cost per hire** can be computed as:

Recruiting Cost per Hire = (Total Recruiting Costs)/(Total Number of Recruits Hired)

Recruiting Cost per External Source Employee = (Total Recruiting Costs for External Sources)/(Total Number of Recruits Hired from External Sources)

❑ Learning Objective 5.4: UNDERSTAND THE EMPLOYEE SELECTION PROCESS

Employee selection is the process of choosing the best individual from a group of applicants who are well suited for a specific job.

Several factors affect the employee selection process, such as (1) competing with other organization's HR functions in terms of compensation package and safety and health conditions in a company, (2) meeting legal and regulatory requirements in terms of not discriminating against gender, race, and ethnicity, (3) speed of decision making in terms of filling the job quickly, (4) the type of job that is being filled (e.g., clerk versus senior manager), (5) the type of organization recruiting (e.g., private, government, or not-for-profit), and (6) the length of the probationary period (e.g., 60 to 90 days).

Applicant pool is the number of qualified applicants recruited for a particular job. The expansion and contraction of the labor market affects the size of the applicant pool (i.e., a low unemployment rate leads to a small size and a high unemployment rate leads to a large size).

Selection ratio is the number of individuals hired for a particular job compared to the total number of individuals in the applicant pool. This ratio is computed as:

Selection Ratio = (Number of Individuals Hired)/(Number of Individuals in the Applicant Pool)

The validity of the selection process can impact the selection ratio.

The goal is to have several qualified applicants available. The selection ratio should be interpreted as follows:

A selection ratio of 1.00 means that there was only one qualified applicant available for one open job.

A selection ratio of 0.10 means that there were 10 qualified applicants available for one open job.

A selection ratio of less than 1.00 means more choices are available to make an effective selection decision.

Other metrics related to the employee selection process include **acceptance rate** and **yield rate**:

Acceptance Rate = [(Number of Applicants Accepted a Job Offer)/(Total Number of Applicants with a Job Offer Made)] × 100

A low acceptance rate increases recruiting costs and vice versa.

Yield Rate = [(Number of Job Applicants Moved to Next Stage of Selection Process from Recruiting Source and Method)/(Total Number of Job Applicants from Recruiting Source and Method)] × 100

The yield rate reveals the effectiveness of a recruiting source and method.

❏ Learning Objective 5.5:
UNDERSTAND THE EMPLOYEE SELECTION TESTS AND THEIR CHARACTERISTICS

Traditional employee selection tools, such as preliminary interview (i.e., telephone or videotaped), employment application, and/or the applicant resume, are not foolproof due to their shortcomings.

Additional **selection tests** are needed to supplement traditional selection tools in order to determine how employees fit the job and the organization's culture. These additional tests (pre-employment tests) rate aptitude, personality, abilities (i.e., a can-do attitude), and motivation levels (a will-do attitude), and they have been found to be reliable and accurate predictors of on-the-job performance.

Pre-employment tests can expose employers to legal liabilities in terms of a lawsuit from rejected applicants claiming that the test was unrelated to the job or that the test was unfairly discriminated against a protected group. A negligent-hiring lawsuit can also be filed by rejected applicants claiming that they are the victims of a company's misbehavior or incompetence.

Hiring costs can be costly, especially when there is a judgment error associated with it. There are two types of **hiring errors**: (1) **No-Hire error** exists when rejecting a qualified job candidate and (2) **Yes-Hire error** exists when accepting an unqualified or less qualified job candidate. Properly designed, developed, and validated tests administered by competent and reputable professionals can minimize such hiring errors.

Important characteristics of properly designed selection tests include standardization, objectivity, norms, reliability, and validity. **Standardization** is the uniformity of the procedures and conditions related to administering tests. **Objectivity** occurs when everyone taking a test obtains the same results. A **norm** is a standard frame of reference for comparing an applicant's performance with that of others. **Reliability** is the extent to which a selection test provides consistent results. **Validity** is the extent to which a test measures what it claims to do, which should be job related.

Three approaches to validating selection tests are as follows:

1. The **criterion-related validity approach** compares the scores on selection tests to some aspects of job performance measures, such as quality and quantity of work, turnover, and absenteeism. A close relationship means that the test is valid.

2. The **content validity approach** is a sensible and straightforward method and requires thorough job analysis and well-documented job descriptions since the approach is not based on statistical concepts. The approach can be either performing certain job-related tasks or completing a paper-and-pencil test that measures relevant job knowledge. For example, a data entry operator is given a test to enter data into a computer.

3. The **construct validity approach** determines whether a test measures certain traits (e.g., creative or aggressive) relating to the job analysis. This approach needs to be supplemented with other approaches because it is not a primary validating method by itself.

Six types of **employment tests** include cognitive aptitude tests, psychomotor-abilities tests, job-knowledge tests, work-sample tests, vocational interest tests, and personality tests. These tests measure differences in an individual's characteristics related to job performance. **Cognitive aptitude tests** determine general reasoning ability, memory, vocabulary, verbal fluency, and numerical ability. **Psychomotor-abilities tests** measure strength, coordination, and dexterity. **Job-knowledge tests** measure specific knowledge items required of a job, derived from job analysis. **Work-sample tests** focus on doing some specific tasks (e.g., use of spreadsheets) required of the job and these tests are valid and acceptable to applicants. **Vocational interest tests** indicate the occupation a person is most interested in and the one likely to provide satisfaction. **Personality tests** are self-reported measures of traits, temperaments, or dispositions.

Four unique forms of employment testing methods include genetic testing, graphoanalysis, polygraph testing, and online testing. **Genetic testing** identifies predisposition to inherited diseases, such as cancer, heart disease, neurological disorders, and congenital diseases. **Graphoanalysis** is the use of handwriting analysis. The **polygraph test** (lie detector test) confirms or refutes the essential information contained in the job application. **Online testing** is using the Internet to test various job-related skills required by the job applicants, and these tests are convenient, affordable, and fast.

An **assessment center** is a selection approach that requires candidates to perform activities similar to those found in an actual job of a manager.

Potential managerial employees are first interviewed and later evaluated in real work situations. It is a job-simulated environment with in-basket exercises (an alternative to paper-and-pencil test), management games, leaderless discussion groups, or mock interviews. The assessment centers focus on prioritizing (organizing), delegating, and decision-making skills:

Assessment Center Approach = Interview + Evaluation

Assessment Center Focus = Organizing Skills + Delegating Skills + Problem-Solving and Decision-Making Skills

The assessment center approach is reliable and valid, and the in-basket exercise is a good predictor of management performance.

❑ Learning Objective 5.6:
UNDERSTAND THE EMPLOYMENT INTERVIEW PROCESS

The **employment interview** is a goal-oriented conversation between the interviewer and the applicant to exchange meaningful information related to a job. Historically, interviews have been poor predictors for making employee selection decisions, but they are getting better due to sophisticated design and application.

The employment interview occurs after the preliminary interview, after the application was reviewed, and after scoring satisfactorily on selection tests. The focus of the employment interview is to assess whether an individual is willing to work and can adapt to the organization culture and work ethics.

The first step in the employment interview process is interview planning in terms of time and location. The interviewer then prepares a job profile based on the job description to use as a checklist in the interview.

The next step is to decide on the content of the interview, including work experience, academic preparation, interpersonal skills (getting along with others), personal qualities (e.g., appearance, vocabulary, and poise), and organizational fit with the firm's culture or values:

Employment Interview = Interview Planning + Interview Content

Three types of interviews exist: structured, unstructured, and behavioral. In the **structured interview,** the same series of job-related questions are asked of all the applicants to ensure consistency. These series of questions focus on situations, job-knowledge, job-sample simulation, and worker requirements. In the **unstructured interview,** open-ended questions are asked. The use of structured interviews increases reliability and accuracy by reducing subjectivity and inconsistency of unstructured interviews. The **behavioral interview** is a structured interview where applicants are asked to relate actual incidents from their past experiences relevant to the target job. The behavioral interviews are equally applicable to both lower-level and higher-level jobs because past behavior is the best predictor of future behavior. A positive feature about behavioral interviewing is the ability to use the results as a tiebreaker, and a negative feature is that some applicants can deliberately misrepresent themselves.

Interviewing methods include one-on-one interview, group interview, panel interview, multiple interviews, stress interview, and realistic job preview (RJP). The focus of RJP is to convey both positive and negative aspects of job information to the applicant in an unbiased manner, which in turn reduces an applicant's unrealistic expectations about the job and the employer.

Potential **interviewing problems** that should be avoided include using inappropriate questions, making premature judgments, interviewer domination, permitting non-job-related information to be discussed, interviewer's contrast (halo) effect, lack of interviewer's training, and nonverbal communication (body language) between the interviewer and the interviewee.

❑ Learning Objective 5.7:
UNDERSTAND THE PRE-EMPLOYMENT SCREENING PROCESS

The **pre-employment screening process** starts after a job candidate completes an employment application, submits a resume, takes the required selection tests, and undergoes an employment interview. At this point, the candidate is being considered for the job and requires further work prior to hiring.

Two types of pre-employment screening include background investigations and reference checks, where the latter supplements the former.

The focus of the **background investigation** is to determine the accuracy of information submitted or to determine whether the required information was not submitted. Background investigations involve collecting data from various sources, such as previous employers, business associates, credit bureaus, government agencies, academic institutions, and the applicant's mode of living and the nature of character. Some sensitive jobs require fingerprinting and security clearances.

Reference checks from outsiders verify the accuracy of information provided by the applicant. A problem with reference checks is that they do not tell the whole truth about an applicant. Another problem is that previous employers are reluctant to reveal information about the applicant due to privacy reasons.

HR management needs to be concerned about three legal liabilities when hiring, which provide additional justification for conducting a thorough background investigation of the job applicant:

1. **Negligent hiring** is the liability of the current employer when he fails to conduct a reasonable investigation of a job applicant's background and then hires a potentially dangerous person who can damage company property and/or harm employees and others. The definition of **reasonable investigation** depends on the nature of the job and requires due diligence in conducting background investigations. The hiring organization must be able to foresee the harm resulting from a dangerous employee being hired.
2. **Negligent referral** is the liability of the former employer when he fails to warn the potential employer about a severe problem with a past employee.
3. **Negligent retention** is the liability of the current employer if he keeps an employee on the payroll whose records indicate strong potential for wrongdoing and fails to take necessary steps to defuse a possibly violent situation.

Negligent Hiring versus Negligent Referral versus Negligent Retention

Negligent hiring is a legal liability for the current employer.

Negligent referral is a legal liability for the former employer.

Negligent retention results from negligent hiring.

❑ Learning Objective 5.8: UNDERSTAND THE EMPLOYEE TRAINING AND DEVELOPMENT PROCESS

The goal of training and development (T&D) is to improve employee competencies and to increase organizational performance continuously. Competencies are a broad range of knowledge, skills, and abilities (KSAs), traits, and behaviors that could be labeled as hard skills and soft skills.

Training provides learners with the KSAs needed to perform their current jobs. **Development** involves learning and education that goes beyond the current job and prepares for the future job(s).

Employee Training versus Employee Development

Employee training focuses on achieving short-term goals.

Employee development focuses on achieving long-term goals.

Significant benefits accrue to both employees and employers when an employee's personal growth strategies are aligned with corporate strategies. These benefits include greater employee satisfaction, which in turn increases customer satisfaction; improved employee morale; higher employee retention; and lower employee turnover. To achieve these benefits, many firms are becoming **learning organizations** by recognizing the importance of continuous improvement and continuous learning to deliver continuous performance. The learning organization should turn every learner into a teacher and every teacher into a learner to sustain knowledge levels in the organization.

Several factors that can impact and are impacted by T&D include top management support (budget and active role), commitment from specialists and generalists (i.e., line versus staff), technological advances (e.g., the Internet and computer), organization complexity (i.e., flat versus tall organization structure), and learning styles (e.g., just-in-time training). For example, a company that hires marginally qualified employees needs to plan for extensive T&D programs. Similarly, companies with competitive pay systems or comprehensive healthcare benefit packages and progressive safety programs attract competent employees requiring less T&D work.

The T&D process consists of a series of steps, including determining specific T&D needs, establishing specific T&D objectives, selecting specific T&D learning methods, identifying specific T&D delivery systems, implementing T&D programs, and evaluating T&D programs.

Determining specific T&D needs focuses on organizational analysis using corporate mission, goals, and plans and HR plans; task analysis using job descriptions; and individual analysis to strengthen the employees' KSAs.

Establishing specific T&D objectives starts with defining the purpose and developing specific learning objectives to achieve organizational goals.

Selecting specific T&D learning methods includes instructor-led courses, case study, behavior modeling, role-playing, business games, in-basket training, on-the-job training (OJT), job rotation, internships, and apprenticeship training

Identifying specific T&D delivery systems includes corporate universities, colleges and universities, community colleges, distance learning, videoconferencing, vestibule systems, video media, e-learning for online instruction, virtual reality, and simulators.

Implementing T&D programs is difficult, as it requires the cooperation of both managers and employees. Managers must try to implement the T&D programs on an incremental basis, meaning showing success rates in one area and extending them into other areas of the company. Employees resist training because it implies a change. Employee feedback and record-keeping are vital to correct and improve any gaps in the program.

Evaluating T&D programs is even more difficult because it is a soft issue to measure objectively. Various methods exist for evaluation, including (1) soliciting the training participants' opinions and suggestions, (2) designing pre-test and post-test control group studies, (3) requesting a 360-degree feedback from managers, employees, trainers, and colleagues, (4) assessing whether stated training objectives have been achieved and that they have resulted in an improved job performance, (5) calculating the return on training (ROT) investment, and (6) benchmarking with other companies regarding training costs and ratio of training staff to total employees in a department, division, or company.

Return on training (ROT), expressed as a percentage, is computed as:

$$ROT = [(\text{Net Present Value of Training Benefits})/(\text{Net Present Value of Training Costs})] - 1.00$$

The result is multiplied by 100 to get the percentage.

All benefits and costs are multiplied with the corresponding present value factors to result in NPV of benefits and costs respectively.

Orientation is of two types: employee orientation and executive orientation. **Employee orientation** is the initial T&D effort for new employees to inform them about the organization (i.e., policies, procedures, and rules), the job (i.e., how his jobs fits into the organizational structure and goals), the work environment (i.e., rewards, career management, employee development, and teamwork), and the work culture (i.e., dress code and ethics). **Executive orientation** focuses on learning an organization's structure, mission, products and services, competition, culture, and organizational politics to bring the executive up to speed for early contributions. This requires senior management's commitment to make the executive orientation program work. All orientation efforts can establish positive working relationships between the employee and the employer.

Various special training programs are identified for supervisors, managers, and employees to avoid potential risks and legal liabilities. These programs include (1) diversity training to handle protected groups such as women and minorities properly, (2) ethics training, dealing with fair play, respecting laws and rules, rewarding ethical behavior, punishing unethical behavior, and ways to prevent and detect fraud, (3) telecommuter training, dealing with employees working from home where the supervisor's focus is changed from task-based management to results-based management, (4) customer service training, requiring communication and listening skills to handle customers with care, (5) conflict resolution training where conflicts may occur between employees and between customers and employees, (6) teamwork training to teach employees how to work in groups for better performance, (7) empowerment training, dealing with problem-solving and decision-making skills, taking responsibility for results, and not abusing the empowerment privilege, and (8) anger-management training to prevent workplace violence.

❏ Learning Objective 5.9: UNDERSTAND THE MANAGEMENT DEVELOPMENT PROCESS

Management development (MD) is a broad term encompassing elements such as upgrading the KSAs required for a manager or a professional to apply them either in the current job or in a future job.

The managerial talent is a complex group consisting of first-line supervisors, middle-level managers, and higher-level executives and as such requires a different type of MD programs to cater to the needs of each level in the management hierarchy. For example, as the level goes up in the hierarchy, there should be a strong focus on soft skills and general business knowledge, less focus on hard skills and vice versa.

The MD programs can be conducted either inside or outside the company. The reasons for conducting the program outside the company are that it brings new viewpoints, different perspectives, and broad exposure to outside experts. The reasons for conducting the program inside the company are that customized courses can be developed in less time and at a reduced cost, the course content is controlled, teamwork is facilitated, and the company culture is known.

Five related concepts in the MD program include mentoring, reverse mentoring, coaching, job rotation, and delegation, all with the similar purpose of learning and growing personally and professionally with the advice and experience of others.

Mentoring is advising, coaching, and nurturing a protégé to enhance his career development. The mentor can be anywhere in the same organization as the protégé or may work in another organization or another industry. The mentor or the sponsor could be the same or different gender as the protégé. Sometimes, a protégé may have more than one mentor to learn the unwritten rules to make it to the top.

Implications of Mentoring

Mentoring can break the glass-ceiling obstacle facing women and minorities.

Research has shown that women who have women mentors have done well in enhancing their careers.

Research has shown that African-American women who have one mentor are **more likely** to get promoted.

Research has shown that African-American women who have more than one mentor are **most likely** to get promoted.

Reverse mentoring is where older employees learn from younger ones because the latter group has some special skills that the former group does not have.

This approach will keep the older employees more productive with special skills and thus more useful to the company.

Coaching is the responsibility of the immediate supervisor, who provides assistance much like a mentor. Coaching is more direct than mentoring.

Although mentoring and coaching concepts sound good in theory, there are some practical problems in selecting and pairing the right mentor and the right protégé, the amount of attention given by the mentor to the protégé, the temperament of both parties, and the personality conflicts between the two parties.

Job rotation is a T&D method, which can also be used as a part of the MD program, where new or current employees move from one job to another in order to broaden their work experience and to increase their KSAs.

Delegation is a higher-level management right to transfer authority and responsibility to lower-level management, where the latter group develops managerial skills such as problem solving and decision making and learns how to take responsibility and accountability for achieving results. As a part of the MD program, delegation involves developing and empowering lower-level management. Although managers are encouraged to delegate, they often find it difficult to do so.

❑ Learning Objective 5.10: UNDERSTAND THE ORGANIZATION DEVELOPMENT PROCESS

Organization development (OD) seeks big change in the corporate culture either at the organization level or at the division level. OD requires change in the organizational structures, systems, and processes to achieve the desired goals.

T&D Efforts versus OD Efforts

T&D efforts are small in size and scope (e.g., change in an employee's skillsets).

OD efforts are large in size and scope (e.g., change in the corporate culture or employee's work behavior).

Examples of OD intervention techniques include survey feedback, quality circles, team building, and sensitivity training. These techniques together can achieve the OD goals.

Survey feedback requires collection of data from questionnaires, interviews, productivity records, and employee turnover and absenteeism data. This feedback data helps in diagnosing the problem areas, developing action plans to increase employee productivity and company profits, and improving overall working relationships.

Quality circles consist of groups of voluntary employees who meet with their supervisors regularly to discuss problems, investigate root causes, recommend solutions, and take corrective actions. The group as a whole must be familiar with problem-solving and decision-making processes and tools to be effective. Both financial and nonfinancial rewards must be available to this group to keep them motivated and productive.

Team building can boost employee morale, increase employee retention, and increase company profits. The team-building concept uses self-directed teams consisting of a small group of employees responsible for an entire work process or part of it. Together, they improve their operation or product, plan and control their workload, and resolve day-to-day problems on their own. They may even get involved in solving vendor quality and safety-related problems.

Sensitivity training (T-group training) is designed to help individuals learn how others perceive their behavior. Sensitivity training is different from the traditional mode of training (i.e., learning a predetermined set of concepts) in that there is no agenda, no rules, no authority, no power positions, and no leaders. Individuals are gathered and start talking about work-related and common issues they face in an unstructured environment, where the trainer is just a facilitator. The T-group training increases interpersonal skills of the participants and increases self-awareness and sensitivity to the behavior of others. A drawback of the sensitivity training program is that it focuses on changing individuals, instead of changing the work environment in which they work.

❏ Learning Objective 5.11: UNDERSTAND THE CAREER PLANNING AND DEVELOPMENT PROCESS

Key elements of career planning and development include career, individual career planning, organizational career planning, succession planning, career path, career development, and career security.

A **career** is a general course that an individual chooses to pursue throughout his working life. It is a sequence of work-related positions an individual has occupied during his lifetime, whether with one organization or more than one.

Individual career planning is an ongoing process in which a person establishes personal goals and identifies the means to achieve them.

Organizational career planning is the planned succession of jobs mapped out by an organization's management to develop its employees in order to take on increased responsibilities. The organization identifies career paths and developmental programs to meet the challenges of increased responsibilities. Individual career plans and organizational career plans must be synchronized for maximum benefit to both the employee and the employer.

Succession planning is the process of ensuring that qualified individuals are ready to assume key managerial positions once these positions are available to fill. The need for succession planning arises due to untimely deaths, resignations, terminations, or retirements of higher-level senior managers. Succession planning should reach lower levels of management in addition to higher levels of management due to delayering of management hierarchy, implying the importance of lower levels of management for continued business operations. In this sense, the succession plan should accommodate the development of lower level management talent for readiness.

A **career path** is the line of progression through which a person makes job changes within a company or moves from company to company and from position to position in order to gain greater knowledge and experience. Usually, career paths focus on upward mobility, which is not guaranteed because of business uncertainties. Alternative career paths include **network** (vertical jobs with horizontal opportunities), **lateral** (learning new skills in other functions), **dual-career** (a technical specialist will stay as a specialist without becoming a manager), and **downward mobility** (i.e., demotion if money is not a problem). Some may opt to be **free agents**, being their own boss.

Career development is a formal approach to ensure that employees with the proper qualifications and experiences are available when needed. Career development programs ensure the availability of highly motivated and committed employees.

Individual career planning must start with a self-assessment of interests and match them against the job requirements because self-assessment is the process of learning about oneself. Tools are available to facilitate the self-assessment exercise, including identifying personal strengths (assets) and weaknesses (liabilities) through a balance sheet approach, taking a personal survey of likes and dislikes, and taking a professional self-assessment of KSAs to enrich a person's professional career in terms of pursuing college/advanced education or acquiring professional certifications.

An individual must focus on adding value to his career by increasing his toolbox with continual personal and professional development programs to meet the needs defined by the marketplace.

Ideally speaking, the employee must drive his career plans (i.e., objectives and actions) and career development programs (courses and milestones) because he knows best or he should know what he wants and how to achieve them. The employee, of course, can seek the advice and assistance of his immediate supervisor and work together in developing career paths and development programs.

Self-Assessment → Self-Development

Organizational career planning must focus on increasing the talent pool of qualified men and women who can take on increased opportunities in the future. When an employee believes that his employer is interested in his career planning, he is likely to remain with the company (loyal) and become motivated and productive. The output of the career plans is used to determine the employee's training and development (T&D) needs.

There can be several inputs to an employee's **career development plan,** including the employee's own career plan and development list, employee–supervisor mutually identified and agreed-on career path and development guidelines, employee job description document to determine the necessary education, skills, and experience required to do the job, and employee performance appraisal report describing the employee's strengths and weaknesses documented by the supervisor.

Specific **career development programs** include attending colleges and universities for specific courses or degree programs, educational workshops of short duration, trade seminars and conferences, in-house or outside training courses, or earning professional certifications with continuing education requirements.

The individual employee career plans and development programs should complement and supplement the organizational career plans and development programs to enhance their value to the individual employee and to the organization.

It is human nature to desire career/job security. **Career security** can be obtained by developing marketable KSAs that help ensure continued employment within a range of careers either inside or outside of a company.

❑ Learning Objective 5.12: UNDERSTAND THE EMPLOYEE PERFORMANCE APPRAISAL PROCESS

Similar to corporations wanting to grow in sales and market share to increase profits and stakeholder value, employees need to grow personally and professionally to reach their career goals and make a positive contribution to the company they work for and to reach the company's goals. Goal congruence is at play here.

Although neither employees nor supervisors like to give or receive performance appraisal evaluations for delicate reasons, it is a very important part of employee career growth plans, can be used in justifying employee termination and promotion decisions, and can help in identifying employee training and development needs.

Characteristics of an effective appraisal system include job-related criteria, performance expectations, standardization, trained appraisers, continuous open communications, periodic performance reviews, and due process to appeal appraisal results.

Results from the employee performance appraisal process can be put to several good uses, such as input into human resource planning, recruitment and selection, training and development, career planning and development, compensation programs, employee relations, and assessment of employee potential in the company.

Two **external factors** affecting the employee performance appraisal system are: (1) government legislation requiring nondiscriminatory practices to follow and (2) labor unions preferring seniority as the basis for promotions instead of performance. A major **internal factor** that affects the performance appraisal is the organization's culture, where nontrusting culture does not encourage high performance.

The employee performance appraisal process is divided into a series of steps, including identifying specific performance appraisal goals, establishing performance criteria and communicating them to employees (e.g., traits, behaviors, competencies, goal achievement, and improvement potential), examining employees' work performed, appraising employees' performance, and discussing appraisal results with employees.

Individuals responsible for conducting the employee performance appraisal include self-appraisal, immediate supervisor, senior managers, subordinates, peers and team members, and internal and external customers, called a **360-degree feedback** evaluation method. The biggest risk with 360-degree feedback is confidentiality, whether the evaluation is done internally or externally.

A **720-degree review** focuses on the big picture at the company level for all of its employees, not at the individual employee level. The review is all about senior managers and their performance. The participants in the review include senior managers, subordinates, customers, and investors. This is because senior managers deal more with external parties such as customers and investors.

Performance appraisal methods include 360-degree feedback, 720-degree review, rating scales method, critical incident method, essay method, work standard method, ranking method, forced distribution method, behaviorally anchored rating scales (BARS) method, and results-based system.

Problems associated with the performance appraisal process include appraiser discomfort, lack of objectivity, **halo/horn error**, leniency/strictness effect, central tendency error, recent behavior bias, personal bias (stereotyping), manipulating the evaluation, and employee anxiety.

Halo Error versus Horn Error

Halo error occurs when a manager projects one positive performance feature or incident onto the rest, resulting in a higher rating.

Horn error occurs when a manager projects one negative performance feature or incident onto the rest, resulting in a lower rating.

❑ Learning Objective 5.13: UNDERSTAND THE EMPLOYEE RELATIONS ISSUES

Employees constantly move in and out of an organization—some for good reasons and others for not-so-good reasons. Examples of employee movements internal to the organization include promotion (upward), transfer (lateral), and demotion (downward). Examples of employee movements external to the organization include resignation, termination (discharge), layoff, and retirement. Demotion can be an alternative to termination.

There is an unwritten (implied) employment contract created when an employee agrees to work for an employer with no end date for employment, called the **employment-at-will doctrine.** In other words, these at-will employees depend on the goodwill of their employers for continued employment due to lack of an explicit contract. This means, employees can be terminated at the will of the employer, and employees can leave the employer at the will of the employee. Most non-union employees fall under the employment-at-will employee category.

For example, union members, who have a collective bargaining agreement, and teachers, who have a contract, are not at-will employees. Employees with an implicit employment contract and who report an illegal act, like whistleblowers, are not subject to the employment-at-will doctrine because they are protected under the provisions of the U.S. Sarbanes-Oxley Act of 2002.

Employment applications, employee handbooks, policy manuals, and other employee-related documents should not contain or imply words such as job security or permanent employment because a discharged employee can use these documents against an employer in a lawsuit of wrongful discharge. Other protective measures that an employer can take include employee's signed acknowledgment of the at-will disclaimer, developing clearly written job descriptions, conducting regular employee performance appraisals, and giving frequent verbal performance feedback to employees.

An employer can invoke a penalty against an employee who was subject to disciplinary action and consequently discharged with the reason that the employee failed to meet certain established employment standards.

To handle **disciplinary actions** properly, organizations should follow a structured approach in terms of defining specific steps. These steps include setting organizational goals, establishing employment rules, communicating the rules to employees, observing employee actual performance, comparing actual performance with rules, and taking appropriate disciplinary actions. These steps are needed to avoid legal and financial risks.

Three important approaches are available to handle disciplinary actions: **hot-stove rule** (i.e., advance warning), **progressive disciplinary action** (minimum penalty), and **disciplinary action without punishment** (i.e., time off with pay). The progressive disciplinary action approach is designed to impose a minimum penalty appropriate to the offense and requires the employer to follow specific steps in sequence:

Oral Warning → Written Warning → Suspension → Termination
(Least Severe)   (Most Severe)

Many organizations are rethinking their approach to disciplinary actions, deciding to abandon warnings (oral and written) and suspensions (unpaid time off) and going strictly with disciplinary action without punishment (i.e., time off with pay). This rethinking is attributed to avoiding or reducing legal and financial risks.

Employers must be consistent in their disciplinary actions against employees from the beginning to the end; that is, actions cannot be too lenient in the beginning and too strict at the end. Consistent action means a long-term employee might receive merely a suspension notice, whereas a short-term employee might be terminated for the same serious violation.

Grievance procedures under a collective bargaining agreement (union organization) are handled differently than in a non-union organization. A grievance is an employee's dissatisfaction or feeling of injustice relating to his job (e.g., getting fired). Arbitrators, mediators, and union stewards are involved in union organizations to solve grievance problems. Non-union organizations are encouraged to develop and implement formal grievance procedures so that an employee can make complaints without fear of reprisal.

Firing costs are expensive, especially when there is a judgment error associated with it. There are two types of **firing errors**: (1) **Yes-Fire error** exists when the employer decides to fire when the employee does not deserve firing. (2) **No-Fire error** exists when the employer does not fire when the employee deserves firing.

The U.S. Office of Personnel Management (OPM) developed alternative dispute resolution (ADR) guidelines to help employers and employees avoid going to courts because the court system is costly, uncertain, and untimely. The ADR is a procedure whereby the employee and the employer agree ahead of time that any problems will be addressed by agreed-upon means, as follows:

Alternative Dispute Resolution = Arbitrator or Mediator or Ombudsperson

An **arbitrator** is an impartial third party who enters into a dispute case between a labor union and company management for a binding resolution. He acts as judge and jury.

A **mediator** is a neutral third party who enters into a dispute case between a labor union and company management when a bargaining impasse has occurred. He acts like a facilitator and informal coach to ensure that bargaining discussions are fair and effective. Mediation is a voluntary process.

An **ombudsperson** is a complaint officer in a company who has access to top management and who hears employee complaints, investigates, and recommends appropriate action.

Arbitrators and mediators are involved in handling disputes in private-sector organizations with labor unions and in public-sector organizations. Use of an ombudsperson is seen more in private-sector, non-union organizations.

Termination is the most severe penalty, requiring careful consideration on the part of the employer. Termination of nonmanagerial and nonprofessional employees is handled differently from the termination of higher-level executives and middle-level/lower-level managers and professionals.

For example, termination procedures for nonmanagerial and nonprofessional employees (e.g., truck drivers and waiters) are dictated by whether these employees belong to a union.

Usually, executive jobs are protected under a contract, if there is one. They have no formal appeal rights because the termination could be due to valid business reasons (e.g., economic downturn, reorganization and downsizing, and decline in performance and productivity). However, executives involved in illegal activities such as management fraud, insider trading, or a sexual harassment suit can be terminated. Terminated executives can be costly to replace and can make negative statements about the company to the press in order to damage its reputation.

Middle-level and lower-level managers and professionals are most vulnerable to termination, unless they belong to a union, because their employment depends on the will and whim of their immediate supervisor.

Resignations occur on a voluntary basis by the employee or are forced by the employer. When an employee resigns on a voluntary basis, the employer must determine the reasons for leaving through the use of an exit interview (before an employee departs) and post-exit questionnaire (after an employee has departed).

Exit interviews, which are face-to-face meetings, can identify the reasons for leaving, which can be used to change the HR planning process, modify training and development programs, and address other areas needing improvement. A major problem with the face-to-face exit interview is that the departing employee may not tell the interviewer the real reasons for leaving due to their sensitivity.

Post-exit questionnaires are sent to former employees several weeks after they leave the company to determine the real reasons they left, which can negate problems with exit interviews. The departed employee may respond freely to the questionnaire because he is not in front of the interviewer.

The best way to manage employee relations is to conduct a periodic **attitude survey** of current employees to determine their feelings, issues, and concerns related to their jobs and to seek their ideas for improvement. The scope of the survey can include nature of the work, supervisor relations, work environment (tools and materials), flexibility in the work schedules, opportunities for job advancement, training and development opportunities, pay and benefits, and workplace safety and security concerns. The results from the survey can benefit the employer in correcting the identified gaps on a proactive basis before problems get out of hand. If uncorrected, they can result in employees leaving the company.

The Nature of Employee Feedback

Employee attitude surveys are proactive in nature and timely.

Exit interviews and post-exit questionnaires are reactionary in nature and untimely.

All of the above focus on the same thing except for differences in timing and results.

❑ Learning Objective 5.14:
COMPUTE THE HUMAN CAPITAL METRICS

Human capital metrics provides an objective evaluation of the efficient and effective utilization of financial and human resources allocated for managing the HR function in an organization.

Several human capital metrics are available from the *Saratoga Review*:

Examples of Human Capital Metrics

Revenue per Employee = Total Revenues/Total Number Fulltime Equivalent Employees (FTEs)

Labor Cost Revenue Percent = (Regular Compensation Costs + Benefits Costs)/Total Revenues

Labor Cost Expense Percent = (Employee Compensation Costs + Benefits Costs Excluding Payments for Time Not Worked)/Total Operating Costs

Profit per Full-time Employee = (Total Revenues − Total Operating Costs)/Total Number FTEs

HR Headcount Ratio = Total Headcount/Direct HR Headcount

HR Spend per Employee = Total HR Budget/Total Number FTEs

Number of Qualified Candidates per Requisition = Qualified Applications/Total Number Approved Requisitions

Time to Fill = Total Days to Fill/Total Number of Hires

Rehire Percent = Number of Rehires/Total Number of External Hires

Learning & Development (L&D) Hours per Employee = Total Number L&D Hours/Total Number FTEs

HR Outsourcing Costs per Employee Served = Direct HR Outsourcing Costs/Total Headcount

Average Time to Promotion = Total Number Months to Promotion/Total Number Promotions

First Year of Service Turnover Rate = Total Turnover with One Year of Service/Total Headcount with One Year of Service

Internal Management Hiring Source = Number Internal Management Hires/Total Management Requisitions Filled

Percent of Management with No Direct Reports = Management Headcount with No Direct Reports/Total Management Headcount

Key Position Pipeline Utilization = Key Positions Filled by Succession Planning Candidates/ Total Number Key Positions Filled

One or More Candidate Succession Planning Depth = Total Number Key Roles with One or More Unique Successors/Total Number Key Roles

Executive Stability Ratio = Executive Headcount with Greater Than Three Years of Service/ Total Executive Headcount

Source: *U.S. Saratoga Review:* Monthly Benchmarking and Human Capital Newsletters, PricewaterhouseCoopers, July 2006 to September 2008 (www.pwc.com).

 Self-Assessment Exercise

Online exercises are provided for the learning objectives in this module. Please visit www.mbaiq.com to complete the online exercises and to calculate your MBA IQ Score.

Accounting

Learning Objective 6.1: Understand the Basic Concepts of Financial Accounting — **120**
Business Entity Concept — 120
Cost Concept — 120
Matching Concept — 120
Other Concepts — 120
Accounting Principles — 121
Qualities of Accounting Information — 121

Learning Objective 6.2: Understand the Purpose of the Accounting Cycle — **121**
Cash-Basis versus Accrual-Basis — 122
Steps in the Accounting Cycle — 122

Learning Objective 6.3: Understand the Types and Contents of Financial Statements — **122**
Types of Financial Statements — 122
Contents of Financial Statements — 123
Balance Sheet — 125

Learning Objective 6.4: Understand the Intermediate Concepts of Financial Accounting — **128**
Bonds and Notes — 128
Leases — 129
Pensions — 130

Learning Objective 6.5: Understand the Advanced Concepts of Financial Accounting — **132**
Business Combinations — 132
Consolidated Financial Statements — 132
Partnerships — 132
Foreign Currency Transactions — 132

Learning Objective 6.6: Learn How to Analyze Financial Statements — **133**
Income Statement — 133
Balance Sheet — 134
Statement of Retained Earnings — 134
Statement of Cash Flows — 135
Common Size Analysis — 136
Trend Analysis — 136
Comparative Ratios — 136

Single Ratios — 136
Limitations of Financial Statement Ratios — 139

Learning Objective 6.7: Understand Various Cost Concepts and Cost Behaviors — **140**
Absorption and Variable Costs — 140
Cost Behavior — 143

Learning Objective 6.8: Understand the Principles and Techniques of Operating Budgets — **143**
Benefits of Operating Budgets — 144
Different Dimensions in Operating Budgets — 144
How Operating Budgets are Prepared — 144
Operating Budgeting Techniques — 145
Advantages of Operating Budgets — 146
Limitations of Operating Budgeting Techniques — 146

Learning Objective 6.9: Understand the Application of Transfer Pricing — **146**
Methods for Determining Transfer Prices — 147
Criteria Affecting Transfer Pricing Methods — 147
International Transfer Pricing — 147

Learning Objective 6.10: Understand the Application of Cost-Volume-Profit Analysis — **148**
Equation Method — 148
CM Method — 148
Graphic Method — 148
CVP Assumptions and Their Limitations — 148
Ways to Lower the Breakeven Point — 149
Sensitivity Analysis in CVP — 149
Changes in Variable and Fixed Costs — 149
Contribution Margin and Gross Margin — 149
Profit-Volume Chart — 149
Effect of Sales Mix on BEP — 150

Learning Objective 6.11: Understand the Meaning and Application of Relevant Costs — **150**
Application of Relevant Cost Concept — 150

Learning Objective 6.12: Understand Various Costing Systems for Products and Services — **151**
Target Costing — 151

Traditional Costing   151
Activity-Based Costing   151
Standard Costing   151

Learning Objective 6.13: Understand
the Meaning and Application of
Responsibility Accounting   152

❑ Learning Objective 6.1: UNDERSTAND THE BASIC CONCEPTS OF FINANCIAL ACCOUNTING

Financial accounting is the language of business. All business transactions will eventually end up in financial statements. Accounting principles are used to classify, record, post, summarize, and report business transactions between various parties involved. Accountants apply their professional standards to analyze business transactions, prepare estimations, and report business events. The business transactions data accumulated in the chart of accounts are used to prepare the financial statements of an organization.

The scope of basic concepts in financial accounting includes accounting concepts, accounting principles, and quality of accounting information. The scope of accounting concepts includes business entity, cost, matching, and others (i.e., materiality, accounting period, and revenue recognition).

Business Entity Concept

The individual business unit is the business entity for which economic data are needed. This entity could be an automobile dealer, a department store, or a grocery store. The business entity must be identified so that the accountant can determine which economic data should be analyzed, recorded, and summarized in reports.

The **business entity concept** is important because it limits the economic data in the accounting system to data related directly to the activities of the business. In other words, the business is viewed as an entity separate from its owners, creditors, or other stakeholders. For example, the accountant for a business with one owner (a proprietorship) would record the activities of the business only, not the personal activities, property, or debts of the owner. The business entity concept can be related to the **economic entity assumption**, which states that economic activity can be identified with a particular unit of accountability; **going-concern assumption**, where the

accountant assumes, unless there is evidence to the contrary, that the reporting entity will have a life long enough to fulfill its objectives and commitments; and **monetary unit assumption**, where it provides that all transactions and events can be measured in terms of a common denominator—the dollar.

Cost Concept

The **historical cost concept** is the basis for entering the exchange price or cost of an asset into accounting records. Using the cost concept involves two other important accounting concepts: (1) objectivity and (2) the unit of measure. The **objectivity concept** requires that accounting records and reports be based upon objective evidence. In exchanges between a buyer and a seller, both try to get the best price. Only the final agreed-upon amount is objective enough for accounting purposes. If the amounts at which properties were recorded were constantly being revised upward and downward based on offers, appraisals, and opinions, accounting reports would soon become unstable and unreliable. The **unit-of-measure concept** requires that economic data be recorded in dollars. Money is a common unit of measurement for reporting uniform financial data and reports.

Matching Concept

The **matching concept**, which is based on accrual accounting, refers to the matching of expenses and revenues (hence net income) for an accounting period. Under the accrual basis, revenues are reported in the income statement in which they are earned. Similarly, expenses are reported in the same period as the revenues to which they relate. Under the cash basis of accounting, revenues and expenses are reported in the income statement in the period in which cash is received or paid.

Other Concepts

The **materiality concept** implies that errors, which could occur during journalizing and posting transactions, should be significant enough to affect the decision-making process. All material errors should be discovered and corrected. The **accounting period concept** breaks the economic life of a business into time periods and requires that accounting reports be prepared at periodic intervals. The **revenue recognition concept,** which is based on accrual accounting, refers to the recognition of revenues in the period in which they are earned.

Accounting Principles

If the management of a company could record and report financial data as it saw fit, comparisons among companies would be difficult, if not impossible. Thus, financial accountants follow **generally accepted accounting principles (GAAP)** in preparing reports. These reports allow investors and other stakeholders to compare one company to another. GAAP are developed from research, accepted accounting practices, and pronouncements of authoritative bodies.

Qualities of Accounting Information

The accounting function collects the raw data from business transactions and converts them into information useful to the decision maker. In this regard, the accounting information should contain two qualitative characteristics: (1) primary and (2) secondary qualities.

Primary Qualities

The two primary qualities that distinguish useful accounting information are relevance and reliability. If either of these qualities is missing, accounting information will not be useful. **Relevance** means the information must have a bearing on a particular decision situation. Relevant accounting information possesses at least two characteristics: timeliness and predictive value or feedback value. **Timeliness** means accounting information must be provided in time to influence a particular decision. **Predictive value** means accounting information can be used to predict the future and timing of cash flows. **Feedback value** means the accounting function must provide decision-makers with information that allows them to assess the progress or economic worth of an investment.

To be considered reliable, accounting information must possess three qualities: verifiability, representational faithfulness, and neutrality. Information is considered **verifiable** if several individuals, working independently, would arrive at similar conclusions using the same data. **Representational faithfulness** means accounting information must report what actually happened. **Neutrality** means accounting information must be free of bias or distortion.

Secondary Qualities

"Secondary qualities" does not mean that these characteristics are of lesser importance than the primary qualities. If a secondary characteristic is missing, the accounting information is not necessarily useless. The secondary qualities of useful information are comparability and consistency. **Comparability** means the accounting reports generated for one firm may be easily and usefully compared with the accounting reports generated for other firms. If the two firms use totally different accounting methods, it would be very difficult to make a useful comparison of their data and information. **Consistency** means that a firm systematically uses the same accounting methods and procedures from one accounting period to the next accounting period.

In addition to the primary and secondary qualities, the accounting information must be understandable to economic decision-makers. "Earnings management" strategy can destroy the primary and secondary qualities of accounting information.

❑ Learning Objective 6.2: UNDERSTAND THE PURPOSE OF THE ACCOUNTING CYCLE

Financial accounting provides accounting information for use by those outside and inside the organization. This information is used by current investors and potential investors to determine future benefits they will receive if they hold or acquire ownership in a business. Creditors and lenders use this information to assess the creditworthiness of an organization. Other users of this information include employees, unions, customers, the general public, and governmental units.

Transactions, in accounting, are the result of the exchange of goods and/or services. Two factors allow the recording of a transaction—**evidence** and **measurement**. An exchange is an observable event and, therefore, provides evidence of business activity. This exchange takes place at a set price and, thus, provides an objective measure of the economic activity. The accounting cycle is one of four business cycles; the other three are sales, finance, and production.

With the traditional accounting model, a **double-entry system** of recordkeeping is used. The fundamental equation used with this system is:

$$Assets = Liabilities + Owners' Equity$$

All transactions are analyzed and then recorded based on their effect on assets, liabilities, and owners' equity. The increases and decreases in these accounts are recorded as debits or credits. In recording these transactions, the total amount of debits must equal the total amount of credits. The requirement that debits and credits must be equal gives rise to the double-entry method of recordkeeping. In account form, the rules of debits and credits include the following:

Debits	Credits
Increase assets	Decrease assets
Decrease liabilities	Increase liabilities
Decrease owners' equity	Increase owners' equity
Increase owners' drawing	Decrease owners' drawing
Decrease revenues	Increase revenues
Increase expenses	Decrease expenses

Cash-Basis versus Accrual-Basis

The two approaches of accounting are cash-basis accounting and accrual-basis accounting. With **cash-basis of accounting,** revenues are recognized when cash is received, and expenses are recognized when cash is paid out. The primary advantages of cash-basis accounting are the increased reliability due to the fact that transactions are not recorded until complete and the simplicity due to the fact that fewer estimates and judgments are required.

For most businesses, the cash-basis of accounting for a period requires recognition and measurement of noncash resources and obligations. Cash-basis accounting is not in accordance with GAAP.

With the **accrual-basis of accounting,** revenues are recognized when sales are made or services are performed, and expenses are recognized as incurred. Revenues and expenses are recognized in the period in which they occur rather than when cash is received or paid out.

The attempt to record the financial effect of transactions that have cash consequences in the periods in which those transactions occur rather than in the periods in which cash is received or paid pertains to accrual accounting.

Steps in the Accounting Cycle

The accounting cycle records the effect of economic transactions on the assets, liabilities, and owners' equity of an organization. The accounting cycle involves eight steps: (1) analysis of transactions, (2) journalizing of transactions, (3) posting to the ledger, (4) trial balance and working papers, (5) adjusting journal entries, (6) closing journal entries, (7) preparing financial statements, and (8) reversing journal entries.

❑ Learning Objective 6.3: UNDERSTAND THE TYPES AND CONTENTS OF FINANCIAL STATEMENTS

Every business manager at one time or another will get involved in analyzing his company's financial statements or other firms'. These analyses will reveal trends and patterns, which will provide period-to-period comparisons as well as with other firms in the industry.

Types of Financial Statements

The following is the sequence of preparing four different types of financial statements:

1. **Income statement.** After preparing the adjusting journal entries and posting them to the working papers, an income statement can be prepared using the income statement numbers from the working papers.
2. **Statement of Retained Earnings and Statement of Stockholders' Equity.** After preparing the closing journal entries and posting them to the working papers, the only accounts with balances should be the asset, liability, and owners' equity accounts. At this time, a Statement of Retained Earnings or Statement of Stockholders' Equity should be prepared. This statement summarizes the transactions affecting the owners' capital account balance or retained earning. Such a statement shows the beginning capital account, plus net income or less net loss, less owners' withdrawals or dividends. The ending capital account is then carried forward to the balance sheet, which helps to relate income statement information to balance sheet information.
3. **Balance sheet**. The balance sheet is divided into assets, liabilities, and stockholders' equity and

reflects the balances in these accounts at the end of the year.

4. **Statement of Cash Flows.** A Statement of Cash Flows is prepared either in conjunction with the balance sheet or separately. It directly or indirectly reflects an entity's cash receipts classified by major sources and its cash payments classified by major uses during a period, including cash flow information about its operating, financing, and investing activities.

Contents of Financial Statements

The full set of four financial statements discussed in this section is based on the concept of financial capital maintenance. For a period, the full set should show the following:

Income Statement

The **income statement,** also known as the Statement of Income, Statement of Earnings, or Statement of Operations, summarizes the results of an entity's economic activities or performance for a period of time (i.e., an accounting period). It also measures a firm's profitability over a specific period. Management of the enterprise is concerned with the income statement since it is curious to find out how efficiently or effectively resources are used and how investors and creditors view the income statement.

A simplified format of income statement is shown here, as it may not contain all the components.

DV Knowledge Corporation

Income Statement

Gross sales

Less: Returns and allowances
Net sales
Less: Cost of goods sold
    Fixed costs
    Variable costs

Gross profit or margin

Less: operating expenses
    Fixed expenses
    Variable expenses

Operating income (EBIT)

Less: Interest expenses
Net income before taxes
Less: Taxes

Net income after taxes
Less: Cash dividends to preferred stockholders

Net income (loss)

Earnings per share (EPS) to common stockholders

Notes: Total revenues can include revenues from gross sales of products and services, dividend revenues, and rental revenues. Cost of goods sold includes wages, materials, rent, supplies, and utilities to manufacture goods. Operating expenses include selling, general, administrative, lease, and depreciation expenses, classified as fixed or variable. Operating income is same as earnings before interest and taxes (EBIT). Net income or loss is posted to retained earnings account on the balance sheet. Net income is earnings available to common stockholders. EPS is calculated as net income divided by the number of common shares outstanding.

Major components and items required to be presented in the income statement include: income from continuing operations, results from discontinued operations, extraordinary items, accounting changes, net income, and earnings per share.

Income from Continuing Operations **Sales** or **revenues** are charges to customers for the goods and/or services provided during the period. Both gross and net sales/revenues should be presented by showing discounts, allowances, and returns.

Cost of goods sold is the cost of inventory items sold during the period for a manufacturing or retail company.

Operating expenses are primary recurring costs associated with business operations to generate sales or revenues. They do not include cost of goods sold but include selling expenses (e.g., salesperson salaries, commissions, advertising) and general and administrative expenses (e.g., salaries, office supplies, telephone, postage, utilities, accounting and legal services). An expense is to be recognized whenever economic benefits have been consumed.

Gains and losses stem from the peripheral transactions of the enterprise. Examples are write-downs of inventories and receivables, effects of a strike, and foreign currency exchange gains and losses.

Losses result from peripheral or incidental transactions, whereas expenses result from ongoing major or central operations of the entity. Expense accounts are costs related to revenue, whereas loss accounts are not related to revenue.

Other revenues and expenses are revenues and expenses not related to the operations of the enterprise. Examples include gains and losses on the disposal of equipment, interest revenues and expenses, and dividend revenues. A material gain on the sale of a fully depreciated asset should be classified on the income statement as part of other revenues and gains. Since the sale of an asset is not an operating item, it should be classified as other revenues and gains.

Income tax expense relates to continuing operations.

Results from Discontinued Operations It contains two components. The first component, income (loss) from operations, is disclosed for the current year only if the decision to discontinue operations is made after the beginning of the fiscal year for which the financial statements are being prepared. The second component, gain (loss) on the disposal, contains income (loss) from operations during the phaseout period and gain (loss) from disposal of segment assets. **Discontinued operations** are presented after income from continuing operations and before extraordinary income on the income statement. The disposal of a line of business is normal and any loss should be treated as an ordinary loss.

Extraordinary Items Two criteria must be met to classify an event or transaction as an **extraordinary item**: unusual nature (high degree of abnormality, clearly unrelated to, or only incidentally related to) and infrequency of occurrence (not reasonably expected to recur in the foreseeable future).

Accounting Changes A **change in accounting principles** (including methods of applying them) results from adoption of GAAP different from the ones previously used for reporting purposes. The effect on net income of adopting the new accounting principle should be disclosed as a separate item following extraordinary items in the income statement. **Changes in accounting estimates** (lives of fixed assets, adjustments of the costs) are *not* considered errors or extraordinary items; instead, they are considered as prior-period adjustments.

Net Income Obviously, net income is derived by subtracting "results from discontinued operations," "extraordinary items," and "cumulative effect of changes in accounting principles" from "income from continuing operations."

Earnings per share **Earnings per share (EPS)** is a compact indicator of a company's financial performance. It is used to evaluate a firm's stock price, in assessing the firm's future earnings potential, and in determining the ability to pay dividends. *EPS is calculated as net income minus preferred dividends divided by the weighted-average of common shares outstanding.* EPS must be disclosed on the face of the income statement. EPS may be disclosed parenthetically when only a one-per-share amount is involved.

EPS is required to be reported for the following items:

- Income from continuing operations
- Income before extraordinary items and cumulative effect of changes in accounting principles
- Cumulative effect of changes in accounting principles
- Net income
- Results from (gain/loss on) discontinued operations (optional)
- Gain or loss on extraordinary items (optional)

The following are limitations of income statements:

- Items that cannot be quantified with any degree of reliability were not included in determining income (i.e., economic income versus accounting income).
- Income numbers are often affected by the accounting methods employed (e.g., depreciation).
- Increases in income may result from a nonoperating or nonrecurring event that is not sustainable over a period of time (e.g., one-time tax forgiveness, exchange of preferred stock).

The following are limitations of accrual-based accounting for earnings:

- Information about the liquidity and potential cash flows of an organization is absent.
- The income statement does not reflect earnings in current dollars.
- Estimates and judgments must be used in preparing the income statement.

Statement of Retained Earnings and Statement of Stockholders' Equity

The **Statement of Retained Earnings** is a reconciliation of the balance of the retained earnings account from the beginning to the end of the year. This statement tells the reader how much money management is plowing back into the business. Prior-period adjustments, including correction of errors (net of taxes), are charged or credited to the opening balance of retained earnings.

Net income is added and dividends declared are subtracted to arrive at the ending balance of retained earnings. This statement may report two separate amounts: retained earnings free (unrestricted) and retained earnings appropriated (restricted).

A simplified format of retained earnings statement is shown here, as it may not contain all the components.

DV Knowledge Corporation

Statement of Retained Earnings

Retained earnings balance at the beginning of the period
Prior period adjustments, net of taxes (+/−)
Correction of an error, net of taxes (+/−)
Net income (loss) for the period (+/−)
Cash dividends declared (−)
Retained earnings balance at the end of the period (=)

Notes: Retained earnings are increased by revenues, decreased by expenses, and decreased by dividends; they can be restricted or unrestricted. Cash dividends declared includes dividends on preferred stock and common stock.

The **Statement of Stockholders' Equity** shows investments by and distributions to owners as it reflects an entity's capital transactions during a period—the extent to which and in what ways the equity of the entity increased or decreased from transactions with investors as owners.

A simplified format of stockholders' equity statement is shown here, as it may not contain all the components.

DV Knowledge Corporation

Statement of Stockholders' Equity

Preferred stock at par (+)
Common stock at par (+)
Treasury stock (−)
Paid-in-capital (+)
Property and stock dividends (−)
Retained earnings (+/−)
Total stockholders' equity (=)

Notes: Paid-in-capital is in excess of par. Stockholders' equity is increased by sale of preferred and common stock, decreased by purchase of treasury stock, and decreased by property and stock dividends.

Balance Sheet

The **Statement of Financial Position** (balance sheet) presents assets, liabilities, and shareholders' equity. The balance sheet provides a basis for assessing the liquidity and financial flexibility of an entity, computing rates of return on investments, and evaluating the capital structure of an entity. It reflects the financial status (health) of an enterprise in conformity with GAAP. The balance sheet reports the aggregate (and cumulative) effect of transactions at a point in time, whereas the Statement of Income, Statement of Retained Earnings, and the Statement of Cash Flows report the effect of transactions over a period of time. The balance sheet is based on historical cost, the exchange price principle, or the acquisition price.

A simplified format of balance sheet is shown here, as it may not contain all the components.

DV Knowledge Corporation

Balance Sheet

Assets	Liabilities and Stockholders' Equity
Current assets	**Current liabilities**
Cash (1)	Accounts payable (20)
Marketable securities (2)	Taxes payable (21)
Net accounts receivable (3)	Notes payable (22)
Notes receivable (4)	Interest payable (23)
Inventories (5)	Accruals (24)
Prepaid expenses (6)	Total current liabilities (25 = 20 + 21 + 22 + 23 + 24)
Total current assets (7)	
Gross non-current assets	**Long-term liabilities**
Vehicles and leases (8)	Bonds/loans/notes (26)
Land and buildings (9)	Mortgage payable (27)
Machinery and equipment (10)	Total long-term liabilities (28 = 26 + 27)
Furniture and fixtures (11)	Total liabilities (29 = 25 + 28)
Total gross non-current assets (12)	Stockholders' equity
Less: Accumulated depreciation (13)	Preferred stock at par (30)
	Common stock at par (31)
Net non-current assets (14 = 12 − 13)	Treasury stock (32)
	Paid-in capital (33)
	Property and stock dividends (34)
	Retained earnings (35)
Intangible assets (15)	Total stockholders' equity (36)
Total assets (16 = 7 + 14 + 15)	
	Total liabilities and stockholders' equity (37)

Notes: Total assets must be equal to total liabilities and stockholders' equity. Net accounts receivable is gross accounts receivable minus allowance for doubtful accounts. Inventories include raw materials, work-in-process, and finished goods. Total current assets are 7 = 1 + 2 + 3 + 4 + 5 + 6.

(Continued)

Non-current assets are fixed or long-term assets. The book value of a fixed asset is historical cost minus accumulated depreciation. Total gross non-current assets are $12 = 8 + 9 + 10 + 11$. Intangible assets include patents, copyrights, trademarks, and franchises. Paid-in capital is excess of par on common and preferred stock. Retained earnings are coming from the income statement, thus providing a link between the balance sheet and the income statement. Total stockholders' equity is $36 = 30 + 31 + 32 + 33 + 34 + 35$. Total liabilities and stockholders' equity is $37 = 29 + 36$.

Assets **Assets** are classified as "current" if they are reasonably expected to be converted into cash, sold, or consumed either in one year or in the operating cycle, whichever is longer.

Current assets include cash, short-term investments, receivables, inventories, and prepaid expenses. The key criterion to include in current assets is the length of the operating cycle. When the cycle is less than one year, the one-year concept is used. When the cycle is very long, the usefulness of the concept of current assets diminishes.

Noncurrent assets include long-term investments; property, plant, and equipment; and intangible assets.

Other assets include accounts that do not fit in the above asset categories. Examples include long-term prepaid expenses, deferred taxes, bond issue costs, noncurrent receivables, and restricted cash.

Liabilities **Liabilities** are classified as "current" if they are expected to be liquidated through the use of current assets or the creation of other current liabilities. Liabilities are presented in the balance sheet in the order of payment. It is grouped into three categories: current, noncurrent, and other.

Current liabilities include: obligations arising from the acquisition of goods and services entering the operating cycle, collections of money in advance for the future delivery of goods or performance of services, and other obligations maturing within the current operating cycle to be met through the use of current assets.

Noncurrent liabilities include: obligations arising through the acquisition of assets, obligations arising out of the normal course of operations, and contingent liabilities involving uncertainty as to possible losses.

Other liabilities include: deferred charges, noncurrent receivables, intangible assets, deferred income taxes, or deferred investment tax credits.

Classification of Shareholders' Equity **Shareholders' equity** arises from the ownership relation and is the source of enterprise distribution to the owners. Equity is increased by owners' investments and comprehensive income and is reduced by distributions to the owners.

Shareholders' equity is the interest of the stockholders in the assets of an enterprise. It shows the cumulative net results of past transactions. Specific components include capital stock (e.g., common stock and preferred stock), additional paid-in capital, donated capital, retained earnings, treasury stock, dividends, and adjustments of equity.

Limitations of Balance Sheets
The following are limitations of the balance sheet:

- It does not reflect current values. Items are recorded at a mixture of historical cost and current values. Historical cost used to record assets and liabilities does not always reflect current value. Monetary assets such as cash, short-term investments, and receivables closely approximate current values. Similarly, current liabilities closely approximate current value and should be shown on the balance sheet at face value.
- Fixed assets are reported at cost less depreciation, depletion, or amortization. Inventories and marketable equity securities are exceptions to historical cost, where they are allowed to be reported at lower of cost or market. Similarly, certain long-term investments, which is another exception, are reported under the equity method. Long-term liabilities are recorded at the discounted value of future payments.
- Judgments and estimates are used to determine the carrying value or book value of many of the assets. Examples include determining the collectability of receivables, salability of inventory, and useful life of fixed (long-term) assets. Estimations are not necessarily bad except there is no accounting guidance available.
- Appreciation of assets is not recorded except when realized through an arm's-length transaction.
- Internally generated goodwill, customer base, managerial skills and talent, reputation, technical innovation, human resources, and secret processes and formulas are not recorded in the balance sheet. Only assets obtained in a market transaction are recorded.
- It ignores the time value of its elements. Most items are stated at face value regardless of the

timing of the cash flows that they will generate. Exceptions are certain long-term receivables and payables, which are discounted.
- It omits off-balance-sheet items (mostly liabilities) such as sales of receivables with recourse, leases, throughput arrangements, and take-or-pay contracts.

Statement of Cash Flows

The Statement of Cash Flows (SCF) requires three classifications:

1. **Operating activities** include all transactions that are not investing and financing activities. It includes delivering or producing goods for sale and providing services to customers. It involves cash effects of transactions that enter into the determination of net income for the period.
2. **Investing activities** show the acquisition and disposition of long-term productive assets or securities that are not considered cash equivalents. It also includes the lending of money and collection of loans.
3. **Financing activities** include obtaining resources from and returning resources to the owners. It also includes resources obtained from creditors and repaying the amount borrowed.

A simplified format of cash flows statement is shown here, as it may not contain all the components.

DV Knowledge Corporation

Statement of Cash Flows

Cash flows from operating activities

Net income after taxes	+
Depreciation, amortization, or depletion	+
Decrease in accounts receivable	+
Decrease in inventories	+
Increase in accounts payable	+
Decrease in accruals	−
Total net cash flows from operating activities (1)	=

Cash flows from investment activities

Increase in gross fixed assets	−
Proceeds from sale of fixed assets	+
Total net cash flows from investment activities (2)	=

Cash flows from financing activities

Decrease in notes payable	−
Increase in long-term debt	+
Proceeds from sale of common stock	+
Cash dividends paid	−
Total net cash flows from financing activities (3)	=

Net increase or decrease in cash (4 = 1 + 2 + 3)

Add: Cash at the beginning of the year
Cash at the end of the year

Notes: Cash at the end of the year must be equal to the cash account in the balance sheet. Retained earnings are excluded here because they were already included in the net income after taxes and cash dividends paid. Operating cash flows affect current assets and current liabilities, investing cash flows affect long-term assets, and financing cash flows affect long-term liabilities and stockholder's equity on the balance sheet.

The following tables present examples of the SCF classifications in terms of cash inflows and cash outflows:

Cash Inflows

Operating	Investing	Financing
Cash receipts exceed cash expenditures	Principal collections from loans	Proceeds from issuing equity securities
Receipts from sale of goods or services	Sale of long-term debt or equity securities	Proceeds from issuing short-term or long-term debt (e.g., bonds and notes)
Returns on loans (interest)	Sale of property, plant, and equipment	
Returns on equity securities (dividends)		

Cash Outflows

Operating	Investing	Financing
Cash expenditures exceed cash receipts	Loans made to others	Payment of dividends
Payments for inventory	Purchase of long-term debt or equity securities	Repurchase of entity's capital stock (e.g., treasury stock)
Payments to employees	Purchase of property, plant, and equipment	Repayment of debt principal
Payments of taxes		
Payments of interest		
Payments to suppliers		

Noncash exchange gains and losses recognized on the income statement should be reported as a separate item when reconciling net income and operating activities.

Specifically, the SCF should help investors and creditors assess:

- Ability to generate future positive cash flows
- Ability to meet obligations and pay dividends
- Reasons for differences between income and cash receipts and cash payments
- Both cash and noncash aspects of entities' investing and financing transactions

Noncash Investing and Financing Activities

Cash may not be required in all cases to acquire assets or to pay off debts; instead, a debt or stock might be involved. Under these conditions, a separate schedule is needed to show the noncash investing and financing activities.

A simplified format of noncash flows schedule is shown here, as it may not contain all the components.

DV Knowledge Corporation

Schedule of Noncash Investing and Financing Activities

Acquisition of building by issuing common stock	+
Acquisition of land by issuing notes payable	+
Payment of note payable by issuing common stock	+
Total noncash investing and financing activities	=

❏ Learning Objective 6.4:
UNDERSTAND THE INTERMEDIATE CONCEPTS OF FINANCIAL ACCOUNTING

The scope of intermediate concepts in financial accounting includes bonds, notes, leases, pensions, intangible assets, and research and development.

Bonds and Notes

Bonds result from a single agreement. However, a bond is divided into various subunits. Notes and bonds have similar characteristics. These include a written agreement stating the amount of the principal to be paid, the interest rate, when the interest and principal are to be paid, and the restrictive covenants.

The stated interest rate on a note or bond often differs from the market interest rate at the time of issuance. When this occurs, the present value of the interest and principal payments will differ from the maturity, or face value. Possible scenarios include the following:

- When the market rate exceeds the stated rate, the instrument is sold at a discount, meaning that the cash proceeds are less than the face value.
- When the stated rate exceeds the market rate, the instrument is sold at a premium, meaning that the cash proceeds are more than the face value.
- When the market and stated rates are the same at the time of issuance, no discount or premium exists and the instrument will be sold at its face value.

The proper valuation is the present value of the future payments using the market rate of interest, either stated or implied in the transaction, at the date the debt was incurred.

Nominal rate, stated rate, or coupon rate are all names for the interest rate stated on a bond. The periodic interest payments on a bond are determined by this rate. However, the price at which the bonds are sold determines the actual interest expense incurred on the bond issue. The actual rate of interest incurred is called the **effective rate,** the **yield rate,** or the **market rate** and is determined by the investment market.

When a bond sells at par value or face amount, the effective interest rate and the stated rate are equal. When a bond sells at a discount (below par), the effective rate is greater than the stated rate. When a bond sells at a premium (above par), the stated rate is greater than the effective rate of the bond; then the bond will sell at a discount. If the prevailing market rate of interest is less than the stated rate, then the bond will sell at a premium.

When a note is issued solely for cash, the present value of the note is the cash proceeds. The present value of the note minus its face amount is the amount of the discount or premium. The interest expense on such a note is the stated or coupon interest plus or minus the amortization of any discount or premium.

When a note is issued in a noncash transaction and no interest rate is stated, and if the stated interest rate is unreasonable or if the stated face amount of the note is materially different from the current cash sales price for similar items or from the market value of the note at the date of the transaction, then the note issued and the property, goods, or services received should be recorded at the fair value of the property, goods, or services. If the fair value of the noncash item cannot be determined, then the market value of the note should be used.

A discount or premium is recognized when there is a difference between the face amount of the note and its fair value. This discount or premium should be amortized over the life of the note. If neither the fair value of the noncash item nor the market value of the note is determinable, then the present value of the note should be determined by discounting all future payments on the note using an imputed interest rate.

Short-term obligations that are expected to be refinanced on a long-term basis may be classified as long-term liabilities on the balance sheet. The requirements for classification as long-term are as follows: management intends to refinance the obligations on a long-term basis and demonstrates the ability to obtain the refinancing.

Bondholders have a prior claim to the earnings and assets of the issuing organization. They rank ahead of preferred and common stockholders. Interest must first be paid to bondholders before dividends can be distributed to stockholders. Bondholders have a prior claim on assets in the case of dissolution or bankruptcy.

Leases

A lease agreement involves at least two parties (lessor, lessee) and an asset. The **lessor**, who owns the asset, agrees to allow the **lessee** to use it for a specified period of time for rent payments. *The key point in leases is the transfer of risk of ownership.* If the transaction effectively transfers ownership to the lessee, then it should be treated as a sale even though the transaction takes the form of a lease. Here, the substance, not the form, dictates the accounting treatment. Two types of leases exist: capital and operating lease.

Suggested disclosures for the lessee include the following:

For Capital Leases

- The gross amount of assets recorded
- Future minimum lease payments in the aggregate
- Total of minimum sublease rentals to be received
- Total contingent rentals actually incurred for each period
- Depreciation

For Operating Leases

- Future minimum lease payments in the aggregate
- Total of minimum rentals that will be received under noncancelable subleases
- Rental expenses separated into minimum rentals, contingent rentals, and sublease rentals

Suggested disclosures for the lessor include the following:

For Sales-Type and Direct Financing Leases

- Components of the net investment in leases including future minimum lease payments, unguaranteed residual values, initial direct costs for direct financing leases, and unearned interest revenue
- Future minimum lease payments
- Total contingent rentals included in income

For Operating Leases

- The cost and carrying amount of property leased
- Minimum rentals on noncancelable leases in the aggregate
- Total contingent rentals included in income

A lessor has four types of choices in classifying a lease:

1. Sales-type leases
2. Direct financing leases
3. Operating leases
4. Participation by third parties

Leases involving Real Estate

Leases involving real estate can be divided into four categories: (1) leases involving land only, (2) leases involving land and buildings, (3) leases involving equipment as well as real estate, and (4) leases involving only part of a building.

Sale-Leaseback Transactions

Sale-leaseback transactions involve the sale of property by the owner and a lease of the property back to the seller. The seller-lessee must account for the lease as a capital lease or an operating lease.

Accounting and Reporting for Leveraged Leases

From the standpoint of the lessee, leveraged leases shall be classified and accounted for in the same manner as nonleveraged leases. The balance of this section deals with leveraged leases from the standpoint of the lessor.

Leveraged lease is defined as one having all of the following characteristics:

- Direct financing and sales-type leases are not included.
- It involves at least three parties: a lessee, a long-term creditor, and a lessor (commonly called the **equity participant**).
- The financing provided by the long-term creditor is nonrecourse as to the general credit of the lessor. The amount of the financing is sufficient to provide the lessor with substantial leverage in the transaction.
- The lessor's net investment declines during the early years once the investment has been completed and rises during the later years of the lease before its final elimination. Such decrease and increase in the net investment balance may occur more than once.

Pensions

The principal focus in pensions is the present value of the pension obligation, the fair value of plan assets, and the disclosure of the makeup of net pension costs and of the projected benefit obligation. The critical accounting issues are the amount to be expensed on the income statement and the amount to be accrued on the balance sheet.

Employer commitment to employees takes the form of contributions to an independent trustee. The trustee then invests the contributions in various plan assets such as Treasury bills and bonds, certificates of deposit, annuities, marketable securities, corporate bonds, and stock. The plan assets generate interest and/or appreciate in asset value. The return on the plan assets provides the trustee the money to pay the benefits to which the employees are entitled. These benefits are defined by the terms of the pension plan using a plan's benefit formula. The formula is used to determine the pension cost for each year. The formula takes into account factors such as employee compensation, service length, age, and other factors to determine pension costs.

Pension expense is determined by adding up five components, which affect the pension expense amount as follows:

Component	Effect
1. Service cost	Increases
2. Interest cost	Increases
3. Actual return on plan assets	Generally decreases
4. Prior service cost	Generally decreases
5. Net total of other components (gain or loss) $5 = 1 + 2 + 3 + 4$	Increases or decreases

Intangible Assets

Typically **intangible assets** lack physical existence and have a high degree of uncertainty regarding their future benefits. These assets have value because of the business advantages of exclusive rights and privileges they provide. The two sources of intangible assets are:

1. **Exclusive privileges** granted by authority of the government or legal contract, which includes patents, copyrights, trademarks, franchises, and organization costs (e.g., legal fees) for incorporating a new business.
2. Superior entrepreneurial capacity or management know-how and customer loyalty, that is, **goodwill.**

Intangible assets are initially recorded at cost. Therefore, the costs of intangible assets, except for goodwill, are relatively easy to determine. These assets must be amortized over their expected useful life but not to exceed 40 years. An organization must use straight-line amortization, unless it can prove that another method is more appropriate. The amortization of intangible assets over their useful lives is justified by the **going-concern assumption.**

Summary of Amortization Periods

- Copyrights not to exceed 40 years
- Trademarks not to exceed 40 years
- Patents not to exceed 17 years
- Organization costs not to exceed 40 years
- Goodwill not to exceed 40 years

Some intangible assets, since they cannot be separated from the business as a whole, are not specifically identifiable. **Goodwill** is a prime example of this type of intangible.

Goodwill arises when an organization's value as a whole exceeds the fair market value of its net assets. This typically occurs when an organization generates more income than other organizations with the same assets and capital structure. Superior management, a superior reputation, or valuable customer lists are examples of factors that may contribute to these excess earnings.

Product R&D Costs

The scope of **research and development (R&D)** deals with manufacturing a product and developing software.

Accounting standards require R&D costs to be expensed as incurred except for intangible or fixed assets purchased from others having alternative future uses. Thus, the cost of patents and R&D equipment purchased from third parties may be deferred, capitalized, and amortized over the assets' useful life. However, internally developed R&D may not be deferred and therefore should be expensed. R&D done under contract for others is not required to be expensed. The costs incurred would be matched with revenue using the completed-contract or percentage-of-completion method. The key accounting concept is: expense R&D costs as incurred and disclose total R&D expenses per period on face of income statement or notes.

R&D activities included in the standard are laboratory research to discover new knowledge, formulation, and design of product alternatives (e.g., testing and modifications); preproduction prototypes and models (e.g., tools, dies, and pilot plants); and engineering activity until product is ready for manufacture.

R&D activities excluded from the standard are (1) engineering during an early phase of commercial production, (2) quality control for commercial production, (3) troubleshooting during commercial production breakdowns, (4) routine, ongoing efforts to improve products, (5) adaptation of existing capability for a specific customer, (6) seasonal design changes to products, (7) routine design of tools and dies, (8) design, construction, and startup of equipment except that used solely for R&D, and (9) legal work for patents or litigation. Item 9 is capitalized, whereas the other eight items are expensed.

Elements of R&D costs include: materials, equipment, and facilities, salaries, wages, and related costs, intangibles purchased from others, which are treated as materials, R&D services performed by others, and a reasonable allocation of indirect costs, excluding general and administrative costs not clearly related to R&D.

Software Developed for Sale or Lease

The costs incurred internally to create software should be expensed as R&D costs until technological feasibility is established. Thereafter, all costs should be capitalized and reported at the lower of unamortized cost or net realizable value. Capitalization should cease when the software is available for general release to customers.

The annual amortization of capitalized computer software costs will be the greater of the ratio of current revenues to anticipated total revenues or the straight-line amortization, which is based on the estimated economic life. Once the software is available for general release to customers, the inventory costs should include costs for duplicating software and for physically packaging the product. The cost of maintenance and customer support should be charged to expense in the period incurred.

Software Developed for Internal Use

Software must meet two criteria to be accounted for as internally developed software. First, the software's specifications must be designed or modified to meet the reporting entity's internal needs, including costs to customize purchased software. Second, during the period in which the software is being developed, there can be no plan or intent to market the software externally, although development of the software can be jointly funded by several entities, each of which plan to use the software internally.

In order to justify capitalization of related costs, it is necessary for management to conclude that it is probable that the project will be completed and that the software will be used as intended. Absent that level of expectation, costs must be expensed currently as R&D costs are required to be. Entities that historically were engaged in both research and development of software for internal use and for sale to others would have to carefully identify costs with one or the other activity, since the former would be subject to capitalization, while the latter might be expensed as R&D costs until technological feasibility was demonstrated.

Under terms of the standard, cost capitalization commences when an entity has completed the conceptual formulation, design, and testing of possible project alternatives, including the process of vendor selection for purchased software, if any. These early-phase costs (i.e., preliminary project stage costs) are similar to R&D costs and must be expensed as incurred.

Costs incurred subsequent to the preliminary project stage and that meet the criteria under GAAP as long-lived assets can be capitalized and amortized over the asset's expected economic life. Capitalization of costs will begin when both of two conditions are met. First, management having the relevant authority approves and commits to funding the project and believes that it is probable that it will be completed and that the resulting software will be used as intended. Second, the conceptual formulation, design, and testing of possible software project alternatives (i.e., the preliminary project stage) have been completed.

☐ Learning Objective 6.5: UNDERSTAND THE ADVANCED CONCEPTS OF FINANCIAL ACCOUNTING

The scope of advanced concepts in financial accounting includes business combination, consolidated financial statements, partnerships, and foreign currency transactions.

Business Combinations

A **business combination** occurs when an entity acquires net assets that constitute a business or acquires equity interests of one or more other entities and obtains control over that entity or entities. Business combinations may be friendly or hostile takeovers. Purchase accounting is the only acceptable accounting method for all business combinations; the pooling-of-interest method is not.

Consolidated Financial Statements

The purpose of **consolidated financial statements** is to present for a single accounting entity the combined resources, obligations, and operating results of a group of related corporations such as parent and subsidiaries. Only subsidiaries not actually controlled should be exempted from consolidation. Usually, an investor's direct or indirect ownership of more than 50 percent of an investee's outstanding common sock has been required to evidence the controlling interest underlying a parent–subsidiary relationship. Actual control is more important than the controlling interest in situations such as liquidation or reorganization (bankruptcy) of a subsidiary or control of a foreign subsidiary by a foreign government. GAAP require the use of the cost method of accounting for investments in unconsolidated subsidiaries because the subsidiaries generally are neither controlled nor significantly influenced by the parent company.

Assets, liabilities, revenues, and expenses of the parent company and its subsidiaries are totaled; intercompany transactions and balances are eliminated; and the final consolidated amounts are reported in the consolidated balance sheet, income statement, Statement of Stockholders' Equity, Statement of Retained Earnings, and Statement of Cash Flows.

Partnerships

A **partnership** is an association of two or more people to carry on as co-owners of a business for profit. Competent parties agree to place their money, property, or labor in a business and to divide the profits and losses. Each person is personally liable for the debts of the partnership. Express partnership agreements may be oral or written.

Partnerships are not subject to the income tax. The partnership net profit or loss is allocated to each partner according to the partnership's profit-sharing agreement. Each partner reports these items on his own tax return. Several separately reported items (e.g., capital gains, charitable contributions) retain their character when passed through to the partners.

If a firm is insolvent and a court of equity is responsible for the distribution of the partnership assets, the assets are distributed in accordance with a rule known as **marshalling of assets.** The firm's creditors may seek payment out of the firm's assets and then the individual partner assets. The firm's creditors must exhaust the firm's assets before recourse to the partners' individual assets. *The descending order of asset distribution of a limited partnership is as follows:*

1. To secured creditors other than partners
2. To unsecured creditors other than partners
3. To limited partners in respect of their profits
4. To limited partners in respect of their capital contributions
5. To general partners in respect of any loans to the partnership
6. To general partners in respect of their profits
7. To general partners in respect of their capital contributions

The asset distribution hierarchy of a limited partnership is shown in the figure.

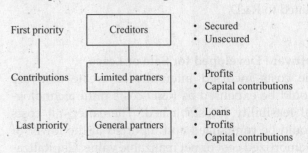

Foreign Currency Transactions

The buying and selling of **foreign currency transactions** result in variations in the exchange rate between the currencies of two countries. The **selling spot rate** is charged by the bank for current sales of the foreign currency. The bank's **buying spot rate** for the currency is less than the selling spot rate; the **spread** between the selling and buying spot rates represents gross profit to a trader in foreign currency. Factors influencing fluctuations in exchange rates include a nation's balance of payments surplus or deficit, differing global rates of inflation, money-market variations such as interest rates, capital investment levels, and monetary policies and actions of central banks.

A multinational corporation (MNC) headquartered in the United States engages in sales, purchases, and loans with foreign companies as well as with its own branches, divisions, investees, and subsidiaries in other countries. If the transactions with foreign companies are denominated in terms of the U.S. dollar, no accounting problems arise for the U.S.-based MNC. If the transactions are negotiated and settled in terms of the foreign companies' local currency unit, then the U.S. company must account for the transaction denominated in foreign currency in terms of U.S. dollars. This foreign currency translation is accomplished by applying the appropriate exchange rate between the foreign currency and the U.S. dollar.

In addition to spot rates, **forward rates** apply to foreign currency transactions to be completed on a future date. Forward rates apply to forward exchange contracts, which are agreements to exchange currencies of different countries on a specified future date at the forward rate in effect when the contract was made. Forward rates may be larger or smaller than spot rates for a foreign currency, depending on the foreign currency dealer's expectations regarding fluctuations in exchange rates for the currency.

Increases in the selling spot rate for a foreign currency required by a U.S.-based MNC to settle a liability denominated in that currency generate transaction losses to the company because more dollars are required to obtain the foreign currency. Conversely, decreases in the selling spot rate produce transaction gains to the company because fewer U.S. dollars are required to obtain the foreign currency. In contrast, increases in the buying spot rate for a foreign currency to be received by a U.S.-based MNC in settlement of a receivable denominated in that currency generate transaction gains to the company; decreases in the buying spot rate produce transaction losses.

☐ Learning Objective 6.6: LEARN HOW TO ANALYZE FINANCIAL STATEMENTS

Financial statement analysis requires a comparison of the firm's performance with that of other firms in the same industry, comparison with its own previous performance, and/or both. Three major parties who analyze financial statements from their own perspectives are: (1) managers of the firm, to gauge performance, (2) potential investors, who want to invest in the firm by purchasing stocks and bonds, and (3) creditors and lenders (e.g., bankers), who analyze data in financial statements to assess the financial strength of the firm and its ability to pay interest and principal for the money they lent to the firm. Investors use data in financial statements to form expectations about future earnings and dividends and about the riskiness of these expected values. *The real value of financial statements is in their predictive power about the firm's future earnings potential and dividends payment strength.*

Who Looks for What?

- Investors look for earnings and dividends, and this is reflected in security values. Therefore, cash flows are the major basis for security values.
- Creditors look for asset strength and the ability to pay off debt.
- Financial statements report accounting profits.
- High accounting profits generally mean high cash flows and the ability to pay high dividends and make debt payments.

A company's annual report presents four basic financial statements: a Statement of Income (income statement), a Statement of Financial Position (balance sheet), a Statement of Retained Earnings, and a Statement of Cash Flows. The income statement summarizes the firm's revenues and expenses over an accounting period.

Income Statement

The income statement presents the results of operations for a given time period. Net sales are shown at the top; after which various costs, including income taxes, are subtracted to obtain the net income available to common stockholders. A report on earnings and dividends per share is given at the bottom of the statement. A sample income statement is shown here.

DV Knowledge Corporation

Income Statement

Gross sales

Less: Returns and allowances
Net sales
Less: Cost of goods sold
Fixed costs
Variable costs

Gross profit or margin

Less: operating expenses
Fixed expenses
Variable expenses

Operating income (EBIT)

Less: Interest expenses
Net income before taxes
Less: Taxes
Net income after taxes
Less: Cash dividends to preferred stockholders

Net income (loss)

Earnings per share (EPS) to common
stockholders

Notes: Total revenues can include revenues from gross sales of products and services, dividend revenues, and rental revenues. Cost of goods sold includes wages, materials, rent, supplies, and utilities to manufacture goods. Operating expenses include selling, general, administrative, lease, and depreciation expenses, classified as fixed or variable. Operating income is same as earnings before interest and taxes (EBIT). Net income or loss is posted to retained earnings account on the balance sheet. Net income is earnings available to common stockholders. EPS is calculated as net income divided by the number of common shares outstanding.

Balance Sheet

The **balance sheet** is a statement of the firm's financial position at a specific point in time. The firm's assets are shown on the left-hand side of the balance sheet while liabilities and equity (the claims against these assets) are shown on the right-hand side. The assets are listed in the order of their liquidity or the length of time it takes to convert assets into cash. The liabilities are listed in the order in which they must be paid. A sample balance sheet is shown here.

DV Knowledge Corporation

Balance Sheet

Assets	Liabilities and Stockholders' Equity
Current assets	**Current liabilities**
Cash (1)	Accounts payable (20)
Marketable securities (2)	Taxes payable (21)
Net accounts receivable (3)	Notes payable (22)
Notes receivable (4)	Interest payable (23)
Inventories (5)	Accruals (24)
Prepaid expenses (6)	Total current liabilities (25 = 20 + 21 + 22 + 23 + 24)
Total current assets (7)	
	Long-term liabilities
Gross non-current assets	Bonds/loans/notes (26)
Vehicles and leases (8)	Mortgage payable (27)
Land and buildings (9)	Total long-term liabilities (28 = 26 + 27)
Machinery and equipment (10)	Total liabilities (29 = 25 + 28)
Furniture and fixtures (11)	Stockholders' equity
Total gross non-current assets (12)	Preferred stock at par (30)
	Common stock at par (31)
Less: Accumulated depreciation (13)	Treasury stock (32)
	Paid-in capital (33)
Net non-current assets (14 = 12 − 13)	Property and stock dividends (34)
	Retained earnings (35)
Intangible assets (15)	Total stockholders' equity (36)
Total assets (16 = 7 + 14 + 15)	**Total liabilities and stockholders' equity (37)**

Notes: Total assets must be equal to total liabilities and stockholders' equity. Net accounts receivable is gross accounts receivable minus allowance for doubtful accounts. Inventories include raw materials, work-in-process, and finished goods. Total current assets are 7 = 1 + 2 + 3 + 4 + 5 + 6. Non-current assets are fixed or long-term assets. The book value of a fixed asset is historical cost minus accumulated depreciation. Total gross non-current assets are 12 = 8 + 9 + 10 + 11. Intangible assets include patents, copyrights, trademarks, and franchises. Paid-in capital is excess of par on common and preferred stock. Retained earnings are coming from the income statement, thus providing a link between the balance sheet and the income statement. Total stockholders' equity is 36 = 30 + 31 + 32 + 33 + 34 + 35. Total liabilities and stockholders' equity is 37 = 29 + 36.

Statement of Retained Earnings

The **Statement of Retained Earnings** shows how much of the firm's earnings were not paid out in dividends. Retained earnings represent a claim against assets, not assets per se. Retained earnings do not represent cash and are not "available" for the payment of dividends or anything else. A positive retained earnings means that the firm has earned an income, but its dividends have been less than its reported income. Due to differences between accrual and cash accounting practices, a firm may earn money, which shows an increase in the retained earnings, but still could be short of cash. A sample Statement of Retained Earnings is shown here.

DV Knowledge Corporation

Statement of Retained Earnings

Retained earnings balance at the beginning of the period
Prior period adjustments, net of taxes (+/−)
Correction of an error, net of taxes (+/−)
Net income (loss) for the period (+/−)
Cash dividends declared (−)
Retained earnings balance at the end of the period (=)

Notes: Retained earnings are increased by revenues, decreased by expenses, and decreased by dividends; they can be restricted or unrestricted. Cash dividends declared includes dividends on preferred stock and common stock.

Statement of Cash Flows

The **Statement of Cash Flows** reports the impact of a firm's operating, investing, and financing activities on cash flows over an accounting period. This statement shows how the firm's operations have affected its cash flows and presents the relationships among cash flows from operating, investing, and financing activities of the firm. It presents net income, depreciation, and operating, investing, and financing activities. A sample Statement of Cash and Noncash Flows is shown here.

DV Knowledge Corporation

Statement of Cash Flows

Cash flows from operating activities

Net income after taxes	+
Depreciation, amortization, or depletion	+
Decrease in accounts receivable	+
Decrease in inventories	+
Increase in accounts payable	+
Decrease in accruals	−
Total net cash flows from operating activities (1)	=

Cash flows from investment activities

Increase in gross fixed assets	−
Proceeds from sale of fixed assets	+
Total net cash flows from investment activities (2)	=

Cash flows from financing activities

Decrease in notes payable	−
Increase in long-term debt	+
Proceeds from sale of common stock	+
Cash dividends paid	−
Total net cash flows from financing activities (3)	=

Net increase or decrease in cash (4=1+2+3)
Add: Cash at the beginning of the year
Cash at the end of the year

Notes: Cash at the end of the year must be equal to the cash account in the balance sheet. Retained earnings are excluded here because they were already included in the net income after taxes and cash dividends paid. Operating cash flows affect current assets and current liabilities, investing cash flows affect long-term assets, and financing cash flows affect long-term liabilities and stockholder's equity on the balance sheet.

DV Knowledge Corporation

Schedule of Noncash Investing and Financing Activities

Acquisition of building by issuing common stock	+
Acquisition of land by issuing notes payable	+
Payment of note payable by issuing common stock	+
Total noncash investing and financing activities	=

Four types of measures that are used to analyze a company's financial statements and its financial position are common size analysis, trend analysis, comparative ratios, and single ratios.

Common Size Analysis

Common size analysis expresses items in percentages, which can be compared with similar items of other firms or with those of the same firm over time. For example, common size balance sheet line items (both assets and liabilities) are expressed as a percentage of total assets (e.g., receivables as X percent of total assets). Similarly, common size income statement line items are expressed as a percentage of total sales (e.g., cost of goods sold as X percent of total sales).

Variations of common size analysis include vertical analysis and horizontal analysis. **Vertical analysis** expresses all items on a financial statement as a percentage of some base figure, such as total assets or total sales. Comparing these relationships between competing organizations helps to isolate strengths and areas of concern.

In **horizontal analysis**, the financial statements for two years are shown together with additional columns showing dollar differences and percentage changes. Thus, the direction, absolute amount, and relative amount of change in account balances can be calculated. Trends that are difficult to isolate through examining the financial statements of individual years or comparing with competitors can be identified.

Trend Analysis

Trend analysis shows trends in ratios, which gives insight whether the financial situation of a firm is improving, declining, or stable. It shows a graph of ratios over time, which can be compared with a firm's own performance as well as that of its industry.

Comparative Ratios

Comparative ratios show key financial ratios, such as current ratio and net sales to inventory, by industry, such as beverages and bakery products. These ratios represent average financial ratios for all firms within an industry category. Many ratio data-supplying organizations are available and each one designs ratios for its own purpose, such as small firms or large firms. Also, the focus of these ratios is different too, such as creditor's viewpoint or investor's viewpoint. Another characteristic of the ratio data-supplying organization is that each has its own definitions of the ratios and their components. A caution is required when interpreting these ratios due to these differences.

Another type of comparative analysis is comparing the financial statements for the current year with those of the most recent year. Also, by comparing summaries of financial statements for the last five to ten years, an individual can identify trends in operations, capital structure, and the composition of assets. This comparative analysis provides insight into the normal or expected account balances or ratios, information about the direction of changes in ratios and account balances, and insight into the variability or fluctuation in an organization's assets or operations.

Single Ratios

Single ratios or simple ratios show logical relationships among certain accounts or items in financial statements, expressed as fractions. These ratios are grouped into five categories: liquidity ratios, asset management ratios, debt management ratios, profitability ratios, and market value ratios.

Liquidity Ratios

Liquidity ratios measure an organization's debt-paying ability, especially in the short term. These ratios indicate an organization's capacity to meet maturing current liabilities and its ability to generate cash to pay these liabilities. Examples include current ratio and quick ratio.

- **Current ratio (working capital ratio):** *current assets divided by current liabilities.* Current ratio indicates an organization's ability to pay its current liabilities with its current assets and, therefore, shows the strength of its working capital position. A high current ratio indicates a strong liquidity and vice versa. While a high current ratio is good, it could also mean excessive cash, which is not good.

  Both short-term and long-term creditors are interested in the current ratio because a firm unable to meet its short-term obligations may be forced into bankruptcy. Many bond indentures require the borrower to maintain at least a certain minimum current ratio.

- **Quick ratio (acid-test ratio):** *quick assets divided by current liabilities.* Quick assets are cash, marketable securities, and net receivables. This ratio is particularly important to short-term creditors since it relates cash and immediate cash inflows to immediate cash outflows. Purchases of inventory on account would make the quick ratio decrease since it does not include inventory. Current liabilities increase, not current assets. Quick assets are current assets minus inventory.

Asset Management Ratios

Asset management ratios or **activity ratios** measure the liquidity of certain assets and relate information on how efficiently assets are being utilized. Examples include inventory turnover ratio, days sales outstanding ratio, fixed assets turnover ratio, and total assets turnover ratio.

- **Inventory turnover ratio:** *sales divided by average inventory or cost of goods sold divided by average inventory.* The inventory turnover indicates how quickly inventory is sold. Typically, a high turnover indicates that an organization is performing well. This ratio can be used in determining whether there is obsolete inventory or whether pricing problems exist. The use of different inventory valuation methods (LIFO, FIFO, etc.) can affect the turnover ratio. It is also called **inventory utilization ratio.** As the obsolete inventory increases, the inventory turnover decreases.

- **Days sales outstanding ratio:** *receivables divided by average sales per day.* Days sales outstanding (DSO) ratio indicates the average length of time that a firm must wait to receive cash after making a sale. It measures the number of days sales are tied up in receivables. If the calculated ratio for a company is 45 days, its sales terms are 30 days, and the industry average ratio is 35 days, it indicates that customers, on the average, are not paying their bills on time. In the absence of a change in the credit policy about sales terms, the higher the company's actual ratio, the greater the need to speed up the collection efforts. A decrease in the DSO ratio is an indication of effective collection efforts.

  Another related ratio is **accounts receivable turnover ratio**, which is net credit sales divided by average net trade receivables outstanding. The average receivables outstanding can be calculated by using the beginning and ending balance of the trade receivables. This ratio provides information on the quality of an organization's receivables and how successful it is in collecting outstanding receivables. A fast turnover lends credibility to the current ratio and acid-test ratio.

- **Fixed asset turnover ratio:** *net sales divided by net fixed assets.* Fixed asset turnover ratio shows how effectively the firm uses its fixed assets such as plant, equipment, machinery, and buildings. A caution should be noted here that inflation erodes the historical cost base of old assets thus reporting a higher turnover. This inflation problem makes it hard to compare fixed asset turnover between old and new fixed assets. Assets reported on current value basis would eliminate the inflation problem. Fixed asset turnover is also called **fixed assets utilization ratio** and is similar to the inventory utilization ratio. A high fixed asset turnover ratio may mean either that a firm was efficient in using its fixed assets or that the firm is undercapitalized and could not afford to buy enough fixed assets.

- **Total assets turnover ratio:** *net sales divided by average total assets.* The total assets turnover indicates how efficiently an organization utilizes its capital invested in assets. A high turnover ratio indicates that an organization is effectively using its assets to generate sales. This ratio relates the volume of a business (i.e., sales, revenue) to the size of its total asset investment. In order to improve this ratio, management needs to increase sales, dispose of some assets, or a combination of both.

Debt Management Ratios

Debt management ratios or **coverage ratios** are used in predicting the long-run solvency of organizations. Bondholders are interested in these ratios, because they provide some indication of the measure of protection available to bondholders. For those interested in investing in an organization's common stock, these ratios indicate some of the risk since the addition of debt increases the uncertainty of the return on common stock. Examples include debt-to-total-assets ratio, times-interest-earned ratio, fixed charge coverage ratio, and cash flow coverage ratio.

- **Debt ratio:** *total debt divided by total assets.* Debt ratio impacts an organization's ability to obtain additional financing. It is important to creditors because it indicates an organization's ability to withstand losses without impairing the creditor's interest. A creditor prefers a low ratio since it means there is more cushion available to creditors if the organization becomes insolvent. However, the owner(s) prefer high debt ratio to magnify earnings due to leverage or to minimize loss of control if new stock is issued instead of taking on more debt. Total debt includes both current liabilities and long-term debt.

The capitalization of a lease by a lessee will result in an increase in the debt-to-equity ratio. If a firm purchases a new machine by borrowing the required funds from a bank as a short-term loan, the direct impact of this transaction will be to decrease the current ratio and increase the debt ratio.

- **Times-interest-earned ratio:** *earnings before interest and taxes divided by interest charges.* Times-interest-earned ratio provides an indication of whether an organization can meet its required interest payments when they become due and not go bankrupt. This ratio also provides a rough measure of cash flow from operations and cash outflow as interest on debt. This information is important to creditors, since a low or negative ratio suggests that an organization could default on required interest payments. This ratio measures the extent to which operating income can decline before the firm is unable to meet its annual interest costs. The ability to pay current interest is not affected by taxes since interest expense is tax deductible. In other words, the interest expense is paid out of income before taxes are calculated.

- **Fixed charge coverage ratio:** *earnings before interest and taxes plus lease payments divided by interest charges plus lease payments.* Fixed charge coverage ratio is similar to times-interest-earned ratio except that the former ratio includes long-term lease obligations. When a company's ratio is less than the industry average, the company may have difficulty in increasing its debt.

- **Cash flow coverage ratio:** *earnings before interest and taxes plus lease payments plus depreciation divided by interest charges plus lease payments plus preferred stock dividends (before tax) plus debt repayment (before tax).* The cash flow coverage ratio shows the margin by which the firm's operating cash flows cover its financial obligations. This ratio considers principal repayment of debt, dividends on preferred stock, lease payments, and interest charges. The reason for putting the dividends on preferred stock and debt repayment amounts on before the tax basis is due to their nontaxdeductibility, meaning that they are paid out of the income before taxes are paid.

Profitability Ratios

Profitability ratios are the ultimate test of management's effectiveness. They indicate how well an organization operated during a year. They are a culmination of many policies and decisions made by management during the current year as well as previous years. Typically these ratios are calculated using sales or total assets. Profitability ratios show the combined effect of liquidity, asset management, and debt management performance on operating results. Examples include profit margin on sales ratio, basic earning power ratio, return on total assets ratio, return on common equity ratio, earnings per share ratio, and payout ratio.

- **Profit margin on sales ratio:** *net income available to common stockholders divided by sales.* Profit margin on sales ratio indicates the proportion of the sales dollar that remains after deducting expenses. Here, the net income after taxes is divided by sales to give the profit per dollar of sales.

- **Basic earning power ratio:** *earnings before interest and taxes divided by total assets.* Basic earning power ratio shows the raw earning power of the firm's assets before the influence of taxes and impact of the financial leverage. It indicates the ability of the firm's assets to generate operating income. A low "total asset turnover" and low "profit margin on sales" gives a low "basic earning power ratio." **Return on investment (ROI)** may be calculated by multiplying total asset turnover by profit margin.

- **Return on total assets ratio:** *net income available to common stockholders divided by total assets.* Return on total assets (ROA) ratio measures the return on total assets after interest and taxes are paid. The net income used in the equation is the net income after taxes. A low ratio indicates a low "basic earning power ratio" and a high use of debt.

  Another way of looking at the ROA ratio is by breaking it down into subcomponents as shown below: net income divided by net sales (i.e., profit margin on sales) as one component and net sales divided by total average assets (i.e., total asset turnover) as another component. This breakdown helps in pinpointing problems and opportunities for improvement.

- **Return on common equity ratio:** *net income available to common stockholders divided by common equity.* Return on common equity (ROE) measures the rate of return on common stockholders' investments. The net income used in the equation is the net income after taxes, and common equity is the average stockholders' equity. A low ratio compared to the industry indicates high use of debt. This ratio reflects the return earned by an organization on each dollar of owners' equity invested.

- **Earnings per share ratio:** *net income minus current year preferred dividends divided by weighted-average* *number of shares outstanding.* Earnings per share (EPS) ratio is probably the most widely used ratio for evaluating an organization's operating ability. The complexity of the calculation of EPS is determined by a corporation's capital structure.

An organization with no outstanding convertible securities, warrants, or options has a simple capital structure. An organization has a complex structure if it has such items outstanding. The investor should be careful not to concentrate on this number to the exclusion of the organization as a whole. One danger in concentrating on this number is that EPS can easily be increased by purchasing treasury stock that reduces the outstanding shares.

- **Payout ratio:** *cash dividends divided by net income or dividends per share divided by earnings per share.* Payout ratio indicates the ability to meet dividend obligations from net income earned. There is a relationship between the payout ratio and the need for obtaining external capital. The higher the payout ratio, the smaller the addition to retained earnings, and hence, the greater the requirements for external capital. This says that dividend policy affects external capital requirements. If *d* is the dividend payout ratio, $(1 - d)$ is called the earnings retention rate.

Depending on their tax status, certain investors are attracted to the stock of organizations that pay out a large percentage of their earnings, and others are attracted to organizations that retain and reinvest a large percentage of their earnings. Growth organizations typically reinvest a large percentage of their earnings; therefore, they have low payout ratios.

Market Value Ratios

Market value ratios relate the firm's stock price to its earnings and book value per share. It shows the combined effects of liquidity ratios, asset management ratios, debt management ratios, and profitability ratios. The viewpoint is from outside in, that is, from an investors' view about the company's financial performance—past and future. Examples include price/earnings ratio, book value per share, and market/book ratio.

- **Price/earnings ratio:** *price per share divided by earnings per share.* Price/earnings (P/E) ratio shows how much investors are willing to pay per dollar of reported profits. Financial analysts, stock market analysts, and investors in general use this value

to determine whether a stock is overpriced or underpriced. Different analysts have differing views as to the proper P/E ratio for a certain stock or the future earnings prospects of the firm. Several factors such as relative risk, trends in earnings, stability of earnings, and the market's perception of the growth potential of the stock affect the P/E ratio.

- **Book value per share:** *common equity divided by shares outstanding.* Book value per share ratio is used as an intermediate step in calculating the market/book ratio. Book value per share ratio is used in evaluating an organization's net worth and any changes in it from year to year. If an organization were liquidated based on the amounts reported on the balance sheet, the book value per share would indicate the amount that each share of stock would receive. If the asset amounts on the balance sheet do not approximate fair market value, then the ratio loses much of its relevance.

- **Market/book ratio:** *market price per share divided by book value per share.* Market/book ratio reveals how investors think about the company. Market/book ratio is related to ROE ratio in that high ratio of ROE gives high market/book ratio and vice versa. In other words, companies with higher ROE sell their stock at higher multiples of book value. Similarly, companies with high rates of return on their assets can have market values in excess of their book values. A low rate of return on assets gives low market/book value ratio.

Limitations of Financial Statement Ratios

Because ratios are simple to compute, convenient, and precise, they are attractive, and a high degree of importance is attached to them. Since these ratios are only as good as the data on which they are based, the following limitations exist:

- The use of ratio analysis could be limiting for large, multidivisional firms due to their size and complexity—two conditions that mask the results. However, they might be useful to small firms.
- Typically, financial statements are not adjusted for price-level changes. Inflation or deflation can have a large effect on the financial data.
- Since transactions are accounted for on a cost basis, unrealized gains and losses on different asset balances are not reflected in the financial statements.
- Income ratios tend to lose credibility in cases where a significant number of estimated items exist, such as amortization and depreciation.

- Seasonal factors affect and distort ratio analysis, which can be minimized by using average figures in calculations.
- Be aware of "window dressing" and "earnings management" techniques used by firms to make them look financially better than they really are. Management may manipulate financial statements to impress credit analysts and stock market investors (i.e., management fraud).
- Certain off-balance-sheet items do not show up on the financial statements. For example, leased assets do not appear on the balance sheet, and the lease liability may not be shown as a debt. Therefore, leasing can improve both the asset turnover and the debt ratios.
- Attaining comparability among organizations in a given industry is an extremely difficult problem, since different organizations apply different accounting procedures. These different accounting procedures require identification of the basic differences in accounting from organization to organization and adjustment of the balances to achieve comparability.
- Do not take the ratios on their face value since a "good" ratio does not mean that the company is a strong one; nor does a "bad" ratio mean that the company is a weak one. This implies that ratios should be evaluated and interpreted with judgment and experience and considering the firm's characteristics and the industry's uniqueness.

□ Learning Objective 6.7: UNDERSTAND VARIOUS COST CONCEPTS AND COST BEHAVIORS

The scope of cost concepts includes a discussion of absorption and variable costs and other varieties of cost concepts. Cost behavior in terms of how costs change with volume is also presented. An understanding of these cost concepts and cost behavior patterns can help organizations establish an optimum cost structure, consisting of the amounts and proportions of variable costs and fixed costs as part of total costs.

Absorption and Variable Costs

The cost of goods sold, which is larger than all of the other expenses combined in a product cost, can be determined under either the absorption costing or variable costing method.

Under **absorption costing**, all manufacturing costs are included in finished goods and remain there as an inventory asset until the goods are sold. Management could misinterpret increases or decreases in income from operations, due to mere changes in inventory levels to be the result of business events, such as changes in sales volume, prices, or costs. Absorption costing is necessary in determining historical costs for financial reporting to external users and for tax reporting.

Variable costing may be more useful to management in making decisions. In variable costing (direct costing), the cost of goods manufactured is composed only of variable manufacturing costs—costs that increase or decrease as the volume of production rises or falls. These costs are the direct materials, direct labor, and only those factory overhead costs that vary with the rate of production. The remaining factory overhead costs, which are fixed or nonvariable costs, are generally related to the productive capacity of the manufacturing plant and are not affected by changes in the quantity of product manufactured. Thus the fixed factory overhead does not become a part of the cost of goods manufactured but is treated as an expense of the period (period cost) in which it is incurred.

The income from operations under variable costing can differ from the income from operations under absorption costing. This difference results from changes in the quantity of the finished goods inventory, which are caused by differences in the levels of sales and production.

The following decision rules apply:

- If units sold are less than units produced, then variable costing income is less than absorption costing income.
- If units sold are greater then units produced, then variable costing income is greater than the absorption costing income.

Many accountants believe that the variable costing method should be used for evaluating operating performance because absorption costing encourages management to produce inventory. This is because producing inventory absorbs fixed costs and causes income from operations to appear higher. In the long run, building inventory without the promise of future sales may lead to higher costs such as handling, storage, financing, and obsolescence costs.

Management's Use of Absorption and Variable Costing Methods

Management's use of variable costing and absorption costing includes controlling costs, pricing products, planning production, analyzing market segments (sales territory and product profitability analysis), and analyzing contribution margin. Preparing comparative reports under both concepts provides useful insights.

Other Varieties of Cost Concepts

The following list provides a brief description about cost concepts other than absorption or variable costs:

Actual costs. The amounts determined on the basis of cost incurred for making a product or delivering a service to customers.

Average cost. The total cost divided by the activity, that is, number of units.

Budgeted costs. Costs that were predetermined for managerial planning and controlling purposes.

Common costs. Costs of facilities and services shared by several functional departments. These are costs incurred for the benefit of more than one cost objective.

Conversion costs. A combination of direct labor costs, indirect material costs, and factory overhead. Assembly workers' wages in a factory are an example of conversion costs since their time is charged to direct labor.

Current costs. Costs that represent fair market value at current date.

Direct costs. Costs that can be directly identified with or traced to a specific product, service, or activity (e.g., direct labor and direct materials). In a manufacturing operation, direct material costs would include wood in a furniture factory since it is a basic raw material of furniture. Direct labor costs are wages paid to workers. Examples include insurance on the corporate headquarters building since it is not a cost of production, depreciation on salespersons' automobiles, salary of a sales manager, commissions paid to sales personnel, and advertising and rent expenses.

Expired cost. This is the portion of cost that is expensed. An expired cost is a period cost, and it is either an expense or loss.

Fixed costs. Costs that remain constant in total, but change per unit, over a relevant range of production or sales volume (e.g., rent, depreciation). It is a unit cost that decreases with an increase in activity. A fixed cost is constant in total but varies per unit in direct proportion to changes in total activity or volume. It is a cost that remains unchanged in total for a given period despite fluctuations in volume or activity. A fixed cost remains constant in total for a given period despite variations in activity as long as the production is within the relevant range. A fixed cost may change in total between different periods or when production is outside the relevant range. Therefore, unit fixed cost decreases as output increases at a given relevant range.

Full costs. A combination of direct costs and a fair share of the indirect costs for a cost objective. Full costs refer to a unit of finished product. They consist of prime costs and overhead. It is the entire sacrifice related to a cost objective.

Historical costs. Costs that were incurred at the time of occurrence of a business transaction. They represent what costs were.

Indirect costs. Costs that cannot be identified with or traced to a specific product, activity, or department (e.g., salaries, taxes, utilities, machine repairs). An example is a factory manager's salary. Another term for indirect costs is **factory overhead.** It consists of all costs other than direct labor and direct materials associated with the manufacturing process.

Joint costs. Costs of manufactured goods of relatively significant sales values that are simultaneously produced by a process.

Long-run costs. Costs that vary as plant capacity changes over a long period of time.

Marginal cost. The cost to make an additional unit or the last unit. It is the incremental or variable costs of producing an additional or extra unit.

Mixed costs. Costs that fluctuate with volume, but not in direct proportion to production or sales. Mixed costs (semivariable or semifixed costs) have elements of both fixed and variable costs (e.g., supervision and inspection). A salesperson's compensation is an example of mixed costs since salary is fixed and commissions are variable.

Period costs. Costs that can be associated with the passage of time, not the production of goods. Period costs are always expensed to the same period in which they are incurred, not to a particular product. Period costs are not identifiable with a product and are not inventoried. Only product costs are included in manufacturing overhead. Period costs are those costs deducted as expenses during the current period without having been previously classified as costs of inventory.

Prime costs. A combination of direct labor and direct material costs. Overhead is not a part of it. Prime costs refer to a unit of finished product. They can be identified with and physically traceable to a cost objective.

Product costs. Costs that can be associated with production of certain goods or services. Product costs are those that are properly assigned to inventory when incurred. Inventoriable costs are those costs incurred to produce the inventory and stay with the inventory as an asset until they are sold. Product costs are expensed (as cost of goods sold) in the period the product is sold. Examples include property taxes on a factory in a manufacturing company, direct materials, direct labor, and factory overhead. Product costs include direct labor, direct material, and plant manufacturing overhead.

Short-run costs. Costs that vary as output varies for a short period or for a given production capacity.

Standard costs. Predetermined or engineered costs that should be attained under normal conditions of operations. They represent what costs should be.

Step cost. A step cost is constant over small ranges of volume (output) but increases in discrete steps as volume increases. A supervisor of the second shift is an example of a step cost. If the range of the step cost is narrow, it is equal to variable cost. If the range of the step cost is wide, then it is equal to fixed cost.

Sunk cost. A past cost that has already been incurred (e.g., installed factory machinery and equipment) or committed to be incurred. It is not relevant to most future costs and decisions since it cannot be changed by any decision made now or in the future. It is irreversible. It cannot be affected by the choices made.

Unexpired cost. The portion of cost that remains as assets and continues to generate future benefits.

Variable costs. Costs that fluctuate in total, but remain constant per unit, as the volume of production or sales changes. A variable cost is constant per unit produced but varies in total in direct proportion to changes in total activity or volume. The cost of cable fabricator wages should be considered variable because they change in total in direct proportion to the number of similar cables fabricated. General and administrative and other indirect costs can be either fixed or variable. In general, variable costs vary directly with volume or activity. For example, if indirect materials vary directly with volume, then indirect materials can be classified as variable costs.

Avoidable costs. Costs that will not be incurred or costs that may be saved if an ongoing activity is discontinued, changed, or deleted, such as in a make-or-buy decision. These costs are relevant costs.

Unavoidable costs. Opposite of avoidable costs—costs that are irrelevant; they are sunk costs.

Controllable costs. Costs that can be definitely influenced by a given manager within a given time span. Examples include office supplies purchased by an office manager. In the long run, all costs are controllable. In the short run, costs are controllable too, but they are controlled at different management levels. The higher the management level, the greater the possibility of control.

Noncontrollable costs. Opposite of the controllable costs—costs that are unaffected by a manager's decision (e.g., plant rent expense by a plant foreman).

Out-of-pocket costs. Costs that require the consumption of current economic resources (e.g., taxes, insurance). It is the current or near-future expenditure that will require a cash outlay to execute a decision.

Embodied cost. It measures sacrifices in terms of their origins, reflecting what was originally given up to acquire and convert the object being costed.

Displaced costs. These measure sacrifices in terms of their ultimate effects upon the group making the sacrifice, reflecting the opportunity lost by, or the adverse consequences resulting from, the sacrifice in question. They are also called **opportunity costs.**

Discretionary costs. Costs that arise from periodic budgeting decisions and which have no strong input/output relationship.

Opportunity cost. The maximum net benefit that is forgone by the choice of one course of action over another course of action. It is the economic sacrifice attributable to a given decision. It is the loss associated with choosing the alternative that does not maximize the benefit.

Incremental costs. The increase in total sacrifice identifiable with the specific object, or group of objects, being costed, recognizing that fixed and otherwise joint sacrifices may be increased little, if at all, because of what was done to or for the specific object being costed. These are also called **differential costs.**

Differential costs. The difference in total costs between alternatives.

Replacement cost. The cost that would have to be incurred to replace an asset.

Implicit costs. Implicit costs are imputed costs and used in the analysis of opportunity costs.

Imputed costs. Costs that can be associated with an economic event when no exchange transaction has occurred (e.g., the rent for a building when a company "rents to itself" a building).

Committed costs. Two types: (1) manageable and (2) unmanageable. **Manageable committed costs** are sacrifices influenced to an important degree by managers' decisions and actions, but these influences have already had most of their effect, setting in motion the chain of events that largely determine the sacrifice in question. Most fixed costs are committed costs. **Unmanageable committed costs** are sacrifices largely influenced by factors or forces outside managers' control and already set in motion to such an extent that influences have had most of their effect.

Uncommitted costs. Two types: (1) manageable and (2) unmanageable. **Manageable uncommitted costs** are sacrifices influenced to an important degree by managers' decisions and actions with plenty of time for these influences to have their effect. **Unmanageable uncommitted costs** are sacrifices largely influenced by factors or forces outside managers' control with plenty of time for these influences to have their effect.

Rework costs. Costs incurred to turn an unacceptable product into an acceptable product and sell it as a normal finished good.

Engineered costs. Costs resulting from a measured relationship between inputs and outputs.

Cost Behavior

Costs have a behavior pattern. For example, costs vary with volumes of production, sales, or service levels, with the application of the amount of resources, and with the timeframe used. Knowing the cost-behavior information helps in developing budgets, interpreting variances from standards, and making critical decisions. The manager who can predict costs and their behavior is a step ahead in planning, budgeting, controlling, product pricing, nonroutine decisions (i.e., make-or-buy, keep or drop), and separating cost into its components (i.e., fixed, variable, and mixed costs). In order to make more accurate cost predictions, the manager needs superior cost estimates at his disposal.

Techniques to separate costs into variable and fixed components include statistics using regression analysis, scatter graphs, and least squares methods; the high-low method; spreadsheet analysis; sensitivity analysis; and managerial judgment.

Approaches to estimate costs include the following:

1. The **industrial engineering method** analyzes relationships between inputs and outputs in physical terms.
2. The **conference method** incorporates analysis and opinions gathered from various departments of the firm.
3. The **account analysis method** classifies cost accounts in the ledger as variable, fixed, or mixed costs.
4. **Quantitative analysis method** uses time-series data based on past cost relationships and regression analysis.

The first three methods require less historical data than do most quantitative analyses. Therefore, cost estimations for a new product will begin with one or more of the first three methods. Quantitative analysis may be adopted later, after experience is gained. These cost estimation approaches, which are not mutually exclusive, differ in the cost of conducting the analysis, the assumptions they make, and the evidence they yield about the accuracy of the estimated cost function.

❑ Learning Objective 6.8: UNDERSTAND THE PRINCIPLES AND TECHNIQUES OF OPERATING BUDGETS

A budgeting system includes both expected results and historical or actual results. A budgeting system builds on historical, or actual, results and expands to include consideration of future, or expected, results. A budgeting system guides the manager into the future:

Budget System → Forward Looking
Historical Cost System → Backward Looking

A budget is a quantitative expression of a plan of action. It will aid in the coordination of various activities or functions throughout the organization. The master budget by definition summarizes the objectives of all subunits of an organization. The master budget helps in coordinating activities, implementing plans, authorizing actions, and evaluating performance.

The master budget captures the financial impact of all the firm's other budgets and plans. Although the master budget itself is not a strategic plan, it helps managers to implement the strategic plans. The master budget focuses on both operating decisions and financing decisions. Operating decisions concentrate on the acquisition and use of scarce resources.

Financing decisions center on how to get the funds to acquire resources.

Benefits of Operating Budgets

The following are benefits to be derived from budgets:

- Budgets are planning tools. Budgets force managers to look into the future and make them prepare to meet uncertainties and changing business conditions.
- Budgets provide a starting point for discussing business strategies. In turn, these strategies direct long-term and short-term planning. Therefore, strategic plans and budgets are interrelated and affect one another.
- Budgeted performance is better than historical data for judging or evaluating employee performance. This is because employees know what is expected of their performance. A major drawback of using historical data is that inefficiencies and bad decisions may be buried in past actions.
- Budgets can be a valuable vehicle for communication with interested parties. Budgets help coordinate activities of various functions within the organization to achieve overall goals and objectives.
- Budgets are control systems. Budgets help to control waste of resources and to search out weaknesses in the organizational structure.
- A budget should be implemented so as to gain acceptance by employees. This requires buy-in by employees, senior management support, and lower-level management involvement.
- A budget should be set tight, but attainable and flexible. A budget should be thought of as a means to an end, not the end in itself.
- A budget should not prevent a manager from taking prudent action. Nonetheless, he should not disregard the budget entirely.

Different Dimensions in Operating Budgets

The time period for budgets varies from one year to five or more years. The common budget period is one year and broken down by quarters and months. Four types of budgets emerge from the time-coverage-and-update point of view:

1. **Short-term budgets** (operating budgets) have a timeframe of one to two years.
2. **Long-term budgets** (strategic budgets) have a timeframe of three to five or more years.
3. **Static budgets** are the original budgeted numbers, which are not changed. The timeframe does not change.
4. **Continuous budgets** are also called **rolling budgets,** where a 12-month forecast is always available by adding a month in the future as the month just ended is dropped. The timeframe keeps changing in the continuous budgets.

Budgets should be viewed positively, not negatively. Although budget preparation is mechanical, its administration and interpretation require patience, education, and people skills. Budgets are a positive device designed to help managers choose and accomplish objectives. However, budgets are not a substitute for bad management or poor accounting system.

How Operating Budgets are Prepared

The **master budget** (static budget) is developed after the goals, strategies, and long-range plans of the organization have been determined. It summarizes the goals of the subunits or segments of an organization. This information summarizes, in a financial form, expectations regarding future income, cash flows, financial position, and supporting plans. The functions of the master budget include planning, coordinating activities, communicating, evaluating performance, implementing plans, motivating, and authorizing actions. It contains the operating budget.

A detailed budget is prepared for the coming fiscal year along with some less-detailed amounts for the following years. Budgets may be developed with the **top-down** or the **bottom-up approach**. With the top-down approach, upper management determines what it expects from subordinate managers. Subordinate managers may then negotiate with upper management concerning the items they feel are unreasonable. With the bottom-up approach, lower-level managers propose what they expect to accomplish and the required resources. Upper management then makes suggestions and revisions. Budgets may be used for long-range planning, but the typical planning-and-control budget period is one year. This annual budget may be broken down into months or quarters and continuously updated.

The following are various types of budgets:

- **Budgeted balance sheet.** This budget reflects the expected balance sheet at the end of the budget period. The budgeted balance sheet is determined by combining the estimate of the balance sheet at the beginning of the budget period with the estimated results of operations for the period obtained from the budgeted income statements and estimating changes in assets and liabilities. These changes in assets and liabilities result from management's decisions regarding capital investment in long-term assets, investment in working capital, and financing decisions.
- **Budgeted income statement or operating budget.** This budget reflects the income expected for the budget period.
- **Budgets for other expenses.** These budgets may be broken down according to expense category depending on the relative importance of the types of expenses (i.e., selling, administrative, research and development, etc.).
- **Cash budget.** The cash budget summarizes cash receipts and disbursements and indicates financing requirements. This budget is important in assuring an organization's solvency, maximizing returns from cash balances, and determining whether the organization is generating enough cash for current and future operations.
- **Cash disbursements budget.** This budget is dependent on the pattern of payments for expenses. Cash disbursements do not typically match costs in a period, since expenses are typically paid later than they are incurred.
- **Cash receipts budget.** The collection of sales depends on an organization's credit policies and its customer base. Most organizations must obtain cash to pay current bills while waiting for payment from customers. This cash represents an opportunity cost to the organization.
- **Labor budget.** This budget may be broken down by type of worker required in hours or number of workers.

- **Production cost budget.** This budget may be broken down by product or plant.
- **Production budget.** This budget may be broken down by product or plant. Production must meet current sales demand and maintain sufficient inventory levels for expected activity levels during the budget period and on into the next period. This budget is reviewed with production managers to determine if the budget is realistic. If the budget is not attainable, management may revise the sales forecast or try to increase capacity. If production capacity will exceed requirements, other uses of the idle capacity may be considered.
- **Purchases budget.** This budget is typically broken down by raw materials and parts. An organization's inventory policy determines its level of purchases.
- **Sales budget.** This budget may be broken down by product, territory, plant, or other segment of interest.

Operating Budgeting Techniques

Budgets are a necessary component of financial decision making because they help provide an efficient allocation of resources. A budget is a profit planning and a resource-controlling tool. It is a quantitative expression of management's intentions and plans for the coming year(s) to meet their goals and objectives within resource constraints. Budgets are prepared at the beginning of each year. Departmental or functional budgets are summarized and compared with revenue forecasts and revised as necessary.

Five budgeting techniques are available:

1. Incremental budgeting (adds a percentage or fixed amount to the previous budget)
2. Flexible budgeting (reflects variation in activity levels)
3. Zero-based budgeting (uses "decision packages" to specify objectives and workloads)
4. Program planning budgeting (presents budget choices more explicitly in terms of objectives)
5. Performance budgeting (links performance levels with specific budget amounts)

Incremental budgeting is a traditional approach to budgeting focusing on incremental changes in detailed categories of revenues and expenses, called **line items,** to represent sales, salaries, travel, supplies, and so forth. The incremental approach to budgeting does not take variation in volume or change in activity levels into account. It operates on the principle of management by exception.

Flexible budgeting (variable or dynamic budgeting) is a budget that is adjusted for changes in the unit level of the cost or revenue. It is also called a **variable budget.** The flexible budget is based on the knowledge of how revenues and costs should behave over a range of activity. Thus, it is appropriate for any relevant level of activity. The master budget is not adjusted after it is developed, regardless of changes in volume, cost, or other conditions during the budget period.

Zero-based budgeting, especially in the public sector, attempts to analyze the incremental change in a program's output at different levels of funding. For each program, a "decision package" would specify objectives and measures of efficiency, effectiveness, and workload for alternative levels of funding.

Planning, programming, and budgeting systems (PPBSs) attempt to further advance budgeting techniques, especially in the public sector, by presenting budget choices more explicit in terms of public objectives. With PPBS budgets, the cost and effectiveness of programs would be evaluated in a multi-year framework and alternative approaches would be considered.

Performance budgeting, again focusing on the public sector, links performance measures directly to agency missions and program objectives. Under the performance budgeting model, budgets would be developed based on unit costs and service expectations followed by analysis of actual work performed compared with budget estimates.

Advantages of Operating Budgets

Budgets are commonly used in both large and small organizations. No matter what the size of the organization, typically the benefits of budgeting exceed the costs. The advantages of budgets are that they:

- *Compel planning.* Management must have targets, and budgets reflect expected performance. Budgets affect strategies that are the relatively general and permanent plans of an organization that change as conditions and/or objectives change. Budgets can give direction to operations, point out problems, and give meaning to results.
- *Provide performance criteria.* The budget allows employees to know what is expected of them. Comparing actual results to budgeted amounts instead

of past performance provides more useful information. Comparison with past performance may be hampered by past inefficiencies or changes in technology, personnel, products, or general economic conditions.

- *Promote communication and coordination.* Coordination deals with the interests of the organization as a whole, meshing and balancing the factors of production and other departments and functions so that objectives can be achieved. Budgets aid coordination because they require well-laid plans and isolate any problems.

Limitations of Operating Budgeting Techniques

The following are peculiarities and limitations of budgets:

- Be aware that budgeted items are a mixture of fixed and variable cost components. Accordingly, mixed costs cannot be used for linear projection.
- Be aware that budgeted items include some direct costs and some allocated costs. Direct costs are more useful for decision making than allocated costs. Responsibility accounting favors direct and controllable costs, not allocated and uncontrollable costs.
- The nature of volume levels needs to be understood. Most budgets are based on a single level of volume (point estimates, whereas multiple volume levels (range estimates) would be better for decision making.
- The kinds of assumptions made during the budget development process need to be known. Understand the budget preparer's state of mind: optimistic, most likely, or pessimistic outcomes. Each of these outcomes would bring a different type of realism to the budget numbers.
- The variances from budgets need to be analyzed very carefully. Performance reports show the variations between the actual and the budgets—an element of control. Corrective action requires determination of underlying causes of variation. Variances could be favorable or unfavorable.

❑ Learning Objective 6.9: UNDERSTAND THE APPLICATION OF TRANSFER PRICING

Transfer pricing involves inter- or intracompany transfers, whether domestic or international. A transfer price is the price one unit of a corporation charges for a product or service supplied to another unit of the same corporation. The units involved could be either domestic or international, and the products involved could be intermediate products or semifinished goods.

The following are reasons for establishing transfer pricing in either domestic or international operations:

- Performance evaluation of decentralized operations
- Overall minimization of taxes to a corporation
- Minimization of custom duties and tariffs
- Minimization of risks associated with movements in foreign currency exchange rates
- Circumventing restrictions on profit remittance to the corporate headquarters
- Motivation of business unit managers

Methods for Determining Transfer Prices

Three methods are available for determining transfer prices: market based, cost based, and negotiation based. The choice of transfer pricing method affects the operating income of individual units.

1. **Market-based transfer prices.** The price appearing in a trade journal or other independent (outside) sources establishes the transfer price of a product or service. Difficulty in obtaining market price forces corporations to resort to cost-based transfer prices. This method is widespread in use.
2. **Cost-based transfer prices.** The costs used could be either actual costs or standard costs and include variable manufacturing costs or absorption (full) costs. Use of full cost-based prices leads to suboptimal decisions in the short run for the company as a whole. This method is also widespread in use. Standard costs are used more widely than actual costs to motivate the seller to produce efficiently. If transfer prices are based on actual costs, sellers can pass along costs of inefficiency to the buyers.
3. **Negotiation-based transfer prices.** These are the negotiated prices between units of a corporation and may not have any relation to either market or cost data. Unit autonomy is preserved. Drawbacks include time-consuming and drawn-out negotiations, which may not lead to goal congruence. Weak bargaining units may lose out to the strong.

Criteria Affecting Transfer Pricing Methods

The criteria of goal congruence, managerial effort, and unit autonomy affect the choice of transfer-pricing methods.

Goal congruence exists when individual goals, group goals, and senior management goals coincide. Under these conditions, each unit manager acts in his own best interest, and the resulting decision is in the long-term best interest of the company as a whole. A transfer price method should lead to goal congruence.

A sustained high level of **managerial effort** can lead to achievement of goals. A transfer price method promotes management effort if sellers are motivated to hold down costs and buyers are motivated to use the purchased inputs efficiently.

Senior management should allow a high level of **unit autonomy** in decision making in a decentralized organization. This means that a transfer price method should preserve autonomy if unit managers are free to make their own decisions and are not forced to buy or sell products at a price that is unacceptable to them.

Dual pricing uses two separate transfer-pricing methods to price each inter-unit transaction. This is because seldom does a single transfer price meet the criteria of goal congruence, managerial effort, and unit autonomy. An example of dual pricing is when the selling unit receives a full-cost-plus-markup-based price and the buying unit pays the market price for the internally transferred products.

The dual pricing method reduces the goal-congruence problems associated with a pure cost-plus-based transfer-pricing method. Some of the drawbacks of dual pricing include:

- The manager of the supplying unit may not have sufficient incentives to control costs.
- It does not provide clear signals to unit managers about the level of decentralization senior managers are seeking.
- It tends to insulate managers from the frictions of the marketplace, that is, knowledge of units' buying and selling market forces.

International Transfer Pricing

The multinational corporation (MNC) must deal with transfer pricing and international taxation, and, therefore, a knowledge of international laws related to these areas is important. A transfer is a substitute for a market price and is recorded by the seller as revenue and by the buyer as cost of goods sold. The transfer-pricing system should motivate unit managers not to make undesirable decisions at the expense of the corporation as a whole. The ideal manager would act in the best interests of the company as a whole, even at the expense of the reported profits of his own unit. For this to happen, the manager must be rewarded when he chooses companywide goal congruence over his unit performance.

❑ Learning Objective 6.10: UNDERSTAND THE APPLICATION OF COST-VOLUME-PROFIT ANALYSIS

Cost-volume-profit (CVP) analysis helps managers who are making decisions about short-term duration and for specific cases where revenue and cost behaviors are linear and where volume is assumed to be the only cost and revenue driver. CVP is an approximation tool and a low-cost tool.

CVP analysis is a straightforward, simple-to-apply, widely used management tool. CVP analysis answers questions such as, How will costs and revenues be affected if sales units are up or down by x percent? What if price is decreased or increased by x percent? A decision model can be built using CVP relationships for choosing among courses of action. *CVP analysis tells management what will happen to financial results if a specific level of production or sales volume fluctuates or if costs change.*

An example of a decision model is the **breakeven point (BEP),** which shows the interrelationships of changes in costs, volume, and profits. It is the point of volume where total revenues and total costs are equal. No profit is gained or loss incurred at the BEP.

Three methods available for calculating the BEP include equation method, contribution margin (CM) method, and graphic method. An increase in the BEP is a red flag for management to analyze all its CVP relationships more closely.

Equation Method

The **equation method** is more general and thus is easier to apply with multiple products, with multiple costs and revenue drivers, and with changes in the cost structure. At breakeven point, the operating income is zero. The formula is:

(Unit Sales Price × Number of Units) − (Unit Variable Cost × Number of Units) − Fixed Costs = Operating Income

or

$$\text{Sales} - \text{Variable Costs} - \text{Fixed Costs} = \text{Operating Income}$$

CM Method

Contribution-margin (CM) is equal to sales minus all variable costs. BEP is calculated as follows:

$$\text{BEP} = \text{Fixed Costs}/\text{Unit Contribution Margin}$$

A desired target operating income can be added to the fixed costs to give a new BEP that tells how many units must be sold to generate enough CM to cover total fixed costs plus target operating income.

The BEP tells how many units of product must be sold to generate enough contribution margin to cover total fixed costs. The CM method is valid only for a single product and a single cost driver. The CM method is a restatement of the equation method in a different form. Either method can be used to calculate the BEP.

Graphic Method

A **CVP chart** results when units are plotted on the x-axis and dollars on the y-axis. The breakeven point is where the total-sales line and total-cost line intersect. The total sales line begins at the origin because if volume is zero, sales revenue will be zero too.

CVP Assumptions and Their Limitations

CVP relationships hold true for only a limited range of production or sales volume levels. This means that these relationships would not hold if volume fell below or rose above a certain level.

The following are assumptions:

- The behavior of total revenues and total costs is linear over the relevant range of volume.
- Selling prices, total fixed costs, efficiency, and productivity are constant.
- All costs can be divided neatly into fixed and variable components. Variable cost per unit remains constant.
- A greater sales mix will be maintained as total volume changes.
- Volume is the only driver of costs.
- The production volume equals sales volume, or changes in beginning and ending inventory levels are zero.

There are many limitations to these CVP assumptions. Volume is only one of the factors affecting cost behavior. Other factors include unit prices of inputs, efficiency, changes in production technology, civil wars, employee strikes, laws, and regulations. *Profits are affected by changes in factors besides volume.* A CVP chart must be analyzed together with all assumptions and their limitations.

Ways to Lower the Breakeven Point

The following strategies should help in lowering the BEP, which means fewer units need to be sold, which in turn contributes more to profits (the strategies are not order ranked):

- Reducing the overall fixed costs
- Increasing the CM per unit of product through increase in sales prices
- Increasing the CM per unit of product through decreases in unit variable costs
- Increasing the CM per unit through increase in sales prices and decreasing unit variable costs together
- Selecting a hiring freeze for new employees
- Limiting merit increase for senior executives
- Cutting the annual percentage salary rate increase for all salaried employees
- Reducing overtime pay for all employees to reduce labor costs
- Reducing the number of employees on payroll
- Improving employee productivity levels
- Increasing machine utilization rates

Sensitivity Analysis in CVP

A CVP model developed in a dynamic environment determined that the estimated parameters used may vary between limits. Subsequent testing of the model with respect to all possible values of the estimated parameters is termed a **sensitivity analysis.**

Sensitivity analysis is a management tool that will answer questions such as, What will operating income be if volume changes from the original prediction? What will operating income be if variable costs per unit decrease or increase by x percent? If sales drop, how far can they fall below budget before the BEP is reached? This last question can be answered by the margin-of-safety tool. The **margin of safety** is a tool of sensitivity analysis and is the excess of budgeted sales over the breakeven volume.

Sensitivity analysis is a **what-if technique** aimed at asking how a result will be changed if the original predicted data are not achieved or if an underlying assumption changes. It is a measure of changes in outputs resulting from changes in inputs. It reveals the impact of changes in one or more input variables on the output or results.

Changes in Variable and Fixed Costs

Organizations often face a trade-off between fixed and variable costs. Fixed costs can be substituted for variable costs and vice versa. This is because variable costs and fixed costs are subject to various degrees of control at different volumes—boom or slack. For example, when a firm invests in automated machinery to offset increase in labor rates, its fixed costs increase, but unit variable costs decrease.

Contribution Margin and Gross Margin

Contribution margin (CM) is the excess of sales over all variable costs, including variable manufacturing, marketing, and administrative categories. **Gross margin (GM),** also called **gross profit,** is the excess of sales over the cost of the goods sold. Both CM and GM would be different for a manufacturing company. They will be equal only when fixed manufacturing costs included in cost of goods sold are the same as the variable nonmanufacturing costs, which is a highly unlikely event.

CM versus GM

- Variable manufacturing, marketing, and administrative costs are subtracted from sales to get CM, but not GM.
- Fixed manufacturing overhead is subtracted from sales to get GM, but not CM.
- Both the CM and GM can be expressed as totals, as an amount per unit, or as percentages of sales in the form of ratios.

Profit-Volume Chart

The **profit-volume (PV) chart** is preferable to the CVP chart because it is simpler to understand. The PV chart shows a quick, condensed comparison of how alternatives on pricing, variable costs, or fixed costs affect operating income as volume changes. The operating income is drawn on the y-axis and the x-axis represents volume (units or dollars).

Due to operating leverage, profits increase during high volume because more of the costs are fixed and do not increase with volume. Profits decrease during low volume because fixed costs cannot be avoided despite the lower volume.

Effect of Sales Mix on BEP

Sales mix is the relative combination of quantities of products that constitute total sales. A change in sales mix will cause actual profits to differ from budgeted profits. It is the combination of low-margin or high-margin products that causes the shift in profits, despite achievement of targeted sales volume.

There will be a different BEP for each different sales mix. A higher proportion of sales in high contribution margin products will reduce the BEP. A lower proportion of sales in small contribution margin products will increase the BEP. Shifting marketing efforts to high contribution margin products can increase the operating income and profits.

Management is interested in the effect of various production and sales strategies on the operating income, not so much on BEP. Both the operating income and BEP are dependent on the assumptions made (i.e., if the assumptions change, the operating income and the BEP will also change).

❑ Learning Objective 6.11: UNDERSTAND THE MEANING AND APPLICATION OF RELEVANT COSTS

The relevant revenues and costs focus on the difference between each alternative. Managers must consider the effects of alternative decisions on their businesses. We discuss differential analysis, which reports the effects of alternative decisions on total revenues and costs. Planning for future operations involves decision making. For some decisions, revenue and cost data from the accounting records may be useful. However, the revenue and cost data for use in evaluating courses of future operations or choosing among competing alternatives are often not available in the accounting records and must be estimated. These estimates include relevant revenues and costs. The relevant revenues and costs focus on the differences between each alternative. Costs that have been incurred in the past are not relevant to the decision. These costs are called **sunk costs.**

Differential revenue is the amount of increase or decrease in revenue expected from a course of action as compared with an alternative. To illustrate, assume that certain equipment is being used to manufacture calculators, which are expected to generate revenue of $150,000. If the equipment could be used to make digital clocks, which would generate revenue of $175,000, the differential revenue from making and selling digital clocks is $25,000.

Differential cost is the amount of increase or decrease in cost that is expected from a course of action as compared with an alternative. For example, if an increase in advertising expenditures from $100,000 to $150,000 is being considered, the differential cost of the action is $50,000.

Differential income or loss is the difference between the differential revenue and the differential costs. Differential income indicates that a particular decision is expected to be profitable, while a differential loss indicates the opposite.

Differential analysis focuses on the effect of alternative courses of action on the relevant revenues and costs. For example, if a manager must decide between two alternatives, differential analysis would involve comparing the differential revenues of the two alternatives with the differential costs.

Differential analysis can be used in analyzing the following alternatives:

- Leasing or selling equipment
- Discontinuing an unprofitable segment
- Manufacturing or purchasing a needed part (make-or-buy analysis)
- Replacing usable fixed assets
- Processing further or selling an intermediate product
- Accepting additional business at a special price

Application of Relevant Cost Concept

When deciding whether to accept a special order from a customer, the best thing to do is to compare the total revenue to be derived from this order with the total relevant costs incurred for this order. The key terms are incremental relevant costs and incremental relevant revenues. The relevant costs are those that vary with the decision.

The long-term fixed costs should be excluded from the analysis since they will be incurred regardless of whether the order is accepted. Direct labor, direct materials, variable manufacturing overhead, and variable selling and administrative costs are relevant because they will not be incurred if the special order is not accepted. Incremental fixed costs would be relevant in short-term decision making under certain situations.

❏ Learning Objective 6.12: UNDERSTAND VARIOUS COSTING SYSTEMS FOR PRODUCTS AND SERVICES

One of the goals of cost accounting is to provide information for management planning and control and determination of product or service costs. This is achieved through the accumulation of costs by department and/or by product. Although the terminology differs between manufacturing and service industries, the principles of cost accounting are the same.

Product cost control systems can be viewed in terms of target costing and traditional costing a product.

Target Costing

Target costing is a new way of controlling a product's cost. A target cost is the allowable amount of cost that can be incurred on a given product and still earn the required profit margin. It is a market-driven cost in which cost targets are set by considering customer requirements and competitive environment. Cost targets are achieved by focusing and improving both process design and product design. Market research indicates the target price customers are willing to pay:

$$\text{Target Price} - \text{Profit Margin} = \text{Target Cost}$$

The need for target costing arises due to sophisticated customers demanding better-quality products with more features and functions at an affordable price. This is made real by aggressive competitors who are willing to take risks and provide a product at target price with the hope of achieving efficiencies in cost management and production operations.

Target costing is not exactly the same as **design to cost** or **design for manufacturability,** which are issues for engineering and manufacturing management respectively. Target costing integrates strategic business planning with cost/profit planning. To achieve this integration, a target-costing system requires cross-functional teams to take ownership and responsibility for costs. These teams consist of representatives from finance/accounting, marketing, engineering, manufacturing, and other functions.

Traditional Costing

Traditional costing systems use a cost-plus approach, where production costs are first estimated, then a profit margin is added to it to obtain a product price that the market is going to pay for it. If the price is too high, cost reductions are initiated. It is a cost-driven approach where customer requirements and competitive environment are not considered:

$$\text{Traditional Production Cost} + \text{Profit Margin}$$
$$= \text{Traditional Product Price}$$

The cost to manufacture a product is necessary for external reporting (e.g., inventory valuation and cost of goods sold determination) and internal management decisions (e.g., price determination, product mix decisions, and sensitivity analysis).

Two methods to **accumulate product costs** include job order costing system and process (operations) costing system. Both methods help management in planning and control of business operations. A **job order cost system** provides a separate record for the cost of each quantity of product that passes through the factory. A job order cost system is best suited to industries that manufacture custom goods to fill special orders from customers or that produce a high variety of products for stock (job shops). Under a **process cost system,** costs are accumulated for each of the departments or processes within the factory. A process cost system is best suited for manufacturers of units of products that are not distinguishable from each other during a continuous production process (e.g., oil refineries and food processing).

Activity-Based Costing

Activity-based costing (ABC) is a management system that focuses on activities as the fundamental cost objects and uses the costs of these activities as building blocks for compiling the costs of other cost objects. ABC helps management in controlling costs through its focus on cost drivers. ABC can provide more accurate product cost data by using multiple cost drivers that more accurately reflect the causes of costs. Inaccurate product cost information can lead to cross-subsidization of products. This results in systematic undercosting of products due to lower overhead rate. These cost drivers can be non-volume-based as well as volume-based drivers.

Standard Costing

Standard costs are predetermined costs or estimated costs requiring a startup investment to develop them. Ongoing costs for maintenance of standards can be lower than for an actual-cost system. Standard costs should be attainable and are expressed on a per-unit basis. Without standard costs, there is no flexible budgeting system since the latter is developed at different volumes of production using standard costs per unit.

Standard costs, flexible budgets, and standards are equally applicable to manufacturing and nonmanufacturing firms. Standard costs and flexible budgets are interrelated. A **flexible budget** is a budget that is adjusted for changes in the unit level of the cost driver or revenue driver. In a standard cost system, the concept of flexible budget is key to the analysis of variances.

A powerful benefit of standard costing is its feedback mechanism, where actual costs are compared with standard costs, resulting in variances. This feedback helps explore better ways of adhering to standards, of modifying standards, and of accomplishing production goals. Standard costs can be developed for material, labor, and overhead. One drawback of a standard cost system is that actual direct material costs and actual direct labor costs cannot be traced to individual products.

Types of standards include perfection (ideal or theoretical) standards and currently attainable standards. Types of variances include price, efficiency, direct materials, direct labor, and overhead variances.

❑ Learning Objective 6.13: UNDERSTAND THE MEANING AND APPLICATION OF RESPONSIBILITY ACCOUNTING

Managers are responsible and accountable for their decisions and actions in planning and controlling the resources of the organization. Resources include physical, human, and financial resources. Resources are used to achieve the organization's goals and objectives. Budgets help to quantify the resources required to achieve goals.

The concept of responsibility accounting emerged since a few senior managers at the top cannot run all parts of a business effectively. To improve performance, the organization is divided into centers, product lines, divisions, and units so that a lower-level manager is responsible for a specific center, product line, division, or unit.

Each manager is in charge of a responsibility center and is accountable for a specified set of activities and operations within a segment of the organization. The degree of responsibility varies directly with the level of the manager. Responsibility accounting is a system that measures the plans and actions of each responsibility center. Four types of responsibility centers include cost, revenue, profit, and investment center.

In a **cost center,** a manager is accountable for costs only (e.g., a manufacturing plant). In a **revenue center,** a manager is accountable for revenues only (e.g., a product manager or brand manager). In a **profit center,** a manager is accountable for revenues and costs (e.g., a division). In an **investment center,** a manager is accountable for investment (e.g., a division's revenues and costs).

A major advantage of the responsibility accounting approach is that costs can be traced to either the individual who has the best knowledge about the reasons for cost increase or the activity that caused the cost increase. A major disadvantage is its behavioral implications for managers whose performance is to be evaluated.

A manager should be held accountable for the costs that he has control over. Controllability is the degree of influence that a specific manager has over costs, revenues, and investment. A controllable cost is any cost that is subject to the influence of a given manager of a given responsibility center for a given time span. Controllable costs should be separated from uncontrollable costs in a manager's performance report.

In responsibility accounting, feedback is crucial. When budgets are compared with actual results, variances occur. The key is to use variance information to raise questions and seek answers from the right party. Variance information should not be abused—in other words, it should not be used to fix the blame on others. *Variances invoke questions as to why and how, not who.*

 Self-Assessment Exercise

Online exercises are provided for the learning objectives in this module. Please visit www.mbaiq.com to complete the online exercises and to calculate your MBA IQ Score.

Finance

Learning Objective 7.1: Understand the Need for Financial Plans and Controls — **154**
Financial Plans — 154
Cash Budget — 154
Financial Control — 156

Learning Objective 7.2: Understand the Principles and Techniques of Cash Management — **157**
Cash Presentation — 157
Cash Items Excluded — 157
Controls Over Cash — 157
Management of Cash — 158
Advantages of Holding Adequate Cash and Near-Cash Assets — 158
Cash Management Efficiency Techniques — 159

Learning Objective 7.3: Understand the Techniques of Managing Current Assets — **160**
Cash Conversion Cycle Model — 160
Approaches to Shorten the Cash Conversion Cycle — 161
Working Capital Asset Investment Policies — 161
Working Capital Financing Policies — 161
Management of Marketable Securities — 161
Criteria for Selecting Marketable Securities — 162
Risks in Marketable Securities — 162

Learning Objective 7.4: Understand the Various Types of Debt and Equity in a Capital Structure — **163**
Types of Debt — 163
Short-Term Debt — 163
Use of Security in Short-Term Financing — 165
Long-Term Debt — 165
Factors Influencing Long-Term Financing Decisions — 167
Types of Equity — 167

Learning Objective 7.5: Understand the Techniques for Evaluating the Cost of Capital — **169**
Cost of Debt — 169
Cost of Preferred Stock — 169
Cost of Retained Earnings — 170
Cost of Common Stock — 170

Weighted-Average and Marginal Cost of Capital Concepts — 171
Issues in Cost of Capital — 171

Learning Objective 7.6: Understand the Principles and Techniques of Capital Budgeting — **171**
Methods to Rank Investment Projects — 172
Postaudit of Capital Projects — 176
Project Cash Flows — 176
Project Risk Assessment — 177
Techniques for Measuring Standalone Risk — 177
Techniques for Measuring Market/Beta Risk — 178
Project Risks and Capital Budgeting — 178
Capital Rationing — 178
International Capital Budgeting — 178

Learning Objective 7.7: Understand the Various Types and Risks of Financial Instruments — **179**
Forward Contracts — 179
Futures Contracts — 179
Currency Options — 179
Currency Swaps — 180
Hidden Financial Reporting Risk — 181
Financial Engineering — 181

Learning Objective 7.8: Understand the Various Types of Valuation Models — **182**
Inventory Asset Valuation — 182
Financial Asset Valuation — 182
Business Valuation — 183

Learning Objective 7.9: Understand the Nature of Business Mergers and Acquisitions — **185**
Types of Mergers — 185
Merger Tactics — 185
Merger Analysis — 186

Learning Objective 7.10: Understand the Implications of Dividend Policies, Stock Splits, Stock Dividends, and Stock Repurchases — **187**
Dividend Policy in Theory — 187
Dividend Policy in Practice — 188
Dividend Payment Procedures — 189
Stock Splits, Stock Dividends, and Stock Repurchases — 189

☐ Learning Objective 7.1: UNDERSTAND THE NEED FOR FINANCIAL PLANS AND CONTROLS

The scope of financial plans consists of cash planning (i.e., developing pro forma cash budgets) and profit planning (i.e., preparing pro forma financial documents such as income statement and balance sheet) for internal (management) and external purposes (creditors and lenders).

Financial Plans

Financial planning takes place in two time horizons: long-term (2 to 10 years) and short-term (1 to 2 years). Factors such as business operating risks, business and economic cycles, and product lifecycles determine the planning horizon in that high risk and/or short cycles require shorter planning horizons and vice versa.

Long-term financial plans have a strategic focus, supporting the organization's goals and objectives. **Short-term financial plans** have an operating focus, supporting the long-term financial plans.

The inputs to long-term financial plans include capital structure (i.e., the percentage of debt and equity); financing sources (i.e., the amount of bonds and stocks); acquisition of plant, property, and equipment (fixed assets); marketing actions; research and development actions; repayment of debt and reacquisition of stock; and disposal of plants, product lines, and lines of business. The outputs include a series of annual budgets, with contingencies factored into them, that are highly linked to the organization's strategic plans and highly connected with all the managers and executives in the organization.

The inputs to short-term financial plans include sales forecasts, production plans, fixed assets acquisition plans, current period balance sheet, and financing plans. The outputs include cash budget and pro forma financial statements (i.e., income statement and balance sheet).

Cash Budget

The **cash budget** describes cash inflows (cash receipts) and outflows (cash disbursements) in a specific time period, such as one year, one quarter, or one month. Components of cash receipts include cash sales, collections of accounts receivable, and non-sale-related cash (e.g., interest and dividends received; cash from the sale of equipment, stocks, and bonds; and lease payments). However, credit card sales and sales on account are not a part of cash receipts because they have a time lag and become a part of accounts receivable. Debit card sales are part of cash receipts because cash is immediately deposited into the cash account. Components of cash disbursements include cash purchases; payments of accounts payable; rent, lease, interest, cash dividends, and loan principal; wages and salaries; fixed-asset purchases; and repurchases or retirement of stock.

Net Cash Flow = Cash Receipts − Cash Disbursements

Ending Cash Balance = Net Cash Flow + Beginning Cash Balance

Financing and Investment Needs = Ending Cash Balance − Minimum Cash Balance Required

Shortage of cash exists when the ending cash balance is less than the minimum cash balance. Financing is needed through notes payable. Surplus of cash exists when the ending cash balance is greater than the minimum cash balance. Investment is needed through marketable securities.

Sources of cash (inflows) include decrease in assets, increase in liabilities, net income after taxes, sale of stock and other assets, and noncash charges (e.g., depreciation, amortization, and depletion amounts).

Uses of cash (outflows) include increase in assets, decrease in liabilities, net loss, dividends paid, and repurchase or retirement of stock.

A sample pro forma cash budget is shown here.

DV Knowledge Corporation

Pro Forma Cash Budget

Item	Period 1	Period 2
Cash receipts		
Less: Cash disbursements		
Net cash flow		
Add: Beginning cash balance		
Ending cash balance		
Less: Minimum cash balance required		
Cash shortage		
Cash surplus		

Notes: Cash shortage requires external/internal financing and cash surplus requires external/internal investment.

A pro forma income statement is prepared using the percent-of-sales method in that variable costs and expenses are expressed as a percentage of sales and fixed costs and expenses are expressed as full amounts. A sample pro forma income statement is shown here.

DV Knowledge Corporation

Pro Forma Income Statement

Gross sales

Less: Returns and allowances
Net sales
Less: Cost of goods sold
  Fixed costs
  Variable costs

Gross profit or margin

Less: operating expenses
  Fixed expenses
  Variable expenses

Operating income (EBIT)

Less: Interest expenses
Net income before taxes
Less: Taxes
Net income after taxes
Less: Cash dividends to preferred stockholders

Net income (loss)

Earnings per share (EPS) to common stockholders

Notes: Total revenues can include revenues from gross sales of products and services, dividend revenues, and rental revenues. Cost of goods sold includes wages, materials, rent, supplies, and utilities to manufacture goods. Operating expenses include selling, general, administrative, lease, and depreciation expenses, classified as fixed or variable. Operating income is same as earnings before interest and taxes (EBIT). Net income or loss is posted to retained earnings account on the balance sheet. Net income is earnings available to common stockholders. EPS is calculated as net income divided by the number of common shares outstanding.

A **pro forma balance sheet** is prepared using the percent-of-sales method for certain accounts and the judgmental approach for certain accounts. The difference between the total assets and the total liabilities and stockholders' equity amounts is labeled as "external financing required" (a plug figure). It is understood that growth in sales requires additional investment in assets, which in turn generally requires the firm to raise new funds externally.

If the external financing required is a positive number, it means that the company will not generate enough money internally to support its increased assets. It needs to raise funds externally through debt and/or equity or by reducing dividends.

If the external financing required is a negative number, it means that the company will generate more money internally to support its increased assets. It can pay off debts, repurchase stock, or increase dividends.

A sample pro forma balance sheet is shown here.

DV Knowledge Corporation

Pro Forma Balance Sheet

Assets	Liabilities and Stockholders' Equity
Current assets	**Current liabilities**
Cash (1)	Accounts payable (20)
Marketable securities (2)	Taxes payable (21)
Net accounts receivable (3)	Notes payable (22)
Notes receivable (4)	Interest payable (23)
Inventories (5)	Accruals (24)
Prepaid expenses (6)	Total current liabilities (25 = 20 + 21 + 22 + 23 + 24)
Total current assets (7)	
Gross non-current assets	**Long-term liabilities**
Vehicles and leases (8)	Bonds/loans/notes (26)
Land and buildings (9)	Mortgage payable (27)
Machinery and equipment (10)	Total long-term liabilities (28 = 26 + 27)
Furniture and fixtures (11)	Total liabilities (29 = 25 + 28)
Total gross non-current assets (12)	Stockholders' equity
Less: Accumulated depreciation (13)	Preferred stock at par (30)
Net non-current assets (14 = 12—13)	Common stock at par (31)
	Treasury stock (32)
	Paid-in capital (33)
Intangible assets (15)	Property and stock dividends (34)
Total assets (16 = 7 + 14 + 15)	Retained earnings (35)
	Total stockholders' equity (36)
	External financing required (37)
	Total liabilities and stockholders' equity (38)

Notes: Total assets must be equal to total liabilities and stockholders' equity. Net accounts receivable is gross accounts receivable minus allowance for doubtful accounts. Inventories include raw materials, work-in-process, and finished goods. Total current assets are $7 = 1 + 2 + 3 + 4 + 5 + 6$. Non-current assets are fixed or long-term assets. The book value of a fixed asset is historical cost minus accumulated depreciation. Total gross non-current assets are $12 = 8 + 9 + 10 + 11$. Intangible assets include patents, copyrights, trademarks, and franchises. Paid-in capital is excess of par on common and preferred stock. Retained earnings are coming from the income statement, thus providing a link between the balance sheet and the income statement. Total stockholders' equity is $36 = 30 + 31 + 32 + 33 + 34 + 35$. Total liabilities and stockholders' equity is $38 = 29 + 36 + 37$.

Financial Control

The scope of **financial control** includes determining operating breakeven analysis, operating leverage, financial breakeven analysis, financial leverage, and total leverage. It is important to look at the relationship between sales volume and profitability under different operating conditions. These relationships provide information to plan for changes in the firm's level of operations, financing needs, and profitability. A good control system is essential to ensure that plans are executed properly and to facilitate a timely modification of plans if the assumptions on which the initial plans were based turn out to be different than expected.

Operating breakeven analysis is a method of determining the point at which sales will just cover operating costs—that is, the point at which the firm's operations will break even. It also shows the magnitude of the firm's operating profits or losses if sales exceed or fall below that point.

The operating breakeven point (BEP) in units and dollars can be found by setting the total revenues equal to the total operating costs so that operating income or **net operating income (NOI)** is zero. In equation form, NOI = 0 if

Sales Revenues = Total Operating Costs = Total Variable Costs + Total Fixed Costs

Operating BEP in Units = (Total Fixed Costs)/ (Sales Price per Unit − Variable Cost per Unit)

where sales price per unit minus variable cost per unit equals contribution margin per unit.

Operating BEP in Dollars = (Total Fixed Costs)/ (Gross Profit Margin)

where gross profit margin is $[(1 − (V/P)]$, where V is variable cost per unit and P is sales price per unit.

Operating leverage can be defined in terms of the way a given change in sales volume affects net operating income (NOI) or earnings before interest and taxes (EBIT). The **degree of operating leverage (DOL)** is defined as the percentage change in NOI or EBIT associated with a given percentage change in sales. If a high percentage of a firm's total operating costs are fixed, the firm is said to have a high DOL, meaning that a relatively small change in sales will result in a large change in operating income.

DOL = (Percentage Change in NOI or EBIT)/ (Percentage Change in Sales)

Financial breakeven analysis is a method of determining the NOI or EBIT that covers all of the financing costs and that produces earnings per share (EPS) equal to zero. Financing costs, which are fixed in nature, include interest payments to bondholders and dividend payments to preferred stockholders.

Financial BEP in Dollars = $I + (Dps/1 − T)$

where I is interest payments on debt, Dps is amount of dividends paid to preferred stockholders, and T is the marginal tax rate.

Financial leverage starts after the operating leverage ends, further magnifying the impact of changing sales volume on earnings per share. The **degree of financial leverage (DFL)** is defined as the percentage change in EPS that results from a given percentage change in EBIT. This means that a company with a higher DFL is considered to have greater financial risk than a company with a lower DFL.

DFL = (Percentage Change in EPS)/(Percentage Change in EBIT)

where EPS is net income divided by the number of common shares outstanding.

Operating leverage, which is a first-stage leverage, considers how changing sales volume impacts operating income, thus affecting the operating section of the income statement. Financial leverage, which is a second-stage leverage, considers how changing operating income impacts earnings per share, thus affecting the financing section of the income statement.

Total leverage combines the effects of operating leverage and financial leverage. The **degree of total leverage (DTL)** is defined as the joint effect of operating and financial leverage on earnings per share. DTL can help management evaluate alternative expansion plans regarding the level of operations (e.g., plant automation) and how those operations are financed (e.g., purchasing new equipment for automation with debt).

DTL = (Percentage Change in EPS)/ (Percentage Change in Sales)

or

DTL = DOL × DFL

Note that DTL, DOL, and DFL are expressed as number of times, such as 2.4×.

❑ Learning Objective 7.2: UNDERSTAND THE PRINCIPLES AND TECHNIQUES OF CASH MANAGEMENT

Cash is a very liquid asset and susceptible to fraudulent activities. Controls over cash are very important to protect this financial asset.

Cash Presentation

To be presented as cash on the balance sheet, it must be available to meet current obligations. **Cash** includes such items as coins, currency, checks, bank drafts, checks from customers, and money orders. Cash in savings accounts and cash in certificates of deposit (CDs) maturing within one year can be included as current assets, preferably under the caption of "short-term investments," but not as cash. Petty cash and other imprest cash accounts can be included in other cash accounts.

Current assets are those assets expected to be converted into cash, sold, or consumed within one year or within the operating cycle, whichever is longer. Current assets are properly presented in the balance sheet in the order of their liquidity. Some of the more common current assets are cash, marketable securities, accounts receivable, inventories, and prepaid items.

Cash Items Excluded

The portion of an entity's cash account consisting of a compensating balance must be segregated and shown as a noncurrent asset if the related borrowings are noncurrent liabilities. If the borrowings are current liabilities, it is acceptable to show the compensating balance as a separately captioned current asset.

Certain cash items are not presented in the general cash section of the balance sheet. These include compensating balances, other restricted cash, and exclusions from cash.

Cash requires a good system of **internal control,** since it is so liquid and easy to conceal and transport. Segregation of duties is an important part of the system of internal control for cash. No one person should both record a transaction and have custody of the asset. Without proper segregation, it is easier for an employee to engage in lapping. **Lapping** is a type of fraud in which an employee misappropriates receipts from customers and covers the shortages in these customers' accounts with receipts from subsequent customers. Therefore, the shortage is never eliminated but is transferred to other accounts. Lapping schemes do not require the employee to divert funds for his personal use. The funds can be diverted for other business expenses.

Kiting is a scheme in which a depositor with accounts in two or more banks takes advantage of the time required for checks to clear in order to obtain unauthorized credit. The scheme would be nonexistent if depositors were not allowed to draw against uncollected funds. The use of uncollected funds does not always indicate a kite; such use can be authorized by an officer of the bank. Kiting schemes can be as simple as cashing checks a few days before payday, then depositing the funds to cover checks previously written. Or, they can be as complex as a systematic buildup of uncollected deposits, pyramiding for the "big hit." Kiting can be eliminated or reduced through electronic funds transfer systems. Kiting can be detected when reviewing accounts to determine whether a customer or employee is drawing a check against an account in which he has deposited another check that has not yet cleared.

Float is an amount of money represented by items (both check and noncheck) outstanding and in the process of collection. The amount of float incurred is determined by two factors: the dollar volume of checks cleared and the speed with which the checks are cleared. The relationship between float and these two factors can be expressed as:

$$\text{Float} = \text{Dollar Volume} \times \text{Collection Speed}$$

The cost of float pertains to the potential for earning income from nonearning assets, as represented by items in the process of collection. This cost of float is an opportunity cost—the firm could have fully invested and earned income had the funds been available for investment and not incurred float.

In a financial futures **hedging** transaction, a firm takes a futures position that is opposite to its existing economic, or **cash** position. By taking the opposite position in the financial futures market, the firm can protect itself against adverse interest rate fluctuations by locking in a given yield or interest rate.

Controls Over Cash

Cash is a precious resource in any organization. Cash is required to pay employee wages and salaries, buy raw materials and parts to produce finished goods, pay off debt, and pay dividends, among other things. Cash is received from customers for the sale of goods and the rendering of services. Customer payments come into the organization in various forms, such as checks, bank drafts, wire transfers, money orders, charge cards, and lockboxes. The cash manager's primary job is to ensure that all customer payments funnel into the company's checking accounts as fast as possible with greater accuracy. Payments received at lockboxes located at regional banks flow into cash concentration accounts, preferably on the same day of deposit.

The cash manager should focus on reducing the elapsed time from customer payment date to the day funds are available for use in the company's bank account. This elapsed time is called the "float."

A major objective of the cash manager is to accelerate the cash inflow and slow the cash outflow without damaging the company's reputation in the industry. To do this, the cash manager needs to find ways to accelerate cash flows into the company that in turn reduce investment in working capital. Similarly, the cash manager needs to find ways to slow the outflow of cash by increasing the time for payments to clear the bank. Another major objective is not to allow funds to sit idle without earning interest.

The cash manager needs to focus on the following seven major areas for effective cash management: (1) cash account balances, (2) purchases, (3) payables, (4) manufacturing, (5) sales, (6) receivables, and (7) manual lockbox systems.

Electronic techniques to control cash include electronic lockbox systems, electronic funds transfer (EFT), and electronic data interchange (EDI) systems.

Management of Cash

On one hand, adequate cash serves as protection against a weak economy and can be used to pay off debts and to acquire companies. On the other hand, too much cash makes a firm vulnerable to corporate raiding or takeovers.

> Cash = Currency + Bank Demand Deposits + Near-Cash Marketable Securities
>
> Near-Cash Marketable Securities = U.S. Treasury Bills + Bank Certificates of Deposit

Effective cash management is important to all organizations, whether profit-oriented or not. The scope of cash management encompasses cash gathering (collection) and disbursement techniques and in-

vestment of cash. Since cash is a "nonearning" asset until it is put to use, the goal of cash management is to reduce cash holdings to the minimum necessary to conduct normal business.

There are four reasons for holding cash by organizations: transaction balance, compensating balance, precautionary balance, and speculative balance.

1. **Transaction balance.** Payments and collections are handled through the cash account. These routine transactions are necessary in business operations.
2. **Compensating balance.** A bank requires the customer to leave a minimum balance on deposit to help offset the costs of providing the banking services. It is compensation paid to banks for providing loans and services. Some loan agreements also require compensating balances.
3. **Precautionary balance.** Firms hold some cash in reserve to accommodate for random, unforeseen fluctuations in cash inflows and outflows. These are similar to the "safety stocks" used in inventories.
4. **Speculative balance.** Cash may be held to enable the firm to take advantage of any bargain purchases that might arise. Similar to precautionary balances, firms could rely on reserve borrowing capacity and on marketable securities rather than on cash for speculative purposes.

A total desired cash balance for a firm is not simply the addition of cash in transaction, compensating, precautionary, and speculative balances. This is because the same money often serves more than one purpose. For example, precautionary and speculative balances can also be used to satisfy compensating balance requirements. A firm needs to consider these four factors when establishing its target cash position.

Advantages of Holding Adequate Cash and Near-Cash Assets

In addition to the motives for transaction, compensating, precautionary, and speculative balances, firms do have other advantages for holding adequate cash and near-cash assets. These advantages include:

- Taking trade discounts. Suppliers offer customers trade discounts—a discount for prompt payment of bills. Cash is needed to take advantage of trade discounts. Cost of not taking trade discounts could be high.

- Keeping current ratios and acid-test ratios in line with those of other firms in the industry requires adequate holdings of cash. Higher ratios give a strong credit rating. A strong credit rating enables the firm both to purchase goods and services from suppliers and to provide favorable terms and to maintain an ample line of credit with the bank. A weak credit rating does the opposite.
- Holding an ample supply of cash could help to acquire another firm, to handle contingencies such as a labor strike, to attack competitors' marketing campaigns, and to take advantage of special offers by suppliers.

Cash Management Efficiency Techniques

A **cash budget**, showing cash inflows and outflows and cash status, is the starting point in the cash management system. The techniques used to increase the efficiency of management include cash flow synchronization, use of float, speeding collections, slowing disbursements, and transfer mechanisms.

Cash Flow Synchronization

By coinciding cash inflows with cash outflows, the need for transaction balances will be low. The benefits would be reduced cash balances, decreased bank loan needs, reduced interest expenses, and increased profits.

Use of Float

Two kinds of float exist: disbursement float and collection float. The difference is net float. **Disbursement float** arises when one makes a payment by a check and is defined as the amount of checks that one has written but that are still being processed and thus have not yet been deducted from one's checking account balances by the bank. **Collection float** arises when one receives a check for payment and is defined as the amount of checks that one has received but that are in the collection process. It takes time to deposit the check, for the bank to process it, and to credit one's account for the amount collected.

Net Float = Disbursement Float − Collection Float

Net Float = One's Checkbook Balance − Bank's Book Balance

A positive net float is better than a negative net float because the positive net float collects checks written to a firm faster than clearing checks written

to others. The **net float** is a function of the ability to speed up collections on checks received and to slow down collections on checks written. The key is to put the funds received to work faster and to stretch payments longer.

Speeding Collections

Funds are available to the receiving firm only after the check-clearing process has been satisfactorily completed. There is a time delay between a firm processing its incoming checks and its making use of them. Three parties are involved in the check-clearing process: the payer, payee, and the U.S. Federal Reserve System (requires a maximum of two days to clear the check). The length of time required for checks to clear is a function of the distance between the payer's and the payee's banks. The greater the distance, the longer the delay due to mail. If the payer's and the payee's bank are the same, there is less delay than otherwise.

Slowing Disbursements

Three techniques are available to slow down disbursements. These include delaying payments, writing checks on banks in different locations, and using drafts. Delaying payments has negative consequences, such as a bad credit rating. A firm can be sued by a customer for writing checks on banks in distant locations (e.g., playing West Coast banks against eastern banks in the United States). Speeding the collection process and slowing down disbursements have the same objective. Both keep cash on hand for longer periods.

Use of draft seems normal. A check is payable on demand; a draft is not. A draft must be transmitted to the issuer, who approves it and then deposits funds to cover it, after which it can be collected.

Money Transfer Mechanisms

A **transfer mechanism** is a system for moving funds among accounts at different banks. Three types of transfer mechanisms are (1) depository transfer checks, (2) wire transfers, and (3) electronic depository transfer checks:

1. A **depository transfer check (DTC)** is restricted for deposit into a particular account at a particular bank. A DTC is payable only to the bank of deposit for credit to the firm's specific account. DTCs provide a means of moving money from

local depository banks to regional concentration banks and to the firm's primary bank.

2. **Wire transfer.** A wire transfer is the electronic transfer of funds via a telecommunications network that makes funds collected at one bank immediately available from another bank. The wire transfer eliminates transit float and reduces the required level of transaction and precautionary cash balances.

3. The **electronic depository transfer check (EDTC)** is a combination of a wire transfer and a DTC. EDTC provides one-day availability in check clearing-time because it avoids the use of the mail. EDTC is a paperless transaction. EDTC is also called **automated clearinghouse (ACH),** which is a telecommunication network that provides an electronic means of sending data from one financial institution to another. Magnetic tape files are processed by the ACH and direct computer-to-computer links are also available.

❏ Learning Objective 7.3: UNDERSTAND THE TECHNIQUES OF MANAGING CURRENT ASSETS

Effective management of current assets requires a working capital policy, which refers to the firm's policies regarding the desired level for each category of current assets and how current assets will be financed. The **components of current assets** in the order of liquidity are:

- Cash (most liquid and easy to conceal and transport)
- Marketable securities
- Accounts receivable
- Prepaid expenses
- Inventories (least liquid and can be damaged, spoiled, or stolen)

Current assets fluctuate with sales and represent a large portion (usually greater than 40%) of total assets. Working capital management is important for both large and small firms alike.

Working Capital versus Net Working Capital

- Working capital means current assets (also gross working capital).
- Net working capital is current assets minus current liabilities.

- Working capital management involves the administration of current assets and current liabilities.

For financing current assets, most small firms rely on trade credit and short-term bank loans, both of which affect working capital by increasing current liabilities. Accounts payable represents "free" trade credit when discounts are taken. This is similar to an interest-free loan. However, current liabilities are used to finance current assets and in part represent current maturities of long-term debt. Large firms usually rely on long-term capital markets such as stocks. The **components of current liabilities** are shown here with their associated costs:

- Accounts payable (free trade credit)
- Accrued wages
- Accrued taxes
- Notes payable (not free)
- Current maturities of long-term debt

The relationship between sales and the need to invest in current assets is direct:

- As sales increase, accounts receivable increases, inventory increases, and cash needs increase.
- Any increase in an account on the left-hand side of the balance sheet (e.g., assets) must be matched by an increase on the right-hand side of the balance sheet (e.g., liabilities).

This involves matching maturities of assets and liabilities. That is, current assets are financed with current liabilities and fixed assets are financed with long-term debt or stock. This is to reduce interest rate risk.

Cash Conversion Cycle Model

The **cash conversion model** defines the length of time from the payment for the purchase of raw materials to the collection of accounts receivable generated by the sale of the final product. It is an important model since it focuses on the conversion of materials and labor to cash.

Cash Conversion Cycle = Inventory Conversion
    Period (1) + Receivables Conversion Period (2)
    −Payables Deferral Period (3)

where (1) **inventory conversion period** is the length of time required to convert raw materials into finished goods and then to sell these goods;

(2) **receivables conversion period** is the length of time required to convert the firm's receivables into cash; and (3) **payables deferral period** is the average length of time between the purchase of raw materials and labor and the payment of cash for them.

The cash conversion cycle begins the day a bill for labor and/or supplies is paid and runs to the day receivables are collected. The cycle measures the length of time the firm has funds tied up in working capital. The shorter the cash conversion cycle, the smaller the need for external financing and thus the lower the cost of such financing. This would result in increase in profits.

Approaches to Shorten the Cash Conversion Cycle

The following list provides approaches to shorten the cash conversion cycle:

- Reduce the inventory conversion period by processing and selling goods more quickly.
- Reduce the receivables conversion period or days sales outstanding by speeding up collections.
- Lengthen the payables deferral period by slowing down payments.

Working Capital Asset Investment Policies

Appropriate **working capital asset investment policies** are needed to support various levels of sales. Three such policies are:

1. **Relaxed (liberal) working capital policy.** Sales are stimulated by the use of a credit policy that provides liberal financing to customers, which results in a high level of accounts receivable. This is a policy that maximizes the current assets. Accounts receivable will increase as the credit sales increase for a relaxed policy, and the opposite is true for the restricted policy.
2. **Moderate working capital policy.** This is a policy that falls between liberal and tight working capital policy.
3. **Restricted (tight) working capital policy.** This is a policy that minimizes current assets. A tight policy lowers the receivables for any given level of sales or even the risk of a decline in sales. This policy provides the highest expected return on investment and entails the greatest risk. The firm would hold minimal levels of safety stocks for cash and inventories.

Working Capital Financing Policies

A good working capital financing policy is needed to handle seasonal or cyclical business fluctuations and a strong or weak economy. When the economy is strong, working capital is built up and inventories and receivables go up. When the economy is weak, the working capital goes down, along with inventories and receivables. Current assets are divided into permanent and temporary, and the manner in which these assets are financed constitutes the firm's working capital financing policy.

A firm's working capital asset investment policy, including the cash conversion cycle, is always established in conjunction with the firm's working capital financing policy. Three financing policies are available to manage working capital: maturity matching, aggressive approach, and conservative approach.

The **maturity matching** or "self-liquidating" approach requires that asset maturities are matched with liability maturities. This means permanent assets are financed with long-term capital to reduce risk. Each loan would be paid off with the cash flows generated by the assets financed by the loan, so loans would be self-liquidating. Uncertainty about the lives of assets prevents exact matching in an *ex post* sense.

The three working capital financing policies discussed above differ in the relative amount of short-term debt financing each uses, as shown in the figure.

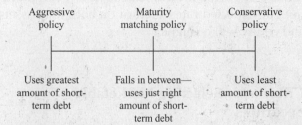

Management of Marketable Securities

Two basic reasons for holding marketable securities (e.g., U.S. Treasury bills, commercial paper, and certificates of deposit) are: (1) they are used as a temporary investment and (2) they serve as a substitute for cash balances. Temporary investment occurs when the firm must finance seasonal or cyclical operations; when the firm must meet some known financial requirements such as new plant construction program, a bond about to mature, or quarterly tax payments; and when the proceeds from stocks and bonds are used to pay for operating assets.

Actually, it is a choice between taking out short-term loans or holding marketable securities. There is a trade-off between risks and return. Similar to cash management policy, a firm's marketable security policy should be an integral part of its overall working capital policy. The policy may be conservative, aggressive, or a moderate working capital financing policy.

If the firm has a **conservative working capital financing policy,** its long-term capital will exceed its permanent assets and it will hold marketable securities when inventories and receivables are low. This is a less risky one. There is no liquidity problem since the firm has no short-term debt. However, the firm incurs higher interest rates when borrowing than the return it receives from marketable securities. It is evident that a less risky strategy costs more.

If the firm has a **moderate working capital financing policy,** the firm will match permanent assets with long-term financing and meet most seasonal increases in inventories and receivables with short-term loans. The firm also carries marketable securities at certain times. With this policy, asset maturities are matched with those of liabilities. No risk exists, at least theoretically.

If the firm has an **aggressive working capital financing policy,** it will never carry any securities and will borrow heavily to meet peak needs. This is the riskiest, and it will face difficulties in borrowing new funds or repaying the loan, due to its low current ratio. The expected rate of return on both total assets and equity will be higher.

Criteria for Selecting Marketable Securities

The selection criteria for a marketable security portfolio include default risk, taxability, and relative yields. Several choices are available for the financial manager in selecting a marketable securities portfolio, and they all differ in risk and return. Most financial managers are averse to risk and unwilling to sacrifice safety for higher rates of return. The higher a security's risk, the higher its expected and required return and vice versa. A trade-off exists between risk and return.

Large corporations tend to make direct purchases of U.S. Treasury bills, commercial paper, certificates of deposit, and Eurodollar time deposits. Small corporations are more likely to use money market mutual funds as near-cash reserves (because they can be quickly and easily converted to cash). Interest rates on money market mutual funds are lower and net returns are higher than is the case with the Treasury bills.

Risks in Marketable Securities

Let us review the four different types of risk (i.e., default risk, interest rate risk, purchasing power risk, and liquidity risk) facing the financial manager in managing the portfolio of marketable securities:

1. **Default risk.** The risk that a borrower will be unable to make interest payments or to repay the principal amount upon maturity is known as default risk. For example, the default risk for securities issued by the U.S. Treasury is negligible, whereas securities issued by a corporation and others have some degree of default risk. *The higher the earning power of a firm, the lower its default risk and vice versa.*

2. **Interest rate risk.** The risk to which investors are exposed due to rising interest rates is known as interest rate risk. It is the interest rate fluctuations that cause interest rate risk. Even U.S. Treasury bonds are subject to interest rate risk. *Bond prices vary with changes in interest rates. Long-term bonds have more interest rate risk. Short-term bonds have less interest rate risk.*

3. **Purchasing power risk.** The risk that inflation will reduce the purchasing power of a given sum of money is known as purchasing power risk. Purchasing power risk is lower on assets whose returns tend to rise during inflation. Purchasing power risk is higher on assets whose returns are fixed during inflation. So it is the variability of returns during inflation that determines the purchasing power risk. *Real estate, short-term debt, and common stocks are better hedges against inflation. Bonds and other long-term fixed-income securities are not the best hedges against inflation.*

4. **Liquidity (marketability) risk.** The risk that securities cannot be sold at close to the quoted market price on short notice is known as liquidity risk. For example, securities issued by the U.S. Treasury and larger corporations have little liquidity risk, whereas securities issued by small and unknown companies are subject to liquidity risk. Illiquidity of a firm is the situation where the firm's maturing obligations are greater than the cash immediately available to pay. *An asset that can be sold quickly for close to its quoted price is highly liquid. An asset that cannot be sold quickly and is sold at a reduced price is not highly liquid.*

❏ Learning Objective 7.4: UNDERSTAND THE VARIOUS TYPES OF DEBT AND EQUITY IN A CAPITAL STRUCTURE

The capital structure of a firm consists of amounts and proportions of debt and equity as part of total capital.

Types of Debt

Debt is of two types: (1) short-term debt and (2) long-term debt. Debt maturities affect both risk and expected returns. For example:

- Short-term debt is riskier than long-term debt if the debt cannot paid off when due.
- Short-term debt is less expensive than long-term debt.
- Short-term debt can be obtained faster than long-term debt.
- Short-term debt is more flexible than long-term debt.

There is a trade-off between risk and profits in using short-term debt.

Short-Term Debt

By definition, **short-term debt (credit)** is any liability originally scheduled for payment within one year. The four major sources of short-term credit are: (1) accruals, (2) accounts payable, (3) bank loans, and (4) commercial paper. The order of short-term credit sources is shown here from both cost and importance viewpoints:

In the Order of Importance	In the Order of Cost
A. Trade credit (most important)	A. Trade credit (free, no interest paid)
B. Bank loans	B. Accruals
C. Commercial paper	C. Commercial paper
D. Accruals (least important)	D. Bank loans (not free, interest paid)

(A) Trade Credit

Trade credit is granted by the suppliers of goods as a sales-promotion device. All firms, regardless of their size, depend on accounts payable or trade credit as a source of short-term financing. Small firms do rely more heavily on trade credit than larger firms due to the former's inability to raise money from other sources. Trade credit, a major part of current liability, is an interfirm debt arising from credit sales and recorded as an account receivable by the seller and as an account payable by the buyer. Trade credit is a spontaneous source of financing arising from the normal course of business operations.

When payment terms are extended, the amount in accounts payable is expanded to provide an additional source of financing. Therefore, lengthening the credit period generates additional financing.

Payment terms vary and usually call for **net 30**, meaning that it must pay for goods 30 days after the invoice date. Other terms include **1/10, net 30**, which means that a 1% discount is given if payment is made within 10 days of the invoice date, but the full invoice amount is due and payable within 30 days if the discount is not taken. The finance manager has a choice of taking or not taking the discount, and he needs to calculate the cost of not taking discounts on purchases. The equation is:

$$\text{Percentage Cost of Not Taking Discount}$$
$$= \frac{\text{Discount Percent}}{100\% - \text{Discount \%}} \times \frac{360}{A - B}$$

where A = days credit is outstanding and B = discount period.

A firm's policy with regard to taking or not taking trade discounts can have a significant effect on its financial statements. A dichotomy exists in terms of taking discounts or not taking discounts. Careful analysis needs to be performed showing relevant costs and its effects on net income:

Decision Conditions in Discounts:

1. If the company does not take discounts (i.e., uses maximum trade credit), its interest expense will be zero (i.e., no borrowing is necessary), but it will have an expense equivalent to lost discounts.
2. If the company does take discounts (i.e., borrows money from bank), it will incur interest expense on the loan, but it will avoid the cost of discounts lost. The company gives up some of the trade credit, and it has to raise money from other sources such as bank credit, common stock, or long-term bonds.

Decision Rules in Discounts:

1. If the discount amount lost exceeds the interest expense, the "take-discounts" policy would result in a higher net income and eventually a higher stock price.
2. If the interest expense exceeds the discount amount lost, the "do-not-take-discounts" policy would result in a higher net income and eventually a higher stock price.

(B) Bank Loans

Bank loans appear on firms' balance sheets under the notes payable account category. A **promissory note** is signed by the borrower (customer) specifying the amount borrowed, the percentage interest rate, the repayment schedule, any collateral, and any other terms and conditions. Banks require a compensating balance in the form of a minimum checking account balance equal to a specified percentage (i.e., 10 to 20%) of the face amount of the loan. A compensating balance raises the effective interest rate on the loan.

Examples of Bank Loan Features:

- Promissory note
- Compensating balance
- Line of credit
- Revolving credit agreement

Banks also give a line of credit to a borrower, and it works like a credit card limit. A line of credit can be based on either formal or informal understanding. It includes the maximum amount of credit the bank will extend to the borrower. A revolving credit agreement, which is similar to a line of credit, is a formal line of credit often used by large firms. The bank has a legal obligation to honor a revolving credit agreement while no legal obligation exists under the line of credit.

The cost of a bank loan (i.e., interest rate) varies depending on economic conditions and U.S. Federal Reserve (Fed) money supply policy. Generally, interest rates are higher for riskier borrowers and for smaller loans due to fixed costs of servicing the loan. If a firm is financially strong, it can borrow at the prime rate, which has traditionally been the lowest rate banks charge. If a firm is financially weak, the bank will charge higher than prime rate to compensate for the risk involved.

Interest rates on bank loans are quoted in three ways: (1) simple interest, (2) discount interest, and (3) add-on interest. Each method is briefly discussed:

1. **Simple (regular) interest.** In a simple interest loan, the borrower receives the face value of the loan and then repays the principal and interest at maturity. Effective Rate = Interest/Amount Received. If a loan period is one year or more, the nominal (stated) rate equals the effective rate. If a loan period is less than one year, the effective rate is higher than the nominal (stated) rate.

2. **Discount interest.** In a discount interest loan, the borrower receives less than the face value of the loan since the bank deducts the interest in advance. Effective Rate = Interest/Amount Received. Because of discounting, the effective rate is always higher than a simple interest loan regardless of the loan period. However, the discount interest imposes less of a penalty on a shorter-term than on a longer-term loan because the interest is paid closer to the average date of use of the funds (half the life of the loan).

3. **Add-on interest.** Small installment loans employ the add-on interest method. The interest is calculated based on the nominal rate and then added to the amount received to obtain the loan's face value. Effective Rate = Interest/0.5 (Amount Received). The effective rate can be almost double the stated rate since the average amount actually outstanding is less than the original amount of the loan.

The situation is different when compensating balances are introduced to the simple interest method and discount interest method. In general, compensating balances tend to raise the effective interest rate on a loan because some money is tied up in a checking account (i.e., cannot be used). There are two exceptions: (1) if the firm can use transaction balances as compensating balances, the effective interest rate will be less than otherwise and (2) if the firm can earn interest on its bank deposits, including the compensating balance, the effective interest rate will be decreased.

(C) Commercial Paper

Commercial paper represents short-term, unsecured promissory notes of large, strong firms and is highly liquid in nature. The interest rate charged on commercial paper is somewhat below the prime rate, and its maturity ranges from two to six months. Even though compensating balances are not required for commercial paper, its effective interest rate is higher due to the loan commitment fees involved.

Firms issuing commercial paper are required by commercial paper dealers to have unused revolving credit agreements to back up their outstanding commercial paper. A commitment fee is charged on the unused credit line.

The commercial paper market is impersonal, unlike bank loans. However, the commercial paper market is flexible and provides a wide range of credit sources generally available to financially strong firms with low credit risks.

(D) Accruals

Accruals are short-term liabilities arising from wages owed to employees and taxes owed to government. These accruals increase automatically as a firm's operations expand, and hence little control exists over their levels. No explicit interest is paid on funds raised through accruals.

Use of Security in Short-Term Financing

The security agreement of the U.S. Uniform Commercial Code (UCC) provides guidelines for establishing loan security. Secured loans are expensive due to recordkeeping costs. Financially weak companies are required to put up some type of collateral to protect the lender, while financially strong companies generally are not, even though they are encouraged to do so. The most commonly used collateral for short-term credit is accounts receivable and inventories as described here:

Collateral for Short-Term Loans	Collateral for Long-Term Loans
Examples of collateral used for short-term loans include accounts receivable, inventories, stocks, and bonds.	Examples of collateral for secured long-term loans include land, building, equipment, stocks, and bonds.

- **Accounts receivable financing.** Accounts receivable (A/R) financing involves either the pledging of receivables or the selling of receivables (i.e., factoring) to obtain a short-term loan. Either commercial banks or industrial finance companies are usually involved in pledging and factoring, and a legally binding agent is established between the borrower and the lender.
- **Inventory financing.** Inventory financing involves the use of inventory as a security to obtain a short-term loan. Three methods exist: (1) inventory blanket liens, (2) trust receipts, and (3) warehouse receipts.

Long-Term Debt

Long-term debt is often called **funded debt,** a term used to define the replacement of short-term debt with securities of longer maturity (e.g., stocks and bonds). Many types of long-term debt instruments are available including term loans, bonds, secured notes, unsecured notes, marketable debt, and non-marketable debt.

Term Loans

A **term loan** is a contract under which a borrower agrees to make a series of payments (interest and principal) at specific times to the lender. Most term loans are amortized, which means they are paid off in equal installments over the life of the loan, ranging from 3 to 15 years. Amortization protects the lender against inadequate loan provisions made by the borrower.

Since the agreement is between the lender and the borrower, documentation requirements are lower, the speed and future flexibility are greater, and the cost is lower compared to a public offering involved in a stock or bond issue. The interest rate on a term loan can either be fixed or variable, and lenders will be reluctant to make long-term, fixed-rate loans.

Bonds

A **bond** is a long-term contract (seven to ten years or more) under which a borrower agrees to make payments (interest and principal) on specific dates to the holder of the bond. The interest rates paid on bonds can be fixed or variable (floating-rate bonds) and are generally fixed.

Some debts have specific contractual requirements to meet. The effective cost of the debt is high, and many restrictions are placed in the debt contracts, which limit a firm's future flexibility. In order to protect the rights of the bondholders and the issuing firm, a legal document called **indenture** is created, and it includes **restrictive covenants.** A trustee, usually a bank, is assigned to represent the bondholders and to enforce the terms of the indenture and to ensure compliance with restrictive covenants.

Most bonds contain a call provision that gives the issuing firm the right to call the bonds before maturity for redemption. The bondholder is paid an amount greater than par value (call premium) for the bond when it is called. The call premium is set equal to one year's interest if the bond is called during the first year, and the premium declines at a constant rate of I/N each year thereafter, where I equals annual interest and N equals original maturity in years.

Another example of specific debt contract features is sinking fund requirements. A **sinking fund** is a provision that requires annual payment designed to amortize a bond or preferred stock issue. It retires a portion of the bond issue each year. It can also be viewed as buying back a certain percentage of the issue each year. Annual payments are a cash drain on the firm, and nonpayment could cause default or force the company into bankruptcy. The firm may deposit money with a trustee who will retire the bonds when they mature.

The sinking fund retirement is handled either by calling in for redemption (at par) a certain percentage of the bonds each year or by buying the required amount of bonds on the open market. A sinking fund call requires no call premium, whereas a refunding operation does. A sinking fund requires that a small percentage of the issue is callable in any one year.

The refunding operation works as follows: when a firm sold bonds or preferred stock at high interest rates, and if the issue is callable, the firm could sell a new issue at low interest rates. Then the firm could retire the expensive old issue. This refunding operation reduces interest costs and preferred dividend expenses.

Relationships between Bond Prices and Interest Rates

- There is an inverse relationship between bond prices and interest rates.
- If interest rates increase, the firm will buy bonds in the open market at a discount.
- If interest rates decrease, the firm will call the bonds.

Examples of various types of long-term bonds are described next.

Mortgage bonds. Under a mortgage bond, the corporation pledges certain fixed assets as security for the bond. Mortgage bonds can be of two types: (1) senior (first) mortgage bonds and (2) junior (second) mortgage bonds. Second mortgage bondholders are paid only after the first mortgage bondholders have been paid off in full. All mortgage bonds are written subject to an indenture. Details regarding the nature of secured assets are contained in the mortgage instrument. From the viewpoint of the investor, mortgage bonds provide lower risk, and junk bonds provide greater risk.

Bond rating criteria include:
- Debt ratio
- Times-interest-earned ratio
- Current ratio
- Fixed charge coverage ratio
- Mortgage or other provisions
- Sinking fund requirements

Debentures. A debenture is an unsecured bond. Consequently, it provides no lien against specific property as security for the obligation. Debenture holders come under "general creditors." Financially strong companies do not need to put up property as security when they issue debentures. Debentures can be subordinate or not. In the event of liquidation, reorganization, or bankruptcy, subordinate debt has claims on assets only after senior debt has been paid off. Subordinate debentures may be subordinated either to designated notes payable or to all other debt.

Convertible bonds. Convertible bonds are securities that are convertible into shares of common stock, at a fixed price, at the option of the bondholder. Convertible bonds have a lower coupon rate than nonconvertible debt and have a chance for capital gains.

Warrants. Warrants are options, which permit the holder to buy stock for a stated price, thereby providing a capital gain if the price of the stock rises. Bonds that are issued with warrants, like convertible bonds, carry lower coupon rates than straight bonds.

Income bonds. As the name implies, income bonds pay interest only when interest is earned. These bonds are safer to a company but riskier to an investor than "regular" bonds.

Putable bonds. Putable bonds may be turned in and exchanged for cash at the holder's option. The put option can be exercised only if the issuer is being acquired or is increasing its outstanding debt or other specified action.

Treasury bonds. A Treasury bond will have the lowest risk and low opportunity for return to an investor. Compare the Treasury bond to a junk bond, which has the highest risk and high opportunity for return.

Indexed bonds. Countries faced with high inflation rates issue indexed bonds, also known as purchasing power bonds. The interest paid is based on an inflation index (e.g., consumer price index) so that the interest paid rises automatically when the inflation rate rises. This bond protects the bondholder against inflation.

Floating-rate bonds. The interest rate on floating-rate bonds fluctuates with shifts in the general level of interest rates. The interest rate on these bonds is adjusted periodically, and it benefits the investor and the lender. Corporations also benefit from not having to commit themselves to paying a high rate of interest for the entire life of the loan.

Zero coupon bonds. Capital appreciation is the major attraction in zero coupon bonds rather than interest income. Therefore, zero coupon bonds pay no interest and are offered at a discount below their par values. Both private and public organizations are offering zero coupon bonds to raise money. Zero coupon bonds are also called **original issue discount bonds.**

Junk bonds. Junk bonds are high-risk, high-yield bonds issued to finance a leveraged buyout, a merger, or a troubled company. In junk bond deals, the debt ratio is high, so bondholders share as much risk as stockholders would. Since interest expense on bonds is tax deductible, it increases after-tax cash flows of the bond issuer.

The reason for the availability of so many different types of long-term securities is that different investors have different risk/return trade-off preferences. Different securities are issued to accommodate different tastes of investors and at different points in time. Short-term U.S. Treasury bills are risk-free and low-return (which act as a reference point), while warrants are high-risk and high-return securities.

Factors Influencing Long-Term Financing Decisions

Long-term financing decisions require a great deal of planning since a firm commits itself for many years to come. The long-term nature combined with uncertainty makes long-term financing risky, requiring careful consideration of all factors involved. Examples of important factors include:

Target capital structure. A firm should compare its actual capital structure to its target structure and keep it in balance over a longer period of time. Exact matching of capital structure is not economically feasible on a yearly financing basis due to increased flotation costs involved. It has been shown that small fluctuations about the optimal capital structure have little effect either on a firm's cost of debt and equity or on its overall cost of capital.

Maturity matching. The maturity-matching concept proposes matching the maturity of the liabilities (debt) with the maturity of the assets being financed. This factor has a major influence on the type of debt securities used.

Interest rate levels. Consideration of both absolute and relative interest rate levels is crucial in making long-term financing decisions. The issuance of a long-term debt with a call provision is one example where the interest rate fluctuates. The callability of a bond permits the firm to refund the issue should interest rates drop. Companies base their financing decisions on expectations about future interest rates.

The firm's current and forecasted financial conditions. The firm's financial condition, earnings forecasts, status of research and development programs, and introduction of new products all have a major role in what type of long-term security is issued. For example, the following decision rules apply:

- If management forecasts higher earnings, the firm could use debt now rather than issuing common stock. After earnings have risen and pushed up the stock price, the firm should issue common stock to restore the capital structure to its target level.
- If a firm is financially weak, but forecasts better earnings, permanent financing should be delayed until conditions have improved.
- If a firm is financially strong now but forecasts poor earnings, it should use long-term financing now rather than waiting.
- Restrictions on the current ratio, debt ratio, times-interest-earned ratio and fixed charge coverage ratio can also restrict a firm's ability to use different types of financing at a given time. Also, secured long-term debt will be less costly than unsecured debt. Firms with large amounts of fixed assets (with a ready resale value) are likely to use a relatively large amount of debt.

Types of Equity

When management decides to acquire new assets, it has the option of financing these assets with either equity, debt, or a combination. The following is a good financial management policy:

- Long-term assets should be financed with long-term capital.
- Short-term assets should be financed with short-term capital.

The definition of **common equity** is the sum of the firm's common stock, additional paid-in capital, preferred stock, and retained earnings. Common equity is the common stockholders' total investment in the firm. The sources of long-term capital include common stocks, preferred stocks, debt (e.g., loans, bonds, and notes), leases, and option securities.

Common Stock

The common stockholders are the owners of a corporation. **Common stock** is the amount of stock management has actually issued (sold) at par value. **Par value** is the nominal or face value of a stock and is the minimum amount for which new shares can be issued. The component "additional paid-in capital" represents the difference between the stock's par value and what new stockholders paid when they bought newly issued shares. Retained earnings are the money that belongs to the stockholders and that they could have received in the form of dividends. Retained earnings are also the money that was plowed back into the firm for reinvestment.

Book Value of the Firm = Common Stock
+ Paid-in Capital + Retained Earnings
= Common Equity

Book Value per Share = Book Value of the Firm
÷ Common Shares Outstanding

It should be interesting to note that par value, book value, and market value will never be equal due to conflicting relationships.

Most firms have one type of common stock, whereas others have multiple types of stock called **classified stock.** Usually, newer firms issue classified stock to raise funds from outside sources. For example, Class A stock may be sold to the public with a dividend payment and without voting rights. Class B stock may be kept by the founder of the firm to gain control with full voting rights. A restriction might be placed on Class B stock not to pay dividends until the firm reaches a predesignated retained earnings level.

Legal Rights of Common Stockholders   Since common stockholders are the owners of a firm, they have the following rights: the right to elect the firm's directors and the right to remove the management of the firm if they decide a management team is not effective. Stockholders can transfer their right to vote to a second party by means of an instrument known as a **proxy. A proxy fight** is a situation where outsiders plan to take control of the business by requesting the stockholders transfer their rights to outsiders in order to remove the current management and to bring in a new management team.

Common stockholders have preemptive rights to purchase any additional shares sold by the firm. Preemptive rights protect the power of control of current stockholders and protect stockholders against a dilution of stock value. Selling common stock at a price below the market value would dilute its price. This would transfer wealth from present stockholders to new stockholders. Preemptive rights prevent such transfer.

Put and Call Options   A **put option** is the right to sell stock at a given price within a certain period. A **call option** is the right to purchase stock at a given price within a certain period. Selling a put option could force the company to purchase additional stock if the option is exercised. The holder of a put option for a particular common stock would make a profit if the option is exercised during the option term after the stock price has declined below the put price. A **warrant option** gives the holder a right to purchase stock from the issuer at a given price.

Preferred Stock

Preferred stock is issued to raise long-term capital for many reasons. When neither common stock nor long-term debt can be issued on reasonable terms, during adverse business conditions, a firm can issue preferred stock with warrants when the common stock is depressed. To bolster the equity component of a firm's capital structure, a firm can issue convertible preferred stock in connection with mergers and acquisitions. A firm can also issue a floating-rate preferred stock to stabilize the market price.

Preferred stock is the stock whose dividend rate fluctuates with changes in the general level of interest rates. Thus stock is good for liquidity portfolios (e.g., marketable securities). It is an effective way to obtain new capital at a low cost due to its floating dividend rates, stable market price, and tax exemption for dividends received.

Preferred stock is a hybrid stock, meaning that it is similar to bonds in some respects (e.g., redeemable feature) and similar to common stock in others (e.g., convertibility feature and voting rights). Therefore, preferred stock can be classified either as bonds or common stock.

Preferred stock is usually reported in the equity section of the balance sheet under "preferred stock" or "preferred equity." Accountants and financial analysts treat the preferred stock differently. Accountants treat preferred stock as equity, and financial analysts treat it as equity or debt, depending on who benefits from the analysis being made.

Major Provisions of Preferred Stocks   Major provisions include priority to assets and earnings, par value, cumulative dividends, convertibility into common stock, voting rights, participation in sharing the firm's earnings, sinking fund requirements, maturity date, and call provisions.

Priorities   Preferred stock has an advantage in that it has a higher-priority claim over assets and earnings than common stock but a lower priority than debt holders.

Cumulative Dividends   All preferred dividends in arrears must be paid before common dividends can be paid. This is a protection feature for preferred stock to receive a preferred position and to avoid paying huge common stock dividends at the expense of paying stipulated annual dividends to the preferred stockholders.

Sinking Fund   Most newly issued preferred stocks have sinking fund requirements that call for the purchase and retirement of a given percentage (e.g., 2 to 3%) of the preferred stock each year.

Call Provision   A call provision gives the issuing corporation the right to call in the preferred stock for redemption. A call premium may be attached where a company has to pay more than par value when it calls the preferred stock.

Pros and Cons of Preferred Stock from Issuer and Investor Viewpoints   From an issuer's viewpoint, the advantages of financing with preferred stock are: fixed financial cost, no danger of bankruptcy if earnings are too low to meet fixed charges, and avoidance of sharing control of the firm with new investors.

From an issuer's viewpoint, the disadvantage of financing with preferred stock is a higher after-tax cost of capital than debt due to nondeductibility of preferred dividends. The lower a company's tax bracket, the more likely it is to issue preferred stock.

From an investor's viewpoint, the advantages of financing with preferred stock include steadier and more assured income than common stock, preference over common stock in the case of liquidation, and tax exemption for preferred dividends received.

From an investor's viewpoint, the disadvantages of financing with preferred stock are: no legally enforceable right to dividends, even if a company earns a profit, and, for individual investors, after-tax bond yields could be higher than those on preferred stock, even though the preferred stock is riskier.

❑ Learning Objective 7.5: UNDERSTAND THE TECHNIQUES FOR EVALUATING THE COST OF CAPITAL

Similar to any other resources (e.g., materials, personnel, and machinery), capital has a cost. The rate of return on a security to an investor is the same as the cost of capital to a firm, which is a required return on its investments. Any increase in total assets of a firm's balance sheet must be financed by an increase in one or more capital components (i.e., debt, preferred stock, retained earnings, and common stock). The cost of capital must reflect the average cost of the various sources of long-term funds used, that is, one or more of the capital components used.

Cost of Debt

The **cost of debt** is calculated as Kd $(1-T)$, where Kd is the interest rate on debt and T is the firm's marginal tax rate. The government pays part of the cost of debt (equal to tax rate) because interest is deductible for tax purposes. The value of the firm's stock depends on after-tax cash flows. Here we are interested in acquiring a new debt (marginal cost of debt) to finance a new asset, and past financing is a sunk cost and is irrelevant for cost-of-capital calculation purposes.

The key point is to compare the rate of return with after-tax flows. After-tax cost of debt is less than before-tax cost due to tax savings resulting from an interest expense deduction that reduces the net cost of debt.

Cost of Preferred Stock

The **cost of preferred stock** (Kp) is the preferred dividend (Dp) divided by the net issuing price (Pn) or the price the firm receives after deducting flotation costs. This is $Kp = Dp/Pn$. Since preferred dividends are not tax deductible for the issuer, there are no tax savings, unlike interest expense on debt, which is deductible.

Cost of Retained Earnings

If management decides to retain earnings, then there is an opportunity cost involved: that is, stockholders could have received the earnings as dividends and invested this money somewhere else. Because of this opportunity cost, the firm should earn on its retained earnings at least as much as the stockholders themselves could earn in alternative investments of comparable risk.

Who Requires What?

- The costs of debt are based on the returns investors and creditors require on debt.
- The costs of preferred stock are based on the returns investors require on preferred stock.
- The costs of retained earnings are based on the returns stockholders require on equity capital.

When a stock is in equilibrium, its required rate of return (Ks) should be equal to its expected rate of return (Kes):

$$Ks = Krf = Rp \text{ or } Kes = (D1/Po) + g$$

where Krf is the risk-free rate, Rp = risk premium, $D1/Po$ is the stock's dividend yield, and g is the stock's expected growth rate.

Three methods are commonly used to calculate the cost of retained earnings: (1) the capital asset pricing model (CAPM) approach, (2) the bond-yield-plus-risk-premium approach, and (3) the discounted cash flow (DCF) approach.

CAPM Approach

CAPM provides a basis for determining the investor's expected rate of return from investing in common stock. The equation is:

$$Ks = Krf + (Km - Krf)\, bi$$

where Krf is the risk-free rate (e.g., U.S. Treasury bond or bill rate), ($Km - Krf$) is equal to the risk premium, Km is the expected rate of return on the market or on "average" stock, and bi is the stock's beta coefficient (an index of the stock's risk).

Drawbacks of the CAPM approach include: a stockholder may be concerned with total risk rather than with market risk only. Beta coefficient may not measure the firm's true investment risk. This approach will understate the correct value of the required rate of return on the stock, Ks, and it is dif-

ficult to obtain correct estimates of the inputs to the model to make it operational. Examples include: deciding whether to use long-term or short-term Treasury bonds for risk-free rate, difficulty in estimating the beta coefficient that investors expect the firm to have in the future, and difficulty in estimating the market risk premium.

Bond-Yield-Plus-Risk-Premium Approach

This method provides a ballpark estimate of the cost of equity, not a precise number, since it uses ad hoc, subjective, and judgmental estimates.

$$Ks = \text{Bond Rate} + \text{Risk Premium}$$

A firm's cost on common equity is found by adding a risk premium (say 2 to 4%) based on judgment to the interest rate on the firm's own long-term debt.

Discounted Cash Flow Approach

The **DCF approach** is also called the **dividend-yield-plus-growth rate** approach, and is calculated as:

$$Ks = Kes = D1/Po + \text{Expected Growth } (g)$$

Investors expected to receive a dividend yield ($D1/Po$) plus a capital gain (g) for a total expected return of Kes. At equilibrium, this expected return would be equal to the required return (Ks): $Ks = Kes$.

Cost of Common Stock

The **cost of common stock (Ke)** is higher than the **cost of retained earnings (Ks)** due to flotation costs involved in selling new common stock. The equation is

$$Ke = \frac{D1}{Po(1 - F)} + g$$

where $D1$ is the dividends, Po is the stock price, F is the percentage flotation cost incurred in selling the new stock, and $Po\,(1 - F)$ is the net price per share received by the firm.

The Effects of Cost of Common Stock

- The firm must earn more than the cost of common stock (Ke) due to flotation cost.
- When a firm earns more than Ke, the price of the stock will rise.
- When a firm earns exactly Ke, earnings per share will not fall, expected dividend can be

maintained, and consequently the price per share will not decline.

- When a firm earns less than Ke, then earnings, dividends, and growth will fall below expectations, causing the price of the stock to decline.

Weighted-Average and Marginal Cost of Capital Concepts

An **optimal (target) capital structure** is a mix of debt, preferred stock, and common stock that maximizes a firm's stock price. The goal of the finance manager should be to raise new capital in a manner that will keep the actual capital structure on target over time. The firm's **weighted-average cost of capital (WACC)** is calculated based on the target proportions of capital and the cost of the capital components.

$$WACC = WdKd\,(1 - T) + WpKp + WsKs$$

where Wd, Wp, and Ws are the weights used for debt, preferred stock, and common stock, respectively. T is the marginal tax rate.

The weights could be based on either book values or market values and the latter is preferred over the former. If a firm's book value weights are close to its market value weight, book weights can be used.

As the firm tries to raise more money, the cost of each dollar will at some point rise. The marginal cost concept can be applied here: *The marginal cost of any item is the cost of another unit of that item, whether the item is labor or production. The **marginal cost of capital (MCC)** is the cost of the last dollar of new capital that the firm raises, and the MCC rises as more and more capital is raised during a given period.* The MCC schedule shows how the weighted-average cost of capital changes as more and more new capital is raised during a given year.

The **breakpoint (BP)** is the dollar value of new capital that can be raised before an increase in the firm's weighted-average cost of capital occurs. The BP is computed as:

BP = Total Amount of Lower-Cost of Capital of Given Type ÷ Fraction of This Type of Capital in the Capital Structure

Issues in Cost of Capital

There are three major issues in the cost of capital:

1. **Depreciation-generated funds.** Depreciation is a source of capital and its cash flows can be either reinvested or returned to investors. The cost of depreciation-generated funds is equal to the weighted-average cost of capital in which capital comes from retained earnings and low-cost debt.
2. **Privately owned and small business firms.** The same principles of cost of capital estimation can be applied to both privately held and publicly owned firms. Input data are difficult to obtain for privately owned firms since their stock is not publicly traded.
3. **Measurement problems.** It is difficult to estimate the cost of equity, obtain input data for the CAPM approach, estimate stock growth rate, and assign different risk-adjusted discount rates to capital budgeting projects of differing degrees of riskiness.

Capital budgeting and cost of capital estimates deal with *ex ante* (estimated) data rather than *ex post* (historical) data. Because of this, we can be wrong about the MCC schedule. Consequently, a project that formerly looked good could turn out to be a bad one. Despite these issues, the cost of capital estimates used in this section are reasonably accurate. By solving these issues, refinements can be made.

❏ Learning Objective 7.6: UNDERSTAND THE PRINCIPLES AND TECHNIQUES OF CAPITAL BUDGETING

Capital budgeting decisions deal with the long-term future of a firm's course of action. Capital budgeting is the process of analyzing investment projects and deciding whether they should be included in the capital budget, which in turn outlines the planned expenditures on fixed assets such as buildings, plant, machinery, equipment, warehouses, and offices.

Short-term working capital decisions focus on increasing current assets. Long-term investment (capital budgeting) decisions focus on increasing noncurrent (fixed) assets.

A firm needs to develop capital budget plans several years in advance to synchronize the timing of funds availability with the timing of fixed asset acquisitions. Capital budgeting projects are initiated and selected by company management to be in line with the strategic business plan (e.g., mergers and acquisitions and introduction of new products). Generally, the larger the required investment, the more detailed the analysis, and the higher the level of management approval required to authorize the expenditure.

The process of capital budgeting is similar to securities valuation (i.e., stocks and bonds) in that the value of the firm increases when the asset's present value exceeds its cost. A link between capital budgeting and stock values exists in that the more effective the firm's capital budgeting procedures, the higher the price of its stock. From an economics point of view, an optimal capital budget is determined by the point where the marginal cost of capital is equal to the marginal rate of return on investment.

There are two types of errors in capital budgeting project decisions that must be avoided. These include:

> ### Accept or Reject Error in Capital Budgeting Project Decisions
>
> 1. An accept-error, meaning a project is accepted when it should not
> 2. A reject-error, meaning a project is rejected when it should not

Methods to Rank Investment Projects

Ten methods are used to rank investment projects and to decide whether projects should be accepted for inclusion in the capital budget. They are (1) payback method (regular and discounted), (2) accounting rate of return method, (3) net present value method, (4) benefit–cost ratio or profitability index method, (5) savings investment ratio method, (6) benefit investment ratio method, (7) regular internal rate of return method, (8) modified internal rate of return method, (9) cost–benefit analysis, and (10) cost-effectiveness analysis.

1. Payback Method

Two methods exist: regular and discounted. The **regular payback period** is net investment divided by average annual after-tax operating cash inflows. It is the expected number of years required to recover the original investment in a capital budgeting project. The procedure calls for accumulating the project's net cash flows until the cumulative total becomes positive. The shorter the payback period, the greater the acceptance of the project and the greater the project's liquidity. Risk can be minimized by selecting the investment alternative with the shortest payback period. Initial investment money can be recouped quickly.

Regular Payback Period = Net Investment/ Average Annual After-Tax Operating Cash Inflows

A variation of the regular payback method is the **discounted payback period**, where the expected cash flows are discounted by the project's cost of capital or the required rate of return for the project. A comparison between regular payback and discounted payback is as follows:

- A regular payback period is the number of years required to recover the investment from the project's net cash flows. It does not take account of the cost of capital. The cost of debt and equity used to finance the project is not reflected in the cash flows. It assumes constant annual operating cash inflows.
- A discounted payback period is the number of years required to recover the investment from discounted cash flows. It does take into account the cost of capital. It shows the breakeven years after covering debt and equity costs.
- Both methods are deficient in that they do not consider the time value of money.
- Both methods ignore cash flows after the payback period.
- Neither method measures full profitability of a project.

It is possible for the regular payback and the discounted payback methods to produce conflicting ranking of projects. The payback method is often used as a rough measure of both the liquidity and the riskiness of a project since longer-term cash flows are riskier than near-term cash flows. This method is used as a screening device to weed out projects with high and marginal payback periods. A shorter payback period is preferred. The payback method can be used to reduce the uncertainty surrounding a capital budgeting decision and is often used in conjunction with net present value and internal rate of return methods.

2. Accounting Rate of Return Method

The **accounting rate of return (ARR) method** is based on accounting data and is computed as the average annual profits after taxes divided by the initial cash outlay in the project. This ARR is then compared to the required rate of return to determine whether a particular project should be accepted or rejected. Strengths of the ARR method include that it is simple and that accounting data are readily available. Drawbacks of the ARR method include that it does not consider the project's cash flows, it measures the average rate of return over the asset's entire life, and it ignores the time value of money. The formula for this method is:

ARR = Average Annual Profit After Taxes/Initial Cash Outlay

3. Net Present Value Method

A simple method to accommodate the uncertainty inherent in estimating future cash flows is to adjust the minimum desired rate of return. Discounted cash flow (DCF) techniques, which consider the time value of money, were developed to compensate for the weakness of the payback method. Two examples of DCF techniques include (1) the net present value (NPV) method and (2) the internal rate of return (IRR) method.

NPV is equal to the present value of future net cash flows, discounted at the marginal cost of capital. The approach calls for finding the present value of cash inflows and cash outflows, discounted at the project's cost of capital, and adding these discounted cash flows to give the project's NPV. The rationale for the NPV method is that the value of a firm is the sum of the values of its parts.

NPV = (After-Tax Cash Flows)

× (Present Value of Annuity) − (Initial Investment)

or

NPV = Present Value of Benefits
− Present Value of Costs

NPV decision rules include the following:

- If the NPV is positive, the project should be accepted since the wealth of current stockholders would increase.
- If the NPV is negative, the project should be rejected since the wealth of current stockholders would reduce.
- If the NPV is zero, the project should be accepted even though the wealth of current stockholders is unchanged (the firm's investment base increases but the value of its stock remains constant).
- If two projects are mutually exclusive, the one with the higher positive NPV should be chosen.
- If two projects are independent, there is no conflict in selection. Capital rationing is the only limiting factor.
- If money is available, invest in all projects in which the NPV is greater than zero.
- If a project's return exceeds the company's cost of capital, select the combination of projects that will fully utilize the budget and maximize the sum of the net present values.

4. Benefit–Cost Ratio or Profitability Index (PI) Method

A variation of the NPV approach is the **benefit–cost ratio (BCR)** or **benefit–cost index**. The BCR is the present value of benefits (i.e., cash inflows) divided by the present value of the cost (i.e., cash outflows).

$$BCR = \frac{PV \text{ of Benefits}}{PV \text{ of Costs}}$$

The BCR is a relative measure of an alternative's value. It provides a measure of the benefits obtained per dollar spent. The higher the BCR, the larger the return. NPV, on the other hand, is an absolute measure. In situations where funds are limited, the BCR provides decision-makers with an additional piece of information. In selecting among alternatives, the BCR shows which alternatives provide the largest return relative to costs. As with the use of NPV, non-quantifiable benefits may show that an alternative with a lower BCR may be the most advantageous alternative to the company.

Other names given to the BCR include NPV index, **profitability index (PI)**, or present value (PV) index, which is computed as the present value of after-tax cash inflows divided by present value of the initial investment (cash outflows). When the profitability index or benefit–cost ratio is 1.0, the NPV is zero. The goal is to require that the profitability index or benefit–cost ratio be more than 1.0 so that NPV will be higher than zero. The PI method is used to rank competing projects in the order of their attractiveness when they have different dollar amounts to compare.

As long as the PI is 1.0 or greater, the project is acceptable. For any given project, the NPV method and the PI method give the same accept/reject answer. When choosing between mutually exclusive projects, the NPV method is preferred because the project's benefits are expressed in absolute terms. In contrast, the PI method expresses in relative terms. The formula for the PI method is:

PI = PV of Cash Inflows/PV of Cash Outflows

What Is an Equivalent Uniform Annual Cost?

When the economic lives of alternative investments differ and are shorter than the minimum requirement time period, **equivalent uniform annual cost (EUAC)** allows the alternatives to be compared on a common basis of time. Assuming that alternatives are equal in their ability to fulfill stated objectives, this approach avoids the distortion that would otherwise occur. The EUAC is not appropriate if factors such as technology are involved, the alternatives are not equal in their ability to meet requirements, or the requirement will cease prior to the economic life of one of the alternatives.

EUAC converts each option into an equivalent hypothetical alternative with uniform recurring costs. For example, the yearly costs of system A exceed those of system B, but it functions without major replacements for five years as opposed to system B's three-year economic life. It can be reasonably assumed that the cash flow patterns of each can be repeated; the costs of both alternatives can be extended to a common denominator point of 15 years. The NPV of an alternative is calculated and then divided by the sum of the discount factors for its economic life to yield the EUAC.

5. Savings Investment Ratio Method

Calculating a **savings investment ratio (SIR)** allows organizations to compare the profit (savings) potential of alternatives and helps to answer the question: Do the recurring savings of the proposed investment, compared to the status quo, justify the costs? The ratio is derived by computing the present value (PV) of the savings produced by the investment relative to the costs of the status quo in each year of the analysis. The discounted savings are totaled and divided by the PV of the investment costs. If costs extend over more than one year, these too should be discounted and summed. The resulting ratio indicates the savings resulting from an alternative to the status quo proportionate to the investment required to implement the alternative. An SIR of 1.0 or greater indicates that the NPV of the savings attained by the new investment are equal to or greater than the NPV of the costs incurred to implement the new investment. SIRs can be used to compare multiple investment opportunities, but scale (total costs and savings) must then be considered. When computing SIRs, total annual maintenance and operations costs are not discounted, only the difference between the annual costs of the two alternatives. The formula for SIR is:

$$SIR = PV \text{ of Savings}/PV \text{ of Costs}$$

6. Benefit Investment Ratio Method

Comparing the **benefit investment ratios (BIRs)** of investments may be helpful in situations where the financial analysis scores of alternatives rank closely and an additional viewpoint is desired. Dividing the NPV of benefits by the NPV of costs derives the BIR. The NPV method and the BIR method will always indicate the same accept/reject decision for independent projects but can reflect different rankings of alternatives. The formula for this ratio is:

$$BIR = NPV \text{ of Benefits}/NPV \text{ of Costs}$$

7. Regular Internal Rate of Return (IRR) Method

In the regular IRR method, the discount rate that equates the present value of future cash inflows to the investment's cost is found. In other words, the IRR method is defined as the discount rate at which a project's NPV equals zero.

$$IRR = PV \text{ of Cash Inflows} = PV \text{ of Cash Outflows}$$

Similarities between the NPV and IRR methods include the following:

• Both NPV and IRR methods consider the time value of money.
• Both methods use the same basic mathematical equation for solving the project's problems.

Differences between NPV and IRR methods include the following:

• In the NPV method, the discount rate is specified, and the NPV is found.
• In the IRR method, the NPV is specified to equal zero, and the value of IRR that forces this equality is determined.
• The NPV method assumes reinvestment of project cash flows at the cost of capital.
• The IRR method assumes reinvestment of project cash flows at the internal rate of return.

When a project's IRR is greater than its marginal cost of capital, it increases the value of the firm's stock since a surplus remains after paying for the capital. Similarly, when a project's IRR is less than its marginal cost of capital, it decreases the value of the firm's stock since the project reduces the profits of the existing stockholders.

Two kinds of projects exist: (1) normal and (2) nonnormal. A **normal project** is one that has one or more cash outflows followed by a series of cash inflows. No difficulties are encountered when evaluated by the IRR method. However, a **nonnormal project** (i.e., a project that calls for a large cash outflow either sometime during or at the end of its life) can give unique difficulties when evaluated by the IRR method.

The payback method, NPV method, and IRR method all show an investment breakeven point for the project in an accounting sense, which would be useful in evaluating capital projects. The IRR method, NPV method, and NPV index consider risk only indirectly through the selection of a discount rate used in the present value computations.

Which Method Is Best: Payback, NPV, or IRR? Any capital budgeting method should meet the following three criteria in order to produce consistent and correct investment decisions:

1. The method must consider all cash flows throughout the entire life of a project. The payback method does not meet this property while the NPV and IRR methods do.
2. The method must consider the time value of money. A dollar received today is more valuable than a dollar received tomorrow. The payback method does not meet this property while the IRR and NPV methods do.
3. The method must choose the project that maximizes the firm's stock price when faced with selecting from a set of mutually exclusive projects. The payback method and the IRR methods do not meet this property while the NPV method meets this property all the time.

The NPV method is better for evaluating mutually exclusive projects. However, when two projects are independent, both the NPV and the IRR criteria always lead to the same accept/reject decision.

The critical issue in resolving the NPV/IRR conflicts between mutually exclusive projects is the different reinvestment rate assumptions made. The reinvestment rate is the opportunity cost rate at which a firm can invest differential early year's cash flows generated from NPV or IRR methods.

The following are assumptions in NPV and IRR methods:

- *NPV assumptions.* The cash flows generated by a project can be reinvested at the cost of capital. The NPV method discounts cash flows at the cost of capital.

- *IRR assumptions.* The cash flows generated by a project can be reinvested at the IRR. The IRR method discounts cash flows at the project's IRR.

It has been demonstrated that the best assumption is that projects' cash flows are reinvested at the cost of capital. Therefore, the NPV method is better.

8. Modified Internal Rate of Return (MIRR) Method

Academics prefer the NPV method, whereas business executives favor the IRR method. The reason business executives prefer the IRR method is that they find IRR "more natural" to analyze investments in terms of percentage rates of return rather than dollars of NPV.

The regular IRR method can be modified to make it a better indicator of relative profitability and hence better for use in capital budgeting. The **MIRR** is the discount rate at which the present value of a project's cost is equal to the present value of its terminal value. The **terminal value** is the sum of the future values of the cash inflows, compounded at the firm's cost of capital. In other words, the MIRR is the discount rate that forces the present value of the costs to equal the present value of the terminal value.

The MIRR method is better than the regular IRR method because MIRR assumes that cash flows from all projects are reinvested at the firm's cost of capital, whereas the regular IRR method assumes that the cash flows from each project are reinvested at the project's own IRR. Therefore, the MIRR method is a better indicator of a project's true profitability.

9. Cost–Benefit Analysis

Cost–benefit analysis (CBA) or **benefit–cost analysis (BCA)** is used for many purposes, such as a planning tool, a decision-making criterion, and a means to evaluate investments. CBA has four major elements that should be factored in for consideration: (1) total business and system costs with the IT investment in a new system, (2) total business costs without the IT investment in a new system, (3) tangible benefits, and (4) intangible benefits.

There are many advantages to performing a CBA that reach far beyond its ability to facilitate ultimate decision-making processes. A comprehensive CBA will include a documented path that clearly reveals the rationale behind a decision. When a CBA is performed correctly, all assumptions, theories, methods, and procedures are labeled and can be easily extracted from the decision or traced to the decision itself. This allows for the modification or clarification of any of the individual elements throughout the life of the project.

The CBA itself is structured as a systematic and organized collection of facts underlying a decision being made about a particular set of alternatives. It ensures that there is standardization and objectivity in the decision-making process. The CBA is a particularly accommodating tool when evaluating seemingly noncomparable alternatives or solutions.

10. Cost-Effectiveness Analysis

Cost-effectiveness analysis (CEA) is appropriate to the public sector or wherever it is unnecessary or impractical to consider the dollar value of the benefits provided by the alternatives under consideration. A project or program is cost effective if, on the basis of lifecycle cost analysis of competing alternatives, it is determined to have the lowest costs expressed in present value terms for a given amount of benefits. CEA is appropriate whenever (1) each alternative has the same annual benefits expressed in monetary terms or (2) each alternative has the same annual effects, but dollar values cannot be assigned to their benefits.

CEA does not imply choosing the policy with the smallest dollar price tag. CEA chooses the policy that achieves the policy goal with the smallest loss in social wellbeing. The smallest welfare loss might not be associated with the smallest dollar cost.

A CEA is basically a CBA without the benefits. It entails estimating all lifecycle costs and discounting the annual costs by the appropriate rate to yield the NPV of each alternative. Like the CBA, it should include the rationale for all assumptions and expected key results that can be monitored.

CEA is also useful for comparing alternatives with identical costs but different benefits, although this situation may also require assignment of weighing factors. An example might be the replacement of legacy systems where the alternatives all meet the primary requirements of providing specific functions, but each have different secondary benefits that cannot be separated from the basic product or service. Where all benefits cannot be expressed in dollars, a full listing of such benefits, along with any units of measurement that can be ascertained, should accompany the CEA.

Postaudit of Capital Projects

A **postaudit** is a comparison of the actual and expected results (both costs and savings) for a given capital project and explanation of variances, if any. A postaudit is a good learning exercise and is practiced by most successful organizations. The lessons learned from the postaudit can be used to fine-tune forecasts of costs and benefits and to improve business operations.

The postaudit is a complicated process to review since factors such as demand uncertainty and unexpected deviations from plans occur, which are beyond the control of most managers in the firm. Actual savings may not materialize as expected due to unexpected costs. Despite these problems, it is a good approach to conduct a postaudit of capital projects as long as the blame is on the process, not on the people involved.

Project Cash Flows

It is important to note that capital budgeting decisions must be based on annual cash flows, not accounting income, and that only incremental cash flows are relevant to the accept/reject decision. Cash flows and accounting income can be different due to depreciation expense, which is a noncash expense. Since we are interested in **net cash flows**, it is obtained by adding depreciation expense to the net income after taxes.

Incremental cash flows represent the changes in the firm's total cash flows that occur as a direct result of accepting or rejecting the project. It is the net cash flow that can be traceable to an investment project.

Four special problems occur in determining incremental cash flows:

1. **Sunk costs** are not incremental costs, and they should not be included in the project analysis. A sunk cost is an outlay that has already been committed or has already occurred and hence is not affected by the accept/reject decision under consideration. Only incremental cash flows should be compared with the incremental investment.

2. **Opportunity costs** are the cash flows that can be generated from assets the firm already owns provided they are not used for the project in question. It is the return on the best alternative use of an asset that is forgone due to funds invested in a particular project. Opportunity costs are not incremental costs.

3. **Externalities** are the indirect effects of a project on cash flows in other parts of the firm. Revenues produced from the effects of externalities should not be treated as incremental income.
4. **Shipping and installation costs** incurred on a new fixed asset (e.g., equipment) should be added to the invoice price of the fixed asset. The depreciation base for calculating the depreciation expense is the total invoice price including shipping and installation costs. Therefore, shipping and installation costs should not be treated as incremental cash flows since they would be double-counted.

Project Risk Assessment

Risk analysis is important to capital budgeting decisions. Three separate and distinct types of project risk are: (1) the project's own standalone risk, (2) corporate risk (within-firm risk), and (3) market risk (beta risk).

1. A **project's standalone risk** is measured by the variability of the project's expected returns.
2. A **project's corporate risk** is measured by the project's impact on the firm's earnings variability. It does not consider the effects of stockholders' diversification.
3. A **project's market (beta) risk** is measured by the project's effect on the firm's beta coefficient.

Market risk cannot be eliminated by diversification. If the project has highly uncertain returns and if those are highly correlated with those of the firm's other assets and also with most other assets in the economy, the project will have a high degree of all types of risk. A company whose beta value has decreased due to a change in its marketing strategy would apply a lower discount rate to expected cash flows of potential projects.

Market risk is important because of its direct effect on a firm's stock prices. It has been found that both market risk and capital risk affect stock prices. Corporate risk for weak firms increases significantly compared to strong firms. This is because weak firms would have difficulty in borrowing money at reasonable interest rates, which in turn would decrease profits. The decrease in profits would be reflected in the stock price.

Risk to a company is affected by both project variability and how project returns correlate with those of the company's prevailing business. Overall company risk will be lowest when a project's returns exhibit low variability and negative correlation.

Techniques for Measuring Standalone Risk

Here we are interested in determining the uncertainty inherent in the project's cash flows. Three techniques are available for assessing a project's standalone risk: sensitivity analysis, scenario analysis, and Monte Carlo simulation.

1. **Sensitivity analysis** can provide useful insights into the riskiness of a project. It is a technique that indicates exactly how much the NPV will change in response to a given change in an input variable, other things held constant. For example, if each input variable can be changed by several percentage points above and below the expected value, then a new NPV can be calculated for each of those values. Finally, the set of NPVs can be plotted against the variable that was changed. The slope of the lines in the graphs shows how sensitive NPV is to changes in each of the inputs; the steeper the slope, the more sensitive the NPV is to a change in the variable.
2. **Scenario analysis** is a risk analysis technique that considers both the sensitivity of NPV to changes in key variables and the range of likely variable values. NPV under bad conditions (i.e., low sales, high variable cost per unit) and good conditions (i.e., high sales and low variable cost per unit) are calculated and compared to the expected (i.e., base case) NPV. The following are the highlights of these relationships:

Bad Condition → Worst-Case Scenario → (all input variables are set at their worst forecasted values)

Good Condition → Best-Case Scenario → (all input variables are set at their best forecasted values)

Base Case Condition → Most Likely Scenario → (all input variables are set at their most likely values)

The results of the scenario analysis are used to determine the expected NPV, the standard deviation of NPV, and the coefficient of variation. Even though scenario analysis provides useful information about a project's standalone risk, it is limited in that it considers only a few discrete NPV outcomes for the project. In reality, there are an infinite number of outcomes.
3. **Monte Carlo simulation** ties together sensitivities and input variable probability distributions. Probability distributions of each uncertain cash

flow variable are specified. The computer chooses at random a value for each uncertain variable based on the variable's specified probability distributions. The model then determines the net cash flows for each year, which in turn are used to determine the project's NPV in the first run. Since this is a simulation technique, this model is repeated many times to yield a probability distribution.

The primary advantage of simulation is that it shows a range of possible outcomes along with their attached probabilities. The scenario analysis shows only a few point estimates of the NPV. Both the standard deviation of the NPV and the coefficient of variation are calculated, providing additional information in assessing the riskiness of a project.

It is difficult to obtain valid estimates of probability distributions and correlations among the variables. From both scenario analysis and simulation analysis, no clear-cut decision rule emerges. Both techniques ignore the effects of the project as well as the investor diversification—which is the major drawback.

Techniques for Measuring Market/Beta Risk

Beta risk is that part of a project's risk that cannot be eliminated by diversification. It is measured by the project's beta coefficient. Two methods are available to estimate the betas of individual projects: (1) the pure play method and (2) the accounting beta method.

In the **pure play method**, the company tries to find several single-product firms in the same line of business as the project being evaluated, and it then applies these betas to determine the cost of capital for its own project. A major drawback of the pure play method is that the approach can be applied only for major assets such as whole divisions, not for individual projects. Therefore, it is difficult to find comparable business firms of the size in question.

The **accounting beta method** fills the gap of the pure play method in finding single-product, publicly traded firms by applying against a large sample of firms. The project's beta is determined by regressing the returns of a particular company's stock against returns on a stock market index. Betas determined by using accounting data rather than stock market data are called **accounting betas.** In practice, accounting betas are normally calculated for divisions or other large units, not for single assets, and divisional betas are then imputed to the asset.

Project Risks and Capital Budgeting

Capital budgeting can affect a firm's market risk, its corporate risk, or both. It is difficult to develop a good measure of project risk due to difficulty in quantifying either risk.

Two methods for incorporating project risk into the capital budgeting decision process include (1) the certainty equivalent approach and (2) the risk-adjusted discount rate approach.

Under the **certainty equivalent approach,** the expected cash flows are adjusted to reflect project risk. All unknown cash flows will have low certainty equivalent values. This approach is difficult to implement in practice despite its theoretical appeal.

Under the **risk-adjusted discount rate approach,** differential project risk is dealt with by changing the discount rate. Risk adjustments are subjective and take the following decision paths:

- Average-risk projects are discounted at the firm's average cost of capital.
- Above-average-risk projects are discounted at a higher cost of capital.
- Below-average-risk projects are discounted at a rate below the firm's average.

Capital Rationing

The amount of funds available to a firm is limited even though acceptable capital budget projects are many. A firm will approve an independent project if its NPV is positive. It selects the project with the highest NPV when faced with mutually exclusive projects. Management cannot or would not want to raise whatever funds are required to finance all of the acceptable projects. When the capital budget must be limited, this situation is called **capital rationing.**

Capital rationing is a constraint placed on the total size of the firm's capital investment. A drawback of capital rationing is that it is not maximizing a firm's stock value since it deliberately forgoes profitable projects. Because of this negative effect, only a few firms ration their capital.

International Capital Budgeting

The techniques presented in this section for domestic capital budgeting are equally applicable to the international capital budgeting process. However, three types of risks exist in the international area: (1) **cash flow risk,** that is, cash flow estimation is much more difficult, (2) **exchange rate risk,** that is, exchange rate fluctuations add to the riskiness of the foreign investment, and (3) **sovereignty risk,** that is, the possibility of deliberate foreign government acts that reduce or eliminate cash flows.

In terms of cash flows, the relevant cash flows are the dollar cash flows that the subsidiary can turn over to the parent. Since the foreign currency cash flows turned over to the parent must be converted to U.S. dollar values by translating them at expected future exchange rates, an exchange rate premium should be added to the domestic cost of capital. This is done to reflect the exchange rate risk inherent in the investment. Hedging can minimize the exchange rate risk, which adds to the cost of the project.

Sovereignty risk includes the possibility of expropriation or nationalization without adequate compensation and the possibility of unanticipated restrictions of cash flows to the parent company, such as tighter controls on repatriation of dividends or higher taxes. Generally, sovereignty risk premiums are not added to the cost of capital to adjust for sovereignty risk. Companies can take steps to reduce the potential loss from expropriation in three major ways: (1) by financing the subsidiary with local sources of capital, (2) by structuring operations so that the subsidiary has value only as a part of the integrated corporate system, and (3) by obtaining insurance against economic losses from expropriations. When the insurance is taken, its cost should be added to the project's cost.

❑ Learning Objective 7.7: UNDERSTAND THE VARIOUS TYPES AND RISKS OF FINANCIAL INSTRUMENTS

Financial instruments (currency and credit derivatives) are used by large and small businesses in every industry to hedge against financial risk.

One means to hedge currency exposure and risk is through the currency market, which includes forward contracts, futures contracts, currency options, and currency swaps.

Forward Contracts

In the forward exchange market, one buys a forward contract for the exchange of one currency for another at a specific future date and at a specific exchange ratio. This differs from the spot market, where currencies are traded for immediate delivery. A **forward contract** provides assurance of being able to convert into a desired currency at a price set in advance. A foreign currency sells at a forward discount if its forward price is less than its spot price. If the forward price exceeds the spot price, it is said to sell at a **forward premium.** Forward contracts provide a "two-sided" hedge against currency movements. Forward contracts are settled only at expiration, and they can be issued in any size.

Futures Contracts

A **futures contract** is a standardized agreement that calls for delivery of a currency at some specified future date. These contracts are formed with the clearinghouse, not directly between the two parties. Futures contracts provide a "two-sided" hedge against currency movements.

Each day, the futures contract is marked-to-market, meaning it is valued at the closing price. Price movements affect the buyer and seller in opposite ways. Every day there is a winner and a loser, depending on the direction of price movement. The loser must come up with more margin (a small deposit), while the winner can draw off excess margin. Future contracts come only in multiples of standard-size contracts.

Currency Options

An **option** is a contract that gives its holder the right to buy or sell an asset at some predetermined price within a specified period of time. Pure options (financial options) are created by outsiders (investment banking firms) rather than by the firm itself; they are bought and sold by investors or speculators. The leverage involved makes it possible for speculators to make more money with just a few dollars. Also, investors with sizable portfolios can sell options against their stocks and earn the value of the options (minus brokerage commissions) even if the stocks' prices remain constant. Option contracts enable the hedging of "one-sided" risk. Only adverse currency movements are hedged, either with a call option to buy the foreign currency or with a put option to sell it.

Both the value of the underlying stock and the striking price of the option are very important in determining whether an option is in-the-money or out-of-the-money. If an option has value on its expiration date, it is considered to be **in-the-money;**

otherwise, it is worthless and considered **out-of-the-money.** Therefore, the stock price and the striking price are important for determining the market value of an option. In fact, options are called **derivative securities** because their values are dependent on, or derived from, the value of the underlying asset and the striking price. In addition to the stock's market price and the striking price, the value of an option also depends on the option's time to maturity, the level of strike price, the risk-free rate, and the variability of the underlying stock's price. The higher the strike price, the lower the call option price. The higher the stock's market price in relation to the strike price, the higher will be the call option price. The longer the option period, the higher the option price and the larger its premium. The exercise value of an option is the maximum of current price of the stock minus the strike price. The price of an option is the cost of stock minus the present value of the portfolio. The **Black-Scholes model** is used to estimate the value of a call option.

Warrants are options issued by a company that give the holder the right to buy a stated number of shares of the company's stock at a specified price. Warrants are distributed along with debt, and they are used to induce investors (as a sweetener) to buy a firm's long-term debt at a lower interest rate than otherwise would be required.

Real options are used for investment in real assets and their value is determined as:

$$\text{Project Discounted Cash Flow Value} = (\text{Cash Flows})/(1 + \text{Risk-Free Cash Flow})$$

Currency Swaps

A **swap** exchanges a floating-rate obligation for a fixed-rate one or vice versa. There are two types of swaps: currency swaps and interest-rate swaps. With the currency swaps, two parties exchange interest obligations on debt denominated in different currencies. At maturity the principal amounts are exchanged, usually at an exchange rate agreed upon in advance. With an **interest-rate swap**, interest-payment obligations are exchanged between two parties, but they are denominated in the same currency. There is not an actual exchange of principal. If one party defaults, there is no loss of principal per se. However, there is the opportunity cost associated with currency movements after the swap's initiation. These movements affect both interest and principal payments. In this respect, **currency swaps** are more

risky than interest-rate swaps, where the exposure is only to interest. Currency swaps are combined with interest-rate swaps; there is an exchange of fixed-rate for floating-rate payments where the two payments are in different currencies. Financing hedges provide a means to hedge on a longer-term basis, as do currency swaps.

The swap can be longer term in nature (15 years or more) than either the forward or futures contract (5 years). Swaps are like a series of forward contracts corresponding to the future settlement dates at which difference checks are paid. However, a comparable forward market does not exist nor do lengthy futures or options contracts.

The most common swap is the floating/fixed-rate exchange. The exchange itself is on a net settlement basis. That is, the party that owes more interest than it receives in the swap pays the difference. A basis swap is another popular swap where two floating-rate obligations are exchanged.

Various options exist for swap transactions, which are known as **swaptions.** One is to enter a swap at a future date. The terms of the swap are set at the time of the option, and they give the holder the right, but not the obligation, to take a swap position.

The scope of **credit derivatives** includes total return swaps and credit swaps:

- **Total return swaps.** Credit derivatives unbundle default risk from the other features of a loan. The original lender no longer needs to bear the risk; it can be transferred to others for a price. The party who wishes to transfer is known as the protection buyer. The protection seller assumes the credit risk and receives a premium for providing this insurance. The premium is based on the probability and likely severity of default.

  The protection buyer is assumed to hold a risky debt instrument and agrees to pay out its total return to the protection seller. This return consists of the stream of interest payments together with the change in the instrument's market value. The protection seller agrees to pay some reference rate and perhaps a negative or positive spread from this rate.

- **Credit swaps.** A credit swap, also known as a **default swap,** is similar in concept to the total-return swap, but different in the details. The protection buyer pays a specific premium to the protection seller, insurance against a risky debt instrument deteriorating in quality. The annuity premium is paid each period until the earlier of the maturity of the credit swap agreement or a specific credit event occurring, usually default. If the credit event occurs, the protection seller pays the protection buyer a contingent amount. This often takes the form of physical settlement, where the protection buyer puts the defaulted obligation to the protection seller at its face value. The economic cash flow is the difference between the face value of the instrument and its market value. Thus, the protection buyer receives payment only when a specific credit event occurs; otherwise the cash flow from the protection seller is zero. The periodic premium paid is called the **credit swap spread.** This cost of protection depends on the credit rating of the company, risk mitigation, and likely recovery should default occur.

Other credit derivatives include spread-adjusted notes, credit options, and credit-sensitive notes:

- **Spread-adjusted notes** involve resets based on the spread of a particular grade of security over Treasury securities. An index is specified, and quarterly and semiannual resets occur, where one counterparty must pay the other depending on whether the quality yield spread widens or narrows. Usually the spread is collared with a floor and cap.
- **Credit options** involve puts and calls based on a basket of corporate fixed-income securities. The strike price often is a specified amount over Treasury securities.
- With **credit-sensitive notes,** the coupon rate changes with the credit rating of the company involved. If the company is downgraded, the investor receives more interest income; if upgraded, there is less interest income.

Hidden Financial Reporting Risk

Off-balance-sheet accounting practices include hiding debt with the equity method, hiding debt with lease accounting, hiding debt with pension accounting, and hiding debt with special-purpose entities. In all these cases, debt is underreported, which creates a financial reporting risk. Investors and creditors charge a premium for financial reporting risk. Consequently, the cost of capital goes up, and stock prices and bond prices go down.

The equity method hides liabilities because it nets the assets and liabilities of the investee. Since assets are greater than liabilities, this net amount goes on the left-hand side of the balance sheet. This type of accounting practice hides all of the investee's debts.

Use of operating lease accounting "gains" the managers an understatement of their firm's financial structure by 10 to 15 percentage points. Footnotes to financial statements can help investors, creditors, and analysts to unravel the truth.

Huge amounts of money are involved in pension accounting. Pension expenses include the service cost plus the interest on the projected benefit obligation minus the expected return on plan assets plus the amortization of various unrecognized items, such as the unrecognized prior service cost. The only item found on the balance sheet is the prepaid pension asset or the accrual pension cost, which in turn equals the pension assets minus the projected benefit obligation minus various unrecognized items. The netting of the projected benefit obligations and the pension assets is incorrect; consequently, investors, creditors, and analysts must "unnet" them to gain a better understanding of the truth. Another area of concern is the assumptions about interest rates and the need to assess their appropriateness.

Special-purpose entity debt includes securitizations and synthetic leases. **Securitizations** take a pool of homogeneous assets and turn them into securities. The idea is to borrow money from investors, who in turn are repaid by the cash generated by the asset pool. This process includes mortgages, credit card receivables, transportation equipment, energy contracts, water utilities, and trade accounts receivable. Securitizations are big business and represent a financial risk since these amounts are not shown in the balance sheet. **Synthetic leases** constitute a technique by which firms can assert that they have capital leases for tax purposes but operating leases for financial reporting purposes. They form a way for companies to decrease income taxes without admitting any debt on their balance sheets.

Financial Engineering

The scope of financial engineering involves creating new financial instruments (derivative securities) or combining exiting derivatives to accomplish specific hedging goals (e.g., reduce financial risk). A derivative security is a financial asset that represents a claim to another financial asset (e.g., a stock option gives the owner the right to buy or sell stock). Financial risk may result from changes in interest rates, exchange rates, and commodity prices.

Tools for managing financial risk include hedging with forward contracts, hedging with futures contracts, hedging with currency option contracts, and hedging with currency swap contracts. These tools allow a firm to reduce or even eliminate its exposure to financial risks. Hedging avoids a firm's expensive and troublesome disruptions that result from short-run and temporary price fluctuations. It gives a firm the ability to react and adapt to changing financial market conditions.

Financial engineering can also be applied to insurance and reinsurance areas using captive insurance and alternate risk transfer (ART) methods, as part of a company's risk management and risk mitigation strategy. In the **captive insurance method**, a parent company establishes a subsidiary (called captive insurance company) to finance its retained losses. The type of risk that a captive subsidiary can underwrite for the parent includes property damage, product liability, professional indemnity, employee benefits, employer liability, and motor and medical aid expenses.

The **ART method**, which is an alternative to traditional insurance and reinsurance coverage, provides risk-bearing companies with coverage and protection they need through convergence of insurance and financial markets. The scope of ART methods include risk securitization, catastrophe bonds, dual-trigger or multiple-trigger insurance, financial reinsurance, industry loss warranties, weather derivatives, intellectual property insurance, and enterprise-wide risk insurance coverage.

❑ Learning Objective 7.8: UNDERSTAND THE VARIOUS TYPES OF VALUATION MODELS

The scope of valuation includes physically inventoriable assets, financial assets (e.g., bonds, common stock, and preferred stock), and business valuation (cash flows).

Inventory Asset Valuation

Generally, **historical cost** is used to value inventories and cost of goods sold. In certain circumstances, though, departure from cost is justified. Some other methods of costing inventory include the following:

- **Net realizable value.** Damaged, obsolete, or shopworn goods should never be carried at an amount greater than net realizable value. Net realizable value is equal to the estimated selling price of an item minus all costs to complete and dispose of the item.

- **Lower of cost or market.** If the value of inventory declines below its historical cost, then the inventory should be written down to reflect this loss. A departure from the historical cost principle is required when the future utility of the item is not as great as its original cost. When the purchase price of an item falls, it is assumed that its selling price has fallen or will fall. The loss of the future utility of the item should be charged against the revenues of the period in which it occurred. "**Market**" in this context generally means the replacement cost of the item.

However, market cost is limited by a floor and ceiling cost. Market cannot exceed net realizable value, which is the estimated selling price minus the cost of completion and disposal (**ceiling**). Market cannot be less than net realizable value minus a normal profit margin (**floor**). Lower of cost or market can be applied to each inventory item, each inventory class, or total inventory.

Financial Asset Valuation

Policy decisions that are most likely to affect the value of the firm include: investment in a project with large net present value, sale of a risky operating division that will now increase the credit rating of the entire company, and use of more highly leveraged capital structure that results in a lower cost of capital.

Establishing or predicting the value of a firm is an important task of the financial manager since maximizing the value of his firm is a major goal. Here the focus is on maximizing shareholders' wealth. Similar to capital budgeting decisions, the financial manager can use discounted cash flow (DCF) techniques to establish the worth of any assets (e.g., stocks, bonds, real estate, and equipment) whose value is derived from future cash flows. The key concept of DCF is that it takes time value of money into account. *The financial asset valuation for a firm is a combination of bond valuation, common stock valuation, and preferred stock valuation.*

Bond Valuation

A **bond valuation model** shows the mathematical relationships between a bond's market price and the set of variables that determine the price. For example, bond prices and interest rates are inversely related. Corporate bonds are traded in the over-the-counter market.

Treasuries raise money by issuing bonds and offering common equity. A bond that has just been issued is known as a **new issue.** Newly issued bonds are sold close to par value. A bond that has been on the market for a while is called a **seasoned issue** and is classified as an outstanding bond. The prices of outstanding bonds vary from par value. A bond's market price is determined primarily by its **coupon interest payments**. The coupon interest payment is set at a level that will cause the market price of the bond to equal its par value.

A bond represents an annuity (i.e., interest payments) plus a lump sum (i.e., repayment of the par value), and its value is found as the present value of this payment stream. The equation to find a bond's value is:

Value of Bond = I(Present Value of Annuity)
$+ M$ (Present Value of Lump Sum)

where I is dollars of interest paid each year (i.e., Coupon Interest Rate × Par Value = Coupon Interest Payment) and M is par (maturity) value.

Both the present value of the annuity and the lump-sum amount are discounted at an appropriate rate of interest (Kd) on the bond for a number of years (n) until the bond matures. The value of n declines each year after the bond is issued.

A graph can be drawn to show the values of a bond in relation to interest rate changes. Note that regardless of what the future interest rates are, the bond's market value will always approach its par value as it nears the maturity date except in bankruptcy. If the firm went bankrupt, the value of the bond might drop to zero.

Common Stock Valuation

Investors buy common stock for two main reasons: (1) to receive dividends and (2) to enjoy capital gain. Dividends are paid to stockholders at management's discretion since there is no legal obligation to pay dividends. Usually stockholders have an expectation to receive dividends even though in reality they may not. If the stock is sold at a price above its purchase price, the investor will receive a capital gain. Similarly, if the stock is sold at a price below its purchase price, the investor will suffer capital losses.

The value of a common stock is calculated at the present value of the expected future cash flow stream (i.e., expected dividends, original investment, and capital gain or loss). Different aspects of these cash flow streams is the determination of the amount of cash flow and the riskiness of the amounts and knowing what alternative actions affect stock prices.

Preferred Stock Valuation

Preferred stock is a hybrid stock—it has elements of both bonds and common stock. Most preferred stocks entitle their owners to regular fixed dividend payments. The value of preferred stock can be found as follows:

$$Vps = Dps/Kps$$

where Vps is the value of the preferred stock, Dps is the preferred dividend, and Kps is the required rate of return on preferred stock.

Business Valuation

Business valuation is valuing the worth of a business entity, whether in whole or part. The value of a business is derived from its ability to generate cash flows consistently period after period over the long term. Business valuation can be performed at various milestones, such as new product introduction; mergers, acquisitions, divestitures, recapitalization, and stock repurchases; capital expenditures and improvements; joint venture agreements; and ongoing review of performance of business unit operations.

There are 11 models to help management in making sound decisions during valuation of a business opportunity. These models, in the order of importance and usefulness, are (1) book value model, (2) liquidation value model, (3) replacement cost model, (4) discounted abnormal earnings model, (5) price multiples model, (6) financial analysis model, (7) economic-value-added model, (8) market-value-added model, (9) economic profit model, (10) net present value model, and (11) discounted cash flow model.

1. **Book value model.** The book value (net worth, net assets, or stockholders' equity) of a company's stock represents the total assets of the company less its liabilities. The book value per share has no relation to market value per share, as book values are based on historical cost of assets, not on the current value at which they could be sold. Book values are not meaningful because they are distorted by inflation factors and different accounting assumptions used in valuing assets. One use of book value is to provide a floor value, with the true value of the company being some amount

higher. Sales prices of companies are usually expressed as multiples of book values within each industry.

2. **Liquidation value model.** Liquidation value of a firm is total assets minus all liabilities and preferred stock minus all liquidation costs incurred. Liquidation value may be a more realistic measure of a firm than its book value in that liquidation price reflects the current market value of the assets and liabilities if the firm is in a growing, profitable industry. Depending on the power of negotiations, the liquidation prices may be set at fire-sale levels.

3. **Replacement cost model.** The replacement cost model is based on the estimated cost to replace a company's assets, which include both tangible (plant, equipment) and intangible assets (patents, copyrights). Only tangible assets are replaceable, not the intangible ones. Because of this, the replacement cost is lower than the market value of the company; sometimes it could be higher than the market value.

4. **Discounted abnormal earnings model.** If a firm can earn only a normal rate of return on its book value, then investors will pay no more than the book value. Abnormal earnings are equal to total earnings minus normal earnings. The estimated value of a firm's equity is the sum of the current book values plus the discounted future abnormal earnings.

5. **Price multiples model.** The value of a firm is based on price multiples of comparable firms in the industry. This model requires calculation of the desired price multiples and then applying the multiple to the firm being valued. Examples of price multiples include price-to-earnings (P/E) ratio, price-to-book ratio, price-to-sales ratio, price-to-cash-flow ratio, and market-to-book ratio.

6. **Financial analysis model.** Financial analysis includes ratio analysis and cash flow analysis. In ratio analysis, the analyst can compare ratios for a firm over several years, compare ratios for the firm and other firms in the industry, and compare ratios to some benchmark data. While **ratio analysis** focuses on analyzing a firm's income statement or its balance sheet, the cash flow analysis will focus on operating, investing, and financing policies of a firm by reviewing its Statement of Cash Flows. **Cash flow analysis** also provides an indication of the quality of the information in the firm's income statement and balance sheet.

7. **Economic-value-added (EVA) model.** EVA is operating profit minus a charge for the opportunity cost of capital. An advantage of the EVA method is its integration of revenues and costs of short-term decisions into the long-term capital budgeting process. A disadvantage of EVA is that it focuses only on a single period and that it does not consider risk. The EVA model can be combined with the market-value-added model to address this disadvantage. The formula for calculating the EVA is: Operating Profit – (Weighted-Average Cost of Capital × Capital Invested).

8. **Market-value-added (MVA) model.** MVA is the difference between the market value of a company's debt and equity and the amount of capital invested since its origin. The MVA measures the amount by which stock market capitalization increases in a period. Market capitalization is simply the number of shares outstanding multiplied by share price. MVA is calculated as follows: Present Value of Debt + Market Value of Equity – Capital Invested.

9. **Economic profit model.** According to the economic profit model, the value of a company equals the amount of capital invested plus a premium equal to the present value of the cash flows created each year. Economic profit measures the value created in a company in a single period, and it is calculated as follows: Invested Capital × (Return on Invested Capital – Weighted-Average Cost of Capital).

10. **Net present value model.** Basically, the net present value (NPV) model compares the benefits of a proposed project or firm with the costs, including financing costs, and approves those projects or firms whose benefits exceed costs. The NPV model incorporates the time value of money and the riskiness of cash flows, which are the vital elements of a valuation model. The approach is to calculate the NPV of each alternative and then select the alternative with the highest NPV. NPV is calculated as follows: present value of all cash inflows minus present value of all cash outflows.

11. **Discounted cash flow model.** The total value of a firm is the value of its debt plus the value of its equity. The discounted cash flow (DCF) model goes beyond the NPV model and uses free cash flows. The DCF model focuses on discounting cash flows from operations after investment in working capital, less capital expenditures. The model does not consider interest expenses and cash dividends. The calculation involves the

generation of detailed, multiple-year forecasts of cash flows available to all providers of capital (debt and equity). The forecasts are then discounted at the weighted-average cost of capital to arrive at an estimated present value of the firm. The value of debt is subtracted from the total value of firm to arrive at the value of equity.

❑ Learning Objective 7.9: UNDERSTAND THE NATURE OF BUSINESS MERGERS AND ACQUISITIONS

A **merger** is defined as the combination of two firms to form a single firm. A merger can be a friendly merger or a hostile merger. In a **friendly merger**, the terms and conditions of a merger are approved by the management of both companies, while in a **hostile merger**, the target firm's management resists acquisition. It has been pointed out that many mergers today are designed more for the benefit of managers of the firm than for that of stockholders—who are really the owners of the firm.

Five motives are given to account for the high level of U.S. merger activity: (1) synergy, (2) tax considerations, (3) purchase of assets below their replacement cost, (4) diversification, and (5) maintaining control.

1. **Synergy** is seen as the whole is greater than the sum of the parts (i.e., $2 + 2 = 5$). It is the basic rationale for any operating merger. Synergistic effects can arise from four sources: (a) operating economies of scale in production or distribution, (b) financial economies, which include a higher price/earnings ratio, a lower cost of debt, or a greater debt capacity, (c) differential management efficiency (one firm's management is seen as inefficient), and (d) increased market power resulting from reduced competition.

2. **Tax considerations** include using tax status to the firm's advantage and using excess cash in mergers. Using excess cash to acquire another firm has no immediate tax consequences for either the acquiring firm or its stockholders.

3. When the **replacement value of a firm's assets** is considerably higher than its market value, the firm becomes an acquisition candidate. Purchase price will be less than the replacement value of the assets.

4. **Diversification** was thought to be a stabilizing factor on a firm's earnings and thus reduces risk.

There is a controversy about this practice. Stabilization of earnings is beneficial to a firm's employees, suppliers, and customers, but its value to stockholders and debt holders is not clear. This is because investors can diversify their risk on their own; a merger is not the answer.

5. **Maintaining control** is a major motivation and based on human psychology. The managers of the acquired companies generally lose their jobs or lose their autonomy. Therefore, managers who own less than 51 percent of the stock in their firms look to mergers that will lessen the chances of their firm being taken over. Defensive merger tactics are practiced by using much higher debt to acquire other firms so that it will be hard for any potential acquirer to digest.

Types of Mergers

Economists classify mergers into five groups:

1. A **horizontal merger** occurs when one firm combines with another in its same line of business. It can occur between a producer and another producer in the same industry. This kind of merger provides the greatest synergistic operating benefits and is the target of investigation by the U.S. Department of Justice. It is most likely to be attacked as a restraint of trade.

2. A **vertical merger** occurs between a firm and one of its suppliers or customers. It can occur between a producer and its supplier.

3. A **congeneric merger** is a merger of firms in the same general industry, but for which no customer or supplier relationship exists.

4. A **conglomerate merger** occurs when unrelated enterprises combine.

5. A **beachhead merger** takes on a new risk and opportunity entering a new industry.

Merger Tactics

Management uses the following terms and tactics during the merger and acquisition (M&A) process either to delay the process or to deny the offer, especially if it is a hostile one. (In M&A, one firm is targeting to buy another firm either in part or whole with an offer to start the process.)

• A **friendly merger** involves amicable terms that are approved by the management and board of both firms.

- A **tender offer** occurs when one firm is buying the stock of another firm by going directly to the stockholders in an effort to bypass the target firm's management.
- In a **hostile merger,** the target firm's management opposes the proposed M&A offer and uses various defensive tactics. Examples of defensive tactics include greenmail, poison pill, poison put, shark repellent, scorched earth (crown jewel), white knight, and pac-man defense.
- **Greenmail** involves acquiring the common stock currently owned by the prospective combinor at a price greater than the combinor's cost, with the stock thus acquired placed in the treasury or retired stock status.
- A **poison pill** is an action that can damage a target firm if it is acquired by a hostile firm. It may require an amendment of the "articles of incorporation or bylaws" to make it more difficult to obtain stockholders' approval for a hostile takeover.
- A **poison put** is a variation of the poison pill as it forces a firm to buy its securities back at some set price.
- **Shark repellent** is any tactic (e.g., a poison pill) designed to discourage hostile or unwanted merger offers. It may involve acquiring common stock in exchange for treasury stock or incurring long-term debt in exchange for common stock.
- Target firms either sell or threaten to sell their major assets **(crown jewels)** when faced with a hostile takeover threat. This tactic often involves a lockup, which is called a **scorched earth** strategy. It can also involve disposal of assets either by sale or by spinoff to stockholders.
- A target firm facing an unfriendly merger offer might arrange to be acquired by a different, friendly firm, called the **white knight.**
- When white knights or others are granted exceptional merger terms or otherwise well compensated, it is referred to as **whitemail.**
- A **pac-man defense** is a threat to undertake a hostile takeover of the prospective combinor.
- A **lockup** is an option granted to a friendly suitor (e.g., a white knight) giving it the right to purchase stock or some of the major assets (e.g., crown jewels) of a target firm at a fixed price in the event of an unfriendly takeover.
- A **golden parachute** is a large payment incentive to senior management of a firm if it is acquired in a hostile takeover. This payment is based on a contract.

Merger Analysis

The acquirer is the firm that obtains control of the other firm—the acquiree. Whatever type of merger is used, the underlying theory of merger analysis is capital budgeting techniques. The objective is to determine whether the present value of the cash flows expected to result from the merger exceeds the price that must be paid for the target company. The acquiring firm performs the capital budgeting analysis.

A merger can be either an operating merger or a financial merger or a combination of both. An **operating merger** is a merger in which operations of the firms involved are integrated in the hope of achieving synergistic benefits. Accurate estimates of future cash flows, although difficult to obtain, will be required.

Analytical Techniques Used in Mergers:

- Investment analysis (capital budgeting)
- Sensitivity (what-if) analysis
- Scenario analysis
- Simulation analysis
- Due diligence reviews

A **financial merger** is one in which the merged companies will be operated independently and from which no significant operating economies are expected. The postmerger cash flows are simply the sum of the expected cash flows of the two companies if they had continued to operate independently.

A value of the target firm should be assessed in order to determine an educated price. Both cash flows and a discount rate are essential in valuing the target firm. Cash flows can be developed using a set of pro forma income statements for a number of years (say five years). These net cash flows are discounted at the overall cost of capital, if both debt and equity are used to finance the merger. If only equity is used, then the cost of equity should be used. The price paid to acquire the target firm is a summation of the discount net cash flows at the appropriate cost of capital.

Other types of merger and acquisition activities include the following:

- **Spinoff** is when a company sells one of its operating divisions to its existing shareholders, and the shareholders receive new stock representing separate ownership rights in the division.
- **Divestiture** is when a large U.S. company sets up a new corporation based on the assets from one of

its divisions. The stock of the new corporation is titled to the stockholders of the original firm.

- Often, a **leveraged buyout (LBO)** is an alternative to a merger. There is controversy whether LBOs are a good or a bad idea for a company or the economy as a whole. Some argue that LBOs might destabilize the economy because of the disruptive forces involved in the deal. Others argue that LBOs can stimulate lethargic or complacent management. The existence of potential bargains, situations in which companies were using insufficient leverage, and the development of the so-called "junk bond market" all facilitated the use of leverage in takeovers.

- A **holding company** is a company that owns stock in another company and exercises control. The holding company is called the **parent company** and the controlled companies are called **subsidiaries** or **operating companies.** A holding company is taxed on profits, cannot issue tax-free bonds, and is subject to normal government regulations.

- A formation of a **joint venture** or the acquisition of an asset or a group of assets that does not constitute a business are not business combinations, as per the accounting standards.

❏ Learning Objective 7.10: UNDERSTAND THE IMPLICATIONS OF DIVIDEND POLICIES, STOCK SPLITS, STOCK DIVIDENDS, AND STOCK REPURCHASES

Dividend policy involves the decision whether to pay out earnings or retain them for reinvestment in a firm. If the firm pays out more cash dividends, it will tend to increase the price of the stock. The result is that not much money is available for reinvestment, the expected future growth rate will be lowered, and this will depress the price of the stock. Thus, changing the dividend has two opposing effects. *The optimal dividend policy for a firm strikes that balance between current dividends and future growth that maximizes the price of the stock.*

Dividend Policy in Theory

Four theories exist for dividend policy:

1. The **dividend irrelevance theory.** A dividend policy is irrelevant when it has no effect on either the price of a firm's stock or its cost of capital. Modigliani and Miller (MM), who are proponents of the dividend irrelevance theory, argued that the value of the firm is determined only by its basic power and its business risk. Stated differently, the value of the firm depends only on the income produced by its assets, not on how this income is split between dividends and retained earnings.

   MM argued that (a) financial leverage has no effect on the cost of capital, (b) the distribution of income between dividends and retained earnings has no effect on the firm's cost of equity, and (c) a firm's capital budgeting policy is independent of its dividend policy. Clearly these assumptions do not hold true in the real world.

2. The **"bird-in-hand" theory.** Gordon and Linter (GL) counteracted MM's theory that dividend policy does not affect investors' required rate of return on equity. GL said that investors should value a dollar of expected dividends more highly than a dollar of expected capital gains because dividend yield is less risky than stock growth. MM disagreed and argued that the required rate of return on equity is independent of the dividend policy and implies that investors are indifferent between dividends and capital gains. In MM's view, most investors plan to reinvest their dividends in the stock market. MM argued that the riskiness of the firm's cash flows to investors in the long-run is determined only by the riskiness of its investors' operating cash flows and not by its dividend-payout policy.

   GL argued that a dividend "in the hand" is less risky than a possible capital gain "in the bush," so investors require a larger total return if that return has a larger capital gains component than dividend yield. GL argued that more than 1 percent of additional stock growth is required to offset a 1 percent reduction in dividend yield.

   Empirical test results to determine the true relationship between dividend yield and required return have been unclear in that either of the two theories could be correct or incorrect. The capital asset pricing model (CAPM)-based empirical test results were inconclusive about which dividend theory is correct.

   The CAPM studies hypothesized that required returns are a function of both market risk, as measured by beta, and dividend yield. The issue is still unresolved in that nobody can tell how dividend policy affects stock prices and capital costs.

3. The **information content theory.** MM and others state that a larger-than-expected dividend increase is taken by investors as a signal that the firm's management forecasts improved future earnings reflected in a stock price increase, whereas a dividend reduction signals a forecast of poor earnings reflected in a stock price decline. The strong price changes indicate that important information is contained in dividend amounts. This theory is known as the **information content** or **signaling hypothesis.** MM claims that investors' reactions to changes in dividend payments do not show that investors prefer dividends to retained earnings.

4. The **clientele effect theory.** A firm attracts certain types of investors—clientele who like the firm's particular dividend policy. MM concluded that those investors who desired current cash income would own shares in high-dividend-payout firms, whereas those who did not need current cash income would invest in low-payout firms. This means (a) retired individuals prefer current cash income to future capital gains and (b) younger individuals prefer future capital gains to current cash income.

It is advised that firms should follow a specific, stable dividend policy to prevent the **investor switching effect**. This switching is costly because of brokerage cost, capital gains taxes, and a possible shortage of investors.

Dividend Policy in Practice

The four specific practices that prevail today include:

1. Residual Dividend Policy

The **residual dividend policy** states that investors prefer to have the firm retain and reinvest earnings rather than pay them out in dividends if the rate of return the firm can earn on reinvested earnings exceeds the rate investors on average can themselves obtain on other investments of comparable risk. It implies that dividends should be paid only out of leftover earnings and are influenced by investment opportunities and by the availability of funds with which to finance new investments. A firm will pay dividends only if earnings exceed the amount needed to support an optimal capital budget.

The cost of retained earnings is an opportunity cost, which reflects rates of return available to equity investors. If a firm's stockholders can buy other stocks of comparable risk and obtain a 15 percent dividend-plus-capital-gains yield, then 15 percent is the firm's cost of retained earnings.

Strict adherence to the residual dividend policy would result in dividend variability due to investment opportunities and fluctuating earnings. Some investors prefer steady and stable dividends.

Ways to reduce dividend variability include delaying some investment projects, departing from the target capital structure during a particular year, issuing new common stock, and using retained earnings for dividends.

2. Constant Dividends

In order to adjust for inflation, some firms adopted a "stable growth rate" dividend payment policy. A certain amount of growth rate for dividends is established, and the dividends are increased by this amount each year. This policy provides investors with a stable, real income as long as the firm's earnings are growing at about the same rate.

There are two sound reasons for paying a stable, predictable dividend rather than following the residual dividend policy:

1. A **fluctuating dividend policy** would lead to greater uncertainty, which lowers stock price. A **stable dividend policy** would do the opposite.
2. Those stockholders depending on current dividend cash income would be put to trouble and expense if they had to sell part of their shares to obtain cash if the company cut the dividend.

3. Constant Payout Ratio

Some firms make it a practice to pay out a constant percentage of earnings as dividends. Since earnings fluctuate, the dollar amount of dividends will vary using a constant percentage.

4. Regular Dividend Plus Extras

Some firms follow paying low, regular dividends plus a year-end extra in a good year. This would be the best choice for firms experiencing volatile earnings and cash flows. This is a compromise between a stable dividend based on stable growth rate and a constant payout rate. Such a policy gives firms flexibility; yet investors can count on receiving at least a minimum dividend.

Dividend Payment Procedures

There are four dates that are important when paying dividends to stockholders for their investment: (1) declaration date, (2) holder-of-record date, (3) ex-dividend date, and (4) payment date.

The **declaration date** is the date on which a firm's directors issue a statement declaring a dividend. For accounting purposes, the declared dividend becomes an actual liability (i.e., current liability) on the declaration date, and retained earnings would be reduced by the amount of current liability established.

If the company lists the stockholder as an owner on the **holder-of-record date,** then the stockholder receives the dividend. **Ex-dividend date** is the date on which the right to the current dividend no longer accompanies a stock. The ex-dividend date is usually four working days prior to the holder-of-record date. **Payment date** is the date on which a firm actually mails dividend checks. Payment date is after the holder-of-record date.

Stock Splits, Stock Dividends, and Stock Repurchases

Stock splits and stock dividends are related to the firm's cash dividend policy. A **stock split** is an action taken by a firm to increase the number of shares outstanding and to decrease the price of the stock when the current stock price is close to or above the optimal price range. Stock splits can be of any size (e.g., two-for-one, three-for-one). On the other hand, **reverse splits** reduce the shares outstanding and increase the stock price. It is done when the current stock price is below the optimal range.

When a stock price is within the optimal range, the price/earnings (P/E) ratio, and hence the value of the firm, will be maximized.

Stock dividends are similar to stock splits without offsetting the financial position of the current stockholders. The effect of a stock dividend is an increase in the total number of shares and a decrease in earnings, dividends, and price per share.

Stock repurchase is a transaction in which a firm buys back shares of its own stock. It is also called **treasury stock.** The effects of treasury stock are to decrease shares outstanding, to increase earnings per share, and to increase market price of the stock.

The firm engages in stock repurchases when it has surplus cash and when its capital structure is too heavily weighted with equity. The firm sells debt and uses the proceeds to buy back its stock. When a firm buys back its stock, it is providing capital gain to the stockholder on the stock price appreciation instead of cash dividends.

Some of the characteristics of treasury stock include: it cannot receive assets upon liquidation, it cannot exercise preemptive rights, it reduces a firm's capitalization amount, it is not an asset, it has no voting rights, it is not eligible for dividends, it is not to record profits from its trading, and it may be sold to obtain funds.

 Self-Assessment Exercise

Online exercises are provided for the learning objectives in this module. Please visit www.mbaiq.com to complete the online exercises and to calculate your MBA IQ Score.

Information Technology

Learning Objective 8.1: Understand How to Plan and Manage the Information Technology Function — 192
IT Strategies — 192
Elements of the Strategic IT Planning Framework — 192
IT Strategic Planning — 193
Strategic Initiatives — 193
IT Planning Process — 194
Assessing IT Plans — 196

Learning Objective 8.2: Understand How Business Application Systems are Developed and Maintained — 196
Initiation Phase — 196
Development/Acquisition Phase — 197
Implementation Phase — 197
Operations/Maintenance Phase — 197
Disposal Phase — 197
Security Considerations in SDLC — 198

Learning Objective 8.3: Understand How Business Application Systems are Operated and Improved — 198
Data Origination, Preparation, and Input — 199
Data Processing — 199
Data Output — 200
Documentation — 200
Data Integrity — 200

Learning Objective 8.4: Understand the Need for Contingency Plans to Ensure the Continuity of Business Operations — 201
Step 1: Develop Contingency Planning Process — 201
Step 2: Conduct Business Impact Analysis — 201
Step 3: Identify Preventive Controls — 201
Step 4: Develop Recovery Strategies — 202
Step 5: Develop Contingency Plan — 206
Step 6: Plan Testing, Training, and Exercises — 206
Step 7: Plan Maintenance — 207

Learning Objective 8.5: Understand How Information Technology Operations Are Managed — 207
Data Control (Input and Output) Procedures — 208
Production Control (Program Execution) Procedures — 208

Job Scheduling Practices — 208
Production Job Turnover Procedures — 208
Console Operations — 209
System Backups — 209
Preventive Maintenance — 210
System Logs — 210
Help-Desk Function — 210

Learning Objective 8.6: Understand the Technology Behind Computer Network Management — 211
Computer Network Types — 211
Connectivity Hardware — 214
Network Management — 216
Network Changes — 216
Network Interoperability — 217
Network Architecture — 217

Learning Objective 8.7: Understand How to Manage the Information Technology Security Function — 217
Information Security Strategic Planning — 217
General Security Plans — 218
System Security Plans — 218
Security Concepts in Planning — 218
Basic Computer Security Practices — 219
Security Goals and Objectives — 219
Interdependence — 220
Security Controls and Safeguards — 221

Learning Objective 8.8: Understand How Databases are Designed and Managed — 223
Database Design Approaches — 224
Data Warehouse — 227
Data Marts — 227
Data Mining — 227
Information Engineering — 228

Learning Objective 8.9: Understand How Electronic Commerce is Facilitated and Managed — 228
The Internet — 228
Common Internet Services — 229
Internet Protocols — 229
Internet Security-Related Problems — 229
Intranet — 230

Extranet	230	Information Transactions Security Issues	231
Web Management Issues	230	Financial Transactions Security Issues	231
Electronic Commerce	230	E-Commerce Software	232
E-Mail Security Issues	231	E-Commerce Infrastructure	232
EDI Security Issues	231		

❑ Learning Objective 8.1: UNDERSTAND HOW TO PLAN AND MANAGE THE INFORMATION TECHNOLOGY FUNCTION

The **IT function** in an organization should be treated as an asset, not as an expense. **IT planning** can be strategic (long-term), tactical (mid-term), and operational (short-term) in nature. The **IT strategic plan** is a stable document, whereas the operational plan is not. The IT strategic plan deals with assessment of internal and external environments. The scope of the **IT tactical plan** includes budget plans, application system development and maintenance plans, and technical support plans. The scope of the **IT operational plan** includes project descriptions, resource estimates, and implementation schedules. An important measure of success for any IT project is whether the project has achieved its estimated benefits.

IT Strategies

The IT function is no longer a backroom operation. Strategic information systems management is now a critical, integrated part of any general management framework. Strategic information systems management typically involves defining a mission based on customer segments and needs, establishing core processes that accomplish the mission, understanding the key decisions that guide mission delivery processes, supporting those decisions with the right information available to the right people at the right time, and using technology to collect, process, and disseminate information in ways that improve the delivery of products, goods, and services to customers.

One of the goals of IT management is to reduce cycle time, improve quality, reduce costs, and increase productivity.

Although there are many critical success factors, three factors can summarize all of them: **people**, **process**, and **tools**. People and process need to be related to each other to improve quality and increase productivity. A process is a sequence of steps or operations used to accomplish a certain goal. People perform operations. For example, all processes need to be identified for improvement, methodologies need to be changed where needed, and applications of tools need to be evaluated. In all these activities, people are an integral part.

Other examples of common critical success factors include top-management support, long-term commitment, high-quality staffing, "business-is-the-driver strategy," substantial customer input, coordination between organizations, appropriate use of technology, good up-front planning, and the ability to change corporate culture.

Elements of the Strategic IT Planning Framework

The strategic information systems planning framework is generally designed so that it can be applied to any kind of IT acquisition. The rigor with which an organization applies the framework and the amount of detail generated when applying the framework depend in large part on the complexity of the system to be acquired. Also, high technical risks and the application of relatively immature technologies require more detailed analyses and risk management, even though the process to be followed and the factors to be considered are the same as for less risky acquisitions.

The framework involves a structured, orderly process of obtaining and analyzing key information before initiating system acquisition. The framework is made up of eight steps:

1. Identifying the mission and the strategy (e.g., organizational mission, operational concept, and operational requirements)
2. Identifying the functions to be performed in carrying out that mission (e.g., functions and subfunctions)
3. Identifying information needed to perform those functions (e.g., information architecture)
4. Identifying data needed to perform those functions (e.g., data architecture)
5. Identifying application architecture needed to provide that information

6. Specifying a logical system definition (e.g., relationships between the functional, information, data, and application architectures and criteria for analyzing various alternative hardware, software, communications, security, and data management architectures)
7. Exploring alternative architectures (involves hardware, software, communications, security, and data management considerations)
8. Selecting a target architecture (e.g., managers, users, operators, maintainers, and designers)

Since the process is iterative, any major change in mission or requirements during any of the steps may require restarting the process from the top to ensure that the acquired system will meet user needs and be developed within budget and on schedule. Further, each step in the process builds on the previous step.

IT Strategic Planning

Most organizations use IT to manage, manipulate, and disseminate information, as information is one of the resources of an organization. Strategic planning can help organizations achieve these goals. Strategic planning is the process of deciding organizational direction. Managers apply analytical techniques, creativity, and sound judgment to anticipate the requirements of the future. When properly executed, IT strategic planning helps an organization to efficiently and effectively carry out its mission. By recognizing the value of strategic thinking and developing the resulting strategic plans, managers can better position their organization to meet tomorrow's challenges. Strategic planning is a key tool for moving from where one is to where one wants to be.

An IT strategic plan supports an organizational strategic plan. It describes how an organization will manage information and other resources to support the manufacture of products and the delivery of services to its customer base. An IT strategic plan should be a part of the organization strategic plan. Due to their long-term nature, strategic plans are not updated frequently. External or internal changes within an organization are often the catalyst for organization strategic planning.

The seven key components of an IT strategic plan are: (1) a mission statement that defines the organization's purpose, (2) a vision to support the mission, (3) goals to achieve the vision and mission, (4) an environmental analysis to identify internal strengths and weaknesses and external challenges and op-

portunities (i.e., strengths, weaknesses, opportunities, and threats (SWOT) analysis), (5) strategies to meet the vision and goals, (6) a risk assessment that contrasts the impacts of change versus those of no change, and (7) critical success factors that highlight key elements for achieving organization goals.

For strategic planning to succeed, managers must commit to and participate in the planning process, nurture strategic thinking, communicate with all parties affected by the plan, gain staff and customer/client support for the plan, and develop operational plans to guide the implementation of the strategic vision.

Approaches to the Development of IT Strategic Plans:

- Enterprise models
- Work process redesign
- Business reengineering
- IT planning models

A successful IT plan factors in other functional departments' planning, presents a cohesive information architecture that promotes appropriate data sharing, and seeks IT solutions where appropriate, but not as a cure for every problem.

Strategic planning allows senior management to take a proactive role in anticipating organizational direction and communicating that direction throughout the organization. It provides senior management with a foundation for decision making based on an organization-wide plan rather than many individual initiatives.

Strategic Initiatives

The essence of strategy is innovation, so competitive advantage often occurs when an organization tries a strategy that no one has tried before. Eight strategic initiatives to obtain a competitive advantage are as follows:

1. **Reduce costs.** A company can gain advantage if it can sell more units at a lower price while providing quality and maintaining or increasing its profit margin. Examples include online tracking of packets (UPS and FedEx), web-based frequently asked questions (FAQs), and online retailing (e-tailing).
2. **Raise barriers to entrants.** A company can gain advantage if it deters potential entrants into the market, enjoying less competition and bigger market share. Examples include Amazon.com's

"one-click" purchases and Microsoft's copyrighting and patenting software.

3. **Establish high switching costs.** A company can gain advantage if it creates high switching costs, making it economically infeasible for customers to buy from competitors. Examples include Microsoft's Office suite and SAP's ERP software.

4. **Create new products or services.** A company can gain advantage if it offers a unique product or service. Examples include Lotus's 1-2-3 software, Amazon.com's one-click service, and FedEx's online package tracking.

5. **Differentiate products or services.** A company can gain advantage if it can attract customers by convincing them its product differs from the competition's product. Examples include Internet-based electronic commerce.

6. **Enhance products or services.** A company can gain advantage if its product or service is better than anyone else's. Examples include stock brokerage companies offering online stock transaction services.

7. **Establish alliances.** Companies from different industries can help each other gain advantage by offering combined packages of goods or services at special prices. Examples include airline companies partnering with hotels and car rental companies providing vacation packages.

8. **Lock in suppliers or buyers.** A company can gain advantage if it can lock in either suppliers or buyers, making it economically impractical for suppliers or buyers to deal with competitors. Another way to lock in customers is creating a standard in the field. Examples include Wal-Mart's partnership with its suppliers, Microsoft's Internet Explorer, and ERP software vendors in terms of providing training and software updates to their customers.

IT Planning Process

The planning cycle is an iterative process, and its results are dynamic. Resources are required to develop, implement, and maintain the plan. When successfully executed, these efforts yield substantial and tangible benefits.

The IT planning process links organization strategic planning and IT strategic planning, uses information to maximize an organization's usefulness, preserves information integrity, availability, and confidentiality, encourages IT to meet anticipated needs, reflect budget constraints, and form the basis for budget requests, examines the ultimate impact of information resources on operations through work process redesign, and moves from traditional procedure-based and rule-based planning to mission-driven and broad-based strategic thinking.

Four types of planning exist: strategic planning, tactical planning, operational planning, and information systems planning. **Strategic planning** defines the mission, goals, and objectives of the organization. It also identifies the major IT activities to be undertaken to accomplish the desired direction. **Tactical planning** identifies, schedules, manages, and controls the tasks necessary to accomplish individual IT activities. It involves planning of projects, procurement, and staffing. **Operational planning** integrates tactical plans and supportive activities and describes the short-term tasks that must be accomplished in order to achieve the desired results. **Information systems planning** provides a phased, structured approach to systematically define, develop, and implement all aspects of an organization's near- and long-term information needs. More is said about these plans later.

Planning is the formulation of future courses of action. Being the primary management function, planning provides purpose and direction to the organization. The planning horizon consists of three types: strategic (long-term), tactical (intermediate), and operational (short-term). Plans and forecasts are interrelated, since the latter is used in the former. Forecasts are predictive in nature, whereas plans are goal-oriented.

IT Strategic Plan

The **IT strategic plan** sets the broad direction and goals for managing information within the organization and supporting the delivery of services to customers. It produces a high-level strategy for pursuing the organization's information needs.

Members of the strategic planning team should include high-level management staff and representatives of the functional departments and divisions. The participants in the strategic planning process should have direct access to the decision-makers of the organization.

Strategic plans evaluate how well individual IT plans fit together to meet the overall needs of the organization. Strategic plans examine current areas of IT applications, identify opportunities for improvement in the organization, monitor costs associated with technology and services, help organizations avoid a crisis-oriented approach to the management of technologies, reflect current and future needs, reflect budget constraints, form the basis for budget requests, and serve as the foundation for tactical and operational planning.

IT Tactical Plan

Tactical planning is the identification, scheduling, management, and control of tasks necessary to accomplish the individual activities identified in the strategic plan. It involves planning of projects, procurement, and staffing. The **IT tactical plan** is concerned with the management of one IT activity, which may be scheduled over a period longer than one year.

IT Operational Plan

Operational planning integrates individual tactical IT plans and drives the day-to-day supportive activities of the line operations. An IT operational plan typically covers a period of one year or less and identifies, defines, schedules, and provides for control of all activities that support the organization's strategic and tactical plans. The operational plan integrates tactical plans for individual activities.

An **IT operational plan** describes how an organization will implement the strategic plan. Usually, this plan answers the following questions: How do we get there?, When will it be done?, Who will do it?, and How much will it cost?

How Long Is What?

- Strategic planning may cover five years or longer (i.e., long-range planning).
- Tactical planning may cover one year or longer (i.e., mid-range planning).
- Operational planning may cover one year (i.e., short-range planning).
- IS planning may cover a few months to a few years.

The plan identifies logical steps (e.g., Gantt chart) for achieving the IT strategic visions. It may present an implementation schedule, identify key milestones, define project initiatives, and include resource (funding and personnel) estimates. The IT operational plan should identify dependencies among IT strategies and present a logical sequence of project initiatives to assure smooth implementation.

Project initiatives should describe key tasks that an organization must undertake in order to achieve its vision. The following are examples of project initiatives that may be found in an IT operational plan:

- Define how IT architecture will be achieved through the use of technology.
- Conduct a thorough analysis of the organization's information requirements to determine the information architecture and how to effectively support this architecture through technology.
- Develop a cohesive organization-wide acquisition strategy for obtaining IS resources to support the organization's near-term needs and to prepare for the future.

The components of an operational plan include information plans, security plans, acquisition plans, and training plans. **Information plans** may document the information architecture, define how an organization plans to use information throughout its lifecycle, and discuss the protection and use of information within the organization. Typically, these plans address data collection techniques, privacy, standardization, distribution, and disposition.

Security plans should be developed for an organization or an individual system. These plans document the controls and safeguards for maintaining information integrity and for preventing malicious or accidental use, destruction, or modification of information resources within the organization. Coordinated **acquisition plans** present a consolidated description of the major IT resources that an organization plans to acquire over a designated period of time. **Training plans** document the types of training the IT staff will require to effectively perform their duties.

Information Systems Plan

Information systems planning is a three-phased process. The **definition phase** (phase 1) defines the major business activities (processes) and information groups (data classes) required by an organization and produces a high-level blueprint of the organization's information needs (i.e., the information architecture). The **architecture development phase** (phase 2) develops separate but closely related views of the organization's information requirements in the form of the data, application, and geographic architectures, each of which further defines the information requirements of the organization. During this phase, a prioritized slate of projects necessary to accomplish the identified improvements is also developed. The **implementation phase** (phase 3) involves the development of detailed plans to implement the project slate developed in phase 2.

Once these plans are completed, the actual development of databases and applications may begin based on the information requirements identified in phases 1 and 2.

Assessing IT Plans

Theoretically, an organization's execution of IT strategic and operational plans moves it closer to its vision of the future. However, this may not always be true. An organization should periodically assess its progress during the execution of the plans to determine whether it is truly moving toward its vision. Based on the progress to date, the organization may decide either that its vision and direction are still accurate or that it needs a midcourse correction. Organizations need a mechanism for evaluating the success and usefulness of IT plans.

An organization should develop criteria for evaluating the execution of its IT plans. These criteria may differ for each stage of the planning cycle. For example, an organization can develop performance standards to be used as quantifiable measures during the implementation effort. These performance standards can be used to measure the success or failure of a program. Performance standards should be reviewed annually to decide whether the implementation schedule is realistic and to identify problem areas that may recur. These results can be used as input to future evaluation efforts.

Regardless of the mechanism or criteria selected, an organization should carefully review the execution of plans. The feedback obtained from the review will provide the organization with valuable insights that can be applied to other planning efforts such as human resources. For example, an organization's human resource plan can influence the size of an IT staff and the training budget. To be successful, each planning group must consider the planning efforts of the other groups. Functional strategic plans that do not consider other planning efforts are of limited value.

❑ Learning Objective 8.2:
UNDERSTAND HOW BUSINESS APPLICATION SYSTEMS ARE DEVELOPED AND MAINTAINED

A computer system refers to a collection of processes, hardware, and software that perform a specific function. This includes applications, networks, or support systems. A **system development lifecycle (SDLC)** model, which is a structured and standard approach to develop or acquire computer systems, is presented in five phases.

The SDLC is the overall process of developing, implementing, and retiring information systems through a multistep process from initiation, analysis, design, implementation, and maintenance to disposal. There are many different SDLC models and methodologies, but each generally consists of a series of defined steps or phases (NIST SP 800-100 C3.)

Various SDLC methodologies have been developed to guide the processes involved, and some methods work better than others for specific types of projects. Regardless of the type of lifecycle used by an organization, information security features and business controls must be integrated into the SDLC to ensure appropriate protection of the information that the system is intended to transmit, process, and store. Security is most useful and cost-effective when such integration begins with a system development or integration project initiation and is continued throughout SDLC through system disposal.

The SDLC framework can consist of five phases to ensure the selection, acquisition, and use of appropriate and cost-effective security controls:

1. Initiation phase
2. Development/acquisition phase
3. Implementation phase
4. Operations/maintenance phase
5. Disposal phase

Initiation Phase

All IT projects have a starting point, what is commonly referred to as the **initiation phase**. During the initiation phase, the organization establishes the need for a particular system and documents its purpose. The information to be processed, transmitted, or stored is typically evaluated, as well as who requires access to such information and how (in high-level terms). In addition, it is often determined whether the project will be an independent information system or a component of an already-defined system. A preliminary risk assessment is typically conducted in this phase, and initial security planning documents are initiated (system security plan).

Once these tasks have been completed and a need has been recognized for a new or enhanced IT product or service, several processes must take place before the project is approved to include clearly defining project goals and defining high-level information security requirements. Typically, during this phase, the organization defines high-level information security policy requirements as well as the enterprise security system architecture.

Development/Acquisition Phase

During the **development/acquisition phase**, the system is designed, purchased, programmed, developed, or otherwise constructed. This phase often consists of other defined cycles, such as the system development cycle or the acquisition cycle.

During the first part of the development/acquisition phase, the organization should simultaneously define the system's security and functional requirements. These requirements can be expressed as technical features (e.g., access control), assurances (e.g., background checks for system developers), or operational practices (e.g., awareness and training). During the last part of this phase, the organization should perform developmental testing of the technical and security features/functions to ensure they perform as intended prior to launching the implementation and integration phase.

Implementation Phase

In the **implementation phase**, the organization configures and enables system security features, tests the functionality of these features, installs or implements the system, and finally obtains a formal authorization to operate the system. Design reviews and system tests should be performed before placing the system into operation to ensure that it meets all required security specifications. In addition, if new controls are added to the application or the support system, additional acceptance tests of those new controls must be performed. This approach ensures that new controls meet security specifications and do not conflict with or invalidate existing controls. The results of the design reviews and system tests should be fully documented, updated as new reviews or tests are performed, and maintained in the official organization records.

Operations/Maintenance Phase

An effective security program demands comprehensive and continuous understanding of program and system weaknesses. In the **operation and maintenance phase**, systems and products are in place and operating enhancements and/or modifications to the system are developed and tested, and hardware and/or software is added or replaced. During this phase, the organization should continuously monitor performance of the system to ensure that it is consistent with preestablished user and security requirements, and needed system modifications are incorporated.

For configuration management (CM) and control, it is important to document the proposed or actual changes in the security plan of the system. Information systems are typically in a constant state of evolution with upgrades to hardware, software, and firmware and possible modifications to the surrounding environment where the system resides. Documenting information system changes and assessing the potential impact of these changes on the security of a system is an essential part of continuous monitoring and key to avoiding a lapse in the system security accreditation.

Monitoring security controls helps to identify potential security-related problems in the information system that are not identified during the security impact analysis, which is conducted as part of the CM and control process.

Disposal Phase

The **disposal phase** of the system lifecycle refers to the process of preserving (if applicable) and discarding system information, hardware, and software. This step is extremely important because during this phase, information, hardware, and software are moved to another system, archived, discarded, or destroyed. If performed improperly, the disposal phase can result in the authorized disclosure of sensitive data. When archiving information, organizations should consider the need and methods for future retrieval. While electronic information is relatively easy to store and retrieve, problems can arise if the technology used to create the records becomes unavailable as a result of obsolescence or incompatibility with new technologies. Additionally, the organization should consider what measures must be taken for future use of data that has been encrypted, such as taking appropriate steps to ensure the secure long-term storage of cryptographic keys. It is equally important to consider legal requirements for records retention when disposing of information systems.

The removal of information from a storage medium, such as a hard disk or tape, is called **sanitization.** There are four categories of media sanitization: disposal, clearing, purging, and destruction. Because different kinds of sanitization provide different levels of information protection, organizations should use information security requirements as a guide for selecting the sanitization method that best suits their needs.

1. **Disposal** is the act of discarding media (i.e., giving up control) in a manner short of destruction.
2. **Clearing** is the overwriting of classified information on magnetic media such that the media may be reused.
3. **Purging** is the orderly review of storage and removal of inactive or obsolete data files by erasure, by overwriting of storage, or by resetting registers.
4. **Destruction** is the result of actions taken to ensure that media cannot be reused as originally intended and that information is virtually impossible or prohibitively expensive to recover.

Security Considerations in SDLC

Like other aspects of application systems (e.g., features, functions, and business controls), security is most effective and efficient if planned and managed throughout a computer system's lifecycle, from initial planning through design, implementation, and operation. Many security-related events and analyses occur during a system's life.

Planning is used to help ensure that security is addressed in a comprehensive manner throughout a system's lifecycle. Computer security and control management is a part of computer systems management. The benefit of having a distinct computer security plan is to ensure that computer security is not overlooked. A typical plan briefly describes the important security considerations for the system and provides references to more detailed documents, such as system security plans, contingency plans, training programs, accreditation statements, incident handling plans, or audit results. This enables the plan to be used as a management tool without requiring repetition of existing documents.

Although a computer security plan can be developed for a system at any point in the lifecycle, the recommended approach is to draw up the plan at the beginning of the computer system lifecycle. It has long been a tenet of the computer community that it costs ten times more to add a feature in a system after it has been designed than to include the feature at the initial design phase. The principal reason for implementing security during a system's development is that it is more difficult to implement it later

(as is usually reflected in the higher costs of doing so). It also tends to disrupt ongoing operations.

Security also needs to be incorporated into the later phases of the computer system lifecycle to help ensure that security keeps up with changes in the system's environment, technology, procedures, and personnel. It also ensures that security is considered in system upgrades, including the purchase of new components or the design of new modules. Adding new security controls to a system after a security breach, mishap, or audit can lead to haphazard security that can be more expensive and less effective than security that is already integrated into the system. It can also significantly degrade system performance. It is important to keep the computer security plan up-to-date.

Lifecycle management also helps document security-relevant decisions in addition to helping ensure management that security is fully considered in all phases. This documentation benefits system management officials as well as oversight and independent audit groups. System management personnel use documentation as a self-check and reminder of why decisions were made so that the impact of changes in the environment can be more easily assessed. Oversight and independent audit groups use the documentation in their reviews to verify that system management has done an adequate job and to highlight areas where security may have been overlooked. This includes examining whether the documentation accurately reflects how the system is actually being operated.

❑ Learning Objective 8.3:
UNDERSTAND HOW BUSINESS APPLICATION SYSTEMS ARE OPERATED AND IMPROVED

Application-oriented information systems encompass all areas of business and nonbusiness computerized systems. Each application system is designed to perform specific functions, similar to a manual system, with clearly defined input, processing, and output activities.

Examples of Operational Application Systems:

- General ledger
- Insurance claims processing
- Accounts payable
- Demand deposits
- Payroll

- Welfare payments
- Order entry
- Tax administration
- Sales forecasting
- License administration
- Manufacturing scheduling
- Accounts receivable

Most **application systems** are not fully developed all at one time. Rather, they evolve during the course of time. The fact that controls are built into the application systems during software development does not guarantee that they will function properly once the system is operational. Therefore, to ensure a sustained and effective functioning of controls, each application system that is operational requires periodic review, testing, and evaluation of automated and manual internal controls.

Application systems attain operational status after they are either developed in-house or acquired from vendors and then installed into the production area. Application system controls are primarily concerned with data being originated, prepared, entered, processed, stored, accessed, transmitted, secured, controlled, and used. Application systems are usually classified as specific to each industry, such as banking and manufacturing, or across industry, such as general ledger and payroll.

To be effective, one of the major purposes of application systems should be to provide accurate, timely, and relevant data and information to support management decision making at all levels. This will lead to accomplishment of the organization's goals and objectives.

Each operational application system goes through a series of steps to accept data as input and produce reports as output to ensure integrity of both input and output. These steps include (1) data origination, preparation, and input, (2) data processing, and (3) data output. Documentation is needed to operate the system.

Data Origination, Preparation, and Input

There are several approaches to data preparation and data entry into the application system. In some cases, data are captured on a paper (source) document like a sales order or purchase order. The source documents are batched into small groups and entered into the system either by functional users or central data entry operators through the use of terminals. In other cases, there is no externally generated source document since the customer calls in and places an order with the organization.

Regardless of the method used to capture data, the entered data are edited and validated for preventing or detecting errors and omissions. Therefore, access controls and data editing and validation controls are important to ensure that quality data are entered into the application system.

Program-based controls are embedded in online data entry programs in the form of data editing and validation routines. These routines will ensure data integrity. The sequence of events followed by the computer center in a typical batch data entry and batch updating or online data entry and batch updating environment would include:

- Batching records of transactions or source documents
- Converting (keying) transactions or documents to machine-readable form
- Validating input transactions
- Updating the master file with new transactions
- Generating hardcopy reports

Data Processing

Processing controls should satisfy the following objectives: all transactions are authorized prior to processing, all approved transactions are entered quickly in their entirety and accepted by the system, and all transactions are accurately and quickly processed. Understanding the nature of computer processing is critical. Although there are some common controls, controls will be different between batch and online processing. Similar to data input, data editing and validation controls are important during computer processing. Therefore, more use of program-based processing controls is needed to ensure data integrity and security.

The process of carrying forward control totals from one run to another is known as **run-to-run balancing.** Run-to-run control totals are program processing-based controls. Examples could be the number of records in a file and amount totals for certain data fields. The objective is to maintain the accuracy and completeness of data as they pass through computer programs and processing operations (i.e., processing control). It is good to automate the batch report balancing and reconciliation procedures and return this function to functional user departments. Functional user control of the report-balancing activity increases the chances of correcting the source of out-of-balance conditions. This is due to intimate knowledge the users have about the nature of transactions and their interrelationships. Computer operators should not perform run-to-run balancing procedures.

Some data processing rules include the following:

- If an error occurs when processing a transaction, processing should be continued with that transaction, and all errors and rejected transactions should be listed in a report or displayed on a computer terminal.
- When updating a batched file and if end-of-file condition is reached on the master file before end-of-file on the transaction file, then the application program should post the remaining transactions to the master file.

Data Output

There are many output devices in use. Some examples are terminals, printers, plotters, microfilm, microfiche, and voice response units. System output documents are photographed onto a roll of film and stored on microfilm, microfiche, and optical disk. Audio response systems help customers to inquire about a bank balance, get the time and temperature readings, and obtain a telephone number from a directory. Usually, system outputs are in the form of hardcopy reports. Trends indicate that paper will be replaced by online viewing of reports on a terminal.

Balancing, distribution, and retention of system outputs are of major concern to management and the auditor alike since they affect the quality and timeliness of data and usefulness of the system.

Documentation

System documentation is a key element of system operations. Without correct and complete documentation, new users cannot be trained properly, programmers cannot maintain the system correctly, users of the system cannot make any meaningful references to system functions and features, neither management nor anyone else can understand system functions and features, and reviewers of the systems (e.g., auditors) cannot make objective evaluation of system functions and controls.

Application system documentation is classified into six categories: system, program, computer operations, help desk, network control, and user. This classification is based on the major user of the documentation. For example, help desk documentation is used by help desk staff.

Data Integrity

Data and information are not synonymous. **Data** are a collection of facts and figures, and they are raw. **Information** is derived from data in response to a particular need, and it is processed. **Integrity** is binary in nature: it exists or it does not. **Information quality** has a parallel meaning to **data integrity.** Information quality means meeting system user requirements. Quality is a matter of characteristics.

The perception of quality depends on the purpose for which information is to be used. For information to be useful, it should be available where, when, and in the form required with costs equal to or less than benefits to be derived from it.

Data have a certain degree of quality, and the user has some expectations of quality. If data quality equals or exceeds the expectations of quality, data have integrity; otherwise, they do not. Other factors of data quality, in addition to completeness, accuracy, and timeliness, are relevance and validity. **Relevance** is a measure of the appropriateness of the data item in relation to the user's problem or need. **Validity** is a notion of external reference or correspondence. Data may be valid but not relevant or may have low validity but still be relevant.

Data integrity is the heart of any application system. Data integrity controls ensure the reliability and usability of data and information in making management decisions. The higher the integrity of controls, the greater the credibility and reliability of the application system. Here, data integrity refers to **five control attributes:** completeness, accuracy, authorization, consistency, and timeliness.

Which Control Does What?

- A **directive control** will ensure that people follow data integrity rules consistently.
- A **preventive control** will stop a data integrity violation from happening.
- A **detective control** will recognize a data integrity violation.
- A **corrective control** will fix or repair the damage done by a data integrity violation.
- A **recovery control** will help in recovering or restoring from a disaster caused by a data integrity violation.

❏ Learning Objective 8.4: UNDERSTAND THE NEED FOR CONTINGENCY PLANS TO ENSURE THE CONTINUITY OF BUSINESS OPERATIONS

IT contingency planning is one modular piece of a larger contingency and continuity of operations planning program that encompasses IT, business processes, risk management, financial management, crisis communications, safety and security of personnel and property, and continuity of operations. Each piece is operative in its own right, but in concert they create synergy that efficiently and effectively protects the entire organization (NIST SP 800-34).

Contingency planning for information systems is a required process for developing general support systems and major applications with appropriate backup methods and procedures for implementing data recovery and reconstitution against IT risks. Risks to information systems may be natural, technological, or human in nature. Contingency planning consists of a *process* for recovery and documentation of *procedures* for conducting recovery.

A seven-step methodology for developing an IT contingency process and plan is shown below. Planning, implementing, and testing the contingency strategy are addressed by six of the seven steps; documenting the plan and establishing procedures and personnel organization to implement the strategy is the final step.

Step 1: Develop contingency planning process.
Step 2: Conduct business impact analysis.
Step 3: Identify preventive controls.
Step 4: Develop recovery strategies.
Step 5: Develop contingency plan.
Step 6: Plan testing, training, and exercises.
Step 7: Plan maintenance.

The capability to recover and reconstitute data should be integral to the information system design concept during the initiation phase. Recovery strategies should be built into the general support systems or major applications architecture during the development phase. The contingency processes should be tested and maintained during the implementation phase; contingency plans should be exercised and maintained during the operations/maintenance phase. When the information system has reached the disposal phase, the legacy system should remain intact and operational as a contingency to the replaced information system.

Step 1: Develop Contingency Planning Process

When developing an IT contingency plan, the first step is to establish a **contingency planning policy** within the organization. This policy may exist at the department, agency, and/or program level of the organization. The statement should define the organization's overall contingency objectives; identify leadership, roles and responsibilities, resource requirements, and test, training, and exercise schedules; and develop maintenance schedules and determine the minimum required backup frequency.

Step 2: Conduct Business Impact Analysis

A **business impact analysis (BIA)** is a critical step to understanding the information systems components, interdependencies, and potential downtime impacts. Contingency plan strategy and procedures should be designed in consideration of the results of the BIA.

A BIA is conducted by identifying the system's critical resources. Each critical resource is then further examined to determine how long functionality of the resource could be withheld from the information system before an unacceptable impact is experienced.

The impact may be something that materializes over time or may be tracked across related resources and dependent systems (e.g., cascading domino effect). The time identified is called a **maximum allowable outage (MAO).** Based on the potential impacts, the amount of time the information system can be without the critical resource then provides a resource recovery priority around which an organization can plan recovery activities. The balancing point between the MAO and the cost to recover establishes the information system's **recovery time objective (RTO).** Recovery strategies must be created to meet the RTO.

The strategy must also address recovering information system critical components within a priority, as established by their individual RTOs.

Step 3: Identify Preventive Controls

In some cases, implementing preventive controls might mitigate outage impacts identified by the BIA. **Preventive controls** are measures that deter and/or reduce impacts to the system. When cost-effective, preventing an impact is desired over implementing recovery strategies (and therefore risking data loss and impact to the organization). Preventive controls should be documented in the contingency plan, and personnel associated with the system should be trained on how and when to use the controls. These controls should be maintained in good condition to ensure their effectiveness in an emergency. Preventive measures are specific to individual components and the environment in which the components operate. Common controls include:

- Uninterruptible power supply
- Fire-suppression systems
- Gasoline or diesel-powered generators
- Air-conditioning systems with excess capacity to permit failure of certain components
- Heat-resistant and waterproof containers for backup media and vital non-electronic records
- Frequent scheduled data backups

Step 4: Develop Recovery Strategies

When a disruption occurs despite the preventive measures implemented, a **recovery strategy** must be in place to recover and restore data and system operations within the RTO period. The recovery strategy is designed from a combination of methods, which together address the full spectrum of information system risks. Several options may be evaluated during the development phase; the most cost-effective, based on potential impact, should be selected and integrated into the information system architecture and operating procedures.

Recovery strategies provide a means to restore IT operations quickly and effectively following a service disruption. The strategies should address disruption impacts and allowable outage times identified in the BIA. Several alternatives should be considered when developing the strategy, including cost, allowable outage time, security, and integration with larger, organization-level contingency plans.

The selected recovery strategy should address the potential impacts identified in the BIA and should be integrated into the system architecture during the design and implementation phases of the system lifecycle. The strategy should include a combination of methods that complement one another to provide recovery capability over the full spectrum of incidents. A wide variety of recovery approaches

may be considered; the appropriate choice depends on the incident, type of system, and its operational requirements. Specific recovery methods should be considered and may include commercial contracts with cold-, warm-, or hot-site vendors, mobile sites, mirrored sites, reciprocal agreements with internal or external organizations, and service-level agreements (SLAs) with the equipment vendors. In addition, technologies such as Redundant Arrays of Independent Disks (RAID), automatic failover, uninterruptible power supply, and mirrored systems should be considered when developing a system recovery strategy.

Systems and Data Backup

Systems and data must be backed up regularly; therefore, all IT contingency plans should include a method and frequency for conducting data backups. The frequency of backup methods—daily or weekly, incremental or full—should be selected based on system criticality when new information is introduced. The backup method selected should be based on system and data availability and integrity requirements (as defined in the BIA). Data that are backed up may need to be stored offsite and rotated frequently, depending on the criticality of the system.

Backup Methods

Policies should specify the frequency of backups (e.g., daily or weekly, incremental or full), based on data criticality and the frequency with which new information is introduced. Data backup policies should designate the location of stored data, filenaming conventions, media rotation frequency, and method for transporting data offsite. Data may be backed up on magnetic disk, tape, or optical disks (such as compact disks). The specific method chosen for conducting backups should be based on system and data availability and integrity requirements. These methods include electronic vaulting and mirrored disks (using direct-access storage devices or RAID).

It is good business practice to store backed-up data offsite. Commercial data storage facilities are specially designed to archive media and protect data from threatening elements. When using offsite storage, data is backed up at the organization's facility and then labeled, packed, and transported to the storage facility. If data are required for recovery or testing purposes, the organization contacts the storage facility requesting specific data to be transported to the organization or to an alternative facility. Backup tapes should be tested regularly to ensure that data are being stored correctly and that the files may be retrieved without errors or lost data. Also, the Contingency Planning Coordinator should test the backup tapes at the alternative site, if applicable, to ensure that the site supports the same backup configuration that the organization has implemented. Commercial storage facilities sometimes offer media transportation and response and recovery services. When selecting an offsite storage facility and vendor, geographic area, accessibility, security, environment (i.e., temperature or humidity), and cost factors should be considered.

Major disruptions to system operations may require restoration activities to be implemented at an alternative site. The type of alternative site selected must be based on RTO requirements and budget limitations. Equipment for recovering and/or replacing the information system must be provided as part of the recovery strategy. Cost, delivery time, and compatibility factors must also be considered when determining how to provide the necessary equipment. Organizations must also plan for an alternative site that, at a minimum, provides workspace for all contingency plan personnel, equipment, and the appropriate IT infrastructure necessary to execute IT contingency plan and system recovery activities.

The level of operational readiness of the alternative site is an important characteristic to determine when developing the recovery strategy.

Alternative Sites

Although major disruptions with long-term effects may be rare, they should be accounted for in the contingency plan. Thus, the plan must include a strategy to recover and perform system operations at an alternative facility for an extended period. In general, three types of alternative sites are available:

1. Dedicated site owned or operated by the organization
2. Reciprocal agreement or memorandum of agreement with an internal or external entity
3. Commercially leased facility

Regardless of the type of alternative site chosen, the facility must be able to support system operations as defined in the contingency plan. The three alternative site types may be categorized in terms of their operational readiness. Based on this factor, sites may be identified as cold sites, warm sites, hot sites, mobile sites, and mirrored sites. Progressing from basic to advanced, the five sites are described here.

1. **Cold sites** typically consist of a facility with adequate space and infrastructure (electric power, telecommunications connections, and environmental controls) to support the IT system. The space may have raised floors and other attributes suited for IT operations. The site does not contain IT equipment and usually does not contain office automation equipment, such as telephones, facsimile machines, or copiers. The organization using the cold site is responsible for providing and installing necessary equipment and telecommunications capabilities.

2. **Warm sites** are partially equipped office spaces that contain some or all of the system hardware, software, telecommunications, and power sources. The warm site is maintained in an operational status ready to receive the relocated system. The site may need to be prepared before receiving the system and recovery personnel. In many cases, a warm site may serve as a normal operational facility for another system or function; in the event of contingency plan activation, normal activities are temporarily displaced to accommodate the disrupted system.

3. **Hot sites** are office spaces appropriately sized to support system requirements and configured with the necessary system hardware, supporting infrastructure, and support personnel. Hot sites are typically staffed 24/7. Hot-site personnel begin to prepare for the system arrival as soon as they are notified that the contingency plan has been activated.

4. **Mobile sites** are self-contained, transportable shells custom-fitted with specific telecommunications and IT equipment necessary to meet system requirements. These are available for lease through commercial vendors. The facility often is contained in a tractor-trailer and may be driven to and set up at the desired alternative location. In most cases, to be a viable recovery solution, mobile sites should be designed in advance with the vendor, and an SLA should be signed between the two parties. This is necessary because the time required to configure the mobile site can be extensive, and without prior coordination, the time to deliver the mobile site may exceed the system's allowable outage time.

5. **Mirrored sites** are fully redundant facilities with full, real-time information mirroring. Mirrored sites are identical to the primary site in all technical respects. These sites provide the highest degree of availability because the data are processed and stored at the primary and alternative site simultaneously. These sites typically are designed, built, operated, and maintained by the organization.

There are obvious cost and ready-time differences among the five options. The mirrored site is the most expensive choice, but it ensures virtually 100 percent availability. Cold sites are the least expensive to maintain; however, it may require substantial time to acquire and install necessary equipment. Partially equipped sites, such as warm sites, fall in the middle of the spectrum. In many cases, mobile sites may be delivered to the desired location within 24 hours. However, the time necessary for installation can increase this response time. The selection of fixed-site locations should account for the time and mode of transportation necessary to move personnel there. In addition, the fixed site should be in a geographic area that is unlikely to be negatively affected by the same disaster event (e.g., weather-related impacts or power grid failure) as the organization's primary site. Sites should be analyzed further by the organization based on specific requirements defined in the BIA. As sites are evaluated, the Contingency Planning Coordinator should ensure that the system's security, management, operational, and technical controls are compatible with the prospective site. Such controls may include firewalls and physical access controls, data remanence controls, and security clearance level of the site and staff supporting the site.

These alternative sites may be owned and operated by the organization (*internal recovery*), or commercial sites may be available under contract. If contracting for the site with a commercial vendor, adequate testing time, workspace, security requirements, hardware requirements, telecommunications requirements, support services, and recovery days (how long the organization can occupy the space during the recovery period) must be negotiated and clearly stated in the contract. Customers should be aware that multiple organizations may contract with a vendor for the same alternative site; as a result, the site may be unable to accommodate all of the customers if a disaster affects enough of them simultaneously. The vendor's policy on how this situation should be addressed and how priority status is determined should be negotiated.

Two or more organizations with similar or identical IT configurations and backup technologies may enter a formal agreement to serve as alternative sites for each other or enter into a joint contract for an alternative site. This type of site is set up via a **reciprocal agreement** or **memorandum of understanding (MOU).** A reciprocal agreement should be entered into carefully because each site must be able to support the other, in addition to its own workload, in the event of a disaster. This type of agreement requires the recovery sequence for the applications from both organizations to be prioritized from a joint perspective, favorable to both parties. Testing should be conducted at the partnering sites to evaluate the extra processing thresholds, compatible system and backup configurations, sufficient telecommunications connections, compatible security measures, and the sensitivity of data that might be accessible by other privileged users, in addition to functionality of the recovery strategy.

An MOU, **memorandum of agreement (MOA),** or a **service-level agreement (SLA)** for an alternative site should be developed specific to the organization's needs and the partner organization's capabilities. The legal department of each party must review and approve the agreement. In general, the agreement should address, at a minimum, each of the following elements:

- Contract/agreement duration
- Cost/fee structure for disaster declaration and occupancy (daily usage), administration, maintenance, testing, annual cost/fee increases, transportation support cost (receipt and return of offsite data/supplies, as applicable), cost/expense allocation (as applicable), and billing and payment schedules
- Disaster declaration (i.e., circumstances constituting a disaster, notification procedures)
- Site/facility priority access and/or use
- Site availability
- Site guarantee
- Other clients subscribing to same resources and site, and total number of site subscribers, as applicable
- Contract/agreement change or modification process
- Contract/agreement termination conditions
- Process to negotiate extension of service
- Guarantee of compatibility

- IT system requirements (including data and tele-communication requirements) for hardware, software, and any special system needs (hardware and software)
- Change management and notification requirements, including hardware, software, and infrastructure
- Security requirements, including special security needs
- Staff support provided/not provided
- Facility services provided/not provided (e.g., use of onsite office equipment and cafeteria)
- Testing, including scheduling, availability, test time duration, and additional testing, if required
- Records management (onsite and offsite), including electronic media and hardcopy
- Service-level management (performance measures and management of quality of IT services provided)
- Workspace requirements (e.g., chairs, desks, telephone, and PCs)
- Supplies provided/not provided (e.g., office supplies)
- Additional costs not covered elsewhere
- Other contractual issues, as applicable
- Other technical requirements, as applicable

Equipment Replacement

If the IT system is damaged or destroyed or the primary site is unavailable, necessary hardware and software will need to be activated or procured quickly and delivered to the alternative location. Three basic strategies exist to prepare for equipment replacement. (When selecting the most appropriate strategy, note that the availability of transportation may be limited or temporarily halted in the event of a catastrophic disaster.)

1. **Vendor agreements.** As the contingency plan is developed, SLAs with hardware, software, and support vendors may be made for emergency maintenance service. The SLA should specify how quickly the vendor must respond after being notified. The agreement should also give the organization priority status for the shipment of replacement equipment over equipment being purchased for normal operations. SLAs should further discuss what priority status the organization will receive in the event of a catastrophic disaster involving multiple vendor clients. In such cases, organizations with health- and safety-dependent processes will often receive the highest priority for shipment. The details of these negotiations should be documented in the SLA, which should be maintained with the contingency plan.

2. **Equipment inventory.** Required equipment may be purchased in advance and stored at a secure offsite location, such as an alternative site where recovery operations will take place (warm or mobile site) or at another location where they will be stored and then shipped to the alternative site. This solution has certain drawbacks, however. An organization must commit financial resources to purchase this equipment in advance, and the equipment could become obsolete or unsuitable for use over time because system technologies and requirements change.

3. **Existing compatible equipment.** Equipment currently housed and used by the contracted hot site or by another organization within the agency may be used by the organization. Agreements made with hot sites and reciprocal internal sites stipulate that similar and compatible equipment will be available for contingency use by the organization.

When evaluating the choices, the Contingency Planning Coordinator should consider that purchasing equipment when needed is cost-effective but can add significant overhead time to recovery while waiting for shipment and setup; conversely, storing unused equipment is costly but allows recovery operations to begin more quickly. Based on impacts discovered through the BIA, consideration should be given to the possibility of a widespread disaster requiring mass equipment replacement and transportation delays that would extend the recovery period. Regardless of the strategy selected, detailed lists of equipment needs and specifications should be maintained within the contingency plan.

The recovery strategy requires personnel to implement the procedures and test operability. Generally, a member of the organization's senior leadership is selected to activate the plan and lead overall recovery operations. Appropriate teams of personnel (at least two people to ensure there is a primary and alternative available to execute procedures) are identified to be responsible for specific aspects of the plan.

Personnel should be chosen to staff the teams based on their normal responsibilities, system knowledge, and availability to recover the system on an on-call basis. A line of succession should be defined to ensure that someone can assume the role of senior leadership if the plan leader is unable to respond.

Having selected choices for each component of the recovery strategy, the final consideration should be given to cost. The recovery strategy must meet criticality, availability, and RTO requirements while remaining within budget. Less obvious costs—such as shipping, awareness programs, tests and exercises, travel, labor hours, and contracted services—must also be incorporated into the evaluation.

Step 5: Develop Contingency Plan

Procedures for executing the recovery strategy are outlined in the **contingency plan.** The plan must be written in a format that will provide the users (recovery team leadership and members) with the context in which the plan is to be implemented and the direct procedures, based on role, to execute.

The procedures are documented in the notification/activation phase, recovery phase, and reconstitution phase components of the plan. The supporting information and appendices components provide supplemental information necessary to understand the context in which the plan is to be used and give additional information that may be necessary to execute procedures (e.g., emergency contact information and the BIA).

Step 6: Plan Testing, Training, and Exercises

Organizations should maintain their IT plans so that they will be prepared to manage and recover from adverse events that could disrupt their operations. Computer contingency and computer-security incident response plans, which are part of an organization's IT planning framework, are examples of plans that address recovery from adverse events (NIST SP 800-84).

It is recommended that organizations should develop **test, training, and exercise (TT&E)** programs that combine training, exercise, and testing activities. These activities are closely related but offer different ways of identifying problems with IT plans and procedures. The TT&E program should include a TT&E plan, policy, event methodology, and procedures. It should address resource and budget requirements and provide a schedule for conducting types of TT&E events. The TT&E plan should document the projected schedule of activities to be performed within the TT&E program. TT&E events should be conducted periodically, following organi-

zational changes, updates to an IT plan, or the issuance of new TT&E guidance. TT&E events should be conducted as needed, and organizations should evaluate the required frequency of their events and document the frequency of each event in a TT&E schedule. The TT&E program should include several types of events to ensure the availability of a wide range of methods for validating various planning elements in the context of cyber-attacks or incidents.

A TT&E program contributes to the effective maintenance of all IT plans through the following activities.

Tests

These are evaluation tools that use quantifiable metrics to validate the operability of a system or system components in an operational environment as specified in an IT plan. Tests could include activities such as checking whether call tree cascades can be executed within prescribed time limits or removing power from a system or system component. Quantifiable metrics can be collected when these activities are performed. The organization should develop a test plan to identify the systems or components to be tested and the overall test objectives. Test results could indicate problems in personnel training or in IT plans and procedures, and systems/components malfunctioning or becoming inoperable. Tests often focus on recovery and backup operations; however, testing can be conducted to accomplish other goals, depending on the specific IT plans.

Plan testing should include:

- Notification procedures
- System recovery on an alternative platform from backup media
- System performance using alternative equipment
- Coordination among recovery teams
- Restoration of normal operations
- Internal and external connectivity

Training

This includes advising personnel of their roles and responsibilities within a particular IT plan, such as decision making, and teaching them skills related to those roles and responsibilities. These training activities prepare staff members for participation in exercises, tests, and actual emergency situations related to the IT plan. Staff members are trained on their roles and responsibilities before an exercise or test event. Discussions at these training events enable staff members to demonstrate their understanding of the subject matter.

Personnel training should include:

- Purpose of the plan
- Cross-team coordination and communication
- Reporting procedures
- Security requirements
- Team-specific processes
- Individual responsibilities

Exercises

Exercises are simulations of an emergency designed to validate the viability of one or more aspects of an IT plan. Exercises help to identify gaps and inconsistencies within IT plans and procedures, as well as cases where personnel need additional training or when training needs to be changed. In an exercise, personnel with roles and responsibilities in a particular IT plan meet to validate the content of a plan through discussion of their roles and their responses to emergency situations. The responses may be executed in a simulated operational environment or through other means of validating responses that do not involve using the actual operational environment for deployment of personnel. Exercises are scenario driven; for example, an exercise might be concerned with a power failure in one of the organization's data centers or a fire that causes certain systems to be damaged.

Two types of exercises are tabletop and functional:

1. **Tabletop exercises** are discussion-based exercises enabling personnel to meet in a classroom setting or in breakout groups to discuss their roles during an emergency and their responses to a particular emergency situation. A facilitator presents a scenario and asks the exercise participants questions related to the scenario. The questions initiate discussion among the participants of roles, responsibilities, coordination, and decision making. A tabletop exercise is discussion based only and does not involve deploying equipment or other resources.
2. **Functional exercises** allow personnel to validate their operational readiness for emergencies in a simulated operational environment. Functional exercises are designed to exercise the roles and responsibilities of specific team members, procedures, and assets involved in one or more functional aspects of an IT plan, such as communications, emergency notifications, or IT equipment

setup. Functional exercises vary in complexity and scope and range from validation of specific aspects of a plan to full-scale exercises that address all plan elements. Functional exercises allow staff members to execute their roles and responsibilities as they would in an actual emergency situation but in a simulated manner.

Step 7: Plan Maintenance

The IT contingency plan must always be maintained in a ready state for use immediately upon notification. Periodic reviews of the plan must be conducted for currency of key personnel and vendor information, system components and dependencies, the recovery strategy, vital records, and operational requirements. While some changes may be obvious (e.g., personnel turnover or vendor changes), others will require analysis. The BIA should be reviewed periodically and updated with new information to identify new contingency requirements and priorities. Changes made to the plan are noted in a **record of changes,** dated, and signed or initialed by the person making the change. The revised plan (or plan sections) is circulated to those with plan responsibilities. Because of the impact that plan changes may have on interdependent business processes or information systems, the changes must be clearly communicated and properly annotated in the beginning of the document.

❏ Learning Objective 8.5: UNDERSTAND HOW INFORMATION TECHNOLOGY OPERATIONS ARE MANAGED

The scope of **IT operations** includes computer operating environment, computer operations, change and problem management, service-level management, and separation of duties. The goals of the IT (data center) operations management should be to:

- Stabilize the production environment and limit negative impact (e.g., system outages, errors, backouts, and downtime) due to changes or problems.
- Maintain the integrity and security of all program modules, hardware devices, and network components within the production environment.
- Prioritize those changes that are critical to business function versus those changes that can be deferred.

- Coordinate all problems and changes in a controlled and coordinated manner.
- Promote a proactive mode of computer operations instead of a reactive one.

The scope of **computer operating environment** includes data control procedures, production control procedures, job scheduling practices, and production job turnover procedures.

Data Control (Input and Output) Procedures

The data control or production control function is the first line of defense in the computer center against possible delays, errors, omissions, and irregularities. This is due to the fact that many front-end activities such as data entry, job setup, and job scheduling are performed prior to executing production jobs for application systems. The things that data/production control staff do and how well they do them will have a great impact on subsequent activities such as computer operations, backup and recovery, storage media management, help-desk, and report delivery. Consequently, there are many potential risks and exposures in the data control/production control work area.

Production Control (Program Execution) Procedures

Production control activities include scheduling of jobs and controlling production job turnover procedures, among other things. Some typical activities of a computer operator include execution of production jobs and programs; monitoring of system resources including computer consoles, hardware preventive maintenance, and operational changes; backing up of program and data files; mounting/unmounting of tapes, cartridges, and disks; recording of operational problems; monitoring of physical security and environmental controls; and housekeeping activities and logging of system activities.

Job Scheduling Practices

The operations manager has a difficult task in balancing between a certain amount of scheduling work to do and a certain amount of resources with which to do it. Consequently, work must be prioritized based on user business needs. In this regard, the most important considerations are peripheral devices (e.g., tape or disk drives) required, job execution time, and memory required. The least important consideration is how the operator interacts with the user. Most production jobs will have a predecessor and successor job to be run.

Usually, when a new application system is being developed, runtimes and other resource requirements (e.g., disk and memory space) are estimated for each job by the system development group. Operations management then determines how best to accommodate these requirements in light of other job needs.

Production Job Turnover Procedures

Production problems stem from hardware failures (10%), systems software failures (20%), and applications software failures (70%).

Applications software failures are usually the result of problems originating in or unaddressed by the applications software development and maintenance work area. The most prevalent causes of those failures are:

- Incomplete software testing by programmers and functional end users for new application systems development work
- Inappropriate software **regression testing** by programmers for existing application systems maintenance work
- Inappropriate changes made in common program modules such as copy and macros
- Unreliable paper records and manual procedures in the user and IT departments
- Lack of production/operation acceptance testing by computer operations staff
- Lack of or inadequate quality assurance review by production scheduling and control staff
- Overall poor-quality job turnover procedures
- Inexperienced programmers, production control analysts, and computer operators

Some ways to reduce or eliminate the business risk are to automate the production turnover process and to focus on software configuration management. Online approvals and automatic transfer of programs from test to production via **quality assurance (QA) libraries** or from test to production directly will dominate the automation process. A QA library is a staging library where final quality reviews and production setup procedures take place. Software configuration management helps in identifying the locations and the number of computer machines and in determining the networks that need to be propagated with new or changed software (see the figure).

The scope of **computer operations** includes console operations, system backups, preventive maintenance, system logs, and help-desk function, which constitute a major responsibility of a computer operator.

Console Operations

An important task for the computer operator is operating the system console. The operating system sends questions and messages to the operator for a response. It is estimated that 90 percent or more of these messages are trivial in nature and do not require the operator's attention. Yet, they consume valuable operator time and cause frustration to the operator due to their speed in presentation. Software is available to automate console operations and to suppress trivial messages so that the operator responds only to important questions and messages.

Computer operators should have access to system console and operator manuals, not program documentation. They should not perform run-to-run balancing procedures. The console log should contain operator commands, operator messages, and system abends, not data entry errors.

System Backups

Hardware failures, disk crashes, power outages, software failures, and other disruptions are normal in computer center operation. Periodic system backups would provide the ability to recover and restart from a failure or disaster and prevent the destruction of information. *System backups include backing up of operational application programs, data files, databases, systems software products, system development programs, utility programs, and others.*

Timely system backups help in reconstructing any damaged files (recovery) and resuming computer program execution (restart). For example, online and real-time systems and database systems require duplicate backup arrangements and extensive backup and recovery and restart procedures.

For online systems, restart procedures identify transactions that were lost when the online process failed. Another related backup mechanism is **checkpoints,** which allow program restarts. Checkpoints would be most effective for batch (sequential processing) online data entry and batch update processing and multiprogramming and least effective for online real-time systems due to their instant access and updates. Checkpoints are needed to recover from hardware failures and are usually applicable to sequential files, direct (random) access files, and tape or disk files (see the figure).

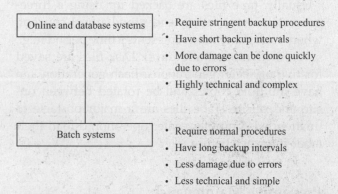

A prerequisite to the performance of timely system backups is the availability of accurate and up-to-date operations documentation (run books), which includes runtime instructions, backup schedules, and recovery/restart procedures for each application system in the production environment. The decision regarding how often to back up a file is dependent on cost of backup versus expected cost of failure, capability of recreating the file without a backup, and time needed to create a copy.

System backup alternatives include full-volume backups and incremental backups.

Full-volume backups, which are common, involve compressing the image copy of an entire magnetic disk volume to a tape/cartridge. This is also known as the brute-force approach since it takes copies of all files regardless of the need or file changes. It takes less time to back up and is less error-prone but requires more magnetic media to store and more manual intervention.

This method is most applicable to database programs and data files due to the logical relationships between data. System recovery is achieved by restoring the database and reapplying transactions from the journal or log. Journals and logs are records of all the transactions that have been processed against a database. The log contains before-and-after images of transactions for all changes. In the event of a failure, the database is restored, and all the changes that have occurred up to the point of failure are reapplied to the database. Some databases are so large that record-level backup is performed whenever a change to the logical database record occurs.

Incremental backups, a new approach, focus only on backing up datasets that have changed since the last full backup. The need for continuous, uninterrupted online system availability leaves a reduced time-window for full backups, which in turn justifies the use of incremental backups.

Usually, tape files are backed up using a three-generation (son, father, and grandfather) concept, where each generation represents a time period (e.g., seven or five operating days). Disk files are saved for five or seven generations. Each generation can have multiple copies and be rotated between on-site and offsite. Tape files are a major obstacle to unattended computer center operation due to their labor-intensive nature.

Preventive Maintenance

The regular practice of preventive maintenance of computer equipment and other system components will provide the assurance of continuity of computing services to end users. Here, computer equipment includes CPU, printers, terminals, and disk/tape drives; other system components include physical channels, control units, cables, air-conditioning units, uninterrupted power supply machines, and other mechanical/electrical devices.

The operations manager first needs to analyze the failure rates for each piece of computer equipment and system component parts. After knowing the failure rates, the manager should determine the impact of failing equipment or a component on the completion of the application system production job schedule. Component failure rates and impact analysis will allow the manager to shift the processing schedules either manually or automatically to balance the workload. Mean time between failures should be determined for each piece of computer equipment and the system components.

The output of component failure rates and impact analysis can be used to establish system availability objectives and service levels between hardware

vendors and computer operations management. Some examples of system availability objectives include:

- The CPU should be available for 99 percent of all scheduled production time.
- Disk/tape drives should be available for 98 percent of scheduled time.
- Terminals and printers should be available 95 percent of the time.

A preventive maintenance log would help the operations manager and the hardware vendor in tracking problems. The log can be maintained by computer operators or supervisors.

System Logs

Another important task performed by computer operations staff is logging and monitoring various systems activities. A **transaction log** is a processing control, provides an audit trail, and is good for online systems. It is useful for file reconstruction and error tracing if errors occur in updating online files.

Help-Desk Function

In order to provide quality and timely support and service to end users, many computer centers are establishing an end-user support function. This includes an information center, help-desk, 24-hour hotline services, telephone voice response system, and automated problem and change management systems.

A help-desk function can implement telephone hotline services so that end users can call in with their problems and ask pertinent questions. These problems could be related to problems as diverse as printer/terminal operations, operating system malfunctions, telecommunications software incompatibilities, or applications software glitches. The help-desk person will try to solve a problem; if he cannot, he will hopefully route the problem to the right person. Problem logging, routing, and escalation procedures are needed to resolve problems in a timely and proper manner.

Recent innovations such as voice response systems could supplement the help desk function in terms of directing the end user to the appropriate person. Other developments include the implementation of expert systems that aid the help-desk staff in terms of problem diagnosis and resolution.

Installation of a **change and problem management system** or service is another end-user service and support tool where problems and changes are logged, tracked, reported, resolved, and implemented.

Often, incorrectly implemented changes cause problems. There should be a cross-reference between a change and a problem caused by a change. To some extent, integrity, liability, and availability of computer systems depend on the way the problems and changes are managed, controlled, and secured. Problem management is critical to online processing due to high visibility of problems to end users. Changes can be classified into standard change requests, mandatory change requests, and emergency change requests so that priorities can be established and resources can be allocated accordingly.

Service-level management is a better way for computer center management to improve quality of computing services to system users. Computer center management must define a set of user service levels or service objectives that describe application systems, volume of transactions, processing windows, online system response times, and batch job turnaround times. Without defined service levels to monitor against actual performance determined in the resource utilization function, a computer system's capacity limit is difficult to identify. Without service levels, the computer center management will consider that the capacity of a computer is near its limits when the users begin to complain about computer performance.

By monitoring performance against service levels, the computer center management can identify approaching problems in meeting service objectives. In order to achieve these goals, computer center management needs to develop service-level objectives for internal use.

It is important to remember that these service-level agreements are not static. They require adjustments and refinements periodically, such as at least once a year or preferably at the time of renegotiation of the agreement with customers (users).

The objective of **separation of duties** is to ensure that no one person has complete control over a transaction throughout its initiation, authorization, recording, processing, and reporting. The rationale is to minimize the incompatible functions, which are not conducive to good internal control structure, and to prevent and detect irregular activities such as fraud.

❏ Learning Objective 8.6: UNDERSTAND THE TECHNOLOGY BEHIND COMPUTER NETWORK MANAGEMENT

Computers operating on different vendor hardware and software platforms at various locations are connected through networks to facilitate data transfers and voice communications. Examples of connectivity hardware include protocol converters, gateways, backbones, bridges, routers, brouters, repeaters, concentrators, switches, and network interface cards. These complex networks need to be managed due to their constant changes to ensure interoperability, flexibility, integrity, and reliability.

Computer Network Types

There are at least nine types of computer networks available today:

1. **Local-area networks.** Local-area networks (LANs) connect computers with other computers, peripherals (e.g., printers), and workstations that are fairly close in proximity. It is a type of network that is used to support interconnections within a building or set of buildings (e.g., a campus).

   Wireless LANs provide a hand-held spread-spectrum workstation for temporary situations or out-of-office environments. These LANs transfer files, provide electronic mail, and offer other data services. Each wireless LAN unit contains a radio transceiver, processor, and memory. Interference is possible even with wireless LANs. Transmission is affected by thick concrete walls and metal fixtures but is not affected by office partitions and normal wooden walls. A risk in wireless LAN is that anyone with the appropriate receiver device can capture the signal transmitted from one unit to another.

2. **Metropolitan-area networks.** Metropolitan-area networks (MANs) link an organization's factory or office buildings within a small geographic area such as a town or a city. MANs cover a distance up to 50 km (30 miles) and fill the technical or operational gap between WANs and LANs.

3. **Wide-area networks.** A wide-area network (WAN) is a network that interconnects systems located in a large geographic area, such as a city,

a continent, or several continents. A complex network can consist of WANs that span continents or geographic regions within continents and connect smaller, more localized LANs or MANs. WANs provide system users with access to any connected computer for fast interchange of information among the users of the network.

WANs connect intelligent terminals, workstations, personal computers, minicomputers, mainframe computers, LANs, and MANs. They use public telecommunication facilities to accomplish this connection. For example, a WAN data-link interconnection can be used to connect two or more physical LANs in different geographic locations. Devices that are available for network interconnection include bridges, repeaters, routers, switches, front-end processors, communication controllers, and protocol converters.

Connections among LANs, MANs, and WANs

A LAN can be connected to a WAN. A WAN can be used as an intermediary to interconnect two separate LANs. A WAN can be used to geographically disperse subnetworks, some of which can be LANs and others MANs. LANs can be interconnected directly or through higher-level MANs or WANs. MANs can be used to interconnect groups of LANs.

4. **Virtual private networks**. A virtual private network (VPN) is a private network composed of computers owned by a single organization that share information with each other in that organization (e.g., LAN or WAN). However, a public network is a large collection of organizations or computers that exchange information with each other (e.g., a public telephone system and the Internet).

A VPN blurs the line between a private and public network. With a VPN, a secure, private network can be created over a public network such as the Internet. A VPN can be created using software, hardware, or a combination of the two that provides a secure link between peers over a public network. Control techniques such as encryption, packet tunneling, and firewalls are used in a VPN. Tunneling encapsulates a packet within a packet to accommodate incompatible protocols. The packet within the packet could be either of the same protocol or of a completely different one.

The private network is called "virtual" because it uses temporary connections that have no real physical presence, but consist of packets routed over various computers on the Internet on an ad hoc basis. Secure virtual connections are created between two computers, a computer and a network, or two networks. A VPN does not physically exist.

5. **Value-added networks.** Value-added network (VAN) vendors operate in a secondary network market. They lease communication facilities from primary common carriers. They add equipment such as multiplexors and computers and provide time-sharing, routing, and information exchange services. A packet-switched network is an example of a VAN.

Value-added carriers lease channels from other common carriers and then provide additional services to customers, using these leased channels. They operate a public data network, where the equipment breaks up the user's data into packets, routes the packets over its network between one location and another, and reassembles them into their original form on the other end. Value-added networks take advantage of economies of scale. Usually, they share a wider bandwidth, which gives faster response time. Some examples of services provided by VANs include bulletin board services, Internet, electronic data interchange, and dial-in services.

Differences among WANs, LANs, MANs, and VANs

WANs, used across geographic locations, are usually static in nature in that changes to them mean that maintenance crews have to go out and climb telephone poles, reroute lines, install new modems, and the like. But LAN topologies, used across and within buildings, are reconfigured in real time (i.e., lines go up and down more easily, gateways to host computers are installed often, system users change frequently, and departments reroute cables frequently).

The dynamic nature of **LANs** require the presence and use of high-level protocol analyzers, problem diagnostic tools, testing instruments, and network monitoring software to recognize potential problems before they become failures. This approach eliminates or reduces the need for trial-and-error practice. For WANs, there is not yet much testing equipment available in the way of control logic, recovery, or repairs.

MANs are aimed at consolidating business operations spread out in a town or city. MANs fill the gap between LANs and WANs.

VANs provide networking and computing services between user organization computers and third-party service organizations (e.g., EDI).

6. **Virtual networks.** Long-distance telephone carriers are offering virtual network (VN) services, controlled by software, as a good intermediate step between private networks and dialup access. The benefits of VN are that it allows carriers to route more traffic over existing facilities, offer volume discounts, support ISDN, and control remote access.

7. **Multicorporate networks.** Certain kinds of organizations operating in specific industries, such as banks and airlines, have developed their own networks to tie computers in multiple separate organizations. Examples include SITA network for passing messages between airline computers around the world and SWIFT network for transferring electronic funds between banks. The SWIFT system uses a message-switching network. Transactions can be entered into the system regardless of whether the recipient bank's terminals are busy.

8. **Integrated services digital networks.** An integrated services digital network (ISDN) may be defined as an end-to-end digital network that provides customer services using existing subscriber loops. It allows integrated access to voice and data services including video and other types of services by using circuit- and/or packet-switching services.

   The main feature of ISDN is the provision of a wide range of service capabilities with the promise of great potential in future applications. ISDN is intended to provide easier access both to knowledge and to distributed processing, including better customer service applications. ISDN operates in a multivendor environment.

9. **Voice communication networks.** Voice-over-Internet Protocol (VoIP)—the transmission of voice over packet-switched IP networks—is one of the most important emerging trends in telecommunications. As with many new technologies, VoIP introduces both security risks and oppor-

tunities. Lower cost and greater flexibility are among the promises of VoIP for the enterprise, but the technology presents security administrators with significant security challenges. Administrators may mistakenly assume that some digitized voice travels in packets; they can simply plug VoIP components into their already-secure networks and remain secure. Unfortunately, the process is not that simple.

VoIP systems take a wide variety of forms, including traditional telephone handsets, conferencing units, and mobile units. In addition to end-user equipment, VoIP systems include a variety of other components, including call processors/call managers, gateways, routers, firewalls, and protocols. Most of these components have counterparts used in data networks, but the performance demands of VoIP mean that ordinary network software and hardware must be supplemented with special VoIP components. Not only does VoIP require higher performance than most data systems; critical services such as Emergency 911 (E-911) must be accommodated. One of the main sources of confusion for those new to VoIP is the (natural) assumption that because digitized voice travels in packets just like other data, existing network architectures and tools can be used without change. Unfortunately, VoIP adds a number of complications to existing network technology, and these problems are magnified by security considerations.

Quality of service (QoS) is fundamental to the operation of a VoIP network that meets users' quality expectations. Unfortunately, the implementation of various security measures can cause a marked deterioration in QoS. These complications range from firewalls delaying or blocking call setups to encryption-produced latency and delay variation (jitter). Because of the time-critical nature of VoIP and its low tolerance for disruption and packet loss, many security measures implemented in traditional data networks are simply not applicable to VoIP in their current form. Current VoIP systems use either a proprietary protocol or one of two standards, H.323 or the Session Initiation Protocol (SIP). Although SIP seems to be gaining in popularity, neither of these protocols has become dominant in the market yet, so it often makes sense to incorporate components that can support both. An extension of SIP, the SIP for Instant Messaging and Presence Leverage Extensions (SIMPLE) standards, is being incorporated into products that support instant messaging. In addition to H.323 and SIP, there are two other standards, Media Gateway Control Protocol (MGCP) and Megaco/H.248, which may be used in large deployments for gateway decomposition. These standards may be used to ensure message handling with media gateways, or they can be easily used to implement terminals without any intelligence, similar to today's phones connected to a private branch exchange (PBX) system, utilizing a stimulus protocol. Until a truly dominant standard emerges, organizations moving to VoIP should consider gateways and other network elements that support both H.323 and SIP. Such a strategy helps to ensure a stable and robust VoIP network in the years to come, no matter which protocol prevails.

Firewalls are a staple of security in today's IP networks. Whether protecting a LAN or WAN, encapsulating a demilitarized zone (DMZ) or just protecting a single computer, a firewall is usually the first line of defense against would-be attackers. Firewalls work by blocking traffic deemed to be invasive, intrusive, or just plain malicious from flowing through them. Acceptable traffic is determined by a set of rules programmed into the firewall by the network administrator. The introduction of firewalls to the VoIP network complicates several aspects of VoIP, most notably dynamic port trafficking and call-setup procedures.

Network address translation (NAT) is a powerful tool that can be used to provide security and enable several endpoints within a LAN to share the same IP address. The benefits of NATs come at a price. For one thing, an attempt to make a call into the network becomes very complex when a NAT is introduced. The situation is analogous to a phone network where several phones have the same phone number (e.g., a house with multiple phones on one line). There are also several issues associated with the transmission of voice data across the NAT, including an incompatibility with IPsec protocol.

Firewalls, gateways, and other such devices can also help keep intruders from compromising a network. However, firewalls are no defense against an internal hacker. Another layer of defense is necessary at the protocol level to protect the data. In VoIP, as in data networks, this can be accomplished by encrypting the packets at the IP level using IPsec or at the transport level with secure remote transport protocol (RTP). However, several factors, including the expansion of packet size, ciphering latency, and a lack of QoS urgency in the cryptographic engine itself can cause an excessive amount of latency in the VoIP packet delivery. This leads to degraded voice quality, again highlighting the trade-off between security and voice quality, and emphasizing a need for speed.

Designing, deploying, and securely operating a VoIP network is a complex effort that requires careful preparation. The integration of a VoIP system into an already-congested or overburdened data network could be problematic for an organization's technology infrastructure. An organization must investigate carefully how its network is laid out and which solution best fits its needs.

Connectivity Hardware

Networks are connected through various hardware devices such as protocol converters, gateways, backbones, bridges, routers, brouters, repeaters, concentrators, switches, and network interface cards.

Protocol Converters

Protocol converters are devices that change one type of coded data to another type of coded data for computer processing. Conversion facilities allow an application system conforming to one network architecture to communicate with an application system conforming to some other network architecture.

Gateways

Gateways are used to interconnect dissimilar network architectures from competing computer network manufacturers. They are also used to connect LANs to host computers.

The integration of WANs, MANs, VANs, LANs, and private branch exchange (PBX) to the backbone network is becoming an absolute requirement. Modern networks can be interconnected through gateways. Typically, gateways are located between the backbone network and other subnetworks (e.g., WANs and LANs).

A gateway, a hardware device, is an example of a protocol converter and performs three major functions: message format conversion, address translation, and protocol conversion.

A gateway translates the address and document content to conform to the standards of the receiving environment. In other words, gateways act as translators between networks using incompatible transport protocols. A gateway is used to interconnect networks that may have different architectures.

Gateways offer the greatest flexibility in network interconnections. The gateway's job is to receive a message and translate it into a form that the next message-handling service can understand. The gateway can be a potential bottleneck, considering the number of stations to handle and the amount of traffic going through the gateway. To overcome performance limitations, an organization might need more than one gateway, which in turn complicates the station software. There are trade-offs associated with gateways. On extended LANs and networks, they can introduce substantial packet-queuing delays, which could be longer than in either a bridge or router. This is due to traffic passing up one protocol stack and out another. Simple checksums are calculated at each gateway to ensure data integrity.

Backbone

A **backbone network** is a central network to which other networks connect. Users are not attached directly to the backbone network; they are connected to the access networks, which in turn connect to the backbone. A backbone network provides connection between LANs and WANs. Dumb terminals can be attached directly to the backbone through terminal servers.

The backbone network is a high-speed connection within a network that connects shorter, usually slower circuits. It is also used in reference to a system that acts as a **hub** for activity, but that is no longer common.

Bridges and Routers

Bridges and **routers** are lower-level network interconnection devices. Typically network interconnection strategies will involve some combination of bridges and routers. The decision about when to use a bridge and when to use a router is a difficult one.

A bridge is a device that connects similar or dissimilar LANs together to form an extended LAN. It can also connect LANs and WANs. Bridges are protocol-independent devices and are designed to store and then forward frames destined for another LAN. Bridges are transparent to the end-stations that are connecting through the bridge. Bridges can reduce total traffic on the extended LAN by filtering unnecessary traffic from the overall network.

Routers offer a complex form of interconnectivity. The router keeps a record of node addresses and current network status. Routers are known to the end-stations as they are device dependent. LANs connect personal computers, terminals, printers, and plotters within a limited geographic area. An extended LAN is achieved through the use of bridges and routers. In other words, the capabilities of a single LAN are extended by connecting LANs at distant locations.

Routers convert between different data-link protocols and resegment transport-level **protocol data units (PDUs)** as necessary to accomplish this. These PDUs are reassembled by the destination end-point transport protocol entity.

There are several routing protocols in common use. Routers must have more detailed knowledge than bridges about the protocols that are used to carry messages through internetwork. The following is a comparison between bridges and routers:

- Bridges are generally considered to be faster than routers since the processing they perform is simpler.
- Routers are limited to particular routing protocols, whereas bridges may be transparent to most routing protocols.
- Bridging protocols are semiautomatic. Routers are automatic and depend on routing tables, which typically must be maintained.
- Bridge protocols limit the size of any extended LAN network, whereas routers do not.
- Routers are used to connect LANs and WANs.

Brouters

Brouters are routers that can also bridge; they route one or more protocols and bridge all other network traffic. Routing bridges are those capable of maintaining the protocol transparency of a standard bridge while also making intelligent path selections, just like a router. Brouters merge the capabilities of bridges and routers into a single, multifunctional device.

$$Brouters = Bridges + Routers$$

Repeaters

Repeaters offer the simplest form of interconnectivity. They merely generate or repeat data packets or electrical signals between cable segments. Repeaters perform data insertion and reception functions. They receive a message and then retransmit it, regenerating the signal at its original strength. In their purest form, repeaters physically extend a network. They also provide a level of fault tolerance by isolating networks electrically, so problems on one cable segment do not affect other segments. However, repeaters exert stress on a network's bandwidth due to difficulty in isolating network traffic. Repeaters are independent of protocols and media.

Concentrators

The major function of **concentrators** is to gather together several lines in one central location. Concentrators are the foundation of a **fiber distributed data interface (FDDI) network** and are attached directly to the FDDI dual ring. Concentrators provide highly fault-tolerant connections to the FDDI rings.

The concentrator allows stations to be inserted and removed with minimal effect on the operation of the ring. One of the functions of the concentrator is to ensure ports (stations) are automatically bypassed in response to a detected fault connection or a high error rate or when a user powers down the station. This bypass function of the concentrator enhances the reliability of the FDDI ring.

Switches

Bridges and repeaters share the same physical transmission medium to interconnect or extend a LAN. **Switches** and hardware devices are designed for the opposite purpose to that of bridges and repeaters. Switches, in the form of routers, interconnect when the systems forming one workgroup are physically separated from the systems forming other workgroups. Switches do not extend LANs as bridges and repeaters do. Switches are primarily used to implement multiple parallel transmission-medium segments to which different groups of workstations can be connected and to provide full network bandwidth to multiple groups of systems.

In a switched network, connections are established by closing switches through dialing. Ethernet switches establish a data link in which a circuit or a channel is connected to an Ethernet network.

Network Interface Cards

Network interface cards (NICs) are circuit boards used to transmit and receive commands and messages between a PC and a LAN. When the network interface card fails, workstations and file servers also fail. Network adapters establish a connection to other computers or peripherals, such as a printer in the network. Network adapters function similarly to NICs.

Network management, changes, interoperability, and architecture are discussed next.

Network Management

Network management deals with six categories:

1. Network architecture specifies network management functions that are essential building elements for a network management system from an architectural point of view.
2. Configuration management is concerned with initializing a network and gracefully shutting down part of or entire network.
3. Fault management encompasses fault detection, isolation, and the correction of abnormal operations.
4. Security management supports the application of security policies.
5. Performance management allows evaluation of the behavior of resources in the open system and of the effectiveness of communication activities.
6. Accounting management enables charges to be established for the use of resources in the open system and costs to be identified for the use of those resources.

Network Changes

Network changes are many and common in any computer center. Unauthorized, incomplete, or incorrect network changes can have an adverse effect on a computer center's security, integrity, and operations. Adequate and timely procedures are needed to define clearly who should do what, when, and how. The following are some examples of network changes:

- Adding, changing, or deleting a user's access to computer systems and data files (e.g., application systems, databases, electronic mail, utility programs)
- Adding, changing, or removing a VDU/CRT terminal, printer, or PC connection or its location
- Adding, changing, or removing network data lines and circuits
- Adding, changing, or removing a modem (dial-in) connection to inter- and intraorganization computers
- Adding a person to use the voice-mail and voice-answering telephone system
- Adding, changing, or removing other related network devices, connections (e.g., gateways, LANs, WANs, MANs, and VANs), and their definitions

A network change request can come from many sources, either on paper or via phone or other media. Regardless of request media, basic information such as user name, user/terminal/controller ID, hardware device model/serial number and location, modem type (external/internal), network port number, logical address of the hardware device, control unit address, request date, and date service needed are required for effective and timely service.

If the current paper-based network change request mechanism is slow and ineffective, a computer-based approach should be considered. The change request can be entered electronically by the requester, can be routed to various personnel who process the request, and can be updated by the person who completed it. The status (e.g., closed, open, deferred, pending, and waiting) can be inquired by the requester or other interested parties.

Network Interoperability

Many organizations' computing environment today consists of hardware, systems software, applications software, printers, protocols, and terminals acquired from different vendors with different platforms. Problems abound in terms of computers' ability to talk to each other. Data cannot be extracted from these systems easily and quickly, so management can get a consolidated view of the business operations and performance. Decisions are made without complete information, and available information is normally out-of-date.

The question is how to integrate data from a vast array of dissimilar systems of mainframe, midrange, mini-, and microcomputers acquired from different vendors. **Interoperability** of systems is becoming a prerequisite to operate and manage in local and global markets and to handle competition. A major stumbling point in the struggle toward interoperability today is the lack of global distributed naming standards and directory services that would help users find services in geographically dispersed networks.

The ideal goal for network management in providing network interoperability is to:

- Minimize the costs of handling data.
- Minimize the learning curve in accessing new data.
- Increase data integrity.
- Increase system reliability.

Network Architecture

Network architecture is a plan describing the design of software, firmware, and hardware components that make up a data communication system. The functions performed by software or firmware are divided into independent **layers.** Each layer isolates the layers above it from the complexities below. The network architecture also defines protocols, rules, standards, and message formats to which different hardware and software vendors must conform in order to satisfy given customer data communication needs and objectives.

❏ Learning Objective 8.7: UNDERSTAND HOW TO MANAGE THE INFORMATION TECHNOLOGY SECURITY FUNCTION

Similar to protecting physical assets, good security is important to protecting intangible assets such as IT assets. **Information security strategic planning** is a part of IT strategic planning, which in turn becomes a part of the organization's strategic planning.

Information Security Strategic Planning

Each organization should define the information security strategy for its information security program, as follows:

- Clear and comprehensive mission, vision, goals, and objectives and how they relate to organization mission
- High-level plan for achieving information security goals and objectives, including short- and midterm objectives and performance targets, specific for each goal and objective, to be used throughout the life of this plan to manage progress toward successfully fulfilling the identified objectives
- Performance measures to continuously monitor accomplishment of identified goals and objectives and their progress toward stated targets

Regardless of how the information security strategy is documented, its contents should be aligned with the overall organization strategic planning activities. The document should be revisited when a major change in the organization information security environment occurs, including:

- Change in applicable legislation, regulations, or directives
- Change in organization mission priorities
- Emerging information security issues, such as changes in threat and vulnerability environment or the introduction of new technologies

General Security Plans

Similar to other functions, the IT security function should have appropriate plans to manage that function properly. The essential elements of a security management function include the following: a responsible individual (a security manager), a security policy, a mission (function) statement, long-term strategies, a compliance program, and a liaison with internal groups. The security objectives must be achievable.

A **security manager or director** should be selected as the IT security program manager. The program should be staffed with able personnel and linked to the other IT functions. The security program requires a stable base in terms of staffing, funding, and other support.

A **security policy** provides the foundation for the IT security program and is the means for documenting and promulgating important decisions about IT security. The security function should publish standards, procedures, regulations, and guidelines that implement and expand on policy.

A published **mission and function statement** grounds the IT security program into the organization's unique operating environment. The statement should clearly establish the function of the IT security program, define responsibilities for the IT security program and other related programs and entities, and provide the basis for evaluating the effectiveness of the IT security program. The **security mission statement** should be linked to the IT function as well as the organization's mission statement.

Long-term strategies should be developed to incorporate security into the next generation of information technology. Since the IT field moves rapidly, planning for future operating environments is essential.

A **compliance program** enables the organization to assess conformance with organization-specific policies and requirements.

Liaisons should be established with internal groups such as personnel, physical security, safety, quality assurance, internal audit, and legal. These relationships must be more than just sharing information; these internal groups must influence each other to ensure that security is considered in the organization plan for information technology.

System Security Plans

The purposes of **system security plans** are to provide an overview of the security requirements of the system, describe the controls in place or planned for meeting those requirements, and delineate responsibilities and expected behavior of all individuals who access the computer system. "Expect the unexpected" is an example of the **lessons learned concept**.

Security Concepts in Planning

Two security concepts in planning deal with establishing a defense-in-depth strategy and avoiding single points of failure.

Establishing a Defense-in-Depth Strategy

Securing data/information and computer systems against the full spectrum of threats requires the use of multiple overlapping protection approaches addressing the people, technology, and operational aspects of IT. This is due to the highly interactive nature of the various systems and networks and to the fact that any single system cannot be adequately secured unless all interconnecting systems are also secured.

By using multiple overlapping protection approaches, the failure or circumvention of any individual protection approach will not leave the system unprotected. Through user training and awareness, well-crafted policies and procedures, and redundancy of protection mechanisms, layered protections enable effective protection of IT assets for the purpose of achieving its objectives. The concept of layered protections is called **security-in-depth** or **defense-in-depth** strategy, and it has a synergistic effect.

Avoiding Single Points of Failure

A **single point of failure** is a security risk due to concentration of risk in one place, system, and process, or with one person. Compensating controls, backup personnel, alternative facilities, fallback procedures, and/or redundancy features are required to ensure that damage or loss resulting from a single point of failure is minimized.

Basic Computer Security Practices

In practice, certain basic actions are necessary for all organizations. These include:

- **Develop computer security policies and procedures.** Computer security policies and procedures are needed to define the overall framework for implementing and sustaining an efficient and cost-effective computer security program at the overall organization level. The policy establishes lines of authority, roles and responsibilities, and basic principles and requirements that define the computer security program. The procedures contain implementation and compliance instructions and management processes.
- **Institute computer security planning.** Computer security planning must provide a consistent approach for determining short- and long-range management objectives, developing security enhancement proposals, mapping proposals to budget requests, and ensuring the implementation of cost-effective measures.
- **Institute a sensitivity identification process.** This process determines the sensitivity of computer systems and when data classification and declassification procedures must be implemented.
- **Define and implement a risk analysis program.** This program ensures the performance of risk analysis on the computer system. It is important to continually identify and analyze potential threats to the computing and telecommunications environments and take action to reduce risk exposure to acceptable levels.
- **Establish a protective measure baseline.** A combination of technical, personnel, administrative, environmental, and telecommunications protective measures must be considered. These can be translated into preventive, detective, and corrective controls as well as management, technical, and operational controls.
- **Ensure the conduct of certifications and/or accreditation.** Computer security certifications and/or accreditation are a management control for ensuring that installed security safeguards are adequate.

- **Oversee a multilayer compliance assurance mechanism.** Management and compliance reviews should be conducted periodically to sustain optimal security levels.
- **Develop an incident response and reporting mechanism.** Organizations should develop appropriate responses to security incidents and provide feedback information to senior management on significant incidents. This reporting also supports the tracking of organization-wide trends.
- **Ensure continuous awareness, training, and education.** Continuous awareness, training, and education are necessary to elevate and sustain management and personnel awareness and to provide specific guidance for personnel who design, implement, use, or maintain computer systems.
- **Ensure contingency planning.** Contingency, disaster recovery, and continuity of operations plans provide continued processing capability when other safeguards have failed to maintain system reliability or availability. Such plans should be in place and tested periodically.
- **Ensure personnel screening.** Personnel who participate in managing, using, designing, developing, operating, or maintaining computer systems should be appropriately screened. The level of screening should be commensurate with the loss or harm that could be caused by these individuals.
- **Develop appropriate security requirements.** In contracts for hardware, software, and computer-related services, organizations must ensure that appropriate security requirements and specifications are included in the statement of work (SOW) documents and that security requirements and specifications are implemented properly before the system goes live.

Security Goals and Objectives

The fundamental purpose for IT security is to provide value by enabling an organization to meet all mission/business objectives while ensuring that system implementations demonstrate due care consideration of risks to the organization and its customers. This purpose is achieved by accomplishing the five security goals, properties, objectives, or requirements:

1. **Integrity.** Integrity (of system and data) is commonly an organization's most important security objective after availability. Integrity deals

with both the system and data. It is the security goal that generates the requirement or protection against either intentional or accidental harmful acts. Integrity has two facets: (a) **data integrity** (the property that data have not been altered in an unauthorized manner while in storage, during processing, or while in transit) and (b) **system integrity** (the quality that a system has when it performs its intended function in an unimpaired manner, free from unauthorized manipulation). Examples of integrity services include authorization, access control enforcement, proof of wholeness, intrusion detection and containment, and restore to secure state.

2. **Confidentiality.** Confidentiality (of data and system information) is the requirement that private and confidential information not be disclosed to unauthorized individuals. Confidentiality protection applies to data in storage, during processing, and while in transit. Examples of confidentiality services include authorization, access control enforcement, and transaction privacy.

3. **Availability.** Availability is frequently an organization's foremost security objective. It is a requirement intended to ensure that systems work promptly and service is not denied to authorized users. This objective protects against (a) intentional or accidental attempts to either perform unauthorized deletion of data or otherwise cause a denial of service or data and (b) attempts to use the system or data for unauthorized purposes. Examples of availability services include authorization, access control enforcement, proof of wholeness, intrusion detection and containment, and restore to secure state.

4. **Accountability.** Accountability (at the individual level) is the requirement that actions of an entity may be traced uniquely to that entity. This directly supports nonrepudiation, deterrence, fault isolation, intrusion detection and prevention, and after-action recovery and legal action. Examples of accountability services include nonrepudiation, access control enforcement, and audit.

5. **Assurance.** Assurance is the basis for confidence that security measures, both technical and operational, work as intended to protect the system and the information it processes. The fifth goal of assurance is taken care of when the other four goals are satisfactory. The other four security goals (integrity, availability, confidentiality, and accountability) have been adequately met by a specific implementation when (a) required functionality is present and correctly implemented, (b) there is sufficient protection against unintentional errors by users or software, and (c) there is sufficient resistance to intentional penetration or bypass. Assurance is essential; without it the other objectives are not met. However, assurance is a continuum; the amount of assurance needed varies between systems. Examples of assurance services include authentication, audit, access control enforcement, proof of wholeness, intrusion detection and containment, and restore to secure state.

Interdependence

The five security goals and objectives are **interdependent**. Achieving one objective without consideration of the others is seldom possible.

Integrity is dependent on confidentiality, in that if confidentiality of certain information is lost (e.g., the superuser password), then integrity mechanisms are likely to be bypassed.

Confidentiality is dependent on integrity, in that if the integrity of the system is lost, then there is no longer a reasonable expectation that the confidentiality mechanisms are still valid.

Availability and accountability are dependent on confidentiality and integrity, in that (1) if confidentiality is lost from certain information (e.g., superuser password), the mechanisms implementing these objectives are easily bypassable and (2) if system integrity is lost, then confidence in the validity of the mechanisms implementing these objectives is also lost.

All of the above four objectives are interdependent with assurance. When designing a system, a design architect or engineer establishes an assurance level as a target. This target is achieved by both defining and meeting the functionality requirements in each of the other four objectives and doing so with sufficient quality. Assurance highlights the fact that for a system to be secure, it must not only provide the intended functionality, but also ensure that undesired actions do not occur.

In addition to the above five goals and objectives, information security objectives include **safety** and **reliability**. For example, safety (defect-free) is required within avionic and transportation control systems. In addition to integrity, medical systems require greater reliability to ensure their correct operation.

Security Controls and Safeguards

The following is a list of security controls and safeguards to ensure proper security:

- **Rules of behavior.** The rules of behavior are a form of security control that should clearly delineate responsibilities and expected behavior of all individuals with access to the system. The rules should state the consequences of inconsistent behavior or noncompliance and be made available to every user prior to receiving authorization for system access. It is required that the rules contain a signature page for each user to acknowledge receipt, indicating that they have read, understand, and agree to abide by the rules of behavior. Electronic signatures are acceptable for use in acknowledging the rules of behavior. The following is an example of rules of behavior:
  - Delineate responsibilities, expected use of system, and behavior of all users.
  - Describe appropriate limits on interconnections.
  - Define service provisions and restoration priorities.
  - Be clear on consequences of behavior not consistent with rules.
  - Cover the following topics:
    - Work at home.
    - Dial-in access.
    - Connection to the Internet.
    - Use of copyrighted work.
    - Unofficial use of organization equipment.
    - Assignment and limitations of system privileges and individual accountability (i.e., password usage and searching databases and divulging information).
- **Virus scanners.** Virus scanners are a popular means of checking for virus infections. These programs test for the presence of viruses in executable program files.
- **Check-summing software.** Check summing presumes that program files should not change between updates. They work by generating a mathematical value based on the contents of a particular file. When the integrity of the file is to be verified, a checksum is generated on the current file and compared with the previously generated value. If the two values are equal, the integrity of the file is verified. Program check summing can detect viruses, Trojan horses, accidental changes to files caused by hardware failures, and other changes to files. However, they may be subject to covert replacement by a system intruder. Digital signatures can also be used.
- **Password checkers.** Password checkers or crackers check passwords against a dictionary (regular or specialized) and also check whether passwords are common permutations of the user ID. Examples of special dictionary entries could be the names of regional sports teams and stars; common permutations could be the user ID spelled backwards.
- **Integrity checkers.** Integrity verification programs can be used by such applications to look for evidence of data tampering, errors, and omissions. Techniques include consistency and reasonableness checks and validation during data entry and processing. These techniques can check data elements, as input or as processed, against expected values or ranges of values; analyze transactions for proper flow, sequencing, and authorization; or examine data elements for expected relationships. These programs comprise a very important set of processes because they can be used to convince people that, if they do what they should not do, accidentally or intentionally, they will be caught. Many of these programs rely on logging of individual user activities.
- **Intrusion detectors.** Intrusion detectors analyze the system audit trail, especially logons, network connections, operating system calls, and various command parameters, for activity that could represent unauthorized activity. Intrusion detection refers to the process of identifying attempts to penetrate a system and gain unauthorized access. Intrusions can be detected in real time, by examining audit records as they are created (or through the use of other kinds of warning flags/notices) or after the fact (e.g., by examining audit records in a batch process).

  Real-time intrusion detection is primarily aimed at outsiders attempting to gain unauthorized access to the system. It may also be used to detect changes in the system's performance indicative of, for example, a virus or worm attack. After-the-fact identification may indicate that unauthorized access was attempted or was successful. Attention can then be given to damage assessment or reviewing controls that were attacked.

- **Software metering product.** A computer system-user can be an employee, a contractor, a computer system, and a computer. System-users are defined to the software metering product, and the product controls and monitors who is using the system and determines whether the user is authorized to use the system. Unauthorized users will be denied access to the system. Multiuser application systems allow several workstations to access and alter the same data files at the same time through the use of logical record/file locks. These locks synchronize multiuser access. System/data owners are best to determine the sensitivity of an application system and its data.
- **System analyzers.** System performance-monitoring analyzers analyze system performance logs in real time to look for availability problems, including active attacks such as Internet worm and system and network slowdowns and crashes.
- **Configuration management.** From a security point of view, configuration management provides assurance that the system in operation is the correct version (configuration) of the system and that any changes to be made are reviewed for security implications. Configuration management can be used to help ensure that changes take place in an identifiable and controlled environment and that they do not unintentionally harm any of the system's properties, including its security. Some organizations, particularly those with very large systems, use a configuration control board for configuration management.

  Changes to the system can have security implications because they may introduce or remove vulnerabilities and because significant changes may require updating the contingency plan, risk analysis, or accreditation.
- **Security audit.** A common approach for measuring the security posture of an organization is a formal security audit. Audits ensure that policies and controls already implemented are operating correctly and effectively. Audits can include static analysis of policies, procedures, and safeguards as well as active probing of the system's external and internal security mechanisms. The results of an audit identify the strengths and weaknesses of the security of the system and provide a list of noted deficits for resolution, typically ranked by degree of severity. Because the security posture of a system evolves over time, audits are most effective when done on a recurring basis.

While periodic formal audits are useful, they are not a replacement for day-to-day management of the security status of a system. Enabling system logs and reviewing their contents manually or through automated report summaries can sometimes be the best means of uncovering unauthorized behavior and detecting security problems.

- **System logs.** A periodic review of system-generated logs can detect security problems, including attempts to exceed access authority or gain system access during unusual hours.
- **Checklists.** Checklists can also be used to verify that changes to the system have been reviewed from a security point of view. A common audit examines the system's configuration to see whether major changes (such as connecting to the Internet) have occurred that have not yet been analyzed from a security point of view.
- **Penetration testing.** Penetration testing can use many methods to attempt a system break-in. In addition to using active automated tools, penetration testing can be done manually. The most useful type of penetration testing is to use methods that might really be used against the system. For hosts on the Internet, this would certainly include automated tools. For many systems, lax procedures or a lack of internal controls on application systems are common vulnerabilities that penetration testing can target. While penetration testing is a very powerful technique, it should preferably be conducted with the knowledge and consent of IT management as well as the organization's senior management. Unknown penetration attempts can cause a lot of stress among IT operations staff and may create unnecessary disturbances to system users. Penetration testing is conducted using red-team and blue-team approaches. Another approach is using a "social engineering" technique, which includes getting system users or IT administrators to divulge information about systems, including their passwords.
- **Red-team testing** is done without the knowledge and consent of IT management and the organization's senior management. A red team takes an adversarial approach to assessing security posture.
- **Blue-team testing** is done with the knowledge and consent of IT management and the organization's senior management. A blue team does not take an adversarial approach to assessing security posture.

❏ Learning Objective 8.8:
UNDERSTAND HOW DATABASES ARE DESIGNED AND MANAGED

A **database** contains facts and figures on various types of information such as sales, costs, and personnel. These files are collectively called the firm's database. A database is a collection of related data about an organization, intended for sharing among multiple users. A **database management system (DBMS)** is comprised of software, hardware, and procedures. The DBMS acts as a software controller enabling different application systems to access a large number of distinct data records stored on direct-access storage devices (e.g., disk).

The DBMS should be compatible with the operating system environment as it handles complex data structures. Unauthorized access to data elements is a major concern in a database system due to concentration of data. The DBMS helps in providing the user interface with the application system through increased accessibility and flexibility by means of **data views.**

Some advantages (objectives) of a DBMS are:

- Provides minimum data redundancy, resulting in data consistency.
- Provides data independence from application programs, except during computer processing.
- Provides consistent and quality information for decision-making purposes.
- Provides adequate security and integrity controls.
- Facilitates uniform development and maintenance of application systems.
- Ensures that all applicable standards (e.g., documentation, data naming, data formats) are observed in the representation of the data.
- Provides shared access to data.
- Improves program maintenance due to separation of data from programs.
- Provides a single storage location for each data item.
- Separates file management tasks from application programs.
- Programs access data according to predefined subschema.
- Provides built-in backup and recovery procedures.

Some disadvantages of a DBMS are:

- Can be expensive to acquire, operate, and maintain.
- Requires additional main memory.
- Requires additional disk storage.
- Requires knowledgeable and technically skilled staff (database administrator).
- Results in additional system overhead, thereby slowing down the system response time.
- Needs additional CPU processing time.
- Requires sophisticated and efficient security mechanisms.
- Difficult to enforce security protection policies.

Redundancy of data is sometimes necessary when high system performance and high data availability are required. The trade-off here is the cost of collecting and maintaining the redundant data and the system overhead it requires to process the data. Another concern is synchronization of data updates in terms of timing and sequence. Ideally, the synchronization should be done at the system level, rather than the application level.

A DBMS understands the structure of the data and provides a language for defining and manipulating stored data. The primary functions of the DBMS are to store data and to provide operations on the database. The operations usually include creating, deleting, updating, and searching of data. It is generally known that most DBMS products require extensive file backup-and-recovery procedures and require more processing time.

Some essential features supported by most DBMSs are:

- **Persistence.** Persistence is the property wherein the state of the database survives the execution of a process in order to be reused later in another process.
- **Data sharing.** Data sharing is the property that permits simultaneous use of the database by multiple users. A DBMS that permits sharing must provide some concurrency control (locking) mechanism that prevents users from executing inconsistent actions on the database.
- **Recovery.** Recovery refers to the capability of the DBMS to return its data to a consistent and coherent state after a hardware or software failure.
- **Database language.** The database language permits external access to the DBMS. The database language may include the **Data Definition Language (DDL)**, the **Data Manipulation Language (DML)**, the **Data Control Language (DCL)**, and an ad-hoc query language. The DDL is used to define the database schema and subschema. The DML is used to examine and manipulate contents of the database. The DCL is used to specify parameters

needed to define the internal organization of the database, such as indices and buffer size. Ad-hoc query language is provided for interactive specification of queries.

- **Security and integrity.** Security and authorization control, integrity checking, utility programs, backup/archiving, versioning, and view definition are other features of most DBMSs. Integrity checking involves two types: semantic and referential. Semantic integrity refers to the declaration of semantic and structural integrity rules (e.g., typing constraints, values of domain constraints, uniqueness constraints) and the enforcement of these rules. Semantic integrity rules may be automatically enforced at program runtime or at compile time or may be performed only when a message is sent. Referential integrity means that no record may contain a reference to the primary key of a nonexisting record. Cascading of deletes, one of the features of referential integrity checking, occurs when a record is deleted and all other referenced records are automatically deleted.

Database Design Approaches

First, user requirements are specified to the **conceptual model,** which represents "user views" of the database. When the conceptual model is presented to the DBMS, it becomes a logical model, external model, or schema/subschema. The type of DBMS is not a factor in designing a conceptual model, but the design of a logical model is dependent on the type of DBMS to be used. This means that the conceptual model is, or should be, independent of a DBMS.

Second, the **logical model** is converted to a physical model in terms of physical storage media such as magnetic disk, tape, cartridge, or drum. The **physical model,** which is also called an **internal model,** considers the type of access methods needed, the type of indexing techniques required, and the data distribution methods available.

Schema versus Subschema

- A logical view of an entire database is called a **schema.** Schemas may be external, conceptual, or internal. A synonym for schema is **view.**
- A **subschema** is a part of a schema. In other words, a schema is made up of one or more subschemas.
- A logical data model presents a view of data.

Logical database design is the process of determining an information system structure that is independent of software or hardware considerations. It produces logical data structures consisting of a number of entities connected by one-to-one or one-to-many relationships, subject to appropriate integrity checking. The objective is to improve the effectiveness of an information system by maximizing the accuracy, consistency, integrity, security, and completeness of the database.

Physical database design is the implementation of a logical design in a particular computer system environment. It deals with retrieval and update workloads for the system and the parameters required (i.e., average time required for random/sequential access to a track, length of a track, and disk cylinder sizes) for the hardware environment. The objective is to improve the performance of the information system by minimizing the data entry time, data retrieval time, data update time, data query time, and storage space and costs.

For large, logically complex databases, physical design is an extremely difficult task. Typically, an enormous number of alternatives must be explored in searching for a good physical design. Often, optimal or near-optimal designs cannot be discovered, resulting in the creation of inefficient and costly databases. Following are the action steps required in a physical database design (see the figure):

- Analyze workload complexity and characteristics.
- Translate the relationships specified in the logical data structures into physical records and hardware devices, and determine their relationships. This includes consideration of symbolic and direct pointers. Symbolic pointers contain the logical identifier of the other. Direct pointers contain the physical address of the other. Both pointers can coexist.
- Fine-tune the design by determining the initial record loading factors, record segmentations, record and file indexes, primary and secondary access methods, file block sizes, and secondary memory management for overflow handling.

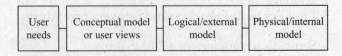

Prior to developing a full-scale database, a prototype may be undertaken to finalize user/technical requirements of the application system. Later, the prototype can be merged into the normal system design phase for security, controls, recovery, and performance considerations.

Another way of looking at the database models is from the design focus and features of the database itself, described as follows:

Physical Data Model	Logical Data Model
Concerned with physical storage of data (internal schema)	Concerned with user-oriented data views (external schema)
Concerned with the entities for which data are collected	Concerned with entities for which data are collected
Describes how the data are arranged in the defined storage media (e.g., disk) from program and programmer viewpoints	Describes how the data can be viewed by the designated end user
Physical in nature in the sense that it describes the way data are physically located in the database	Conceptual in nature (conceptual schema) in the sense that it describes the overall logical view of the database

A **data model** describes relationships between the data elements and is used as a tool to represent the conceptual organization of data. A relationship within a data model can be one-to-one (e.g., between patient and bed in a hospital environment—at any given time, one bed is assigned to one patient), one-to-many (e.g., between hospital room and patients—one hospital room accommodates more than one patient), and many-to-many (e.g., between patient and surgeon—one surgeon may attend to many patients and a patient may be attended by more than one surgeon). A data model can be considered as consisting of three components:

1. **Data structure**—the basic building blocks describing the way data are organized
2. **Operators**—the set of functions that can be used to act on the data structures
3. **Integrity rules**—the valid states in which the data stored in the database may exist

The primary purpose of any data model is to provide a formal means of representing information and a formal means of manipulating the representation. A good data model can help describe and model the application effectively. A DBMS uses one or more of six data models as described below.

1. Relational Data Model

The **relational data model** (e.g., DB2) consists of columns, equal to data fields in a conventional file, and rows, equal to data records in a conventional file, represented in a table. Data are stored in tables with keys or indexes outside the program. For example, in a hospital environment, a patient table may consist of columns (patient number, name, and address) and the values in the column (patient number, 1234; patient name, John Jones; patient address, 100 Main Street, Any Town, USA) are represented in rows.

The columns of the table are called **attributes,** and the rows are called **tuples.** A set of actual values an attribute may take is drawn from a **domain.** The primary key to the patient table is patient number. The following is a description of properties of a relational data model:

- All key values are defined.
- Duplicate rows do not exist.
- Column order is not significant.
- Row order is not significant.

Some major advantages of a relational model are its simplicity in use and true data independence from data storage structures and access methods. Some major disadvantages are low system performance and operational efficiency compared to other data models.

2. Hierarchical Data Model

From a comparison point of view, the **hierarchical data model** (e.g., IMS) can be related to a family tree concept, where the parent can have no children, one child, or more than one child. Similarly, a tree is composed of a number of branches or nodes. A number of trees or data records form a database. Every branch has a number of leaves or data fields. Hence, a hierarchical tree structure consists of nodes and branches. The highest node is called a **root** (parent—level 1), and its every occurrence begins a logical database record. The dependent nodes are at the lower levels (children—levels 2, 3, . . .).

The following is a description of the properties of a hierarchical data model:

- A model always starts with a **root node.**
- A parent node must have at least one dependent node.
- Every node except the root must be accessed through its parent node.

- Except at level 1, the root node, the dependent node can be added horizontally as well as vertically with no limitation.
- There can be a number of occurrences of each node at each level.
- Every node occurring at level 2 must be connected with one and only one node occurring at level 1 and is repeated down.

Some major advantages of a hierarchical data model are its proven performance, simplicity, ease of use, and reduction of data dependency. Some major disadvantages are that addition and deletion of parent/child nodes can become complex and that deletion of the parent results in the deletion of the children.

3. Network Data Model

The **network data model** (e.g., IDMS/R) is depicted using blocks and arrows. A block represents a record type or an entity. Each record type in turn is composed of zero, one, or more data elements/fields or attributes. An arrow linking two blocks shows the relationship between two record types. A network database consists of a number of areas. An area contains records, which in turn contain data elements or fields. A set, which is a grouping of records, may reside in an area or span a number of areas. Each area can have its own unique physical attributes. Areas can be operated independently of, or in conjunction with, other areas.

The following is a description of the properties of a network data model:

- A set is composed of related records.
- There is only a single "owner" in a set.
- There may be zero, one, or many members in a set.

Some major advantages of a network data model are its proven performance and the accommodation of many-to-many relationships that occur quite frequently in real life. Some major disadvantages are its complexity in programming and loss of data independence during database reorganization and when sets are removed.

4. Inverted File Data Model

In the **inverted file data model** (e.g., ADABAS), each entity is represented by a file. Each record in the file represents an occurrence of the entity. Each attribute becomes a data field or element in the file. Data fields are inverted to allow efficient access to individual files. To accomplish this, an index file is created containing all the values taken by the inverted field and pointers to all records in the file.

Some major advantages of the inverted file data model are its simplicity, data independence, and ease of adding new files and fields. A major disadvantage is difficulty in synchronizing changes between database records/fields and index file.

5. Object Data Model

The **object data model** is developed by combining the special nature of **object-oriented programming languages** (e.g., Lisp, C++) with DBMS. Objects, classes, and inheritance form the basis for the structural aspects of the object data model. Objects are basic entities that have data structures and operations. Every object has an object ID that is a unique system-provided identifier. Classes describe generic object types. All objects are members of a class. Classes are related through inheritance. Classes can be related to each other by superclass or subclass relationships, similar to the entity-relationship-attribute model, to form class hierarchies. Class definitions are the mechanism for specifying the database schema for an application. For example, the class PERSON has an attribute SPOUSE whose data type is also PERSON.

Object DBMS also supports data sharing, provides concurrency controls and system recovery, and handles cooperative transaction processing and data versioning. Engineering applications such as computer-aided design systems, office information systems, and artificial intelligence (knowledge-based) systems require the use of cooperative transaction processing and data versioning techniques.

Version management is a facility for tracking and recording changes made to data over time through the history of design changes. The version management system tracks version successors and predecessors. When objects constituting a portion of the design are retrieved, the system must ensure that versions of these objects are consistent and compatible. System development efficiency and handling of complex data structures are some advantages of the object data model. Some disadvantages include new technology and new risks, which require training and learning curves.

6. Distributed Data Model

The **distributed database model** can be thought of as having many network nodes and access paths between the central and local computers and within local computer sites. Database security becomes a major issue in a truly distributed environment, where data are distributed and there are many access paths to the data from far-flung locations.

Data in a distributed database reside in more than one physical database in the network. Location transparency, in which the user does not need to know where data are stored, is one of the major goals of a distributed database data model. Similarly, programmers do not have to rewrite applications and can move data from one location to another, depending on need.

Data Warehouse

The purpose of a data warehouse is information retrieval and data analysis. It stores precomputed, historical, descriptive, and numerical data. It is the process of extracting and transferring operational data into informational data and loading it into a central data store or warehouse. Once loaded, users can access the warehouse through query and analysis tools. The data warehouse can be housed on a computer different from the production computer.

A **data warehouse** is a storage facility where data from heterogeneous databases are brought together so that users can make queries against the warehouse instead of against several databases. The warehouse is like a big database. Redundant and inconsistent data are removed from the databases, and subsets of data are selected from the databases prior to placing them in a data warehouse. Usually, summary data, correlated data, or otherwise massaged data are contained in the data warehouse.

Data integrity and security issues are equally applicable to warehouses as they are to databases. One issue is: What happens to the warehouse when the individual databases are updated?

Data modeling is an essential task for building a data warehouse along with access methods, index strategies, and query language. For example, if the data model is relational, then a **structured query language (SQL)**-based language is used. If the data model is object oriented, an object-based language may be appropriate.

Metadata management is another critical technology for data warehousing. Metadata will include the mapping between the data sources (databases) and the warehouse. Another issue is whether the warehouse can be centralized or distributed.

Database versus Data Warehouse

- A database contains raw data.
- A data warehouse contains massaged (cleaned up) data.
- Users query many points with heterogeneous databases.
- Users query only a single point with a data warehouse.

Data Marts

A **data mart** is a subset of a data warehouse. It brings the data from transaction processing systems (TPSs) to functional departments (i.e., finance, manufacturing, and human resources) or business units or divisions. Data marts are scaled-down data warehouses, where targeted business information is placed into the hands of more decision-makers.

Data Mart versus Data Warehouse

- A data mart provides detailed data for a specific function of a business.
- A data warehouse provides summary data for the entire business.

Data Mining

Data mining can be applied to databases as well as to data warehouses. A warehouse structures the data in such a way as to facilitate query processing. **Data mining** is a set of automated tools that convert the data in the warehouse into some useful information. It selects and reports information deemed significant from a data warehouse or database.

Data mining is the process of posing a series of queries to extract information from the databases. A data warehouse itself does not attempt to extract information from the data contained in the warehouse. One needs a data mining tool to do this.

There are several types of data mining applications, including data classifications, data sequencing, data dependencies, and deviation analysis. Data records can be grouped into clusters or classes so that patterns in the data can be found. Data sequencing can be determined from the data. Data dependencies such as relationships or associations between the data items can be detected. Deviation analysis can be performed on data. Fuzzy logic, neural networks, and set theory are some techniques used in data mining tools.

Data mining techniques can also be used in intrusion detection, fraud detection, and auditing the databases. One may apply data mining tools to detect abnormal patterns in data, which can provide clues to fraud. A security problem can be created when a user poses queries and infers sensitive hypotheses. That is, the inference problem occurs via a data mining tool. A data mining tool can be applied to see whether sensitive information can be deduced from the unclassified information legitimately obtained. If so, then there is an inference problem. An inference controller can be built to detect the motives of the users and prevent the inference problem from occurring. The inference controller can be placed between the data mining tool and the database. Since data mining tools are computationally intensive, parallel-processing computers are used to carry out data mining activities.

Examples of application of data mining include: market segmentation, where it identifies the common characteristics of customers who buy the same products; customer defection, where it predicts which customers are likely to leave the company; fraud detection, where it identifies which transactions are most likely to be fraudulent; direct marketing, where it identifies which prospects are the target for mailing; market basket analysis, where it identifies what products or services are commonly purchased together; and trend analysis, where it reveals the difference between a typical customer this month versus last month.

Uses of Data Mining

- Data mining is a user tool to select information from a data warehouse.
- Data mining is an auditing tool to detect fraud, intrusions, and security problems in a data warehouse.

Information Engineering

Information engineering (IE) has many purposes, including organizational planning, business re-engineering, business application development, information systems planning, and system re-engineering (www.wikipedia.org).

IE was first developed to provide data analysis and database design techniques that could be used by database administrators and by systems analysis to develop database designs and systems based upon an understanding of the operational processing needs of organizations. Later, IE was used in rapid application development (RAD), business process re-engineering (BPR), computer-aided software engineering (CASE) tools, and object oriented design and development methodologies.

Seven stages of IE include information strategy planning, summary business area analysis, detailed business area analysis, business system design, technical design, construction, and transition.

Techniques used during an IE project include entity analysis, functional analysis and process dependency, process logic analysis, entity type lifecycle analysis, matrix cross-checking, normalization, cluster analysis, and data flow and data analysis.

❑ Learning Objective 8.9:
UNDERSTAND HOW ELECTRONIC COMMERCE IS FACILITATED AND MANAGED

Electronic commerce is facilitated on the World Wide Web (WWW, or simply Web). The Web infrastructure consists of hardware, software, services, networks, protocols, policies, and procedures. It is described in terms of the Internet, intranet, and extranet. Web management issues in terms of security, privacy, and service bottlenecks are presented. The scope of e-commerce is discussed, including electronic data interchange (EDI) and electronic funds transfer (EFT) systems.

The Internet

The Internet is a worldwide "network of networks" that uses the **Transmission Control Protocol/Internet Protocol (TCP/IP)** suite for communications.

Connection to the Internet is accomplished in three different ways: (1) a user may obtain an account on a host connected to the Internet and access the Internet services through that host; (2) through a commercial online service provider, a user may connect a PC or workstation directly to the Internet with that PC or workstation becoming an Internet host with its own Internet address; and (3) an organization may connect its own network to the Internet and become a network on the Internet, referred to as an **Internet subnet.** Routers and modems are used in the connection to the Internet.

Internet hosts are one of two types: (1) **client hosts**, generally a Windows PC, which accesses only services on the Internet provided by other hosts; or (2) **server hosts**, generally Unix PCs or workstations, which provide services on the Internet to other hosts but may also access services from other hosts.

Pull Technology versus Push Technology

Pull technology or client pull is a style of network communication where the initial request for data originates from the client and then is responded to by the server. Pull requests form the foundation of network computing, where many clients request data from centralized servers. Pull technology is used extensively on the Internet for hypertext transfer protocol (HTTP) page requests from websites. Most web feeds, such as really simple syndication (RSS) feeds and other streaming media sites, are technically pulled by the client or receiver (www.wikipedia.org).

Push technology or server push describes a style of Internet-based communication where the publisher or central server initiates a request for a given transaction. Examples of push technology applications include e-mail, synchronous conferencing, market data distribution (stock tickers), online chat/messaging systems (Webchat), online betting and gaming, sport results, monitoring consoles, and sensor network monitoring (www.wikipedia.org).

Common Internet Services

There are a number of services associated with TCP/IP and the Internet. The most commonly used service is electronic mail, implemented by the **Simple Mail Transfer Protocol (SMTP)**, terminal emulation for remote terminal access (Telnet), and File Transfer Protocol (FTP). Beyond that, there are a number of services and protocols used for remote printing, remote login, remote file and disk sharing, management of distributed databases, and information-based services. Although TCP/IP can be used equally well in a LAN or WAN environment, a common use is for file and printer sharing at the LAN level and for electronic mail and remote terminal access at both the LAN and WAN levels.

Gopher and Mosaic are increasingly popular; both present problems to firewall designers.

Internet Protocols

TCP/IP is more correctly a suite of protocols including TCP and IP, UDP (User Datagram Protocol), ICMP (Internet Control Message Protocols), and several others. The TCP/IP protocol suite, which is a four-layer model, does not conform exactly to the open systems interconnection's seven-layer model.

IP

The IP layer receives packets delivered by lower-level layers, (e.g., an Ethernet device driver) and passes the packets up to the higher-level TCP or UDP layers. Conversely, IP transmits packets that have been received from the TCP or UDP layers to the lower-level layer. **IP packets** are unreliable datagrams in that IP does nothing to ensure that IP packets are delivered in sequential order or are not damaged by errors. IP does contain an option known as **IP Source Routing,** which can be used to specify a direct route to a destination and return path back to the origination. However, this option can be used by intruders to trick systems into permitting connections from systems that otherwise would not be permitted to connect. Thus, since a number of services trust and rely on the authenticity of the IP source address, this is problematic and can lead to break-ins and intruder activity.

TCP

If IP packets contain encapsulated TCP packets, IP software will pass them up to the TCP software layer. TCP sequentially orders the packets, performs error correction, and implements virtual circuits or real connections between hosts. The TCP packets contain sequence numbers and acknowledgments of received packets so that a packet received out of order can be reordered, and damaged packets can be retransmitted.

Internet Security-Related Problems

Some of the problems with Internet security are a result of inherent vulnerabilities in the services (and the protocols that the services implement), while others are a result of host configuration and access controls that are poorly implemented or overly complex to administer.

Security problems include installation of sniffer programs to monitor network traffic for user-names and static passwords typed in by users; use of weak, static, or reusable passwords; ease of spying and spoofing, where an attacker's host can masquerade as a trusted host or client; and poor configuration of host systems, which can result in intruders gaining access. A solution is to install an Internet firewall, which is a device that sits between the user organization network and the outside Internet. It limits access into and out of the user network based on the user organization's access policy. A firewall can be set up to allow access only from specific hosts and networks or to prevent access from specific hosts. In addition, one can give different levels of access to various hosts; a preferred host may have full access, whereas a secondary host may have access to only certain portions of the user host's directory structure.

Intranet

An **intranet** is simply Internet technology put to use on a private network. Intranet is an internal network within an organization to facilitate employee communications and information sharing. Organizations are posting information to their internal web sites and using web browsers as a common collaborative tool. An example of an intranet application is a customer database accessible via the Web. Sales staff could use this database to contact customers about new product offerings and send them quotes. Other applications include internal phone books, procedures manual, training manual, and purchase requisition forms.

A **virtual private network (VPN)** can allow employees to connect to the intranet securely, so there are no fears of sensitive information leaving the network unprotected. The Internet alone cannot remove this fear.

Extranet

Whereas the scope of an intranet is limited to a customer organization, the scope of an **extranet** includes vendor or customer organizations that do business with the suppler organization. Extranets are intranet-based networks restricted to select audiences such as vendors, clients, and other interested parties outside the organization. In other words, intranets talk to extranets through Internet-based technology.

Security and performance concerns are different for an extranet than for a web site or network-based intranet. Authentication and privacy are critical on an extranet so that information is protected from unauthorized users. Performance in terms of response time must be good for customers and suppliers. Secured intranet and extranet access applications require the use of a VPN.

Web Management Issues

Managing the Web is not easy since no one owns it on a global basis in terms of access, security, hardware, software, privacy, and control. The Web is managed at the local level as there is no centralized governing body. Service bottlenecks occur due to overloaded routers, slow modems, and the use of twisted pairs of copper wires. Suggested solutions include: upgrading the backbone links by installing bigger, faster "pipes," improving routers with increased hardware capacity and efficient software to provide quick access to addresses, prioritizing traffic going through the backbone, and installing digital subscriber line (DSL) and cable modems to speed Internet access.

Regarding privacy, many Internet sites use cookies to gather information about users who visit their web sites. A **cookie** is a text file that an Internet company places on the hard disk of a computer system. These text files keep track of visits to the site and the actions users take. This tracking can be disabled with special software.

Regarding security, cryptography, firewalls, encryption, and digital signatures can be used to protect web resources from unauthorized access.

Electronic Commerce

Electronic commerce (e-commerce) is defined as a place where buyers and sellers are connected using computers and networks (the Internet) to buy and sell goods and services. The term **electronic business (e-business)** is much broader than e-commerce because the former includes distribution of information and customer support, which are lacking in the latter. In other words, e-commerce is a subset of e-business.

E-commerce is a web-enabled value chain with the Internet as the enabling technology. Business applications are located on web servers for wide access to employees and selective access to customers and suppliers.

E-commerce can be grouped into three models: business to consumer (B2C), business to business (B2B), and government to citizen (G2C). Online stores selling goods directly to consumers is an example of the B2C model. EDI is a critical component of the sales process for many online retailers. B2B e-commerce involves "Internet-enabling" of existing relationships between two companies in exchanging goods and services. EDI is the underlying technology enabling online catalogs and continuous stock-replenishment programs. For example, in the G2C model, the U.S. federal government uses the Internet to reach its citizens for a variety of information-dissemination purposes and transactions (e.g., Internal Revenue Service, U.S. Postal Service, and Social Security Administration). A value chain is created in e-commerce between demand planning, supply planning, and demand fulfillment. The demand planning consists of analyzing buying patterns and developing customer demand forecasts. The supply planning consists of supply allocation, inventory planning, distribution planning, procurement planning, and transportation planning. The demand fulfillment consists of order capturing, customer verification, order promising, backlog management, and order fulfillment.

An important application of e-commerce is in electronic procurement through **reverse auctions,** where (1) an industrial buyer invites bids from multiple suppliers (sellers) to find the lowest price and (2) a consumer names his price for a hotel room, airline ticket, or mortgage interest rate to get the lowest price. In both examples, sellers compete with each other and the buyer benefits from the low price.

For the purposes of exploring relevant security issues, one can divide e-commerce into four basic classes: (1) e-mail, (2) EDI, (3) information transactions, and (4) financial transactions.

E-Commerce Security Issues = E-Mail Security Issues + EDI Security Issues + Information Transaction Security Issues + Financial Transaction Security Issues

E-Mail Security Issues

The use of Internet e-mail to carry business-critical communications is growing exponentially. While e-mail provides a low-cost means of communication with customers, suppliers, and partners, a number of security issues are related to the use of e-mail. The security issues include: Internet e-mail addresses are easily spoofed. It is nearly impossible to be certain who created and sent an e-mail message based on the address alone. Internet e-mail messages can be easily modified. Standard SMTP mail provides no integrity checking, there are a number of points where the contents of an e-mail message can be read by unintended recipients, and there is usually no guarantee of delivery with Internet e-mail. While some mail systems support return receipts, when such receipts work at all they often only signify that the user's server (not necessarily the user) has received the message. These weaknesses make it important for organizations to issue policies defining acceptable use of e-mail for business purposes.

EDI Security Issues

Traditional EDI systems allow preestablished trading partners to electronically exchange business data through **value-added networks (VANs)**. The Internet can provide the connectivity needed to support EDI at substantial cost savings over VAN. However, the Internet does not provide the security services (integrity, confidentiality, and nonrepudiation) required for business EDI. Similar to e-mail over the Internet, EDI transactions are vulnerable to modification, disclosure, or interruption when sent over the Internet. The use of cryptography to provide the required security services has changed this; consequently, many companies and government agencies are moving to Internet-based EDI.

Information Transactions Security Issues

Providing information (e.g., stock quotes, news) is a major and costly element of commerce. Using the Internet to provide these services is substantially less expensive than fax, telephone, or postal mail services. Integrity and availability of the information provided are key security concerns that require security controls and policy.

Financial Transactions Security Issues

Computer networks have been used to process financial transactions such as checks, debit cards, credit cards, and electronic funds transfer (EFT). Similar to EDI over VANs, the connectivity options have been limited, and the leased lines are expensive. The Internet provides an opportunity for cost savings in electronic financial transactions. The use of the

Internet to carry these types of transactions replaces the physical presentation or exchange of cash, checks, or debit/credit cards with the electronic equivalent. Each of these forms of transactions involves the use of cryptography to provide for integrity, confidentiality, authentication, and nonrepudiation. For example, a standard known as **Secure Electronic Transactions (SET)** is used for processing credit card transactions over public networks. Use of SET involves three-way transactions between the buyer, the seller, and a financial institution (a bank).

E-Commerce Software

E-commerce software should support the following five tasks:

1. **Catalog management.** Catalog management software combines different product data formats into a standard format for uniform viewing, aggregating, and integrating catalog data into a central repository for easy access, retrieval, and updating of pricing and availability changes.
2. **Product configuration.** Customers need help when an item they are purchasing has many components and options. Buyers use the new web-based product configuration software to build the product they need online with little or no help from salespeople.
3. **Shopping cart facilities.** Today many e-commerce sites use an electronic shopping cart to track the items selected for purchase, allowing shoppers to view what is in their cart, add new items to it, or remove items from it.
4. **E-commerce transaction processing.** E-commerce transaction processing software takes data from the shopping cart and calculates volume discounts, sales tax, and shipping costs to arrive at the total cost.
5. **Web-site traffic data analysis.** Web-site traffic data analysis software captures visitor information, including who is visiting the web site, what search engine and key words they used to find the site, how long their web browser viewed the site, the date and time of each visit, and which pages were displayed. These data are placed into a we-blog file for future analysis to improve the web site's performance.

E-Commerce Infrastructure

Key technology infrastructure for e-commerce applications includes web server hardware, server operating system, server software, e-commerce software, VPN, VAN, and the Internet, intranet, or extranet. Strategies for successful e-commerce include developing an effective web site that creates an attractive presence and that meets the needs of its visitors (customers), contracting out with web-site hosting service providers or storefront brokers, building traffic into the web site through meta tag, which is a special **HyperText Markup Language (HTML)** tag that contains keywords about the web site, and analyzing web-site traffic to identify which search engines are effective for your business.

Electronic data interchange (EDI) systems provide computer-to-computer communication. EDI systems are becoming a normal way of exchanging or transmitting documents, transactions, records, quantitative and financial information, and computer-related messages from one computer to another. Some examples of transactions and documents involved are purchase orders, invoices, shipping notices, receiving advice, acknowledgments, and payments. When payment is involved, the EDI system can be referred to as an Electronic Funds Transfer (EFT) system.

EDI is replacing manual data entry with electronic data entry. The objective of EDI is to eliminate manual data entry work and to eliminate or reduce paper mailing and processing delays between two trading parties, for example, buyer and seller or manufacturer and supplier.

Traditional paper-driven systems such as order entry, purchase order, billing, and accounts payable systems are changing significantly with the introduction of EDI-based systems. Some problems with traditional paper-driven application systems are low accuracy, increased mailing and processing times, and high labor and processing costs.

Basically, the transmission of information between two parties can take place in three ways. The first is direct, the second is via a third-party service provider, and the third is in the form of computer tapes and disks.

EDI System

Essentially, the EDI system works as follows:

1. The buyer identifies the item to be purchased. Data are entered into the purchasing application system. Translation software creates an EDI purchase order, which is sent electronically to the supplier. The same order is sent to the buyer's accounts payable and goods-receiving system.

2. A functional acknowledgment, indicating receipt of the order, is automatically generated and electronically transmitted to the buyer.

3. The supplier's computer sends the order information to his shipping and invoicing systems.

4. Upon receipt by the buyer of the ship notice, the data are electronically entered into the receiving system file.

5. The receipt notice is electronically transmitted to the accounts payable application system.

6. The ship notice is electronically transmitted to the invoicing application system.

7. An invoice is electronically generated by the supplier and transmitted to the buyer. The same information is sent to the supplier's accounts receivable system.

8. The invoice is received by the buyer's computer and is translated into the buyer's format. The invoice, receiving notice, and purchase order are electronically matched and reconciled.

9. The buyer electronically transmits payment to the supplier's bank through its own bank. An electronic remittance advice is transmitted to the supplier.

10. Upon receipt of the remittance and notice of payment, the data are transmitted to the accounts receivable system, and the buyer account is updated. The buyer is given credit for payment.

Components of an EDI System

The components of an EDI system are standards, software, and networks. **EDI standards** consist of formatting standards and communication standards. **Formatting standards** deal with the type, sequence, and content of an electronic document. **Communication standards** cover baud rate, protocols, electronic envelopes, and message-transmission times. Standards provide a set of common rules, in terms of syntax and formatting, for the development of electronic communications.

In terms of software, a translation program is needed to translate company-specific data to EDI standard format for transmission. A reverse translation is performed when data arrive at the organization from external sources.

In terms of networks, there are two approaches in common use. In a direct network, the computers of the trading partners are linked directly, usually through dialup modems. A direct network is effective for a limited number of trading partners. As the number of trading partners increases, it is difficult to maintain open lines for all trading partners. The

second choice is to use a third-party network (i.e., a VAN) that acts as an intermediary between trading partners. A VAN maintains a mailbox for both the sender and the receiver.

The VAN receives purchase orders from the sender (buyer), sorts them by seller, and places each seller's purchase orders in its own mailbox. At a later time, the seller can dial into the VAN and retrieve its mail in the form of electronic purchase orders. This approach allows each trading partner to create only one electronic transmission to the VAN rather than having to create a separate electronic transmission for each trading partner.

Benefits of EDI

A major benefit is being able to load data, without rekeying, from various formats and placing them where they are needed in a different format for further processing. Besides savings due to reductions in document mailing and processing costs, decreases in data entry personnel costs, and reductions in inventory stock levels, organizations are realizing other significant benefits.

These added benefits include improved operational efficiency in warehousing, shipping, purchasing, and receiving areas; increased sales; increased customer responsiveness; increased ability to compete; and quick access to better information in a timely manner. The users of EDI include organizations in the trucking, retail, shipping, grocery, health-care, pharmaceutical, and automotive industries, government, and others.

Electronic Funds Transfer

An **electronic funds transfer (EFT)** system transfers money and other information electronically from one institution to another. A byproduct of this service is the reduction of mountains of paper and time delays, thereby gaining cost efficiencies. For example, banks can transfer money from an account in one bank to another account in another bank, and the federal government can deposit benefits directly into recipients' bank accounts.

A new trend in the EFT system is the transmittal of tax information electronically to tax authorities at a central processor. Information such as the amount, tax due, and employer identification number would be provided to the central processor. Some advantages of this approach include fewer errors, lower costs, more timely deposits, and increased elimination of float associated with delays in moving funds.

Some U.S. state governments distribute public-aid benefits electronically. Benefit recipients who use this system are given magnetic cards with their photographs, which they insert in special electronic devices at the participating check-cashing centers or banks. The cards access computer records to tell the agents the amounts of benefits due.

Other applications include payment of unemployment insurance benefits. Claimants can call the government agency and enter their Social Security number and personal identification number (PIN). After successfully answering certification questions, claimants are informed that they are to receive their benefits. Participants then gain access to their weekly payments with a plastic card and a PIN through automated teller machines (ATMs) or point-of-sale

(POS) terminals. Those who already have a bank account are given the option to directly deposit their benefits, and those who prefer to receive state-issued checks may continue to do so. This is a clear example of integration of such diverse technologies as POS, EFT, and ATMs.

 Self-Assessment Exercise

Online exercises are provided for the learning objectives in this module. Please visit www.mbaiq .com to complete the online exercises and to calculate your MBA IQ Score.

Corporate Control, Law, Ethics, and Governance

Learning Objective 9.1: Understand the Nature and Types of Corporate Control Systems   **236**

Control Characteristics   236
Control Design   236
Control Placement   236
Control Costs and Benefits   237
Control Implementation   237
Controls Classification   237
Control Requirements   241
Control Assessment   241
Control Responsibilities   241

Learning Objective 9.2: Understand the Nature and Types of Corporate Risks   **241**

Risk Management Methodology   242
Risk Management Tools   243
Managing Corporate Risks   246

Learning Objective 9.3: Understand the Scope and Nature of Business Law, Policy, and Ethics, Including Social Responsibility   **247**

Contract Defined   247
Antitrust Laws   248
Environmental Laws   250
Consumer Product Safety Laws   250
Food and Drug Administration Laws   250
Investment Securities Laws   250
Intellectual Property Laws   250
Employment Laws   251
Bankruptcy Laws   251
Compliance Management   251
Business Policy   252
Business Ethics   253
Corporate Social Responsibility   253
The Pyramid of Corporate Social Responsibility   255

Learning Objective 9.4: Understand the Various Issues in Corporate Governance   **256**

Components of Corporate Governance   256
Corporate Governance Standards   256
Roles of the Board of Directors   257
Roles of CEOs and Senior Executives   258
Need for Board Independence   259
Insider Trading Scandals   259
Improving Corporate Governance   260

Learning Objective 9.5: Understand the Nature and Types of Corporate Audits   **260**

Construction/Contract Audit   260
Quality Audit   261
Due-Diligence Audit   261
Security Audit   262
Safety Audit   262
Privacy Audit   262
Performance Audit   262
Operational Audit   263

Learning Objective 9.6: Understand the Nature and Types of Corporate Fraud   **263**

Types of Fraud   263
Degree of Fraud   264
Red Flags for Fraud   264
Symptoms of Management Fraud   264
Symptoms of Employee Fraud   265
Management Representations versus Risk   265
Review of Accounting Estimates   266

Learning Objective 9.7: Understand the Issues in Corporate Law Regarding Agency Problems and Costs   **266**

❑ Learning Objective 9.1: UNDERSTAND THE NATURE AND TYPES OF CORPORATE CONTROL SYSTEMS

Four critical elements supporting corporate management infrastructure are control systems, laws, ethics, and governance mechanisms. When one of these elements is broken, the other three elements are also broken because they are all tightly intertwined and closely connected. The infrastructure chain is as strong as its weakest link. The goal is to create a control-rich, law-abiding, fraud-free, ethics-full, and governance-compliant environment that is as strong as possible. This requires taking full responsibility and owning complete accountability for both actions and inactions, which are the cornerstones of corporate management.

Control Characteristics

Control is any positive and negative actions taken by management that would result in accomplishment of the organization's goals, objectives, and mission. Controls are described in the form of policies, procedures, standards, and rules (i.e., do's and don'ts). Controls should not lead to compulsion or become a constraint on employees. Controls should be natural and should be embedded in the organizational functions, systems, and operations. More so, controls should be accepted by the employees using or affected by them. Use and implementation of controls should be inviting, not inhibiting. Controls should be seen as beneficial from the employee's personal and professional viewpoints. Ideally, controls should facilitate the achievement of employees' and organizational goals and objectives (i.e., ensure the goal-congruence principle). In other words, any control that does not promote achieving the goals and objectives should not be implemented. Controls should be effective and efficient. Controls should not cost more than the benefits derived. Controls prevent or reduce the adverse effects of risks. Moreover, **controlling** is the result of proper planning, organizing, and directing activities—all are major functions of management. This means that controls ensure that targeted plans are achieved.

Controls work in an additive way, meaning that their combined effect is far greater than the sum of each individual effect. Two examples follow:

Example 1: Business control A is effective 90 percent of the time, and business control B is effective 90 percent of the time. What is the combined effect of control A and B?

Answer 1: The combined effect is 99 percent. In combination, both controls are ineffective only 1 percent of the time (i.e., $0.1 \times 0.1 \times 100 = 1\%$). This means the combined controls are effective 99 percent of the time (i.e., $100\% - 1\%$).

Example 2: Security control A misses 30 percent of attacks, and security control B also misses 30 percent of attacks. What percentage of attacks will be caught when both controls are working together?

Answer 2: The combined effect is 91 percent. In combination, both controls should only miss 9 percent of attacks (i.e., $0.3 \times 0.3 \times 100 = 9\%$). This means 91 percent of attacks should be caught (i.e., $100\% - 9\%$).

Control Design

The complexity of an entity and the nature and scope of activities affect its control activities. Complex organizations with diverse activities may face more difficult control issues than simple organizations with less varied activities. An entity with decentralized operations and an emphasis on local autonomy and innovation presents different control circumstances than a highly centralized one. A major factor that can affect controls negatively is situations such as downsizing, outsourcing, and business slowdown, resulting in loss of revenues, profits, and employees, in that controls are either relaxed or turned off. Management can override controls because they do not see the need for controls under these situations, when in fact more controls are needed to counterbalance the adverse effects of these situations. Other factors that influence an entity's complexity and, therefore, the nature of its controls include location and geographic dispersion, the extensiveness and sophistication of operations, and information processing methods. All these factors affect an entity's control activities, which need to be designed accordingly to contribute to the achievement of the entity's objectives. Simply stated, the nature and amount of controls needed depends on the level of risk. High-risk business situations require stronger controls and vice versa. Controls that are designed but not implemented are of no use.

Control Placement

Controls should be placed where control-related activities are taking place and where risks are the greatest. Examples of control activities include management approvals, authorizations, verifications, reconciliations, reviews of operating budgets and performance, security of assets, mergers and acquisitions, and segregation of duties.

Control Costs and Benefits

A cost–benefit analysis is advised during the process of designing each type of control into business functions and systems. Ideally, costs should never exceed the benefits to be derived from installing controls. However, costs should not always be the sole determining factor because it may be difficult or impractical to quantify benefits such as timeliness, improved quality and relevance of data and information, and improved customer service and system response time. Sometimes, controls are simply needed to comply with government regulation without any measurable benefit.

When controls are properly planned, designed, developed, tested, implemented, and followed, they should meet as many as possible of the following attributes: practical, reliable, simple, complete, operational, usable, appropriate, cost-effective, timely, meaningful, reasonable, and consistent.

Control Implementation

Costs of controls vary with their implementation time and the complexity of the system or operation. **Control implementation** time is important to realize benefits from installing appropriate controls. For example, it costs significantly more to correct a design problem in the implementation phase of an application system under development than it does to address it in the early planning and design phases.

There are trade-offs among costs, controls, and convenience factors as they affect a system's usability, maintainability, auditability, controllability, and securability. For example:

- High-risk systems and complex systems and operations require more controls and cost more.
- Excessive use of tight-security features and control functions can be costly and may complicate procedures, degrade system performance, and impair system functionality, which could ultimately inhibit the system's usability.
- System users prefer as few integrity and security controls as possible—only those needed to make the system really usable.

- The greater the maintainability of the system, the easier it is for a programmer to modify it. Similarly, the greater the maintainability of the system, the less expensive it is to operate in the long run.

Controls Classification

Controls are classified in several ways because controls work in different locations and functions, at different times with different results, and all achieving different objectives set by various managers.

Classifying Controls by Their Nature

One way of classifying controls is by their nature, such as management controls, technical controls, and operational controls.

Management controls, in the broadest sense, include the plan of organization, methods, and procedures adopted by management to ensure that its goals and objectives are met (i.e., ensure the goal-congruence principle). Management controls, also known as **internal controls,** include accounting and administrative controls. **Internal control** is a process within an organization designed to provide reasonable assurance regarding the achievement of these five primary objectives: (1) reliability and integrity of information, (2) compliance with policies, plans, procedures, laws, regulations, and contracts, (3) safeguarding of assets, (4) economical and efficient use of resources, and (5) accomplishment of established objectives and goals for operations and programs. Internal controls include procedural checks and balances that safeguard assets and ensure data integrity. The internal control system is intertwined with an entity's operating activities and exists for fundamental business reasons. Internal controls are most effective when they are built into the entity's infrastructure and are part of the essence of the enterprise. They should be "built in" rather than "built on." Building in controls can directly affect an entity's ability to reach its goals and supports businesses' quality initiatives. The quest for quality is directly linked to how businesses are run.

As discussed in Learning Module 1, "General Management, Leadership, and Strategy," management controls are divided into feed-forward, concurrent, and feedback.

Management control systems must be integrated with ongoing management practices and, where appropriate and effective, with other management initiatives, such as productivity improvement, quality improvement, business process improvement, reengineering, and performance measures and standards. Examples of management practices include periodic staff meetings, quarterly management reviews, budget planning and execution, and variance analysis.

Management control systems must be effective and efficient—balancing the costs of control mechanisms and processes with the benefits the systems are intended to provide or control. They should identify who is accountable and provide accountability for all activities.

Traditional management controls include the process for planning, organizing, directing, and controlling the entity's operations. They include the management control systems for measuring, reporting, and monitoring operations. Specifically, they include automated and manual systems, policies and procedures, rules of behavior, individual roles and responsibilities, and other ongoing management activities that help ensure risks are managed and controlled. Internal auditing is an important part of management control.

Several contemporary management controls have evolved over the years, including economic-value-added, market-value-added, activity-based costing, open-book management, and the balanced scorecard system.

Technical controls focus on engineering specifications for manufacturing a product or security controls over computer systems. The controls can provide automated protection for unauthorized access or misuse, facilitate detection of security violations, and support security requirements for application systems and data. The topical areas to review include identification and authentication mechanisms, logical access controls, and audit trails. Technical controls are hardware and software controls used to provide automated protection to the IT system or applications. They operate within the technical system and applications.

Operational controls are the day-to-day procedures and mechanisms used to control operational activities, such as scheduling, shipping, and billing, to ensure that they are carried out effectively and efficiently. They also address computer security methods focusing on mechanisms primarily implemented and executed by people as opposed to computer systems. These controls are put in place to improve the security of a particular computer system or group of systems. They often require technical or specialized expertise and often rely on management controls and technical controls.

Classifying Controls by Time Dimension

Another way of classifying controls is by **time dimension,** using three different dimensions of timing: precontrol, concurrent control, and postcontrol.

Precontrol (e.g., policy) anticipates problems and is proactive in nature. **Concurrent control** is exercised through supervision and monitoring and is ongoing. **Postcontrol** identifies deviations from standards or budgets and calls for corrective action and is similar to feedback control. Precontrol and feed-forward controls are interrelated since they deal with future-directed actions. Forecasting, budgeting, and real-time computer systems are examples of feed-forward controls. Precontrol is the most preferred action; the least preferred action is postcontrol. The difference is *when* a corrective action is taken—the sooner the better. The following is a comparison between controls by nature and controls by time:

Feed-forward control	Precontrol
Concurrent control	Concurrent control
Feedback control	Postcontrol

Classifying Controls by Their Location

Another way of classifying controls is by their location, such as centralized control and decentralized control.

Centralized control means control is located at the headquarters from which senior management works. Centralized control, another name for **bureaucratic control,** involves monitoring and influencing employee behavior through extensive use of rules, policies, hierarchy of authority, written documentation, reward systems, and other formal mechanisms. Many traditional companies use top-down budgeting, which means that the budgeted amounts for the coming year are literally imposed by senior managers on middle and lower-level managers.

Decentralized control is located at the field (e.g., local factory, office, warehouse, and department) where operating and division management works. Decentralized control relies on cultural values, traditions, shared beliefs, and trust to foster compliance with organizational goals. Managers operate on the assumption that employees are trustworthy and willing to perform effectively without extensive rules and standards and with little or no supervision. The movement toward employee empowerment, participation, and learning means that many organizations are adopting bottom-up budgeting, a process in which middle and lower-level managers anticipate their departments' resource needs and pass them up to senior managers for approval.

Classifying Controls by Their Measuring Strength

Another way of classifying controls is by their **measuring strength,** such as hard controls and soft controls.

Hard controls are formal, tangible, and easier to measure and evaluate. Examples of hard controls include budgets, dual controls, written approvals, reconciliations, authorization levels, verifications, and segregation of duties. Tools to evaluate hard controls include flowcharts, system narratives, testing, and counting.

Soft controls are informal, intangible, subjective, and difficult to measure and evaluate. Examples of soft controls include an organization's ethical climate, integrity, values, culture, and vision; people's behaviors, attitudes, and commitment to competence; tone at the top; management philosophy; management's operating style, level of understanding, and commitment; and communication. Tools to evaluate soft controls include self-assessments, questionnaires, interviews, and workshops.

Generally speaking, senior managers most often use soft skills and soft controls to achieve their objectives; middle and lower-level managers most often use hard skills and hard controls. **Soft skills** include written/oral and listening communication skills, and people skills such as interpersonal, motivation, implementation, teamwork, negotiation, and leadership skills. **Hard skills** include analytical, technical, mathematical, problem-solving, decision-making, and functional skills.

However, managers at all levels in the hierarchy deal with **soft issues** (e.g., handling employee low-morale issues, employee high-job-turnover issues, employee disciplinary actions, and labor union grievance issues) and **hard issues** (e.g., handling tough competitors, increasing revenues, decreasing costs, increasing profits, increasing market share, and increasing stock price of a company).

Classifying Controls by Their Action, Objective, or Function

Another way of classifying controls is by their action, objective, or function, such as directive controls, preventive controls, detective controls, corrective controls, recovery controls, manual controls, and computer controls.

Directive controls are actions, policies, procedures, directives, standards, circulars, regulations, or guidelines that cause or encourage a desirable event to occur. By their broad nature set by management, directive controls affect the entire business unit, function, system, or operation, and have far-reaching and long-lasting effects.

A specific example of a directive control is requiring all accountants and auditors to be certified. Another specific example of directive control is providing management with assurance of achieving the specified minimum gross margins on sales.

Preventive controls are actions taken to deter undesirable events from occurring. Examples include segregation of duties, use of checklists, use of systems development methodology, competent staff, use of passwords, authorization procedures, and documentation. Segregation of duties means duties are divided among different people to reduce the risk of errors, fraud, or inappropriate actions. For example, it includes dividing the responsibilities for authorizing transactions, recording them, and handling the related asset. A manager authorizing credit sales would not be responsible for maintaining accounts receivable records or handling cash receipts. Similarly, salespersons would not have the ability to modify product price files or commission rates. It calls for a separation of the functional responsibilities of custodianship, record keeping, operations, and authorization.

In general, sound prevention is better than detection and correction. However, prevention is not always possible or cost effective. Prevention, although expensive sometimes, is the primary control function. It is good to implement a dual-control concept in that two-person control, two physical keys, or two encryption keys are better than one-person control or one key.

Detective controls are actions taken to detect undesirable events that have occurred. The installation of detective controls is necessary to provide feedback on the effectiveness of directive and/or preventive controls or whether standards or guidelines have been met. Examples include reviews and comparisons, bank reconciliations, account reconciliations, and physical counts. They detect computer attacks, crime, fraud, errors, omissions, and irregularities and identify aspects of system quality, control, and security features that need management's attention. Detective controls include both manual and automated tools and techniques and measure the effectiveness of preventive steps.

Usually, general-purpose detection and correction is better than special-purpose detection and correction due to its cost effectiveness and broad usage.

Corrective controls are actions taken to correct undesirable events that have occurred. They fix both detected and reported errors. Examples include correction procedures, documentation, and control and exception reports. Corrective controls provide information, procedures, and instructions for correcting detected attacks, errors, omissions, and irregularities. They may simply identify the areas where corrective action is required, may actually facilitate the corrective action, and include both manual and automated tools and techniques.

Recovery controls are actions taken to ensure the continuity of business operations and computer systems. They facilitate application system backup, restoration, recovery, and restart after any attacks or interruption in information processing. They promote an orderly environment in which all required resources are readily available to ensure a reasonably smooth recovery from disaster. This permits continuation of a specific activity or of the entire operation of the organization.

Manual controls include budgets, forecasts, policies, and procedures; reporting; and physical controls over equipment, inventories, securities, cash, and other assets, which are periodically counted and compared with amounts shown on control records.

Computer controls include general controls and application controls. **General controls** include data center operations controls, system software controls, access security controls, and application system development and maintenance controls. **Application controls** are designed to control application processing, helping to ensure the completeness and accuracy of transaction processing, authorization, and validity. Many application controls depend on computerized edit checks. These edit checks consist of format, existence, reasonableness, and other checks on the data, which are built into each application during its development. When these checks are designed properly, they can help provide control over the data being entered into the computer system. Computer controls are performed to check accuracy, completeness, and authorization of transactions.

Classifying Controls by How They Interact

Another way of classifying controls is how they interact with each other. This includes combination controls, complementary controls, compensating controls, contradictory controls, and risk avoidance controls.

Rarely would a single control suffice to meet control objectives. Rather, a **combination of controls** is needed to make up a whole and to provide a magnifying effect. For example, supervisory reviews and approvals are combined with the organization's policies, procedures, and standards.

An example of a combination of controls is a situation where fire-resistant materials are used in the computer center (a preventive control) to prevent a fire, while smoke and fire detectors are used to detect smoke and fire (a detective control), and fire extinguishers are used to put out the fire (a corrective control). Here a single preventive control would not be sufficient. All three controls are needed to be effective.

Complementary controls (hand-in-hand controls) have an important place in both the manual and the automated control environment. Complementary controls are different from compensating controls where in the latter category weak controls in one area or function are balanced by strong controls in other areas or functions and vice versa. A function or an area need not be weak to use complementary controls.

Complementary controls can enhance the effectiveness of two or more controls when applied to a business function, computer system, or operation. Examples of complementary controls include access profiles, user IDs, and passwords, where these controls together can provide a moderate level of access control mechanism. These individual controls are effective as standalone and are maximized when combined or integrated with each other. These individual controls have an additive nature to produce a synergistic effect. These complementary controls should fit with each other in order to obtain maximum benefit.

The purpose of **compensating controls** is to balance weak controls in one area with strong controls in another related area and vice versa. If actions of individuals or systems were not recorded before, implementing a log now to record such actions is an example of compensating control. Another dimension is that automated controls compensate for the weaknesses in or lack of manual controls. For example, if manual controls over program changes were weak, automated software management is a compensating control.

Contradictory controls are those controls that act against each other. Such controls should be eliminated or reassessed because they confuse employees and are counterproductive. An example is one policy encouraging employees to do telecommuting work (one control) and another policy restricting employees from carrying software home from work (contradictory control).

The rationale behind the **risk avoidance control** is that the management view of a resource has to be isolated from the implementation of that resource. Resources are entities within a system or network of systems that require management. Resources can include physical entities (e.g., printers, libraries, and routers) or logical entities (e.g., users, groups). The goal of risk avoidance controls is to separate two entities from each other so that they are safe and secure and that potential risk from their being together is avoided. Examples include separating assets from threats to avoid potential risk, separating computer equipment from radio receivers to avoid the spread of electromagnetic signals for possible interception by outsiders, separating production libraries from test libraries to avoid possible contamination of program code and corruption of data, separating system development procedures from data entry procedures, and separating system components from each other.

Control Requirements

The auditor needs to understand the control requirements of a business function operation before assessing control strengths and weaknesses. In other words, there should be a basis or baseline in place (i.e., standards, guidelines, and benchmarks) prior to control measurement and assessment. In the absence of a baseline of standards, auditor's findings, conclusions, and recommendations will be questioned and will not be accepted by the auditee. Usually the basis is:

- Technical standards
- Operations standards
- Administrative standards
- Industry standards

Control Assessment

During an assessment of control strengths and weaknesses, the auditor might run into situations where a business function, system, or manual/automated procedure is overcontrolled or undercontrolled. This means that there may be too many controls in one area and not enough controls in other areas. Also, there may be duplication or overlapping of controls between two or more areas. Under these conditions, the auditor should recommend to eliminate some

functional user controls, some information system controls, some manual controls, some automated controls, or a combination of them. The same may be true of situations where a system or operation is oversecured or undersecured and where an application system is overdesigned or underdesigned. This assessment requires differentiating between relevant and irrelevant information, considering compensating controls, considering interrelationships of controls, and judging materiality and significance of audit findings taken separately and as a whole.

Control Responsibilities

Who is responsible for establishing and ensuring an adequate and effective internal control environment within the organization? It is the company management, the audit committee, and the board of directors—not the auditors (internal or external). Here "company management" refers to senior management, operating management, and department/division management, who are responsible for ensuring the adequacy of disclosures in the financial statements of a publicly held company. Auditors are responsible for ensuring an adequate and effective system of internal control in the organization. Simply put, management establishes controls, and auditors evaluate such controls. External parties also influence controls indirectly (e.g., customers, suppliers, legislators, regulators, financial analysts, bond raters, and news media).

❑ Learning Objective 9.2: UNDERSTAND THE NATURE AND TYPES OF CORPORATE RISKS

Risk is the possibility of something adverse happening to an organization. **Risk management** is the process of assessing risk, taking steps to reduce risk to an acceptable level, and maintaining that level of risk. Risk management encompasses three processes: risk assessment, risk mitigation, and risk evaluation.

Risk Management = Risk Assessment
+ Risk Mitigation + Risk Evaluation

Risk assessment includes identification and evaluation of risks and risk impacts and recommendation of risk-reducing measures. **Risk mitigation** refers to prioritizing, implementing, and maintaining the appropriate risk-reducing measures recommended from the risk assessment process. **Risk evaluation** is a continual process for implementing a successful risk management program. Management is responsible for determining whether the remaining risk (residual risk) is at an acceptable level or whether additional controls should be implemented to further reduce or eliminate residual risk.

A successful risk management program will rely on critical success factors such as senior management's commitment; the full support and participation of team members; the competence of the risk assessment team, which must have the expertise to apply the risk assessment methodology to a specific process or system, identify mission risks, and provide cost-effective safeguards that meet the needs of the organization; the awareness and cooperation of members of the functional user community, who must follow procedures and comply with the implemented controls to safeguard the mission of their organization; and an ongoing evaluation and assessment of mission risks.

Minimizing negative impact on an organization and need for a sound baseline in decision making are the fundamental reasons organizations implement a risk management process.

Risk Management Methodology

As stated earlier, risk management encompasses three processes: risk assessment, risk mitigation, and risk evaluation. These processes are further expanded next.

Risk Assessment

Risk assessment is the first process in the risk management methodology. Organizations use risk assessment to determine the extent of the potential threat and the risk associated with a process or system. The output of the process helps to identify appropriate controls for reducing or eliminating risk during the risk mitigation process. Major activities in the risk assessment process include vulnerability identification, threat identification, control analysis, impact analysis, risk determination, and control recommendations.

Risk Mitigation

Risk mitigation, the second process of risk management, involves prioritizing, evaluating, and implementing appropriate risk-reducing controls recommended from the risk assessment process. Because the elimination of all risk is usually impractical or close to impossible, it is the responsibility of senior management and functional and business managers to use the least-cost approach and implement the most appropriate controls to decrease mission risk to an acceptable level, with minimal adverse impact on the organization's resources and mission.

Risk mitigation can be achieved through any one or a combination of the following risk mitigation options:

- **Risk rejection.** Risk rejection or risk ignorance is not a wise choice, as all major risks must be managed.
- **Risk assumption (acceptance).** Risk acceptance is recognizing a risk and its potential consequences and accepting that risk. This usually occurs when there is no alternative risk mitigation strategy that is more cost effective or feasible.

  To accept the potential risks and continue operating the system or process, management needs to decide at some point whether the operation or the function or the system is acceptable, given the kind and severity of remaining risks. Risk acceptance is linked to the selection of safeguards since, in some cases, risk may have to be accepted because safeguards (countermeasures) are too expensive (in either monetary or nonmonetary factors).

  Merely selecting safeguards does not reduce risk; those safeguards need to be effectively implemented. Moreover, to continue to be effective, risk management needs to be an ongoing process. This requires a periodic assessment and improvement of safeguards and reanalysis of risks.
- **Risk avoidance.** To avoid the risk means eliminating the risk cause and/or consequence (e.g., add controls that prevent the risk from occurring, remove certain functions of the system, or shut down the system when risks are identified).
- **Risk reduction (limitation).** To limit risk means implementing controls that minimize the adverse impact of a threat's exercising a vulnerability (e.g., use of supporting, preventive, and detective controls) or authorizing operation for a limited time during which additional risk mitigation by other means is being put into place. Risk reduction affords an opportunity to decrease the likelihood a risk will occur.
- **Risk transfer.** To transfer the risk means using other options to compensate for the loss, such as purchasing insurance, coinsurance, or outsourcing. Risk transfer is finding another person or organization that can manage the project risk(s) better. Risk protection can be referred to as

"insurance" against certain events. Risk protection involves doing something to allow the project to fall back on additional or alternative resources should the scheduled resource(s) fail.

- **Risk contingency.** This means to define the necessary alternative steps needed if an identified risk event should occur.
- **Risk compliance.** It is necessary to comply with all the applicable laws and regulations in a timely and proper manner in order to reduce compliance risk.
- **Residual risk.** Organizations can analyze the extent of the risk reduction generated by new or enhanced controls in terms of the reduced threat likelihood or impact. The risk remaining after the implementation of new or enhanced controls is residual risk. Practically no system or process is risk free, and not all implemented controls can eliminate the risk they are intended to address or reduce the risk level to zero.

Implementation of new or enhanced controls can mitigate residual risk by:

- Eliminating some of the system's vulnerabilities (flaws and weaknesses), thereby reducing the number of possible threat-source/vulnerability pairs
- Adding a targeted control to reduce the capacity and motivation of a threat-source (e.g., if technical controls are expensive, then consider administrative and physical controls)
- Reducing the magnitude of the adverse impact (e.g., limiting the extent of a vulnerability or modifying the nature of the relationship between the IT system and the organization's mission)

If residual risk has not been reduced to an acceptable level, the risk management cycle must be repeated to identify a way of lowering the residual risk to an acceptable level.

Risk Evaluation

Risk evaluation, the third and final process of risk management, is a continual evaluation process since change is a constant thing in most organizations. Possible changes include: new businesses are acquired, new products are introduced, new services are provided, networks are updated and expanded, network components are added or removed, applications software is replaced or updated with newer versions, personnel changes are made, and security policies are updated. These changes mean that new risks will surface and risks previously mitigated may

again become a concern. Thus, the risk evaluation process is ongoing and evolving.

Risk Management Tools

Measuring risk can be difficult, and in practice a variety of approaches are used, ranging from simply adjusting costs up or benefits down or adjusting risk levels, dollar amounts, and probabilities to the use of statistical modeling and Monte Carlo simulation. A few of the more commonly used tools and techniques include business impact analysis; cost–benefit analysis; strengths, weaknesses, opportunities, and threats (SWOT) analysis (situation analysis); sensitivity analysis; gap analysis; option analysis; economic analysis; expected value analysis; and subjective scoring. It is a good business practice to combine quantitative methods with qualitative techniques to obtain broad perspectives.

Business Impact Analysis

A **business impact analysis (BIA)** is a critical step in understanding the impact of various threats, exposures, and risks facing an organization. This analysis can be applied to any business function, operation, or mission. The results of the BIA are then integrated into business strategies, plans, policies, and procedures.

Example of BIA Application

An example of BIA application includes determining objective risk resulting from fire incidents for two warehouses of a major corporation. Each warehouse has the same area (one million square feet), and each warehouse has a total of 100 minor and major fire incidents per year. The Corporate Risk Management department estimated the number of fire incidents during the next year as follows:

Fire incidents for Warehouse 1 can range from 95 to 105, based on the most likely estimate.
Fire incidents for Warehouse 2 can range from 80 to 120, based on the most likely estimate.

What is the degree of risk for each warehouse? Which warehouse has the higher degree of risk?

Degree of Risk for Warehouse 1
$$= (105 - 95)/100 = 10\%$$
Degree of Risk for Warehouse 2
$$= (120 - 80)/100 = 40\%$$ *(Continued)*

> The degree of risk for Warehouse 2 is four times that for Warehouse 1, even though the chances of fire incidents are the same for both warehouses.

Cost–Benefit Analysis

To allocate resources and implement cost-effective security controls, organizations, after identifying all possible controls and evaluating their feasibility and effectiveness, should conduct a cost–benefit analysis for each proposed control to determine which controls are required and appropriate for their circumstances.

The **cost–benefit analysis** can be qualitative and quantitative. Its purpose is to demonstrate that the costs of implementing the controls can be justified by the reduction in the level of risk. A cost–benefit analysis for proposed new controls or enhanced control encompasses the following:

- Determining the impact of implementing the new or enhanced controls.
- Determining the impact of not implementing the new or enhanced controls.
- Estimating the costs of the implementation. These may include hardware and software purchases; reduced operational effectiveness if system performance or functionality is reduced for increased security; cost of implementing additional policies and procedures; cost of hiring additional personnel to implement proposed policies, procedures, or services; and training and maintenance costs.
- Assessing the implementation costs and benefits against system and data criticality to determine the importance to the organization of implementing the new controls, given their costs and relative impact.

The organization will need to assess the benefits of the controls in terms of maintaining an acceptable mission posture for the organization. Just as there is a cost of implementing a needed control, there is a cost of not implementing it. By relating the result of not implementing the control to the mission, the organization can determine whether it is feasible to forgo its control implementation.

SWOT Analysis

The scope of situation or **SWOT analysis** includes an assessment of an organization's key strengths (S), weaknesses (W), opportunities (O), and threats (T). It considers several factors, such as the firm itself, the organization's industry, the competitive position, functional areas of the firm, and management of the firm.

Sensitivity Analysis

Sensitivity analysis includes scenario (what-if) planning and simulation studies. Sensitivity analysis indicates how much change in outputs will occur in response to a given change in inputs. As applied to investments, it indicates how much an investment's return (or net present value, NPV) will change in response to a given change in an independent input variable, with all other factors held constant. This technique can be used on one variable at a time or on a group of variables (sometime referred to as **scenario analysis**). Typically, investment returns are more sensitive to changes in some variables than to changes in others.

Gap Analysis

Gap analysis determines the difference between the actual outcome and the expected outcome. The gap can be reduced, though not eliminated, through strategies, contingency plans, and specific action steps after identifying the root causes of the gap.

Option Analysis

Option (choice) analysis is more a framework for critical thinking than a model, requiring analysts to ask whether all options for managing uncertainty have been considered. Option analysis may be subdivided into sequential decision analysis and irreversible investment theory.

Economic Analysis

The scope of **economic analysis** includes breakeven analysis, capital budgeting analysis (e.g., payback period, net present value (NPV), internal rate of return (IRR), and profitability index), and financial ratio analysis such as return on investment (ROI), return on quality (ROQ), return on assets (ROA), return on training (ROT), and return on sales (ROS). These deal with quantitative data in terms of dollars and ratios.

Expected Value Analysis

Expected value analysis involves the assignment of probability estimates to alternative outcomes and summing the products of the various outcomes. For example, the price of crude oil per barrel today is $10.80 and there is a 25 percent probability of the price rising to $11.50 in the next year, a 25 percent chance it will fall to $10.50, and a 50 percent chance of a slight increase to $11.00. The expected value (EV) of the future price of one barrel of crude oil would be:

$$EV = 0.25 \times \$11.50 + 0.25 \times \$10.50 + 0.50 \times \$11.00$$
$$= \$11.00$$

Subjective Scoring

Subjective scoring involves assigning weights to responses to questions addressing areas that might introduce elements of risk. The resulting risk score may be just one component of an overall subjective project or investment evaluation. Evaluation criteria are individually weighted to reflect their concept of inherent risk. Identified risk factors should be limited to a few points for manageability and understandability and for meaningful interpretation of the results.

Quantitative Methods

Organizations should use both quantitative and qualitative methods to obtain a comprehensive picture of risks. Examples of quantitative methods include five specific approaches:

1. **Exposure factor.** This risk metric provides a percentage measure of potential loss—up to 100 percent of the value of the asset.
2. **Single-loss exposure value.** Single-loss exposure value is computed by multiplying the asset value with the exposure factor. This risk metric presents the expected monetary cost of a threat event. For example, an earthquake may destroy critical information technology and communications resources, thereby preventing an organization from billing its clients for perhaps a week—until replacement resources can be established—even though the necessary information may remain intact.

   Financial losses from a single event could be devastating. Alternatively, the threat of operational errors costing individually from hundreds to a few thousands of dollars—none devastating or even individually significant—may occur many times a year with a significant total annual cost and loss of operational efficiency.
3. **Annualized rate of occurrence**. Threats may occur with great frequency, rarely, or anywhere in between. Seemingly minor operational threats may occur many times every year, adding up to substantial loss, while potentially devastating threats, such as a 100-year flood, a fire, or a hacker who destroys critical files, may occur only rarely. Annualizing threat frequency allows the economic consequences of threat events to be addressed in a sound fiscal manner, much as actuarial data enable insurance companies to provide valuable and profitable services to their clients.
4. **Probability of loss**. Probability of loss is the chance or likelihood of expected monetary loss attributable to a threat event. For example, loss due to operational error may extend from a 1/10 chance of losing $10 million annually to a 1/100 chance of losing $1 billion annually, provided the right combinations of conditions are met. Note that there is little utility in developing the probability of threat events for anything but relatively rare occurrences. The annualized probable monetary loss can be useful in budgeting.
5. **Annualized loss expectancy.** The simplest expression of annualized loss expectancy is derived by multiplying the annualized rate of occurrence (i.e., threat frequency) with the single-loss exposure value. For example, given an annual rate of occurrence of 1/10 and a single-loss exposure of $10 million, the expected loss annually is 1/10 × $10 million = $1 million. This value is central in the cost–benefit analysis of risk mitigation and in ensuring proportionality in resources allocated to protection of assets.

Qualitative Methods

Examples of qualitative methods include judgment and intuitive (gut feel) approach, checklists, self-assessments, focus groups, interviews, surveys, and Delphi technique. In the Delphi technique, subject matter experts (SMEs) present their own view of risks independently and anonymously, which are then centrally compiled. The process is repeated until consensus is obtained. The Delphi technique is a method used to avoid groupthink, as SMEs do not meet face-to-face to make decisions.

Managing Corporate Risks

The following five plans and controls should be implemented to manage corporate risks on an ongoing basis:

1. *Manage existing safeguards and controls.* The day-to-day management of existing safeguards and controls ranges from the robust access control for information assets, to enforcement of systems development standards, and to awareness and management of the physical environment and associated risks. Many other essential areas of safeguard and control must be administered and practiced daily. These include, but are not limited to, personnel procedures, change control, information valuation and classification, and contingency planning.

2. *Periodically assess risks.* In order to determine whether all necessary and prudent safeguards and controls are in place and efficiently administered, associated risks must be assessed periodically, preferably with quantitative risk assessment. An insecure information technology environment may appear on the surface to be securely administered, but quantitative risk assessment can reveal safeguard or control inadequacies. Effective application of the results of that assessment, through risk mitigation and associated cost–benefit analysis, can lead to the assurance of efficient safeguard or control of organization assets and improved bottom-line performance.

3. *Mitigate risks by implementing and efficiently administering safeguards and controls.* It is important to remedy situations where risk assessment shows that safeguards or controls are not in place or are not effectively administered.

4. *Do risk assessment and strategic planning.* Quantitative risk assessment, applied in the consideration of alternative strategic plans, can reveal unacceptable risks in an otherwise-sound business case. Failure to assess the risks associated with alternative strategic plans can result in the implementation of plans at significant monetary loss. That loss is a consequence of being unaware of, or inadequately considering, risks.

5. *Implement a **enterprise risk management (ERM)** program.* Traditionally, corporate risk management focused on a partial portfolio of risks (silo approach), specifically on financial and hazard risks. The scope was narrow, ignoring all the other risks impacting the organization. It did not exploit the "natural hedges" and "portfolio effects" in the collective. It tended to treat risk as a downside phenomenon.

Now ERM focuses on the total portfolio of risks, including financial, hazard, strategic, and operational risks. The scope of ERM is much broader than the traditional view with the objective of creating, protecting, and enhancing shareholder value. The ERM treats risk as both an upside and downside phenomenon since it integrates all risks.

Five alternative risk-transfer tools, other than traditional insurance, are (1) captives, (2) financial insurance, (3) multiline/multiyear insurance, (4) multiple-trigger policies, and (5) securitization. Multiple-trigger policies and securitization tools are more commonly used.

1. **Captives** are where a noninsurance firm for the purpose of accepting the risk of the parent firm owns an insurer. Captives combine risk transfer and risk retention.

2. **Financial insurance contracts** are based on spreading risk over time, as opposed to across a pool of similar exposures. These contracts usually involve a sharing of the investment returns between the insurer and the insured.

3. **Multiline/multiyear insurance contracts** combine a broad array of risks (multiline) into a contract with a policy period that extends over multiple years (multiyear). For example, a pure risk may be combined with a financial risk.

4. **Multiple-trigger policies** reflect the source of the risk, which is not as important as the impact of the risk on a firm's earnings. A pure risk is combined with a financial risk. The policy is triggered, and payment is made, only upon the occurrence of an adverse event.

5. **Securitization** involves the creation of securities such as bonds, or derivatives contracts, options, swaps, and futures, which have a payout or price movement that is linked to an insurance risk. Examples include catastrophe options, earthquake bonds, catastrophe bonds, and catastrophe equity puts.

Scorecards, action plans, and monitoring are part of the ERM approach. Scorecards include metrics, a timeframe for managing the risk, and a link to shareholder value. Action plans include identifying a risk champion and determining milestones. Monitoring includes progress reviews and review for validity of metrics.

❑ Learning Objective 9.3: UNDERSTAND THE SCOPE AND NATURE OF BUSINESS LAW, POLICY, AND ETHICS, INCLUDING SOCIAL RESPONSIBILITY

Business laws are presented in terms of contract law, antitrust laws, environmental laws, consumer product safety laws, food and drug administration laws, investment securities laws, intellectual property laws, employment laws, and bankruptcy laws. Business law is related to business policy and ethics, which in turn are related to social responsibility.

Contract Defined

U.S. contracts are governed by state common law. A **contract** is a binding agreement that the courts will enforce. It is a promise or a set of promises for the breach of which the law gives a remedy, or the performance of which the law in some way recognizes a duty. A promise manifests or demonstrates the intention to act or to refrain from acting in a specified manner.

Those promises that meet all of the essential requirements of a binding contract are contractual and will be enforced. All other promises are not contractual, and usually no legal remedy is available for a breach of, or a failure to properly perform, these promises. The remedies provided for breach of contract include compensatory damages, equitable remedies, reliance damage, and restitution. Thus, a promise may be contractual (and therefore binding) or noncontractual. In other words, all contracts are promises, but not all promises are contracts.

Requirements of a Contract

The four basic requirements of a contract are (1) mutual assent, (2) consideration, (3) legality of object and subject matter, and (4) capacity (competent parties).

1. **Mutual assent.** The parties to a contract must manifest by words or conduct that they have agreed to enter into a contract. The usual method of showing mutual assent is by offer and acceptance. An offer is a proposal or expression by one person that he is willing to do something for certain terms. A contract does not exist until the offer is formally accepted, either verbally or in written form. The offer and acceptance have to match. If they match, there is an agreement leading up to a contract. If they do not, it is more like a negotiation, to which someone responds with a counteroffer rather than an acceptance, which continues until both parties reach an agreement or a "meeting of the minds."

2. **Consideration.** Each party to a contract must intentionally exchange a legal benefit or incur a legal detriment as an inducement to the other party to make a return exchange. Consideration is a form of "mutual obligation." In the business world, mutual promises in a contract of sale, whether express or implied, are generally sufficient consideration.

3. **Legality of object and subject matter.** The purpose of a contract must not be criminal, tortious, or otherwise against public policy. If the purpose is illegal, the resulting contract is null and void. The performance of a party in regard to the contract must not be an unlawful act if the agreement is to be enforceable. However, if the primary purpose of a contract is legal, but some terms contained within the agreement are not, then the contract may or may not itself be illegal, depending on the seriousness of the illegal terms and the degree to which the legal and illegal terms can be separated.

4. **Capacity (competent parties).** The parties to a contract must have contractual capacity. Certain persons, such as adjudicated incompetents, have no legal capacity to contract, while others, such as minors, incompetent persons, and intoxicated persons, have limited capacity to contract. All others have full contractual capacity. The parties can be principals or qualified agents. The parties cannot engage in any fraudulent activities. The use of force or coercion to reach an agreement is not acceptable in signing a contract because both parties must enter into the agreement of their own free will. Both parties must indicate a willingness to enter into the agreement and be bound by its terms.

In addition, though in a limited number of instances a contract must be evidenced in writing to be enforceable, in most cases an oral contract is binding and enforceable. Moreover, there must be an absence of invalidating conduct, such as duress, undue influence, misrepresentation, or mistake. A promise meeting all of these requirements is contractual and legally binding. However, if any requirement is unmet, the promise is noncontractual.

Classification of Contracts

Contracts can be classified according to various characteristics, such as method of formation, content, and legal effect. The standard classifications are (1) express or implied contracts; (2) bilateral or unilateral contracts; (3) valid, void, voidable, or unenforceable contracts; and (4) executed or executory contracts. These classifications are not mutually exclusive. For example, a contract may be express, bilateral, valid, executory, and informal.

1. **Express and implied contracts.** A contract formed by conduct is an implied or, more precisely, an implied-in-fact contract. In contrast, a contract in which the parties manifest assent in words is an express contract. Both are contracts, equally enforceable. The difference between them is merely the manner in which the parties manifest their assent.
2. **Bilateral and unilateral contracts.** When each party is both a promisor (a person making a promise) and a promisee (the person to whom a promise is made), the contract is a bilateral one. A unilateral contract is one where only one of the parties makes a promise.
3. **Valid, void, voidable, and unenforceable contracts.** A **valid contract** is one that meets all of the requirements of a binding contract. It is an enforceable promise or an agreement. A **void contract** is an agreement that does not meet all of the requirements of a binding contract. It has no legal effect and it is merely a promise or agreement. An example is an agreement entered by a person whom the courts have declared incompetent. A contract that is neither void nor voidable may nonetheless be unenforceable. An **unenforceable contract** is one for the breach of which the law provides no remedy. After the statutory time period has passed, a contract is referred to as unenforceable, rather than void or voidable.
4. **Executed and executory contracts.** A contract that has been fully carried out and completed by all of the parties to it is an executed contract. By comparison, the term "executory" applies to contracts that are still partially or entirely unperformed by one or more of the parties.

Other Types of Contracts

Two other types of contracts that occur in common are the doctrine of promissory estoppel and quasi-contracts.

1. **Doctrine of promissory estoppel.** In certain circumstances, the courts enforce noncontractual promises under the doctrine of promissory estoppel in order to avoid injustice. A noncontractual promise is enforceable when it is made under circumstances that should lead the promisor reasonably to expect that the promisee, in reliance on the promise, would be induced by it to take definite and substantial action or to forbear, and the promisee does take such action or does forbear.
2. **Quasi-contracts.** A quasi (meaning "as if") contract is not a contract at all. A quasi-contract is based neither on an express nor on an implied-in-fact contract. Rather, a quasi-contract is a contract implied in law, which is an obligation imposed by law to avoid injustice. Infrequently, quasi-contracts are used to provide a remedy when the parties enter into a void contract, an unenforceable contract, or a voidable contract that is voided. In such a case, the law of quasi-contracts will determine what recovery is permitted for any performance rendered by the parties under the invalid, unenforceable, or invalidated agreements.

Antitrust Laws

The goals of antitrust laws are to ensure free and fair competition in the marketplace; prohibit anticompetitive practices such as price fixing, deceptive pricing, price discrimination, and promotional pricing; and prevent unreasonable concentration of economic power that can weaken competition. Examples of federal laws in this category include: the Sherman Antitrust Act, the Clayton Act, the Federal Trade Commission Act, the Robinson-Patman Act, the Wheeler-Lea Act, and the Celler Antimerger Act.

These federal statutes when combined with state legislation intend to promote and preserve competition in a free enterprise system and to prevent monopoly power. The coverage of these acts extends to interstate commerce among the several states, but not intrastate activity. All states have antitrust statutes applicable to intrastate activity.

Sherman Antitrust Act

The **Sherman Act of 1880** is the primary tool of antitrust enforcement. The Act declares any combination, contract, or conspiracy in restraint of trade made among the states or with foreign countries illegal. The Act also makes it illegal to monopolize, attempt to monopolize, or conspire to monopolize any portion of interstate commerce or any portion of trade with foreign nations. However, the Sherman Act does not state exactly what types of action are prohibited.

Clayton Act

The **Clayton Act of 1914** was designed to strengthen and clarify the provisions of the Sherman Act. It defines specifically what constitutes monopolistic or restrictive practices, whereas the Sherman Act does not.

The Clayton Act makes price discrimination illegal unless it can be justified because of differences in costs. It prohibits the use of exclusive or tying contracts when their use "substantially lessens competition or tends to create a monopoly." Exclusive or tying contracts are contracts in which the seller agrees to sell a product to a buyer on the condition that the buyer will not purchase products from the seller's competitors. It also makes intercorporate stockholdings illegal if they tend to greatly reduce competition or to create a monopoly. In addition, the Clayton Act makes interlocking directorates (having the same individual on two or more boards of directors) illegal if the corporations are competitive and if at least one of the corporations is of a certain minimum size.

The goal of the Clayton Act is to curb anticompetitive practices in their incipiency. Under the Clayton Act, simply showing a probable, rather than actual, anticompetitive effect would be enough cause for a violation of the Act. This means the Clayton Act is more sensitive to anticompetitive practices than the Sherman Act.

The scope of the Clayton Act in mergers includes both asset and stock acquisitions. The Act now covers both mergers between actual competitors and vertical and conglomerate mergers having the requisite anticompetitive effect.

Federal Trade Commission Act

Like the Clayton Act, the **Federal Trade Commission Act** was designed to prevent abuses and to sustain competition. The Federal Trade Commission Act declares as unlawful "unfair methods of competition in commerce."

The Act also established the Federal Trade Commission (FTC) in 1914 and gave it the power and the resources to investigate unfair competitive practices. The FTC Act authorizes the FTC to issue "cease-and-desist" orders prohibiting "unfair methods of competition" and "unfair or deceptive acts or practices." These orders provide injunctive relief by preventing or restraining unlawful conduct. *One of the goals of the FTC is to enforce antitrust laws and to protect consumers.*

The FTC has a dual role in prohibiting unfair methods of competition and anticompetitive practices. *The FTC Act supplements the Sherman and the Clayton Acts.* The FTC protects consumers who are injured by practices such as deceptive advertising or labeling without regard to any effect on competitors.

Although not explicitly empowered to do so, the FTC frequently enforces the Sherman Act indirectly and enjoins conduct beyond the reach of either the Sherman or Clayton acts.

Robinson-Patman Act

The U.S. Congress passed the **Robinson-Patman Act** in 1936 to protect small competitors by amending the Clayton Act. It is often called the **chain store act.** The Robinson-Patman Act amends the price discrimination section of the Clayton Act. It was aimed at protecting independent retailers and wholesalers from "unfair discriminations" by large chain stores and mass distributors, which were supposedly obtaining large and unjustified price discounts because of their purchasing power and bargaining position.

Both the Department of Justice and the FTC can proceed against violators of the Robinson-Patman Act. The Robinson-Patman Act prohibits price discrimination (where a seller charges one buyer more than another for the same product). It makes it unlawful for sellers to grant concessions to buyers unless concessions are granted to all buyers on terms that are proportionally equal. The Act reaches the quantity discount, a major form of price discrimination.

The Act applies only to sales, not to leases, agency/consignment arrangements, licenses, or refusals to deal (selling to one firm while refusing to deal with another). The scope of the Robinson-Patman Act applies to tangible personal property (commodities) and in the sale of services or intangibles such as advertising.

Wheeler-Lea Act

In 1938, the **Wheeler-Lea Act** was passed as an amendment to the FTC Act. The Wheeler-Lea Act makes "unfair or deceptive acts or practices" in interstate commerce illegal; thus, it was designed to protect consumers rather than competitors. Now, the FTC has the authority to prohibit false and misleading advertising and product misrepresentation.

Celler Antimerger Act

The **Celler Antimerger Act** of 1950 also amended the Clayton Act by making it illegal for a corporation to acquire the assets, as well as the stock, of a competing corporation if the effect is to greatly reduce competition or to tend to create a monopoly.

Environmental Laws

The U.S. Environmental Protection Agency (EPA) protects and enhances the environment today and for future generations to the fullest extent possible under the laws enacted by the U.S. Congress. The agency's mission is to control and abate pollution in the areas of air, water, solid waste, pesticides, radiation, and toxic substances. Its mandate is to mount an integrated, coordinated attack on environmental pollution in cooperation with state and local governments. Examples of laws in this category include the National Environmental Policy Act, the Clean Air Act, and the Clean Water Act.

Consumer Product Safety Laws

The Consumer Product Safety Commission enforces the Consumer Product Safety Act, which covers safety of any consumer product not addressed by other regulatory agencies.

Product liability is a liability of manufacturers and distributors for defective products that cause injury and death to consumers, resulting from the use of unsafe products. It focuses on negligence and strict liability. If a person knows a product is defective and uses it anyway (assumption of risk), there is no strict liability. Two types of negligence exist: **contributory negligence** (negligence of a plaintiff) and **comparative negligence** (sharing of fault between the plaintiff and the defendant). **Compensatory damage** is of two types: **special damages** (i.e., paying for out-of-pocket costs) and **general damages** (paying for pain and suffering, and loss of a limb). **Punitive damages** are awarded only for gross negligence due to conduct that is reckless and wanton. Different jurisdictions handle these negligences and damages differently.

The **Magnuson-Moss Warranty Act** is the U.S. federal law that governs consumer product warranties. The Act requires manufacturers and sellers of consumer products to provide consumers with detailed information about warranty coverage. In addition, it affects both the rights of consumers and the obligations of warrantors under written warranties.

Food and Drug Administration Laws

The Food and Drug Administration (FDA) agency enforces laws and develops regulations to prevent distribution and sale of adulterated foods, drugs, cosmetics, and hazardous consumer products. The manufacturer is usually liable for dangerous and unsafe products.

Investment Securities Laws

The primary purpose of federal securities regulation is to prevent fraudulent practices in the sale of investment securities and thereby to foster public confidence in the securities market. Two statutes include the **Securities Act of 1933**, which focuses on the issuance of original securities (primary transactions) and the **Securities Exchange Act of 1934**, which deals with trading in already-issued securities (secondary transactions). These secondary transactions greatly exceed in volume and value the original offerings. The 1933 Act mainly focuses on information provided to investors to prohibit misrepresentation and deceit, whereas the 1934 Act primarily focuses on disclosure requirements and regulates tender offers and proxy solicitations.

Intellectual Property Laws

Intellectual property (IP) is a type of intangible personal property that includes trade secrets, trade symbols, copyrights, and patents. These interests are protected from infringement or unauthorized use by others. Such protection is essential to the conduct of personal or corporate business. Examples of laws in this category include the Uniform Trade Secrets Act, the Economic Espionage Act, the Federal Trademark Act (the Lanham Act), the Federal Copyright Act, and the Patent Act.

Employment Laws

Three categories of government regulation of the employment relationship are labor laws, employment discrimination laws, and employee protection laws.

Labor laws are aimed at protecting both labor unions and employers with defined unfair practices. Examples of unfair union practices include forcing an employee to join the union, refusing to bargain in good faith, picketing an employer to require recognition of an uncertified union, discriminating against a nonunion employee, causing an employer to pay for work not performed (called **featherbedding**), and charging excessive or discriminatory membership dues. Examples of unfair employer practices include interfering with the right to unionize (called **yellow-dog contracts**), refusing to bargain in good faith, discriminating against union members, dominating the union, and discriminating against an employee who has filed charges or testified against the employer. Examples of laws in this category include the Norris-La Guardia Act, National Labor Relations Act (a pro-union act), Labor-Management Relations Act (Taft-Hartley Act, a pro-employer act), and Labor-Management Reporting and Disclosure Act (Landrum-Griffin Act to eliminate corruption in labor unions).

Employment discrimination laws prohibit discrimination in employment on the basis of race, sex, religion, national origin, age, and disability. Examples of laws in this category include the Civil Rights Act, Equal Pay Act, Age Discrimination in Employment Act, Rehabilitation Act, and Americans with Disabilities Act.

Employee protection laws are intended to provide a limited right not to be unfairly dismissed from the job, a right to a safe and healthy workplace, compensation for injuries sustained in the workplace, and financial security upon retirement or loss of employment. Examples of laws in this category include Employee Termination at Will, Occupational Safety and Health Act (OSHA), Privacy Laws, Workers' Compensation Laws, Social Security and Unemployment Insurance Act, Fair Labor Standards Act, Worker Adjustment and Retraining Notification Act (WARN Act), and Family and Medical Leave Act.

Bankruptcy Laws

The U.S. bankruptcy law is governed by federal law, which describes the procedures used by debtors and creditors when debtors cannot meet their financial obligations to creditors. The purpose of the law is to legally relieve debtors of the burdens of being unable to pay debts, while protecting the rights of creditors to any nonexempt assets that the debtor might have. A debtor can keep exempt assets, but not nonexempt assets. The debtor must pay child-support money and taxes because they are not dischargeable. Several bankruptcy procedures exist, including one in which the debtor can ask the court to approve a payment plan that may include payment of a lesser amount than is owed.

Compliance Management

Various governmental authorities at local, state, and federal levels pass various laws, rules, and regulations to control the conduct of business organizations for the good of the society and to collect tax revenues for proper functioning of government to provide services to citizens and businesses. Corporate management can get a reasonable assurance about compliance with laws, rules, and regulations through audits. Government has the right to fine and punish business organizations for failing to comply with the required laws, rules, and regulations.

Compliance Process

The compliance program requires a three-step process, as follows.

Step 1: Understand Relevant Laws, Rules, and Regulations Auditors may obtain an understanding of laws, rules, and regulations through review of relevant documents and inquiry of attorneys. Generally, more audits of compliance with laws and regulations take place in the public sector than in the private sector. For example, understanding relevant laws and regulations can be important to planning a performance audit because government programs are usually created by law and are subject to more specific rules and regulations than the private sector. What is to be done, who is to do it, the goals and objectives to be achieved, the population to be served, and how much can be spent on what, are usually set forth in laws and regulations. Thus, understanding the laws establishing a program can be essential to understanding the program itself. Obtaining that understanding may also be a necessary step in identifying laws and regulations that are significant to audit objectives.

Step 2: Test Compliance with Laws, Rules, and Regulations   Auditors should design the audit to provide a reasonable assurance about compliance with laws, rules, and regulations that are significant to audit objectives. This requires determining whether laws and regulations are significant to the audit objectives and, if they are, assessing the risk that significant illegal acts could occur. Based on that risk assessment, the auditors design and perform procedures to provide reasonable assurance of detecting significant illegal acts.

Step 3: Develop Action Plans to Comply with Laws, Rules, and Regulations   Based on the audit report, management should develop action plans showing the timetables and resources required to conform with the missed laws, rules, and regulations. A checklist describing who should do what and when would help management in implementing the action plans.

Management and auditors should look for the following red flags as signs of noncompliance:

- Poor records or documentation
- Complex transactions
- Activities that are dominated and controlled by a single person or small group
- Unreasonable explanations to inquiries by auditors
- Auditee annoyance at reasonable questions by auditors
- Employees' refusal to give others custody of records
- Employees' refusal to take vacations and/or accept promotions
- Extravagant lifestyle of employees
- A pattern of certain contractors bidding against each other or, conversely, certain contractors not bidding against each other
- Use of materials on commercial contracts that were intended for use on government contracts
- A high default rate on government-backed loans

Management and auditors should understand the following terms for the proper meaning of compliance:

- **Noncompliance** is a failure to follow requirements or a violation of prohibitions, contained in laws, rules, regulations, contracts, governmental grants, or organization's policies and procedures.
- **Illegal acts** are a type of noncompliance; specifically, they are violations of laws, rules, or regulations. They are failures to follow requirements of laws or implementing regulations, including intentional and unintentional noncompliance and criminal acts.
- **Criminal acts** are illegal acts for which incarceration, as well as other penalties, is available if the organization obtains a guilty verdict.
- **Civil acts** are illegal acts for which penalties that do not include incarceration are available for a statutory violation. Penalties may include monetary payments and corrective actions.
- **Fraud** is the obtaining of something of value, illegally, through willful misrepresentation. Thus, fraud is a type of illegal act.
- **Abuse** occurs when the conduct of an activity or function falls short of expectations for prudent behavior. Abuse is distinguished from noncompliance in that abusive conditions may not directly violate laws or regulations. Abusive activities may be within the letter of the laws and regulations but violate either their spirit or the more general standards of impartial and ethical behavior.
- **Errors** are unintentional noncompliance with applicable laws and regulations and/or misstatements or omissions of amounts or disclosures in financial statements.
- **Irregularities** are intentional noncompliance with applicable laws and regulations and/or misstatements or omissions of amounts or disclosures in financial statements.

Compliance Costs and Benefits

Corporate management says it costs a significant amount of resources to comply with the often confusing and duplicating laws, rules, and regulations in terms of recordkeeping and monitoring activities. Management does not readily see a direct and positive benefit from compliance. On the other hand, regulators say these laws, rules, and regulations are developed with a purpose for the benefit of the entire society. Regulators say that the cost of compliance should be treated as a cost of doing business. This is a never-ending debate, but in the end the government wins due to its constitutional power.

Business Policy

Business objectives are derived from a company's vision and mission statements (ends). Business strategy is designed to achieve those objectives (means). **Business policy**, along with budgets, is a part of strategy execution and implementation in that the policy supports the strategy. Business policies can be established either at high level (e.g., ethical behavior and pollution control) or low level (e.g., policy of requiring signed contracts prior to acquisition of assets or start of projects and policy on employee compensation, benefits, and training). Similar to business strategy, business policy can be both proactive (intended and deliberate) and reactive (adaptive). Moreover, business strategy precedes business policy, whereas business ethics succeeds business policy. Also, note that business ethics precedes social responsibility.

> **Business Strategy** → **Business Policy**
> → **Business Ethics**
> → **Social Responsibility**

Business Ethics

Ethics can be defined broadly as the study of what is right or good for people. It attempts to determine what people ought to do or what goals they should pursue. **Business ethics**, as a branch of applied ethics, is the study and determination of what is right and good in business settings and includes the moral issues that arise from business practices, institutions, and decision making. Unlike legal analyses, analyses of ethics have no central authority, such as courts or legislatures, upon which to rely; nor do they follow clear-cut, universal standards. Nonetheless, despite these inherent limitations, it is still possible to make meaningful ethical judgments.

Examples of key ethical principles include the following:

- **The Golden Rule.** The Golden Rule means putting oneself in others' shoes. It includes not knowingly doing harm to others.
- **The means–ends cycle.** The means–end cycle states that when ends are of overriding importance, unscrupulous means may be used to reach the ends.
- **The might-equals-right principle.** The might-equals-right principle states that justice is defined as the interest of the stronger, meaning that stronger people have an upper hand over weaker people.
- **The professional principle.** The professional principle states that a true professional will do things

in such a way that he can explain them before a committee of peer professionals.
- **Goal-congruence principle.** The goal-congruence principle states that actions, wills, and needs of employees should be subordinated to the greater good of the organization they work for. An employee should ask himself whether his goals are consistent with the organization's goals. This principle is similar to (1) the utilitarian ethic, meaning the greatest good should be done for the greatest number and (2) the organization ethic, meaning that employees do things for the good of the organization.
- **Prudent-person concept.** The prudent person, who is not infallible or perfect, has the ability to govern and discipline himself by the use of reason, does not neglect his duty, and applies his knowledge, skills, and sound judgment in the use of the organization's resources. The prudent-person concept is related to the goal-congruence principle.

Corporate Social Responsibility

We would like to present Archie Carroll's (1979) four-part definition of **corporate social responsibility (CSR)** that focuses on the types of social responsibilities it might be argued that business has. Carroll's definition helps us to understand the component parts that make up CSR:

> *The social responsibility of business encompasses the economic, legal, ethical, and discretionary (philanthropic) expectations that society has of organizations at a given point in time.*

Carroll's four-part definition attempts to place economic and legal expectations of business in context by relating them to more socially oriented concerns. These social concerns include ethical responsibilities and philanthropic (voluntary/discretionary) responsibilities.

Economic Responsibilities

First, there are business's economic responsibilities. It may seem odd to call an economic responsibility a social responsibility, but in effect this is what it is. First and foremost, the U.S. social system calls for business to be an economic institution. That is, it should be an institution whose orientation is to produce goods and services that society wants and to sell them at fair prices—prices that society thinks represent the true values of the goods and services delivered and that provide business with profits adequate to ensure its perpetuation and growth and to reward its investors. While thinking about its economic responsibilities, business employs many management concepts that are directed toward financial effectiveness—attention to revenues, costs, strategic decision making, and the host of business concepts focused on maximizing the long-term financial performance of the organization.

Legal Responsibilities

Second, there are business's legal responsibilities. Just as society has sanctioned our economic system by permitting business to assume the productive role mentioned earlier, as a partial fulfillment of the social contract, it has also laid down the ground rules—the laws—under which business is expected to operate. Legal responsibilities reflect society's view of **codified ethics** in the sense that they embody basic notions of fair practices as established by our lawmakers. It is business's responsibility to society to comply with these laws. If business does not agree with laws that have been passed or are about to be passed, our society has provided a mechanism by which dissenters can be heard through the political process. In the past 30 years, our society has witnessed a proliferation of laws and regulations striving to control business behavior.

As important as legal responsibilities are, legal responsibilities do not cover the full range of behaviors expected of business by society. The law is inadequate for at least three reasons. First, the law cannot possibly address all the topics, areas, or issues that business may face. New topics continually emerge, such as Internet-based business (e-commerce) and genetically engineered foods. Second, the law often lags behind more recent concepts of what is considered appropriate behavior. For example, as technology permits more exact measurements of environmental contamination, laws based on measures made by obsolete equipment become outdated but not frequently changed. Third, laws are made by lawmakers and may reflect the personal interests and political motivations of legislators rather than appropriate ethical justifications. A wise sage once said: "Never go to see how sausages or laws are made." It might not be a pretty picture.

Ethical Responsibilities

Third, because laws are important but not adequate, ethical responsibilities embrace those activities and practices that are expected or prohibited by societal members even though they are not codified into law. Ethical responsibilities embody the full scope of norms, standards, and expectations that reflect a belief of what consumers, employees, shareholders, and the community regard as fair, just, and in keeping with the respect for or protection of stakeholders' moral rights (Carroll 1979).

In one sense, changes in ethics or values precede the establishment of laws because they become the driving forces behind the initial creation of laws and regulations. For example, the civil rights, environmental, and consumer movements reflected basic alterations in societal values and thus may be seen as ethical bellwethers foreshadowing and leading to later legislation. In another sense, ethical responsibilities may be seen as embracing and reflecting newly emerging values and norms that society expects business to meet, even though they may reflect a higher standard of performance than that currently required by law. Ethical responsibilities in this sense are often ill-defined or continually under public scrutiny and debate as to their legitimacy and thus are frequently difficult for business to agree on. Regardless, business is expected to be responsive to newly emerging concepts of what constitutes ethical practices.

Superimposed on these ethical expectations emanating from societal and stakeholder groups are the implied levels of ethical performance suggested by a consideration of the great ethical principles of moral philosophy, such as justice, rights, and utilitarianism (Carroll 1979).

For the moment, let us think of ethical responsibilities as encompassing those areas in which society expects certain levels of moral or principled performance that have not yet been articulated or codified into law.

Philanthropic Responsibilities

Fourth, there are business's voluntary/discretionary or philanthropic responsibilities. These are viewed as responsibilities because they reflect current expectations of business by the public. These activities are voluntary, guided only by business's desire to engage in social activities that are not mandated, not required by law, and not generally expected of business in an ethical sense. Nevertheless, the public has an expectation that business will engage in philanthropy, and thus this category has become a part of the social contract between business and society. Such activities might include corporate giving, product and service donations, volunteerism, partnerships with local government and other organizations, and any other kind of voluntary involvement of the organization and its employees with the community or other stakeholders.

The distinction between ethical responsibilities and philanthropic responsibilities is that the latter typically are not expected in a moral or an ethical sense. Communities desire and expect business to contribute its money, facilities, and employee time to humanitarian programs or purposes, but they do not regard firms as unethical if they do not provide these services at the desired levels. Therefore, these responsibilities are more discretionary, or voluntary, on business's part, although the societal expectation that they be provided is always present. This category of responsibilities is often referred to as good "corporate citizenship."

In essence, then, our definition forms a four-part conceptualization of corporate social responsibility that encompasses the economic, legal, ethical, and philanthropic expectations placed on organizations by society at a given point in time. The implication is that business has accountability for these areas of responsibility and performance. This four-part definition provides us with categories within which to place the various expectations that society has of business. With each of these categories considered as indispensable facets of the total social responsibility of business, we have a conceptual model that more completely describes the kinds of expectations that society expects of business. One advantage of this model is that it can accommodate those who have argued against CSR by characterizing an economic emphasis as separate from a social emphasis. This model offers these two facets along with others that collectively make up corporate social responsibility.

The Pyramid of Corporate Social Responsibility

A helpful way of graphically depicting the four-part definition is envisioning a pyramid composed of four layers. The pyramid portrays the four components of CSR, beginning with the basic building block of economic performance (making a profit) at the base. At the same time, business is expected to obey the law because the law is society's codification of acceptable and unacceptable behavior. Next

is business's responsibility to be ethical. At its most basic level, this is the obligation to do what is right, just, and fair and to avoid or minimize harm to stakeholders (employees, consumers, the environment, and others). Finally, business is expected to be a good corporate citizen—to fulfill its voluntary/discretionary or philanthropic responsibility to contribute financial and human resources to the community and to improve the quality of life.

Pyramid Layers of Corporate Social Responsibility

A socially responsible firm should strive to:

- Be a good corporate citizen (top).
- Be ethical.
- Obey the law.
- Make a profit (base).

The most critical tensions, of course, are those between economic and legal, economic and ethical, and economic and philanthropic. The traditionalist might see this as a conflict between a firm's "concern for profits" and its "concern for society," but it is suggested here that this is an oversimplification. A CSR or stakeholder perspective would recognize these tensions as organizational realities but would focus on the total pyramid as a unified whole and on how the firm might engage in decisions, actions, policies, and practices that simultaneously fulfill all its component parts. This pyramid should not be interpreted to mean that business is expected to fulfill its social responsibilities in some sequential fashion, starting at the base. Rather, business is expected to fulfill all its responsibilities simultaneously.

In summary, the total social responsibility of business entails the concurrent fulfillment of the firm's economic, legal, ethical, and philanthropic responsibilities. In equation form, this might be expressed as:

Total Corporate Social Responsibility

= Economic Responsibilities

+ Legal Responsibilities

+ Ethical Responsibilities

+ Philanthropic Responsibilities

❑ Learning Objective 9.4: UNDERSTAND THE VARIOUS ISSUES IN CORPORATE GOVERNANCE

The issue of corporate governance is a direct outgrowth of the question of legitimacy. For business to be legitimate and to maintain its legitimacy in the eyes of the public, its governance must correspond to the will of the people.

Corporate governance refers to the method by which a firm is being governed, directed, administered, or controlled and to the goals for which it is being governed. Corporate governance is concerned with the relative roles, rights, and accountability of such stakeholder groups as owners, boards of directors, managers, employees, and others who assert to be stakeholders.

Components of Corporate Governance

To appreciate fully the legitimacy and corporate governance issues, it is important to understand the major groups that make up the corporate form of business organization because it is only by so doing that one can appreciate how the system has failed to work according to its intended design.

The four major groups needed in setting the stage are (1) shareholders (owners or stakeholders), (2) board of directors, (3) managers, and (4) employees. Overarching these groups is the charter issued by the state, giving the corporation the right to exist and stipulating the basic terms of its existence.

Under U.S. corporate law, **shareholders** are the owners of a corporation. As owners, they should have ultimate control over the corporation. This control is manifested primarily in the right to select the board of directors of the company. Generally, the number of shares of stock owned determines the degree of each shareholder's right.

Because large organizations may have hundreds of thousands of shareholders, they elect a smaller group, known as the **board of directors,** to govern and oversee the management of the business. The board is responsible for ascertaining that the manager puts the interests of the owners (i.e., shareholders) first. The third major group in the authority hierarchy is **management**—the group of individuals hired by the board to run the company and manage it on a daily basis. Along with the board, top management establishes overall policy. Middle-and lower-level managers carry out this policy and conduct the daily supervision of the operative employees. **Employees** are those hired by the company to perform the actual operational work. Managers are employees too, but in this discussion we use the term "employees" to refer to nonmanagerial employees.

Corporate Governance Standards

The Business Roundtable supports the following eight guiding principles as part of good corporate governance practices (Business Roundtable 2005, pp. 2–3):

1. The paramount duty of the board of directors of a public corporation is to select a chief executive officer (CEO) and to oversee the CEO and senior management in the competent and ethical operation of the corporation on a day-to-day basis.

2. It is the responsibility of management to operate the corporation in an effective and ethical manner to produce value for shareholders. Senior management is expected to know how the corporation earns its income and what risks the corporation is undertaking in the course of carrying out its business. The CEO and board of directors should set the "tone at the top" that establishes a culture of legal compliance and integrity. Management and directors should never put personal interests ahead of or in conflict with the interests of the corporation.

3. It is the responsibility of management, under the oversight of the audit committee and the board, to produce financial statements that fairly present the financial condition and results of operations of the corporation and to make the timely disclosures investors need to assess the financial and business soundness and risks of the corporation.

4. It is the responsibility of the board, through its audit committee, to engage an independent accounting firm to audit the financial statements prepared by management, issue an opinion that those statements are fairly stated in accordance with generally accepted accounting principles (GAAP), and oversee the corporation's relationship with the outside auditor.

5. It is the responsibility of the board, through its corporate governance committee, to play a leadership role in shaping the corporate governance of the corporation. The corporate governance committee also should select and recommend to the

board qualified director candidates for election by the corporation's shareholders.

6. It is the responsibility of the board, through its compensation committee, to adopt and oversee the implementation of compensation policies, establish goals for performance-based compensation, and determine the compensation of the CEO and senior management.

7. It is the responsibility of the board to respond appropriately to shareholders' concerns.

8. It is the responsibility of the corporation to deal with its employees, customers, suppliers, and other constituencies in a fair and equitable manner.

These eight responsibilities and others are critical to the functioning of the modern public corporation and the integrity of the public markets. No law or regulation alone can be a substitute for the voluntary adherence to these principles by corporate directors and management.

The Business Roundtable continues to believe that corporate governance should be enhanced through conscientious and forward-looking action by a business community that focuses on generating long-term shareholder value with the highest degree of integrity.

The principles discussed here are intended to assist corporate management and boards of directors in their individual efforts to implement best practices of corporate governance, as well as to serve as guideposts for the public dialogue on evolving governance standards.

Roles of the Board of Directors

An effective system of corporate governance provides the framework within which the board and management address their respective responsibilities (Business Roundtable 2005, pp. 7–10):

- The business of a corporation is managed under the direction of the corporation's board. The board delegates to the CEO—and through the CEO to other senior management—the authority and responsibility for managing the everyday affairs of the corporation. Directors monitor management on behalf of the corporation's shareholders.

- Making decisions regarding the selection, compensation, and evaluation of a well-qualified and ethical CEO is the single most important function of the board. The board also appoints or approves other members of the senior management team.

- Directors bring to the corporation a range of experience, knowledge, and judgment. Directors should not represent the interests of particular constituencies.

- Effective directors maintain an attitude of constructive skepticism; they ask incisive, probing questions and require accurate, honest answers; they act with integrity and diligence; and they demonstrate a commitment to the corporation, its business plans, and long-term shareholder value.

- In performing its oversight function, the board is entitled to rely on the advice, reports, and opinions of management, corporate counsel, auditors, and expert advisors. The board should assess the qualifications of those it relies on and hold managers and advisors accountable. The board should ask questions and obtain answers about the processes used by managers and the corporation's advisors to reach their decisions and recommendations, as well as about the substance of the advice and reports received by the board. When appropriate, the board and its committees should seek independent advice.

- Given the board's oversight role, shareholders and other constituencies can reasonably expect that directors will exercise vigorous and diligent oversight of a corporation's affairs. However, they should not expect the board to micromanage the corporation's business by performing or duplicating the tasks of the CEO and senior management team.

- The board's oversight function carries with it a number of specific responsibilities in addition to that of selecting and overseeing the CEO. These responsibilities include:
  - *Planning for management development and succession.* The board should oversee the corporation's plans for developing senior management personnel and plan for CEO and senior management succession. When appropriate, the board should replace the CEO or other members of senior management.
  - *Understanding, reviewing, and monitoring the implementation of the corporation's strategic plans.* The board has responsibility for overseeing and understanding the corporation's strategic plans from their inception through their development and execution by management. Once the board reviews a strategic plan, it should regularly monitor implementation of the plan to determine whether it is being implemented effectively and whether changes are needed. The board also

should ensure that the corporation's incentive compensation program is aligned with the corporation's strategic plan.

- *Understanding and approving annual operating plans and budgets.* The board is responsible for understanding, approving, and overseeing the corporation's annual operating plans and for reviewing the annual budgets presented by management. The board should monitor implementation of the annual plans to assess whether they are being implemented effectively and within the limits of approved budgets.
- *Focusing on the integrity and clarity of the corporation's financial statements and financial reporting.* The board, assisted by its audit committee, should be satisfied that the financial statements and other disclosures prepared by management accurately present the corporation's financial condition and results of operations to shareholders and that they do so in an understandable manner. To achieve accuracy and clarity, the board, through its audit committee, should have an understanding of the corporation's financial statements, including why the accounting principles critical to the corporation's business were chosen, what key judgments and estimates were made by management, and how the choice of principles and the making of these judgments and estimates affect the reported financial results of the corporation.
- *Advising management on significant issues facing the corporation.* Directors can offer management a wealth of experience and a wide range of perspectives. They provide advice and counsel to management in formal board and committee meetings, and they are available for informal consultation with the CEO and senior management.
- *Reviewing and approving significant corporate actions.* As required by state corporate law, the board reviews and approves specific corporate actions, such as the election of executive officers, the declaration of dividends, and (as appropriate) the implementation of major transactions. The board and senior management should have a clear understanding of what level or types of decisions require specific board approval.
- *Reviewing management's plans for* **business resiliency**. As part of its oversight function, the board should designate senior management who will be responsible for business resiliency. The board should periodically review management's plans to address this issue. Business resiliency can include such items as business risk assessment and management, business continuity, physical and cyber-security, and emergency communications.
- *Nominating directors and committee members and overseeing effective corporate governance.* It is the responsibility of the board, through its corporate governance committee, to nominate directors and committee members and oversee the composition, independence, structure, practices, and evaluation of the board and its committees.
- *Overseeing legal and ethical compliance.* The board should set a tone at the top that establishes the corporation's commitment to integrity and legal compliance. The board should oversee the corporation's compliance program relating to legal and ethical conduct. In this regard, the board should be knowledgeable about the corporation's compliance program and should be satisfied that the program is effective in preventing and deterring violations. The board should pay particular attention to conflicts of interest, including related-party transactions.

Roles of CEOs and Senior Executives

The Business Roundtable defines the following specific roles and responsibilities for the CEO and other senior executives (Business Roundtable 2005, pp. 10–12):

- It is the responsibility of the CEO and senior management (senior executives), under the CEO's direction, to operate the corporation in an effective and ethical manner. As part of its operational responsibility, senior management is charged with the following tasks:
- *Operating the corporation.* The CEO and senior management run the corporation's day-to-day business operations. With a thorough understanding of how the corporation operates and earns its income, they carry out the corporation's strategic objectives within the annual operating plans and budgets, which are reviewed and approved by the board. In making decisions about the corporation's business operations, the CEO considers the long-term interests of the corporation and its shareholders and necessarily relies on the input and advice of others, including senior management and outside advisors. The CEO keeps the board apprised of significant

developments regarding the corporation's business operations.

- *Strategic planning*. The CEO and senior management generally takes the lead in strategic planning. They identify and develop strategic plans for the corporation; present those plans to the board; implement the plans once board review is completed; and recommend and carry out changes to the plans as necessary.
- *Annual operating plans and budgets*. With the corporation's overall strategic plans in mind, senior management develops annual operating plans and budgets for the corporation and presents the plans and budgets to the board. Once the board has reviewed and approved the plans and budgets, the management team implements the annual operating plans and budgets.
- *Selecting qualified management and establishing an effective organizational structure*. Senior management is responsible for selecting qualified management and implementing an organizational structure that is efficient and appropriate for the corporation's particular circumstances.
- *Identifying and managing risk*. Senior management identifies and manages the risks that the corporation undertakes in the course of carrying out its business. It also manages the corporation's overall risk profile.
- *Accurate and transparent financial reporting and disclosures*. Senior management is responsible for the integrity of the corporation's financial reporting system and the accurate and timely preparation of the corporation's financial statements and related disclosures in accordance with generally accepted accounting principles (GAAP) and in compliance with applicable laws and regulations. It is senior management's responsibility—under the direction of the CEO and the CFO—to establish, maintain, and periodically evaluate the corporation's internal controls and procedures. In accordance with applicable laws and regulations, the CEO and the CFO also are responsible for certifying the accuracy and completeness of the corporation's financial statements and the effectiveness of the corporation's internal and disclosure controls.
- The CEO and senior management are responsible for operating the corporation in an ethical manner. They should never put individual, personal interests before those of the corporation or its shareholders. The Business Roundtable believes that when carrying out this function, corporations should have the following three elements in place:
  1. *A CEO of integrity*. The CEO should be a person of integrity who takes responsibility for the corporation adhering to the highest ethical standards.
  2. *A strong, ethical tone at the top*. The CEO and senior management should set a tone at the top that establishes a culture of legal compliance and integrity that is communicated to personnel at all levels of the corporation.
  3. *An effective compliance program*. Senior management should take responsibility for implementing and managing an effective compliance program relating to legal and ethical conduct. As part of its compliance program, a corporation should have a code of conduct with effective reporting and enforcement mechanisms. Employees should have a means of seeking guidance and alerting management and the board about potential or actual misconduct without fear of retribution, and violations of the code should be addressed promptly and effectively.

Need for Board Independence

Board independence from management is a crucial aspect of good corporate governance. It is here that the difference between inside directors and outside directors becomes most pronounced. **Outside directors** are independent from the firm and its top managers. In contrast, **inside directors** have some sort of ties to the firm. Sometimes they are top managers in the firm; other times insiders are family members or others with close ties to the CEO. To varying degrees, each of these parties is beholden to the CEO and, therefore, might be hesitant to speak out when necessary.

Another problem is managerial control of the board processes. CEOs often can control board perks, such as director compensation and committee assignments. Board members who rock the boat may find they are left out in the cold.

Insider Trading Scandals

Insider trading is the practice of obtaining critical information from inside a company and then using that information for one's own personal financial gain. Not only are shareholders suspicious of what has been going on unbeknownst to them, but small investors and the general public have lost faith in what they had thought was the stable-and-secure financial industry. When companies disclose meaningful information to shareholders and securities professionals, they must now do so publicly so that small investors can enjoy a more level playing field.

Improving Corporate Governance

Efforts to improve corporate governance may be classified into two major categories. First, changes could be made in the composition, structure, and functioning of boards of directors. Second, shareholders—on their own initiative or on the initiative of management or the board—could assume a more active role in governance.

❑ Learning Objective 9.5:
UNDERSTAND THE NATURE AND TYPES OF CORPORATE AUDITS

Auditing is a systematic process of objectively obtaining and evaluating evidence in reaching audit conclusions and reflecting them in the audit reports. The output of the audit work is reports, which are used by management (internal) and investors and creditors (external) stakeholders.

Types of audits include financial audits, operational audits, and information technology (IT) audits. The scope of **financial audit** examines the reliability and integrity of accounting records, financial records, and operational records to express a professional opinion on the financial condition of a firm. The scope of **operational (management) audit** is concerned with the economical and efficient use of an organization's resources and the accomplishment of goals and objectives. The scope of **IT audits** includes the review of controls in computer systems and operations to comply with internal control policies and procedures and its effectiveness in safeguarding an organization's technology assets.

Audit work is conducted by two types of individuals: external auditors primarily performing financial and IT audits, and internal auditors primarily performing operational and IT audits.

External auditors play an important role in capital markets. Financial statements audited by external auditors permit the flow of capital to companies in the form of both equity and credit. External auditors owe a duty of due professional care when performing their work since they are accountable primarily to the stakeholders and secondarily to the

company. Full disclosure of accurate and clear financial information should be the goal of external auditors to protect shareholders, investors, and creditors (i.e., stakeholders). External auditors need to establish credibility, honesty, ethical values, and integrity in delivering high-quality financial reporting useful for healthy functioning of the capital market system. External auditors should use professional skepticism when dealing with corporate management assertions and representations. External auditors should act as gatekeepers in preventing and/or detecting client organization management wrongdoings.

Internal auditors play an important role in the organization they work for by adding value to the organization. Internal auditors help the organization in achieving its goals and objectives by reviewing business functions and operations for efficiency and effectiveness. Internal auditors owe a duty of due professional care when performing their work since they are accountable primarily to the company and secondarily to its shareholders. Internal auditors should use professional skepticism when dealing with corporate management assertions and representations. Internal auditors should act as gatekeepers in preventing and/or detecting organization management wrongdoings.

Regardless of the types of audits and the types of auditors, all audit work is done in a systematic process of planning, collecting evidence, evaluating evidence, and reporting the audit results—the **audit process.**

Other varieties of audit work include construction audit, quality audit, due diligence audit, security audit, safety audit, privacy audit, performance audit, and operational audit.

Construction/Contract Audit

Many opportunities exist in construction auditing in terms of cost recovery in such areas as fraud, kickbacks, overcharges, and conflicts of interest. Early participation of the auditor is required in bidding procedures, cost estimates, contractual terms, contractors' accounting (billing) systems, cost control, and project control procedures. There should be a provision in the contract for overall project reviews, billing reviews, progress reviews, and cost recovery audits.

Construction audits generally fall into one of three categories: (1) fixed price (lump sum), (2) cost plus, and (3) unit price. Under the **fixed-price contract,**

contractors agree to work for a fixed amount. The auditor should review escalation clauses, progress payments, incentive provisions, adjustments for excess labor and materials costs, and change orders. Risks in a fixed-price contract include: inadequate insurance and bond coverage; charges for equipment and materials that are not received; overhead cost items included as additional charges; inadequate inspection relative to specifications; and extra costs, changes, and revisions that are already part of the original contract.

Under the **cost-plus contract,** the contractor is reimbursed for costs plus a fixed fee (which is encouraged) or costs plus a fee based on percentage of costs (which is discouraged). Some cost-plus contracts provide for maximum costs and sharing of any savings generated. Risks in cost-plus contracts include: overhead cost items also billed directly; duplication of costs between headquarters and field offices; poor-quality work practices; poor physical protection of materials and equipment; excessive costs incurred due to idle rented equipment; excessive manning of project; and uncontrolled overtime costs.

Unit-price contracts are useful when large amounts of similar work are required from the contractor (e.g., clearing land by the acre and surveillance of a building). A price is agreed on for each unit of work. Risks in the unit-price contract include: excessive progress payment; improper or inaccurate reporting of units completed; unauthorized escalation adjustments; and inaccurate field records.

Quality Audit

Quality audit engagements can take place in two areas: quality audit of a company's products and services and quality audit of an individual business function.

Quality Audit of a Company's Products or Services

Most organizations view quality of a product or service as a competitive weapon. Quality can increase revenues and sales, decrease costs, and increase profits.

The audit scope of the quality function includes review of the charter, organization chart, quality policies and procedures, quality control tools, quality costs (cost of quality), quality management tools, quality standards, applicable laws and regulations, and Six-Sigma metrics.

The auditor needs to understand:

- How quality management tools (affinity diagrams, tree diagrams, process decision program charts, matrix diagrams, interrelationship digraphs, prioritization matrices, and activity network diagrams) are used, including their frequency and applicability
- How Six-Sigma metrics are implemented or planned to be implemented
- How quality control tools (check sheets, histograms, scatter diagrams, Pareto diagrams, flowcharts, cause-and-effect diagrams, and control charts) are used, including their frequency and applicability
- How quality costs (preventive, appraisal, internal failures, and external failures) are accumulated and reported to management and their reasonableness with the industry norms and company targets
- How service-quality characteristics (intangibility, inseparability, heterogeneity, and perishability) are measured and reported

Quality Audit of an Individual Business Function

Many business functions or departments have installed total quality management (TQM) approaches to improve their operations. The department management should perform a self-assessment to ensure compliance with TQM principles and practices.

Due-Diligence Audit

Due-diligence audits provide a safety valve to management that is planning to acquire, manage, or consolidate with other businesses. Joint ventures and environmental audits are also subject to due-diligence audits. These audits are the minimum managerial requirements to ensure that all applicable laws and regulations are met and that risks and exposures are minimized. For example, due-diligence audits are a risk management tool for banks, land buyers, and lending agencies when a buyer is purchasing land or accepting it as a gift. Here the buyer wants to minimize the potential legal liability resulting from land acquisition.

Due-diligence audits are team-based efforts involving internal auditors, external auditors, lawyers, engineers, IT staff, and other specialists. Three phases in this audit include information gathering (phase 1), information analysis (phase 2), and information reporting (phase 3). **Information gathering** involves collecting information through document reviews, interviews, and meetings. **Information analysis** may include analytical reviews, including ratio analysis, regression analysis, and other quantitative techniques. **Information reporting** includes writing a balanced report based on facts with an executive summary. In addition to writing reports, oral reports can be used for immediate response and clarification of issues and findings.

Security Audit

The scope of **security audits**, which can be unannounced audits, includes logical security, physical security, and computer storage medium. **Logical security** focuses on determining whether a person attempting access should be allowed into a computer system and what the user can do once on the system. Specific controls in logical security review include authentication controls such as composition and change of passwords and user identification codes (IDs), encryption methods and routines, and restricting transactions to particular terminals and employees. Terminal-related controls include time-out limits and displaying the last time and date a user ID was used.

The scope of **physical security** audits can include a review of physical access to storerooms, cash vaults, research laboratories, plants and factories, computer centers, preventive maintenance procedures, and environmental controls. Physical access controls include limiting unauthorized access using electronic cards and biometric access devices (voice recognition, electronic signature verification), fire prevention techniques, electric power supply, and air-conditioning for humidity control.

The scope of **computer storage media** audits includes review of rotation of computer files to and from offsite storage, electronic vaulting at remote locations, environmental controls offsite as well as onsite, and adequacy of storage media capacity for future computing needs.

Safety Audit

The scope of **safety audit** includes review of safety policies and procedures and accident statistics and investigations. The auditor needs to make sure that corrective actions for safety problems are proper and timely and that all applicable labor laws are complied with.

The auditor would need to coordinate safety audit activities with other functions, such as qual-

ity, health, security, and industrial engineering. Possible areas of coordination include sharing work plans and schedules, conducting periodic meetings, exchanging reports, developing work statistics, providing control training, and participating in investigations and corrective actions.

Privacy Audit

Privacy is the right to limit access to information regarding oneself. The term **privacy** refers to the social balance between an individual's right to keep information confidential and the societal benefit derived from sharing information and how this balance is codified to give individuals the means to control personal information. The term **confidentiality** refers to disclosure of information only to authorized individuals and entities.

Privacy means that the rights of the accused (suspect) cannot be violated during the investigation. The accused can use protective orders if his privacy rights are ignored or handled improperly. If accused persons can prove that evidence brought against them would do more harm to them than good, the courts will favor the accused in suppressing such evidence from being presented.

The organization can protect itself from privacy and confidentiality problems by developing a **policy statement** and by showing the amount of damage done by the accused.

- A policy statement is a prerequisite to handling privacy issues properly and legally. An incomplete or unclear policy could result in legal action against the organization by employees (suspects) when they find out that their privacy rights are violated.
- The organization must show that the perpetrator actually broke into a computer system, violated its proprietary rights to the system, and show the extent of damage caused. Organizations should have controls such as passwords, encryption, access controls, hidden files, and warning banners to establish proprietary rights to a computer system. A policy statement should define this area.

Performance Audit

Any operation or function, whether it is production or service, needs to be measured in terms of its performance. To measure performance, performance standards, which are tied to the primary objectives of the operation or function, must be developed and monitored. In addition, each performance standard must be expressed in terms of efficiency and effectiveness criteria. If too many performance standards or indicators exist, employees may not be able to handle them properly, which can lead to waste of resources. Therefore, both management and employees should focus on a few meaningful key performance indicators (KPIs).

The auditor needs to be aware that some employees may falsify the KPIs to survive and that performance results may be distorted to receive larger bonuses and promotions. Therefore, the auditor should compare the KPIs with the industry norms as well as with the same company data from period to period. Also, the auditor should be careful in analyzing both KPIs that look too good as well as KPIs that do not meet standards.

Operational Audit

The economic events and business transactions of an entity are usually classified into several operating cycles to manage the audit effectively and efficiently. The scope of operational audit work includes a review of business transactions affecting revenue, expenditure, production (conversion), treasury (financing/investing), and financial reporting (external) cycles.

❑ Learning Objective 9.6: UNDERSTAND THE NATURE AND TYPES OF CORPORATE FRAUD

The legal definition of fraud by most statutes is as follows. **Fraud** is a generic term that embraces all the multifarious means that human ingenuity can devise that are resorted to by one individual to get an advantage over another by false representations. It includes all surprise, trick, cunning, and unfair ways by which another is cheated. Fraud is a term of law, applied to certain facts as a conclusion from them, but is not in itself a fact. It has been defined as any cunning deception or artifice used to cheat or deceive another.

To cheat and defraud means to use every kind of trick and deception, from false representation and intimidation to suppression and concealment of any fact and information, by which a party is induced to part with property for less than its value or to give more than it is worth for the property of another. "Fraud" and "bad faith" are synonymous when applied to the conduct of public offenders.

Three Elements of Fraud:

1. Intent to defraud
2. Commission of a fraudulent act
3. Accomplishment of the fraud

Types of Fraud

There are many types of fraud, limited only by the ingenuity of the perpetrators. Fraud can be classified in a number of ways from a discovery point of view. The reason for this classification is that different approaches and procedures are required to discover each type of fraud and to control each type's occurrence.

Howard Davia and his coauthors (1992) present four types of fraud: (1) theft of assets, (2) fraud by frequency, (3) fraud by conspiracy, and (4) varieties of fraud.

Theft of Assets
Theft of assets is classified into three categories.

1. Theft of assets that appears openly on the books as distinct accounting entries (fraud open on the books is the least difficult to discover).

    Fraud open on the books includes criminal acts that involve discrete entries in the accounting records. Here the term **discrete entry** means that the fraud involves the entire transaction; if that transaction is selected by an auditor for examination, this type of fraud offers the best chance for discovery (e.g., a fraudulent duplicate payment that stands by it).

2. Theft of assets appears on the books but is hidden as a part of other larger, otherwise-legitimate accounting entries (fraud hidden on the books).

    Fraud hidden on the books involves acts of fraud that are included in accounting entries that appear on the books, but are not discrete entries. That is, the amount of the fraud is always buried in a larger, legitimate accounting entry, never appearing as a discrete amount (e.g., kickbacks).

3. Theft of assets not on the books and that never could be detected by an examination of "booked" accounting transactions (fraud off the books is the most difficult to discover).

    In fraud off the books, the amount of the fraud is neither a discrete accounting entry nor a hidden part of an accounting entry. It is the loss of a valuable asset for the victim. Examples include diverting vending-machine sales money and conversion of payments on accounts receivable that have been written off.

Fraud by Frequency

Another way of classifying fraud is by its frequency of occurrence: nonrepeating or repeating. In **nonrepeating fraud**, a fraudulent act, even though repeated many times, is singular in nature in that it must be triggered by the perpetrator each time (e.g., a weekly payroll check requires a timecard every week in order to generate the fraudulent paycheck).

In **repeating fraud**, a defrauding act may occur many times; however, it needs to be initiated only once. It then keeps running until it is stopped. It could possibly recur in perpetuity (e.g., a salaried payroll check that does not require input each time in order to generate the paycheck. It continues until a stop order is issued).

Fraud by Conspiracy

Fraud can be classified as that involving conspiracy, that which does not involve conspiracy, and that involving partial (pseudo-) conspiracy. Here the word **conspiracy** is synonymous with **collusion.** It has been proven that most frauds involve conspiracy, either bona fide or pseudo. In the bona fide conspiracy, all parties involved are fully aware of the fraudulent intent; in the pseudoconspiracy, one or more of the parties to the fraud is innocent of fraudulent intent.

Varieties of Fraud

The varieties of fraud can be grouped in two categories: (1) "specialized" fraud, which is unique to people working in certain kinds of business operations, and (2) "garden-variety" fraud, which anyone is likely to encounter in general business operations.

Examples of **specialized fraud** include: embezzlement of assets entrusted by depositors to financial institutions such as banks, savings and loans, credit unions, and pension funds (called **custodial** fraud), and false insurance claims for life, health, auto, and property coverage.

Examples of **garden-variety fraud** include kickbacks, defective pricing, unbalanced contracts or purchase orders, reopening completed contracts, duplicate payments, double payments, shell payments, and defective delivery.

Degree of Fraud

The degree of fraud can be linked to the environment of an organization:

- **High-fraud environment** is linked to low management integrity, poor control environment, loose accountability, and high pressure for results.

- **Low-fraud environment** is linked to a culture of honesty, management openness, employee-assistance programs, and implementing total quality management (TQM) principles.

Red Flags for Fraud

Red flags do not signal that a fraud has occurred but rather that the opportunity for a fraud exists. Some examples of red flags are:

- Concealed assets
- Missing or destroyed records and documents
- Split purchases
- Excessive "voids" or "refunds"
- Rapid turnover of financial managers and executives

Symptoms of Management Fraud

According to Jack Bologna (1993), **corporate fraud** can be generated internally (perpetrated by directors, officers, employees, or agents of a corporation for or against it or against others) and externally (perpetrated by others—suppliers, vendors, customers, hackers) against the corporation. Bologna includes management fraud as a part of corporate fraud as the intentional overstatement of corporate or division profits. It is inspired, perpetrated, or induced by managers who seek to benefit in terms of promotions, job stability, larger bonuses, and status symbols.

Management fraud tends to involve a number of people with conspiracy in mind. It occurs because senior managers, due to their position of power, circumvent internal controls. According to Bologna, the major symptoms of management fraud are the intentional understatement of losses and liabilities and overstatement of assets or profits. For example:

- Profits can be manipulated by overstating revenues or understating costs.
- Revenues can be overstated by recording fictitious sales, recording unfinalized sales, recording consignments as sales, or recording shipments to storage facilities as sales.
- Costs can be manipulated by deferring them to the next accounting period or understating them in the current period. This is accomplished by such ploys as overstating ending inventories of raw materials, work-in-process, and finished goods, or understating purchases of raw materials.

In almost every case of management fraud, signs (red flags) of the fraud exist for some time before the fraud itself is detected or disclosed by a third party. These signs include:

- Knowledge that the company is having financial difficulties, such as frequent cash flow shortages, declining sales and profits, and loss of market share.
- Apparent management incompetence, such as poor planning, organization, communication, and controls; poor motivation and delegation; management indecision and confusion about corporate mission, goals, and strategies; management ignorance of conditions in the industry and in the general economy.
- Autocratic management, low trust of employees, poor promotion opportunities, high turnover of employees, poorly defined business ethics.
- Accounting-related transaction-based red flags:
  - Cash flow is diminishing.
  - Sales and income are diminishing.
  - Payables and receivables are increasing.
  - Unusual or second endorsements on checks.
  - Inventory and cost of sales are increasing.
  - Income and expense items are continually reclassified.
  - Suspense items are either not reconciled at all or reconciled in an untimely manner.
  - Suspense items are written off without explanation.
  - Accounts receivable write-offs are increasing.
  - Journal entries are heavily adjusted at year-end.
  - Old outstanding checks.
  - Heavy customer complaints.

Accounting Fraud by Higher-Level Managers:

- Early booking of sales
- Expense deferrals
- Inventory overstatement
- Expense account padding

Symptoms of Employee Fraud

Embezzlement is a major type of employee fraud. The crime of embezzlement consists of the fraudulent misappropriation of the property of an employer by an employee to whom the possession of that property has been entrusted. Here is the difference between embezzlement and larceny: embezzlement occurs when the embezzler gains initial possession of property lawfully but subsequently misappropriates it. **Larceny** is committed when property is taken without the owner's consent.

Common embezzlement techniques include these schemes:

- Cash disbursement embezzlement involves the creation of fake documents or false expense entries using phony invoices, timecards, and receipts.
- Cash receipts fraud involves the **lapping** of cash or accounts receivable. Here the embezzler borrows from today's receipts and replaces them with tomorrow's receipts. Other examples are **skimming**, where the proceeds of cash sales are intercepted before any entry is made of their receipts and granting fake credits for discounts, refunds, rebates, returns, and allowances, possibly through collusion with a customer.
- Theft of property involves assets such as tools, supplies, equipment, finished goods, raw materials, and intellectual property such as software, data, and proprietary information.

Corruption is another common type of employee fraud. Vendors, suppliers, service providers, or contractors often corrupt the employees of an organization on both a small-scale level (e.g., gifts and free tickets of nominal value) and a large-scale level (e.g., commissions, payoffs, free trips, free airline tickets and hotel accommodations).

Accounting Fraud by Lower-Level Employees:

- Check kiting
- Lapping of receivables
- Phony vendor invoices
- Phony benefit payment claims
- Expense account padding

Management Representations versus Risk

The auditor needs to assess the risk of management misrepresentations and to consider the effects of such risks in establishing an overall audit strategy and the scope of the audit. Examples of situations (red flags) that could lead to risk of management representations include the following:

- Frequent disputes about aggressive application of generally accepted accounting principles.
- Excessive emphasis on meeting targets upon which management compensation program is based.
- Responses to audit inquiries are evasive.
- Employees lack necessary knowledge and experience, yet develop various estimates including accounting.

- Supervisors of employees generating estimates appear careless or inexperienced in reviewing and approving the estimates.
- A history of unreliable or unreasonable estimates has developed.
- Crisis conditions exist constantly in operating and accounting areas of the organization.
- Frequent and excessive back orders, shortages of materials and products, delays, or lack of documentation of major transactions arise.
- Access to computer-based application systems initiating or controlling the movement of assets is not restricted.
- High levels of transaction processing errors are observed.
- Unusual delays occur in providing operating results and accounting reports.

Review of Accounting Estimates

Many assumptions go into accounting estimates. The auditor should understand these assumptions and should evaluate to determine whether the assumptions are subjective and are susceptible to misstatements and bias.

The auditor should show professional skepticism during the review and evaluation of the reasonableness of accounting estimates. These estimates contain both subjective and objective factors. Professional skepticism is important with respect to subjective factors where personal bias could be significant.

Examples of accounting estimates include: uncollectible receivables; allowance for loan losses; revenues to be earned on contracts; subscription income; losses on sales contracts; professional membership or union dues income; valuation of financial securities; trading versus investment security classifications; compensation in stock option plans and deferred plans; probability of loss; obsolete inventory; net realizable value of inventories; losses in purchase commitments; property and causality insurance accruals; loss reserves; warranty claims; and taxes on real estate and personal property.

In addition to review, the auditor should test management's process of developing accounting estimates or develop an independent estimation. The auditor can compare prior estimates with subsequent results to assess the reliability of the process used to develop estimates. The auditor should also review whether the accounting estimates are consistent with the operational plans and programs of the entity.

❑ Learning Objective 9.7: UNDERSTAND THE ISSUES IN CORPORATE LAW REGARDING AGENCY PROBLEMS AND COSTS

The major condition embedded in the structure of modern corporations that has contributed to the corporate governance problem has been the **separation of ownership from control.** In the precorporate period, owners were typically the managers themselves. Thus, the system worked the way it was intended; the owners also controlled the business. Even when firms grew larger and managers were hired, the owners often were on the scene to hold the management group accountable.

As the public corporation grew and stock ownership became widely dispersed, a separation of ownership from control became the prevalent condition. The dispersion of ownership into hundreds of thousands or millions of shares meant that essentially no one or no one group owned enough shares to exercise control. This being the case, the most effective control that owners could exercise was the election of the board of directors to serve as their representative and watch over management. The shareholders were owners in a technical sense, but most of them perceived themselves to be investors rather than owners.

Other factors that added to management's power were the corporate laws and traditions that gave the management group control over the **proxy process**—the method by which the shareholders elected boards of directors. Over time, it was not difficult for management groups to create boards of directors of likeminded executives who would simply collect their fees and defer to management on whatever it wanted. The result of this process was that power, authority, and control began to flow upward from management rather than downward from the shareholders (owners). **Agency problems** developed when the interests of the shareholders were not aligned with the interests of the manager, and the manager (who is simply a hired **agent** with the responsibility of representing the owner's best interest) began to pursue self-interest instead.

Market forces and **agency costs** aim to prevent or minimize agency problems. Examples of market forces include large shareholders and threat of takeover, where large institutional shareholders put pressure on company management to perform using their voting rights and where a constant threat of a takeover motivates company management to act in the best interest of the corporation owners. Examples of agency costs include cost of management compensation in terms of incentive plans (stock options), performance plans (performance shares), and cash bonuses, and costs imposed by lenders (creditors and bankers) in the form of constraints put on the borrower's actions to protect their investment (e.g., minimum liquidity levels, merger and acquisition activities, executive salaries, and dividend payments).

Not many individuals want board director positions. Concerned about increasing legal hassles emanating from stockholder, customer, and employee lawsuits, people are quitting director positions or refusing to accept them in the first place. Although

courts rarely hold directors personally liable in the hundreds of shareholder suits filed every year, over the past several years there have been a few cases in which directors have been held personally and financially liable for their decisions.

 Self-Assessment Exercise

Online exercises are provided for the learning objectives in this module. Please visit www.mbaiq.com to complete the online exercises and to calculate your MBA IQ Score.

International Business

Learning Objective 10.1: Understand How to Develop and Manage International Business Strategies 269
Organizational Structures 269
Models of MNCs 270
Types of Decision Making in MNCs 270
Types of International Strategies 270
International Strategic and
    Tactical Objectives 271
Learning Objective 10.2: Understand the Various Issues in International Trade and Investment 271
Trade 272
Intellectual Property Rights and International
    Licensing Agreements 273
Foreign Direct Investment 274
Learning Objective 10.3: Understand the Nature of International Production Economics 275
The Terms of Trade 275
Learning Objective 10.4: Understand the Nature of International Trade Laws 276

World Trade Organization 276
North American Free Trade Agreement 278
European Union 278
Regional Groups 279
Learning Objective 10.5: Understand the Various Issues in International Financial Systems 280
Learning Objective 10.6: Understand How to Staff and Manage International Operations 281
Learning Objective 10.7: Understand the Various Issues in Conducting International Business in Cross Cultures 281
Effects of Cultures 282
Global Manager's Dilemma 282
Regional Cultures 282
Global Communication Insights 282
High- and Low-Context Communications 282
Cultural Awareness Learning Program 283
Cross-Cultural Negotiations 283
Global Mindsets 284

❑ Learning Objective 10.1: UNDERSTAND HOW TO DEVELOP AND MANAGE INTERNATIONAL BUSINESS STRATEGIES

The scope of this learning objective includes a discussion of different organizational structures, models, and types of decision making and strategies involved in multinational corporations.

Organizational Structures

The organizational structure of the multinational corporation (MNC) evolves over time due to changes in economic policies, tax laws, government regulations, and political structures. The organizational structure of the MNC varies, in which each manager's level has a varied degree of authority and responsibility.

Mueller suggests five common forms of organizations used by MNCs: (1) the international division/department, (2) organization by product line, (3) functional organization, (4) geographic organization, and (5) the global matrix organization.

The **international division/department** separates foreign operations from domestic operations. This international division is usually evaluated as an independent operation and compared with the domestic division. Information flows occur from subsidiaries to the vice president of the international division.

Organization by product line results in the integration of domestic and foreign operations and the evaluation of product lines based on worldwide results. Information flows occur from subsidiaries to the vice president of the product line.

A company grouped by function (such as marketing, manufacturing, or accounting) is called a

functional organization, and management maintains centralized control over the functions. An example is that the vice president for marketing or manufacturing at U.S. headquarters would be responsible for the marketing or manufacturing function worldwide. This structure is not common but is popular among oil and coal companies, whose products are homogeneous. Information flows occur from subsidiary to headquarters according to specific business function, that is, marketing, manufacturing, or accounting.

Geographic organization separates operations into geographic areas such as North America, Europe, and Asia. A company would use this form of structure when it has substantial foreign operations that are not dominated by a particular country or area of the world. U.S. MNCs do not use this form as often as European and Japanese MNCs do because U.S. MNCs are usually dominated by their domestic markets. Information flows occur from the subsidiary within a geographic area and then sent to headquarters.

The **global matrix organization** blends two or more of the four forms just presented. An example is that the general manager of a German subsidiary will report to the vice president for worldwide product lines and to the area vice president for Europe. The matrix organization avoids the problems inherent in either integrating or separating foreign operations. Information flows occur in two directions: from the subsidiary to the geographic location headquarters and by product line to MNC headquarters.

Models of MNCs

Another dimension to the organization of MNCs is the attitude of headquarters management toward multinational business. These attitudes can be classified into three models: (1) ethnocentric (home-country oriented), (2) polycentric (host-country oriented), and (3) geocentric (world-oriented).

The home country (parent country) refers to that nation in which an MNC establishes a subsidiary in a foreign country. The host country refers to that nation in which an MNC establishes a subsidiary in a local country.

An **ethnocentric management** thinks that home-country standards are superior and therefore applies them worldwide. Automakers are an example of the ethnocentric management model.

A **polycentric management** assumes that host-country cultures are different and, therefore, allows local subsidiaries or affiliates to operate autono-

mously. Standards for performance evaluation and control functions are determined locally. Pharmaceutical companies are an example of the polycentric model.

A **geocentric management** focuses on worldwide objectives and considers foreign subsidiaries as part of a whole. Standards for performance evaluation and control functions are determined both universally and locally. It is an ideal model where decisions are considered globally while, at the same time, individual subsidiaries are able to respond to the demands of host governments and the local customer. People of many different nationalities serve on the board of directors and senior management teams. N.V. Philips and Unilever are good examples of the geocentric management model. *"Think globally and act locally" is the basic tenet.*

Types of Decision Making in MNCs

The attitudes of headquarters management also affect the location of decision making. Basically, three types of decision making may result: (1) centralized, (2) decentralized, and (3) semicentralized or semidecentralized.

If decision-making authority rests with headquarters, an MNC is said to be **centralized.** Even with this structure, an MNC generally does not make all decisions at one location but aims for a collaborative approach between headquarters and other business units.

If an MNC headquarters allows foreign subsidiaries to make important decisions, the corporation is considered to be **decentralized.** This structure is more common when global diversity is considered. Managers of foreign subsidiaries are allowed a great deal of autonomy to plan, control, and evaluate their own operations at the local level.

Not all MNCs are purely centralized or decentralized. Often, a mixture of organizations is necessary. **Semicentralized** or **semidecentralized** decision making arises when an MNC centralizes functions considered critical for success (e.g., research and development) and decentralizes those that are less critical (e.g., marketing and production).

Types of International Strategies

International firms typically develop their core strategy for the home country first. Subsequently, they internationalize their core strategy through international expansion of activities and through adaptation. Eventually, they globalize their strategy by integrating operations across nations. These steps translate into four distinct types of strategies applied by international enterprises:

1. **Ethnocentric strategy.** Following World War II, U.S. enterprises operated mainly from an ethnocentric perspective. These companies produced unique goods and services, which they offered primarily to the domestic market. Lack of international competition offset their need to be sensitive to cultural differences. When these firms exported goods, they did not alter them for foreign consumption—the costs of alterations for cultural differences were assumed by foreign buyers. In effect, this type of company had one strategy for all markets.

2. **Multidomestic strategy.** The multidomestic firm has a different strategy for each of its foreign markets. According to Craig (1976), in this type of strategy, "a company's management tries to operate effectively across a series of worldwide positions with diverse product requirements, growth rates, competitive environments, and political risks. The company prefers that local managers do what is necessary to succeed in research and development, production, marketing, and distribution, but holds them responsible for results." In essence, this type of corporation competes with local competitors on a market-by-market basis.

3. **Global strategy.** The global corporation uses all of its resources against its competition in a very integrated fashion. All of its foreign subsidiaries and divisions are highly interdependent in both operations and strategy. Therefore, whereas in a multidomestic strategy the managers in each country react to competition without considering what is taking place in other countries, in a global strategy, competitive moves are integrated across nations. The same kind of move is made in different countries at the same time or in a systematic fashion. For example, a competitor is attacked in one nation in order to exhaust its resources for another country, or a competitive attack in one nation is countered in a different country—in that instance, the counterattack in a competitor's home market is a party to an attack on one's home market.

4. **Transnational strategy.** The transnational strategy provides for global coordination (like the global strategy) and at the same time it allows local autonomy (like the multidomestic strategy). Nestlé, the world's largest food company, headquartered in Switzerland, follows this strategy.

The challenges that managers of transnational corporations face are to identify and exploit cross-border synergies and to balance local demands with the global vision for the corporation. Building an effective transnational organization requires a corporate culture that values global dissimilarities across cultures and markets.

International Strategic and Tactical Objectives

Organizations generally establish two kinds of measurable objectives:

- **Strategic objectives,** which are guided by the enterprise's mission or purpose and deal with long-term issues, associate the enterprise to its external environment and provide management with a basis for comparing performance with that of its competitors and in relation to environmental demands. Examples of strategic objectives include to increase sales, to increase market share, to increase profits, and to lower prices by becoming an international firm.

- **Tactical objectives,** which are guided by the enterprise's strategic objectives and deal with shorter term issues, identify the key result areas in which specific performance is essential for the success of the enterprise and aim to attain internal efficiency. For example, they identify specifically how to lower costs, to lower prices, to increase output, to capture a larger portion of the market, and to penetrate an international market.

❏ Learning Objective 10.2: UNDERSTAND THE VARIOUS ISSUES IN INTERNATIONAL TRADE AND INVESTMENT

International business is classified into three categories: (1) trade, (2) intellectual property rights (trademarks, patents, and copyrights) and international licensing agreements, and (3) foreign direct investment. To the marketer, these broad categories describe three important methods for entering a foreign market. To the lawyer, they also represent the form of doing business in a foreign country and the legal relationship between parties to a business transaction. Each method brings a different set of problems to the firm because the level of foreign penetration and entanglement in various countries is different.

Trade

Trade consists of the import and export of goods and services. **Exporting** is the term generally used to refer to the process of sending goods out of a country, and **importing** is used to denote when goods are brought into a country. However, a more accurate definition is that exporting is "the shipment of goods or the rendering of services to a foreign buyer located in a foreign country." Importing is then defined as "the process of buying goods from a foreign supplier and entering them into the customs territory of a different country." Every export entails an import and vice versa.

A country will have a **trade deficit** when it consumes more than it produces and imports the difference from other countries. A country will become a debtor nation when there is a huge trade deficit and when it borrows to finance the domestic budget deficit.

Exporting

Trade is often a firm's first step into international business. Compared to the other forms of international business (licensing and investment), trade is relatively uncomplicated. It provides the inexperienced or smaller firm with an opportunity to penetrate a new market or at least to explore foreign market potential, without significant capital investment and the risks of becoming a full-fledged player (that is, citizen) in the foreign country. For many larger firms, including multinational corporations, exporting may be an important portion of their business operations. The U.S. aircraft industry, for example, relies heavily on exports for significant revenues.

Exporting is generally divided into two types: (1) direct and (2) indirect. **Direct exporting** seems similar to selling goods to a domestic buyer. A prospective foreign customer may have seen a firm's products at a trade show, located a particular company in an industrial directory, or been recommended by another customer. A firm that receives a request for product and pricing information from a foreign customer may be able to handle it routinely and export directly to the buyer. With some assistance, a firm can overcome most hurdles, get the goods properly packaged and shipped, and receive payment as anticipated. Although many of these onetime sales are turned into long-term business success stories, many more are not. A firm hopes to develop a regular business relationship with its new foreign customer.

However, the problems that can be encountered even in direct exporting are considerable.

Direct exporting is often done through foreign sales agents who work on commission. It also can be done by selling directly to foreign distributors. Foreign distributors are independent firms, usually located in the country to which a firm is exporting, that purchase goods for resale to their customers. They assume the risks of buying and warehousing goods in their market and provide additional product support services. The distributor usually services the products they sell, thus relieving the exporter of that responsibility. They often train end users to use the product, extend credit to their customers, and bear responsibility for local advertising and promotion.

Indirect exporting is used by companies seeking to minimize their involvement abroad. Lacking experience, personnel, or capital, they may be unable to locate foreign buyers or not yet ready to handle the mechanics of a transaction on their own. There are several different types of indirect exporting. Export trading companies (ETCs) market the products of several manufacturers in foreign markets. They have extensive sales contacts overseas and experience in air and sea shipping. They often operate with the assistance and financial backing of large banks, thus making the resources and international contacts of the bank's foreign branches available to the manufacturers whose products they market. ETCs are licensed to operate under the U.S. antitrust laws.

Export management companies (EMCs), however, are really consultants who advise manufacturers and other exporters. Firms that cannot justify their own in-house export managers use them. They engage in foreign market research, identify overseas sales agents, exhibit goods at foreign trade shows, prepare documentation for export, and handle language translations and shipping arrangements. As in direct exporting, all forms of indirect exporting can involve sales through agents or to distributors.

Importing and Global Sourcing

Here, importing is presented from the perspective of the global firm for which importing is a regular and necessary part of their business. **Global sourcing** is the term commonly used to describe the process by which a firm attempts to locate and purchase goods or services on a worldwide basis. These goods may include, for example, raw materials for manufacturing, component parts for assembly operations, commodities such as agricultural products or minerals, or merchandise for resale.

Methods, Restrictions, and Barriers of International Trade

Tariffs, nontariff barriers, and domestic content laws have a tremendous influence on how firms make their trade and investment decisions. These decisions in turn are reflected in the patterns of world trade and the flows of investment capital.

Tariffs   A **tariff** is a tax imposed on imported goods, usually as a percentage of the product's value. Import duties, or tariffs, have been a source of government revenue far longer than income and value-added taxes. Goods entering a country are taxed on an **ad valorem** (percent of value) basis. Many foreign countries prefer to use tariffs since it is relatively easy to check and control as goods come through designated ports.

Nontariff barriers are all barriers to importing or exporting other than tariffs. Nontariff barriers are generally a greater barrier to trade than are tariffs because they are more insidious. Unlike tariffs, which are published and easily understood, nontariff barriers are often disguised in the form of government rules or industry regulations and are often not understood by foreign companies. Countries impose nontariff barriers to protect their national economic, social, and political interests. Imports might be banned for health and safety reasons. Imported goods usually have to be marked with the country of origin and labeled in the local language, so consumers know what they are buying.

Specific examples of nontariff barriers include the following:

- **Technical barrier to trade or product standard.** Examples of product standards include safety standards, electrical standards, and environmental standards.
- **Embargo.** An embargo is a total or near-total ban on trade with a particular country, sometimes enforced by military action and usually imposed for political purposes.
- **Boycott.** A boycott is a refusal to trade or do business with certain firms, usually from a particular country, on political or other grounds.
- **Export control.** An export control limits the type of product that may be shipped to any particular country. They are usually imposed for economic or political purposes and are used by all nations of the world.
- **Import quotas.** A quota is simply a quantitative restriction applied to imports. Under World Trade Organization (WTO), import quotas are supposed to be banned, but there are so many exceptions that the ban is not that useful. In fact, as tariffs have been reduced as an instrument of protection, the tendency has been to replace them with quotas. Tariffs focus on taxes, while quotas focus on quantities.

Domestic Content Laws   Another way many countries have attempted to assure the participation of domestic producers has been through domestic content laws. These laws stipulate that when a product is sold in the marketplace, it must incorporate a specified percentage of locally made components. These laws must meet "local content requirements."

Intellectual Property Rights and International Licensing Agreements

Intellectual property rights are a grant from a government to an individual or firm of the exclusive legal right to use a copyright, patent, or trademark for a specified time. Copyrights are legal rights to artistic or written works, including books, software, films, and music, or to such works as the layout design of a computer chip. Trademarks include the legal right to use a name or symbol that identifies a firm or its product. Patents are governmental grants to inventors assuring them of the exclusive legal right to produce and sell their inventions for a period of years. Copyrights, trademarks, and patents comprise substantial assets of many domestic and international firms. As valuable assets, intellectual property can be sold or licensed for use to others through a licensing agreement.

International licensing agreements are contracts by which the holder of intellectual property will grant certain rights in that property to a foreign firm under specified conditions and for a specified time. Licensing agreements represent an important foreign market entry method for firms with marketable intellectual property. For example, a firm might license the right to manufacture and distribute a certain type of computer chip or the right to use a trademark on apparel such as bluejeans or designer clothing. It might license the right to distribute Hollywood movies or to reproduce and market word-processing software in a foreign market, or it might license its patent rights to produce and sell a high-tech product or pharmaceutical. U.S. firms have extensively licensed their property around the world and in recent years have purchased the technology rights of Japanese and other foreign firms.

Technology Transfer

The exchange of technology and manufacturing know-how between firms in different countries through arrangements such as licensing agreements is known as **technology transfer.** Transfers of technology and know-how are regulated by government control in some countries. For instance, government regulation might require that the licensor introduce its most modern technology to the developing countries or train workers in its use.

International Franchising

Franchising is a form of licensing that is gaining in popularity worldwide. The most common form of franchising is known as a business operations franchise, usually used in retailing. Under a typical franchising agreement, the franchisee is allowed to use a trade name or trademark in offering goods or services to the public in return for a royalty based on a percentage of sales or other fee structure. The franchisee will usually obtain the franchiser's know-how in operating and managing a profitable business and its other "secrets of success" (ranging from a "secret recipe," to store design, to accounting methods).

Foreign Direct Investment

The term **foreign investment,** or **foreign direct investment,** refers to the ownership and active control of ongoing business concerns, including investment in manufacturing, mining, farming, assembly operations, and other facilities of production. A distinction is made between the home and host countries of the firms involved. The home country refers to that country under whose laws the investing corporation was created or is headquartered. For example, the United States is home to multinational corporations such as Ford, Exxon, and IBM, to name a few, but they operate in host countries throughout every region of the world. Of the three forms of international business, foreign investment provides the firm with the most involvement and perhaps the greatest risk abroad. Investment in a foreign plant is often a result

of having had successful experiences in exporting or licensing, and of the search for ways to overcome the disadvantages of those other entry methods. For example, by producing its product in a foreign country instead of exporting, a firm can avoid quotas and tariffs on imported goods, avoid currency fluctuations on the traded goods, provide better product service and spare parts, and more quickly adapt products to local tastes and market trends. Manufacturing overseas for foreign markets can mean taking advantage of local natural resources, labor, and manufacturing economies of scale. Foreign investment in the United States is often called **reverse investment.**

Multinational corporations wishing to enter a foreign market through direct investment can structure their business arrangements in many different ways. Their options and eventual course of action may depend on many factors, including industry and market conditions, capitalization of the firm and financing, and legal considerations. Some of these options include the startup of a new foreign subsidiary company, the formation of a joint venture with an existing foreign company, or the acquisition of an existing foreign company by stock purchase. For now, keep in mind that multinational corporations are usually not a single legal entity. They are global enterprises that consist of any number of interrelated corporate entities, connected through extremely complex chains of stock ownership. Stock ownership gives the investing corporation tremendous flexibility when investing abroad.

The **wholly owned foreign subsidiary** is a "foreign" corporation organized under the laws of a foreign host country but owned and controlled by the parent corporation in the home country. Because the parent company controls all of the stock in the subsidiary, it can control management and financial decision making.

The **joint venture** is a cooperative business arrangement between two or more companies for profit. A joint venture may take the form of a partnership or corporation. Typically, one party will contribute expertise and another the capital, each bringing its own special resources to the venture. Joint ventures exist in all regions of the world and in all types of industries. Where the laws of a host country require local ownership or where investing foreign firms have a local partner, the joint venture is an appropriate investment vehicle. **Local participation** refers to the requirement that a share of the business be owned by nationals of the host country. These requirements are gradually being reduced in most countries that, in an effort to attract more investment, are permitting wholly owned subsidiaries. Many American companies do not favor the joint venture as an investment vehicle because they do not want to share technology, expertise, and profits with another company.

Another method of investing abroad is for two companies to **merge** or for one company to acquire another ongoing firm. This option has appeal because it requires less know-how than does a new startup and can be concluded without disruption of business activity.

❑ Learning Objective 10.3: UNDERSTAND THE NATURE OF INTERNATIONAL PRODUCTION ECONOMICS

Increased total world output is a good argument for free trade between countries. Incentives exist for trade to develop along the lines of comparative advantage. Countries achieve comparative advantage in certain goods due to international differences in demand or supply.

The **theory of comparative advantage** explains how mutually beneficial trade can occur when one country is less efficient than another county in the production of all commodities. The less-efficient country should specialize in and export the commodity in which its absolute disadvantage is smallest and should import the other commodity.

Countries should specialize when they have their greatest absolute advantage or in their least absolute disadvantage. This rule is known as the **law of comparative advantage.** An absolute advantage is the ability to produce a good using less input than is possible anywhere in the world.

Production of the good with the lower price expands, and the country with a lower relative price of a product has comparative advantage in that product. Therefore, production and trade follow the line of comparative advantage. For trade to occur along the lines of comparative advantage, the relative wage ratio must lie between the extremes of the differences in relative productive advantages.

The **Heckscher-Ohlin (HO) theorem** states that a country will have a comparative advantage in and therefore will export that good whose production is relatively intensive in the factor with which that country is relatively well endowed. For example, a country that is relatively capital-abundant com-

pared with another country will have a comparative advantage in the good that requires more capital per worker to produce.

In a competitive environment, trade flows are determined by profit-seeking firms. If a product is relatively cheap in one country, it will tend to be exported to those places where it is relatively expensive. This practice supports the assumption that trade will flow in the direction of comparative advantage. *Each country exports its comparative advantage good and imports its comparative disadvantage good.*

Which Country Has the Comparative Advantage?

	Labor Hours per Unit of Output	
	Country A	Country B
Cotton	3	12
Automobile	6	8

Note that country A is four times (that is, 12 to 3) more efficient in the production of cotton relative to country B. However, country A is only 4/3 (that is, 8/6) more efficient in the production of automobiles relative to country B. Because country A's greatest absolute advantage is in the production of cotton, it is said to have a comparative advantage in cotton. Because country B's least absolute disadvantage is in the production of automobiles, it is said to have a comparative advantage in automobiles.

The Terms of Trade

The advantages realized as a result of trade are called the **gains from trade,** which are shared among importing and exporting countries through the terms of trade. The terms of trade is related to the quantity of imported goods that can be obtained per unit of goods exported. They are measured by the ratio of the price of exports to the price of imports. A rise in the price of imported goods, with the price of exported goods unchanged, indicates a fall in the terms of trade; it will now take more exports to buy the same quantity of imports. Similarly, a rise in the price of exported goods, with the price of imported goods unchanged, indicates a rise in the terms of trade; it will now take fewer exports to buy the same quantity of imports.

Because international trade involves many countries and many products, it is good to compute a country's terms of trade as an index number:

Terms of Trade = (Index of Export Prices)/
                 (Index of Import Prices) × 100

A rise in the index number is referred to as a favorable change in a country's terms of trade, meaning more goods can be imported per unit of goods exported than before.

A fall in the index number is referred to as an unfavorable change in a country's terms of trade, meaning fewer goods can be imported per unit of goods exported than before. It must export more to pay for any given amount of imports.

Calculation of New Terms of Trade Index

The export price index rises from 100 to 120, and the import price index rises from 100 to 110. What is the new terms of trade number? The new terms of trade index increases from 100 to 109, meaning that a unit of exports will buy 9 percent more imports than at the old terms of trade (i.e., $(120/110) - 1.00 = 9\%$).

❑ Learning Objective 10.4: UNDERSTAND THE NATURE OF INTERNATIONAL TRADE LAWS

The scope of international trade laws includes World Trade Organization (WTO), North American Free Trade Agreement (NAFTA), The European Union (EU), and other regional groups.

World Trade Organization

Trade liberalization refers to the efforts of governments to reduce tariffs and nontariff barriers to trade. In 1995, the Geneva-based WTO was created to administer the rules and to assist in settling trade disputes between its member nations. All WTO nations are entitled to normal trade relations with one another. This is referred to as Most Favored Nation (MFN) trading status. This means that a member country must charge the same tariff on imported goods as, and not a higher one than, that charged on the same goods coming from other WTO member countries. Trade liberalization has led to increased economic development and an improved quality of life around the world.

Implementation of the Uruguay Round agreement is meant to further open markets by reducing tariffs worldwide by one-third; improve WTO procedures over unfair trade practices; broaden WTO coverage by including areas of trade in services, intellectual property rights, and trade-related investment that previously were not covered; and provide increased coverage to the areas of agriculture, textiles and clothing, government procurements, and trade and the environment.

The WTO launched a new round of negotiations in Doha, Qatar in 2001 to conclude in 2004 but collapsed in 2006 due to major differences between parties. The renewed negotiations were designed to lower trade barriers among poor nations and help them in exporting agricultural products and textiles and to improve labor-intensive industries. The goal was to integrate poor nations with rich nations into the global trading system.

Agreement for Market Access

The main contribution of the market access agreements would be to significantly lower, or eliminate, tariff and nontariff barriers and to expand the extent of tariff bindings, on industrial products among WTO signatories. The global economic impact of this agreement is substantial.

Provisions for Subsidies and Countervailing Duties

Subsidies essentially lower a producer's costs or increase its revenues. A subsidy is financial assistance provided to domestic or foreign producers by their respective governments in the form of cash payments, low-interest loans, tax-breaks, and price supports. Consequently, producers may sell their products at lower prices than their competitors from other countries. Subsidies to firms that produce or sell internationally traded products can distort international trade flows.

The United States has historically provided fewer industrial subsidies than most countries, and it has sought to eliminate trade-distorting subsidies provided by foreign governments.

Countervailing duty laws can address some of the adverse effects that subsidies can cause. Countervailing duties are special customs duties imposed to offset subsidies provided on the manufacture, protection, or export of a particular good.

The agreement would create for the first time three categories of subsidies and remedies: (1) prohibited subsidies (known as the "red-light" category); (2) actionable subsidies (known as the "yellow-light" category), and (3) nonactionable subsidies (known as the "green-light" category.

Prohibited subsidies include subsidies to encourage exports, including de facto export subsidies and subsidies contingent on the use of local content. **Actionable subsidies** are domestic subsidies against which remedies can be sought if they are shown to distort trade. **Nonactionable subsidies** include those that are not *specific* (i.e., not limited to an enterprise or industry or group of enterprises or industries). Subsidies also are nonactionable if they fall into three classes: (1) certain government assistance for research and precompetitive development activity, (2) certain government assistance for disadvantaged regions, and (3) certain government assistance to adapt existing plants and equipment to new environmental requirements.

Provision for Antidumping

Dumping is generally considered to be the sale of an exported product at a price lower than that charged for the same or a like product in the "home" market of the exporter. This practice is thought of as a form of price discrimination that can potentially harm the importing nation's competing industries.

Dumping may occur as a result of exporter business strategies that include: trying to increase an overseas market share, temporarily distributing products in overseas markets to offset slack demand in the home market, lowering unit costs by exploiting large-scale production, and attempting to maintain stable prices during periods of exchange rate fluctuations.

Provision for Safeguards

A **safeguard** is a temporary import control or other trade restriction a country imposes to prevent injury to domestic industry caused by increased imports. The new Safeguard Agreement would require that safeguard measures be limited to an eight-year period for developed countries and ten years for developing countries. It provides for suspending the automatic right to retaliate to a safeguard measure for the first three years. However, it would maintain the requirement that safeguards be applied on an MFN basis rather than being applied selectively (applied to just the country or countries causing injury to the domestic industry).

Agreement on Trade-Related Aspects of Intellectual Property Rights

The World Intellectual Property Organizations (WIPO), a UN specialized agency, is a world body whose mission is to promote the protection of intellectual property rights throughout the world through cooperation among countries and, where appropriate, in collaboration with international organizations and to ensure administrative cooperation among the intellectual property unions. WIPO administers a number of international agreements on intellectual property protection, including in particular the Berne Convention for the Protection of Literary and Artistic Works, which provides for copyright protection and the Paris Convention for the Protection of Industrial Property, which provides protection for patents, trademarks, and industrial designs and the repression of unfair competition.

Agreement on Trade in Services

Service industries dominate the U.S. economy and are important contributors to U.S. exports. The U.S. service industry is also the world's largest exporter of services. International trade in services takes place through various channels, including:

- Cross-border transactions, such as transmission of voice, video, data, or other information and the transportation of goods and passengers from one country to another
- Travel of individual consumers to another country (e.g., services provided to nonresident tourists, students, and medical patients)
- Sales of services (e.g., accounting, advertising, and insurance) through foreign branches or other affiliates established in the consuming country
- Travel of individual producers to another country (e.g., services provided to foreign clients by business consultants, engineers, lawyers, etc.)

The Uruguay Round meetings created the **General Agreement on Trade in Services (GATS)**, which is the first multilateral, legally enforceable agreement covering trade and investment in the services sector.

Agreement on Trade-Related Investment Measures

There is consensus among many, primarily developed, countries that foreign direct investment can have a favorable effect on a host country's economy.

The foreign direct investment can create jobs, increase tax revenues, and introduce new technologies. It also increases the host country wages and productivity and seems to have a net positive effect on the competitiveness of the host economy.

Agriculture Provisions of the Uruguay Round

The Uruguay Round represented the first time that WTO contracting parties undertook to substantially reform agricultural trade. The Punta del Este ministerial declaration recognized an urgent need to stabilize the world agriculture market and liberalize trade by reducing import barriers, disciplining the use of direct and indirect subsidies that affect trade, and minimizing the adverse effect of sanitary and phytosanitary regulations and barriers. The declaration recognized that other negotiating areas were likely to improve agricultural trade as well, such as efforts to strengthen the dispute-resolution process. The sanitary and phytosanitary regulations and barriers are measures taken to protect human, animal, or plant life or health.

North American Free Trade Agreement

The **North American Free Trade Agreement (NAFTA)**, which went into effect on January 1, 1994, was intended to facilitate trade and investment throughout North America (United States, Canada, and Mexico). It incorporates features such as the elimination of tariff and nontariff barriers. NAFTA also supports the objective of locking in Mexico's self-initiated, market-oriented reforms. By removing barriers to the efficient allocation of economic resources, NAFTA was projected to generate overall, long-term economic gains for member countries—modest for the United States and Canada and greater for Mexico. For the United States, this is due to the relatively small size of Mexico's economy and because many Mexican exports to the United States were already subject to low or no duties. Under NAFTA, intraindustry trade and coproduction of goods across the borders were expected to increase, enhancing specialization and raising productivity.

NAFTA also included procedures first to avoid and then to resolve disputes between parties to the agreement. Separately, the three NAFTA countries negotiated and entered into two supplemental agreements designed to facilitate cooperation on environment and labor matters among the three countries.

NAFTA will create the largest free trade zone in the world, with 360 million people and an annual gross national product totaling over six trillion dollars.

Major Provisions of NAFTA

Major provisions include "rules of origin"; import and export quotas and licenses; technical standards and certification; escape clauses; telecommunications networks; cross-border trade in services; antidumping and subsidy laws; cross-subsidization; investments; performance requirements; right to convert and transfer local currencies; disputes; intellectual property rights; due process; temporary entry visas; and the side agreements.

Impacts and Implementation of NAFTA

Assessment of NAFTA's effects is a complex undertaking because the provisions last 10 to 15 years. While NAFTA is not yet fully implemented, U.S. trade with NAFTA members has accelerated and is in accordance with pre-NAFTA expectations.

At the sector level, there are diverse impacts from NAFTA. Within sectors, these may include increases or decreases in trade flows, hourly earnings, and employment. Economic efficiency may improve from this reallocation of resources, but it creates costs for certain sectors of the economy and labor force, including job dislocation.

In general, NAFTA or broader trade policies cannot be expected to substantially alter overall U.S. employment levels, which are determined largely by demographic conditions and macroeconomic factors such as monetary policy.

European Union

The **European Union (EU)**, often called the **Common Market,** is a supranational legal regime with its own legislative, administrative, treaty-making, and judicial procedures. To create this regime, many European nations have surrendered substantial sovereignty to the EU. European Union law has replaced national law in many areas and the EU legal system operates as an umbrella over the legal systems of the member states. The EU law is vast and intricate. The EU is the largest market for exports from the United States.

The tasks of EU include creation of an economic and monetary union with emphasis on price stability with the goal of establishing a Europe "without internal frontiers."

The Council, the Commission, the Parliament, the Court of Justice

The Council consists of representatives of the ruling governments of the member states. The European Community Treaty requires the Council to act by a qualified majority on some matters and with unanimity on others.

The Commission is independent of the member states. Its 20 commissioners are selected by council appointment. They do not represent member states or take orders from member state governments. The Commission is charged with the duty of acting only in the best interests of the Union and serves as the guardian of the Treaties. The Commission largely maintains EU relations with the WTO. The Commission proposes and drafts EU legislation and submits to the Council for adoption.

The Parliament historically played an advisory role. The European Parliament has the power to put questions to the Commission and the Council concerning Union affairs. It also has the power, so far unused, to censure the Commission, in which event all the Commissioners are required to resign as a body. As a minimum, the Parliament has a right to be consulted and to give an "opinion" as part of the EU legislative process. The opinion is not binding on the Commission or Council.

The Court of Justice is to ensure that in the interpretation and application of the Treaty "the law" is observed. There are 15 Justices (one from each state) that make up the European Court of Justice. If a conflict arises between Union law and the domestic law of a member state, the Court of Justice has held that the former prevails. When there is no conflict, both Union law and domestic law can coexist.

Major Provisions of the European Union

The major provisions of the EU laws include free movement of goods, free movement of workers, free movement of capital, free movement of payments, establishment of a monetary system, a tax system, and trade rules with nonmember states.

Regional Groups

Many nations are contemplating or have already formed regional economic integration to capture the economic gains and international negotiating strength that regionalization can bring. The following list provides some regions or groups:

- Several groups have been formed in Africa, including UDEA, CEAO, and ECOWAS. The purpose is to establish a common customs and tariff approach toward the rest of the world and to formulate a common foreign investment trade.
- Regional groups have been established in Latin America and the Caribbean (CARICOM, CACM, LAFTA/LAIA). The Latin American Free Trade Association (LAFTA) had small success in reducing tariffs and developing the region through cooperative industrial sector programs. These programs allocated industrial production among the participating states. In 1994, some 37 nations signed the Association of Caribbean States agreement with long-term economic integration goals.
- Gulf Cooperations Council (GCC) was formed between Bahrain, Kuwait, Oman, Qatar, Saudi Arabia, and United Arab Emirates with objectives to establish freedom of movement, a regional armaments industry, common banking and financial systems, a unified currency policy, a customs union, a common foreign-aid program, and a joint, international investment company, the Gulf Investment Corporation. The GCC has already implemented trade and investment rules concerning tariffs on regional and imported goods, government contracts, communications, transportation, real estate investment, freedom of movement of professionals, and development of a Uniform Commercial Code. In 1987, the GCC entered into negotiations with the EU that resulted in a major 1990 trade and cooperation agreement.
- The Andean Common Market (ANCOM) was founded by Bolivia, Chile, Colombia, Ecuador, and Peru in 1969, primarily to counter the economic power of Argentina, Brazil, and Mexico and to reduce dependency on foreign capital. Later, Venezuela joined and Chile left the group. The ANCOM Commission has not been activist on behalf of regional integration like the EU Commission. It mostly reacts to proposals put forth by the Junta, the administrative arm of ANCOM.
- The Association of South East Asian Nations (ASEAN) was formed in 1967 by Indonesia, Malaysia, the Philippines, Singapore, and Thailand. Brunei joined in 1984, Vietnam in 1995. The Bangkok Declaration, establishing ASEAN as a cooperative association, is a broadly worded

document but has little supranational legal machinery to implement its stated goals.

- East Asian Integration, ranging from Japan in the north to Indonesia in the south, has formed Asia-Pacific Economic Cooperation (APEC), consisting of 18 Asian-Pacific nations including the United States. East Asia, unlike Europe, has not developed a formal Common Market with uniform trade, licensing, and investment rules. Late in 1994, the APEC nations targeted free trade and investment for developed countries by the year 2010 and developing countries by the year 2020.

❑ Learning Objective 10.5: UNDERSTAND THE VARIOUS ISSUES IN INTERNATIONAL FINANCIAL SYSTEMS

The main *purposes of international capital markets* are to provide an expanded supply of capital for borrowers, lower the cost of money (interest rates) for borrowers, and lower the risk for lenders. The reasons for growth in this market are due to advances in information technology, deregulation of capital markets, and innovation in financial instruments.

The main *elements of international capital markets* consist of bonds sold by issuers outside their own countries, stocks bought and sold outside the home country of the issuing company, and Eurocurrency banked outside their countries of origin due to lack of government regulation and its lower cost of borrowing.

A **foreign exchange market** exists because individuals and institutions have a need to convert one currency into another, investors can insure against adverse changes in exchange rates, speculators use it to predict an increase in the value of a currency, and investors use it to earn a profit from the instantaneous purchase and sale of a currency.

Financial instruments that exist to reduce exchange-rate risk include a **forward contract**, which requires the exchange of an agreed-on amount of a currency on an agreed-on date at a specific exchange rate; a **currency swap**, which is the simultaneous purchase and sale of foreign exchange for two different dates; a **currency option**, which is the right to exchange a specific amount of a currency on a specific date at a specific rate; and a **currency futures contract**, which requires the exchange of a specific amount of currency on a specific date at a specific

exchange rate. The currency futures contract is the same as the forward contract except for nonnegotiable terms.

World currencies are quoted in a number of different ways, such as an **exchange-rate quote** between currency A and currency B, expressed as (A/B), of 5/1, which means that it takes five units of currency A to buy one unit of currency B; a **cross-exchange rate**, which is a rate between two currencies by using their respective exchange rates with a common currency; a **spot exchange rate**, which requires delivery of the traded currency within two business days; and a **forward exchange rate**, where two parties agree to exchange currencies on a specified future date.

Exchange rates are determined using two concepts: (1) the **law of one price**, which applies to single products selling at identical price with the same content and quality in all countries, and (2) **purchasing power parity**, which applies to a basket of goods based on relative ability of two countries' currencies to buy the same basket of goods in those two countries.

Exchange rates affect the demand for global products in various ways:

- When a country's currency is weak relative to other currencies, the prices of its exports decline, and the prices of its imports increase. Lower prices on exports make the demand for exports increase. Higher prices on imports make the demand for imports decrease.
- When a country's currency is strong relative to other currencies, the prices of its exports increase, and the prices of its imports decrease. Higher prices on exports make the demand for exports decrease. Lower prices on imports make the demand for imports increase.
- A country that is experiencing inflation higher than that of another country should see the relative value of its currency fall, leading to devaluation. **Devaluation** is the intentional decrease of the value of a currency, which decreases the price of exports and increases the price of imports.
- A country that is experiencing inflation lower than that of another country should see the relative value of its currency rise, leading to revaluation. **Revaluation** is the intentional increase of the value of a currency, which increases the price of exports and decreases the price of imports.
- Interest rates affect inflation because the former affects the cost of borrowing money. Low interest

rates encourage more debt, cause more spending, and create inflation. High interest rates discourage debt, cause low spending, and do not create inflation.

Because real interest rates do not consider inflation and hence are equal across countries, any difference in the exchange rates of two countries must be due to different inflation rates.

❏ Learning Objective 10.6: UNDERSTAND HOW TO STAFF AND MANAGE INTERNATIONAL OPERATIONS

The scope of **international production (operations) strategies** includes conducting capacity-planning studies to produce output satisfying demand; performing facilities-location planning for identifying optimal locations after considering the cost–benefit analysis; determining the location of operations decisions, whether it is centralized or decentralized; deciding on production-process planning, whether it is making standardized or customized products; performing facility-layout planning to locate machines, materials, and departments; conducting quality planning to comply with total quality management (TQM) principles and international standards organization (ISO) 9000 supplier certification standards; and making invest-reinvest-divest decisions in manufacturing, retail, office, and warehouse facilities after considering political, legal, economic, and social risks in the host country.

The scope of **international acquisition of materials** includes evaluating make-or-buy decisions for raw materials, parts, and components; making insourcing and outsourcing decisions for raw materials, parts, and components; deciding on quantity and quality of raw materials acquired either from local or outside sources; and making fixed-asset decisions in acquiring plant, property, and equipment from either local or outside sources.

The scope of **international logistics** includes shipping costs by air, sea, or ground to transport raw materials and finished goods in and out of the host country; and keeping inventories at a minimum level using just-in-time (JIT) philosophy in manufacturing.

The scope of **international staffing policies** includes deciding who fits best to the job at hand. These staffing policies should be aligned with the MNC models of organizational structures.

An **ethnocentric staffing policy** states that the home-country nationals should be employed in international operations in the host country.

A **polycentric staffing policy** states that the host-country nationals should be employed in international operations in the host country.

A **geocentric staffing policy** states that the best-qualified individuals worldwide should be employed in the international operations in the host country. This policy usually applies to senior-level managers, who may come from the home country, from the host country, or from a third country.

Culture in a home country could be different from the culture in a host country and vice versa. **Cultural training** helps to cope with culture shock for departing managers and reverse culture shock for returning managers. The ability to adapt to cultural differences is needed in all departing managers.

An effective compensation policy should take into account of local cultures, laws, and practices. Base pay, bonus payments, fringe benefits, cost-of-living adjustments, and cost-of-education adjustments all must be considered.

Most of **labor–management relations** are the same between the home country and the host country, except for cultural differences and political influences in the host country.

❏ Learning Objective 10.7: UNDERSTAND THE VARIOUS ISSUES IN CONDUCTING INTERNATIONAL BUSINESS IN CROSS CULTURES

Culture provides people with identity. Harris summarized characteristics of culture into ten categories: (1) sense of self and space, (2) communication and language, (3) dress and appearance, (4) food and feeding habits, (5) time consciousness, (6) relationships, (7) values and norms, (8) beliefs and attitudes, (9) mental process and learning, and (10) work habits and practices (Harris and Moran 1991).

Corporate culture affects how an organization copes with competition and change, whether in terms of technology, economics, or people. The work culture stimulates or constricts the energies of personnel, whether through slogans and myths or taboos. Now management is more cognizant of its customs and traditions, rules and regulations, policies and procedures—such components of culture are being used to make work more enjoyable, to increase productivity, and to meet customer needs and competitive challenges.

Effects of Cultures

Persons of dissimilar backgrounds usually require more time than those of the same culture to become familiar with each other, to be willing to speak openly, to share sufficiently in common ideas, and to understand one another.

Therefore, education and training of global leaders must include formal learning in the various cultural dimensions. With globalization of business, managers and leaders need to become more transnational and transcultural in their thinking, planning, and involvement with people.

Differences in customs, behavior, and values result in problems that can be managed only through effective cross-cultural communication and interaction. When people have misunderstandings or commit "errors" when working with persons from different cultures, they are often unaware of any problem. Cross-cultural mistakes result when we fail to recognize that persons of other cultural backgrounds have different goals, customs, thought patterns, and values than our own. Differences do not necessarily mean barriers; they can become bridges to understanding and enrichment of human lives.

Global Manager's Dilemma

Global managers operating transnationally are commonly faced with the following situation: in one country something is a lawful or accepted practice, and elsewhere it is illegal. Bribes, for example, may be a common way of doing business to ensure service in the host-country culture but are quite illegal in the home-country culture.

Advances in mass media, transportation, and travel are breaking down the traditional barriers among groups of peoples and their differing cultures so that a homogenization process is underway. Global managers should be alert to serving this new community in human needs and markets with strategies that are transnational.

Global planning not only requires an effective international management information system but input from a variety of locals at different levels of sophistication. Even when there are apparent similarities of peoples in geographic regions, cultural differences may require alteration of strategic market planning.

Regional Cultures

Even in the United States, there are cultural differences between the south and the north and between the east and the west regions. Food habits, language, accent, pace of life, work attitudes, and values are different. Culture affects decision making too.

Global Communication Insights

All behavior is communication because all behavior contains a message, whether intended or not. Communication is not static and passive, but rather it is a continuous and active process without beginning or end. A communicator is not simply a sender or a receiver of messages but can be both at the same time. Culture poses communication problems because there are so many variables unknown to the communicators. *As the cultural variables and differences increase, the number of communication misunderstandings increases.*

High- and Low-Context Communications

Anthropologist Edward Hall makes a vital distinction between high- and low-context cultures and how this matter of context impacts communications. A **high-context culture** uses high-context communications—that is, information is either in the physical context or internalized in the person. Japan, Saudi Arabia, and Africa are examples of cultures engaged in high-context communications, as are the Chinese and Spanish languages. However, a **low-context culture** employs low-context communications—most information is contained in explicit codes, such as words. North American cultures engage in low-context communications, whether in Canada or the United States, and English is a low-context language (Hall 1990).

In the communication process, a low-context culture places the meaning in the exact verbal description of an event. Individuals in such a culture rely on the spoken word. The common statement that typifies this idea is, "Say what you mean." However, in the high-context culture, much of the meaning is not from the words but is internalized in the person. Meaning comes from the environment and is looked for in the relationships between the ideas expressed in the communication process. *High-context cultures tend to be more human-oriented than low-context cultures. The extended-family concept fits into the high-context culture.*

During negotiations or when working with Japanese or Latin Americans, they are looking for meaning and understanding in what is *not* said—in the nonverbal communication or body language, in the silences and pauses, in relationships and empathy. North Americans place emphasis on sending and receiving accurate messages directly, usually by being articulate with words. Specifically, Japanese communicate by not stating things directly, while Americans usually do just the opposite and "spell it all out."

Cultural Awareness Learning Program

The aim of the Canadian International Development Agency's training program is to instill seven skills that could be offered as the objectives of all cultural awareness learning. These skills can be applied to understand people, whether they are local, regional, or international:

1. Communicate respect.
2. Be nonjudgmental.
3. Personalize knowledge and perceptions.
4. Display empathy.
5. Practice role flexibility.
6. Demonstrate reciprocal concern.
7. Tolerate ambiguity.

These seven skills are associated with effective managing and transferring of knowledge in a different culture. The degree to which managers and auditors possess these skills marks their potential effectiveness in working in a multicultural environment.

Cross-Cultural Negotiations

Negotiating across cultures is far more complex than negotiating within a culture because foreign negotiators have to deal with differing negotiating styles and cultural variables simultaneously. In other words, the negotiating styles that work at home generally do not work in other cultures. As a result, cross-cultural business negotiators have one of the most complicated business roles to play in organizations. They are often thrust into a foreign society consisting of what appears to be "hostile" strangers. They are put in the position of negotiating profitable business relationships with these people or suffering the negative consequences of failure. And quite often they find themselves at a loss as to why their best efforts and intentions have failed them.

How to Avoid Failure in International Negotiations

Negotiators in a foreign country often fail because the local counterparts have taken more time to learn how to overcome the obstacles normally associated with international/cross-cultural negotiations. Failure may occur because of time and/or cost constraints. For example, a negotiator may be given a much shorter period of time to obtain better contract terms than was originally agreed to in a country where negotiations typically take a long time. A negotiator may think, "What works in the home country is good enough for the rest of the world," but this is far from the truth. In fact, strategies that fail to take into account cultural factors are usually naive or misconceived. Typically, the obstacles to overcome include:

- Learning the local language
- Learning the local culture
- Arriving well-prepared for the negotiations

How Much Must One Know about the Foreign Culture?

Realistically, it is nearly impossible to learn everything about another culture, although one might come close if one lives in the culture for several years. The reason for this is that each culture has developed, over time, multifaceted structures that are much too complex for any foreigner to understand totally. Therefore, foreign negotiators need not have total awareness of the foreign culture; they do not need to know as much about the foreign culture as the locals, whose frames of reference were shaped by that culture. However, they will need to know enough about the culture and about the locals' negotiating styles to avoid being uncomfortable during (and after) negotiations. Besides knowing enough to not fail, they also need to know enough to win. For example, in negotiations between Japanese and American businesspeople, Japanese negotiators have sometimes used their knowledge that Americans have a low tolerance for silence to their advantage.

In other words, in order for negotiation to take place, the foreigner must at least recognize those ideas and behaviors that the locals intentionally put forward as part of the negotiation process—and the locals must do the same for the foreigners. Both sides must be capable of interpreting these behaviors sufficiently to distinguish common from conflicting positions, to spot movement from positions, and to respond in ways that sustain communication. Ultimately, cross-cultural negotiators must determine their counterparts' personal motivations and agendas and adapt the negotiation style to them.

The purpose of the previous discussion is to develop a cross-cultural negotiating process. The process includes both strategy and tactics. Strategy refers to a long-term plan, and tactics refers to the actual means used to implement the strategy.

Strategic and Tactical Planning for International Negotiations

Strategic planning for international negotiations involves several stages: (1) preparation for face-to-face negotiations, (2) determining settlement range, (3) determining where the negotiations should take place, (4) deciding whether to use an individual or a group of individuals in the negotiations, and (5) learning about the country's views on agreements/contracts.

Tactical planning for international negotiations involves determining how to obtain leverage, use delay tactics, and deal with emotions.

Ethical Constraints

Business ethics and corporate social responsibility place constraints on negotiators. For example, a negotiator's ethical concerns for honesty and fair dealings, regardless of the power status of negotiating parties, will affect the outcome. There is no global standard or view of what is ethical or unethical behavior in business transactions—what is viewed as unethical behavior in one culture may be viewed as ethical in another culture and vice versa. For instance, if a negotiator on one side "pays off" an influential decision maker on the other side to obtain a favorable decision, it would be an unethical business practice in some cultures (and illegal in the United States), but it would be quite acceptable in other cultures.

Global Mindsets

Cultural forces represent another important concern affecting international human resources (HR) management. In addition to organizational culture, national cultures also exist. Culture is composed of the societal forces affecting the values, beliefs, and actions of a distinct group of people. Cultural differences certainly exist between nations, but sig-

nificant cultural differences exist within countries also. One only has to look at the conflicts caused by religion or ethnicity in Central Europe and other parts of the world to see the importance of culture in international organizations. Convincing individuals from different ethnic or tribal backgrounds to work together may be difficult in some parts of the world.

Geert Hofstede conducted research on more than 100,000 IBM employees in 53 countries, and he defined five dimensions useful in identifying and comparing culture. These dimensions include power distance, individualism, masculinity/femininity, uncertainty avoidance, and long-term orientation (Hofstede 1984).

The dimension of **power distance** refers to the inequality among the people of a nation. In countries such as Canada, the Netherlands, and the United States, there is less inequality than in such countries as France, Mexico, and Brazil. As power distance scores increase, there is less status and authority difference between superiors and subordinates.

One way in which differences on this dimension affect HR activities is that the reactions to management authority differ among cultures. A more autocratic approach to managing is more common in many countries, while in the Netherlands and the United States there may be more use of employee participation in decision making.

Another dimension of culture identified by Hofstede is **individualism,** which is the extent to which people in a country prefer to act as individuals instead of members of groups. On this dimension, people in some Asian countries tend to be less individualistic and more group-oriented, whereas those in the United States are more individualistic. An implication of these differences is that more collective action and less individual competition is likely in those countries that deemphasize individualism.

The cultural dimension **masculinity/femininity** refers to the degree to which "masculine" values prevail over "feminine" values. **Masculine values** identified by Hofstede were assertiveness, performance orientation, success, and competitiveness, whereas **feminine values** included quality of life, close personal relationships, and caring. Respondents from Japan had the most masculinity, while those from the Netherlands had more feminine-oriented values. Differences on this dimension may be tied to the role of women in the culture. Considering the different roles of women and what is "acceptable" for women in the United States, Saudi Arabia, Japan, and Mexico suggests how this dimension might affect the assignment of women expatriates to managerial jobs in the various countries.

The dimension of **uncertainty avoidance** refers to the preference of people in a country for structured rather than unstructured situations. A structured situation is one in which rules can be established, and there are clear guides on how people are expected to act. Nations focusing on avoiding uncertainty, such as Japan and France, tend to be more resistant to change. In contrast, people in places such as the United States and Great Britain tend to have more "business energy" and to be more flexible.

A logical use of differences in this factor is to anticipate how people in different countries will react to changes instituted in organizations. In more flexible cultures, what is less certain may be more intriguing and challenging, which may lead to greater entrepreneurship and risk taking than in the more "rigid" countries.

The dimension of **long-term orientation** refers to values people hold that emphasize the future, as opposed to short-term values, which focus on the present and the past. Long-term values include thrift and persistence, whereas short-term values include respecting tradition and fulfilling social obligations. Hofstede developed this dimension a decade after his original studies on dimension. A long-term orientation was more present in Japan and India, while people in the United States and France tended to have more short-term orientations.

Differences in many other facets of culture could be discussed. But it is enough to recognize that international HR managers and professionals must recognize that cultural dimensions differ from country to country and even within countries. Therefore, the HR activities appropriate in one culture or country may have to be altered to fit appropriately into another culture or country.

 Self-Assessment Exercise

Online exercises are provided for the learning objectives in this module. Please visit www.mbaiq.com to complete the online exercises and to calculate your MBA IQ Score.

Project Management

Learning Objective 11.1: Define Project Management and Identify Success Criteria for Projects 287
Project Management Defined 287
Project Success Criteria 288

Learning Objective 11.2: Understand the Various Types of Risks in Project Management 289
Types of Project Risks 289
Risk Management Plan 291

Learning Objective 11.3: Understand the Various Types of Project Structures and Organizations 291
Functional-Type Organization 292
Project-Type Organization 293
Matrix-Type Organization 293
Advantages and Disadvantages
of Project Structures 294

Learning Objective 11.4: Understand the Project Management Process, Including Its Lifecycles 294
The Project Management Process 294

Learning Objective 11.5: Understand the Various Methods in Project

Planning, Estimating, Controlling, and Reporting 296
Project Planning Methods 297
Project Estimating Methods 298
Project Controlling Methods 300
Project Reporting Methods 301
Project Progress 302

Learning Objective 11.6: Understand the Various Methods in Project Scheduling 303
Program Evaluation and Review Technique 303
Critical Path Method 303
CPM versus PERT 304
Work-Breakdown Structure 306
Gantt Chart 306

Learning Objective 11.7: Understand the Project Management Metrics, Problems, and Governance Mechanisms, Including Project Audits 306
Project Management Metrics 307
Problems in Project Management 308
Project Governance Mechanisms 309
Project Management Audit 309

❑ Learning Objective 11.1: DEFINE PROJECT MANAGEMENT AND IDENTIFY SUCCESS CRITERIA FOR PROJECTS

Many projects fail for various reasons—some valid and some invalid. It is important for a project manager to understand what makes a project a success.

The ultimate benefit of implementing project management techniques is having a *satisfied customer*. Usually, a contractor is hired by a customer to perform a project. Completing the full project scope in a quality manner, on time, and within budget provides a great feeling of satisfaction. For a contractor, it could lead to additional business from the same customer or from new customers referred by previously satisfied customers.

Project Management Defined

A **project** is the result of a plan of action to achieve a specific goal within defined resource parameters (e.g., time, cost, materials, quality, and people). Projects must be well managed for them to be successful in utilizing resources. Many organizations apply a variety of project management techniques to optimize project success and enhance the likelihood of meeting project-specific as well as organization-wide goals. These techniques include monitoring project performance, establishing incentives to meet project goals, and developing a project management team with the right people and the right skills. This can help avert cost overruns, schedule delays, and performance problems common to many organizations.

It is important to develop **performance measures** and link project outcomes to business unit and strategic goals and objectives. The key is monitoring project performance and establishing incentives for accountability and using cross-functional teams to involve those with the technical and operational expertise necessary to plan and manage the project.

Project Success Criteria

A **baseline** establishes a standard to decide whether a project is a success or failure. The criteria should be derived from standards.

Baseline

The key in determining the success or failure of a project, program, or function is establishing its current state before any changes are considered or implemented. This is the baseline. The baseline is used in a variety of areas. Gap analysis, for example, uses the baseline to show the difference between the current state and the target goal or objective.

Performance measures, regardless of type, must have a baseline measurement to show the changes or improvements a project undergoes as it achieves its goal. Establishing a baseline measure is essential in establishing the validity of a performance measure. A baseline measure is usually the first measure taken of a system or project. Subsequent measurements may be defined as the new baseline if substantial changes to the system make the earlier baseline obsolete or reduce the effectiveness of the particular performance measure.

Each project manager and functional area manager must choose those performance measures that clearly indicate achievement of goals and mission for their area of responsibility. Some examples of performance measures include customer satisfaction, speed of response, quality, percentage of availability, mean-time-between-failure (MTBF), and percentage of initial budget expended.

An initial baseline document is prepared once as part of the project planning process. This identifies milestones, costs, and schedules that are planned for each project for the next fiscal year. While it is understood that milestones sometimes do run over fiscal years, for accurate reporting purposes, a milestone should be broken up to explain what is being accomplished by fiscal year. After developing the initial baseline, the baseline data should be updated periodically, say monthly or quarterly.

The initial baseline data include project description with milestones, planned start date, planned end date, planned duration hours, and planned cost. The updated baseline data include actual start date, actual end date, actual duration in hours, percent complete, and actual cost.

Project Critical Success Factors

The outcome of any project can be either a success or a failure. There are certain factors leading to success; and not following these success factors can lead to failure. Below are critical success factors useful to project managers, functional managers, and senior managers alike:

- Planning and communication are critical to successful project management. They prevent problems from occurring or minimize their impact on the achievement of the project objective when they do occur.
- Taking the time to develop a well-thought-out plan before the start of the project is critical to the successful accomplishment of any project.
- A project must have a well-defined objective—an expected result or product, defined in terms of scope, schedule, and cost, and agreed on by the customer.
- Involve the customer as a partner in the successful outcome of the project through active participation during the project.
- Effective and frequent personal communication is crucial to successful project management.
- A high degree of face-to-face communication is important early in the project to foster team building, develop good working relationships, and establish mutual expectations.
- Body language and customs reflective of cultural diversity must be considered in communications.
- Be careful not to use remarks, words, or phrases that can be construed to be sexist, racist, prejudicial, or offensive.
- The heart of communication is understanding—not only to be understood, but also to understand. Half of making communication effective is

listening. Failure to listen can cause a breakdown in communication.

- Communication should be straightforward, unambiguous, free of technical jargon, and not offensive.
- Achieving customer satisfaction requires ongoing communication with the customer to keep the customer informed and to determine whether expectations have changed. Regularly ask the customer about the level of satisfaction with the progress of the project.
- Keep the customer and project team informed of the project status and potential problems in a timely manner.
- Project status meetings should be held on a regular basis. Discuss meeting guidelines at a project team meeting at the beginning of the project, so everyone understands what behavior is expected during project meetings.
- Do not confuse busyness and activity with accomplishment when communicating project progress.
- The key to effective project control is measuring actual progress and comparing it to planned progress on a timely and regular basis and taking corrective action immediately, if necessary.
- Reports must be written to address what is of interest to the readers, not what is of interest to the person writing the report.
- Make reports concise. Pay as much attention to format, organization, appearance, and readability as to the content.
- Early in the project, agreement should be reached regarding how changes will be authorized and documented.
- When documents are updated, they should immediately be distributed to all team members whose work will be affected.
- After the conclusion of a project, performance should be evaluated to learn what could be improved if a similar project were to be undertaken in the future. Feedback should be obtained from the customer and the project team.

❏ Learning Objective 11.2: UNDERSTAND THE VARIOUS TYPES OF RISKS IN PROJECT MANAGEMENT

There are several risks facing a project due to cost, time, quality, and performance uncertainties. Risk mitigation strategies can be developed to reduce or minimize project risks.

Types of Project Risks

Having a strategy to deal with the risk that is inherent in large projects, say IT projects, is critical. One of the greatest risk factors to the success of IT projects is the amount of development that is planned. Full-scale development is where the potential is greater for significant cost and schedule overruns and lowered performance goals. In a project environment, cost, benefit, and schedule estimates are typically uncertain.

The types of risks in an IT project, along with risk mitigation strategies, include the following.

Technology Risk

Technology risk is considered as the risk that a product or service may not meet its intended objectives to be able to interface with current processes or software correctly. This form of risk can include both technical feasibility and technical obsolescence. Risk mitigation strategies can include: maximum use of commercial software, practicing open competition, and performing pilot or prototype testing.

A risk exists when these technology risk items are not in place:

- Plan for validating that user needs are met
- Existence of load test in accordance with industry standards
- Evaluation of technology options
- Availability of track record for system
- Maintainability and ability to upgrade key technologies
- Vendor's ability to implement technology

Implementation and Operational Risk

Implementation and operational risk deals with time constraints. This form of risk includes both the amount of time necessary to complete the task and the compatibility between computing platforms. Another risk is whether the project becomes operational in nature. Risk mitigation strategies can include phased implementation, cross-organization involvement, and proven integrated management team.

A risk exists when these operational risk items are not in place:

- Organization's familiarity with proposed hardware and software environment
- Development of system operating procedures

- Experience and ability of existing staff to support a new system
- Impact to organization of a system failure
- Number of business units impacted

Project Management Risk

Project management risk speaks directly to management risk. This human element is difficult to accurately incorporate into a risk assessment but is a critical factor nonetheless. Risk mitigation strategies can include cost estimates prepared by a neutral third party, use of earned value management (EVM) techniques, use of open competition, use of financial incentives for contractor performance, distributing risk between the contractor and the organization, and implementing a sound acquisition plan using modular contracting.

A risk exists when these project management risk items are not in place:

- Experience levels of project management teams
- Number of training days for each team member
- Existence of work plan for the entire project lifecycle
- Degree of development of measurable milestones
- Length of time allowed for project implementation
- Existence of system for tracking unresolved issues
- Definition of user and system development skill requirements
- Number of project milestone reviews

Economic and Financial Risks

Economic risk encompasses such events as miscalculating a discount factor or failing to appropriately quantify other risks such as technology risk. **Financial risk** becomes an issue if budgeted dollars are not available when they are scheduled to be.

A risk exists when these financial risk items are not in place:

- Size of expenditure required
- Existence of cost–benefit analysis
- Existence of defined payback and timeframe of payback
- Reputation and financial status of vendor(s)

Strategic Risk

Strategic risk determines how closely a project is linked with its mission and risks. It is important to be comprehensive and include all risk sources regardless of frequency, probability of occurrence, or magnitude of gain or loss. Risk mitigation strategies can include cross-department or cross-organization efforts, project goals mapped directly to organizational strategic plans, and consistent execution of plans.

A risk exists when these strategic risk items are not in place:

- Alignment with the organization's overall business strategy
- Clarity of expression of anticipated project outcomes
- Presence of metrics to verify the successful completion of each project phase
- Number of or percent of stakeholder participation in projects

Change Management Risk

Change management risk attempts to estimate how easily pilots and prototypes could be incorporated into existing systems. This type of risk also addresses how severely a business would potentially be impacted by a system failure. Risk mitigation strategies can include employee involvement in the project planning process, training and implementation schedules, incentives to use the new system, management leadership, phased implementation, responsive support functions, and outreach communication plan.

A risk exists when these change management risk items are not in place:

- Development of an acceptance plan for new system
- Magnitude and nature of change introduced by system
- Institutionalizing the change risk

Human Capital Risk

Human capital risk results from users' lack of experience with a given technology (i.e., first data warehouse project and first system implementation project).

Dependency Risk

Dependency risk deals with risks between a new project and other projects.

Cost and Schedule Risk

Cost and schedule risk deals with risks where actual cost is more than the budgeted cost and where the actual schedule is longer than the budgeted schedule.

Privacy and Security Risks

Privacy and security risks deal with disclosing sensitive information to unauthorized individuals and unauthorized individuals accessing computer data and information, respectively. Risk mitigation strategies for privacy risk can include authentication method, controlled-access channels and authorization policies, firewalls, and use of secure electronic delivery channels. Risk mitigation strategies for security risk include security plan, consistency with standards, authentication method matching the risk level, and use of secure electronic delivery channels. Risk mitigation strategies for related data and information include use of a data warehouse concept, implementing a backup plan, performing process mapping, and leveraging data-collection efforts.

A risk exists when these security risk items are not in place:

- Performance of risk assessment
- Implementation of security controls
- Security training and awareness
- Contingency planning and disaster recovery
- Compliance with security policy

Risk Management Plan

A risk management plan should be developed that includes information on the types, probability, and impact of risks pertinent to the IT project. This plan should also include the risk that the funding request will not be approved or not approved in its entirety and plans for how to treat and manage the risk, including how to respond to lower funding.

Furthermore, risk can be accommodated by requesting a higher return for projects determined to be of higher risk. Also, risk analysis estimates of the probability that an IT investment project will fail and the impact this would have on the business can be subtracted from the expected benefits to adjust the return on investment (ROI) or net present value (NPV) calculations to reflect risk.

Sophisticated risk assessment methodologies such as probabilistic simulation can be used to estimate ranges for total annual cash flows and other key variables. Probability distributions can then be assigned to the outcomes for each of the variables.

An Example of a Risk Scale and Risk-Adjusted Cost and Value

An organization has established the following risk scale consisting of risk levels (High, Medium, and Low) and associated probabilities along with cost and benefit (value) impacts for the risk factor "failure to maintain project schedule."

Risk Level	Probability	Cost Impact	Benefit Impact
High	50%	25%	–25%
Medium	30%	15%	–15%
Low	25%	5%	–5%

Note that cost impacts and benefit impacts have opposite signs because the cost impact causes the costs to increase and the benefit impact causes the benefits to decrease. Management has estimated the expected cost to be $10,000 with medium probability and high cost impact. It has also estimated the expected value score as 90 with medium probability and medium benefit impact.

Question: What is the risk-adjusted cost and value?

Answer:

$$\text{Probability} \times \text{Impact} \times \text{Expected Cost/Value} = \text{Change Due to Risk}$$

Item	Probability	Impact	Expected Cost/Value	Change Due to Risk
Cost	30%	25%	$10,000	$750
Value	30%	–15%	90	–4.0

Risk-Adjusted Cost = $10,000 + $750 = $10,750

Risk-Adjusted Value = 90.0 – 4.0 = 86.0

❑ Learning Objective 11.3: UNDERSTAND THE VARIOUS TYPES OF PROJECT STRUCTURES AND ORGANIZATIONS

Project structure is a characteristic of all projects that provides for all work being performed in some well-defined order. For example, in research and development and product planning, specifications must be determined before drawings can be made. In advertising, artwork must be made before layouts can be done. **Project organization** is where the reporting relationships and the work location rest predominantly with the project manager. Although there are various ways in which people can be organized to work on projects, the most common types of organization structures are functional, project, and matrix. Each type is discussed next.

Functional-Type Organization

Functional organization structures are typically used in businesses that primarily sell and produce standard products and seldom conduct external projects. For example, a company that manufactures and sells video recorders and players may have a functional organization structure. In the functional organization structure, groups consist of individuals who perform the same function, such as engineering or manufacturing, or have the same expertise or skills, such as electronics engineering or testing. Each functional group, or component, concentrates on performing its own activities in support of the company's business mission. The focus is on the technical excellence and cost competitiveness of the company's products, as well as the importance of the contribution of each functional component's expertise to the company's products.

A company with a functional structure may periodically undertake projects, but these are typically in-house projects rather than projects for external customers. Projects in a functional-type organization might involve developing new products, designing a company information system, redesigning the office floor plan, or updating company policy and procedures manual. For such projects, a **multifunctional project team** or **task force** is formed, with members selected by company management from the appropriate subfunctions in marketing, engineering, manufacturing, and procurement. Team members may be assigned to the project either full-time or part-time, for a part of the project or for the entire project duration. In most cases, however, individuals continue to perform their regular functional jobs while they serve part-time on the project task force. One of the team members or possibly one of the functional vice presidents is designated as the project leader or manager.

In a functional-type organization, the project manager does not have complete authority over the project team, since administratively the members still work for their respective functional managers. Because they view their contribution to the project in terms of their technical expertise, their allegiance remains to their functional managers. If there is conflict among the team members, it usually works its way through the organization hierarchy to be resolved, slowing down the project effort. On the other hand, if the company president does give the project manager the authority to make decisions when there is disagreement among team members, decisions might reflect the interests of the project manager's own functional component rather than the best interests of the overall project. For example, take the situation in which there is disagreement about the design of a new product, and the project manager, who is from the engineering function, makes a decision that reduces the engineering design cost of the product but increases the manufacturing cost. In reporting project progress to the company president, the project manager then makes some biased comments regarding the viewpoints of team members from other functional components, such as, "If manufacturing were more willing to consider other production methods, they could make the product for a lower cost. Engineering has already reduced its design costs." Such a situation could require the company president to get drawn into handling the conflict.

The functional organization structure can be appropriate for internal company projects. However, since projects are not a part of the normal routine, it is necessary to establish a clear understanding of the role and responsibilities of each person assigned to the project task force. If the project manager does not have full authority for project decisions, then he must rely on leadership and persuasion skills to build consensus, handle conflict, and unify the task force members to accomplish the project objective. The project manager also needs to take time to regularly update other functional managers in the company on the project status and thank them for the support of their people assigned to the task force.

There may be situations in which a task force is assigned to work on a project that is strictly within a particular functional component. For example, the manager of technical documentation may form a task force of editors and documentation specialists to develop common standards for all technical documents. In such a case, the particular functional manager has full authority over the project, and conflict can be handled more quickly than when it arises within a multifunctional project team.

Companies with functional organization structures seldom perform projects involving external customers, as such organizations do not have project managers designated to manage customer-funded projects. Rather, functional-type organizations concentrate on producing their products and selling them to various customers.

Project-Type Organization

In the project-type organization, each project is operated like a mini-company. All the resources needed to accomplish each project are assigned full-time to work on that project. A full-time project manager has complete project and administrative authority over the project team. (In the functional-type organization, the project manager may have project authority, but the functional manager retains administrative and technical authority over his people who are assigned to the team.) The project-type organization is well positioned to be highly responsive to the project objective and customer needs because each project team is strictly dedicated to only one project.

A project-type organization can be cost-inefficient both for individual projects and for the company. Each project must pay the salaries of its dedicated project team, even during parts of the project when they are not busy. For example, if a delay in one part of the project leaves some resources with no work to do for several weeks, project funds must cover these costs. If the amount of unapplied time becomes excessive, the project can become unprofitable and drain the profits from other projects. From a company-wide viewpoint, a project-type organization can be cost-inefficient because of the duplication of resources or tasks on several concurrent projects.

Because resources are not shared, they may not be diverted to a similar concurrent project even when they are not busy on or being used for the project to which they are dedicated. Also, there is little opportunity for members of different project teams to share knowledge or technical expertise, since each project team tends to be isolated and focused strictly on its own project. However, there may be some company-wide support functions that serve all the projects such as the human resources function serves all projects.

In a project-type organization, detailed and accurate planning and an effective control system are required to assure optimum utilization of the project resources in successfully completing the project within budget.

Project organization structures are found primarily in companies that are involved in very large projects. Such projects can be of high (multimillion) dollar value and long (several years) duration. Project organization structures are prevalent in construction and aerospace industries. They are also used in the non-business environment, such as a volunteer-managed fundraising campaign, town centennial celebration, class reunion, or variety show.

Matrix-Type Organization

The matrix-type organization is a hybrid (a mix of both the functional and project organization structures). It provides the project and customer focus of the project structure, but it retains the functional expertise of the functional structure. The project and functional components of the matrix structure each have their responsibilities in contributing jointly to the success of each project and the company. The project manager is responsible for project results, while functional managers are responsible for providing resources needed to achieve the results.

The matrix-type organization provides for effective utilization of company resources. The functional components (systems engineering, testing, and so forth), home of the technical staff, provide a pool of expertise to support ongoing projects.

Project managers come under the project component of the organization. When the company receives an order for a new system, the vice president of projects assigns a project manager to the project. A small project may be assigned to a project manager, who is already managing several other small projects. A large project may be assigned a full-time project manager.

The matrix-type organization provides opportunities for people in the functional components to pursue career development through assignment to various types of projects. As they broaden their experience, individuals become more valuable for future assignments and enhance their eligibility for higher-level positions within the company. As each individual in a particular functional component develops a broad base of experience, the functional manager gains greater flexibility to assign individuals to different kinds of projects.

All of the individuals assigned to a given project comprise the project team, under the leadership of a project manager who integrates and unifies their efforts. Individuals assigned to several small projects will be members of several different project teams.

Each member of a project team has a dual reporting relationship; in a sense, each member has two managers: a (temporary) project manager and a (permanent) functional manager. For a person assigned to several concurrent projects, changing work priorities can cause conflict and anxiety.

It is critical to specify to whom the team member reports and for what responsibilities or tasks. Therefore, it is important that project management responsibilities and functional management responsibilities be delineated in a matrix-type organization.

In the matrix organization structure, the **project manager** is the intermediary between the company and the customer. The project manager defines what has to be done (work scope), by when (schedule), and for how much money (budget) to meet the project objective and satisfy the customer. He is responsible for leading the development of the project plan, establishing the project schedule and budget, and allocating specific tasks and budgets to the various functional components of the company organization. Throughout the project, the project manager is responsible both for controlling the performance of the work within the project schedule and budget and for reporting project performance to the customer and to the company's upper management. A project administrator may be assigned to each project to support the project manager and project team in planning, controlling, and reporting.

Each functional manager in a matrix organization structure is responsible for how the assigned work tasks will be accomplished and who (which specific people) will do each task. The functional manager of each organization component provides technical guidance and leadership to the individuals assigned to projects. He is also responsible for ensuring that all tasks assigned to that functional component are completed in accordance with the project's technical requirements, within the assigned budget, and on schedule.

The matrix-type organization provides a checks-and-balances environment. The fact that potential problems can be identified through both its project and its functional structure reduces the likelihood that problems will be suppressed beyond the point where they can be corrected without jeopardizing the success of the project. The matrix organization structure allows for fast response upon problem identification because it has both a horizontal (project) and a vertical (functional) path for the flow of information.

Advantages and Disadvantages of Project Structures

We discussed the characteristics of the functional-, project-, and matrix-type organizations. The following table lists some significant advantages and disadvantages particular to each of the three organization structures:

Project Structure	Advantages	Disadvantages
Functional structure	No duplication of activities Functional excellence	Insularity Slow response time Lack of customer focus
Project structure	Control over resources Responsiveness to customers	Cost-inefficiency Low level of knowledge transfer among projects
Matrix structure	Efficient utilization of resources Functional expertise available to all projects Increased learning and knowledge transfer Improved communication Customer focus	Dual reporting relationships Need for balance of power

❑ Learning Objective 11.4: UNDERSTAND THE PROJECT MANAGEMENT PROCESS, INCLUDING ITS LIFECYCLES

A structured and disciplined approach is needed to manage projects due to their complexity, size, and scope. Dividing a project into phases (lifecycles) can help in managing projects successfully.

The Project Management Process

Succinctly, the **project management process** means *planning the work and then working the plan*. A coaching staff may spend hours preparing unique plans for a game; the team then executes the plans in an attempt to achieve victory. Similarly, project management involves a process of *first establishing a plan and then implementing that plan* to accomplish the project objective.

A **project lifecycle** consists of four phases: identifying needs (phase 1), developing a proposed solution (phase 2), performing the project (phase 3), and terminating the project (phase 4).

Phase 1: Identifying the Needs

The *first phase* involves the identification of a need, problem, or opportunity that is the basis for a customer requesting proposals (the request for proposal, RFP) from internal sources (project team) and/or external parties (e.g., contractors) to address the identified need or solve the problem.

The front-end effort in managing a project must be focused on establishing a baseline plan that provides a roadmap for how the project scope will be accomplished on time and within budget. This planning effort includes the following steps:

1. *Clearly define the project objective.* The definition must be agreed upon by the customer and the individual or organization that will perform the project.
2. *Divide and subdivide the project scope into major "pieces" or work packages.* Although major projects may seem overwhelming when viewed as a whole, one way to conquer even the most monumental endeavor is to break it down. A **work-breakdown structure (WBS)** is a hierarchical tree of work elements or items accomplished or produced by the project team during the project. The work-breakdown structure usually identifies the organization or individual responsible for each work package.
3. *Define the specific activities that need to be performed for each work package in order to accomplish the project objective.*
4. *Graphically portray the activities in the form of a network diagram.* This diagram shows the necessary sequence and interdependencies of activities to achieve the project objective.
5. *Make a time estimate for how long it will take to complete each activity.* It is also necessary to determine which types of resources and how many of each resource are needed for each activity to be completed within the estimated duration.
6. *Make a cost estimate for each activity.* The cost is based on the types and quantities of resources required for each activity.
7. *Calculate a project schedule and budget to determine whether the project can be completed within the required time, with the allotted funds, and with the available resources.* If not, adjustments must be made to the project scope, activity time estimates, or resource assignments until an achievable, realistic baseline plan (a roadmap for accomplishing the project scope on time and within budget) can be established.

Planning determines what needs to be done, who will do it, how long it will take, and how much it will cost. The result of this effort is a baseline plan. Taking the time to develop a well-thought-out plan is critical to the successful accomplishment of any project. Many projects have overrun their budgets, missed their completion dates, or only partially met their requirements because there was no viable baseline plan before the project was started.

Attempting to perform a project without first establishing a baseline plan is foolhardy. The baseline plan for a project can be displayed in graphical or tabular format for each time period (week, month) from the start of the project to its completion. Information should include the:

- Start and completion dates for each activity
- Amounts of the various resources that will be needed during each time period
- Budget for each time period, as well as the cumulative budget from the start of the project through each time period

Once a baseline plan has been established, it must be implemented. This involves performing the work according to plan and controlling the work so that the project scope is achieved within budget and schedule to the customer's satisfaction.

Phase 2: Developing a Proposed Solution

The *second phase* requires the submission of a proposal to the customer with a solution to solve the problem. Potential contractors spend a considerable amount of time and effort in developing RFPs to win the contract from the customer, thus facing a bid/no-bid decision. A bid error can happen as follows:

- **Yes-bid error** can happen when the contractor is not qualified to do the project work and yet decides to submit the RFP.
- **No-bid error** can happen when the contractor is qualified to do the project work and yet decides not to submit the RFP.

Phase 3: Performing the Project

This *third phase* calls for the implementation of the proposed solution and ends when the customer is satisfied that the requirements have been met and the project objective has been accomplished.

Once the baseline plan has been developed, project work can proceed. The project team, led by the project manager, will implement the plan and perform the activities, or work elements, in accordance with the plan. The pace of project activity will increase as more and various resources become involved in performing the project tasks.

While the project work is being performed, it is necessary to monitor progress to ensure that everything is going according to plan. This involves measuring actual progress and comparing it to planned progress. To measure actual progress, it is important to keep track of which activities have actually been started and/or completed, when they were started and/or completed, and how much money has been spent or committed. If, at any time during the project, comparison of actual progress to planned progress reveals that the project is behind schedule, overrunning the budget, or not meeting technical specifications, corrective action must be taken to get the project back on track.

Before a decision is made to implement corrective action, it may be necessary to evaluate several alternative actions to make sure the corrective action will bring the project back within the scope, time, and budget constraints of the objective. Be aware, for instance, that adding resources to make up time and get back on schedule may result in overrunning the planned budget. If a project gets too far out of control, it may be difficult to achieve the project objective without sacrificing the scope, budget, schedule, or quality.

The key to effective project control is measuring actual progress and comparing it to planned progress on a timely and regular basis and taking corrective action immediately, if necessary. Hoping that a problem will go away without corrective intervention is naive. The earlier a problem is identified and corrected, the better. Based on actual progress, it is possible to forecast a schedule and budget for completion of the project. If these parameters are beyond the limits of the project objective, corrective actions need to be implemented at once.

Phase 4: Terminating the Project

The *fourth and final phase* of the project lifecycle is terminating (closing) the project. It starts after project work has been completed and includes various actions to close out the project properly.

The purpose of properly terminating a project is to learn from the experience gained on the project in order to improve performance on future projects. Therefore, the activities associated with terminating the project should be identified and included in the project's baseline plan. They should not be done merely as spontaneous afterthoughts. These activities might include organizing and filing project documents, receiving and making final payments, and conducting post-project evaluation meetings within both the contractor's and the customer's organizations.

The termination phase starts when performance of the project is completed and the customer accepts the result. In some situations, this might be a somewhat formal event in which an automated system satisfies a set of criteria or passes tests that were stated in the contract. Another activity that must be performed during the termination phase is assuring that all payments have been collected from the customer.

During the project termination phase, the project manager should prepare a written performance evaluation of each member of the project team and mention how each has expanded his knowledge as a result of the project assignment, as well as what areas he needs to develop further. If a project team member does not report directly to the project manager within the company's organizational structure, the project manager should provide a copy of the performance evaluation to the person's immediate supervisor.

Finally, no successful project should end without some type of celebration. This can range from an informal pizza party after work to a more formal event, with speakers from the customer's organization and awards or certificates of recognition for project participants.

Another important activity during the termination phase is holding post-project evaluation meetings. These meetings should be conducted internally, within the organization that performed the project, as well as with the customer. The purpose of such meetings is to evaluate performance of the project, to determine whether the anticipated benefits from the project were actually achieved, and to identify what can be done to improve performance on future projects.

❑ Learning Objective 11.5: UNDERSTAND THE VARIOUS METHODS IN PROJECT PLANNING, ESTIMATING, CONTROLLING, AND REPORTING

Typically, a **project plan** is used to manage and control project implementation and includes performance measurement baselines for schedule and cost, major milestones, major deliverables, major assumptions, target dates, and risks and contingencies associated with the project. By tracking cost, schedule, and technical performance, a project team is aware of potential problem areas and is able to determine any impact of the deviation and decide whether corrective action is needed. Regular review of the status of cost, schedule, and technical performance goals by individuals outside the project team allows for an independent assessment of the project and verification that the project is meeting stated goals.

Plans should be separated from scheduling and estimating should be a part of planning. **Project planning** is the act of stating what activities must occur in a project and in what order these activities must take place. **Project scheduling** follows planning and is defined as the act of producing project timetables in consideration of the plan and costs. **Project controlling** is ensuring that plans are accomplished. The correct sequence is:

Planning → Estimating → Scheduling → Controlling → Reporting

After management has approved the project, it is important to estimate the size of the project in terms of time, scope, quality, and resources, which becomes a basis for project planning and controlling work. The time element is related to project complexity, staff training needs, and staff communication complexity. The scope element is related to project size, its difficult level, and the number of affected internal departments and external parties to coordinate. The quality element is related to how well the project requirements are defined, understood, and costed. The resources element is related to human resources (e.g., number of people, their experience, and their performance levels) and computing resources (e.g., computers, their memory, and their storage).

Project Planning Methods

The project plan should specify key points within the project, products to be available at these points, and threats to the delivery of these products at the predicted time. Detailed knowledge of project planning components is essential.

The project plan is a document that describes how the project manager plans to conduct project work. It must define tasks and the resources required to complete the project. Regardless of the size, every project needs to have a plan that clearly defines what is to be accomplished, specifies by whom and when it will be performed, and indicates how much it will cost. The plan defines responsibilities and accountabilities for the people who are involved. The project plan should be viewed as a living document, meaning that it will be updated as needed. Specifically, the planning document needs to have the following items in place:

Milestones
Milestones are a list of major checkpoints for progress review and measurement of work. Milestone charts show achievements by plotting activities against time.

Deliverables
Most project activities can be defined with start and stop points and with clearly measurable deliverables. Each project must have objectives and goals to be achieved with resources assigned to it. Management needs to know what parts of the project are most likely to cause serious delays. This knowledge will lead to management actions that achieve project objectives and deadlines. Deliverables define the specific outcomes (i.e., tangible work products) to be achieved and periodic status-reporting informs management whether agreed-on deliverables will actually be delivered on the expected date.

Baseline
Once approved by management, the project plan becomes a baseline document, which is a starting point for future changes. Any subsequent changes require management approval, thus bringing discipline and structure to the process of change. Also, any subsequent changes will be compared to the baseline, where the latter becomes a standard.

Assumptions
Many assumptions go into the development of a project plan, since the project manager is constantly faced with many uncertainties. Assumptions are required for a good understanding of the project direction. These assumptions need to be spelled out in detail so that the next project manager understands them clearly for reformulating the plan. Management also needs to know what these assumptions

are prior to their approval of the project. Wrong assumptions may cost time and money, in addition to causing poor quality. Such assumptions include:

- Responsibility for providing test data
- Availability of computer time
- Critical schedule milestones
- Programming languages, automated tools, and physical facilities to be used during the project.

Risks

Every project has risks, although risk levels vary from low to high. Significant risks or exposures that may delay or jeopardize the project should be documented and explained. Management is interested in knowing the risks so that they can allocate resources to reduce or eliminate them.

Dependencies

Project tasks depend on each other. The schedules and interrelationships of the tasks and the order in which they must be completed should be included in the project plan. If the starting of task C depends on the completion of tasks A and B, this must be spelled out in the project plan, since doing it in any other way causes quality problems and results in out-of-sequence work.

Contingencies

No matter how carefully the project plan is put together, deviations or disasters occur. Prudent management will plan for contingencies to handle disasters and deviations. Contingencies require allocating additional resources (people, time, money, and facilities) over and beyond the required ones as a cushion against any unpleasant or unexpected outcomes.

Network Diagrams

A network diagram showing what tasks can be done in parallel and what tasks can start only when others are completed helps the project manager plan better. Network diagrams show the time sequence of tasks and how they are related to each other. Techniques such as work-breakdown structure (WBS) and milestones provide input to the development of network diagrams.

Project Estimating Methods

Estimating is an art and a science. It is an essential part of project management, since management ap-proval to proceed with the project and subsequent controlling comes from proper estimations. If estimations deviate too much, it causes the project to go over budget, and time delays lead to user dissatisfaction. Therefore, proper care should be taken during estimating. The element of uncertainty has a major impact on estimating. *The four components of time, scope, quality, and resources are interrelated.* Any change in one component affects the other three. Decisions must be made after considering these four components together.

Time

In a project environment, time is related to cost. There appears to be a schedule threshold for each project that is difficult to estimate. Many development and maintenance tasks are sequential and cannot be arbitrarily compressed or reorganized. Understanding the nature of tasks makes it possible to estimate minimum effective task duration.

For example, adding more people to compensate for a delayed project may increase the complexity of the effort by breaking it in such a way as to be meaningless, increase the training required for the additional personnel, and increase the complexity of project communication. The net effect may be to increase the schedule as well as the cost.

It is important to allocate more time to certain activities, such as requirements analysis and design work. Design deficiencies are much cheaper and easier to fix when discovered early rather than during the testing or implementation stage.

Scope

Project scope focuses on what is included and what is excluded in the project and product. *It consists of features and functions of the product, including factors such as software size, difficulty of product, software reliability, programming language, documentation, development methods, and automated tools.* Any changes in these factors affect the scope of the project, which in turn affects other factors, such as quality, time/cost, and resources.

Software Size   The number of system interfaces, and the number of people involved in a project, affects cost as software size increases.

Difficulty of Product   Project staff productivity varies with the difficulty level of the system being developed or maintained. Some types of applications tend to be more difficult than others. The type of software function, such as real-time or batch, also influences development difficulty.

Software Reliability   Four major criteria exist for determining reliability of software. It must (1) provide continuity of operations, (2) utilize uniform design and implementation techniques, (3) produce accurate output, and (4) be easy for users to understand.

Programming Languages   Project costs are determined to some extent by the type of programming language used. For example, second-generation programming languages are more expensive to use than third- or fourth-generation languages. Programmers experienced in second-generation languages are hard to find and keep and are expensive as well. Development and maintenance costs should both be considered here.

Documentation   It costs money to develop and maintain system documentation. It may be necessary to explore the need for technical writers.

Development Methods   It is generally accepted that a project with the application of structured methods costs less than one with unstructured methods. The scope of the structured methods includes use of top-down design, programming, and the testing and use of structured walkthroughs.

Automated Tools   Automated tools such as compilers, database managers, flowchart packages, utility programs, test data generators, and test drivers affect time and cost factors. Costs associated with tools are a function of tool complexity, features, use, and maturity. Automated tools may reduce the time required, if the staff knows how to use them, or they could increase the time, if the staff is not experienced with their use.

Quality

System requirements drive the entire project, including quality. Inconsistent and incomplete specification of system requirements, and poor translation of these requirements into estimates of time, cost, quality, and resources, are major concerns.

To ensure a quality product, requirements should be well-defined, well-understood, and well-costed. Incomplete definition of requirements is a major cause of cost overruns. If there are too many people in the project, misinterpretation of requirements and related communication problems may occur. Requirements should be firmed up before detailed design work begins. This practice not only increases quality but also leads to accurate costing. Removing unnecessary constraints on project members and stabilizing requirements also increase the quality of the end product.

Resources

The scope of estimating resources covers both human and computing resources. Factors such as number of people, experience of people, and individual performance should be taken into consideration for estimating human resources. On the other hand, computing resources include the availability of computer time for development work and automated tools required during development and maintenance.

- **Number of people.** Too many people on one project may decrease productivity and increase communication problems. On the other hand, too few people will increase the project's elapsed time and further delay the project's completion date. The right number of people should be estimated.
- **Experience of people.** Although there is no direct correlation between years of experience of the project staff and productivity, it has been found that experience with a similar project increases productivity.
- **Individual performance.** Since individuals vary in their performance levels, this factor must be given higher importance in estimate. It is variability in performance that may decide the success of the project.
- **Computing resources.** The amount of computer time required for a given development effort is easily underestimated. Both development and operations time must be accurately estimated.
- **Quantitative and qualitative methods.** Both quantitative and qualitative methods are in use to estimate project variables such as time, resources, and cost. No single method is complete; instead, a combination of methods is suggested. Quantitative methods include models based on techniques such as regression analysis (a method of parametric modeling). The regression method expresses a quantifiable relationship between dependent and independent variables for the current or historical system. New cost estimates may then be made

for the new system, using relationships from historical data.

It should be remembered that models are subject to unreliable and biased results. This may be minimized by performing a detailed decomposition of project tasks (e.g., WBS) so that ambiguities are removed.

Other examples of quantitative methods include comparisons and simple ratios. Quantitative methods should be complemented with qualitative methods such as rules of thumb, heuristics, and trial-and-error methods.

Project Controlling Methods

In any project, there will be at least four types of controls applied:

1. **Time control.** Project network scheduling begins with the construction of a diagram that reflects the interdependencies and time requirements of the individual tasks that make up a project. It calls for work plans prepared in advance of the project. Once the overall schedule is established, weekly or biweekly review meetings should be held to check progress against schedule. Control must be rigorous, especially at the start, so that missed commitments call for immediate corrective action.

2. **Cost control.** Periodic reports showing the budget, the actual cost, and variances is a good start for cost controls. It is necessary to break the comprehensive cost summary reports into work packages or major tasks and focus on major problems and opportunities. The cost reports should be distributed to technical and functional managers alike.

3. **Quality control.** Quality control comprises three elements: defining performance criteria, expressing the project objective in terms of quality standards, and monitoring progress toward these standards. Examples of performance criteria include market penetration of a product line, processing time for customer inquiries, and the like. Both quantitative and qualitative measures need to be defined.

4. **Earned value management (EVM).** EVM provides a standard means of objectively measuring work accomplished based on the budgeted value of that work—it is "what you got for what it cost." EVM is a project management technique that inte-

grates cost, schedule, and technical performance measures to monitor and control project resources and compile results into one set of metrics so that effective comparisons can be made. It also helps evaluate and control project risk by measuring project progress in monetary terms. It provides the project manager with a more complete picture of the health of the entire project, not just certain segments of the project.

The fourth control, EVM, incorporates three vital aspects of effective project/program management: scoping, costing, and scheduling. EVM is a technique aimed at comparing resource planning to schedules and to technical, cost, and schedule requirements.

The EVM technique serves two distinct purposes: it encourages the effective use of internal cost and schedule management systems and it affords the organization the ability to rely on timely data produced by those systems for determining product-oriented contracts status. In order to perform an EVM analysis, one needs to start with a solid baseline schedule that accurately reflects how much work is planned for each time period. After this baseline is determined and captured, work becomes earned in some quantitative form as work is performed. This earned work is then compared to the initial resource allocation estimates in order to determine whether the project or investment has utilized its resources meaningfully and cost-efficiently.

Example of Application of EVM Technique

Schedule and Cost Variances

The **percent complete estimate** method allows for a monthly or quarterly estimate of the percentage of completed work to be made by the project manager in charge of the work package. These estimates are expressed as cumulative values against 100 percent of the milestone value. The earned value is then calculated by applying that percentage to the total budget for that work package.

Project A is authorized with a budget of $1,000,000 over a four-quarter, one-year, time period. The planned value for the first quarter called for an accomplishment of 30 percent or $300,000 (0.30 × $1,000,000) of the value of the work scheduled. Actual costs are $250,000. The earned value estimate based on 20 percent of work completed is \$200,000 (i.e., $0.20 \times \$1,000,000$).

Schedule Variance = Earned Value − Planned Value = \$200,000 − \$300,000 = −\$100,000

where a negative amount means the project is behind schedule.

Cost Variance = Earned Value − Actual Costs = \$200,000 − \$250,000 = −\$50,000

where a negative amount means the project has a cost overrun.

Schedule and Cost Performance Indices

Schedule Performance Index (SPI) = Earned Value/Planned Value = \$200,000/\$300,000 = 0.67

Cost Performance Index (CPI) = Earned Value/ Actual Costs = \$200,000/\$250,000 = 0.80

A project with SPI and CPI of 1.0 is better, less than 1.0 is not good, and the largest negative value should be given top priority to work on it first.

Forecast of Final Project Costs

One can forecast a range of final cost requirements for project A using the SPI and CPI indices:

Low-End Forecast = Total Budget Value/SPI = \$1,000,000/0.67 = \$1,492,537 = \$1.5 million (approximately)

High-End Forecast = Total Budget Value/ (SPI × CPI) = \$1,000,000/(0.67 × 0.80) = \$1,000,000/0.536 = \$1,865,672 = \$1.9 million (approximately)

A range of final cost projections between a minimum of \$1.5 million and a maximum of \$1.9 million are needed to complete project A.

EVM is most effective when implemented using a bottom-up and incremental approach. Examining small, manageable chunks is a more efficient process for identifying problems and root causes and allows the project manager to assess the health and risks of a project more accurately. Generally, small milestones are easier to plan for (their scope can be defined more specifically) and can be measured more objectively than large ones. Project managers should ensure that milestones (or submilestones) are as small and specific as possible, in terms of scheduling. It is good to limit milestone duration to a single fiscal year (or less) instead of multiyear milestones.

Other Types of Project Control

Since a project can have a number of people working on it for a long time, monitoring and control become essential management tools. Formal control techniques include change-management policy, procedures, and forms; logs; checklists; and status reports. Phone conversations and face-to-face communications are examples of informal control techniques. Where possible, formal control techniques should be practiced, since they provide some evidence as to what has been said and when to resolve a question or dispute.

Change Management

Change is a constant aspect of dynamic project management environments, where several people interact with each other. Specifically, project requirements change, design approaches change, business needs change, and team member turnover occurs. Any change in the baseline document is a change. The project manager should define the cost/time and schedule impact so that the change can be given a fair evaluation. If the change justifies the estimated impact on the project, a decision may be made to incorporate it.

A change-management procedure is needed to introduce discipline into the change process. Some basic change-management techniques include: logging all changes with a sequential control number, assigning the change task to the appropriate staff, checking progress periodically, and reporting the status of the change (e.g., completed, deferred or pending). Communication is tied to change-management in that timely communications are important to all parties affected by the change. Communication media should be tied to the importance of the message being communicated.

Project Reporting Methods

Effective and frequent personal communication is crucial to keep the project moving, identify potential problems, solicit suggestions for improving project performance, keep abreast of whether the customer is satisfied, and avoid surprises. Personal communication can occur through words or nonverbal behavior, such as body language. Personal communication can be oral or written.

Oral Communication

Personal oral communication can be face to face or via telephone. It can be by means of voice mail or videoconferencing. Information can be communicated in a more accurate and timely manner through oral communication. Such communication provides a forum for discussion, clarification, understanding, and immediate feedback. Face-to-face communication also provides an opportunity to observe the body language that accompanies the communication. Even phone conversations allow the listener to hear the tone, inflection, and emotion of the voice. Body language and tone are important elements that enrich oral communication. Face-to-face situations provide an even greater opportunity for enriched communication than phone conversations do.

Written Communication

Personal written communication is generally carried out through internal memos to the project team and external letters to the customer or others outside the firm, such as subcontractors. Memos and letters can be transmitted in hardcopy or through e-mail or groupware.

- **Reporting.** Written reports are just as important as oral reports in communicating information about a project. The required types, content, format, frequency, and distribution of reports that the project organization must prepare may be specified by the customer in the contract. There are two types of project reports: progress reports and final report:
  - **Progress reports.** It is important to keep in mind that a progress report is not an activity report. *Do not confuse activity or busyness with progress and accomplishment.* The customer, in particular, is interested in project accomplishments—what progress has been made toward achieving the project's objective rather than what activities the project team was busy doing.
  - **Final report.** The project final report is usually a summary of the project. It is not an accumulation of the progress reports, nor is it a blow-by-blow story of what happened throughout the project.

Project Progress

Management needs to assess the progress of projects. To do that, meaningful and measurable checkpoints are needed, combined with a progress-reporting mechanism to determine whether the project is on schedule. Reporting mechanisms should fit the size of the project, meaning that a small project may not need the elaborate reporting mechanism that a large project would require.

Team members should believe in the periodic progress-reporting mechanism, since they are the ones providing input to management. A 90 percent completion syndrome should be watched for, since the team members may report the task as 90 percent completed week after week. A better approach would be to require estimated times and efforts to complete all tasks. Status-monitoring can be accomplished with periodic status reports and scheduled meetings.

Course Corrections

No project stands still and very few projects proceed according to plan. Therefore, midpoint reviews or some other checkpoint reviews are needed to bring the project back on schedule. During these course corrections, management assesses the situation, identifies the problems, isolates the causes of problems, and allocates resources to fix problems. Timely and proactive action by management is vital to prevent major disasters and delays.

Project Communication

Project communication can take place in several ways in which meetings and reports are a vital part of it. Project management should provide reporting guidelines to project members so that consistency and quality of reporting can be maintained. With this approach, trends and problems can be readily seen due to a standard reporting format.

With regard to meetings, certain guidelines should be followed so that attendees do not consider meetings to be a waste of time. Specific guidelines include defining the purpose of the meeting, informing the attendees in advance with an agenda of what is expected of them, inviting the right people to the meeting, keeping the meeting to a small size (less than 10), limiting the length of the meeting to less than an hour, bringing the meeting to a definite conclusion, and setting a clear direction for future events.

❑ Learning Objective 11.6: UNDERSTAND THE VARIOUS METHODS IN PROJECT SCHEDULING

Two popular project scheduling techniques include program evaluation and review technique (PERT) and critical path method (CPM). Other related tools and techniques include work-breakdown structure (WBS) and Gantt charts.

Program Evaluation and Review Technique

Project management frequently uses network diagrams to plan the project, evaluate alternatives, and control large and complex projects toward completion. The **program evaluation and review technique (PERT)** requires extremely careful plans from the very outset of the project. This allows management to allocate resources to critical areas before they become critical. This will alert a manager to trouble areas or bottlenecks before they become a major problem and the source of a project overrun. PERT also helps to allocate resources but has no influence on the excellence of the end product.

PERT improves communication upward to the manager and the customer (client). It lets the supervisor believe that the project manager is doing a superior job, regardless of how well the project manager is actually performing.

When PERT is used on a project, the three time estimates (optimistic, most likely, and pessimistic) are combined to determine the expected duration and the variance for each activity:

1. **Optimistic.** An estimate of the minimum time an activity will take. This is based on everything "going right the first time." It can be obtained under unusual, "good-luck" situations.
2. **Most likely.** An estimate of the normal time an activity will take—a result that would occur most often if the activity could be repeated a number of times under similar circumstances.
3. **Pessimistic.** An estimate of the maximum time an activity will take—a result that can occur only if unusually "bad luck" is experienced.

The expected times determine the critical path, and the variances for the activities on this path are summed to obtain the duration variance for the project. The **expected completion time** is computed as:

Expected Completion Time = 1/6 $(a + 4m + b)$

where a is optimistic time, m is most likely time, and b is pessimistic time. The expected activity times derived from a three-estimate, PERT-type calculation provide a more accurate estimate and allow the activity time variance to be calculated and included in the estimates of project duration.

Example of Calculation of Expected Completion Time

A company is planning a multiphase construction project. The time estimates for a particular phase of the project are:

Optimistic	2 months
Most likely	4 months
Pessimistic	9 months

Question: Using PERT, what is the expected completion time for this particular phase?

Answer: The expected completion time would be 4.5 months:

$$1/6 (a + 4m + b) = 1/6 (2 + 4 \times 4 + 9) = 27/6 = 4.5$$

Critical Path Method

The **critical path method (CPM)** is a powerful but basically simple technique for analyzing, planning, and scheduling large, complex projects. In essence, the tool provides a means of determining which jobs or activities, of the many that comprise a project, are critical in their effect on total project time and how best to schedule all jobs in the project in order to meet a target date at minimum cost. CPM is an extension of PERT.

Critical path scheduling helps coordinate the timing of activities on paper and helps avert costly emergencies. The network diagram must be developed in detail as much as possible so that discrepancies, omissions, and work coordination problems can be resolved inexpensively, at least to the extent that they can be foreseen.

Project diagrams of large projects can be constructed by sections. Within each section the task is accomplished one arrow at a time by asking and answering the following questions for each job:

- What immediately preceded this job?
- What immediately succeeds (follows) this job?
- What can be concurrent with this job?

If the maximum time available for a job equals its duration, the job is called "critical." A delay in a critical job will cause a comparable delay in the project completion time. A project contains at least one contiguous path of critical jobs through the project diagram from beginning to end. Such a path is called a **critical path**, and there can be only one critical path at a time in a project.

Characteristics of a project for analysis by CPM include the following:

- The project consists of a well-defined collection of jobs or activities that, when completed, mark the end of the project.
- The jobs may be started and stopped independently of each other, within a given sequence.
- The jobs are ordered in a technological sequence (for example, the foundation of a house must be constructed before the walls are erected).

CPM focuses attention on those jobs that are critical to the project time, it provides an easy way to determine the effects of shortening various jobs in the project, and it enables the project manager to evaluate the costs of a "crash" program. **Crashing a project** means reducing its time with increasing cost.

Crashing a project is a subjective decision. The manager needs to decide which activities on the critical path should be crashed first because the activities on the noncritical path need not be crashed at all. It is physically possible to shorten the time required by critical jobs by assigning more people to the jobs; working overtime; and using different equipment, materials, and technology.

Two types of time dimensions are needed to crash a project: normal time and crash time. **Crash time** is the time required by the path if maximum effort and resources are diverted to the task along this path. A balance can be obtained when a manager knows what the normal time and the crash time would be. The goal is to select the activity on the critical path with the least crash cost per day to crash first.

Example of Computation of Crash Cost per Day

Activity	Normal Time	Normal Cost	Crash Time	Crash Cost	Crash Cost/Day
1					
2					
3					
N					

Crash cost per day is computed as:

$$(\text{Crash Cost} - \text{Normal Cost})/(\text{Normal Time} - \text{Crash Time})$$

CPM versus PERT

CPM and PERT methods are essentially similar in general approach and have much in common. However, important differences in implementation details exist. They were independently derived and based on different concepts. Both techniques define the duration of a project and the relationships among the project's component activities. An important feature of the PERT approach is its statistical treatment of the uncertainty in activity time estimates, which involves the collection of three separate time estimates and the calculation of probability estimates of meeting specified schedule dates.

CPM is different from PERT in two areas:

1. The use of only one time estimate for each activity (and thus no statistical treatment of uncertainty)
2. The inclusion, as an integral part of the overall scheme, of a procedure for time/cost trade-off to minimize the sum of direct and indirect project costs

CPM is the same as PERT in two areas:

1. They both use a network diagram for project representation, in which diagram circles represent activities with arrows indicating precedence.
2. They both calculate early and late start and finish times and slack time.

Whereas PERT and CPM are based on different assumptions, they are related to each other because of the obvious relationship between time and cost. The "ideal" network technique would combine the concepts of CPM's crashing strategy with PERT's probability distribution of activity times to derive the optimum project duration and cost.

Some examples of the application of PERT and CPM techniques are:

- Construction and maintenance of chemical plant facilities, highways, dams, buildings, railroads, and irrigation systems
- Planning of retooling programs for high-volume products in plants such as automotive and appliance plants

- Introduction of a new product
- Installation of a computer system
- Acquisition of a company

Application of PERT and CPM Techniques

Example 1

The network in Exhibit 11A describes the interrelationships of several activities necessary to complete a project. The arrows represent the activities. The numbers above the arrows indicate the number of weeks required to complete each activity.

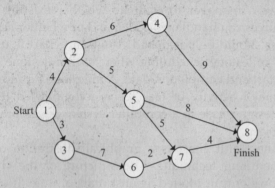

Exhibit 11A   PERT Network

Question 1: What is the shortest time to complete the project?

Answer 1: The longest path from node 1 to node 8 is path 1–2–4–8. Since all other paths are shorter in duration than path 1–2–4–8, the activities along those paths can be completed before the activities along path 1–2–4–8. Therefore, the amount of time to complete the activities along path 1–2–4–8, which is 19 weeks (4 + 6 + 9), is the shortest time to complete the project.

Question 2: What is the critical path for the project?

Answer 2: The critical path is the sequence of activities that constrains the total completion time of the project. The entire project cannot be completed until all the activities on the critical path (the longest path) are completed.

Path 1–2–4–8, which takes 19 weeks, is the critical path. Activities along each of the other three paths can be completed (each requires less than 19 weeks) before the activities along 1–2–4–8 can. The other three paths are: 1–2–5–8 (requires 4 + 5 + 8 = 17 weeks), 1–2–5–7–8 (requires 4 + 5 + 5 + 4 = 18 weeks), and 1–3–6–7–8 (requires 3 + 7 + 2 + 4 = 16 weeks).

Example 2

During an operational audit, an internal auditing team discovers the following document:

	Project Analysis	
Activity	Time in Weeks	Preceding Activity
A	3	—
B	3	A
C	7	A
D	4	A
E	2	B
F	4	B
G	1	C, E
H	5	D

Using the Project Analysis document, the audit supervisor prepares the PERT diagram shown in Exhibit 11B.

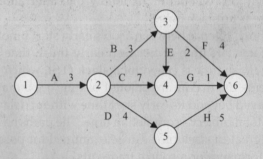

Exhibit 11B   PERT Project Analysis

Question 1: What is the earliest completion time that is indicated by the project analysis?

Answer 1: There are three paths:

Path 1	A–B–F	=	3 + 3 + 4	=	10 weeks
Path 2	A–C–G	=	3 + 7 + 1	=	11 weeks
Path 3	A–D–H	=	3 + 4 + 5	=	12 weeks

Path 3 has the earliest completion time of 12 weeks since it has the longest time to complete.

Question 2: What is the earliest time by which node 4 would be reached?

Answer 2: There are two paths by which node 4 can be reached:

Path A	A–C	=	3 + 7	=	10 weeks
Path B	A–B–E	=	3 + 3 + 2	=	8 weeks

Path A has the earliest time of 10 weeks to reach node 4 since it has the longest time.

Source: Certified Internal Auditor (CIA) Exams from the Institute of Internal Auditors (IIA), Altamonte Springs, Florida, USA.

A time-related concept in PERT/CPM is **slack time,** which is free time associated with each activity in a project as it represents unused resources that can be diverted to the critical path. Noncritical paths have slack time, whereas critical paths have no slack time. Slack is extra time available for all events and activities not on the critical path. A negative slack condition can prevail when a calculated end date does not achieve the planned end date. The slack time is also called a **safety factor** or **float** in that it allows a manager to shorten the lead-times or reevaluate the sequencing of activities along the critical paths or to change the scope of work.

When the earliest time and the latest time for an event are identical, the event has zero slack time—its scheduled start time is automatically fixed; to delay the calculated start time is to delay the whole project. When jobs or operations follow one after another, there is no slack time.

The difference between a job's early start time and its late start time or between early finish time and late finish time is called **total slack (TS),** which represents the maximum amount of time a job may be delayed beyond its early start time without delaying the total project's completion time. The paths having the greatest slack time can be examined for possible performance or resource trade-offs.

For example, jobs with positive total slack allow the project scheduler some discretion is establishing their start times. This flexibility can be applied to smoothing work schedules in that peak loads may be relieved by shifting jobs on the peak days to their late starts.

Total slack time (TS) is computed as:

$$TS = LS - ES \text{ or } LF - EF$$

where LS is latest start time, ES is earliest start time, LF is latest finish time, and EF is earliest finish time.

Another kind of slack is **free slack (FS),** which is the amount of time a job can be delayed without delaying the early start of any other job. A job with positive total slack may or may not also have free slack, but the latter never exceeds the former.

The amount of free slack time (FS) is computed as:

$$FS = EF - ES$$

where EF is earliest finish time and ES is earliest start time of all its immediate successors.

Work-Breakdown Structure

The work-breakdown structure (WBS) was first intended as the common link between schedules and costs in PERT cost application. Later, it became an important tool for conceptual organization of any project. The WBS provides the necessary logic and formalization of task statements. The WBS prepares the work packages, which usually represent the lowest division of the end items.

Gantt Chart

The Gantt chart is a horizontal bar chart that allows a manager to evaluate whether existing resources can handle work demand or whether activities should be postponed. The Gantt chart is used for milestone scheduling where each milestone has a start and completion date. A milestone represents a major activity or task to be accomplished (e.g., a design phase in a computer system development project).

The Gantt chart is a graphical illustration of a scheduling technique. The structure of the chart shows output plotted against units of time. It does not include cost information. It highlights activities over the life of a project and contrasts actual times with projected times using a horizontal (bar) chart. It gives a quick picture of a project's progress in knowing the status of actual timelines and projected timelines.

There may be a lower probability of a cost/schedule overrun if PERT is used because of its sophistication as a scheduling method compared to less sophisticated scheduling methods such as Gantt charts and milestone scheduling. If there is slack time, there is no need to use sophisticated and tight scheduling methods such as PERT.

❑ Learning Objective 11.7: UNDERSTAND THE PROJECT MANAGEMENT METRICS, PROBLEMS, AND GOVERNANCE MECHANISMS, INCLUDING PROJECT AUDITS

A project manager is equipped with metrics, governance mechanisms, cost models, and project audits not only to solve current project-related problems but also to improve performance of future projects.

Project Management Metrics

Management metrics measure how closely a project conforms to development plans and assess whether an acquisition is at risk of delay or cost increases. They provide quantitative information. These techniques require considerable information about the system being developed and can be used only after system design. The metrics will generally be used after contract award, in order to assess how well the organization is managing the system development process.

Software metrics, which use mathematical models to measure elements of the development process, are intended to help organizations better understand and manage the relationships between resource decisions, development schedules, and the cost of software projects. By using software metric tools, an auditor can independently evaluate software development projects by analyzing project budgets, requirements, schedules, and resources, and then confirming or questioning cost, schedule, and resource estimates.

Different metrics may be useful for an audit, depending on the objectives and status of an acquisition. Using cost models to estimate the cost and length of time necessary to develop a new software, for example, is appropriate only after requirements have been defined, a system design has been developed, and the size of the new system has been estimated. The models described here require estimates of either the lines of code or number of function points that the new system will include. Cost models project the time and cost to develop a system on the basis of estimates of the system's size and other pertinent factors. Cost models may be used before a solicitation for software development is issued in order to assess the reasonableness of the project schedule (if a system design has been prepared) or after a contract has been awarded and software development has begun.

Cost Models

Cost models are tools that estimate the effort needed to develop software, based on assumed relationships between the size of a system and the effort needed to design, code, and test the software. These models can help the auditor assess whether the acquisition's estimated cost and schedule are reasonable. Each model uses cost drivers, which are parameters such as the level of experience of the programmers, the reliability requirements of the programs, and the complexity of the project, along with the estimated project size, to derive overall cost and schedule estimates for the acquisition. When a system involving software is being developed, one or more cost models may be useful. A model will be more reliable if it takes into account the organization's historical experience in developing computer-based information systems. Typically cost models are derived using data gathered from years of experience with a wide range of software development projects.

Many cost models are based on industry-recognized models, such as the Constructive Cost Model (COCOMO), PRICE, Putnam, and Jensen. Auditors should use these cost models to look for discrepancies with the cost and schedule estimates established for an acquisition. By varying the estimated values for cost drivers, the auditor may also be able to perform a sensitivity analysis illustrating where project estimates are most susceptible to change. However, cost models have significant limitations in accuracy unless their underlying assumptions of system size and cost drivers are carefully chosen and reflect the organization's previous experience in system development. It is a matter of auditor judgment to decide how discrepant project estimates and estimates provided by cost models should be to raise concerns about risks of cost and schedule overruns. In making this judgment, the project auditor should take into account the uncertainty of estimates and assumptions made in using a cost model.

Project auditors should use a cost model to provide general estimates and not precise figures. This is due to the nature of estimates in that they are based on projections of an inherently uncertain future. Auditors should also ensure that the cost model used is consistent with the software development methodology of the project under consideration. A system developed through rapid prototyping, for example, should be evaluated with a cost model that takes prototyping into account.

Other Project Indicators

In addition to cost models, five indicators such as problem reports, software volatility, development progress, software size, and staff stability are important to assess how effectively an organization is managing system development projects (in-house or contractor developed). These indicators measure differences between what an organization planned for its contractor to accomplish by certain points in the system development lifecycle and the actual results.

In most cases, this comparison is most easily done graphically. Using more than one indicator can give a broader picture of a project's status. Auditors should use indicators appropriate to the project under review and for which data are available. These indicators require that the system development work be underway. A comparison of the actual number of functions successfully tested to the number planned in the acquisition schedule, for example, requires that system testing be underway.

1. **Problem reports.** This indicator involves tracking the number of open and closed problems reported as a system is developed. A problem could be any anomaly discovered during design, coding, testing, or implementation. Problems are distinguished from failures of code, which represent defects discovered during operation. Contracts should specify how problems are to be identified and reported. By reviewing these reports and noting how quickly problems are resolved, auditors can obtain an understanding of how well the contractor is performing.

   A trend chart can be drawn showing the number of new problems reported and the number of problems closed over time and to show any backlog that may be developing. The auditor may also choose to report total problems reported and resolved or break them out by level of priority. Measuring the length of time that problems have remained open will demonstrate how quickly software problems are resolved once found.

2. **Software volatility.** Software volatility refers to the number of additions to, changes in, and deletions from the system requirements. It can be measured graphically to see trendlines for both approved system requirements and cumulative changes where the latter includes additions, deletions, and modifications to requirements. Steady increases in the number of system requirements and changes to requirements may indicate that the project is at risk for delays and cost overruns.

3. **Development progress.** This indicator involves the comparison of actual to expected programs in the design, coding, and integrating of system units. Units can be measured in terms of computer software units or computer software configuration items. If the project team does not complete its design or programming and testing activities as planned, this indicator can show schedule delays before major milestones are reached. The progress

indicator can show all elements of design, coding, testing, and integrating, or it may treat them as separate indicators.

4. **Software size.** This indicator changes in the expected magnitude of the software development effort. The size of the system, measured in source-lines of code as established by the system design, may change as the system is coded. Changes in size can be expressed as total lines of code or can be broken out into new, modified, and reused lines of code. Changes in the estimated system size may indicate that the project was overestimated or underestimated in size and complexity. These changes may also indicate that requirements are changing and may be related to the software volatility presented earlier. Increasing estimates of software size should alert the auditor that the project's schedule and expected cost may be underestimated. Changes in the expected system size may necessitate reestimates of the development cost, using the cost models described earlier.

5. **Staff stability.** Tracking the total number of staff members assigned to a system development effort compared to planned staffing levels provides another indicator of potential problems. The auditor can examine projected versus actual levels of total staff or of key, experienced individuals. Understaffing may result in schedule slippage. Adding staff late in a project can actually cause further slippage—the law of diminishing returns will set in.

Problems in Project Management

Project managers face unusual problems in trying to direct and harmonize the diverse forces at work in the project situation. Their main difficulties arise from three sources:

1. **Organizational uncertainties.** The working relationships between the project manager and functional department managers have not been clearly defined by senior management. Uncertainties arise with respect to handling delays, cost overruns, work assignments, and design changes. Unless the project manager is skillful in handling these situations, senior management may resolve them in the interest of functional departments, at the expense of the project as a whole.

2. **Unusual decision pressures.** When uncertainties are added to the situation, the project manager has

to make his decisions based on limited data and with little or no analysis. He must move fast, even if it means an intuitive decision that might expose him to senior management's criticism. *Decisions to sacrifice time for cost, cost for quality, or quality for time, are common in most projects.* There is a clear indication that the project manager needs support from senior management due to these trade-offs.

3. **Inadequate senior management support.** Senior management can seldom give the project manager as much guidance and support as his line counterpart gets. Delays in initial approval of the project by senior management, inability to resolve conflicts between the project manager and the functional department managers, and delays in allocating resources are the most common issues on which the project manager needs more attention from senior management. Otherwise, project performance can be hampered.

Project Governance Mechanisms

Project governance mechanisms include establishing a project steering committee and project oversight board and conducting a project management audit.

The **project steering committee** is a high-level committee to integrate several functions of the organization. The **project oversight board** is similar to the steering committee except that it is focused on a specific project at hand. The board:

1. Reviews the project request and scope
2. Assesses the project impact
3. Approves the project funding
4. Challenges the costs, schedules, and benefits
5. Monitors the project progress
6. Reviews project deliverables
7. Solves the project-related problems

Regarding the project scope, the board determines what is in scope and what is out of scope so that scope creep does not happen. Any changes in project scope are controlled by change-management procedures.

Project Management Audit

The scope of **project management audit** consists of reviewing project planning, organizing, staffing, leading, and controlling tasks for effectiveness and efficiency and determining whether project objectives and goals are achieved.

The major objective of the project management process, a part of the software assurance process, is to establish the organizational structure of the project and assign responsibilities. The process uses the system requirements documentation and information about the purpose of the software, criticality of the software, required deliverables, and available time and other resources to plan and manage the software development and maintenance processes. The project management process begins before software development starts and ends when its objectives have been met. The project management process overlaps and often reiterates other software assurance processes. It establishes/approves standards, implements monitoring and reporting practices, develops high-level policy for quality, and cites laws and regulations for compliance.

Review the following activities performed by the project manager in the *project planning* area:

1. Set objectives or goals—(a) determine the desired outcome for the project, (b) analyze and document the system and software requirements, (c) define the relationships between the system and software activities, (d) determine management requirements and constraints (resource and schedule limitations), (e) define success criteria, and (f) always include delivery of software that satisfies the requirements on time and within budget.
2. Plan for corrective action.
3. Develop project strategies—decide on major organizational goals (e.g., quality) and develop a general program of action for reaching those goals.
4. Develop policies for the project—make standing decisions on important recurring matters to provide a guide for decision making.
5. Determine possible courses of action—develop and analyze different ways to conduct the project; anticipate possible adverse events and project areas; state assumptions; develop contingency plans; predict results and possible courses of action.
6. Make planning decisions—evaluate and select a course of action from among alternatives. This includes: (a) choosing the most appropriate course of action for meeting project goals and objectives, (b) making trade-off decisions involving costs, schedule, quality, design strategies, and risks, and (c) selecting methods, tools, and techniques (both technical and managerial) by which the output and final product will be developed and assured and the project will be managed.

7. Set procedures and rules for the project—establish methods, guides, and limits for accomplishing the project activities.
8. Select a scheduling process appropriate for development and maintenance methods.
9. Prepare budgets—allocate estimated costs (based on project size, schedule, staff) to project functions, activities, and tasks, and determine necessary resources.
10. Document, distribute, and update project plans.

Review the following activities performed by the project manager in the *project organizing* area:

1. Identify and group required tasks—tasks are grouped into logical entities (e.g., analysis tasks, design tasks, coding tasks, and test tasks) and are mapped into organizational entities.
2. Select and establish organizational structures—define how the project will be organized (e.g., line, staff, or matrix organization) using contractual requirements and principles of independent verification and validation.
3. Create organizational positions—specify job titles and position descriptions.
4. Define responsibilities and authorities—decide who will have the responsibility of completing tasks and who has the authority to make decisions related to the project.
5. Establish position qualifications—identify the qualities personnel must have to work on the project (e.g., experience, education, programming languages, and tool usage).
6. Document organizational structures—document lines of authority, tasks, and responsibilities in the project plan.

Review the following activities performed by the project manager in the *project staffing* area:

1. Fill organizational positions—fill the jobs established during organizational planning with qualified personnel.
2. Assimilate newly assigned personnel—familiarize newly assigned personnel with any project procedures, facilities, equipment, tools, or plans.
3. Educate and train personnel as necessary.

4. Provide for general development of project staff members.
5. Evaluate and appraise personnel.
6. Compensate project personnel (e.g., salary and bonus).
7. Terminate project assignments—reassign or terminate personnel at the end of a project.
8. Document staffing decisions—document staffing plans and training policies adopted.

Review the following activities performed by the project manager in the *project leading* area:

1. Provide leadership—the project manager provides direction to project members by interpreting plans and requirements.
2. Delegate project authority.
3. Build project teams.
4. Coordinate and communicate project activities between in-house and contractor personnel.
5. Resolve project conflicts.
6. Manage changes after considering the inputs, outputs, costs/benefits.
7. Document directing decisions taken.

Review the following activities performed by the project manager in the *project controlling* area:

1. Develop standards of performance—select or approve standards to be used for the software development and maintenance activities.
2. Establish monitoring and reporting systems such as milestones, deliverables, schedules.
3. Analyze results by comparing achievements with standards, goals, and plans.
4. Apply corrective action to bring requirements, plans, and actual project status into conformance.
5. Document the controlling methods used.

 Self-Assessment Exercise

Online exercises are provided for the learning objectives in this module. Please visit www.mbaiq.com to complete the online exercises and to calculate your MBA IQ Score.

Decision Sciences and Managerial Economics

Learning Objective 12.1: Learn How to Apply Quantitative Methods to Business 311

Basic Statistics 312
Basic Probabilities 312
Linear Programming Models 312
Inventory Models 313
Waiting-Line or Queuing Models 313
Decision Analysis Models 313
Forecasting Models 317
Sales Seasonality and Deseasonality 318
Statistical Process Control Methods 318
Simulation Models 319
Sensitivity Analysis 319
The Time Value of Money 319
Simple Ratios 320
Profit Models 320
Discriminant and Multivariate Analysis 320
Cluster Analysis 320
Consumer Research Models 320
Multicriteria Decision Models 321

Learning Objective 12.2: Understand the Basic Principles and Concepts in Economics 321

Learning Objective 12.3: Understand the Basic Principles and Applications of Microeconomics 322

Economic Implications of Competition 322
Economic Implications of Demand and Supply 323
Economic Implications of Utility 323

Economic Implications of Perfect Competition 323
Economic Implications of Monopolistic Competition 324
Economic Implications of Oligopolies 324
Economic Implications of Monopolies 324
Economic Implications of Labor Economics 325
Economic Implications of Structure of Product Markets 325

Learning Objective 12.4: Understand the Basic Principles and Applications of Macroeconomics 325

Economic Implications of Employment, Interest Rates, and Investment Theories 325
Economic Implications of Economic Growth 326
Methods of Measuring Economic Performance 328
Aggregate Demand and Supply 329
Fiscal Policy 330
Monetary Policy 331
Money Supply 332

Learning Objective 12.5: Understand the Basic Principles and Applications of Key Economic Indicators 332

Nature of Key Economic Indicators 332
Specific Types of Key Economic Indicators 333

Learning Objective 12.6: Understand the Nature of Economic Business Cycles and Industry Growth Levels 333

Economic Business Cycles 333
OECD Business Cycles 334
Industry Growth Levels 335

❑ Learning Objective 12.1: LEARN HOW TO APPLY QUANTITATIVE METHODS TO BUSINESS

Quantitative methods in business have different uses depending on the type of business problem to be solved and the type of industry. For example, the banking industry may use waiting-line or queuing models, sensitivity analysis, and simulation techniques in combination more often than other indus-

tries. Usually, quantitative methods involve a combination of mathematical equations, formulas, models, and statistics with computer programs—called **decision sciences.**

Quantitative methods can help managers and executives make better decisions. The focus is on the decision-making process and on the role of quantitative analysis in that process. The difference between the model and the situation or managerial problem it represents is an important point. Mathematical models are abstractions of real-world situations and as such cannot capture all the aspects of the real situation. However, if a model can capture the major relevant aspects of the problem and can then provide a solution recommendation, it can be a valuable aid to decision making.

One of the characteristics of quantitative analysis that will become increasingly apparent is the search for a best solution to the problem. In carrying out quantitative analysis, we shall attempt to develop procedures for finding the best or optimal solution.

Basic Statistics

There are many aspects to basic statistics, including mean, median, mode, mean absolute deviation, variance, standard deviation, coefficient of variation, and mean squared error.

- **Mean** is the simple average of observed measurements.
- **Median** is the halfway point of the data; that is, half of the numbers are above it and half are below.
- **Mode** is the value that occurs most frequently.
- **Mean absolute deviation (MAD)** is a measure of dispersion in the data. This measure is the average of the absolute values of all the forecast errors. A smaller MAD is better.
- **Variance**, similar to MAD, measures the average distance from each number to the mean. We need to square each deviation and then take the average of all the squared deviations. Variance is difficult to interpret.
- **Standard deviation** is the square root of the variance. Assuming normal distribution, 68 percent of the data will be within one standard deviation of the mean, 95 percent of the data will be within two standard deviations of the mean, and 99 percent of the data will be within three standard deviations of the mean.
- The **coefficient of variation** tells us whether the dispersion is large or small relative to the average. It is computed by dividing the standard deviation by the mean. Smaller dispersion is good.
- **Mean squared error (MSE)** measures the average of the sum of the squared differences between the actual time series data and the forecasted data. A smaller MSE is preferred.

The choice between MAD and MSE is up to the individual making the decision. For the same set of data, the value of MSE is larger than that of MAD. Both MAD and MSE measure forecast errors.

Basic Probabilities

A **probability** is a numerical measure of the likelihood that an event or outcome will occur. Basic requirements of probability include that for each experimental outcome, the value must be between 0 and 1 and that all individual probabilities must add up to 1.

There are three methods to assign probabilities: the classical method, the relative frequency method, and the subjective method. The **classical method** assigns probabilities based on the assumption that experimental outcomes are equally likely. The **relative frequency method** assigns probabilities based on experimentation or historical data. The **subjective method** assigns probabilities based on the judgment of the person assigning the probabilities. Business managers and executives use the subjective method more frequently than the other methods.

An important application of probabilities is in the calculation of expected value where each outcome (e.g., payoff) is multiplied with its corresponding probability of occurrence.

Linear Programming Models

Linear programming is a resource allocation and problem-solving model that has been developed for situations involving maximizing or minimizing a linear function subject to linear constraints that limit the degree to which a single objective can be pursued (e.g., maximizing revenues, minimizing costs, or maximizing profits).

The model is built with a linear objective function, a set of linear constraints, and nonnegative decision variables. **Objective function** is the expression that defines the quantity to be maximized or minimized in a linear programming model. **Constraint** is an equation or inequality that rules out certain combinations of decision variables as feasible solutions. A **decision variable** is a controllable input for a linear programming model.

Examples of applications of linear programming include determining the proper mix of ingredients in a food, paint, drug, chemical, or gasoline product, meeting the product specifications, and deciding on the media selection (e.g., newspapers, magazines, radio, television, and direct mail) and marketing research (e.g., conducting customer surveys at a minimum cost).

Extensions to linear programming models include **goal programming,** which is a technique for solving multicriteria decision problems by relaxing the assumption of a single objective; **integer**

programming, where some or all of the decision variables can take only integer values; **nonlinear programming,** where some or all relationships are nonlinear; **transportation model,** which is concerned with shipping goods from a variety of origins to a variety of destinations with the goal of minimizing route miles, shipping costs, and delivery delays; **transshipment model,** which is an extension of the transportation model to product distribution problems involving transfer points and possible shipments between any pair of nodes; and **assignment model,** which is a network flow problem that often involves the assignment of agents to tasks; it can be formulated as a linear program and is a special case of the transportation model.

Inventory Models

Inventory models are used by managers faced with the dual problems of maintaining sufficient inventories to meet demand for goods (e.g., order costs to place the order, receive the order, and inspect the order) and, at the same time, incurring the lowest possible inventory holding costs (e.g., cost of capital tied up in the inventory and storage costs). Examples of applications of inventory models include calculating the economic order quantity (EOQ) that minimizes the total cost (e.g., order costs and holding costs) and calculating the reorder point for inventory replenishment.

If Q is the order quantity, then the how-much-to-order decision involves finding the value of Q that will minimize the sum of ordering and holding costs. The formula for EOQ is:

$$Q = \text{EOQ} = \sqrt{\frac{2DCo}{Ch}}$$

where D is annual sales demand in units, Co is cost of placing one order, and Ch is cost of holding (carrying) one unit in inventory for the year.

The point at which stock on hand must be replenished is called **reorder point (RP).** It is also the inventory level at which an order should be placed. The formula for RP is:

Reorder Point = Lead-Time × Usage Rate

or RP = LT × UR

Waiting-Line or Queuing Models

Waiting-line or queuing models have been developed to help managers understand and make better decisions concerning the operation of systems involving waiting lines. Waiting-line models are applied in a bank teller operation (manual or automated teller machines—ATMs) or a cash register at a department or food store to control the customer's waiting time. A model is developed in terms of customer arrival times, service times, and the number of ATM machines installed.

Decision Analysis Models

Decision analysis models can be used to determine optimal strategies in situations involving several decision alternatives and an uncertain or risk-filled pattern of future events. Uncertain future events are called **chance events** and the outcomes of the chance events are called **states of nature.** The goal of the decision-maker is to maximize profits or minimize losses.

Decision-making is a frequent and important activity for business managers and executives alike and is related to risk levels. With respect to risk, individuals act differently and can be grouped into three categories: risk-takers, risk neutral, and risk-averters. When contrasted with a risk-taking entrepreneur, a professional manager is likely to be more cautious as a risk-taker (i.e., he is either risk neutral or a risk-averter). Another factor is that risks are related to returns. The higher the risk, the greater the return and vice versa. Also, controls are related to risks. The higher the risk, the greater the need for controls and vice versa. Controls reduce or eliminate risks and exposures.

Influence diagrams, payoff tables, decision trees, and market research studies are used to solve decision problems. An **influence diagram** shows the relationships among decisions, chance events, and consequences for a decision problem (nodes). **Payoff tables** show the financial consequences (payoffs) in terms of the alternative decisions (e.g., manufacture domestic, buy abroad, and buy domestic) that can be made and the alternative states of nature that might result (e.g., low, medium, or high volume). The **decision tree** is a diagram showing the logical progression that occurs over time in terms of decisions and outcomes and is particularly useful in sequential decision problems—where a series of decisions need to be made with each in part depending on earlier decisions and outcomes.

Four general types of decisions exist, which require different decision procedures: (1) decisions under certainty, (2) decisions under risk, (3) decisions under uncertainty, and (4) decisions under conflict or competition.

Decision Making under Certainty

A decision-maker is operating in an environment where all of the facts surrounding a decision are known exactly, and each alternative is associated with only one possible outcome. The environment is known as **certainty.**

Five different methods exist: (1) dominance, (2) lexicographic, (3) additive weighing, (4) effectiveness index, and (5) satisficing. The first four methods are optimization methods—that is, they attempt to identify the very best alternative from all available alternatives and are suitable for idealized situations. The fifth method simply looks for the first satisfactory alternative from available alternatives, because it is a nonoptimization and real-world method and the decision-maker accepts the minimum values.

Decision Making under Risk

When a decision-maker is faced with a decision and the probabilities of various outcomes are known, the situation is said to be **decision-making under risk.** Gambling decisions are typical of decisions under risk. An essential feature of decisions under risk is that we can calculate a probability for the effect of the chance event.

Risk is a condition faced by managers when they have to make a decision based on incomplete but reliable information. **Uncertain conditions** exist when little or no reliable information is available. **Certainty conditions** exist when complete, reliable information is available.

Tossing a fair coin, rotating a roulette wheel, and rolling a die are examples of decisions under risk. Examples of decision making under risk can be found in queuing theory, statistical quality control, acceptance sampling, PERT, and so on. Decision trees are used to assist the decision-maker under conditions of risk.

One widely recommended technique for making risky decisions is to choose the action that has the greatest expected value. The **expected value** of an action is the average payoff value we can expect if we repeat the action many times.

Example of Expected Value Computation

Game 1: Win $2.00 whether the coin comes up heads or tails when a fair coin is tossed. What is the expected value for Game 1?

Game 2: Win $10.00 if the coin comes up heads and lose $5.00 if it comes up tails. What is the expected value for Game 2?

Expected Value = Average Payoff = Probability of Heads (PH) × Payoff for Heads (VH) + Probability of Tails (PT) × Payoff for Tails (VT)

$$EV = P(H) \times V(H) + P(T) \times V(T)$$

where $P(H)$ and $P(T)$ have equal chances, that is, 1/2:

$$EV \text{ (for Game 1)} = 1/2\,(2.00) + 1/2\,(2.00)$$
$$= 1.00 + 1.00 = \$2.00$$

$$EV \text{ (for Game 2)} = 1/2\,(10.00) + 1/2\,(-5.00)$$
$$= 5.00 - 2.50 = \$2.50$$

Since the expected value of game 2 is greater than the expected value of game 1, we should choose game 2 in order to maximize our expected value. Whether one chooses to play game 1 or 2 depends on whether he is risk averse.

Managers often make decisions based on little or no information. Sometimes, they are willing to buy information from market research studies. The question is how much is the market research information worth, although it may not be perfect? A concept that can help managers and uses both payoff tables and decision trees is called **expected value of perfect information (EVPI),** which can be computed as:

$$EVPI = EVwPI - EVwoPI$$

where EVwPI is expected value with perfect information, and EVwoPI is expected value without perfect information. The result of EVPI is given in an absolute value, ignoring signs.

If EVPI is greater than the cost to conduct a market research study, management should proceed with the study because they can get additional, hopefully better, information.

Example of Expected Value of Perfect Information

A market research firm approached a company to provide additional information about a new product before developing it at a cost of $3 million. The company estimates that its EVwPI is $20 million and EVwoPI was $15 million. Should the company hire the market research firm to conduct the study?

$$EVPI = EVwPI - EVwoPI = \$20 - \$15$$
$$= \$5 \text{ million}$$

Since EVPI of $5 million is more than the cost to conduct the study of $3 million, the company should hire the market research firm.

Decision Making under Uncertainty

Like decisions under risk, decisions under **uncertainty** involve a chance factor. The unique feature of decision making under uncertainty is that we cannot calculate a probability for the effect of the chance event. This is a situation in which a decision must be made on the basis of little or no reliable factual information. When considering pricing of competitors, actions of regulatory agencies, and strikes of suppliers, the decision-maker is addressing the problem of uncertainty.

Multiple outcomes are possible. The first task is to establish subjective probabilities of occurrence for the multiple outcomes. Under conditions of uncertainty, the rational, economic decision-maker will use expected monetary value (EMV) as the decision criterion. The EMV of an act is the sum of the conditional profit (loss) of each event times the probability of each event occurring.

Four strategies for making decisions under uncertainty are: (1) the minimax strategy, (2) the maximax strategy, (3) the Hurwicz strategy, and (4) and the minimax regret strategy.

The **minimax strategy** is a very conservative, pessimistic strategy that assumes that whatever action we choose, nature is against us and will cause the worst possible outcome (worst payoff). The values of the worst outcomes are the row minima. This strategy calls for choosing the action that gives us the best (largest) of these minima. That is, it chooses the action whose worst possible outcomes are not as bad as the worst possible outcomes of the other actions.

The best examples of applications for uncertainty are in problems of the military, war, and various types of athletic competition, product development, product pricing, collective bargaining, arbitration, foreign policy decisions, contract bidding, and oligopolistic and monopolistic market conditions.

The minimax strategy has a nice property in that it guarantees an outcome that is no worse than the minimum value for the action. The outcome may be better than the minimum, but it will certainly be no worse. However, this strategy, which focuses on preventing disaster, has the unfortunate property that it may eliminate the best outcomes from consideration.

For a maximization problem, the conservative approach is referred to as the **maximin criterion,** which is maximizing the minimum profits.

For a minimization problem, the conservative approach is referred to as the **minimax criterion,** which is minimizing the maximum losses.

The **maximax strategy** is an optimistic strategy that assumes that nature will cooperate with us to provide the best possible outcome for the action we choose—the row maxima. This strategy chooses the action yielding the best of the possible outcomes (best payoff). However, it does not defend the decision-maker against the possibility of containing the worst possible outcome, as does the minimax strategy. When a decision-maker is attracted to large gains, he would most likely use the maximax decision rule.

For a maximization problem, the optimistic approach is referred to as the **maximax criterion,** which is maximizing the maximum profits.

For a minimization problem, the optimistic approach is referred to as the **minimin criterion,** which is minimizing the minimum losses or maximum profits (not worth pursuing).

The **Hurwicz strategy** is a compromise between the very pessimistic minimax strategy and the very optimistic maximax strategy. A value between 0 and 1 is chosen for the coefficient of optimism, A, keeping in mind that low values of A are an indication of pessimism and high values of A are an indication of optimism. The goal is to find both the row minima and the row maxima and choose the activity that yields the maximum of the computed quantities. When A is zero, the Hurwicz is the same as the minimax strategy; when A is 1, the Hurwicz strategy is the same as the maximax strategy.

The **minimax regret strategy** is good for situations where the expected values concept fails. Why does the expected values technique fail? Expected values are averages of values. They are appropriate when we are trying to balance values that are close together, for example, the chance of losing two dollars versus the chance of winning four. Averages are much less appropriate when we balance values that are very different (e.g., the cost of a modest insurance premium versus the risk of being impoverished by a serious car accident).

The **minimax regret decision criterion** chooses the strategy that minimizes the maximum opportunity loss. To measure regret, take the difference between the value of the outcome you actually obtained and the maximum value you could have obtained if you had chosen a different alternative.

The minimax regret approach is minimizing the maximum regret value or opportunity loss. Opportunity loss is the amount of loss (i.e., lower profit or higher cost) from not making the best decision for each state of nature.

Decision Making under Conflict or Competition

Decision making under conflict or competition is referred to as **game theory**, and it uses the minimax strategy. There are two types of games under conflict or competition: (1) a zero-sum game and (2) a non-zero-sum game.

Game theory is used when the states of nature of the decision-maker are the strategies of the opponent. When one opponent gains at the loss of the other, it is called a **zero-sum game**, involving a complete conflict of interest. Games with less than complete conflict of interest are termed **non-zero-sum games.** In non-zero-sum games, the gains of one competitor are not completely at the expense of the other competitors.

The majority of business competitive actions involve non-zero-sum games. Non-zero-sum games require that the payoffs be given for each player since the payoff of one player can no longer be deducted from the payoff of the other, as in zero-sum games. **Prisoner's dilemma** is a type of business game situation where one firm is concerned about the actions of its rivals. Prisoner's dilemma is a classic conflict-of-interest situation. The outcome of the prisoner's dilemma game cannot be predicted conclusively. An example of **payoff table** is shown here:

Alternatives	States of Nature				Expected Profit
	1	2	3	4	
A					
B					
C					

States of nature are uncontrollable future events that can affect the outcomes of a decision. The best examples of applications of zero-sum games are in problems of the military, war, and various types of athletic competition. The best examples of applications of non-zero-sum games are in product development, product pricing, collective bargaining, arbitration, foreign policy decisions, contract bidding, and oligopolistic and monopolistic market conditions.

The simplest type of gain is the two-person zero-sum game. The players, X and Y, are equal in intelligence and ability. The term **zero sum** is used because the sum of gains exactly equals the sum of losses. The sum of player X's gains (or losses) and player Y's losses (or gains) is zero. Such a game, in which the sum of gains and losses added up over all players is zero, is called a zero-sum game.

Game theory is a framework to help decision-makers to decide when a firm's payoffs depend on actions taken by other firms. Game theory is used to develop effective competitive strategies for setting prices, for deciding the level of product quality, for deciding on research and development work, for setting the advertising budget, and for establishing public policy.

There are several concepts in game theory:

- In a simultaneous-move game, each decision-maker makes choices without specific knowledge of his competitor's countermoves.
- In a sequential-move game, each decision-maker makes his move after observing his competitor's moves.
- In a one-shot game, the interaction between competitors occurs only once.
- In a repeat game, the interaction between competitors is continuous.

A game theory strategy is a decision rule that describes the action taken by a decision-maker at any point in time. Prisoner's dilemma is a classic conflict-of-interest situation, as evidenced in a simultaneous-move and one-shot game.

Two strategies exist: dominant strategy and secure strategy. A **dominant strategy** is a decision that gives the best result for either party regardless of the action taken by the other. In this strategy, each party can control the range of outcomes, but no one can control the ultimate outcome. A **secure strategy** (also called the maximum strategy) is a decision that guarantees the best possible outcome given the worst possible scenario.

Nash equilibrium is a set of decision strategies where no firm can improve its own payoff by unilaterally changing its own strategy. Each firm's secure strategy is to offer a discount price regardless of the other firm's actions. The outcome is that both firms offer discount prices and earn relatively modest profit, and this outcome is called a Nash equilibrium.

A **Nash bargaining** game is another application of the simultaneous-move and one-shot game where two competitors or players bargain (haggle) over some items of value, and they have only once chance to reach an agreement.

Pure Strategy and Mixed Strategy

A **pure strategy** exists if there is one strategy for player X and one strategy for player Y that will be played each time. The payoff, which is obtained when each player plays his pure strategy, is called a **saddle point.** The saddle point represents an equilibrium condition that is optimum for both competitors.

The **Wald criterion,** which is a variant of decision making under uncertainty, is a useful technique to determine whether a pure strategy exists. A saddle point can be recognized because it is both the smallest numerical value in its row and the largest numerical value in its column. Not all two-person zero-sum games have a saddle point. When a saddle point is present, complex calculations to determine optimum strategies and game values are unnecessary.

When a pure strategy does not exist, a fundamental theorem of game theory states that the optimum can be found by using a mixed strategy. In a **mixed strategy**, each competitor randomly selects the strategy to employ according to a previously determined probability of usage for each strategy. A mixed strategy involves making a selection each time period by tossing a coin, selecting a number from a table of random numbers, or by using some probabilistic process.

There is a simple test to determine whether a pure or mixed strategy is best. If the maximum of the row minima (the maximin) equals the minimum of the column maxima (the minimax), then a pure strategy is best. Otherwise, use the mixed strategy.

Forecasting Models

Management frequently estimates sales, costs, income, market share, interest rates, inflation, and manufacturing capacity utilization.

Forecasting models are used to predict future aspects of a business operation such as estimating sales volume, short-term cash flow needs, and long-term external funding needs using stocks, bonds, or loans.

There are at least seven forecasting methods available: simple moving-average, weighted moving-average, exponential smoothing, heuristics, conjoint analysis, regression analysis, and Markov process analysis. The simple moving-average, weighted moving-average, and exponential smoothing are examples of time-series models.

The **simple moving-average** method smoothes time series data by averaging each successive group of data points. The **weighted moving-average** method smoothes time series data by computing a weighted average of past time series data. The sum of the weights must equal 1. The **exponential smoothing** method uses a weighted average of past time series data to arrive at smoothed time series data that can be used as forecasts. Smoothing constants are used in the exponential smoothing method. The **smoothing constant** is a parameter that provides the weight given to the most recent time series data. The exponential smoothing method is better than the simple moving average because it uses a weighted average of past time series data to arrive at smoothed time series data.

The **heuristics** method uses rules of thumb that shorten the time or work required to find a reasonably good solution to a complex problem. One aspect of it is a naive approach based on intuition, where it assumes that this month's sales are equal to last month's sales. The heuristics method uses a trial-and-error approach.

Conjoint analysis is a statistical technique where customers' preferences for different attributes (such as product offers or advertising impacts) are decomposed to determine the customer's inferred utility function and relative value for each attribute.

Regression analysis is a causal forecasting method that can be used to develop forecasts when time series data are not available. Regression analysis is a statistical technique that can be used to develop a mathematical equation showing how variables are related. For example, regression models can be used to determine the effect of advertising budget on sales revenue and to estimate manufacturing overhead costs and rates.

Two types of regression analysis are simple linear regression and multiple regression. In simple linear regression, there will be only two variables: one dependent variable and one independent variable. In multiple regression, there will be more than two variables: one dependent variable and more than one independent variable.

The following equation is an example of a simple linear regression model:

$$Y = mx + b$$

where Y is the dependent variable (sales), m is slope, X is the independent variable (disposable income), and b is the intercept.

A **histogram** or a **bar diagram** provides a frequency distribution of the measured data. A **scatter diagram** is used to determine whether a relationship exists between the dependent variable (vertical, y axis) and an independent variable (horizontal, x axis). With the regression equation, management can estimate future period sales by knowing the future period's disposable income.

MSE is an approach to measuring the accuracy of a forecasting model. The MSE is a quantity used in regression to estimate the unknown value of the variance of the error term.

Regression analysis deals with two statistical values: (1) value of the coefficient of determination and (2) value of correlation or correlation coefficient. The value of the coefficient of determination is always between 0 and 1. The higher this value, the better the regression line fits the data. For example, a coefficient of determination value of 0.97 means that 97 percent of the variations in sales can be explained by variations in disposable income. The value of correlation or correlation coefficient is always between -1 and $+1$. A correlation value near -1 or $+1$ indicates that there is a very strong linear relation between the sales and income variables. For example, a correlation coefficient value of 0.985 indicates a very strong linear relation between these two variables.

Markov-process analysis is useful in studying the evolution of certain systems over repeated trials as it shows the probability of moving from a current state to any future state. Markov-process analysis does not optimize a system; instead, it describes the future and steady-state behavior of a system.

Examples of applications of Markov-process analysis include: to describe the probability that a machine, functioning in one period, will function or break down in another period; to determine the market share for a company; to identify changes in the customer's collection experience in accounts receivable (i.e., to determine the amount of bad debts in total accounts receivable amounts); to determine the extent to which customers switch brands; to identify employee fill rates for job openings; and to identify employee succession planning moves.

Sales Seasonality and Deseasonality

Sales for many businesses exhibit seasonality over time. Seasonal index is a measure of the seasonal effect on a time-series. A **seasonalized time-series** is a set of observations measured at successive points in time or over successive periods of time. A seasonal index above 1 indicates a positive effect, a seasonal index of 1 indicates no seasonal effect, and a seasonal index less than 1 indicates a negative effect.

A **deseasonalized time-series** is one that has had the effect of season removed. Deseasonalized sales are calculated by dividing original time-series data by corresponding seasonal index values. The monthly or quarterly forecast is obtained by multiplying the trend forecast by seasonal index values.

Statistical Process Control Methods

All business processes, including production and services, exhibit variation in some dimension (e.g., a deviation from the standard specification of weight, size, and performance) that must be controlled to contain costs and improve quality. Control charts, a part of statistical process control (SPC) methods, can be used in a production environment to determine whether a production process is in control with the use of upper and lower control limits. Similarly, SPC methods can be used to track a call center staff's performance in terms of revenue produced per hour or number of calls attended per hour.

Another application of SPC is in monitoring the cash position of a company, which is subject to fluctuations. The management goal is to invest excess idle cash and to meet ongoing financial obligations. A **lower control limit (LCL)** representing the minimum cash amount and an **upper control limit (UCL)** representing the maximum cash amount can be developed. As long as the **target cash balance (TCB)** is between the LCL and the UCL, no action needs to be taken. The LCL acts as a safety stock in inventory or a required compensating balance. When the actual cash balance reaches the LCL, investment securities worth TCB – LCL are to be sold in order to return the cash balance to the target level. When the actual cash balance reaches the UCL, investment securities worth UCL – TCB are to be bought in order to return the cash balance to the target level.

The formulas used in the cash management model (Miller-Orr model) include the following:

$$UCL = (3 \times TCB) - (2 \times LCL)$$
$$ACB = ((4 \times TCB) - LCL)/3$$

where ACB is average cash balance.

Investment Securities to Be Sold = TCB − LCL
Investment Securities to Be Bought = UCL − TCB

Simulation Models

The primary objective of simulation models is to describe the behavior of a real system. A model is designed and developed, and a study is conducted to understand the behavior of the simulation model. Characteristics that are learned from the model are then used to make inferences about the real system. Later, the model is modified (asking what-if questions) to improve the system's performance. The behavior of the model in response to the what-if questions is studied to determine how well the real system will respond to the proposed modifications. Thus, the simulation model will help the decision-maker by predicting what can be expected in real-world practice. A key requisite is that the logic of the model should be as close to the actual operations as possible. In most cases, a computer is used for simulation models.

Examples of applications of simulation models include: to determine risk levels in a new product development idea, to select an inventory replenishment level that would balance the profit level and customer service level, to identify traffic flow patterns in a highway, to understand a bank's customer waiting lines, and to identify airline ticket overbooking patterns.

Computer simulation should not be viewed as an optimization technique but as a way to improve the behavior or performance of the system through adjusting model parameters.

Sensitivity Analysis

Sensitivity analysis is an evaluation of *how* certain changes in inputs result in *what* changes in outputs of a model or system. Change is inevitable. Prices of raw materials change as demand fluctuates, and changes in the labor market cause changes in production costs. Sensitivity analysis provides the manager with the information needed to respond to such changes without rebuilding the model. For example, bank management can use sensitivity analysis techniques to determine the effects of policy changes on the optimal mix for its portfolio of earning assets.

Computer simulation techniques can be used to perform sensitivity analysis. The capability to ask what-if questions is one of the biggest advantages of computer simulation.

The Time Value of Money

Money received today has a different value in the future, and money to be received in the future has a different value today due to the **time value of money (TVM)**. Both present value and future value techniques use interest rates to bring them to a common money denominator. **Compounding** is the process of determining the future value of present cash flows, which is equal to the beginning principal plus the interest earned. **Discounting** is the process of finding the present value of future cash flows, which is the reciprocal of compounding.

Many applications of TVM include setting up schedules for paying off loans, acquiring new equipment and facilities using capital budgeting techniques, and establishing the value of any asset (e.g., real estate, factories, machinery, oil wells, stocks, and bonds) whose value is derived from future cash flows.

TVM factors for present value of $1 due at the end of n periods ($n = 5$ years) at 4 to 10 percent interest rates are given here:

Period	4%	6%	8%	10%
5	0.8219	0.7473	0.6806	0.6209

TVM factors for present value of an annuity of $1 per period for n periods ($n = 5$ years) at 4 to 10 percent interest rates are given here:

Period	4%	6%	8%	10%
5	4.4518	4.2124	3.9927	3.7908

TVM factors for future value of $1 at the end of n periods ($n = 5$ years) at 4 to 10 percent interest rates are given here:

Period	4%	6%	8%	10%
5	1.2167	1.3382	1.4693	1.6105

TVM factors for future value of an annuity of $1 per period for n periods ($n = 5$ years) at 4 to 10 percent interest rates are given here:

Period	4%	6%	8%	10%
5	5.4163	5.6371	5.8666	6.1051

The present cash flows or the future cash flows are multiplied with the above TVM factors to determine the corresponding total future values or total present values.

Simple Ratios

Simple ratios are used to analyze the relationships between financial statements (e.g., income statement, balance sheet, and cash flow statement) and to calculate depreciation, depletion, and amortization expenses. Depreciation is a cost allocation in the form of an expense for using tangible fixed assets such as plant and equipment. Depletion is a cost allocation for using tangible natural assets such as coal and iron ore resources. Amortization is a cost allocation for using intangible assets such as patents and copyrights.

Profit Models

Profit models establish a quantitative relationship between sales volumes and costs. Management can determine a profit model from revenue-volume and cost-volume models as follows:

$$P(x) = R(x) - C(x)$$

where P is profit, x is volume in units, R is revenue, and C is total cost of producing x units, which includes total fixed costs and variable costs.

For example, total revenue-volume model is R $(x) =$ $\$10x$, where x is sales volume in units and $\$10$ is the selling price per unit (marginal revenue).

For example, total cost-volume model is C $(x) =$ $\$5,000 + \$5x$, where x is production volume in units, $\$5,000$ is total fixed cost, and $\$5$ is variable cost per unit (marginal cost).

Substituting the R (x) and C (x) values in P $(x) =$ R $(x) -$ C (x) equation gives the following result:

$$P(x) = \$10x - (\$5,000 + 5x) = 5x - \$5,000$$

The company needs to sell $x = 1,000$ units (i.e., $\$5,000/\$5$) to cover fixed costs and variable costs with zero profit.

The breakeven point (BEP) is 1,000 units where profit is zero and revenues and costs are equal. The BEP in units can also be calculated as:

BEP = (Total Fixed Costs)/(Selling Price per Unit − Variable Cost per Unit)

BEP = ($\$5,000$)/($\$10 - \$5$) = 1,000 Units

Discriminant and Multivariate Analysis

Discriminant analysis is an identification procedure. This technique can be applied to a wide variety of research and predictive problems, and interpretation and classification of data. It studies the differences between two or more groups and a set of discriminant variables simultaneously. For example, multiple discriminant analysis is used for constructing credit-scoring indexes when granting a personal credit to an individual customer or to a business customer for granting a trade credit, and for identifying businesses that might go bankrupt.

Multivariate analysis is a research technique used to determine how a combination of variables interacts to cause a particular outcome. For example, multivariate analysis can be applied to determine the multiple variables affecting an employee's productivity. Examples of these multiple variables include conscientious personality, high challenging task, and higher satisfaction with job and life. It is called **bivariate analysis** when an employee's productivity is solely based on morale (i.e., one-to-one causal relationship between two variables such as productivity and morale).

Cluster Analysis

Cluster analysis is a statistical technique to identify groups of entities that have similar characteristics that can be applied to data mining and market research areas. For example, cluster analysis can be used by data mining analysts to find groups of customers with similar characteristics from customer order and demographic data and by market researchers to divide the population of subjects to interview into mutually exclusive groups (e.g., city blocks and counties) and draw a sample of the groups from the segmented population.

Consumer Research Models

Marketing engineering is the application of statistical and mathematical models to marketing research in order to study consumer habits, attitudes, and preferences. Marketers use the results of this research in developing new products, evaluating test markets, and allocating advertisement budget to products.

Examples of consumer models include cognitive, attitudinal, compositional (e.g., lexicographic, conjunctive, and linear compensatory), and decompositional (e.g., conjoint analysis) models.

Multicriteria Decision Models

Usually, managers evaluate various alternatives across multiple decision criteria using both quantitative and qualitative methods. **Multicriteria decision models** bring discipline to unstructured and poorly understood problems when there is no clear "best" choice. Examples of application of this model include supplier evaluation criteria, product quality evaluation criteria, and service quality evaluation criteria because these examples need multiple dimensions to consider and require multiple factors to evaluate.

❑ Learning Objective 12.2: UNDERSTAND THE BASIC PRINCIPLES AND CONCEPTS IN ECONOMICS

Economics is the study of making choices in using resources when there is scarcity of resources. The following are major principles and concepts in economics:

- **Opportunity cost** is the cost of a forgone choice when selecting some other choice (i.e., it is the amount of sacrifice to get something). It is a trade-off between two choices and is an example of implicit cost that does not require money payments to acquire inputs. The various principles and concepts in economics are equally applicable to both business and personal situations. Opportunity costs should be considered in decision making.
- **Sunk cost** is a cost that has already been incurred or committed to incur and that cannot be recovered. Sunk costs should not be considered in decision making because they are past costs and have no relevance to current or future costs.
- Profits are maximized when revenues are maximized and costs are minimized. Profits are of two types: economic profits and accounting profits. **Economic profit** is total revenue minus total economic cost. Total revenue is the total money received from selling goods or rendering services. **Accounting profit** is total revenue minus total accounting cost. Accounting profit is always higher than the economic profit since the former does not consider opportunity cost.
- **Economic cost** is the total cost of inputs used in the production of goods and services—equal to explicit costs (accounting costs) plus implicit costs (opportunity costs).
- **Accounting cost** is the explicit costs of production or service inputs, where these costs represent the actual money paid to acquire inputs. The resources (e.g., labor, money, materials, energy, and machinery) used to produce goods and services are known as factors of production or simply production inputs.
- Two concepts related to economic profit include **economic-value-added (EVA)** and **market-value-added (MVA)**. EVA is defined as a company's net operating profit after-tax minus the charges for the use of capital (i.e., invested capital times the cost of capital) invested in the company's tangible assets. MVA measures the total market value of a company's outstanding stock plus the company's debt or total market value minus invested capital. When a company's MVA is positive, it indicates that it has created wealth for its stockholders, and it goes hand in hand with a high EVA measurement.
- **Average fixed cost** is total fixed cost divided by the quantity produced both in short run and long run. Fixed costs are those costs that do not change with quantity produced (e.g., rent).
- **Average variable cost** is total variable cost divided by the quantity produced both in short run and long run. Variable costs are those costs that do change with the quantity produced (e.g., labor wages).
- **Average total cost** is average fixed cost plus average variable cost both in short run and long run. A firm will earn normal profit when price equals average total cost.
- **Average total cost per unit** is total cost divided by the quantity of units produced.
- **Average profit per unit** is total profit divided by the quantity of units produced or sold.
- **Marginal revenue** is the change in total revenue from selling one more unit of output.
- **Marginal cost** is the change in total cost due to a one-unit change in output both in short run and long run.
- **Marginal profit** is marginal revenue minus marginal cost.
- **Marginal revenue** equals marginal cost at the profit-maximizing level of output both in short run and long run.
- **Marginal profit** is the change in total profit due to a one-unit change in output both in short run and long run. Profit is maximized when marginal profit is zero.

- Marginal benefit (additional benefit) should exceed the marginal cost (additional cost).
- The incremental change is the change resulting from a given managerial decision; the change could result in incremental revenue (additional revenue), incremental cost (additional cost), incremental profit (additional profit), or incremental loss (additional loss).
- The term **incremental** focuses on a total level, whereas the term **marginal** focuses on a small (per unit) level. However, both terms deal with "additional" or "change" of something.
- If a manufacturing firm has excess capacity, the incremental profit earned from the production and sale of a new product would be higher than before since the excess capacity is put to good use, instead of wasting it.
- When marginal revenue is greater than average revenue, the average must be increasing. If total revenue increases at a constant rate as output increases, then the average revenue is constant. Marginal revenue equals average revenue at some output level.
- Total revenue increases as long as marginal revenue increases. Total revenue is maximized at the point where marginal revenue equals zero.
- Marginal profit equals average profit when average profit is maximized at some output level.
- When marginal profit is positive, total profit is increasing as output increases. Similarly, when marginal profit is negative, total profit decreases as output increases. The marginal profit increases greater than the average profit due to the averaging effect.
- The optimal output level is determined when marginal revenue equals marginal cost, marginal profit is zero, and total profit is maximized.
- In a perfectly competitive market equilibrium, price equals marginal cost, and marginal revenue equals marginal cost.
- In a monopoly firm, marginal revenue equals marginal cost, and the prices are set at a level where price exceeds marginal revenue in the long-run equilibrium.
- The principle of economies of scale states that the long-run average cost of production decreases as output increases. Diseconomies of scale refer to a situation where the long-run average cost of production increases as output increases.
- The principle of constant returns to scale states that the long-run total cost increases proportionately with output, so average cost is constant.

- The principle of diminishing returns states that as one input increases while other inputs are held constant, output increases at a decreasing rate.
- Consumers are interested in the real value of money or income in terms of its purchasing power (i.e., the quantity of goods the money or income can buy), not the face (nominal) value of money or income.

❑ Learning Objective 12.3: UNDERSTAND THE BASIC PRINCIPLES AND APPLICATIONS OF MICROECONOMICS

The **scope of microeconomics** deals with how an individual firm operates in competitive markets, its demand and supply curves, labor economics, and structure of product markets. It also focuses on the production of individual firms and income of individual consumers in that production leads to income and income leads to production.

Economic Implications of Competition

Competition is the major mechanism of control in a free market system because it forces businesses and resource suppliers to make appropriate responses to changes in consumer wants and needs. Use of scarce resources in a least cost and most efficient manner is good for all—buyers, sellers, resource suppliers, competition, and government.

Competition does more than guarantee responses to consumer needs and wants. It is competition that forces firms to adopt the most efficient production techniques. The firms who do not utilize most efficient, least-cost production techniques will be overpowered by those who do. Inefficient and high-cost firms will eventually be eliminated from the industry and replaced by most efficient and least-cost firms. Therefore, competition provides an environment conducive to technological advance.

Another benefit of competition is when businesses and resource suppliers operating in a highly competitive market system not only seek their own self-interest but also promote the public or social interest. *The key link between self-interest and public-interest is the use of the least expensive combination of resources in producing a given output.* To act otherwise would be to forgo profits or even to risk bankruptcy over a period of time.

Economic Implications of Demand and Supply

To understand how demand and supply forces work, it is important to understand the market in which they operate. A market is an institution or mechanism that brings together buyers and sellers of particular goods and services. *A buyer is a demander. A seller is a supplier.*

The basic determinants of an individual's demand curve for a specific product include preferences or tastes, money income, and the prices of other goods.

Markets assume a wide variety of forms: local, national, or international in scope; personal or impersonal actions by buyers and sellers; and small or large (gas station versus stock market). All these situations, which link the potential buyer with potential sellers, comprise markets.

Changes in Demand and Supply

When a price is changed, it will cause a change in demand, resulting in movement from one point to another on a fixed demand curve. This situation is referred to as "change in the quantity demanded."

When a nonprice determinant of demand is changed, it will cause a change in demand, resulting in shifting the demand curve either left or right of the fixed demand curve. This is referred to as "change in demand."

When a price is changed, it will cause a change in supply, resulting in movement from one point to another on a fixed supply curve. This situation is referred to as "change in the quantity supplied."

When a nonprice determinant of supply is changed, it will cause a change in supply, resulting in shifting the supply curve either left or right of the fixed supply curve. This is referred to as "change in supply."

The equilibrium price and quantity for a product is determined by market demand and supply. It is the point of intersection of the downward-sloping demand curve and the upward-sloping supply curve. Two things can be concluded here:

1. Quantity supplied will exceed quantity demanded when a price is above the equilibrium price. Surplus of goods will occur. This in turn reduces prices and increases consumption.

2. Quantity demanded will exceed quantity supplied when a price is below the equilibrium price. Shortage of goods will occur. This in turn increases prices and increases quantity supplied.

Economic Implications of Utility

The law of demand says that a high price usually discourages consumers from buying a product or service and that a low price encourages them to buy. Three types of explanations exist to represent consumer behavior and the downward-sloping demand curve. These include income and substitution effects, law of diminishing marginal utility, and indifference curves.

The **income effect** indicates that, at a lower price, one can afford more of the good without giving up any alternative goods. The purchasing power of one's money income is increased due to lower prices.

The **substitution effect** states that, at a lower price, one has the incentive to substitute the cheaper good for similar goods that are now relatively more expensive (e.g., beef is substituted for pork or chicken).

A more sophisticated explanation of consumer behavior and consumer equilibrium is based on budget lines and indifference curves.

A **budget line** shows the various combinations of two products A and B, which can be purchased with a given money income. An **indifference curve** shows all combinations of products A and B that will yield the same level of satisfaction or utility to the consumer. Hence, the consumer will be indifferent as to which combination is actually obtained.

Economic Implications of Perfect Competition

A perfect (pure) competition is described as a market with many sellers and buyers of a homogeneous product that has no barriers to market entry, where both buyers and sellers take the market price as given and where the demand is perfectly elastic (e.g., corn and wheat).

The firm operating in a perfectly competitive market need only decide how much to produce given the market price and should be concerned about the market supply curve and the law of supply. Marginal revenue (MR) is constant and equal to marginal cost (MC) and product price (P), where $MR = MC = P$. Perfect competition cannot influence the price of the product it is selling. It assumes that no firm has a significant impact on the market and that it does not matter what the size of the firm is. Cost, price, and product quality information is known to all buyers and sellers.

Economic Implications of Monopolistic Competition

A monopolistic competition is described as a market with many sellers and buyers of a slightly different product that has no barriers to market entry and where the demand is elastic but not perfectly elastic (e.g., grocery stores and coffee shops). The fundamental difference between perfect competition and monopolistic competition is based on the existence of product differentiation. Cost, price, and product quality information is known to all buyers and sellers.

A large firm operating in a monopolistic competition may be able to influence prices. Large numbers of rivals is a characteristic of perfect competition and monopolistic competition (a blend of monopoly and competition). No mutual interdependence exists.

Economic Implications of Oligopolies

The oligopolistic industry is characterized by the presence of a few firms dominating the market with homogeneous or differentiated products or services and with demand being less elastic than the demand facing monopolistic competition. Examples include aluminum and automobile industries and public accounting firms. The primary causes for the existence of oligopolies are economies of scale, large barriers to entry into the industry, and mergers and acquisitions.

When setting prices, the oligopolistic firm should consider the reaction of rivals in addition to cost and demand data. This results in mutual interdependence. A price war can result when one firm cut its prices.

There is no standard model of oligopoly, unlike pure competition and pure monopoly. The latter two refer to clear-cut market arrangements while oligopoly does not. The presence of many variations of oligopoly prevents the development of a simple model describing oligopolistic behavior. It is impossible to estimate the demand and marginal-revenue data when the reaction of rivals is highly uncertain.

Prices change less frequently in oligopoly than they do under pure competition, pure monopoly, or mo-

nopolistic competition. When oligopolistic prices do change, other firms are likely to change their prices. This might suggest a collusion among firms in setting and changing prices. Greater barriers to collusion exist when general economic conditions are recessionary.

Four models of pricing are available for a firm operating in an oligopoly industry: "kinked" demand curve, collusive pricing, price leadership, and cost-plus pricing:

1. In the kinked demand curve, a price increase is ignored, a price cut is followed, and the curve has a gap or break.
2. In collusive pricing, prices are fixed through an unspoken agreement, price war can occur, and entry of new firms is controlled.
3. In price leadership, the dominant firm sets the price or initiates price changes.
4. In cost-plus pricing, a markup is added to costs, it is good for multiproduct firms, and it works with collusive pricing and price leadership situations.

Economic Implications of Monopolies

Absolute or pure monopoly exists when a single firm is the sole producer of a unique product where the firm's demand curve is the same as the market demand curve, meaning the firm is the market and is a price-maker. Examples of monopolies include the gas and electric companies and professional sports. The four characteristics of a pure monopoly include single seller, no close substitutes, price-maker, and barriers to entry and exit. "Barriers to exit" means there is a limit on asset redeployment from one line of business or industry to another. Pure monopoly can be equated to imperfect competition. The absence of rivals is a characteristic of pure monopoly. No mutual interdependence exists.

When a perfectly discriminating monopolist lowers price, the reduced price applies only to the additional unit sold and not to prior units. Hence, price, marginal revenue, and marginal cost are equal for any unit of output (i.e., $P = MR = MC$). The marginal-revenue curve coincides with its demand curve, and there is an incentive to increase production.

When the nondiscriminating monopolist lowers price to sell additional output, the lower price will apply not only to the additional sales but also to all prior units of output. Consequently, marginal revenue is less than price, and the marginal-revenue curve lies below the demand curve. This condition creates a disincentive to increase production. In the long run, monopolies set prices at a level where price exceeds marginal revenue (i.e., P > MR).

Economic Implications of Labor Economics

Labor economics deals with wages, wage rates, and productivity of workers. Wages are the price paid for the use of labor, where labor includes all blue- and white-collar workers, professionals, and owners of small businesses. Wage rate is a price paid for the use of units of labor service.

Basically, there are two types of wages: nominal (money) wages and real wages. Nominal wages are the amounts of money received per unit of time (hour, day, week, month, year). Real wages are the quantity of goods and services that can be obtained with nominal wages. Real wages depend on one's nominal wages and the prices of the goods and services purchased. *Real wages are the "purchasing power" of nominal wages. Nominal wages and real wages need not move together.*

Economic Implications of Structure of Product Markets

The structure of product markets addresses resource pricing and level of employment as factors of production. Production factors cost money to acquire materials and to pay for utilities and wages. Product prices are determined by the interaction of the forces of demand and supply. Similarly, the price of a factor of production is determined by the interaction of the market demand and supply for that factor. The market demand for a factor is derived from the demand curve of a single firm for the factor.

Monopsony refers to one form of imperfect competitive market where there is a single buyer of a particular factor of production such as the sole mining employer in a mining town. Because of the greater factor productivity enjoyed by this firm, it can pay a higher price for the factor and become a **monopsonist.** Monopsony also results from lack of geographic and occupational mobility of factors of production.

Oligopsonistic and monopsonistic competition refers to other forms of imperfect competition in factor markets. An **oligopsonistic competitor** is one of few buyers of a homogeneous or differentiated factor. A **monopsonistic competitor** is one of many buyers of a differentiated factor. Both oligopsonistic and monopsonistic competitors face a rising supply curve of the factor; that is, they must pay higher factor prices for greater quantities of the factor. Their marginal factor cost curve lies above the factor supply curve.

❑ Learning Objective 12.4: UNDERSTAND THE BASIC PRINCIPLES AND APPLICATIONS OF MACROECONOMICS

The **scope of macroeconomics** includes fiscal and monetary policies, employment and unemployment, inflation, interest rates, economic growth, economic performance, government spending, and money supply in the economy. It also focuses on production and income of the economy as a whole.

Economic Implications of Employment, Interest Rates, and Investment Theories

Essentially, there are two theories of employment: classical and Keynesian. Classical economists suggest that full employment is the norm of a market economy and that a laissez-faire (hands-off) policy is best. Keynesian economics holds that unemployment is characteristic of laissez-faire capitalism, and activist government policies are required if one is to avoid the waste of idle resources. Keynesian economists believe that full employment is accidental. The basic question is: Can the market system provide for an efficient allocation of resources and achieve and maintain full employment of available resources?

Classical economists view aggregate supply as determining the full-employment level of real national output while aggregate demand establishes the price-level. Aggregate demand is stable as long as there are no significant changes in the money supply. When aggregate demand declines, the price will fall to eliminate the temporary excess supply and to restore full employment.

Keynesian economists view aggregate demand as unstable and price and wages as downwardly inflexible. A decline in the aggregate demand has no effect on the price level and the real output falls, resulting in unemployment. Volatility of aggregate demand and downward inflexibility of prices mean that unemployment can persist for extended periods of time. An increase in savings will decrease gross national product (GNP).

With a fixed supply of money, higher product price levels increase the demand for money balances, increase the interest rate, and reduce investment. With a fixed supply of money, lower product price levels reduce the demand for money balances, decrease the interest rate, and increase investment.

Interest rate is the major determinant of investment. But other factors or variables determine the location of the investment-demand curve. Changes in these other variables, called **noninterest determinants,** shift the investment-demand curve, either to the right or to the left. Any factor that increases the expected net profitability of investment will shift the investment-demand curve to the right. Any factor that decreases the expected net profitability of investment will shift the investment-demand curve to the left.

Economic Implications of Economic Growth

Growth economics is concerned with the question of how to increase the economy's productive capacity or full employment. Measures of **economic growth** include gross domestic product (GDP), gross national product (GNP), and net national product (NNP). Measures of price changes include consumer price index (CPI) and producer price index (PPI).

GDP is the total market value of all final goods and services produced by a country in a given year. It measures total output of a country. The two main variables that contribute to increases in a nation's real GDP are labor productivity and total worker hours. GDP is computed as:

GDP = Consumption + Investment + Government
   Purchases + Net Exports

where consumption is purchases by consumers, investment is purchases by private sector firms, government purchases include purchases by all levels of government, and net exports are net purchases by the foreign sectors (i.e., net exports are equal to domestic exports minus domestic imports).

Economic growth is the sustained increase in real GDP over a long period of time. **Real GDP** takes price changes into account, whereas **nominal GDP** takes current prices into account.

GDP deflator is the most appropriate inflation index to use when a firm is attempting to estimate the inflation rate on all goods and services over a recent time period. It measures how prices of goods and services included in GDP change over time. GDP deflator is calculated as:

GDP Deflator = [(Nominal GDP)/(Real GDP)] × 100

> ### Example of Computation of GDP Deflator
>
> Real GDP in year 2008 is $50,000, which is the base year with index of 100. Nominal GDP in year 2008 is $60,000. What is the GDP deflator for 2009 and by what percentage did prices increase between the two years?
>
> GDP Deflator for 2009 = ($60,000)/($50,000)
>   × 100 = 112
>
> Price Increase = (112 − 100)/100 = 0.12 = 12%

GNP is GDP plus total income earned worldwide by U.S. firms and its residents. The sale of final goods is included in the GNP and the sale of intermediate goods is excluded from the GNP. *GNP is all-inclusive and better than GDP.*

NNP equals GNP minus depreciation. NNP is composed of the total market value of all final goods and services produced in the economy in one year minus the capital consumption allowance (i.e., depreciation).

Economic growth is defined and measured in two ways: (1) as the increase in real GNP or NNP that occurs over a period of time or (2) as the increase in real GNP or NNP per capita that occurs over time.

Nominal GNP = Real GNP + Inflation

The growth of real output and income per capita is superior for comparisons of living standards among nations or regions. Economic growth is usually calculated in terms of annual percentage rates of growth.

The growth of total output relative to population means a higher standard of living. Similarly, a drop in total output relative to population means a lower standard of living. A growing economy provides an increment in its annual real output, which it can use to satisfy existing needs or to undertake new social programs (e.g., eliminating poverty and cleaning up the environment). Growth lessens the burden of scarcity. This in turn allows a nation to realize existing economic goods and undertake new programs by government. Even a small difference in the rate of growth becomes very important because of the multiplicative, compound interest effect.

The GNP is a quantity measure, not quality. Hence, it measures national economic performance, market-oriented activity, and the size of national output, not improvements in product quality.

Characteristics of GNP

- GNP will rise with an increase in government purchases of services (i.e., government spending).
- GNP will fall following an increase in imports.
- A deficit in the balance of payments occurs when imports exceed exports.
- A surplus in the balance of payments occurs when exports exceed imports.
- The basic source of improvements in real wage rates and in the standard of living is productivity growth.
- When gross investment is less than depreciation, the capital stock of the economy is shrinking.
- An increase in the average hours worked per week of production workers would provide a leading indicator of a future increase in GNP.

The following three items are included in the GNP calculation: (1) capital consumption allowance or goods used up in producing the GNP, (2) Social Security contributions, and (3) undistributed corporate profits. The buying and selling of corporate bonds would not be included in the GNP calculation.

Under the income approach, the GNP is measured as:

Depreciation Charges + Indirect Business Taxes
+ Wages, Rents, Interest, and Profits

Under the output (expenditures) approach, the GNP is calculated as:

Consumption + Investments + Government

Purchases + Expenditures by Foreigners

There are two fundamental ways by which any society can increase its real output and income: (1) by increasing its inputs of resources and (2) by increasing the productivity of those inputs. Real GNP (i.e., total output) in any year depends on the input of labor (measured in worker-hours) multiplied by labor productivity (measured as real output per worker per hour).

Real GNP = Labor Input × Labor Productivity

The hours of labor input (worker-hours) depend on the size of the employed labor force and the length of the average workweek. Labor productivity is de-

termined by technological progress, the quantity of capital goods with which workers are equipped, the quality of labor itself, and the efficiency with which the various inputs are allocated, combined, and managed.

CPI is a statistic used to measure the changes in prices in a market basket of selected items. The CPI is one factor in setting cost-of-living adjustments (COLA) in a country. Critics of CPI argue that it overstates increases in the cost of living. This is due to the constant composition of the market basket of items whose prices are measured. **Chain-weighted index** is a method for calculating changes in prices that uses an average of base years from neighboring years.

The PPI measures the price of a basket of commodities at the point of their first commercial sale. The purchasing managers' index is a composite index based on data from a monthly report on producers' prices.

Example of Application of CPI, Inflation, and Real Income

Assume that in 2005 a business analyst makes $40,000 per year and five years later his income increases to $90,000. The CPI increases from 100 to 250. What is the real income in 2005 prices for the later years? The real income (in 2005 prices) for the later years is as follows:

Inflation Rate = $(250 - 100)/250 = 150/250$
    $= 0.60 = 60\%$

Real Income = Nominal Income − Inflation Rate
    $= 100\% - 60\% = 40\%$

Therefore, real income in 2005 prices is $90,000 × 0.40 = $36,000.

Three ingredients or factors in economic growth are supply factor, demand factor, and allocative factor.

The first, **supply factor,** relates to the physical ability of an economy to grow. These include the quantity and quality of its natural and human resources, the supply or stock of capital goods, and technology. These factors permit an economy to produce a greater real output.

Demand factor is the second ingredient of economic growth. It relates to full employment of its expanding suppliers of resources. This requires a growing level of aggregate demand.

The third factor, the **allocative factor,** requires full production. It is the combination of the actual use of resource suppliers and the allocation of those resources to obtain the maximum amount of useful goods produced.

Supply and demand factors in growth are related to each other. These three factors (supply, demand, and allocative) can also be related to a **production possibilities curve.** This curve shows the various maximum combinations of products that can be produced given the quantity and quality of the natural, human, and capital resources and technology. A negatively sloped curve reflects the concept of opportunity cost. An opportunity cost is the value of a resource in its best alternative use. Opportunity costs are implicit costs and generally are imputed.

Methods of Measuring Economic Performance

The basic goals of the public and private sectors are to achieve both the full employment of resources and a stable price level. *Two major methods exist to measure economic performance of a country: (1) unemployment and (2) inflation.*

Unemployment

The key point is that the level of output depends directly on total or aggregate expenditures. A high level of total spending means it will be profitable for the various industries to produce large outputs, and it will be profitable for various resource suppliers to be employed at high levels. Hence,

Total Spending = Private Sector Spending
+ Public Sector Spending

Private sector spending alone is not enough to keep the economy at full employment. The government's obligation (public spending) is to augment private sector spending sufficient to generate full employment. *Government has two basic economic tools with which to accomplish public spending: (1) spending programs and (2) taxes.* Specifically, government should increase its own spending on public goods and services on the one hand and reduce taxes in order to stimulate private sector spending on the other. Unemployment results when either private sector spending or public sector spending does not measure up to expectations.

There are four variations of employment or unemployment:

1. **Full employment** means that all people 16 years of age or older are employed or are actively seeking employment or that cyclical unemployment is zero. Inflation occurring during a period of full employment is most likely to be demand-pull inflation. In an economy that is near full employment, a decrease in the money supply is likely to decrease the price level.
2. **Frictional unemployment** will always exist in a dynamic economy. It is short-run unemployment that is caused by people voluntarily changing jobs or by frictions that result from lack of knowledge about job opportunities and lack of labor mobility.

   Thus, full employment means that only frictional unemployment exists. In other words, there is no cyclical or structural unemployment when the economy is operating at full employment. There always will be some unemployment at all times caused by workers changing jobs. Frictional unemployment occurs when both jobs and the workers qualified to fill them are available. It is equal to about 5 or 6 percent.
3. **Cyclical employment** is unemployment that results from inadequate aggregate demand during the recession and depression phases of the business cycle.
4. **Structural unemployment** is unemployment that results from an economy's failure to adjust completely and efficiently to basic structural changes such as changes in technology, changes in consumer preferences, and changes in the geographic locations of certain industries. It is equal to about 5 or 6 percent. Structural changes prevent certain people from obtaining jobs because of their geographic location, race, age, inadequate education, or lack of training. *People who are structurally unemployed are often referred to as the "hard-core unemployed."*

Inflation and Deflation

If aggregate spending exceeds full-employment output, excess spending will have the effect of increasing the price level. Therefore, excessive aggregate spending is inflationary. Government intervenes to eliminate the excess spending by cutting its own expenditures and by raising taxes so as to curtail private spending. The inverse relationship between unemployment and inflation is embodied in the **Phillips curve.**

- Total spending should increase to generate full employment.

- Excessive aggregate spending leads to inflation.
- An increase in the price level would tend to decrease consumption.

Inflation is a rise in the general level of prices; deflation is a decline in the general level of prices. When prices rise, purchasing power or the ability to buy goods and services declines. If prices double, purchasing power is reduced to one-half of its previous level. Thus, *inflation reduces the purchasing power of money.* Inflation does not mean that the prices of all goods and services rise. Some prices rise, others fall, and some do not change at all; but on the average, prices rise.

The basic cause of inflation is spending in excess of what an economy can produce. If an economy has unemployed resources, an increase in aggregate demand tends to increase output and employment a great deal and to increase prices only slightly. When an economy is fully employed, an increase in aggregate demand forces prices to increase sharply because resources are scarce and output cannot be increased.

Types of Inflation   There are seven types of inflation:

1. **Cost-push inflation** is a rise in prices brought about by production costs increasing faster than productivity. Since labor is usually the largest cost of production, cost-push inflation is often called **wage-push inflation**. The expected impact is an increase in unemployment.
2. **Demand-pull inflation** is a rise in prices caused by an increase in aggregate demand when an economy's resources are fully employed and production cannot be increased. The expected impact is a decrease in unemployment.
3. **Structural inflation** results when demand increases or costs increase in certain industries even though aggregate demand equals aggregate supply for the nation as a whole.
4. **Profit-push inflation** occurs when corporate profits increase before wages increase. An increase in corporate profits can result from increases in prices or from improvements in productivity that reduce the labor cost per unit.
5. **Hyperinflation or pure inflation** is a rise in prices with a very small, if any, increase in output.
6. **Creeping inflation** is a slow upward movement in prices over a period of several years. Creeping inflation is usually defined as a 1, 2, or 3 percent increase in the general price level each year. Creeping inflation generally accompanies growth and

full employment. Many economists prefer creeping inflation to price stability accompanied by unemployment and lack of economic growth.

7. **Bottleneck inflation** can be associated with an aggregate supply curve that is steep. Before the redistribution effects of inflation can be discussed, a distinction must be made between money income and real income. **Money income** is the amount of money or number of dollars a person receives for the work he does; **real income** is the amount of goods and services the money income will buy or the purchasing power of the money income. Real income is thus a function of money income and the prices of goods and services.

Effects of Inflation   If nominal income increases faster than the price level, then real income will rise. Three classes of people (e.g., fixed-income groups, creditors, and savers) generally suffer from inflation, and three classes of people (e.g., flexible money income groups, debtors, and speculators) generally benefit from inflation.

Nature of Deflation   Deflation is a decrease in prices. Deflation can be induced through contractionary monetary and fiscal policies. If deflation occurs in the United States, it becomes cheaper for other countries to buy U.S. goods. Deflation can arise automatically due to an excess of imports over exports.

Aggregate Demand and Supply

Aggregate demand is the total demand for goods and services in an entire economy (i.e., demand for GDP by individual consumers, private sector firms, the government at all levels, and the foreign sector). The aggregate demand curve, which shows the relationship between the level of prices and the quantity of real GDP demanded, is affected in three different ways: the wealth effect (i.e., a lower price level leads to a higher level of wealth), the interest rate effect (i.e., a lower price level leads to a lower interest rate), and the international trade effect (i.e., a lower price level leads to an increased demand for domestic goods). There are factors other than price level changes that affect the aggregate demand curve, including changes in the supply of money, changes in government spending, changes in taxes, and all other changes in demand (e.g., increase in exports, increase in consumer spending, and increase in private investment spending).

Factors that *increase the aggregate demand* include increase in government spending, decrease in taxes, and increase in the money supply. Factors that *decrease the aggregate demand* include decrease in government spending, increase in taxes, and decrease in the money supply.

The relationship between the level of income and consumer spending is known as the **consumption function,** which states that when consumers have more income, they will purchase more goods and services. Two concepts in this area include **marginal propensity to consume (MPC)** and **marginal propensity to save (MPS)**, with the understanding that whatever income a consumer has not spent (consumed) is saved. The MPC and MPS are computed as:

MPC = Additional Consumption/Additional Income

MPS = Additional Savings/Additional Income

Note that the sum of the MPC and the MPS always equals 1.

There is a **GDP multiplier** effect taking place in the aggregate demand in that small changes in total spending in the economy could lead to large changes in GDP and income. The GDP multiplier is computed in two ways:

GDP Multiplier = Total Shift in Aggregate Demand/Initial Shift in Aggregate Demand

GDP Multiplier = $1/(1 - MPC)$

Increase in GDP and Income = GDP Multiplier × Increase in Spending

Example of Computation of GDP Multiplier Effect

A government increased its spending by $20 billion and the MPC is 0.5. What is the GDP multiplier? What is the total increase in GDP and income?

GDP Multiplier = $1/(1 - MPC) = 1/(1 - 0.5)$
= $1/0.5 = 2.0$

Increase in GDP and Income = GDP Multiplier × Increase in Spending = $2.0 \times \$20$ billion
= 40 billion

Aggregate supply focuses on equating an economy's demand for output with firms' ability to supply output. This concept is similar to an individual firm's demand and supply for its products. The aggregate supply curve shows the relationship between the level of prices and the quantity of output supplied. Two supply curves are in effect: long-run (vertical) and short-run (flat):

- In the **long-run supply curve**, the level of output is dependent solely on the factors of supply (e.g., labor, capital, and technology) and is independent of the price level. The economy is at full employment and changes in the price level do not affect employment.
- In the **short-run supply curve**, the level of output is dependent primarily on demand and is independent of the price level, except for small price changes. The firms are assumed to supply all the output demanded by adjusting their production levels. However, an increase in external events such as an increase in oil prices can increase a firm's costs and reduce its profits, and the firms increase their product prices to cover the increased costs. This is called a **supply shock** because it raises prices and decreases output, resulting in a recession. This phenomenon is called **stagflation** to indicate an increase in prices and a decrease in outputs.

Fiscal Policy

Governments can use fiscal policy as a tool to combat economic downturns and recessions with changes in taxes and spending levels that affect the level of GDP and aggregate demand. Two scenarios can occur from a change in fiscal policy:

Scenario 1: **Expansionary fiscal policy** means an increase in government spending and a decrease in taxes, which increases the aggregate demand and which shifts the aggregate demand curve to the right. This policy action increases the GDP and decreases unemployment when the current level of GDP is below full employment. This expansionary policy increases the money supply.

Scenario 2: **Contractionary fiscal policy** means a decrease in government spending and an increase in taxes, which decreases the aggregate demand and which shifts the aggregate demand curve to the left. This policy action brings the GDP back to full employment when the current level of GDP exceeds full employment, resulting in high inflation associated with an overheated economy. This contractionary policy decreases the money supply.

Both expansionary and contractionary policies are examples of stabilization policies with actions to bring the economy closer to full employment or potential output. However, poorly timed stabilization policies can magnify economic fluctuations with **inside lags** (i.e., the time it takes to formulate and implement a policy change) and **outside lags** (i.e., the time it takes for the policy change to actually work and to see the results). **Automatic stabilizers** are taxes and transfer payments that would stabilize the GDP without government's explicit action.

The **fiscal multiplier** states that the final shift in the aggregate demand curve will be larger than the initial change. Two scenarios can happen here, as follows:

Scenario 1: If government spending increased by $20 billion, that would initially shift the aggregate demand curve to the right by $20 billion and the total shift will be larger, say $30 billion.

Scenario 2: If government spending decreased by $20 billion, that would initially shift the aggregate demand curve to the left by $20 billion and the total shift will be larger, say $30 billion.

Monetary Policy

Governments use monetary policy as a tool to balance the demand for money with the supply of money, which determines the interest rate (i.e., the cost of money). The U.S. Federal Reserve Bank (or Central Bank) can influence the interest rate levels in the economy, as follows:

- In the short run, the Federal Reserve (Fed) can lower interest rates, which increases money supply, which in turn increases investment spending, real GDP, and net exports because the cost of money is cheaper.
- In the short run, the Fed can increase interest rates, which decreases money supply, which in turn decreases investment spending, real GDP, and net exports because the cost of money is higher.
- In the long run, the Fed does not have the power to control real GDP.
- In the long run, changes in the money supply will affect inflation only in that increased money supply will increase inflation and vice versa. When there is inflation, two types of interest rates take on importance: **nominal interest rate**, which is the interest rate quoted in the market, and **real interest rate**, which is the actual rate earned after considering the inflation:

$$\text{Nominal Interest Rate} = \text{Real Interest Rate} + \text{Inflation Rate}$$

The real interest rate determines the investment spending levels in the economy.

Reasons for individuals and firms to demand money include to facilitate short-term transactions, to provide liquidity without incurring excessive costs, and to reduce short-term risk when compared to holding stocks and bonds. The amount of money they want to hold depends on interest rates, real GDP levels, and the price levels.

Ways to increase the money supply include actions taken by the Fed in terms of changing the amount of reserves, changing reserve requirements, and changing the discount rate:

- The Fed changes the amount of reserves frequently through open market operations, which includes open market purchases (i.e., purchasing government bonds from the private sector to increase the money supply, to decrease the interest rates, and to decrease the currency exchange rates) and open market sales (i.e., selling government bonds to the private sector to decrease the money supply, to increase the interest rates, and to increase the currency exchange rates). When private citizens and individual firms write checks to one another, there is no change in the money supply because the total amount of reserves in the banking system is unchanged. Only the Fed has the power to change the total amount of reserves in the banking system.
- The Fed changes the reserve requirements for banks infrequently. It can increase the money supply by reducing the banks' reserve requirements so that banks will have more money to lend out. Similarly, it can decrease the money supply by increasing the banks' reserve requirements so that banks will have less money to lend out.
- The Fed changes the discount rate, which is the interest rate at which individual banks can borrow money from the Fed (the big bank). The big bank can lower the discount rate to increase the money supply because bank borrowing is less costly. Similarly, it can raise the discount rate to reduce the money supply because bank borrowing is more costly. In addition to going to the Fed, individual banks can borrow reserves from other banks, if it is cheaper than the Fed, through the federal funds market using the federal funds interest rate.

Similar to lags in fiscal policy, monetary policy also has lags. The **inside lags** for monetary policy are relatively short compared to those for fiscal policy. However, the **outside lags** for monetary policy are quite long, in part due to changes in interest rates taking a long time to make their effects felt.

Money Supply

Money is used as a medium of economic exchange between buyers and sellers of goods and services. The money supply in the United States is measured in terms of M1 and M2, along with their components:

Components of M1	Components of M2
+ Currency held by the public	+ M1
+ Demand deposits (deposits in checking accounts)	+ Deposits in savings and loans accounts
+ Traveler's checks	+ Deposits in money market mutual funds
	+ Time deposits of less than $100,000

M2 is broader than M1, and all M2 assets need to be converted to M1 before using them. Credit cards are not part of the money supply, but debit cards are because the latter is used like a check, whereas the former eventually uses money from the bank to pay for the purchases. Hence, the credit card is, unlike money, not a medium of exchange, not a unit of account, and not a store of value. Instead, credit cards are convenient and faster because they make business transactions easier and quicker to handle.

Banks create money and in part determine money supply through deposits and loans. Loans and reserves are assets of a bank, whereas deposits and owners' equity are liabilities of a bank. According to law, banks are required to keep an amount of **reserve ratio** as reserves, which are part of deposits and which are not available for loans. The reserve ratio is the ratio of reserves to deposits.

Total Reserves = Required Reserves + Excess Reserves

Law stipulates the required reserves, and banks decide the excess reserves, which are additional reserves beyond the required reserves.

The **money multiplier**, which is 1/reserve ratio, expands the initial cash deposits into several rounds of deposits and loans in the entire banking system:

- Cash deposited into the banking system increases the money multiplier and increases the money supply because more money is available for loans.

- Cash not deposited into the banking system decreases the money multiplier and decreases the money supply because that cash money is not available for loans.
- Cash withdrawals from a bank reduce the money supply because less money is available for loans.
- Excess reserves held by banks also decrease the money multiplier and the money supply because less money is available for loans.
- The banking system as a whole can expand the money supply only if new reserve amounts come into the system.

❑ Learning Objective 12.5: UNDERSTAND THE BASIC PRINCIPLES AND APPLICATIONS OF KEY ECONOMIC INDICATORS

The scope of **key economic indicators** includes describing their nature and specific types, as follows.

Nature of Key Economic Indicators

Business conditions relate to business cycles. The business cycle is the up and down movement of an economy's ability to generate wealth. Business cycles have a predictable structure but variable timing. Decisions such as ordering inventory, borrowing money, increasing staff, and spending capital are dependent on the current and predicted business cycle. For example, decision making in preparation for a recession, such as cost reduction and cost containment, is especially difficult. Also, during a recession, defaults on loans can increase due to bankruptcies and unemployment.

Timing is everything when it comes to making good cycle-sensitive decisions. Managers need to make appropriate cutbacks prior to the beginning of a recession. Similarly, managers cannot get caught short during a period of rapid expansion. Economic forecasting is a necessity for predicting business cycles and swings. Trend analysis, economic surveys, opinions, and simulation techniques are quite useful to managers trying to stay abreast of the latest economic developments.

Businesses use economic forecasts in making investment and production decisions. When they foresee an economic downturn, inventories may be reduced. When prices are expected to rise quickly, they buy goods in advance and add to equipment and plant. These decisions are based on key economic indicators.

Specific Types of Key Economic Indicators

Four types of economic indicators are used in forecasting: leading indicators, coincident indicators, lagging indicators, and composite economic index. They all deal with timing of certain events taking place in the economy.

1. **Leading indicators** change in advance of other variables. These are the least likely to be accurate. However, they are the most useful for business planning because they provide information for action. The consumer price index (CPI) is often used in making plans for inflation and wages because it is a leading economic indicator.

   The index of leading indicators is broadly representative of the economy as its components are drawn from six separate groups of cyclical indicators. Those covered groups include labor force, employment, and unemployment; sales, orders, and deliveries; fixed capital investment; prices; personal income and consumer attitudes; and money, credit, interest rates, and stock prices. The leading index is primarily useful during times of uncertainty.

   Leading indicators include: average workweek of production workers in manufacturing; average initial weekly claims for state unemployment insurance; new orders for consumer goods and materials, adjusted for inflation; vendor performance; new orders for nonmilitary capital goods purchases, adjusted for inflation; new building permits issued; index of stock prices; money supply; spread between rates on 10-year Treasury bonds and federal funds; and index of consumer expectations.

   Diffusion indexes indicate the level of worsening or improving conditions in manufacturing and are highly correlated with growth rates expressed by leading indicators. That is, a low diffusion index is associated with low growth rates, and a high diffusion index is associated with high growth rates. When a diffusion index is 40 percent, it means that 60 percent of the leading indicators have fallen.

2. **Coincident indicators** change at the same time as other variables change. Examples include inflation, unemployment, and consumer confidence. The coincident economic index is primarily used as a tool for dating the business cycle, that is, determining turning points such as cyclical peaks and troughs. Manufacturing and trade sales will determine whether a business cycle is turning into peaks or troughs.

3. **Lagging indicators** change after the other variables change. These are more accurate, but the information is much less useful for decision making. Examples of lagging indicators include average duration of unemployment; inventories to sales ratio for manufacturing and trade; change in labor cost per unit of output, manufacturing; average prime rates; commercial and industrial loans; consumer installment credit to personal income ratio; and change in consumer price index for services.

4. **Composite economic index** is based on the other three indicators: leading, coincident, and lagging.

❑ Learning Objective 12.6: UNDERSTAND THE NATURE OF ECONOMIC BUSINESS CYCLES AND INDUSTRY GROWTH LEVELS

A linkage is shown among business cycles, economic growth of a nation, and industry growth levels. The firm's growth rate is compared to that of the economy.

Economic Business Cycles

Every nation seeks economic growth, full employment, and price level stability, which is not easy to achieve due to business cycles.

The **business cycle** refers to the recurrent ups and downs in the level of economic activity that extends over time. The coincident economic index is primarily used as a tool for dating the business cycle, that is, determining turning points such as cyclical peaks and troughs. Manufacturing and trade sales will determine whether a business cycle is turning into peaks or troughs.

Economists suggest four phases of the business cycle: peak, recession, trough, and recovery. The duration and strength of each phase is variable. Some economists prefer to talk of business fluctuations, rather than cycles, because cycles imply regularity while fluctuations do not.

1. **Peak.** The economy is at full employment, and the national output is close to capacity. The price level is likely to rise.
2. **Recession.** Both output and employment decline, but prices tend to be relatively inflexible in a

downward direction. Depression sets in when the recession is severe and prolonged, and prices fall. In an economy experiencing a recession with low inflation, the central bank could stimulate the economy by purchasing securities in the secondary market, which will increase money supply.

3. **Trough.** Both output and employment bottom-out at their lowest levels.
4. **Recovery.** Both output and employment expand toward full employment. As recovery intensifies, price levels may begin to rise prior to the realization of full employment and capacity production.

Economists suggest many theories supporting the reasons behind the nature of the four phases of the business cycle and its impact on business activity. Examples include:

- Innovations (e.g., computers, drugs, synthetic fibers, and automobiles) have greater impact on investment and consumer spending and therefore on output, employment, and the price level. This innovation is not regular and continued.
- Political and random events such as war have a major impact on increasing employment and inflation followed by slump when peace returns.
- Monetary policy of the government has a major impact on business activity. When government creates too much money, inflation results. When government restricts money supply, it results in lower output and unemployment.
- The level of total expenditures has a major impact on the levels of output and employment, as follows:
  - When total expenditure is low, output, employment, and incomes will be low. Less production will be profitable to the business.
  - When total expenditure is high, output, employment, and incomes will be high. More production will be profitable to the business.
- Many businesses such as retail, automobile, construction, and agriculture are subject to seasonal variations (e.g., pre-Christmas and pre-Easter).
- Business activity is also subject to a secular trend. The secular trend of an economy is its expansion or contraction over a long period of time (i.e., 25 or more years). Both seasonal variations and secular trends are due to noncyclical fluctuations.
- It is important to note that various individuals and various segments of the economy are affected in different ways and in different degrees by the business cycle. For example, consumer durable

and consumer nondurable goods industries are affected in different ways:

- Those industries producing heavy capital goods and consumer durables (e.g., household appliances and automobiles), called **hard goods** industries, are highly sensitive to the business cycle. Both production and employment will decline during recession and increase during recovery. Producers cut the output and employment instead of lowering prices due to their concentration in the industry. Price cuts could be modest, even if they occur. Consumers postpone their purchase decisions and producers postpone their investment decisions.
- Output and employment in consumer nondurable goods industries are less sensitive to the business cycle. This is because food and clothes, which are examples of the consumer nondurable industry, are simply necessities of life. These are called **soft goods** industries. Because it is a highly competitive and low-concentration industry, prices will be cut instead of production and employment. Production decline would be modest, even if it occurs.

OECD Business Cycles

According to the Organization for Economic Cooperation and Development (OECD) at www.oecd.org, business cycles are recurrent sequences of alternating phases of expansion (peak) and contraction (trough) in economic activity. A **phase** is defined as the time span between a peak and a trough. A **cycle** is defined as the time span separating two turning points of the same nature (two peaks or two troughs). A **turning point** occurs in a series when the deviation-from-trend series reaches a local maximum (peak) or a local minimum (trough). **Growth cycle peaks** (end of expansion) occur when activity is furthest above its trend level. **Growth cycle troughs** (end of contraction or recession) occur when activity is furthest below its trend level.

Three different business cycle concepts exist: (1) the **classical cycle** refers to fluctuations in the level of the economic activity (e.g., measured by index of industrial production—IIP), (2) the **growth cycle** refers to fluctuations in the economic activity around the long-run potential level or fluctuations in the output-gap (e.g., measured by the de-trended GDP or IIP), (3) the **growth rate cycle** refers to fluctuations of the growth rate of economic activity (e.g., GDP growth rate).

The **composite leading indicator (CLI)** is an aggregate time-series displaying a reasonably consistent leading relationship with the reference series for the business cycle in a country. The CLI focuses on the growth cycle concept and is constructed by aggregating together component series selected according to multiple criteria, such as economic significance, cyclical behavior, and data quality. Component series are economic time series, which exhibit leading relationship with a reference series at the turning points. Cyclical indicator systems are constructed around a reference series. The reference series is the economic variable whose cyclical movements the CLI intended to predict and include IIP and GDP.

Other related concepts include trend, de-trending, smoothing, and normalization:

- **Trend.** In time-series analysis, a given time-series can be decomposed into four components (i.e., cyclical, trend, seasonal, and irregular).
- **De-trending.** De-trending is a procedure in which the long-term trend, which may obscure cyclical variations in the component or the reference series, is removed.
- **Smoothing.** Smoothing eliminates the noise from time-series, and makes the cyclical signal clearer.
- **Normalization.** Normalization is the transformation of the de-trended component series prior to aggregation into CLI to express the cyclical movements in a comparable form, on a common scale. The method used to calculate normalized indices is to subtract the mean from the observed value and then to divide the resulting difference by the

mean absolute deviation (MAD). Finally the series is relocated to have a mean of 100.

Industry Growth Levels

Another interesting concept is to compare the growth of a firm (industry) with that of the economy. Four growth indicators are:

1. **Supernormal growth** is the part of the lifecycle of a firm in which its growth is much faster than that of the economy as a whole.
2. **Normal growth** is the growth that is expected to continue into the foreseeable future at about the same rate as that of the economy as a whole. The growth rate of a firm is equal to the nominal gross national product (GNP), which is real GNP plus inflation.
3. **Zero growth** indicates that a firm experiences a zero percent growth compared to the economy as a whole.
4. **Negative growth** indicates that a firm experiencing a decline in growth compared to the economy as a whole.

 Self-Assessment Exercise

Online exercises are provided for the learning objectives in this module. Please visit www.mbaiq.com to complete the online exercises and to calculate your MBA IQ Score.

References

Anupindi et al., *Managing Business Process Flows (MBPF): Principles of Operations Management*, 2nd ed. (Upper Saddle River, NJ Pearson/Prentice Hall, 2006), Appendix I, MBPF Checklist, pp. 313–315.

Blake, Robert R., and Jane Srygley Mouton, "A Comparative Analysis of Situationalism and 9, 9 Management by Principle," *Organizational Dynamics*, Spring 1982.

Bologna, Jack, *Handbook on Corporate Fraud* (Stoneham, MA: Butterworth-Heinemann, 1993).

Bolton, Robert, *People Skills* (New York: Simon & Schuster, 1979).

Brinkerhoff, Robert O., and Dennis E. Dressler, *Productivity Measurement: A Guide for Managers and Evaluators*, Applied Social Research Methods Series, Volume 19 (Newbury Park, CA: Sage Publications, 1990).

Business Roundtable, *Business Roundtable's Principles of Corporate Governance* (Washington, DC: 2005), pp. 2–3, 7–10, 10–12.

Carroll, Archie B., "A Three-Dimensional Conceptual Model of Corporate Social Performance," *Academy of Management Review*, Vol. 4, No. 4, 1979, pp. 497–505.

Cohen, Herb, *You Can Negotiate Anything* (Secaucus, NJ: Lyle Stuart, 1980).

Craig, Jack, *Multinational Cooperatives: An Alternative for World Development* (Saskatoon, Saskatchewan, Canada: Western Producers Prairie Books, 1976).

Davia, Howard R., Patrick C. Coggins, John C. Wideman, and Joseph T. Kastantin, *Management Accountant's Guide to Fraud Discovery and Control* (Hoboken, NJ: John Wiley & Sons, 1992).

Hall, E.T., and M.R. Hall, *Understanding Cultural Differences: Keys to Success in West Germany, France, and the United States* (Yarmouth, ME: Intercultural Press, 1990).

Harris, Philip R., and Robert T. Moran, *Managing Cultural Differences*, 3rd ed. (Houston, TX: Gulf Publishing, 1991).

Hofstede, Geert, *Cultural Consequences: International Differences in Work-Related Values* (Beverly Hills: Sage Publishing, 1984).

Kreitner, Robert, *Management*, 9th ed. (Boston: Houghton Mifflin, 2004).

Lewin, Kurt, *Personal Psychology*, Autumn 1989.

Mintzberg, Henry, "Managerial Work: Analysis from Observation," *Management Science*, October 1971.

Gerhard Mueller, Helen Gernon, and Gary Meek, *Accounting: An International Perspective*, 3rd ed. (Burr Ridge, IL: Irwin, 1994).

National Institute of Standards and Technology (NIST), "Contingency Planning Guide for Information Technology Systems (SP 800-34)" (Gaithersburg, MD: U.S. Department of Commerce, 2002).

National Institute of Standards and Technology (NIST), "Information Security Handbook: A Guide for Managers (SP 800-100, Draft)," System Development Life Cycle (Chapter 3) (Gaithersburg, MD: U.S. Department of Commerce, 2006).

National Institute of Standards and Technology (NIST), "Guide to Test, Training, and Exercise Programs for IT Plans and Capabilities (SP 800-84)" (Gaithersburg, MD: U.S. Department of Commerce, 2006).

Porter, Michael E., *Competitive Strategy* (New York: The Free Press, 1980).

Robbins, Stephen P., *Organizational Behavior* (Englewood Cliffs, NJ: Prentice Hall, 1993).

Robbins, Stephen P., and Timothy A. Judge, *Organizational Behavior*, 12th ed. (Upper Saddle River, NJ: Pearson Education, 2007), Chapters 1 and 17.

Schriesheim, Chester, James Tolliver, and Orlando Behling, "Influence Tactics Used by Subordinates," *Journal of Applied Psychology*, June 1990.

Weber, Ann L., *Social Psychology* (New York: Harper-Collins, 1992).

Index

5Ms – resources, 92
5Ws – whys, 50
7-S – McKinsey framework, 8
7Ss – production, 50
7Ws – Waste, 49
360-degree feedback – employee performance, 114
720-degree review – senior managers' performance, 114

A

Absolute advantage, 275
Absorption costing method – production, 140
Accept or reject errors – capital budgeting, 172
Accountability of an individual – IT, 220
Accountability, 11
Accounting cost, 321
Accounting cycle, 121
Accounting estimates, 266
Accounting information qualities, 121
Accounting period concept – accounting, 121
Accounting profit, 321
Accounting rate of return (ARR) method, 172
Accrual-basis accounting, 122
Accruals – financing, 165
Activity network diagram – QM tool, 97
Activity-based costing (ABC) method, 20, 151
Actual cost, 141
Added-value negotiating (AVN), 32
Adverse impact – diversity, 106
Advertising carryover effect, 84
Advertising effectiveness ratio, 84
Advertising elasticity, 84
Advertising response analysis, 84
Affinity diagram – QM tool, 97
Agency costs – employees, 266
Agency problems- employees, 266
Aggregate demand – economics, 329
Aggregate production planning (APP), 60
Aggregate supply – economics, 330
Alternative processing sites – disaster recovery:
 Cold site, 203
 Hot site, 203
 Mirrored site, 204
 Mobile site, 203
 Warm site, 203
Alternative risk transfer (ART) tools and methods, 182, 246
Antitrust laws, 248–250
Application systems, 199
Applications controls, 240
Applications of PERT/CPM, 305
Applications software failures, 208
Appraisal costs – COQ, 94
Arbitrator – labor relations, 115
Assembly time – production, 48
Assessment center – employee, 107
Asset management ratios – financial statements, 137
Assurance services – IT, 220
Attribute chart – SPC, 99
Attribute control chart – SPC, 99
Audit process, 260
Authority – management, 11
Autocratic leader, 14
Automated teller machines (ATMs), 234
Automatic stabilizers – economy, 331
Availability of system and data – IT, 220
Average cost, 141
Average fixed cost, 321
Average profit per unit, 321
Average total cost per unit, 321
Average total cost, 321
Average variable cost, 321
Avoidable cost, 142

B

Backbone – network, 215
Backsourcing – procurement, 64
Backup methods – IT, 202
Balance sheet limitations, 126
Balance sheet, 122, 125, 134
Balanced scorecard system – management, 21
Brand extension, 75
Bank loans, 164
Bankruptcy laws, 251

Bar-coding systems, 68
Basic probabilities, 312
Basic statistics, 312
BATNA – negotiations, 32
BCG matrix model vs. GE model, 9
BCG matrix model:
    Cash cows, 9
    Dogs, 9
    Stars, 9
    Question marks, 9
Benchmarking, 101–102
Benefit-cost analysis (BCA), 175
Benefit-cost-ratio (BCR), 173
Benefit-investment ratio (BIR) method, 174
Best practices, 101
Beta (market) risk, 178
Big Q, little q, 93
Bill of material (BOM) – production, 58
Bivariate analysis, 320
Black belts – Six-Sigma, 96
Blue-ocean strategy, 7
Blue-team testing – IT security, 222
Board independence, 259
Board of directors (BODs), 256
Bond prices vs. interest rates, 166
Bond valuation, 182
Bonds and notes, 128
Bonds, 165
Book value model, 183
Bottleneck inflation, 329
Brainstorming – problem solving tool, 24
Brand dilution, 75
Brand elements, 72
Brand equity, 73, 75
Brand value, 72–73
Branding and packaging, 88
Breakdown maintenance, 65
Breakeven market share, 83
Breakeven point (BEP), 148
Bridges – network, 215
Brouters – network, 215
Budgeted cost, 141
Buffer management – TOC, 62
Bumping procedures – union, 104
Business ethics, 253
Business combinations – accounting, 132
Business entity concept – accounting, 120
Business games – employee, 110
Business impact analysis (BIA) – disaster recovery and risk,
    201, 243
Business laws, 247
Business policy, 252
Business process improvement (BPI), 101
Business process redesign (BPD), 101
Business process reengineering (BPR), 101
Business valuation, 183

C

Call option – stocks, 168
Capability ratio – SPC, 99

Capacity mixing options – production:
    Chase, 60
    Level, 60
    Mixed, 60
Capacity requirements planning (CRP), 60
Capacity utilization – production, 60
Capital asset pricing model (CAPM) approach, 170
Capital budgeting errors – accept or reject, 172
Capital budgeting international, 178
Capital budgeting, 171
Capital rationing, 178
Captive insurance method, 182
Career development plan, 113
Career development programs, 113
Career development, 112
Career path, 112
Career security, 113
Cash budget, 154
Cash conversion cycle model, 160
Cash flow risk, 178
Cash kiting, 157
Cash lapping, 265
Cash management model – Miller-Orr, 318
Cash management techniques, 159
Cash management, 158
Cash presentation on the balance sheet, 157
Cash skimming, 265
Cash-basis accounting, 122
Cause-and-effect diagram – QC tool, 97
Centralized control, 238
Centralized organization, 13
Chain of command – management, 11, 22
Chain-weighted index – prices, 327
Change and problem management – IT, 211
Change management – project, 301
Change management risk – project, 290
Channel operating efficiency, 83
Channel performance, 83
Channel's cost per customer transaction, 82
Channel's transaction value, 82
Charismatic leader, 16
Check float, 157
Check lapping, 157
Check sheets – QC tool, 97
Checklists, 222
Check-summing software, 221
Classical economists, 325
Closed system, 13
Cluster analysis, 320
Coaching, 111
Cobranding, 75
Coincident indicators – economics, 333
Collaboration vs. compromise, 31
Combination controls, 240
Commercial paper – finance, 164
Committed cost, 143
Common cost, 141
Common equity, 167–168
Common Internet services, 229
Common size analysis – financial statements, 136
Common stock valuation, 183

Communication barriers, 34
Communication chain, 33
Communication defined, 33
Communication effectiveness, 35
Comparative ratios – financial statements, 136
Compensating controls, 240
Competitive markets, 77
Competitive strategies, 6
Competitor analysis, 73
Complementary controls, 240
Compliance costs and benefits, 252
Compliance management, 251
Compliance process, 251
Composite economic index, 333
Composite leading indicators, 335
Compromise vs. collaboration, 31
Computer controls, 240
Computer equipment preventive maintenance, 210
Computer integrated manufacturing (CIM), 68
Computer job scheduling practices, 208
Computer network types, 211
Computer operations, 209
Computer production control procedures, 208
Computer production job turnover procedures, 208
Computer security audit, 262
Computer security practices, 219
Computer system logs, 210
Computer-aided design (CAD), 68
Computer-aided manufacturing (CAM), 68
Concentrators – network, 216
Conceptual skill – management, 17
Concurrent control, 20
Concurrent control, 238
Concurrent engineering, 92
Confidentiality of data and system information – IT, 220
Configuration management – IT, 197
Configuration management – IT, 222
Conflict defined, 35
Conflict resolution techniques, 37
Conflict triggers, 37
Conjoint analysis – forecasting, 317
Connectivity hardware, 214
Console operations – computer, 209
Consolidated financial statements, 132
Construction audit, 260–261
Consumer price index (CPI), 326–327
Consumer product safety laws, 250
Consumer research models, 320
Contingency plan – disaster recovery, 206
Contingency plan exercises – disaster recovery, 207
Contingency plan maintenance – disaster recovery, 207
Contingency plan testing – disaster recovery, 206
Contingency plan training – disaster recovery, 206
Contingency planning process- disaster recovery, 201
Continuous improvement – quality, 92
Continuous process improvement (CPI), 101
Contract audit, 260–261
Contract defined, 247–248

Contractionary fiscal policy, 330
Contradictory controls, 240
Contribution margin (CM) method, 148–149
Control assessment, 241
Control characteristics, 236
Control chart – QC and SPC tool, 97–98
Control costs and benefits, 237
Control design, 236
Control implementation, 237
Control placement, 236
Control requirements, 241
Control responsibilities, 241
Controllable cost, 142
Controlling defined, 19
Controls classification, 237
Controls over cash, 157
Controls-by-action, 239
Controls-by-interaction, 240
Controls-by-location, 238
Controls-by-nature, 237
Controls-by-strength, 239
Conversion cost, 141
Convertible bonds, 166
Corporate audits, 260
Corporate culture, 281
Corporate fraud, 263–264
Corporate governance standards, 256–257
Corporate governance, 256
Corporate social responsibility, 253–255
Corrective controls, 240
Correlation analysis – forecasting, 47
Correlation diagram – QC tool, 97
Cost and schedule risk – project, 291
Cost behavior concepts, 141–143
Cost behaviors and patterns, 143
Cost center, 152
Cost concept – accounting, 120
Cost of a lost sale, 77
Cost of capital issues, 171
Cost of common stock, 170
Cost of debt, 169
Cost of goods sold, 123
Cost of preferred stock, 169
Cost of quality (COQ), 92, 94
Cost of retained earnings, 170
Cost-benefit analysis (CBA), 175, 244
Cost-effectiveness analysis (CEA), 176
Cost-of-living adjustment (COLA), 327
Cost-push inflation, 329
Cost-volume-profit (CVP) analysis, 148
CPM and PERT, 303–304
CPM/PERT applications, 305
Credit derivatives, 180
Credit swaps, 180
Creeping inflation, 329
Critical path method (CPM), 303
Critical path, 304
Critical-to-quality (CTO) technique, 94
Cross-cultural negotiations, 283
Cross-exchange rate – foreign, 280
Crossover chart – cost and volume, 48

Cultural awareness learning program, 283
Cultural training – international, 281
Currency futures contract, 280
Currency options, 179, 280
Currency swaps, 180, 280
Current assets, 126
Current cost, 141
Current liabilities, 126, 160
Customer loyalty score, 78
Customer relationship management (CRM), 59
Customer response index (CRI), 84
Customer retention rate, 77
Customer service quality, 83
Customer value, 82
Customer's needs – marketplace:
    Delighted, 94
    Dissatisfied, 94
    Satisfied, 94
Customer-reach, 83
CVP assumptions and limitations, 148
Cycle counting, 56
Cycle sock, 53
Cycle time, 55
Cyclical unemployment, 328

D

Data and systems backup – IT, 202
Data control procedures – IT, 208
Data integrity, 200
Data marts – database, 227
Data mining – database, 227
Data modeling – database, 227
Data origination, preparation, and input, 199
Data output, 200
Data processing, 199
Data sharing- database, 223
Data views – database, 223
Data warehouse – database, 227
Database – computer, 223
Database design approaches, 224
Database management system (DBMS), 223
Debentures – bonds, 166
Debt management ratios – financial statements, 137
Debt types, 163
Decentralized control, 238
Decentralized organization, 13
Decision analysis models, 313
Decision defined, 24
Decision making vs. problem solving, 25
Decision sciences, 311
Decision table, 64
Decision tree, 65, 84, 313
Decision types, 25
Decision-making in MNCs, 270
Decision-making models, 24
Decision-making process, 24
Decision-making under certainty, 314
Decision-making under conflict or competition, 316
Decision-making under risk, 314

Decision-making under uncertainty, 315
Defense-in-depth strategy – IT security, 218
Deflation, 327
Degree of fraud, 264
Delegation, 11, 19, 111
Demand forecasting, 46
Demand-pull inflation, 329
Democratic leader, 14
Dependency risk – project, 290
Dependent demand inventory systems, 53
Derivative securities, 180
Deseasonalized time-series – forecasting, 318
Design capacity – production, 60
Design for manufacturability, 151
Design for Six Sigma model (DCOV), 95
Design of experiments (DOE), 98
Design-to-cost, 151
Detective controls, 239
Deterministic data – decision making, 25
Devaluation of currency, 280
Devil's advocate, 25
Differential analysis, 150
Differential costs, 143, 150
Differential income or loss, 150
Differentiation strategy, 6
Diffusion index – industry growth, 333
Direct cost, 141
Directive controls, 239
Discounted abnormal earnings model, 184
Discounted cash flow (DCF) model, 184
Discretionary cost, 142
Discriminant analysis, 320
Diseconomies of scale, 322
Disparate treatment – diversity, 106
Displaced cost, 142
Distributed data model – database, 226
Distribution requirements planning (DRP), 59
Distribution system, 57
Diversification strategy, 5
Divestiture – business, 3, 186
Dividend payment procedures, 189
Dividend policy in practice, 188
Dividend policy in theory, 187
Division of labor, 11
Double-entry accounting system, 122
Downsizing, 3, 103
Downtime – equipment, 65
Downward communications, 34
Dual branding, 75
Due-diligence audit, 261
Dysfunctional conflict, 36

E

Earned value management (EVM) technique – project, 300
Earnings per share (EPS), 124
E-commerce infrastructure, 232
E-commerce software, 232
Economic analysis, 244
Economic and financial risks – project, 290

Economic business cycles:
   Peak, 333
   Recession, 333
   Recovery, 334
   Trough, 334
Economic cost, 321
Economic entity assumption – accounting, 120
Economic growth, 326
Economic implications of competition, 322
Economic implications of demand and supply, 323
Economic implications of economic growth, 326
Economic implications of employment, interest rates, and
   investment theories, 325
Economic implications of labor economics, 325
Economic implications of monopolies, 324
Economic implications of monopolistic competition,
   324
Economic implications of oligopolies, 324
Economic implications of perfect competition, 323
Economic implications of structure of product markets,
   325
Economic implications of utility, 323
Economic order quantity (EOQ) – inventory, 53–54
Economic profit model, 184
Economic profit, 321
Economic-value-added (EVA) model, 20, 184, 321
Economies of scale, 322
Economy defined, 43
EDI system, 232–233
Effective capacity – production, 60
Effectiveness defined, 43
Effects of international cultures, 282
Efficiency defined, 43
Electronic business (e-business), 230
Electronic commerce (e-commerce), 230
Electronic data interchange (EDI) security issues, 231
Electronic funds transfer (EFT) system, 233
E-mail security issues, 231
Embezzlement, 265
Embodied cost, 142
Empirical decision models, 24
Employee attitude survey, 116
Employee development, 109
Employee disciplinary actions, 114–115
Employee exit interviews, 116
Employee feedback, 116
Employee firing errors, 115
Employee fraud symptoms, 265
Employee hiring errors, 107
Employee orientation, 110
Employee performance appraisal system factors, 113
Employee resignation, 115
Employee selection process, 106
Employee survey feedback, 112
Employee termination, 115
Employee training, 109
Employment interview, 108
Employment laws, 251
Employment tests, 107
Employment-at-will doctrine, 114
Engineered cost, 143

Enterprise resource planning (ERP), 59
Enterprise risk management (ERM) program, 246
Entrepreneurs vs. leaders vs. managers, 19
Entrepreneurs, 19
Environmental quality engineering, 93
Environmental laws, 250
Equipment maintenance, 65
Equity types, 167
Equivalent uniform annual cost (EUAC), 173
Escalation of commitment – decision, 32
European union (EU), 278–279
Evaluating training and development (T&D) programs,
   110
Excess reserves – banks, 332
Exchange rate risk, 178
Executive orientation, 110
Expansionary fiscal policy, 330
Expectancy theory, 21
Expectancy-value model (EVM), 72
Expected monetary value (EMV), 65, 315
Expected value analysis – risk, 245
Expected value of perfect information (EVPI), 314
Expired cost, 141
Exponential smoothing – forecasting, 317
Exporting/importing, 272
External auditors, 260
External failure costs – COQ, 94
External opportunities – environment, 4
External threats – environment, 4
Extranet, 230

F

Facets of decision making, 24
Feedback control, 20, 238
Feed-forward control, 20, 238
Financial analysis model, 184
Financial asset valuation, 182
Financial audit, 260
Financial breakeven analysis, 156
Financial control, 156
Financial engineering – risks, 181
Financial instruments, 280
Financial leverage, 156
Financial plans, 154
Financial statement analysis, 133
Financial statement ratios limitations, 139
Financial statement types, 122
Financial transactions security issues, 231
First-line managers, 18
Fiscal multiplier, 331
Fiscal policy, 330
Fiscal policy lags:
   Inside, 331
   Outside, 331
Fishbone diagram – QC tool, 97
Five focusing steps – TOC, 63
Five resources (5Ms) – organization, 92
Fixed cost, 141
Flexible budget, 152
Flexible manufacturing systems (FMS), 67

Floating-rate bonds, 166
Flow diagram, 48
Flowcharting – QC tool, 97
Focus strategy, 7
Food and drug administration laws, 250
Force-field analysis – problem solving tool, 24
Forecasting HR availability, 103
Forecasting HR requirements, 103
Forecasting models, 317
Foreign currency transactions, 132
Foreign direct investment (FDI), 274
Foreign subsidiary, 274
Foreign-exchange market, 280
Foreign-exchange rate quote, 280
Formal communications, 34
Formal organization chart, 11
Forward contracts, 179, 280
Forward exchange rate, 280
Forward logistics, 58
Fraud – degree of, 264
Fraud red-flags, 264
Fraud types, 263–264
Frictional unemployment, 328
Full cost, 141
Full employment, 328
Full-volume backups – IT, 209
Functional conflict, 35
Functional managers, 18
Functional-type-organization – project, 292–293
Futures contracts, 179

G

Gains from trade, 275
Game theory – decision, 316
Gantt charts, 61, 306
Gap analysis, 244
Gateways – network, 214
GDP deflator, 326
GDP multiplier, 330
GE model vs. BCG matrix model, 9
GE model, 9
General agreement on trade and services (GATS), 277
General controls, 240
General managers, 18
Generally accepted accounting principles (GAAP), 121
Global communication insights, 282
Global manager's dilemma, 282
Global mindsets, 284–285
Global operations, 3
Global sourcing, 272
Goal-setting theory, 22
Going-concern assumption – accounting, 120
Grand strategy, 2
Grapevine – communication, 34
Green belts – Six-Sigma, 96
Grievance procedures- union, 115
Gross domestic product (GDP), 326
Gross margin or profit, 149
Gross national product (GNP), 325–327

Gross rating points (GRPs) – advertising, 84
Group behaviors, 26
Group cohesiveness, 28
Group development stages, 26–27
Group dynamics, 25
Group effectiveness, 27
Group or organizational conflict, 36
Group polarization, 26
Group structures, 28
Groups and individuals, 27
Groupshift, 26
Groupthink, 26

H

Halo error – employee performance, 114
Hard goods, 334
Hard-controls, 239
Hard-issues, 239
Hard-skills, 239
Heckscher-Ohlin (HO) theorem, 275
Help-desk function, 210
Herzberg two-factor theory, 21
Heuristics – forecasting, 317
Hidden financial reporting risks, 181
Hierarchical data model – database, 225
High-context cultural communications, 282
Histogram – QC tool, 97
Historical cost concept – accounting, 120
Historical cost, 141
Holding company, 187
Horizontal communications, 34
Horizontal hierarchy, 11
Horizontal market, 87
Horn error – employee performance, 114
Hoshin planning – Japanese, 91
House of quality (HOQ), 98
Human capital metrics, 116–117
Human capital risk – project, 290
Human resource (HR) planning, 103
Human resource planning process, 103
Human skill – management, 17
Hurwicz strategy – decision, 315
Hyperinflation, 329
HyperText Markup Language (HTML) – Web, 232

I

Implementation and operational risk – project, 289
Implementing training and development (T&D) programs, 110
Implicit cost, 143
Importing/exporting, 272
Imputed cost, 143
In-basket training – employee, 110
Income bonds, 166
Income statement, 122–123, 133
Incremental backups – IT, 209
Incremental cash flows, 176
Incremental change, 322

Incremental cost, 142
Indenture – legal document, 165
Independent demand inventory systems, 52
Indexed bonds, 166
Indifference curves – economics, 323
Indirect cost, 141
Individual career planning, 112–113
Individuals and groups, 27
Industrial engineering, 92
Industry growth levels:
    Negative, 335
    Normal, 335
    Supernormal, 335
    Zero, 335
Inflation rate, 327, 331
Inflation, 327–329
Influence diagrams – decision, 313
Informal communications, 34
Informal organization chart, 11
Information engineering – database, 228
Information plans, 195
Information security strategic plans, 217
Information systems planning, 194–195
Information technology (IT) function, 192
Information transactions security issues, 231
Insider trading scandals, 259–260
Insourcing, 64
Inspection priority index, 100
Integrated service digital networks (ISDN), 213
Integrity checkers – software, 221
Integrity of system and data – IT, 219
Intellectual property (IP) rights, 273
Intellectual property laws, 250
Interactive leader, 16
Interest rates vs. bond prices, 166
Internal auditors, 260
Internal controls, 237
Internal failure costs – COQ, 94
Internal rate of return (IRR) method – modified, 175
Internal rate of return (IRR) method – regular, 174
Internal strengths – strategy, 4
Internal weaknesses – strategy, 4
International acquisition of materials, 281
International businesses, 271
International cultural training, 281
International franchising, 274
International labor-management relations, 281
International licensing agreements, 273
International logistics, 281
International negotiations, 283–284
International production strategies, 281
International staffing policies:
    Ethnocentric, 281
    Geocentric, 281
    Polycentric, 281
International strategies – types, 270–271
International trade barriers, 273
International trade, 272

Internet protocol (IP) – network, 228–229
Internet security-related problems, 229
Internet, 228
Interrelationship digraph – QM tool, 97
Inter-role conflict – groups, 28
Interviewing methods – employee, 108
Interviewing problems – employee, 108
Intranet, 230
Intrusion detectors – IT security, 221
Inventory analysis – ABC system, 55
Inventory asset valuation, 182
Inventory conversion period, 160
Inventory investment, 53
Inventory levels, 53
Inventory models, 313
Inventory-related costs, 54
Inverted file data model – database, 226
Investment center, 152
Investment securities laws, 250
Ishikawa diagram – QC tool, 97
ISO 14000 environmental standards, 93
ISO 14001 environmental standards, 93
ISO 9000 standards, 93
IT acquisition plans, 195
IT audit, 260
IT general security plans, 218
IT operational plan, 192, 194,195
IT operations, 207
IT planning framework, 192
IT planning process, 194
IT planning, 192
IT plans assessment, 196
IT security plans, 195
IT security policy, 218
IT strategic plan, 192–194
IT strategies, 192
IT tactical plan, 192, 194, 195
IT training plans, 195

J

Jidoka – quality, 92
JIT inventory, 51
JIT layout, 52
JIT partnerships, 51
JIT philosophy, 92
JIT production processing, 51
JIT production, 50
JIT purchasing, 50
JIT quality, 51
JIT scheduling, 51
JIT strategy, 50
JIT transportation, 51
Job analysis, 104
Job applicant acceptance rate, 106
Job applicant pool, 106
Job applicant selection ratio, 106
Job applicant selection tests, 107
Job applicant yield rate, 106
Job description, 105

Job design, 104
Job enlargement, 105
Job enrichment, 105
Job order cost systems, 151
Job rotation, 105, 111
Job scheduling methods – production:
    Backward, 161
    Forward, 161
Job sequencing methods – production:
    Critical ratio, 61
    EDD, 61
    FCFS, 61
    Johnson's rule, 61
    LPT, 61
    SPT, 61
Job simplification, 105
Job specification, 105
Joint cost, 141
Joint venture, 187, 274
Junk bonds, 167

K

Kaizen – quality, 92
Kanban system – production, 51
Key economic indicators, 332
Keynesian economists, 325
Knowledge, skills, and abilities (KSAs), 21, 104, 109,
    113

L

Lagging indicators – economics, 333
Lapping of cash, 265
Larceny, 265
Law of comparative advantage, 275
Law of one price – exchange rates, 280
Leaders vs. managers vs. entrepreneurs, 19
Leaders, 19
Leadership categories, 16
Leadership defined, 14
Leadership grid, 14
Leadership theories, 14
Leading indicators – economics, 333
Lean operations, 52
Learning organizations, 109
Learning-curve analysis, 63
Leases, 129–130
Level 5 leader, 16
Leveraged buyout (LBO), 187
Levers in process management, 66
Lifetime value of a customer, 78
Line managers, 18
Linear programming (LP) models, 312–313
Linear regression analysis – forecasting, 47
Liquidation value model, 184
Liquidation – business, 3
Liquidity ratios – financial statements, 136
Loading jobs – production, 61

Local-area network (LAN), 211–212
Logical data model – database, 225
Logistics – international, 281
Logistics management, 57
Long-run costs, 141
Long-run supply curve – economics, 330
Long-term debt, 165
Long-term financing, 167
Low-context cultural communications, 282
Low-cost leadership strategy, 7

M

Machine selection – production, 64
Make-or-buy analysis, 63
Management controls, 20, 237
Management defined, 17
Management development (MD) process, 110
Management fraud symptoms, 264–265
Management functions, 10
Management representation in audit, 265–266
Management skills, 17
Management types, 17
Management, 256
Management-by-objectives (MBO), 22
Management-by-wandering around (MBWA), 34
Manager's information processing styles, 26
Manager's intuitive style, 26
Manager's thinking style, 26
Managerial roles:
    Informational, 18
    Interpersonal, 18
    Decisional, 18
Managers vs. leaders vs. entrepreneurs, 19
Managers, 19
Managing corporate risks, 246
Manual controls, 240
Manufacturing cycle efficiency (MCE), 48
Manufacturing cycle time (MCT), 48
Marginal benefit, 322
Marginal change, 322
Marginal cost, 141, 321
Marginal profit, 321
Marginal propensity to consume (MPC), 330
Marginal propensity to save (MPS), 330
Marginal revenue, 321
Marginal-cost-of-capital (MCC), 171
Market development index (MDI), 80
Market development strategy, 5
Market penetration strategy, 5
Market share index (MSI), 80
Market value ratios – financial statements, 139
Marketable securities management, 161
Marketable securities risks, 162
Marketable securities selection criteria, 162
Marketing budget, 85
Marketing communications mix, 75
Marketing engineering, 320
Marketing mix, 72
Marketing of services, 86

Marketing portfolio analysis, 85
Marketing profitability metrics, 80
Marketing public relations (MPR), 84
Marketing-related financial metrics, 86
Market-value-added (MVA) model, 20, 184, 321
Markov-process analysis – forecasting, 318
Maslow's needs hierarchy theory, 21
Master black belts – Six-Sigma, 96
Master production schedule (MPS), 58
Matching concept -accounting, 120
Material requirements planning (MRP), 58
Materiality concept- accounting, 120
Matrix diagram – QM tool, 97
Matrix organization, 13
Matrix-type organization – project, 293–294
Metropolitan-area network (MAN), 211–212
Maximax strategy – decision, 315
Maximum allowable outage (MAO), 201
McKinsey 7–S framework, 8
Mean time between failures (MTBF), 65
Measuring defined, 20
Mechanistic structure – organization, 13
Mediator – labor relations, 115
Mentoring, 19, 111
Merger analysis, 186
Merger motives, 185
Merger tactics, 185
Merger types:
    Beachhead, 185
    Congeneric, 185
    Conglomerate, 185
    Horizontal, 185
    Vertical, 185
Metadata management – database, 227
Middle managers, 18
Minimax regret strategy – decision, 315
Minimax strategy – decision, 315
Mission statement, 5
Mixed cost, 141
Monetary policy, 331
Monetary policy lags:
    Inside, 332
    Outside, 332
Monetary unit assumption – accounting, 120
Money income, 329
Money multiplier, 332
Money supply – M1 and M2, 332
Money transfer mechanisms, 159
Monopoly firm, 322
Monopsonistic competitor, 325
Monopsony, 325
Monte Carlo simulation, 177
Mortgage bonds, 166
Motivation defined, 21
Motivation strategies, 22
Motivation theories, 21
Multicorporate networks, 213
Multicriteria decision models, 321
Multinational corporations (MNCs) models, 270
Multivariate analysis, 320

N

Nash bargaining game – decision, 317
Nash equilibrium – decision, 316
Natural variation – SPC, 98
Nearshoring – procurement, 64
Negligent hiring, 109
Negligent referral, 109
Negligent retention, 109
Negotiation defined, 30
Negotiation elements, 30
Negotiation modes, 31
Negotiation process, 30
Negotiations – cross-cultural, 283
Negotiations – international, 283–284
Negotiations Do's and Don'ts, 31
Net cash flows, 176
Net marketing contribution (NMC), 78, 79, 83
Net national product (NNP), 326
Net operating income (NOI), 156
Net present value (NPV) method, 173
Net present value model, 184
Net promoter score – marketing, 78
Net working capital, 160
Network architecture, 217
Network changes, 216
Network data model – database, 226
Network interface cards (NICs), 216
Network interoperability, 217
Network management, 216
New-product development errors – drop/go, 76
New-product development process, 75
Nominal GDP, 326
Nominal GNP, 326
Nominal group technique – problem solving tool, 24
Nominal income, 327, 329
Nominal interest rate, 331
Nominal value of money, 322
Nominal wages, 325
Noncontrollable cost, 142
Non-current assets, 126
Non-current liabilities, 126
Nonrealistic conflict, 35
Non-tariff barriers – trade, 273
Non-zero-sum game – decision, 316
Normative decision models, 24
Norms – groups, 28
North American free trade agreement (NAFTA), 278

O

Object data model – database, 226
Objectivity concept – accounting, 120
OECD business cycles:
    Classical, 334
    Growth, 334
    Growth rate, 334
Off-balance sheet accounting practices, 181
Offline quality control, 100
Offshoring – procurement, 64

Oligopsonistic competitor, 325
Ombudsperson – labor relations, 115
Online quality control, 100
On-the-job (OJT) training, 110
Open system, 13
Open-book management, 20
Operating breakeven analysis, 156
Operating budget advantages, 146
Operating budget benefits, 144
Operating budget dimensions, 144
Operating budget limitations, 146
Operating budget preparation, 144
Operating budget techniques 145
Operating budget types, 145
Operating budgets, 143
Operating expenses, 123
Operating leverage, 156
Operational application systems, 198
Operational audit, 260, 263
Operational controls, 238
Operational plan, 10
Opportunity cost, 142, 176, 321
Opportunity loss – decision, 316
Optimal capital structure, 171
Optimal order quantity, 54
Option (choice) analysis – uncertainty, 244
Order qualifier, 72
Order winner, 72
Organic structure – organization, 13
Organization charts, 11
Organization development (OD) intervention techniques, 111
Organization development (OD) process, 111
Organization structure, 11–12
Organizational behavior defined, 38
Organizational career planning, 112–113
Organizational change defined, 39
Organizational change resistance, 40
Organizational change types, 40
Organizational culture defined, 39
Organizational decline defined, 41
Organizational development defined, 41
Organizational effectiveness defined, 41
Organizational mission, 5
Organizational objectives, 5
Organizational or group conflict, 36
Organizational portfolio plan, 5
Organizational strategies, 5
Organizational structures – MNCs, 269–270
Organizing defined, 11
Out-of-pocket cost, 142
Outplacement – job, 104
Output measurement criteria, 43
Outsourcing – procurement, 64

P

Packaging and branding, 88
Pareto diagram – QC tool, 97
Pareto principle, 55
Partnerships, 132

Password checkers – software, 221
Pause strategy –stability, 3
Payables deferred period, 161
Payback method, 172
Payoff tables – decision, 313, 316
Penetration testing – IT security, 222
Pensions, 130
Perfectly competitive market, 322
Performance audit, 262–263
Performance measurement system design, 43
Period cost, 141
Personal conflict, 36
Person-role conflict – groups, 28
PERT and CPM, 303–304
PERT/CPM applications, 305
Phillips curve – economics, 328
Physical data model – database, 225
Plan-do-check-adjust (PDCA) cycle, 92
Planning defined, 10
Planning levels, 10
Planning process, 10
Planning tools, 10
Planning types, 10
Plant selection, 64
Point-of-sale (POS) systems, 68
Point-of-sale (POS) terminals, 234
Poka-yoke – quality, 92
Portfolio strategy – competitive, 8
Portfolio techniques – competitive, 8
Post audit of capital projects, 176
Postcontrol, 238
Post-exit questionnaires – employee, 116
Precontrol, 238
Pre-employment screening process, 108
Pre-employment tests, 107
Preferred stock valuation, 183
Preferred stock, 168–169
Prevention costs – COQ, 94
Preventive controls – disaster recovery, 201
Preventive controls – management, 239
Preventive maintenance, 65
Price multiple model, 184
Price response analysis, 75
Pricing methods, 73–74
Pricing strategies, 73
Prime cost, 142
Principle of constant returns, 322
Principle of diminishing returns, 322
Prioritization matrices – QM tool, 97
Prisoner's dilemma – decision, 316
Privacy and security risk – project, 291
Privacy audit, 262
Pro forma balance sheet, 155
Probabilistic data – decision making, 25
Problem and change management – IT, 211
Problem defined, 23
Problem solving vs. decision making, 25
Problem-solving process, 23
Process capability – SPC, 99
Process capability index (PCI) – SPC, 99
Process chart, 48

Process control systems, 68
Process cost systems, 151
Process decision program chart – QM tool, 97
Process management levers, 66
Process management methods, 101
Process management tools, 101
Process mapping tools, 97
Process mapping, 48
Process time – production or service, 48
Process variation causes – SPC, 98
Producer price index (PPI), 326–327
Product audit, 89
Product classification, 87
Product cost, 142
Product definition, 87
Product development strategy, 5
Product lifecycle concept, 88
Product line, 88
Product management, 87
Product mix, 88
Product profitability, 88
Product quality decision – go/no-go, 99
Product research and development (R&D) costs, 130–131
Product variability, 50
Product's lifecycle cost, 81
Product's relative performance, 81
Product's relative price, 81
Product-by-value analysis, 49
Production economics, 63
Production metrics, 66
Production possibilities curve – economics, 328
Production process flows, 66
Production scheduling methods, 61
Production strategies – international, 281
Production strategies, 47
Production strategy tools, 48
Productivity defined, 42
Productivity improvement criteria, 42
Productivity improvements, 43
Productivity measurement components, 42
Productivity measurement guidelines, 43
Profit center, 152
Profit models, 320
Profitability index (PI) method, 173
Profitability ratios – financial statements, 138
Profit-push inflation, 329
Program evaluation and review technique (PERT), 303
Project assumptions, 297
Project baseline, 288, 297
Project cash flows, 176
Project champions – Six-Sigma, 96
Project change management, 301
Project communication, 302
Project contingencies, 298
Project controlling methods, 300
Project controlling, 297
Project cost control, 300
Project cost models, 307
Project course corrections, 302

Project crashing, 304
Project critical success factors (CSFs), 288
Project deliverables, 297
Project dependencies, 298
Project earned value management (EVM) technique, 300
Project estimating methods, 298
Project float, 306
Project free slack time, 306
Project governance mechanisms, 309
Project indicators, 307–308
Project lifecycle, 294–296
Project management audit, 309–310
Project management defined, 287
Project management metrics, 307
Project management problems, 308–309
Project management process, 294
Project management risk, 290
Project manager, 18, 294
Project milestones, 297
Project network diagrams, 298
Project organization, 292
Project oversight board, 309
Project performance measures, 288
Project plan, 296
Project planning methods, 297
Project planning, 297
Project progress, 302
Project quality control, 300
Project quality, 299
Project reporting methods, 301–302
Project resources, 299
Project risk assessment, 177
Project risk management plan, 291
Project risk types, 289–291
Project risks, 298
Project safety factor, 306
Project scheduling, 297
Project scope, 298
Project slack time, 306
Project steering committee, 309
Project structures – advantages and disadvantages, 294
Project structures, 291
Project success criteria, 288
Project time control, 300
Project time, 298
Project total slack time, 306
Project-bid errors, 295
Project-type-organization, 293
Protocol converters – IT, 214
Proxy fight – stockholder votes, 168
Proxy process – stockholder votes, 266
Pull strategy-marketing expenses, 82
Pull system – manufacturing and distribution, 52
Pull system – throughput, 50
Pull technology – IT, 229
Purchasing power parity – exchange rates, 280
Pure inflation, 329
Push strategy-marketing expenses, 82
Push system – manufacturing and distribution, 52

Push system – throughput, 50
Push technology – IT, 229
Put option – stocks, 168
Putable bonds, 166

Q

Qualitative methods in risk management, 245
Quality assurance, 91
Quality at the source, 101
Quality audit, 91, 261
Quality circles, 91, 112
Quality concepts, 91
Quality control (QC) circles, 22
Quality control (QC) tools, 97
Quality control, 91
Quality cost index – COQ, 94
Quality council, 92
Quality definitions:
    Judgment-based, 93
    Manufacturing-based, 94
    Product-based, 94
    User-based, 94
    Value-based, 94
Quality drivers, 93
Quality engineering, 91, 100
Quality function deployment (QFD), 98
Quality improvements, 92
Quality inspection, 100–101
Quality loss function (QLF), 91, 100
Quality management (QM) tools, 97
Quality of service – VoIP, 213
Quality planning, 91
Quality robustness, 100
Quality tools, 97
Quantitative methods in business, 311
Quantitative methods in risk management, 245
Queuing or waiting-line models, 313

R

Rated capacity – production, 60
Real GDP – economy, 326
Real GNP – economy, 326–327
Real income, 327, 329
Real interest rate, 331
Real value of money, 322
Real wages, 325
Realistic conflict, 35
Reality checks, 25
Receivables conversion period, 161
Reciprocal agreements – disaster recovery, 204
Recovery controls, 240
Recovery strategies, – disaster recovery, 202
Recovery time objective (RTO), 201
Recruiting cost per hire, 106
Recruitment factors, 105
Recruitment for diversity, 106
Recruitment methods, 105
Recruitment sources, 105

Red flags – fraud, 264
Red-ocean strategy, 7
Red-team testing – IT security, 222
Redundant arrays of independent disks (RAID), 202
Regional cultures – national and international, 282
Regional groups – international trade, 279
Regression analysis – forecasting, 317
Relational data model – database, 225
Relevant costs, 150
Reorder point – inventory, 55
Repeaters – network, 215
Replacement cost model, 184
Replacement cost, 143
Required reserves – banks, 332
Reserve ratio – banks, 332
Responsibility accounting, 152
Responsibility – management, 11
Restrictive covenants – bonds, 165
Restructuring – organization, 103
Retailer's transaction value, 82
Retrenchment, 3
Return on quality (ROQ), 96
Return on training (ROT), 110
Revaluation of currency, 280
Revenue center, 152
Revenue management – service, 60
Revenue recognition concept – accounting, 121
Reverse auctions in e-commerce, 231
Reverse innovation – marketing, 76
Reverse investment, 274
Reverse logistics, 58
Reverse marketing, 58
Reverse mentoring, 111
Reverse purchasing, 58
Reverse-splits – stocks, 189
Rework cost, 143
Rightsizing – organization, 103
Risk assessment, 241–242
Risk avoidance control, 241
Risk evaluation, 241, 243
Risk management tools, 243
Risk management, 241
Risk management methodology, 242
Risk mitigation, 241–242
Risk, 241
Role-playing – employee, 110
Roles – groups, 28
Roles of senior executives, 258–259
Roles of the BODs, 257–258
Roles of the CEOs, 258–259
Routers – network, 215
Rules of behavior, 221

S

Saddle point for competitors – decision, 317
Safety audit, 262
Safety stock, 53

Savings investment ratio (SIR) method, 174
Scalar principle – management, 11
Scatter diagram – QC tool, 97
Scenario analysis, 177
Seasonalized time-series – forecasting, 318
Secure electronic transactions (SET), 232
Securitizations, 181
Security audit -IT, 222
Security concepts in planning, 218
Security considerations in SDLC, 198
Security controls and safeguards, 221–222
Security goals and objectives, 219–220
Security-in-depth strategy – IT, 218
Segregation of duties, 211
Self-managed teams, 22
Senior champions – Six-Sigma, 96
Sensitivity analysis, 177, 244, 319
Sensitivity training (T-group training), 112
Separation of duties, 211
Separation of ownership from control, 266
Sequential engineering, 92
Servant leader, 16
Service blueprinting, 48
Service characteristics:
  Inseparability, 86
  Intangibility, 86
Service marketing obstacles, 87
Service quality, 86–87
Service-level agreement (SLA) – disaster recovery, 204
Service-level management – IT, 211
Seven Ss (7Ss) in production, 50
Share development index (SDI), 81
Shareholders, 256
Shareholders' equity, 126
Short-run cost, 142
Short-run supply curve – economics, 330
Short-term debt, 163
Short-term financing, 165
Simple moving-average – forecasting, 317
Simple ratios – financial statements, 320
Simulation models, 319
Single points of failure – IT security, 218
Single ratios – financial statements, 136
Sinking fund – debt, 165
Situation analysis, 3
Situational leadership theory, 15
Six-Sigma improvement model (DMAIC), 95
Six-Sigma players, 96
Six-Sigma, 94
Skimming cash, 265
Slowing cash disbursements, 159
Smoothing constant (beta) – forecasting, 317
Soft goods, 334
Soft-controls, 239
Soft-issues, 239
Soft-skills, 239
Software metering product, 222
Software quality assurance (QA) libraries, 208
Source inspection, 100–101

Sources of cash, 154
Sovereignty risk, 179
Span of control – organization structure, 12
Span of management – organization structure, 12
Speeding cash collections, 159
Spinoff – assets, 186
Stable and unstable processes – SPC, 99
Staff managers, 18
Staffing policies – international, 281
Stagflation, 330
Stakeholder empowerment, 92
Standard cost, 142
Standard costing, 151
Statement of cash flows, 123, 127, 135
Statement of retained earnings, 122, 124, 134
Statement of shareholders' equity, 122, 125
Statistical process control (SPC) methods, 98, 318
Step cost, 142
Stock-dividends, 189
Stock-repurchases, 189
Stock-splits, 189
Strategic business units (SBUs), 8
Strategic control, 4
Strategic initiatives, 193–194
Strategic management defined, 2
Strategic management process, 2
Strategic objectives – international, 271
Strategic plan, 10
Strategic planning process, 5
Strategic planning, 3
Strategic risk – project, 290
Strategy formulation, 3
Strategy implementation, 4
Structural inflation, 329
Structural unemployment, 328
Structured query language (SQL) – database, 227
Subjective scoring – risk, 245
Success-failure analysis, 25
Succession planning – employee, 112
Sunk cost, 142, 176, 321
Supplier certification, 57
Supplier's breakeven analysis, 63
Supply chain, 56
Supply shock – recession, 330
Switches – network, 216
SWOT analysis – company assessment, 244
Symptoms of employee fraud, 265
Symptoms of management fraud, 264–265
Synectics – problem solving tool, 24
Synthetic leases, 181
System analyzers, 222
System backups, 209
System development lifecycle (SDLC):
  Development/acquisition phase, 197
  Disposal phase, 197
  Implementation phase, 197
  Initiation phase, 196
  Operations/maintenance phase, 197
System documentation, 200
System logs – IT, 210, 222

System redundancy, 66
System reliability, 65
System security plans, 218
Systems analysis – problem solving tool, 24
Systems and data backup – IT, 202

T

Tactical objectives – international, 271
Tactical plan, 10
Target costing, 151
Tariffs – trade, 273
TCP/IP framework – network, 228–229
Team building methods:
   Adjourning, 29
   Forming, 29
   Norming, 29
   Performing, 29
   Storming, 29
Team building, 112
Technical controls, 238
Technical skill – management, 17
Technology risk – project, 289
Technology transfer, 274
Term loans, 165
Terms-of-trade index, 276
Terms-of-trade, 275
Theory of comparative advantage, 275
Theory of Constraints (TOC), 62
Theory T employees, 18
Theory T+ employees, 18
Theory X employees, 18
Theory Y employees, 18
Theory Z employees, 18
Throughput – production, 49–50
Time value of money, 319
Time-series models – forecasting, 46
Top managers, 17
Total leverage, 156
Total productive maintenance (TPM), 65
Total quality management (TQM), 93
Total revenue, 322
Total throughput, 48
Toyota production system, 52
Trade credit, 163
Traditional costing systems, 151
Traditional innovation – marketing, 76
Training and development (T&D) delivery systems, 110
Training and development (T&D) learning methods, 110
Training and development (T&D) needs, 110
Training and development (T&D) objectives, 110
Trait leadership theory, 14
Transactional leader, 16
Transfer pricing criteria, 147
Transfer pricing international, 147
Transfer pricing methods, 147
Transfer pricing, 146
Transformational leadership theory, 16

Transmission control protocol (TCP) – network, 228–229
Transnational strategy, 3
Treasury bonds, 166
Treasury stock, 189
Tree diagram – QM tool, 97
Trend analysis – financial statements, 136
Type I statistical error – SPC, 99
Type II statistical error – SPC, 99

U

Unavoidable cost, 142
Uncommitted cost, 143
Unemployment, 328
Unexpired cost, 142
Unit-of-measure concept – accounting, 120
Unity of command, 11
Unstable and stable processes – SPC, 99
Uptime- equipment, 65
Upward communications, 34
Uses of cash, 154

V

Value analysis, 48
Value engineering, 48
Value index, 49
Value research, 48
Value/price ratio, 82
Value-added network (VAN), 212, 231
Value-based location strategy, 49
Values – groups, 28
Value-stream mapping, 48–49
Variability – product, 50
Variable chart – SPC, 98
Variable control chart – SPC, 99
Variable cost, 142
Variable costing method – production, 140
Vendor agreements – disaster recovery, 205
Vertical hierarchy, 11
Vertical market, 87
Virtual leader, 16
Virtual networks, 213
Virtual private network (VPN), 212, 230
Virtual teams, 30
Virus scanners, 221
Visionary leader, 16
Voice communication networks – VoIP, 213
Voice of the customer (VOC), 98

W

Wage-push inflation, 329
Waiting-line or queuing models, 313
Wald criterion in decision making, 317
Warehouses, 57
Warrant options – stock, 166, 168, 180
Web management issues, 230
Weighted moving-average – forecasting, 317

Weighted-average-cost-of-capital (WACC), 171
White belts – Six-Sigma, 96
Wide-area network (WAN), 211–212
Work breakdown structure (WBS) – project, 298, 306
Working capital asset investment policies:
    Relaxed, 161
    Restricted, 161
    Moderate, 161
Working capital financing policies:
    Aggressive, 161
    Conservative, 161
    Maturity matching, 161
Working capital, 160
Working stock, 53

World intellectual property organizations (WIPO), 277
World trade organization (WTO), 276–277

Y

Yellow belts – Six-Sigma, 96
Yield management – service, 60

Z

Zero-coupon bonds, 167
Zero-sum game – decision, 316